T&T Clark Reader in Edward Schillebeeckx

T&T Clark Reader in Edward Schillebeeckx

Edited by
Stephan van Erp & Daniel Minch

t&tclark
LONDON • NEW YORK • OXFORD • NEW DELHI • SYDNEY

T&T CLARK
Bloomsbury Publishing Plc
50 Bedford Square, London, WC1B 3DP, UK
1385 Broadway, New York, NY 10018, USA
29 Earlsfort Terrace, Dublin 2, Ireland

BLOOMSBURY, T&T CLARK and the T&T Clark logo are trademarks of Bloomsbury Publishing Plc

First published in Great Britain 2023

Copyright © Stephan van Erp & Daniel Minch, 2023

Stephan van Erp & Daniel Minch have asserted their right under the Copyright, Designs and Patents Act, 1988, to be identified as Editors of this work.

Cover image: Monastery La Tourette, interior lower church, Eveux-sur-Arbresle, France. © Archimago / Alamy Stock Photo

All rights reserved. No part of this publication may be reproduced or transmitted in any form or by any means, electronic or mechanical, including photocopying, recording, or any information storage or retrieval system, without prior permission in writing from the publishers.

Bloomsbury Publishing Plc does not have any control over, or responsibility for, any third-party websites referred to or in this book. All internet addresses given in this book were correct at the time of going to press. The author and publisher regret any inconvenience caused if addresses have changed or sites have ceased to exist, but can accept no responsibility for any such changes.

A catalogue record for this book is available from the British Library.

A catalog record for this book is available from the Library of Congress.

ISBN: HB: 978-0-5676-8341-0
PB: 978-0-5676-8340-3
ePDF: 978-0-5676-8342-7
eBook: 978-0-5676-8343-4

Typeset by Deanta Global Publishing Services, Chennai, India

To find out more about our authors and books visit www.bloomsbury.com and sign up for our newsletters.

Dedicated to the memory of
Robert J. Schreiter C.PP.S

CONTENTS

Note on the Texts ix

Introduction: Reading Edward Schillebeeckx: Texts and Contexts *Stephan van Erp & Daniel Minch* 1

Timeline of Edward Schillebeeckx's Life and Works 20

PART ONE Sources 25

Introduction *Stephan van Erp* 27

1   Thomas Aquinas and Thomism 32

2   Metaphysics and Phenomenology 42

3   Nouvelle Théologie 60

4   Dominican Spirituality 72

PART TWO The Second Vatican Council and Its Aftermath 87

Introduction *Daniel Minch* 89

5   The Second Vatican Council 94

6   Hermeneutics 108

7   Church and World 127

8   Historical-Critical Method 144

PART THREE Theological Themes 153

Introduction *Julia Feder* 155

9   God 159

10 Creation 167

11 Sacramental Theology 174

12 Theological Anthropology 191

13 Christology 208

14 Grace 223

15 Resurrection 231

16 Mary 243

17 Eschatology 255

18 Magisterium and Authority 269

19 Ministry 284

PART FOUR Theology of Culture 297

Introduction *Elizabeth Pyne* 299

20 Culture 304

21 Secularisation 316

22 Political and Liberation Theology 329

23 Religious Pluralism 342

Index 353

NOTE ON THE TEXTS

This reader contains texts that have been previously published in British and American editions of the works of Edward Schillebeeckx. Some of these translations have been revised and published in the eleven volumes of *The Collected Works of Edward Schillebeeckx* (T&T Clark, 2014). The reference to the full work of each selected text can be found in the first footnote at the beginning of each passage. A reference to the *Collected Works* contains both the pages in the respective volume, and the pages in the original edition, as follows:

> Selected from: Edward Schillebeeckx, 'What is Theology?,' *Revelation and Theology*, trans. N. D. Smith, Collected Works of Edward Schillebeeckx vol. 2 (London: Bloomsbury T&T Clark, 2014), 82–4 [I 124–6].

In most cases we have respected the language and formatting style of the revised translations, and where these were not available, we have used the original translations. We have left the difference in footnote style unchanged. We have also preserved the original uses of italicisation, and capitalisation (e.g. Church/church). Two exceptions were made, however. We have changed the book and journal abbreviations, which were much more common in the twentieth century than they are now, into the full journal titles. Most importantly, we have made the texts gender-neutral as much as possible, and in accordance with the original sense of the Dutch. For example, terms often used by Schillebeeckx, like 'mankind' or 'the salvation of man' have been changed into 'humanity' and 'the salvation of humanity/humankind/all people', as determined by the context. In Dutch, Schillebeeckx employed gender neutral language, using the words *mens* and *menselijkheid*, which mean 'human' and 'humanity' respectively. This change, therefore, is not only a necessary linguistic correction, but it also more accurately articulates the significance of these words in Schillebeeckx's theology.

Introduction

Reading Edward Schillebeeckx: Texts and Contexts

Stephan van Erp & Daniel Minch

A Reader in Edward Schillebeeckx for the twenty-first century

This addition to the series of T&T Clark Readers is dedicated to the groundbreaking Catholic theologian, Edward Schillebeeckx (1914–2009). Schillebeeckx is counted among the giants of twentieth-century modern theology, and he played an especially prominent role in the revolutions in content and method that took place after the Second Vatican Council. During his lifetime, he was well known all over the world for his scholarship as well as for his high-profile conflicts with the authorities in Rome. He founded important international scholarly journals, participated in global conversations about the future of the church, embraced political and theological liberation, and fought for the rights of the laity to be more fully represented in the Catholic world. This is not to reduce him to a media figure or a political agitator. Schillebeeckx was a Flemish Dominican friar and committed priest whose faith in God always remained the guiding star for his life and work, right up until he was united with God in 2009. Schillebeeckx left behind a considerable legacy and an international community of scholars and students inspired by him, both personally and academically. Over the last decade, Schillebeeckx's life and work has reached a new level of prominence in theology, with his work being rediscovered and applied to unique areas that he himself did not fully consider. A new generation of Schillebeeckx scholars is in the process of interpreting his work and legacy for a new century, and we feel that this, combined with the dramatic and often violent changes to the world in the last half-century, warrant the composition of a new *Reader*. Our aim is to provide a guide for reading Schillebeeckx for our own time as a compliment to the work that has come before us. This reader is a stepping stone, an invitation for those who would begin down the road of interpretation and reception.

A number of factors made it opportune for us to compile a new *Reader* for the theology of Edward Schillebeeckx. The first of which is the completion of the *T&T Clark Handbook of Edward Schillebeeckx* (2020) which we are proud to have brought to fruition as editors.[1] In structure and content, the present volume is intended to be a companion piece to the scholarly analysis presented in the *Handbook*. Second, the publication by Bloomsbury of the *Collected Works of Edward Schillebeeckx* series in 2014 edited by Ted Schoof and Carl Sterkens with Robert J. Schreiter and Erik Borgman have made Schillebeeckx's works more available but also present readers with the challenge of eleven large and daunting volumes of scholarship. This series also provided a helpful resource from which to draw on for the practical tasks of composing a *Reader*. These two factors are part of the renewed attention being paid to Schillebeeckx's work and legacy since shortly before his death in 2009 when an international symposium was held in his honour in Leuven, Belgium from 3–6 December 2008. This was followed by the publication of *Edward Schillebeeckx and Contemporary Theology*, edited by Lieven Boeve, Frederiek Depoortere, and Stephan van Erp,[2] which was the precursor for the *T&T Clark Studies in Edward Schillebeeckx* series which has published several collected volumes and monographs on the work and legacy of Schillebeeckx. A number of international conferences, panels, and research colloquia have been held in the last decade in Belgium, the Netherlands, Switzerland, and the United States, involving both universities and organisations such as the Catholic Theological Society of America. All of these factors favour a new *Reader*.

In the Introduction of the *Handbook*, we referred to the roughly three generations of Schillebeeckx scholars who have passed on his work and legacy. The first generation studied with Schillebeeckx himself, or were active during his scholarly career, and therefore directly shaped by him. This includes his most famous students, Erik Borgman, Robert J. Schreiter (who sadly passed away in 2021), Mary Catherine Hilkert, and Philip Kennedy, all of whom have published influential works on Schillebeeckx and are therefore integral to the reception history of his theology. Their work has been an essential source of inspiration for all of us. The second generation began their professional careers in the 1990s and early-2000s, and they have published a wide range of literature on Schillebeeckx over the last decades. They represent a significant cross-section of academic theology in Europe, Asia, Australia, and North America. It is essential to note that this group of scholars began their careers at a time when Schillebeeckx's theological legacy was far from self-evident due to the ecclesial climate of the time. Since the first major international conference on Schillebeeckx in 2008, a third generation of Schillebeeckx scholars have emerged within the drastically changed landscape of academia and theology. They are post-9/11 scholars whose lives have been marked by the conflicts and crises of the early twenty-first century, and this fact influences their interests and how they interpret Schillebeeckx. All three generations are now involved in teaching, research, and

---

[1] Stephan van Erp and Daniel Minch, eds., *T&T Clark Handbook of Edward Schillebeeckx* (London: T&T Clark, 2020).

[2] Lieven Boeve, Frederiek Depoortere and Stephan van Erp, eds., *Edward Schillebeeckx and Contemporary Theology* (London/New York: T&T Clark, 2010).

ministry, and, very likely, the education of an even younger generation of students and scholars who will themselves have new and diverse interests.

This current volume is meant to be a resource for everyone with an interest in the theology of Edward Schillebeeckx, but above all it is meant to be a reference and an accessible introduction to the many areas of his expertise for the younger generations. We hope that this volume will be well-used and widely read by teachers and students alike, as well as by anyone who is interested in knowing what it was that Schillebeeckx actually thought regarding his own attempts at 'faith seeking understanding'. Like most of the towering intellectual figures of history, Schillebeeckx's positions are often cited, both negatively and positively, based on a caricature or overly simplistic image of what he in fact wrote. This *Reader* is meant, therefore, to provide access to the core points of his theology while still preserving as much of the nuance and detail as possible.

It is important to acknowledge that this is indeed a new *Reader*, and distinct from *The Schillebeeckx Reader* edited in 1984 by Robert J. Schreiter.[3] Schreiter was a former holder of the Edward Schillebeeckx Chair in Theology at Radboud University Nijmegen (RU Nijmegen) and Vatican Council II Professor of Theology at Catholic Theological Union in Chicago. This volume has had a long and influential life as a sourcebook and introduction to Schillebeeckx, and it was approved by Schillebeeckx himself in a short foreword. Unfortunately, it is increasingly difficult to find as it was published over thirty-five years ago and is long out of print. The date of its publication presents a second problem since it does not reflect the entirety of Schillebeeckx's publishing career. Although he retired in 1982, he continued to publish books and articles, albeit with diminishing frequency, until 2000. At least two major works, *Church with a Human Face* (1985) and *Church: The Human Story of God* (1989) appeared after Schreiter's volume, as did several minor works and important essays. Finally, as with the *Handbook*, the current volume should reflect the needs of the moment and the state of theology in the twenty-first century.

We now have more than a decade of distance from Schillebeeckx's death. We cannot and will not present an entirely up to date volume, since that would not be possible or even desirable, but we do seek to acknowledge the changes in interest and interpretation of Schillebeeckx's work since Schreiter's *Reader* was published. In the mid-1980s, Schillebeeckx was a modern theologian when that movement was still the dominant school in systematic theology. Since then, we have passed the end of modernity and run through the postmodern era and now find ourselves in another situation entirely. The field of theology has further fragmented, making it at once more specialised and more alienating, while also perhaps more able to productively incorporate critical movements and marginalised voices. That does not diminish the importance or place of his work for 'Schillebeeckx studies' as a field and we are greatly indebted to him personally and professionally. His work, published in Schillebeeckx's lifetime, played a significant role in the reception history of Schillebeeckx's work and perhaps even had an impact on the thought and scholarly trajectory of Schillebeeckx himself.

---

[3] Edward Schillebeeckx, *The Schillebeeckx Reader*, ed. Robert J. Schreiter (New York: Crossroad, 1984).

Other forerunners to the present volume include the previously mentioned *T&T Clark Handbook of Edward Schillebeeckx* and *Edward Schillebeeckx and Contemporary Theology*, as well as the revised and expanded second edition of *The Praxis of the Reign of God*, edited by Mary Catherine Hilkert and Robert Schreiter.[4] There are also two significant books by Philip Kennedy, one simply called *Schillebeeckx*, which is an introduction to his life and theology, and a second, nearly exhaustive study of Schillebeeckx's philosophical theology, *Deus Humanissimus: The Knowability of God in the Theology of Edward Schillebeeckx*.[5] Each of these has, in some way, influenced the preparation of this current *Reader*.

It should be noted that although Edward Schillebeeckx was a gifted essayist, he had difficulty with writing full monographs. Although he composed many of the latter in his long career, they were often made up of previously published articles, as with his book *The Eucharist* and the *Theological Soundings* series, or they tended to become extremely long and at times unwieldy. This is especially true for *Jesus: An Experiment in Christology* (1974) and *Christ: The Christian Experience in the Modern World* (1977), which in the new English editions total over 1500 pages combined. His other books, including the third *Jesus*-volume, *Church: The Human Story of God* (1989), are much shorter and are generally more recognisably composed of sections that were previously published as essays and articles.[6]

With this in mind, we have attempted preserve the form of Schillebeeckx's style to the best of our ability. Instead of trying to cut very short sections of a paragraph or two on single topics, we have focused on short sections or excerpts that form a narrative whole. Admittedly, this is difficult in part due to the density of his work – Schillebeeckx was very often weaving together several threads at one time or developing multiple themes. This is especially the case for his *Jesus*-volumes. Nevertheless, we feel that it is better to present slightly longer selections of text in order to both preserve the character and complexity of his thought and in order to give the reader a better sense of how Schillebeeckx worked. Where possible, we have preserved the original headings and titles of the text selections or the nearest subheading under which the selection falls. The footnotes, when they are used, have also been preserved in an amended form in order to make them clearer to the contemporary reader and particularly to those not immediately familiar with the abbreviations common to French, Dutch, and German scholarship of the middle of the last century.

---

[4] Mary Catherine Hilkert and Robert J. Schreiter, eds., *The Praxis of the Reign of God: An Introduction to the Theology of Edward Schillebeeckx*, 2nd ed. (New York: Fordham University Press, 2002).

[5] Philip Kennedy, *Schillebeeckx* (Collegeville, MN: Liturgical Press, 1993); Philip Kennedy, *Deus Humanissimus: The Knowability of God in the Theology of Edward Schillebeeckx* (Fribourg: Presses universitaires de Fribourg, 1993).

[6] *Church* includes material previously published in *Jesus in Our Western Culture: Mysticism, Ethics and Politics*, trans. John Bowden (London: SCM Press, 1987), and *Theologisch geloofsverstaan anno 1983* (Baarn: Nelissen, 1983).

Introducing Edward Schillebeeckx: his life and context

Edward Schillebeeckx was born in Antwerp, Belgium on 12 November 1914. He was the sixth child in a family of fourteen, which at that time was not uncommon for Catholic families. For the Schillebeeckx family, the church was a focal point for daily life. The young Edward attended the Jesuit college and boarding school in Turnhout, and although he felt drawn to religious life, he chose the Dominicans over the Jesuits. After writing to the Dominican novitiate in Ghent in May 1933, he received a letter from the superior with the reply that 'St. Dominic's white habit would not look amiss on you'.[7] At his boarding school, Schillebeeckx had experienced the Jesuits as rigid and inflexible, inward-looking and oriented towards principles rather than people. In the Dominicans, he found a different attitude and spirituality which nourished him. He made his profession on 21 September 1935 and began to train for the priesthood, which would involve studies in philosophy and theology.[8]

In Ghent, Schillebeeckx studied philosophy under Dominicus De Petter, who founded the *Tijdschrift voor Filosofie* in 1939. De Petter was a philosopher and neo-Thomist who had become influential in the Low Countries because of his article 'Impliciete Intuïtie', which was an attempt to harmonise Thomist positions with the modern philosophies of Descartes and Kant.[9] His course of study was strongly Thomistic and classical, but he was also in touch with the contemporary philosophical debates of the moment and an expert in modern' philosophy. This made De Petter controversial, but also an important influence for Schillebeeckx, especially in the realm of epistemology. As a Thomist, De Petter went beyond narrow neoscholasticism, and was clear about the need for a modern reading of Thomas, and he was well versed in the works of Edmund Husserl and the existentialist philosophers.

This training certainly influenced Schillebeeckx's early scholarly trajectory, wherein he was much more interested in philosophy than theology. He wrote early articles on Thomas' philosophy on God, knowledge, and language. Consonant with both with Dominican tradition and the spirit of the age, Schillebeeckx read Thomas himself rather than relying on than the 'authoritative' commentaries on his work.[10] Already at this point in his career, Schillebeeckx was part of a theological *ressourcement*.

In the midst of the Second World War, Schillebeeckx became a lecturer at the Dominican study house in Leuven in 1943, where he lectured on theological topics for the students.[11] After the war was over, he went to Paris for doctoral studies at the

---

[7]Edward Schillebeeckx, *I Am a Happy Theologian: Conversations with Francesco Strazzari*, trans. John Bowden (London: SCM Press, 1994), 86–8.
[8]Erik Borgman, *Edward Schillebeeckx: A Theologian in His History*, trans. John Bowden (London/New York: Continuum, 2003), 37.
[9]Edward Schillebeeckx, *I Am a Happy Theologian: Conversations with Francesco Strazzari*, trans. John Bowden (London: SCM Press, 1994), 86–8.
[10]These essays have been collected in Edward Schillebeeckx, *Revelation and Theology*, Collected Works of Edward Schillebeeckx vol. 2 (London: Bloomsbury T&T Clark, 2014).
[11]Borgman, *Edward Schillebeeckx*, 61.

famed Dominican study house, Le Saulchoir, outside of Paris. There he came under the mentorship of the great Dominicans Marie-Dominique Chenu and Yves Congar. He learned a great deal from both theologians, but he certainly took different lessons from each, with Congar providing formal historical and theological lectures, while Chenu was a source of more personal inspiration and a dynamic spirit. During this time he also attended lectures in Paris at the Sorbonne.

In 1952, Schillebeeckx published his dissertation on Thomas' doctrine of the sacraments, *The Sacramental Economy of Salvation* (*De sacramentele heilseconomie. Theologische bezinning op S. Thomas' sacramentenleer in het licht van de traditie en van de hedendaagse sacramentsproblematiek*). Its subtitle can be translated as 'a theological reflection on St. Thomas's teaching on the sacraments in light of the tradition and contemporary sacramental problematic', which speaks to Erik Borgman's thesis that Schillebeeckx was primarily concerned in his early career with a 'theology of culture'. He was attempting to locate the encounter with God in history between tradition and situation.[12] This dissertation already evidences Schillebeeckx's talent for detailed historical and biblical analysis – here applied to the concept of 'sacrament' before he moves on to a consideration of the Thomist theology of the sacraments. He continued to work on a renewed interpretation of the sacraments in his later books on marriage and Christology, the latter of which, *Christ the Sacrament of the Encounter with God*, became an international bestseller, translated into nine languages.[13]

In 1958, Schillebeeckx was appointed as professor of Dogmatics and the History of Christianity at the Catholic University of Nijmegen in the Netherlands (now Radboud University Nijmegen). Almost at the same moment, the announcement came that an ecumenical council would soon be held in Rome. The Catholic Church under Pope John XXIII had entered a period of *aggiornamento*, opening up to the world. The preparations began in 1958 for the Second Vatican Council (1962–5), and the expectations that many people had had of this council led to a renewed enthusiasm for theology. This, among other factors, inspired Schillebeeckx to found a new theological journal in 1961 for the Netherlands and Flanders: *Tijdschrift voor theologie*. This journal was published continuously from 1961 until 2020, and was essentially the journal for *nouvelle théologie* and the successors of that movement in the Low Countries. In the introduction of the first issue, Schillebeeckx wrote: 'There is much talk of what is new in Catholic theology these days. This should not baffle us or raise our suspicion. What is meant is not a different theology, but the old theology of the church itself which has possessed itself more strongly of the realities

---

[12]Henricus Edward Schillebeeckx, *De sacramentele heilseconomie. Theologische bezinning op S. Thomas' sacramentenleer in het licht van de traditie en van de hedendaagse sacramentsproblematiek* (Antwerp/Bilthoven: 't Groeit/H. Nelissen, 1952). A French translation was published in 2004: Edward Schillebeeckx, *L'économie sacramentelle du salut: réflexion théologique sur la doctrine sacramentaire de saint Thomas, à la lumière de la tradition et de la problématique sacramentelle contemporaine*, Studia Friburgensia 95 (Fribourg: Presses universitaires de Fribourg, 2004).
[13]Edward Schillebeeckx, *Christ the Sacrament*, Collected Works of Edward Schillebeeckx vol. 1 (London: Bloomsbury T&T Clark, 2014); Edward Schillebeeckx, *Marriage: Human Reality and Saving Mystery*, trans. N. D. Smith, vol. 1 & 2 (New York: Sheed and Ward, 1965).

of faith'.[14] This sentiment is unsurprisingly quite similar to the tone of the landmark pastoral letter issued by the Dutch bishops in 1961 concerning the coming council. The bishops anticipated that it would bring an 'internal renewal and reformation of Catholic life'.[15] In a postscript, the document explicitly thanks 'professor dr. E. Schillebeeckx' for his contributions to the text, which in reality was nearly all of it.[16] Already at this stage he was marked out to play a major role at the council, both as an advisor to the Dutch bishops and as lecturer and informal expert for the many prelates gathered in Rome from all over the world.

Schillebeeckx always presented the work of the council in terms of reform and continuity with tradition, but he was not overly optimistic about its results. He certainly praised the new openness of the church to the world and to the modern age. He was clear that the importance of Scripture as a symbol of the church, the recognition of freedom of religion and conscience, and the emphasis on salvation as also occurring within history rather than exclusively after death, were all significant and positive steps. However, immediately after the council and much later, he was quite critical of it for the places where it had failed to make significant changes or left dogmatic possibilities open and able to be ignored by later interpreters. He also recognised that the council had come too late, taking up the issues of modernity at a moment when modernity was no longer the dominant paradigm in the world. He also feared that the pastoral aspects of the Vatican II would be emphasised, but merely in the sense of psychological and consoling and not in the dogmatic and magisterial senses of the term.

Like other major theological figures who had taken part in the council, Schillebeeckx saw clearly that the work begun in Rome was not yet finished. Together with Karl Rahner, Yves Congar, Hans Küng, Johann Baptist Metz and others, he founded the international theological journal *Concilium* in 1965. The journal was meant to take the council documents as a starting point for further reflection and reform. *Concilium* continues this mission, carrying on the spirit of Vatican II, to this day.

The Dutch church concretely attempted to implement Vatican II with the publication of a new catechism – which provoked a strong reaction from Rome – and the convocation of the Dutch Pastoral Council (1966–70). Schillebeeckx acted as the Dutch bishops' advisor at the council and was part of the discussions on reform. The Pastoral Council took the international spotlight due to the discussion on priestly celibacy. In the final session, it was even decided to abandon celibacy for priests. Although that particular reform was not implemented, the Pastoral Council began a process of polarisation in the Netherlands between progressive and conservative Catholics. Although Schillebeeckx is often portrayed as part of the progressive movement in the Netherlands, and even as a radical, during the discussion he was quite restrained, frequently pointing to the legitimacy of practices that were associated with the traditional, conservative side.

Schillebeeckx's own theology changed following the Second Vatican Council, especially in terms of his use of methodology and the integration of philosophy

---

[14]"Ter Oriëntering', *Tijdschrift voor theologie* 1 (1961), 1.
[15]'De Bisschoppen van Nederland over het concilie', *Tijdschrift voor theologie* 1 (1961), 71–90, at 72.
[16]He later commented on this in Schillebeeckx, *I Am a Happy Theologian*, 17.

into theological reflection. He especially focused on contemporary philosophical hermeneutics as a tool for interpreting tradition and the contemporary situation. The use of hermeneutics, already current in Protestant theology, became a way of explaining Christian faith and interpretation to people who no longer shared the narrow scholastic metaphysical presuppositions of a previous age. In the rapidly secularising context of post-Second World War Europe, this was very necessary, but it also made his work more accessible to people from other contexts and socio-religious backgrounds. His goal was both to articulate a proper understanding of tradition, and to make the relevance of faith clear to people living in the contemporary situation. More than just a rephrasing of older language or repackaging of propositions of doctrine, Schillebeeckx uncovered a new theological foundation in the dual reality of experience and interpretation. In the experience and interpretation of faith, God's self-revelation was at work in history, making that history a *locus theologicus*. Ultimately, the deep connection between revelation and experience makes hermeneutics more than a methodology used for *post factum* interpretation. It is essential to the process and structure of revelation within creation, and is therefore a fundamental part of how reality functions. This turn to experience, along with his participation in the Dutch Pastoral Council brought Schillebeeckx to consider the political aspects of theology. By engaging with the critical theory of society of Jürgen Habermas and the political theology of Johann Baptist Metz, Schillebeeckx also began to articulate the theo-political aspects of Christian faith. Here, his political concerns were more fundamentally a product of his theological concerns about the world, and we should see the legacy of Vatican II as the ultimate impetus behind this turn in his work.

The new importance of history, experience, and interpretation for theology had a major influence on the direction of Schillebeeckx's later career. After 1968, he began to distance himself from the neo-Thomism of his mentor, De Petter, and the metaphysical framework of his own pre-Conciliar theology. As a result, he abandoned the *Theological Soundings* series after volume five (*The Understanding of Faith*), despite having originally planned ten volumes. His turn to experience and hermeneutics had convinced him that a new approach was needed, and as part of that he started to prepare a book on Christology. He planned three volumes on the subject, which, after his methodological and fundamental theological writings of the late 1960s, came as something of a surprise to his readers. His first volume, entitled *Jesus, the story of one who is alive* (1974), appeared in English as *Jesus: An Experiment in Christology*, and it included an impressive synthesis of historical critical research.[17] He had taken biblical exegesis and combined it with a hermeneutical framework for interpretation and used this to develop a systematic theology. In this way, he was very much in line with *Dei verbum*, the Dogmatic Constitution on Revelation, which called biblical study 'the soul of sacred theology.'[18] The second volume appeared in 1977 with the title *Justice and love, Grace and liberation* (1977) in Dutch. In English, it was alternatively known as *Christ: The Experience of Jesus as Lord* in North

---

[17]Edward Schillebeeckx, *Jezus, het verhaal van een levende*, Baarn 1974; trans. Edward Schillebeeckx, *Jesus*, Collected Works of Edward Schillebeeckx vol. 6 (London: Bloomsbury T&T Clark, 2014).
[18]*Dei verbum* (18 November 1965) 24, http://www.vatican.va/archive/hist_councils/ii_vatican_council/documents/vat-ii_const_19651118_dei-verbum_en.html.

America, and *Christ: The Christian Experience in the Modern World* in the United Kingdom.[19] This second volume, often referred to simply as *Christ*, is widely seen as one of Schillebeeckx's most important works. In it he moves away from exegesis, which is still a significant part of the volume, and into a political theology of grace and liberation. Its core issues are grace, salvation coming from God, and the mystery of human suffering in history. The two books are together often counted as two of the most important Christological works of the twentieth century, and certainly of post-Vatican II theology.

Prior to Vatican II, Schillebeeckx's work for the Dutch bishops had drawn scrutiny from Rome with the result that he was not able to be an official expert, a *peritus*, at the council. In some ways, this gave him more freedom to be in touch with a larger audience, but it was a clear act of exclusion. In 1968, it became public that an official investigation had been opened against Schillebeeckx, although it is likely that the roots of it went back much further. This first case was resolved the next year, but after the publication of *Jesus: An Experiment in Christology* in 1974, new questions arose. In 1976, the Sacred Congregation for the Doctrine of the Faith sent him a number of questions regarding his Christology.[20] The questions were largely methodological, and they concerned his use of the historical critical method, the humanity of Jesus, and prophetic and messianic characteristics of Jesus, the virginal conception of Christ, and the Trinity. Schillebeeckx answered the questionnaire and then after the *Christ* volume had been published, composed a short defence of his work known as *Interim Report*.[21] This short book, which summarises and clarifies his positions on method and Christology, became a classic in its own right and a frequent tool for teachers of theology thanks to its straightforward and compact nature. The affair with Rome culminated with a colloquium in December of 1979. In reality, the meeting had the character of a trial wherein he attempted once again to clarify his methodology to an unsympathetic audience. Finally, in 1980, Schillebeeckx was asked to publish his answers to the Congregation along with a declaration of his obedience.[22] Evidently the Congregation still had questions about the relation between revelation and experience in his theology. The case drew international media attention and a great deal of public sympathy for Schillebeeckx because of the perception of how he was treated by Rome, even more so because the case against

---

[19]Edward Schillebeeckx, *Gerechtigheid en liefde: Genade en bevrijding*, Baarn 1977; trans. Edward Schillebeeckx, *Christ*, Collected Works of Edward Schillebeeckx vol. 7 (London: Bloomsbury T&T Clark, 2014).
[20]Ted Mark Schoof, ed., *The Schillebeeckx Case: Official Exchange of Letters and Documents in the Investigation of Fr. Edward Schillebeeckx, O.P. by the Sacred Congregation for the Doctrine of the Faith, 1976-1980*, trans. Matthew J. O'Connell (New York: Paulist Press, 1984); Leo Kenis and Lieven Boeve, 'The Schillebeeckx Case: Three Acts and an Open Ending', in *T&T Clark Handbook of Edward Schillebeeckx*, ed. Stephan van Erp and Daniel Minch (London: T&T Clark, 2020), 208–20. Also see the special issue of *Tijdschrift voor theologie*: 'De zaak Schillebeeckx: reflecties en reacties', *Tijdschrift voor theologie* 20 (1981).
[21]Edward Schillebeeckx, *Tussentijds verhaal over twee Jezusboeken*, Bloemendaal 1978; Edward Schillebeeckx, *Interim Report on the Books Jesus & Christ*, Collected Works of Edward Schillebeeckx vol. 8 (London: Bloomsbury T&T Clark, 2014).
[22]The letter containing the final judgment of the Congregation is included in *The Schillebeeckx Case*, 141–4.

Hans Küng was happening at the same time, albeit with a very different outcome. This would not be the last of Schillebeeckx's difficulties with the Congregation for the Doctrine of the Faith.

In 1984, Schillebeeckx received a letter dated from 13 June of that year that demanded he renounce views on ministry that he had published in the late 1970s.[23] His book, titled *Ministry* in English, was a response to the extraordinary situation in the Netherlands and a prophetic prediction of the current situation in western nations regarding the chronically low numbers of priestly vocations. The letter mandated that he agree to the doctrine set out by a letter from the Congregation to the bishops concerning ministers of the eucharist, *Sacerdotium ministeriale* which was dated 6 August 1983.[24] Schillebeeckx's responded by telling Joseph Ratzinger, the prefect of the Congregation since 1982, during an informal meeting in Rome that he would address the concerns in a new book, which was published in 1985 as *The Church with a Human Face* (*Pleidooi voor mensen in de kerk*).[25] Despite this, Ratzinger issued a notification dated 15 September 1986, claiming that Schillebeeckx persisted in holding to an conception of priestly ministry that was out of step with the doctrine of the church.[26] An explicit condemnation of Schillebeeckx, however, was never issued and the matter eventually faded away, but not without longstanding effects for the freedom of theologians.

As all of this was happening, Schillebeeckx did not stand still. In 1982, he had retired from his position as professor in Nijmegen.[27] In 1983 he delivered his farewell lecture, wherein he unfolds a vision for a theology that is able to move critically between tradition and situation. The mutually critical interrelation between tradition and situation outlined in this essay by Schillebeeckx attempted to open up both the horizons of the past and present as sites of continuing interpretation; neither is closed off or entirely determined, and neither can be absolutised as an supra-historical objective position from which we can read history or salvation history. Further, '[u]nderstanding the past presupposes interpretation of the present', while that same interpretation is conditioned by the history of meaning that comes to us through tradition.[28] The gospel itself is trans-cultural precisely because it is not directly bound to any one culture, but it can only be definitively encountered in

---

[23] Edward Schillebeeckx, *Basis en ambt: Ambt in dienst van nieuwe gemeentevorming*, Bloemendaal 1979.
[24] The dating is important because the Congregation essentially condemns writings based on a law that was not in force at the time of their publication. This violates canon 10 of the Pio-Benedictine *Code of Canon Law* (CIC/1917) in force in 1979 and canon 9 of the revised *Code* (CIC/1983) which came into force in November 1983.
[25] Edward Schillebeeckx, *The Church with a Human Face*, Collected Works of Edward Schillebeeckx vol. 9 (London: Bloomsbury T&T Clark, 2014).
[26] Congregation for the Doctrine of the Faith, *Notification on the book Pleidooi voor mensen in de kerk. Christelijke identiteit en ambten in de kerk (Nelissen, Baarn 1985), by Professor Edward Schillebeeckx, O.P.* (15 September 1985), http://www.vatican.va/roman_curia/congregations/cfaith/documents/rc_con_cfaith_doc_19860915_libro-schillebeeckx_en.html.
[27] His farewell lecture has been published as Edward Schillebeeckx, 'Theological Interpretation of Faith in 1983', *Essays*, Collected Works of Edward Schillebeeckx vol. 11 (London: Bloomsbury T&T Clark, 2014), 51–68.
[28] Ibid., 60.

concrete cultural forms.[29] The transformative and liberating characteristics of the Christian tradition are made evident not through a reproducible set of propositions or identity between past and present horizons of meaning, but rather in the *'proportional equality'* between the contemporary religious interpretation and the contemporary socio-historical context that preserves the Christian message.[30] This is a difficult task, and it requires a great deal of critical reflection on the actual socio-historical context, and especially the historically determined ideological elements embedded in social structures that often masquerade as eternal truths. This *critical* element enables the gospel to be liberative for people who experience it as salvation coming from God, whether in ancient Palestine, in the Netherlands in 1983, or in the twenty-first century.

In 1982, the year of his retirement, Schillebeeckx was awarded the prestigious Erasmus Prize, recognising significant contributions to culture, the arts, the humanities, and society, both in Europe and beyond. In receiving this award, he joined the ranks of important artists, scholars, politicians, and public figures, including Marc Chagall, Romano Guardini, Martin Buber, Claude Lévi-Strauss, Simon Wiesenthal, Mary Robinson, Jürgen Habermas and many others. The Erasmus Prize was a significant acknowledgement of Schillebeeckx's impact on the world outside of the Catholic Church. His publications were bestsellers in several languages, reaching far beyond scholarly or even Catholic circles. He delivered the Abraham Kuyper Lectures in Amsterdam in 1986, responding to particular questions about Christianity and politics that were current at the time. The resulting book, *Jesus in Our Western Culture: Mysticism, Ethics and Politics*, became part of the preparation for his final *Jesus*-volume.[31]

In 1989, *Church: The Human Story of God*, the long anticipated third volume of his *Jesus* trilogy appeared in Dutch and was translated into other languages.[32] Here Schillebeeckx deviated from his original plan, and although the book does deal with the church and ecclesiology, this part of the book follows a lengthy reworking and clarification of his hermeneutics, theology of revelation, and theological anthropology. Working more firmly in a pluralistic situation, Schillebeeckx also confronts the role of Christology for a context in which there are many religions and world-views. This is perhaps his most approachable and comprehensive book while also being one of his most forward-looking works. Many sections in the book have produced the source material for theologies of ministry, revelation, interreligious dialogue, inculturation, and mysticism. *Church* is a popular source for students and it continues to be popular in teaching to this day. It is the true capstone to Schillebeeckx's academic career, but it is not his final work and it is not the point at which he ceased to innovate.

---

[29]Ibid., 57.
[30]Ibid., 63.
[31]Edward Schillebeeckx, *Jesus in Our Western Culture: Mysticism, Ethics and Politics*, trans. John Bowden (London: SCM Press, 1987).
[32]Edward Schillebeeckx, *Mensen als verhaal van God*, Baarn 1989; trans. Edward Schillebeeckx, *Church*, Collected Works of Edward Schillebeeckx vol. 10 (London: Bloomsbury T&T Clark, 2014).

Schillebeeckx's final major work is what he called his *Theological Testament* (*Theologisch testament*), with the seemingly paradoxical subtitle, roughly translated, 'a record that is not yet in the past' (*Notarieel nog niet verleden*).[33] The book is something of a patchwork, including a short autobiography in the first part, followed by several short essays on dogma, creation and grace, eschatology, and the doctrine of God. In the end, Schillebeeckx's theology was focused in dogmatics – the core truths of the Christian. He drew the fields of fundamental and dogmatic theology closer together, however, because he recognised the need to rethink the foundations of Christian faith before explicating the content of faith. His groundbreaking work on hermeneutics, exegesis, and political theology was still part and parcel of his attempts to express the nature of the relationship between God and humanity. In particular, he saw that hermeneutics and politics were linked in the expression of a contemporary understanding of faith. We believe that this intuition was correct, and even prescient for our own time. theological task. It is, in fact, perhaps truer for the early twenty first century than it was in the late twentieth century.

In an article published in *Tijdschrift voor theologie* in 2000, Schillebeeckx returned to his original interest in the sacraments, but he did so by building on new insights on ritual studies and sacramentality.[34] This became one of his final published works, and it marks both continuity and an innovative rupture for his theology. The article was announced as part of his preparations for a new book on the sacraments. In the last decade of his life, he spent a great deal of time on notes for the book, but he was not able to complete it.

After a long illness, Edward Schillebeeckx died on 23 December 2009 at the age of ninety-six. His passing was not unnoticed by the international press, and he eulogised in newspapers, academic journals, and in Catholic publications. Long after the end of his academic and publishing career, and in a drastically different social and religious context, his work continues to be read and received by new generations of scholars. Many scholars, ministers, and lay people marked his passing by acknowledging his influence and importance for their lives and work. At the time of his death, Schillebeeckx was not alone. His long-time friend Hadewych (Dory) Snijdewind O.P. was there, having cared for him during his illness. She recorded his last words: 'Dory, God is calling me.'[35] At 5:15pm, Edward Schillebeeckx answered God's call, returning to his creator after a life of faithful service to the church and to the Lord.

---

[33]The second half of *Theologisch testament* (pp. 69–137) has been translated as Edward Schillebeeckx, 'Theological Quests', *Essays*, Collected Works of Edward Schillebeeckx vol. 11 (London: Bloomsbury T&T Clark, 2014), 111–61. For the events during Schillebeeckx's final years, see Ted Schoof, 'Edward Schillebeeckx: de laatste twintig jaar', in *Trouw aan Gods toekomst: de blijvende betekenis van Edward Schillebeeckx*, ed. Stephan van Erp (Amsterdam: Boom, 2010), 144–52.

[34]Edward Schillebeeckx, 'Naar een herontdekking van de christelijke sacramenten: Ritualisering van religieuze momenten in het alledaagse leven', *Tijdschrift voor theologie* 40 (2000): 164–87; trans. Edward Schillebeeckx, 'Towards a Rediscovery of the Christian Sacraments', *Essays*, Collected Works of Edward Schillebeeckx vol. 11 (London: Bloomsbury T&T Clark, 2014), 183–210.

[35]Edward Schillebeeckx, *Verhalen van een levende: theologische preken van Edward Schillebeeckx*, ed. Hadewych Snijdewind (Nijmegen: Valkhof Pers, 2015), 439.

The structure and content of the *Reader*

We have structured this *Reader* in four main parts encompassing what we consider to be fundamental organising principles of Schillebeeckx's thought and his body of work. These four parts, *Sources*, *The Second Vatican Council and its Aftermath*, *Theological Themes*, and *Theology of Culture*, reflect mixed categories with both thematic and chronological continuity. They are not attempts to simply begin with Schillebeeckx's earliest writings and then move to his later work, although *Sources* necessarily contains early work while part four indeed includes significant sections from his final *Jesus*-volume. Each section and the individual chapters that comprise them show internal development and, we believe, an overarching consistency that cuts across time and the topic of consideration. This is therefore a mixed approach, but it leans heavily on emphasising themes over biographical developments or chronological movement.

Part One, *Sources*, encompasses Schillebeeckx's use of and adaptation to foundational principles for his own theology. In part, these are the sources of his own life. The chapters presented here encompass his use of Thomism, metaphysics, and phenomenology, *Nouvelle Théologie*, and Dominican Spirituality. Interestingly, each of these chapters is intimately related to the others. The work of St. Thomas Aquinas was the ocean in which theologians of Schillebeeckx's era swam, and the neo-Thomism that he learned at Le Saulchoir from his Dominican mentors Chenu and Congar was integral to the *ressourcement* theology that came to be called *nouvelle théologie*. At first this was named 'new theology' in a pejorative sense, but quickly it became the fertile ground for the reform of the church and theology that occurred at Vatican II. As a return to the sources it was deeply connected to the theology of Aquinas. Metaphysics was and remains an important topic of discussion for Catholic theology, and is also intimately related to the scholastic and neo-scholastic metaphysical synthesis that came into crisis in the twentieth century. Schillebeeckx's adoption of new philosophical methods, in particular existential phenomenology and hermeneutics, came to define his response to this crisis and how he sought to rethink the relation between church and world. Dominican spirituality likewise has much to do with Thomism and *nouvelle théologie*, in the sense that Thomas is a source of inspiration for Dominican life and many of Schillebeeckx's confreres in the Order were also Dominicans who lived their vocation as he did. We would be remiss in overlooking the inheritance of St. Dominic and the Order of Friars Preachers in his life and the evolution of his thought. Therefore, we present texts that make this relationship clear. Stephan van Erp (KU Leuven/ACU Melbourne) gives an insightful introduction to Part One, addressing four sources in Schillebeeckx's early work: Thomism, metaphysics and phenomenology, ressourcement theology, and Dominican spirituality.

Part Two begins with the council itself, including Schillebeeckx's writings during the course of the historic gathering of the church, as well as some of his reflections on the aftermath and meaning of the council. With some hindsight, we can now identify that Vatican II and what came immediately after it is a major turning point for Schillebeeckx's use of theological method. It is not that the council produced a massive change in direction for Schillebeeckx, but it accelerated the pace of change and brought him into contact with a new international audience beyond the Low Countries and France. His post-conciliar writings are especially revealing and we have found it interesting to juxtapose his reflections immediately after the event and those that were composed many years later. Among the most significant methodological developments, already underway in his writings on the council, is the integration of existential hermeneutics as a tool for theological reflection and especially for formulating a contemporary understanding of Christian faith. This was augmented in the late 1960s with neo-Marxist Critical Theory drawn from Max Horkheimer, Theodor Adorno, and Jürgen Habermas. This body of work gave Schillebeeckx the tools to more critically engage with critiques of tradition and the discontinuities that are indeed present in history, but it also allowed him to develop the category of 'negative contrast experience', which is one of his most lasting contributions to systematic theology. Part Two therefore includes chapters on the Second Vatican Council, hermeneutics, church and world, and the historical critical method. In his introduction, Daniel Minch (Ruhr University Bochum) moves through the history and context of Schillebeeckx's participation in the council, his adoption of critical hermeneutics and later use of the historical critical method for the first volumes of his groundbreaking Christology in the 1970s. Included in this section are both pre- and post-conciliar texts on the nature and constitution of the church in the modern world, the latter of which reflect Schillebeeckx's later understanding of what happened at Vatican II and how the council fell short of what was perhaps needed for a more thorough theological renewal.

Part Three, *Theological Themes*, collects Schillebeeckx's positions on the core issues of Christian faith, both fundamental and dogmatic. Although Schillebeeckx held the chair of Dogmatics and the History of Christianity at the Catholic University of Nijmegen, it would be reductive to simply say he was a dogmatic theologian. Certainly, he began his career as an expert on the sacraments and Aquinas, and his courses from his teaching prior to Vatican II reflect very traditional themes and approaches. However, his writings touched nearly every area of theology, from biblical studies and historical critical methodologies, ecclesiology, to practical theology and ministry. Most of all, we know him as a fundamental theologian who grappled with issues of theological anthropology and epistemology, but the more classical areas of Catholic theology did not go unneglected in both his pre- and post-conciliar work. In fact, his final published academic article was a reflection on the sacraments in light of ritual studies, and Schillebeeckx even planned to write a new book on the subject prior to his death. This section is the longest, comprising eleven chapters. The topics covered are: theology of God, creation, sacramental theology, theological anthropology, Christology, grace, the resurrection of Jesus, Mariology, eschatology, the magisterium, and ministry. Julia Feder (Creighton University) has provided an introduction for this section which revolves around three key themes: salvation, the person of Jesus, and the church. All of these are core elements of Schillebeeckx's theology and they are foundation of each chapter in Part Three.

Part Four, *Theology of Culture*, reflects, in part, the contemporary concerns of scholars who continue to turn to Schillebeeckx as a resource for engagement of faith with culture while also Schillebeeckx's own attempts to formulate a 'theology of culture'. Schillebeeckx's student, the influential Dutch theologian Erik Borgman, made this a key part of his theological biography of Schillebeeckx, *Edward*

Schillebeeckx: A Theologian in His History (English 2003; Dutch 1999). In the rapidly secularising post-Second World War context of Northern Europe, a theology that could critically engage with the changing culture was seen by Schillebeeckx as a necessity. The entire Catholic cultural milieu was on the move, and theology could not afford to fall behind. In addition to the chapters on culture and secularisation, issues still relevant to our time but with different points of emphasis, we have included texts on Political and Liberation Theology and Pluralism. The latter two topics are of increased relevance for the contemporary moment, given the emergence of Catholicism after Vatican II as a global church which must necessarily be in dialogue with other religions and world views while also maintaining the liberative core of the gospel. In the contemporary age marked by seemingly endless conflicts, climate change, and a resurgent authoritarianism, politics and liberation may well prove to be the necessary pillars for a truly dynamic form of fundamental theology. Elizabeth M. Pyne (Mercyhurst University) gives a short analysis of the complexities of the term 'culture' and how it plays a foundational role in each of the chapters of Part IV. She clarifies the relation between each of the chapters, since they build on one another in Schillebeeckx's progression of thought: theology of culture was concerned with secularisation, and later the focus became political and theological liberation. However, liberation had to occur against an increasingly pluralised background thanks to the evolution of Western culture and the increasingly globalised world of the late-twentieth century.

Suggestions for further reading

Ultimately, there is no substitute for reading Edward Schillebeeckx's original work, which is now much more accessible thanks to the publication of the *Collected Works of Edward Schillebeeckx*.[36] Even so, the sheer volume of literature that he wrote during his life and career is often quite daunting, and indeed the *Collected Works* currently totals eleven volumes of between roughly 125 and 900 pages each. This combined with the length and complexity of his most well-known books, *Jesus: An Experiment in Christology* and *Christ: The Christian Experience in the Modern World*, make it

---

[36]Edward Schillebeeckx, *The Collected Works of Edward Schillebeeckx*, ed. Ted Mark Schoof and Carl Sterkens, with Erik Borgman and Robert J. Schreiter (London: Bloomsbury, 2014). The volumes are: I. *Christ the Sacrament of the Encounter with God*, The Collected Works of Edward Schillebeeckx vol. 1, trans. Paul Barrett and Lawrence Bright; II. *Revelation and Theology*, The Collected Works of Edward Schillebeeckx vol. 2, trans. N. D. Smith; III. *God the Future of Man*, The Collected Works of Edward Schillebeeckx vol. 3, trans. N. D. Smith; IV. *World and Church*. The Collected Works vol. 4, trans. N. D. Smith; V. *The Understanding of Faith*, The Collected Works of Edward Schillebeeckx vol. 5, trans. N. D. Smith; VI. *Jesus: An Experiment in Christology*, The Collected Works of Edward Schillebeeckx vol. 6, trans. Hubert Hoskins and Marcelle Manley; VII. *Christ: The Christian Experience in the Modern World*, The Collected Works of Edward Schillebeeckx vol. 7, trans. John Bowden; VIII. *Interim Report on the Books Jesus and* Christ, The Collected Works of Edward Schillebeeckx vol. 8, trans. John Bowden; IX. *The Church with a Human Face*, The Collected Works of Edward Schillebeeckx vol 9, trans. John Bowden; X. *Church. The Human Story of God*, The Collected Works of Edward Schillebeeckx vol. 10, trans. John Bowden; XI. *Essays. Ongoing Theological Quests*, The Collected Works of Edward Schillebeeckx vol. 11, trans. Marcelle Manley, Edward Fitzgerald and Peter Tomlinson.

difficult for students and scholars alike to know where to begin. With that said, there are several excellent collected volumes and monographs that serve as introductions to his work as well as a voluminous body of more specialised secondary literature in the form of scholarly books and articles. The field of Schillebeeckx studies is a few generations old, but a few authors have acted as the stewards of Schillebeeckx's legacy and their works can generally be seen as sure points of reference for readers looking for guidance.

The first suggestions for further reading are the well-worn and authoritative reference points provided by Schreiter, Hilkert, and Kennedy. *The Praxis of the Reign of God* continues to be one of the most accessible and reliable introductions to Schillebeeckx's thought on different topics. Philip Kennedy's *Schillebeeckx* presents more of the development of Schillebeeckx's thought and gives some more biographical detail. His *Deus Humanissimus* is a scholarly work that is really suited to researchers due to its density and length, and, as it is out of print, it is increasingly hard to find even in reference libraries. Erik Borgman's theological biography, *Edward Schillebeeckx: A Theologian in His History* is an engaging and meticulous telling of Schillebeeckx's life and theological development from 1914–65.[37] Envisioned as 'Part One' of two, Borgman's biography leaves off just at the end of Vatican II, leaving a great deal of the story yet to be told.[38] It is important to note that all of the works mentioned above come from the first generation of Schillebeeckx scholarship, edited or authored by theologians who studied with him and knew him personally. However, a renewed attempt at a foundational introduction to Schillebeeckx's work is now available in the form of the *T&T Clark Handbook of Edward Schillebeeckx*, edited by Stephan van Erp and Daniel Minch, the editors of this volume. The twenty-eight chapters of the *Handbook* span a full range of topics, from historical-biographical studies to in-depth analyses of his theology in different periods or on different theological topics. The *Handbook* includes an international group of authors from all three generations of Schillebeeckx scholars and so gives a unique and updated perspective on the significance and continuing reception of his theology.

A second category of volumes include collected volumes published after Schillebeeckx's death, most of which are associated with international conferences dedicated to his theology. The volume *Edward Schillebeeckx and Contemporary Theology*, edited by Lieven Boeve, Frederiek Depoortere, and Stephan van Erp, is a forward-looking collection of essays that attempt to gauge the ongoing reception of Schillebeeckx's work and apply it in distinct areas.[39] This volume features a large cross-section of scholars from the first and second generations of Schillebeeckx

---

[37]Borgman, *Edward Schillebeeckx*.

[38]Part Two of the biography, written by Stephan van Erp and Brian Heffernan, is expected to be published in 2023. There is a short biography in Dutch and English available: Stephan van Erp and Maarten van den Bos, *Een gelukkige theoloog: Honderd jaar Edward Schillebeeckx/A Happy Theologian: A Hundred Years of Edward Schillebeeckx* (Nijmegen: Valkhof Pers, 2014). There is a recent biography available in German: Ulrich Ruh, *Edward Schillebeeckx: Leben und Denken* (Freiburg: Herder, 2019).

[39]A related volume appeared in Dutch as a special edition of *Tijdschrift voor theologie* dedicated to Schillebeeckx in 2010. It has some overlap with *Edward Schillebeeckx and Contemporary Theology*: Stephan van Erp, ed., *Trouw aan Gods toekomst: de blijvende betekenis van Edward Schillebeeckx* (Amsterdam: Boom, 2010).

scholars and those inspired by him in areas including philosophical theology, hermeneutics, political theology, interreligious dialogue, and theologies of suffering. In cooperation with the Marie-Dominique Chenu Institute in Berlin, the bilingual volume *Edward Schillebeeckx: Impulse für Theologien im 21. Jahrhundert/Impetus Towards Theologies in the 21st Century* gives both some interesting insights into Schillebeeckx's work and more contemporary appraisals of how it has been received, particularly in Europe.[40] The majority of the contributions are in German, but several, including chapters from Borgman, Schreiter, and van Erp offer English speakers valuable insights. In 2014 a conference was held in the Netherlands in honour of Schillebeeckx's 100th birthday which gave us two edited volumes, dedicated respectively to the junior and senior scholars who attended and participated. The senior volume, *Grace, Governance and Globalisation*, edited by Stephan van Erp, Lieven Boeve, and Martin Poulsom, is a focused study by scholars on four major areas pioneered by Schillebeeckx: theological hermeneutics, Christology, eschatology, and ecclesiology.[41] It features a diverse group of leading scholars in contemporary theology. The second volume, *Salvation in the World: The Crossroads of Public Theology*, edited by Stephan van Erp, Christopher Cimorelli, and Christiane Alpers, presents fifteen chapters from the newer generation of scholars from different backgrounds.[42] These contributions are a bit more focused on Schillebeeckx's work, but they range from in depth appreciations of his use of metaphysics to the possibilities of his work for theologies of sexual trauma and victimisation. These two books comprise the first volumes in the *T&T Clark Studies in Edward Schillebeeckx* series, which has become an important repository for new studies in this area.

The third category of literature on Schillebeeckx include monographs on various specific aspects of his work. These are often still quite fundamental in nature, but they do not seek to be as comprehensive as the works in the first category. These can be subdivided into dedicated studies of one area of theology such as hermeneutics, creation theology, or theology of suffering; comparative works that place Schillebeeckx in dialogue with other authors; and monographs that either situate Schillebeeckx or fundamental aspects of his theology in a new context or seek to apply his work.

In the first group, we must mention Kathleen McManus' *Unbroken Communion: The Place and Meaning of Suffering in the Theology of Edward Schillebeeckx*, Daniel Speed Thompson's *The Language of Dissent: Edward Schillebeeckx on the Crisis of Authority in the Catholic Church*, Jennifer Cooper's *Humanity in the Mystery of God: The Theological Anthropology of Edward Schillebeeckx*, and Kathleen Dolphin's *Praxis-Oriented Theology and Spirituality in the Sermons of Edward*

---

[40]Thomas Eggensperger, Ulrich Engel and Angel F. Méndez Montoya, eds., *Edward Schillebeeckx: Impulse Für Theologien Im 21. Jahrhundert/ Impetus Towards Theologies in the 21st Century* (Ostfildern: Grünewald, 2012).

[41]Stephan van Erp, Lieven Boeve and Martin G. Poulsom, eds., *Grace, Governance, and Globalization*, T&T Clark Studies in Edward Schillebeeckx (London: Bloomsbury T&T Clark, 2017).

[42]Stephan van Erp, Christopher Cimorelli and Christiane Alpers, eds., *Salvation in the World: The Crossroads of Public Theology*, T&T Clark Studies in Edward Schillebeeckx (London: Bloomsbury T&T Clark, 2017).

Schillebeeckx.⁴³ The subtitles of each of these make their purpose relatively clear, and they are important resources for scholars, especially in the places where these authors bring out aspects of Schillebeeckx's theology that are implicit in his work. We should also mention that many unpublished dissertations fall under this category, especially on hermeneutics and Christology, but we have restricted ourselves to published works that can be easily accessed.

Comparative works that place Schillebeeckx in conversation with another author include Marguerite Thabit Abdul-Masih's interesting study, *Hans Frei and Edward Schillebeeckx: A Conversation on Method and Christology*, Steven M. Rodenborn's *Hope in Action: Subversive Eschatology in the Theology of Edward Schillebeeckx and Johann Baptist Metz*, *The Dialectics of Creation: Creation and the Creator in Edward Schillebeeckx and David Burrell* by Martin M. Poulsom, and *Metaphysics of Mystery: Revisiting the Question of Universality through Rahner and Schillebeeckx* by Marijn de Jong.⁴⁴ As with the previous category, there are a number of unpublished dissertations that are also essentially comparative studies which can be found in university databases.

The third grouping of major book-length works on Schillebeeckx are those monographs that take a more constructive approach, examining the continuing relevance of Schillebeeckx's work in a changed context. Antonio D. Sison's unique book, *Screening Schillebeeckx: Theology and Third Cinema in Dialogue* certainly deserves to be placed in this category.⁴⁵ In the fields of intercultural and interreligious dialogue, Edmund Kee-Fook Chia's *Edward Schillebeeckx and Interreligious Dialogue: Perspectives from Asian Theology* and Kevin M. Considine's *Salvation for the Sinned-Against: Han and Schillebeeckx in Intercultural Dialogue* are the most important examples.⁴⁶ The *T&T Clark Studies in Edward Schillebeeckx* series has provided two volumes that locate and apply Schillebeeckx's work within contemporary social and economic trends. The first of these, by Christiane Alpers, is called *A Politics of Grace: Hope for Redemption in a Post-Christendom Context*.⁴⁷

---

⁴³Kathleen Anne McManus, *Unbroken Communion: The Place and Meaning of Suffering in the Theology of Edward Schillebeeckx* (Lanham, MD: Rowman & Littlefield Publishers, 2003); Daniel Speed Thompson, *The Language of Dissent: Edward Schillebeeckx on the Crisis of Authority in the Catholic Church* (Notre Dame, IN: University of Notre Dame Press, 2003); Jennifer Cooper, *Humanity in the Mystery of God: The Theological Anthropology of Edward Schillebeeckx* (London: T&T Clark, 2011); Kathleen Dolphin, *Praxis-Oriented Theology and Spirituality in the Sermons of Edward Schillebeeckx* (Lewiston, NY: The Edwin Mellen Press, 2014).
⁴⁴Marguerite Thabit Abdul-Masih, *Hans Frei and Edward Schillebeeckx: A Conversation on Method and Christology*, Editions SR 26 (Waterloo, ON: Wilfrid Laurier University Press, 2001); Steven M. Rodenborn, *Hope in Action: Subversive Eschatology in the Theology of Edward Schillebeeckx and Johann Baptist Metz* (Minneapolis, MN: Fortress Press, 2014); Marijn De Jong, *Metaphysics of Mystery: Revisiting the Question of Universality through Rahner and Schillebeeckx*, T&T Clark Studies in Edward Schillebeeckx (London: T&T Clark, 2020).
⁴⁵Antonio D. Sison, *Screening Schillebeeckx: Theology and Third Cinema in Dialogue* (New York: Palgrave Macmillan, 2014).
⁴⁶Edmund Kee-Fook Chia, *Edward Schillebeeckx and Interreligious Dialogue: Perspectives from Asian Theology* (Eugene, OR: Pickwick Publications, 2012); Kevin P. Considine, *Salvation for the Sinned-against: Han and Schillebeeckx in Intercultural Dialogue* (Eugene, OR: Pickwick Publications, 2015).
⁴⁷Christiane Alpers, *A Politics of Grace: Hope for Redemption in a Post-Christendom Context*, T&T Clark Studies in Edward Schillebeeckx (London: T&T Clark, 2018).

The second, *Eschatological Hermeneutics: The Theological Core of Experience and Our Hope for Salvation*, by Daniel Minch, is both a study of Schillebeeckx's hermeneutics and an application of his theology within the contemporary economic framework.[48]

Next to the many monographs and edited volumes on Schillebeeckx, there are theological works that have been heavily influenced by him, such as Lieven Boeve's *God Interrupts History: Theology in a Time of Upheaval*, and those that place him in his historical context. He is present in most major works on Vatican II, or is at least briefly mentioned, and there are two collections of primary documents related to his issues with the Congregation for the Doctrine of the Faith in the 1970s, one of which has been reprinted in 2011.[49] In addition, there are numerous articles in scholarly journals or edited volumes (not including contributions to the volumes enumerated above) that delve deeply into various aspects of Schillebeeckx's theology and theological legacy.

---

[48]Daniel Minch, *Eschatological Hermeneutics: The Theological Core of Experience and Our Hope for Salvation*, T&T Clark Studies in Edward Schillebeeckx (New York: T&T Clark, 2018).
[49]T. M. Schoof, ed., *The Schillebeeckx Case: Official Exchange of Letters and Documents in the Investigation of Fr. Edward Schillebeeckx, O.P. by the Sacred Congregation for the Doctrine of the Faith, 1976-1980*, trans. Matthew J. O'Connell (Eugene, OR: Wipf & Stock, 2011); Peter Hebblethwaite, *The New Inquisition?: The Case of Edward Schillebeeckx and Hans Küng* (San Francisco: Harper & Row, 1980).

Timeline of Edward Schillebeeckx's Life and Works

1914
12 November – Edward Cornelis Florentius Alfonsus Schillebeeckx is born in Antwerp, Belgium.

1934
20 September – Joins the Belgian province of the Dominican Order in Ghent and receives the religious name of Henricus.
Studies philosophy under Dominicus De Petter OP.

1939
Starts theological formation in Leuven.

1941
Ordained a priest.

1945
Summer – Starts doctoral studies at Le Saulchoir in Étiolles, near Paris, and at the Sorbonne.

1947
Starts to teach dogmatic theology at the Dominican house of studies in Leuven.
Appointed master of students for the Dutch speaking Dominican theology students.

1952
Awarded doctorate for *De sacramentele heilseconomie. Theologische bezinning op S. Thomas' sacramentenleer in het licht van de traditie en van de hedendaagse sacramentsproblematiek* (The Sacramental Economy of Salvation: Theological Reflection on the Sacramental Theology of St. Thomas in the Light of Tradition and of Contemporary Sacramental Issues).

1957
Appointed to the Chair of Dogmatics and the History of Christianity at the Catholic University of Nijmegen, the Netherlands.
Publication of *De Christusontmoeting als sacrament van de godsontmoeting* (*Christ the Sacrament of the Encounter with God*).

1958
Moves to Nijmegen to take up professorship.

1959
9 May – Inaugural lecture in Nijmegen: 'In Search of the Living God'.

1961
Founds new journal for theology: *Tijdschrift voor theologie*, which runs until 2020.
January – The Dutch bishops publish their pastoral letter on the coming council, written primarily by Schillebeeckx.

1962
11 October – Opening of the first session of the Second Vatican Council.

1965
Co-founds the journal *Concilium*.

1966
Publication of *De nieuwe katechismus* (*A New Catechism: Catholic Faith for Adults*).
27 November – Opening of the Dutch Pastoral Council in Noordwijkerhout (continues until 1970).

1967
November – December – First lecture tour in North America.

1968–1969
First Schillebeeckx case and investigation by the Congregation for the Doctrine of the Faith.

1974
Publication of *Jezus het verhaal van een levende* (*Jesus: An Experiment in Christology*).

1976
October – Start of the second Schillebeeckx case. Schillebeeckx receives questions from the Congregation for the Doctrine of the Faith concerning his book *Jesus*.

1977
April – Submits answers to the Congregation for the Doctrine of the Faith.
Publication of *Gerechtigheid en liefde. Genade en bevrijding* (*Christ: The Christian Experience in the Modern World*).

1978
6 July – Receives an *appreciation* from Rome acknowledging his answers.
Publication of *Tussentijds verhaal over twee Jezusboeken* (*Interim Report on the Books Jesus and Christ*).

1979

8 May – Delivers *laudatio* at the conferring of honorary doctorate upon Gustavo Gutiérrez by the Catholic University of Nijmegen.

13–15 December – Attends meeting with the Congregation for the Doctrine of the Faith in Rome.

1980

Publication of *Kerkelijk ambt* (*Ministry: Leadership in the Community of Jesus Christ*).

25 November – Receives letter from the Congregation for the Doctrine of the Faith requesting clarifications on his Christology.

1981

26 June – *Note annexe* published in *L'Osservatore Romano*, concluding the second Schillebeeckx case.

1982

Awarded the Erasmus Prize.

1 September – Retires as professor in Nijmegen.

27 October – Receives a letter from Cardinal Joseph Ratzinger, new Prefect of the Congregation for the Doctrine of Faith; start of third Schillebeeckx case.

20 November 1982 – Replies to Ratzinger and the Congregation for the doctrine of Faith.

1983

11 February – Valedictory lecture, *Theologisch geloofsverstaan anno 1983* (*Theological Interpretation of Faith in 1983*).

1984

13 June – Receives word from the Congregation for the Doctrine of Faith that his previously published views on ministry conflict with the doctrine of the church as expressed in *Sacerdotium ministeriale*.

24 July – Brief 'informal conversation' with Ratzinger in Rome.

1985

Publication of *Pleidooi voor mensen in de Kerk* (*Church with a Human Face*), in which he clarifies his position on ministry.

11 January – *L'Osservatore Romano* publishes the 13 June 1984 letter.

22 January – Holds press conference denying that he changed his views.

8 May – First '8 May' protest for reform in the church in response to upcoming papal visit to the Netherlands; leads to establishment of Acht Meibeweging (8 May Movement).

1986
15 September – Official *Notification* published by the Congregation for the Doctrine of the Faith about Schillebeeckx's theology of ministry.

1989
Publication of *Mensen als verhaal van God* (*Church: The Human Story of God*).

1994
Publication of 'Theological Testament' (*Theologisch testament. Notarieel nog niet verleden*).

2000
Publication of final article, on the sacraments, in *Tijdschrift voor theologie*, 'Naar een herontdekking van de christelijke sacramenten: Ritualisering van religieuze momenten in het alledaagse leven' ('Towards a Rediscovery of the Christian Sacraments: Ritualising Religious Elements in Daily Life').

2008
3–6 December – International Symposium *Theology for the 21st Century: The Enduring Relevance of Edward Schillebeeckx for Contemporary* Theology, organised in Leuven.

2009
23 December – Edward Schillebeeckx dies at age 96.

31 December – Buried in Nijmegen.

PART ONE

Sources

Introduction

Stephan van Erp

The theology of Edward Schillebeeckx is inspired by many different intellectual sources. This is partly due to the period in which he published his work – between the 1930s and the early 2000s. During this period, church and theology underwent major changes, with the Second Vatican Council halfway through as an important turning point. For Schillebeeckx, the council could also be seen as the moment when the style and content of his work started to change. This was not necessarily due to the council, because according to Schillebeeckx himself, the council only brought the church up to date with the pre-conciliar cultural and theological developments. From the second half of the 1960s onwards, his work was influenced by the hermeneutics of Hans-Georg Gadamer, and the critical theory of Jürgen Habermas and Theodor Adorno. In the first volume of his trilogy, *Jesus*, Schillebeeckx famously claimed that his own work had undergone a radical shift, from Thomist metaphysics with its focus on truth and unity, to critical hermeneutics and political theology with a key role for the history of human suffering. Some interpreters of Schillebeeckx's theology follow him in this and confirm that there is a noticeable break in the development of his work. Others see more continuity in his thought, and argue that the Thomist principles of his early work are still visible in his later writings. The question of continuity or discontinuity in Schillebeeckx's theology is an important part of the current debate on the development of modern Catholic theology. This is why it is necessary to have a closer look at Schillebeeckx's intellectual sources in his early period.

Thomism

Schillebeeckx's Dominican formation came with a solid philosophical education. Even though he did not believe that faith could be proven by philosophy, he was of the opinion that philosophy offers a major contribution to making faith and theology comprehensible. He studied philosophy when Thomism was the official philosophy of the Roman Catholic Church, which had been the case since Leo XIII had recommended it in *Aeterni patris* (1879). Schillebeeckx was underwhelmed by his neo-Thomist teachers, and was more interested in reading Thomas Aquinas in his own historical context. During the time he studied at Le Saulchoir, the Dominican house of studies, the historical method was taught, especially by Marie-Dominique Chenu. Chenu's Thomism was critical of the Platonist and speculative elements in Aquinas' thought, and his own interpretation of Thomas was deeply rooted in Aristotelianism. Chenu interpreted the Angelic Doctor's work as an example of how medieval philosophers responded to the challenges of their own situation. Aquinas himself, Chenu argued, should be seen as a teacher and a commentator, who was inspired by the gospel. Rather than intending to write a definitive handbook for theology, he responded intellectually to the questions of his own age. Contemporary theology, according to Chenu, should do likewise and react to the challenges of the present, rather than merely repeat the dogmas of the past. This was an explicit critique of the neoscholasticism and the neo-Thomist manuals of the nineteenth and twentieth centuries. In his theological program *Une école de théologie,* Chenu wrote: 'The stuff of revelation is not intended to reinforce the Thomistic system, rather the Thomistic system is at the service of the faith – which transcends it – in an intelligible manner.'

Schillebeeckx wrote his doctoral dissertation, *De sacramentele heilseconomie: Theologische bezinning op S. Thomas' sacramentenleer in het licht van de traditie en van de hedendaagse sacramentsproblematiek,* in a Thomistic style. In it, he explores the role of the sacraments in Aquinas's *Summa theologiae*. He argues that the history of salvation through Christ becomes present in the sacraments and that they form an extension of God's incarnation and an integral part of the movement of human beings toward God. Therefore, Christology and sacramental theology, according to him, are two closely connected theological fields of study. As part of his earlier work, he wrote several articles on the epistemology and metaphysics of Aquinas, which are collected in *Revelation and Theology*. In these articles, Schillebeeckx's interest in negative theology becomes clear when he writes about the non-conceptual dimension of our knowledge of God. In a sharp analysis of Aquinas's concept of analogy, he concludes that although we transfer names onto God based on a real relationship with God, we cannot attribute any concept to God. The analogy between God and the human language about God can only be found in the names for God, and not in the concepts. Therefore, although knowing and naming God is limited, these activities nevertheless participate in God in a creaturely way.

Metaphysics and phenomenology

In the 1930s and 1940s, phenomenology and existentialism were gaining influence, also at the houses of formation of the religious orders and congregations. Phenomenology was considered difficult to reconcile with neo-Thomism and this problem alone made it attractive for atheist or secular philosophers. Catholics made an effort to study these new developments in philosophy by generating a critical mass that brought phenomenology to the attention of well-known thinkers in Catholic education. In turn, philosophers interested in phenomenology could not ignore this Catholic reception. Phenomenology emerged at a time when neo-Thomists were searching for an apologetic strategy for their debates with secular philosophers. Phenomenology fascinated them because there were examples of people who converted to Catholicism because of it, while it also caused others turn away from Catholicism. The fascination and frustration with these conversions in two directions led to an intense Catholic study of phenomenology, which is still present in continental philosophy today, and has had an impact on the following characteristics of Catholic philosophy: a critique of Cartesian dualism, a rejection of naturalism and other totalising forms of rationality, an interest in limit concepts and in the porous boundaries between the transcendent or the so-called '(wholly) Other' on the one hand, and the immanent or the existential on the other hand.

These developments have had a significant influence on Catholic theology in the second half of the twentieth century, and Schillebeeckx's theology is no exception. The most significant metaphysical influence on his thought, however, is quite unique, since it was the work of his philosophy professor and fellow Dominican in Leuven, Dominicus De Petter. De Petter founded the well-known journal for philosophy *Tijdschrift voor Filosofie*. In the first issue of that journal, De Petter published an article on the concept of 'implicit intuition'. 'Implicit intuition', as De Petter defines it, is the direct intellectual grasping of the concrete. 'Intuition' should not be understood as a sudden, accidental insight, which at best can be trained as if it is a certain type of sensibility or something to which one can open one's mind. Nor should it be understood as a preparatory phase, from which all knowledge develops. Implicit intuition is therefore not a pre-reflexive given, which precedes active and conscious knowledge. It is performed by the intellect, De Petter claims, while, on the other hand, it enables the intellectual act to have a true grasp of reality. Implicit intuition is not an epistemic characteristic that is present in the intellect. It is a condition for knowledge that, rather than serving as a capstone for a naive realist philosophy, needs to be realised by the act of knowing itself. This metaphysics, a mixture of Thomist, Kantian and phenomenological philosophies, in which reality is both a condition for and a performance of human judgment, became foundational for Schillebeeckx's theology of revelation, and for his theological hermeneutics. According to him, we can only know of revelation and creation by means of interpretation, yet revelation and creation are at the same time the conditions for interpretation. His hermeneutics of experience was deeply influenced by the phenomenology of Maurice Merleau-Ponty, who pointed at the double edge of human experience, being both individual and universal. The hermeneutics in Schillebeeckx's later work builds on that phenomenological analysis, in which experience and interpretation are never reduced to either a merely universal or a merely particular perspective.

Ressourcement theology

While existentialist phenomenology emerged and had its impact on Catholic theology, the Jesuits and Dominicans in France and Belgium developed what came to be known as ressourcement theology, or *nouvelle théologie*. The latter was once a negative term, first used by the editors of the *Osservatore Romano* in 1942 and later becoming widely known through the title of a very critical article by the neo-Thomist Réginald Garrigou-Lagrange OP: 'La nouvelle theologie où va-t-elle?'. Famous *ressourcement* theologians studied at the Jesuit study house at Fourvière near Lyon, among whom were Henri de Lubac, Jean Daniélou and Henri Bouillard, and at that of the Dominicans in Belgium near the French border at Tournai. It was called Le Saulchoir, and was later relocated to France, near Paris, and was the place where Marie-Dominique Chenu and Yves Congar taught.

The development of modern Catholic theology in the interwar period is driven both by Maurice Blondel's reformulation of metaphysics and tradition, and by the Catholic responses to *laïcité* in France, which formed a first generation of ressourcement thinkers. The famous, second ressourcement generation of the 1930s was influenced by the shock of the First World War, which shaped their ideas about the cultural crisis, such as Henri de Lubac's opposition to atheistic humanism. The theology of that generation was not entirely original, but the combination of several characteristics was quite innovative: a theological renewal that had already begun in the work of John Henry Newman and Blondel in the nineteenth century, a historical use of patristic and medieval sources, and a social critique prompted by the cultural and political situation.

Schillebeeckx studied at Le Saulchoir in the 1940s, where he heard Congar lecture on the theology of Karl Barth. He also attended lectures at the Sorbonne in Paris, where he went to Chenu's lectures. It was a period when Schillebeeckx's Thomism, his metaphysics and his theology was being influenced by the ressourcement theologians. In an interview, published under the title *I Am a Happy Theologian*, he describes the significance of this period as follows:

> Under the guidance of Chenu I read St. Thomas from a historical perspective and not just literally, in the context of the philosophy of the time. At Le Saulchoir I learned to tackle problems from a historical perspective. In my courses, in succession, I went through the Old and New Testament, the teaching of the Fathers, of St. Thomas and the post-Tridentine era. I was convinced that faith and reflection on the faith should be in close contact with the tradition.

Dominican spirituality

Besides the philosophical and theological sources of Schillebeeckx's education, one should not underestimate the significance of the formation and spirituality of the Dominican Order, which have been equally influential for his thought. His religious name was 'Henricus', after the Rhineland mystic and Dominican Henry Suso. His main influences, Aquinas, De Petter, Congar and Chenu were all Dominicans. After his studies in Paris, he returned to Leuven, where he became Professor of Dogmatic Theology at the Dominican house of studies, and the master of the Dutch speaking students in formation. Throughout his life, he reflected on the nature and content of Dominican spirituality. Similar to his study of Thomas Aquinas, he approached it historically. Unlike the Benedictines or the Jesuits, the Dominicans did not have concrete texts from their founder that needed to be interpreted again by every new generation. So they were left with the spirit of Saint Dominic, a spirit that, according to Schillebeeckx, was characterised by God's grace, which invites all Dominicans to be open to God's promised future. This focus on God is qualified by Christ's humanity, which Schillebeeckx saw embodied in the Dominican brotherly life and in the apostolate, directed towards the salvation of souls. In his early work on Dominican spirituality, we can already see the theological themes – God's initiative, grace, the life of Christ, the salvation of humanity – that he would develop further in his later work.

Questions for discussion

1. According to Schillebeeckx, what is the balance between positive (cataphatic) and negative (apophatic) theology in the thought of Thomas Aquinas?
2. What is the relationship between experience and concept in theology? How do experiences and concepts relate to the truth?
3. Why does Schillebeeckx believe it is important to address the Bible and the Church Fathers in the development of theology that is relevant for people today?
4. What are the main characteristics of Dominican spirituality? How has this spirituality shaped Schillebeeckx's theology?

1

Thomas Aquinas and Thomism

Aquinas and positive theology[1]

It has frequently happened that Aquinas has been falsely interpreted because of his differently orientated terminology. Aquinas was a great theologian above all because of his positive theological output. It was astonishing for his period, especially as he was often unable easily to obtain certain positive works – such as, for example, the commentaries of a father of the church. I have already pointed out in the introduction to this article that it is characteristic of Aquinas that he seldom used the term *theology*, but usually employed the term *sacra doctrina*. And for him, *sacra doctrina* included very much more than pure speculative theology. Every scientific activity that was concerned with 'Holy Scripture' was, for Aquinas, genuine theology. I have no need to outline here the development of the medieval concept of *sacra doctrina*. This has already been dealt with in an excellent manner.[2] Holy Scripture was really the centre of all theological activity. But the method of dealing with it was always dependent on the new techniques of thought, as these came to be used in the *facultas artium* ('arts faculty'). As the growth of human awareness brought about a renewal of this method, there was at the same time a renewal of the theological method, until finally the Aristotelian technique of the *scientia conclusionum* came to be used, when the discursive function of theology was stressed in addition to all the other theological functions. When Aquinas asked the question, 'Utrum sacra doctrina sit scientia',[3] what this *quaestio* meant was whether theology, in addition to its many other functions, also possessed a discursive function. His affirmative answer meant that, in addition to the many other *scientific* activities of theology (here taken in the modern sense), theology also had a definite function in which it realised, in

---

[1] Selected from: Edward Schillebeeckx, 'What is Theology?', *Revelation and Theology*, trans. N. D. Smith, Collected Works of Edward Schillebeeckx vol. 2 (London: Bloomsbury T&T Clark, 2014), 82–4 [I 124–6].
[2] See especially the article referred to above by J. de Ghellinck, and the great works of M. D. Chenu: *La théologie comme science au XIIIe siècle*, Paris, 1957³; *Introduction à l'étude de saint Thomas d'Aquin*, Ottawa and Paris, 1950; *La théologie au XIIe siècle*, Paris, 1957.
[3] 'Whether holy doctrine is a science' (*ST* [*Summa Theologiae*] I, q. 1, a. 1).

accordance with the medieval view, the Aristotelian concept of *scientia*. It was very far from Aquinas' mind to define the whole of theology in this answer. He did not see the drawing of conclusions as the most important function of theology (I shall discuss later what he meant by this); for him the most important function was quite simply the *intelligentia fidei*, the understanding of the faith:

> Reason led by the hand of faith develops to the point at which it more fully takes hold of the objects of faith and then in a certain measure understands them.[4]

The master in theology was, then, a *Magister in Sacra Pagina*, a biblical theologian par excellence. He was also a patristic theologian, because Scripture was studied in the light of the fathers' study of the Bible. The church's pronouncements were also studied in this perspective, and *consuetudines Ecclesiae* ('usages of the church') were looked for – these had a normative value for Aquinas. A good example of this broad view of theology can be found in articles 8 to 10 of the *Summa Theologiae* I, q. 1,[5] in which Aquinas examines the procedures of theological study. It is clear from these articles that the science of theology included – for Aquinas – in addition to the speculative aspect, everything that we should call positive theology. It was only after Aquinas that the division occurred between positive and speculative theology. A relic of this pernicious division still persists in the organisation of programmes of theological study, in which separate courses exist in speculative theology and in the history of dogma. The grave danger inherent in this system is that speculative theology tends to become sterile, while positive theology tends to become pure history.

Thomas' Christological interpretation of sacramental *ex opere operato* causality[6]

As far as we have been able to discover, St. Thomas uses the term *ex opere operato* [from the work performed] twenty times in a sacramental context in the *Scriptum super Sententiis*, but in the *Summa* not at all. This is an indication that St. Thomas, in whose day *ex opere operato* was already a traditional technical term, found that it was not really needed in order to present a genuine view of Catholic sacramental doctrine, for the truth which this terminology was intended to bring out was presented satisfactorily, and even in finer detail, in his Christological appreciation of the sacraments. The passages in which St. Thomas has used this term can be classified under four headings according to the precise sense in which it is employed.

---

[4] "Ratio manducta per fidem excrescit in hoc ut credibilia plenius comprehendat at tunc ipsa ipsa quodammodo intelligat' (*I Sent.* [*First Book of the Commentary on the Sentences*] Prol., q. 1, a. 3, sol. 3).
[5] See also *I Sent.* Prol., q. 1, a. 5, in which these three articles still form one single article.
[6] Selected from: Edward Schillebeeckx, *Christ the Sacrament of the Encounter with God*, trans. Paul Barrett, Lawrence Bright, Collected Works of Edward Schillebeeckx vol. 1 (London: Bloomsbury T&T Clark, 2014), 58–60 [100–3].

First we have those passages in which it has the old meaning given it by the earlier masters. The sacrament itself is the *opus operatum*; the use of the sacrament is the *opus operans*.[7] In this, the old sense, the term is used especially in connection with different aspects of Christ's death on the Cross; indefensible murder and a meritorious death of reconciliation.[8]

In other passages St. Thomas contrasts *ex opera operato* with 'faith alone' on the part of the recipient. The 'sacraments of nature' are not efficacious *ex opere operato*, but by faith alone; the Christian sacraments, on the other hand, have their effect *ex opera operato*.[9] Elsewhere he makes a similar but already more profound distinction between the part played by personal faith (and hope) with regard to the sacrament, and with regard to the bestowal of grace – the *res sacramenti*. The personal faith of the recipient has considerable effect upon the measure of what the sacrament brings about, but it has no effect on the sacrament itself; in other words, the validity of a sacrament does not depend upon the faith of the recipient, 'because the sacraments of the New Law are efficacious by the very fact that the rite is performed'.[10] The particularly Thomist use of the term is very often found to convey this meaning; the sacrament as an 'outward sign' – the objective embodiment in a sign of God's will to bestow grace, or as an objective source of power – is in fact realised quite independently of personal faith. 'In baptism, as far as the work done [*opus operatum*] is concerned, the merit of the person baptised has no effect.'[11] In other words, sacramentality, or the *veritas signi*, is quite independent of the subjective religious purposefulness of the one for and upon whom the sacrament is being performed. In this context St. Thomas usually contrasts the *opus operatum* with the *opus operans* as well, so that we already see that this terminology does not concern or convey a relationship between the gift of grace (the *res sacramenti*) and the personal act of the minister (the *opus operands*), and this is of capital importance for a correct appreciation of sacramental efficacy *ex opere operato*.[12]

In passages of the third group, *ex opere operato* indicates that the efficacy of sacramental grace does not depend on the moral and religious dispositions of the minister.[13] The contrasting of the *opus operantis* and the *opus operatum* also sometimes refers to this independence of the sacrament with regard to the minister's dispositions.[14]

---

[7] *IV Sent.*, d. I, q. 1, a. 5, sol. 1 (p. 41) and sol. 2 (p. 42): St. Thomas says: 'dicitur a quibusdam...' (Note: the pagination refers to the critical edition of E. Moos, Paris (1947), vol. 4, for texts from *IV Sent.*, d. 1-d. 22. Other loci in *IV Sent.* are from the *Opera Omnia*, Parma (1858), vol. 7.
[8] *III Sent.*, d. 20, a. 5, sol. 2, ad 3. (Moos, vol. 3, p. 627).
[9] *IV Sent.*, d. 2, q. 1, a. 4, sol. 4, ad 2 (p. 92).
[10] *IV Sent.*, d. 2, q. 2, a. 4 (p. 101).
[11] *IV Sent.*, d. 4, q. 2, a. 2, qla. 2, ob. 1 (p. 171); cf. also d. 45, q. 2, a. 3, sol. I, ad 3 (Parma ed., vol. 7, p. 1126), and compare d. 45, q. 2, a. 2, sol. 2, and 4 (p. 1124).
[12] *IV Sent.*, d. 1, q. 2, a. 4, sol. 2 (p. 58); d. 4, q. 3, a. 3, qla. 3, ob. 1 (p. 191) and ad 1 (p. 194); d. 5, q. 2, a. 2. qla. 3, ob. 1 (p. 216) in connection with sol. 1 (pp. 218-19).
[13] *IV Sent.*, d. 13, q. I, a. I, sol. 5 (p. 550); d. 5, q. 2, qla. 3, ob. 2 (p. 216); d. 13, q. I, a. 3, qla. 3, ob. 3 (p. 560).
[14] *IV Sent.*, d. 5, q. 1, a. 2 (p. 204); d. 6, q. 1, a. 2, sol. 2, ad 2 (p. 238). In this latter text *ex opere operato* does not appear, but the *bonitas ex opere operante* is distinguished from the *bonitas* of the sacrament of baptism itself.

A final category of texts shows us the fundamental idea underlying the term *ex opere operate*: the idea upon which die two previous senses (B and C) are based. In these passages it is precisely the Christological character of the sacrament as the 'work of God' and the 'work of Christ' that is emphasised. 'Baptism justifies *ex opere operato*: this is not people's work, but God's.'[15] Elsewhere the same thing is said in a different way: 'Baptism does not have its effect because of the merits of the person being baptised, but because of the merits of Christ';[16] '...baptism with water [is efficacious] 'because of the passion of Christ'.[17] Thus in these last two texts the notion *ex opere operato* (the term itself is not used, but the meaning is clearly there) refers to efficacy in virtue of the passion of Christ.

From all this we have a clear idea of the many shades of meaning St. Thomas gives to the term *ex opere operato*[18] – a term which was later to be taken over and used in official definitions by the Church.[19] In no place at all does it imply a contrast between the bestowal of grace (the *res sacramenti*) and the subjective religious intention of the person; the contrast is found only between the constitution of the sacrament or the outward sacramental sign and the subjective state of the minister or the recipient. It is not the *opus operantis* of the minister, nor of the recipient, that constitutes the sacramental sign; the *opus operantis* is quite external to sacramentalism in this sense (i.e., as the actual administration and reception of a sacrament). However, the *opus operantis* of the recipient does have a part to play in sacramentalism considered as the actual reception of grace bestowed sacramentally. With regard to the sacramental sign, all that is necessary on the part of the minister is to do what the Church does; all that is necessary on the part of the recipient is to receive this. Hence *ex opera operato* efficacy means that the sacrament, as an act which is done in virtue of a character, is objectively and ministerially an act of Christ, an objective celebration in mystery of the historical, redemptive mystery of Christ, in such a way that it brings about the unmerited application of the Redemption, a work of pure mercy, to *this* person. In this sense *ex opere operato* is a reference to the universal causality of Christ's grace, to the unicity of Christ's mediation, to the pure gratuity of redemption; it says, in other words, *gratis estis salvati* by sacramental means; sacraments effect what they signify.

In consequence it is not possible to agree with the purely juridical interpretation of a correct administration of the sacraments which many moralists attach to the term *ex opere operato*, and in which they are altogether silent about its profound Christological sense. Prummer, for example, writes: 'The term "ex opere operato" is explained in two ways: (a) as the valid administration of the sacrament itself, provided there is no obstacle... (b) as the work of redemption done by Christ. This

---

[15]*IV Sent.*, d. 15, q. 1, a. 3, sol. 3, ad 2 (p. 656).
[16]*IV Sent.*, d. 6, q. 1, a. 3, sol. 2 (p. 242).
[17]*IV Sent.*, d. 4, q. 3, qla. 4, ob. 1 (p. 191).
[18]As far as I know, we have seen all the in stances in which the term is used in the Sentences. Apart from the Sentences I have found it used only once in a sacramental context by St. Thomas: in *Commentum in Johannem*, c. 6, lect. 6 *in fine*. The search, however, could not be exhaustive.
[19]Selected from: Edward Schillebeeckx, *Christ the Sacrament of the Encounter with God*, trans. Paul Barrett, Lawrence Bright, Collected Works of Edward Schillebeeckx vol. 1 (London: Bloomsbury T&T Clark, 2014), 62 [106–7].

latter explanation, proposed by few theologians [he cites Möhler and Hilgers], is not so correct [*minus est recta*].'[20] St. Thomas, on the contrary, unites both meanings in one fundamental notion, in which the central and essential factor is the meritorious and efficient activity of the historical mystery of Christ. A sacrament, the *opus operatum*, is valid when the ministerial act is an act of Christ (*opus Christi*); it is valid therefore when it is authentic sacramental representation of the acts of the mystery of Christ in and through his ecclesial community. The constitution of the sacramental symbolic act is not dependent on the disposition of the minister or recipient, as long as each has the required intention. Already in principle any tendency towards a magical or mechanical concept of *ex opera operato* efficacy is excluded. Loyal human care for correctness concerning the 'matter' and the 'form' is quite simply care authentically to extend Christ's work of redemption in and through the sacrament; contact with the saving mystery of Christ comes about only when the sacrament is really valid, only when the sacramental act is really a symbolic act of Christ himself through his Church. If 'bringing together matter and form correctly' gives grace efficiently, this happens in virtue of the fact that, through this correctly performed action, the ecclesial symbolic act really becomes an act of Christ through the minister and really is, therefore, the representation of his effective work of redemption. This beyond doubt is St. Thomas's view of sacramental efficacy *ex opere operate*. Since the time of the Council of Trent some theologians, as far as their systematic treatises are concerned, have separated their sacramental doctrine far too much from the mystery of Christ; the term *ex opere operato* thus degenerated into an emphasis of one element only of the scholastic, and especially Thomist, doctrine, and gave the impression of a purely materialist juridical approach to the sacraments. However, this is no more than an impression; it was not the deliberate intention of these writers, and certainly was never the intention of the Church, to approach the sacraments in this way.

Truth or relevance for the Christian life in scholastic theology[21]

There has been a tendency in recent years to go back more than in the past to Albert the Great and Bonaventure, in the belief that they represent the substance of the patristic theology, and thus the substance of authentically Christian theology, more excellently than Aquinas, who, it is felt, deviated from the theology of the fathers in

---

[20] D. Prummer, *Manuale Theologiae Moralis*, 12th ed., Freiburg and Barcelona (1955), vol. 3, p. 29. As his reason, the writer gives: 'Etenim Chri stus Redemptor per suam passionem est quidem causa meritoria gratiae sacramenta lis... [blithe omission of the *causa instrumentaliter efficiens* of which St. Thomas speaks], sed in sacramentis no vae legis gratia causatur effective (licet instrumenttaliter) per ipsum signum sensible, i.e. per debitam applicationem formae ad materiam'. This is the headless corpse of sacramentalism if St. Thomas's explanation is the right one.

[21] Selected from: Edward Schillebeeckx, 'Scholasticism and Theology', *Revelation and Theology*, trans. N. D. Smith, Collected Works of Edward Schillebeeckx vol. 2 (London: Bloomsbury T&T Clark, 2014), 174 [I 266–7].

favour of a pure and abstract Aristotelian approach. I shall attempt here to clarify only two aspects that are characteristic of the pre-Thomist theology of the so-called *Summa Alexandrina*, of Albert the Great and of Bonaventure, in order to ascertain to what extent these two characteristics are present in Aquinas as well. It should then be possible to establish whether Aquinas really broke with the theology of the fathers or whether he synthesised all these elements in a higher unity.

These two aspects, which I propose to consider briefly here, are the saving aspect and the affective aspect. Both are given considerable prominence in the present renewal of theology, and it is possible that we may learn something from these older theologians here since, to judge from the prologues to the works of Alexander, Albert, and Bonaventure, it is precisely these two aspects that define theology. For them, theology was not a science – and here I mean a science in the Aristotelian sense – but a 'wisdom'.[22] Wisdom, too, should not be understood here in the Aristotelian sense, for this would include science,[23] but in the affective sense. It was, for these theologians, *sapientia, sapida scientia*, 'a tasteful science' – an 'affective science' as Alexander called it, or a *scientia secundum pietatem* ('science in accordance with religion') in the words of Albert.

Aquinas on theology[24]

Thus we come to the attractive definition of theology according to the *Summa Alexandrina*:

> Theology is the science of understanding the divine substance by means of Christ in his work of reparation.[25]

Theology, in other words, knows God through the mystery of Christ. Because everything in theology is seen, according to the *Summa Alexandrina*, from the aspect of salvation, and so not in an abstract and metaphysical light, but in the concrete light of the history of salvation, therefore Christ is also directly involved in the very definition of theology.

This brief outline of the theological thought of Alexander, Albert, and Bonaventure may serve to sum up the theological situation at the time of Aquinas. It is certainly possible to see in this situation the continuation of a very old patristic tradition. Recent works on the theology of Augustine, for example, confirm this. They

---

[22]In the Aristotelian sense, science is the insight into the connection between principles and the conclusions that are necessarily illuminated by them.

[23]In the Aristotelian sense, all that wisdom adds to the concept of science is that the conclusions are being related to the deepest and ultimate principles.

[24]Selected from: Edward Schillebeeckx, 'Scholasticism and Theology', *Revelation and Theology*, trans. N. D. Smith, Collected Works of Edward Schillebeeckx vol. 2 (London: Bloomsbury T&T Clark, 2014), 175–9 [I 268–75].

[25]*Summa Alexandrina* I, q. 1 (ed. Quaracchi, 6): 'theologia est scientia de substantia divina cognoscenda per Christum in opere reparationis'. Or: 'scientia de Deo cognoscendo per Christum redemptorem' ('the science of understanding God by means of Christ the redeemer').

emphasise the central importance of the saving aspect, the affective character, in the theological thought of this doctor of the church as well, and the fact that his theology consequently also has a patristic and apostolic and thus, ultimately, a 'kerygmatic' orientation. What we have here is, in other words, an authentic Christian inheritance which was treated by Alexander, Albert, and Bonaventure only in a more systematic and consciously reflective way, because at this time a consciously devised methodology had been achieved in theology, a reflection about the theological method as already practised in living experience.

But, as I have already indicated, the charge of breaking with this patristic tradition has been made against Aquinas. He is said to have spurned the warm traditional example of 'Christian wisdom' and to have modelled his theology on the cold reason of an Aristotelian science. From the historical point of view, it cannot of course be denied that Aquinas did appeal to the traditional, patristic *sacra doctrina*. This accounts for the fact that he was able to call theology a science in an analogous but real sense, at least formally as far as its reasoning function is concerned. He certainly did not consequently call it a science in respect of everything that it is and does.[26] But this is not our main concern here – what does concern us is the fact that it is not true that the authentically patristic elements were simply banished by Aquinas' vision. I propose to show that he, on the contrary, did not leave out any single essential element. By this I do not mean that he took these elements over eclectically, as, for example, Albert did, but that he accorded a place to them either in theology (the saving aspect) or outside theology, but in immediate association with it (the affective aspect).

According to Aquinas, theology is a science of faith, a reflection about faith, that is demanded by the structure of faith itself. We may say that the life of faith includes not only an element of firm resolution, of repose or settled assent or resolute acceptance of faith, but also an element of reflection which is in motion. The fact that this reflection about faith is not at rest does not in any way invalidate the resolution of our consent to faith. It is rather the result both of the fact that the datum of faith is not self-evident and of the special nature of the human intellect, which is inclined towards quidditative insight. This natural attitude of the intellect moreover reaches an apogee here, as the 'object' is one that at the same time offers itself as the highest value in life – God himself, 'the first truth and salvation'. That is why, together with the tension of the 'natural desire to see God', an unpleasant resentment on the part of the intellect is also revealed in this aspect of reflection – our mind feels itself to have been 'made captive' when confronted with the 'obscurity' of the datum of faith.[27] Consequently, if it is the purpose of theology to be a reflection about faith, then the structure of faith itself must also be relevant for the structure of theology.

If, then, we consider the material object of our catholic faith, that is, what we believe, we come to the conclusion that, according to Aquinas, saving truths

---

[26] Theology could be called a science (in the modern sense) in respect of all its functions – that is, a knowledge that is critically justified, methodically conducted, and systematically planned.

[27] Aquinas, *Verit.* (*De Veritate*) q. 14, a. 1: 'Intellectus credentis dicitur captivatus, quia tenetur principiis alienis et non propriis' ('the intellect of the believer is called "captive" in that it is bound by principles foreign to it rather than its own').

constitute this object. We have been raised to the level of the supernatural order, that is, to God as the 'content of our salvation'. In addition, this activity is also raised to this level, so that we may attain this transcendent destiny in a vital way, that is, through activity that is strictly human, but which has been made supernatural. Since the dynamic force of humanity has an intellectual character, knowledge of this destiny and of the means of attaining it must also already be provided in advance. Consequently, revelation is a necessary element in the supernatural order of salvation. It is the good news of our elevation to a supernatural destiny – God reveals himself as humanity's supernatural destiny. God reveals himself as God, because he gives himself to us precisely as the content of our salvation. He makes himself known to us as our salvation. 'Notum fecit Dominus salutare suum.' We may therefore say that, according to Aquinas, the real object of our faith is the God of our salvation or, expressed in a different way, 'Deus qui sub ratione Deitatis est salus nostra: Veritas prima salutaris' – that is, God as God-for-us.

Aquinas therefore placed the God of Salvation, *Deus salutaris*, at the very beginning of the *Summa*, in the first article. As known by us, the God of salvation is, it is true, 'plurified' in various conceptual truths.[28] These truths do not, however, thereby lose their saving character – 'actus credentis non terminatur ad enuntiabile sed ad rem' ('the act of the believer terminates, not at the object of the profession, but at the reality'),[29] that is, it is not the conceptual ideas that are the aspect of repose in the act of faith, but the reality of salvation. As a result, Aquinas was able to speak in this first article of the *Summa* of saving truths, 'truths that are necessary to salvation'. He is therefore really writing about God who is God-for-us precisely in his being God. Moreover, if we maintain that this saving aspect should not be included in the object of faith, the question can be raised as to exactly what the criterion should be for the extension of the material object of faith. If our answer is formal revelation, then we are simply shifting the difficulty. What, then, is the criterion by which God reveals certain supernatural truths and not others? For, as Aquinas said explicitly in his commentary on the *Sentences* of Peter Lombard (the writings of Aquinas which are of particular interest for his teaching on faith):

> Not everything that, in God's wise knowledge, transcends our human intellect, is an object of faith.[30]

Aquinas consequently put the criterion for the extension of the material object of faith in the *beatitudo humana*, salvation of humanity – for him, it was the relevance for human life, the saving significance of a truth that decided whether God revealed this truth or not:

---

[28] *Verit.*, q. 14, a. 12: 'plurificatur per diversa enuntiabilia' ('he is "plurified" in the various objects of the profession of faith').
[29] *ST* II-II, q. 1, a. 2, ad 2.
[30] *Sent.*, d. 24, a. 3, sol. 1, ad 3.

Not everything that, in God's wise knowledge, transcends our human intellect, is an object of faith, but only what is necessary to our knowledge of our supernatural destiny and of everything that directs us in a supernatural manner towards it.

All truths of faith are therefore saving truths by the very fact that they are truths of faith. To maintain, as some 'kerygmatic theologians' do, that prominence ought only to be given, in faith and therefore in preaching and theology, to those truths that are saving truths and are relevant to human life, and that other truths may be neglected, would be to misjudge the real nature of every truth of faith formally as a truth of faith and thus to betray a too pragmatic, utilitarian conception of value and relevance for life. In Aquinas' view, it was God himself who, by the very fact that he revealed the truths of faith *propter nostram salutem*, for our salvation, determined their relevance. The totality of faith as such has a saving value and, within this totality, so does each separate truth of faith. On pain of falling into error (*ST* II-II, q. 5, a. 3), consent to faith refers to this totality as such, to the entire complex of salvation. One of theology's many tasks must therefore be to attempt to make this saving value and this relevance for life – in the Christian sense of the word – of every separate truth of faith within the totality of faith intelligible. This was clearly expressed by the First Vatican Council:

> When reason illuminated by faith searches with diligence, piety, and prudence, it attains – through the gift of God – a certain understanding of the mysteries [of faith], and an abundantly fruitful understanding at that:... from the interconnection of these very mysteries with each other and with the final end and purpose of humanity.[31]

According to this council, one of the main functions of speculative theology was to discover the reference towards salvation and modestly to attempt to make it intelligible, as well as to investigate the mutual connections between the mysteries of faith. As I have said, theology is reflection about the data that we accept in divine faith – positive theology attempts to describe these data of faith, in the light of the church's teaching authority, according to their pure factuality, whereas speculative theology attempts to find their aspect of intelligibility. Theology formally considers the 'first truth' that brings salvation (and, as it is known by us, this therefore means the 'truths that are necessary to salvation'), not as believed in – this is assumed –, but as intelligible. This does not, however, mean that the inner reference of these truths of faith towards salvation is thereby set aside – because it is a reflection about the objective, present, and implicit content of faith, theology is at the same time a reflection about the reference towards salvation which is inseparable from the content of faith. Theology is therefore bound to throw light scientifically on the saving value of all the data of faith.

---

[31]DS 3016 (=DR 1796) [DH 3016]. For the Latin text see p. [84 (I 127)].

We practise theology in order to become more holy and to bring those who believe to holiness.[32] The aim of theology is practical and apostolic, too, and indeed essentially so – but only *extensione*, by 'repercussion'. It is here that Aquinas differs from Albert and Bonaventure. It is precisely our reflection about the dogmatic truths of salvation, about the *Deus salutaris*, that enables us to appreciate the relevance of the truths of faith for the Christian life. Action is enlightened and guided by this insight, and our practical, apostolic activity can only gain from it if we respect the distinctive nature of faith and theology, which is in principle speculative that is, disinterested and contemplative, and not utilitarian and pragmatic. That is why Aquinas stated in the first article of the *Summa* that knowledge, that is, knowledge of God as a value for human life, the knowledge of 'those truths that are necessary to salvation', must be presupposed if this relevance for life is really to be a norm for life.

It is therefore evident that Aquinas fully maintained the saving aspect of the truths of faith and their relevance for the Christian life – values which the whole Christian tradition had always stressed – but that he provided them, with the help of Aristotle, with a different basis.

Selected literature

- Aquinas and Positive Theology, Selected from: Edward Schillebeeckx, 'What is Theology?', *Revelation and Theology*, trans. N. D. Smith, Collected Works of Edward Schillebeeckx vol. 2 (London: Bloomsbury T&T Clark, 2014), 82–4 [I 124–6].
- St. Thomas' Christological Interpretation of Sacramental Ex-Opere-Operato Causality; Selected from: Edward Schillebeeckx, *Christ the Sacrament of the Encounter with God*, trans. Paul Barrett, Lawrence Bright, Collected Works of Edward Schillebeeckx vol. 1 (London: Bloomsbury T&T Clark, 2014), 58–63 [100–9], 58–60 [100–3], 62 [106–7].
- Truth or Relevance for the Christian Life in Scholastic Theology; Selected from: Edward Schillebeeckx, 'Scholasticism and Theology', *Revelation and Theology*, trans. N. D. Smith, Collected Works of Edward Schillebeeckx vol. 2 (London: Bloomsbury T&T Clark, 2014), 174 [I 266–7], 175–9 [I 268–75], 180–1 [I 276–7].

---

[32]Selected from: Edward Schillebeeckx, 'Scholasticism and Theology', *Revelation and Theology*, trans. N. D. Smith, Collected Works of Edward Schillebeeckx vol. 2 (London: Bloomsbury T&T Clark, 2014), 180–1 [I 276–7].

2

Metaphysics and Phenomenology

The concept of truth[1]

Our present thinking is characterised by a critical attitude towards the rationalism of previous centuries. Long before even the emergence of existentialism, thought which, in the Hellenistic climate of Western civilisation, was to a very great extent orientated towards the consideration of abstract and universal and unchangeable truths had changed course and was moving in a direction whose motto was *vers le concret*, back to the concrete, shifting reality. It was from this background of modern thought that both existentialism and phenomenology emerged; but from it also emerged a great variety of attempts on the part of neo-Thomist thinkers to reassess human thought as a faculty of truth whereby reality could be meaningfully encountered, according to the way in which this reality discloses itself to the activity of human thought which both extracts and gives meaning. Conceptual, rational thought is contrasted with lived experience, *l'expérience vécue*. Present-day thought is clearly reacting on the one hand against idealism, according to which human thought itself creatively produces its contents and therefore truth, and on the other hand against the 'representational realism' of scholasticism, which regards the content of our concepts as an exact reflection of reality without any reference to a human act which confers meaning. This reaction against these two trends of thought clearly moves in two directions. On the one hand, it tends in the direction of phenomenology, one of the basic affirmations of which is that the world is essentially a 'world-for-me'. In other words, reality has no independent, absolute meaning, but many different significations in relation to human beings, and these significations vary according to the standpoint from which they approaches or deals with reality. Indeed, according to many modern phenomenologists, the objective signification of a reality can be found only in the meaning that this reality has in relation to a person. On the other hand, there is also the trend of thought followed by certain Catholic philosophers (especially De Petter and Strasser) who claim that,

---

[1]Selected from: Edward Schillebeeckx, 'The Concept of "Truth"', *Revelation and Theology*, trans. N. D. Smith, Collected Works of Edward Schillebeeckx vol. 2 (London: Bloomsbury T&T Clark, 2014), 189–91 [II 5–9].

implicit in the relative meanings given by someone, there is an absolute meaning in reality. This meaning is, in their view, independent of human thought and acts, in its absolute value, as the norm for all meanings given by someone. This second movement attempts to gear what is true in phenomenological thought to what may be called the insights of the *philosophia perennis*, but this perennial philosophy is consequently placed in a perspective which is entirely different from that in which it was seen in scholastic thought.

The notion of truth has thus become much more 'supple' in modern thought – so supple, in fact, that it has in many cases moved in the direction of complete relativism. The modern insight that the essence of humanity is inseparable from his historicity has, of its very nature, resulted in a more flexible view of truth than the traditional one, according to which humanity is seen in terms of a human nature that has been permanently defined once and for all time and is incapable of being inwardly conditioned by concrete, changing circumstances. In the modern view, insofar as it accepts an absolute reality at all, reality (as truth) is seen as the never-wholly-to-be-deciphered background of all our human interpretations. The ontological basis, as the mysterious source of a still-hidden fullness of meaning, remains the same and does not change, but the human interpretation of this basis, and thus the human possession of truth, grows and evolves. This is, however, drawn in one definite direction by this implicit ontological significance, so that truth is always approached more and more concretely, even though it is never completely apprehended.

If we disregard the relativist views, according to which no absolute truth exists (a view which is, of course, implicitly atheistic), we are nonetheless forced, by experience itself, to affirm – against the background of the absolute truth that determines our thought as a norm – the imperfection and the evolving and relative nature of our possession of truth, and consequently the fact that our earlier insights are capable of inexhaustible amplification. It is the fundamental orientation to the absolute implicit in all our knowledge which gives continuity to our human and constantly changing consciousness. From a finite, limited, constantly changing, and historical standpoint, we have a view of absolute truth, although we never have this in our power. In this sense, we cannot say that truth changes. We cannot therefore say that what was true before is now untrue, for even our affirmation of truth does not change or become obsolete. The standpoints from which we approach truth, however, are changing continuously and our knowledge is thus always growing inwardly. The whole of our human knowledge is, in its orientation towards the absolute, also coloured by these standpoints. It is, however, at the same time apparent from the fact that we are aware of the existence of these perspectives from which we view absolute truth that we rise above relativism. We do not possess a *conscience survolante*, an awareness that is able to transcend all relative standpoints and thus survey objective reality. Yet this is still the view held in many scholastic circles with regard to truth. The consequence of this is that differences of view are frequently confused with the relativist tendencies that are in fact present in modern thought.

It is at the same time clear, from this 'perspectivism' of our knowledge (which is orientated towards absolute reality and also regulated by it), that insights into truth will never lead to complete unanimity. Our maintaining an open and receptive attitude in our affirmation of the truth towards what is true in the views of others is, anyway, a condition for the attainment of the highest possible degree of unanimity.

We have also achieved in recent years a more modulated insight into the multi-dimensional nature of the human world of truth.[2]

> Thus there is, for example, the truth of the everyday, practical world, the truth of modern positive science, the truth to which philosophy aspires, and finally the truth which we attain and love in religious faith.[3]

Thus the truth of the positive sciences is confined to the world of phenomena. These sciences are therefore concerned only with the verifiable aspects of reality. As a result, these sciences do not cover the whole of reality and therefore cannot claim to replace metaphysical and religious truths. But neither should someone who is convinced of his affirmations of metaphysical and religious truths simply play these off against the partial values of the positive sciences. The first attitude would lead to dogmatic positivism and scientism, and the second to a religious dogmatism that denies different levels of truth. In the problem of truth, we have therefore to take into account the multi-dimensional character of truth, which cannot be reduced to one single type of truth. This view too has not yet generally penetrated into every Catholic circle.

The relationship between experience and concept in modern Catholic theology[4]

As we have already seen, the representational conceptualism of scholasticism subsequent to Scotus, according to which conceptual contents were directly applicable both to worldly and to supramundane realities, led to an impasse in modern neoscholasticism. More fundamental attempts – more fundamental than, for example, the rather passing comments made by Bouillard on the affirmation of truth and its presentation already referred to – to solve the problem of the conceptual nature of our knowledge have been made in recent years. These have followed two different directions. On the one hand, there has been the direction taken by Blondel and made explicit in Thomist perspective by Maréchal (whose work resulted in a school, among whose members I would include, for example, Karl Rahner). On the other hand, there is the direction taken by De Petter (who has been followed in the theological field by the present writer).

The school of Maréchal: the dynamism of the spirit

Confronted with Kant's criticism of speculative knowledge, and under the influence, at the same time, of M. Blondel, who regarded all human knowledge as supported

---

[2] See A. Dondeyne, *Geloof en wereld*, Antwerp and Bilthoven, 1962, 147 ff.
[3] Dondeyne, 148.
[4] Selected from: Edward Schillebeeckx, 'The Concept of "Truth"', *Revelation and Theology*, trans. N. D. Smith, Collected Works of Edward Schillebeeckx vol. 2 (London: Bloomsbury T&T Clark, 2014), 196–200 [II 17–22].

by affective experience, J. Maréchal, S.J.,[5] seeing the impasse into which scholastic conceptualism had got itself (for which Modernism had been unable to find a satisfactory alternative) proceeded to deny that conceptual knowledge as such, in and of itself, could reach reality. We cannot, therefore, reach God with our human concepts, because their representational content is creaturely and hence is not applicable to God. If we say God is good, then the representational content of this goodness is inevitably a creaturely goodness. How, then, can we call God good? From what does this affirmation derive its validity, in spite of the creaturely – and thus relative – character of its conceptual content? If there is to be any truth in the affirmation 'God is good', an implicit confrontation must take place somewhere between creaturely goodness and the reality of God.

Maréchal provided a solution to this problem by basing the reality and validity of our knowledge of God not on these concepts in themselves, but on a non-intellectual, dynamic element – the dynamism of the human spirit towards the infinite. The conceptual contents are taken up in this dynamism of the spirit, and so this conceptual content is transcended and projected towards God. Our knowledge of God is, therefore, according to Maréchal, a projective act by means of which I reach out beyond the concept in the direction of God, thanks to the dynamic impulse of the spirit which animates the concept. Human beings are thus able to reach towards God via the conceptual content – towards God as the aim of the human capacity to know.[6]

What is unsatisfactory about Maréchal's solution is that it does not explain the distinctive meaning of every conceptual content; that the reality and validity of knowledge is based on an extra-intellectual element; and, finally, that while it does establish that human knowledge cannot remain stationary at anything finite, but must always be continuing to search and to explore other territories, it does not establish that human beings, in their knowledge, really attains a positive and infinitive end, God himself.

The school of De Petter: the 'non-conceptual' dimension of knowledge

The school of De Petter is in accord with that of Maréchal in affirming that concepts as such cannot reach reality or truth, and therefore that they can do so only as elements of a greater whole. In addition, this trend of thought also affirms that a non-conceptual aspect is the basis of the validity of our conceptual knowledge. Maréchal did not, however, situate this non-conceptual aspect formally in a real intellectual element, but in an extra-intellectual element – that is, in the dynamism of the human spirit. De Petter and his followers, on the other hand, speak of a

---

[5] *Le point de départ de la métaphysique*, Louvain and Paris, 1927², Cahier I, 207 ff. See also 'Le dynamisme intellectuel dans la connaissance objective', *Revue néo-scolastique de philosophie* (1927), 137–65; and *Mélanges J. Maréchal*, Brussels and Paris, 1950, pt. 1.

[6] See chapter 12 [of *Revelation and Theology*, 207–38 (II 157–206)]: 'The non-conceptual intellectual dimension in our knowledge of God according to Aquinas'.

non-conceptual dimension of knowledge itself, and thus of an 'objective dynamism' – that is, of an objective dynamic element in the contents themselves of our knowledge, which themselves refer to the infinite. According to De Petter, the concept is

> ... a limited expression of an awareness of reality that is in itself unexpressed, implicit, and pre-conceptual.[7]

This pre-conceptual awareness of reality is in itself not open to appropriate expression. Our concepts refer to this non-conceptual awareness essentially as to something that they aim to express, but to which they can only give inadequate and limited expression. It is therefore not an extra-intellectual dimension – the dynamism of the human spirit – that enables us to reach reality in our concepts, but a non-conceptual consciousness through which we become aware of the inadequacy of our concepts, and thus transcend our conceptual knowledge and approach reality, although in a manner that is no longer open to expression. According to this view, the concept, or the 'conceived', has the value of a definite *reference* to the reality, which is, however, not grasped or possessed by it. By virtue of the inexpressible and non-conceptual consciousness which is implied in our explicit or conceptual knowledge, or in which this conceptual knowledge is included, the concept indicates the objective direction in which reality is to be found, and – what is more – indicates a *definite* direction – the direction which is inwardly pointed out by the abstract conceptual content. Therefore, although concepts are insufficient and even do not reach reality in themselves – that is, seen in their exclusive abstract character[8] – they have a certainly inadequate but nonetheless real truth and validity as included in the non-conceptual consciousness, because they – and they alone – impart a direction and meaning to the transcending beyond the concepts to reality. Experience and conceptual thought thus together constitute our single knowledge of reality.

I have shown, in a historical study of Aquinas,[9] that he had already defended, although not in a fully elaborated manner, the proposition that we cannot apply our concepts as such to God, as though one and the same concept (goodness, for example) might analogously but equally apply both to the creature and to God, but that the conceptual content of goodness is only the perspective in which we must situate God's goodness, without knowing how this content really also applies to God. Our knowledge therefore only comes into contact with God in conscious unknowing (the wholly Other). We know that God is good, although the conceptual content of this goodness is only a creaturely goodness and the divine mode of this goodness therefore escapes us. The typical intellectual value of our conceptual knowledge of God is therefore situated in a projective act in which we reach out towards God via the conceptual contents. In this, we cannot grasp God conceptually, although we

---

[7] See D. De Petter, *Begrip en werkelijkheid: Aan de overzijde van het conceptualisme*, Hilversum, 1964, esp. 25–136 and 168–73.
[8] This is because what an abstract concept makes known is concretely, and therefore differently, realised in the concrete reality.
[9] See chapter 12 [of *Revelation and Theology*, 207–38 (II 157–206)]: 'The non-conceptual intellectual dimension in our knowledge of God according to Aquinas'.

do know that he is present in the objective and definite direction that is indicated by the contents of the concept.[10] In this way, the agnosticism that is inherent in the purely symbolic value of conceptualism according to Modernism (E. Le Roy) is overcome, and the older, Thomistic affirmation according to which the highest human knowledge is to be found in conscious unknowing (*theologia negativa*) is reasserted.

This applies even more to our supernatural knowledge of faith. If our concepts are, in the case of our natural knowledge of God, naturally open to the transcendent, then our natural concepts are, in the case of the concepts of faith, made open by positive revelation to the expression of supernatural truths. The God who revealed himself in human form has given a new dimension to human contents of knowledge – a new objective perspective which these contents do not in themselves have for our human intellect as such, but which they only derive from revelation and thus from the non-conceptual aspect of our act of faith. This natural intellectual content, which is included in the supernatural act of faith, directs our spirit by virtue of revelation (and thus by virtue of the non-conceptual element in the act of faith) objectively to God's intimate life, which is not attainable by purely human knowledge. Thus, the fatherhood and sonship of God, for example, are really an extension of the reality, father and son, of our human experience, but we cannot grasp conceptually the manner in which this fatherhood and sonship is realised in God. In this, our concepts of faith are not purely symbols that are interchangeable with other symbols (as the Modernists believed), nor are they a purely pragmatic knowledge in the sense that we must behave towards God as a son behaves towards his father. We do not in fact apply the purely conceptual representational content of *father* and *son* to God, but we can, by extending that and no other conceptual content (that is, father and son), really reach God. Consequently, God is in himself Father and Son, although in such a way that we cannot form any real conception of this divine fatherhood and sonship.[11] Thus mystery and objective intelligibility are intimately connected with each other.

This view provides us, in my opinion, with the true perspective within which we can affirm both the absolute character of the truth of faith and the high degree of relativity and thus of growth in our reflection about faith. And all this is contained within the one human consciousness – this is not to be reduced exclusively to conceptual knowledge.

The biblical view of the world: the cosmos[12]

We use the word 'cosmos', world, in a very different sense from the Bible. Since the Greek translation of the Hebrew Bible, the general Greek meaning of *kosmos*,

---

[10]See chapter 5 [of *Revelation and Theology*, 65–118 (I 95–181)]: 'What is Theology?'.
[11]See chapter 5 [of *Revelation and Theology*], 'What Is Theology?', the section on the basis of the possibility of a speculative theology.
[12]Selected from: Edward Schillebeeckx, 'Religion and the World: Renewing the Face of the Earth', *World and Church*, trans. N. D. Smith, Collected Works of Edward Schillebeeckx vol. 4 (London: Bloomsbury T&T Clark, 2014), 4–7 [5–9].

the universe ('heaven and earth' is what appears in the original Hebrew), the good creator of which is believed to be God,[13] has entered the Old and New Testaments, in which *kosmos* is also used in the neutral sense of the earth or the human world as such, without any religious qualification at all (as in John 13.1). In addition to these meanings, however, John and Paul especially used *kosmos* in a characteristically biblical sense which was essentially religious and, at the same time, fundamentally non-Greek and non-Roman. Their vision was neither cosmological nor metaphysical, but historical, i.e. in accordance with the history of salvation. In this context, then, *kosmos*, the world, means fallen humanity, not, however, as a static entity, like scholastic 'fallen nature', but as a historical, dynamic reality. *Kosmos* in John and Paul is the world of human beings under God's 'anger', in other words, humanity in its deepest foundation, the religious significance of which human beings cannot change themselves. The reality of human existence as life in the world was here given the religious meaning of an existence opposed to salvation, the antipode of the kingdom of God. In John and Paul, everything belonging to this *kosmos*, its spirit and mentality,[14] its wisdom[15] and even its grief,[16] in a word, the whole of the *kosmos* itself,[17] is diametrically opposed to everything that comes to us from Christ. Whether sound elements worthy of humanity are present in this existence without salvation is a question which only arises incidentally and very exceptionally in the mind of Paul and never in the case of John.[18] I insist, moreover, that this view is purely *religious*, that is to say, it does not consider humanity in itself, but in its relationship to God which has been broken. But this relationship with God is not one relationship beside many other relationships – it penetrates all the others and gives them their deepest and ultimate meaning. As a result, a religious dislocation, via our moral life, also causes a terrestrial catastrophe *within this world*. The religious is given a 'cosmic' resonance. The *fundamental situation* itself is infected, distorted, affected at its root and confused – 'we were by nature children of wrath' (Eph 2.3). The very meaning of human existence is lost and then the fine aspects which are still to be found lose their real and ultimate, all-determining meaning. The whole cosmos is therefore, according to Paul, 'held accountable to God' (Rom 3.19) – it is subject to God's judgement.[19] John formulated this drastically: 'the whole world is in the power of the evil one' (1 John 5.19). It was evident to both John and Paul that the devil was the 'prince of this world' who was responsible for this situation without salvation.

---

[13] In the New Testament, for example: Acts 17.24; John 1.10; 1 Cor 3.22; Rom 1.20.
[14] 1 Cor 2.12.
[15] 1 Cor 1.20-1; 3.19; 2.6ff; 2.14; 1.26.
[16] 2 Cor 7.10.
[17] 1 John 4.4f.
[18] Neither John nor Paul deny the goodness and the value of the world of creation as praised by the Old Testament. What they say, however, is that these values have been misused. The very fact that this misuse goes against the inner promptings of things themselves (see Rom 8.22; Phil 3.21) shows that they are not bad, but positively good. The New Testament, however, is not so much in the perspective of the optimistic Old Testament faith in creation as in that of the salvation of humanity, involved in sin, by Christ. The New Testament does not provide a systematic exposition of every aspect of the human predicament and my exposition of the New Testament concept of 'cosmos' is intended as no more than an introduction.
[19] Rom 3.6; 1 Cor 6.2; 1 Cor 11.32.

They were, however, both fully conscious of the other side of the coin. God nonetheless loved this world – 'God so loved the world that he gave (us) his only Son', not 'to condemn the world', but to pronounce the liberating *absolvo* over it.[20] God had compassion on this world, which we have called a world 'without salvation'. He became the *sōtēr tou kosmou*,[21] the saviour of unredeemed humanity. He came to share our situation without salvation. Because of their situation without salvation, Paul used a very strong word and called people *douloi*, slaves or servants,[22] and said explicitly (in Phil 2.7) that the Word took precisely this form of a servant, that is, he entered a world where the evil one ruled. In the form of a servant, however, Christ broke this rule and gave a new meaning to the world and to being a 'servant'. This is so true that Paul could boldly assert that, had the prince of this world known that he was having the 'Lord of glory' crucified, he would have frustrated this plan (1 Cor 2.8), since this crucifixion marked the end of the rule of the evil one. But this wise divine plan of salvation eluded him (ibid).

Just as the first Adam was tempted by the devil and involved in the fall of the evil angels, so too did the evil one try, at the very beginning of Christ's public life, to lead the second Adam astray and establish his kingdom (Mark 1.12). But his plan failed: 'The light shone in the darkness, and the darkness was not able to take it in its grip.'[23] 'Since therefore the children share in flesh and blood, he himself likewise partook of the same nature, that through death he might destroy him who has the power of death, that is, the devil' (Heb 2.14). Christ's love overcame the situation without salvation: 'I have overcome the world' (John 16.33). The entry of God himself into this world brought meaning and sense into the human world and the result of this redeeming entry of God into the world in the person of Jesus Christ went to the very root of human existence. In this context, Paul said explicitly: 'If anyone is in Christ, he is a new creation' (2 Cor 5.17), meaning not only that human beings have acquired a new reality, grace, but also that the whole person has, as a human being in the world, been renewed in and through grace in Christ, in other words, that the mystery of Christ and our incorporation into this mystery through baptism marked the end of the 'cosmos' in the biblical sense of the word. 'By the cross of our Lord Jesus Christ', Paul said, 'the world has been crucified to me, and I to the world' (Gal 6.14). The believing, baptised person, the Christian, thus lives concretely in a new world. The whole of his being human in this world is baptised and Christianised. By Christ, the optimistic faith in creation is once again situated in its original sphere of life in which it can freely breathe. The world of creation is, in Christians, as Christians, withdrawn from the yoke of evil. As though it were a second day of creation, God pronounces his approval over humanity in Christ: 'He saw that it was good'. Paul said this explicitly: 'There is now no condemnation for those who are in Christ Jesus' (Rom 8.1). The redeemed world ceases to be 'cosmos' and is now called the kingdom of God. 'Just as we have borne the image of the man of dust, we shall

---

[20] John 3.16f; 12.47.
[21] John 4.42; 1 John 4.14; also 2 Cor 5.19; Rom 11.15.
[22] Rom 6.16, 17, 19, 20; 6.6; 15.21.
[23] This is a more correct translation perhaps of what John intended to say when he used the Greek word *katalambanein* in John 1.5. See also John 12.35.

also bear the image of the man of heaven' (1 Cor 15.49). Anyone who lives in Christ has, like Christ, overcome the world. 'For whatever is born of God overcomes the world', said John (1 John 5.4) and he added, 'Who is it that overcomes the world but he who believes that Jesus is the Son of God?' (1 John 5.5).

This, then, is how the Bible sees human existence, and this biblical view is not metaphysical, but ethical and religious. Outside of Christ, human existence lacks ultimate meaning. In Christ, on the other hand, the whole of human existence has commenced a new life.[24] The whole of Christian humanism is contained in this and it is in her growing awareness of this datum of faith that the church has become more sharply conscious, in this biblical view of life, of the real place of humanism within the mystery of Christ, just as understanding the meaning of human beings in the world has grown and matured in the human mind.

Human beings in their bodily world: death[25]

Light is thrown, from the perspective of experience and faith, on the distinctive mode of being that human being are not only by their origin in this world, but also by their disappearance from the world.[26] If we regard death as a biological event, it appears to us as something normal. Death simply points to the fact that a human being, in his or her body, is a piece of nature. If, however, we take the *humanity* of this body into account and thus regard death as an event in a human being, human experience can scarcely be reconciled with this fact. This is clear in the case of the death of someone with whom we have had a personal relationship. The death of a person who is dear to us is something that we regard as impossible and absurd. The fact that we are allowing our personal relationships with the dying person to be related to the experience of his or her death does not mean that our experience of the absurdity of their death is therefore subjective. On the contrary – in this experience, we are reflecting about the death of a person precisely as a person, because it is only in a personal relationship with a fellow human being that someone is encountered as a person, as more than an 'abstract case'. This experience of the death of a person precisely as a person makes clear that there is a disproportion between the biological event and its consequences, which are on an entirely different plane, of the end of personal relationships with this particular dead person.

The experience of the death of fellow human beings, then, causes us to protest against the absurdity of the fact that personal relationships, and thus the persons

---

[24] I do not propose to discuss the question of pre-Christian religious human beings here.
[25] Selected from: Edward Schillebeeckx, 'Man and His Bodily World', *World and Church*, trans. N. D. Smith, Collected Works of Edward Schillebeeckx vol. 4 (London: Bloomsbury T&T Clark, 2014), 188–92 [245–50].
[26] For death as a biological phenomenon, see M. d'Halluin, *La mort, celte inconnue*, Paris 1952²; for death from the philosophical point of view, D. De Petter, 'De onsterfelijkheid', *Kultuurleven* 23 (1956), 11–22, later included in *Begrip en werkelijkheid*, 217–33; for death from the philosophical and theological point of view, E. Schillebeeckx, 'The Death of a Christian', *Vatican II, a Struggle of Minds and Other Essays*, Dublin, 1963 (published in the USA as *The Layman in the Church*, Staten Island, NY, 1963), 61–91; see also P. L. Landsberg, *Essai sur l'expérience de la mort*, Paris (1951).

themselves, should have ceased to exist simply and solely because of a chance or a necessary biological event, such as the breaking of a muscle in the heart or a diseased stomach, liver or kidneys. But to the evident experience of this disproportion can be added a certainty of a different kind which seems to contradict the first – the undeniable reality of humanity's essential incarnation. In the case of a person's death, we are also confronted with the evident fact that cannot be denied – that this person has been taken away from us, that, for us at least, they are no longer there, and this arouses in us the fear that they are no longer there at all. It is clear that we cannot escape from the experience that personal contact and human intercourse, although these are of quite a different kind from those of purely bodily and organic activities, are only possible through the body. The affection that the deceased person had for us existed only insofar as it appeared before us and addressed us in that person's bodily presence and appearance. We may go even farther and say that the body is not simply the medium through which our fellow human beings orientate themselves towards us –human persons also give their own inner life form only in their body, in the expressions and effects which bodily activity bestows on personal activity. But death eliminates this body and the result of this is that personal contacts with the deceased person are cut off and new contacts are impossible, so that we live only on memories of the dead person. The human spirit is, in life, essentially directed, in and through its own bodiliness, towards the bodily world and towards other persons; death, rather than, as Platonic and Cartesian dualism claims, the body is its 'prison'. In death it is really as if the soul went to sleep. Even though we are bound to affirm a human being's continued existence as a person, we can, because of the essential incarnation, only regard the continued existence of the dead person *naturally*, that is, without the help of the light of revelation, as a continued existence in a state of spiritual lethargy, isolation and non-activity, as a pale, helpless, reduced and inferior kind of existence. This was indeed the way in which death was spontaneously regarded by all primitive peoples and even the way in which it was originally regarded within the pagan religious view of the Greeks and the Romans. Sheol, Hades or the underworld – these were universally regarded as a twilight realm of the departed spirits in which only a shadowy existence was possible. The despair that is present in the experience of the death of a beloved fellow-man is attributable to the contradiction between these two evident facts – on the one hand, that we cannot accept the fact that a purely biological event should cause the person to cease to exist and, on the other hand, the experience of the fact that he no longer exists for us in any case because of the cessation of bodily life.

If we analyse the implicit content of this experience of despair, the result has two elements. In the first place, the person – and let me say here, the soul, although this is inaccurate – must continue to exist because this continued existence is simply another name for the person's transcendence of bodily life. Once it has been called into existence, with and in a body, the spirit can no longer be affected, *in its existence*, by the fortunes of the body and cannot even be affected by death. On the other hand, however, we cannot, naturally, form any positive idea as to how the spirit continues to exist after death. This leads consequently to our feeling that the so-called 'departed soul' cannot be comprehended or grasped, that it is not essential, to our experience of emptiness with regard to it.

It is, of course, this feeling that makes it difficult for us to be certain that the dead person still continues to live outside our terrestrial world. But, if a truth presents itself to us in conditions that are less satisfactory from the psychological point of view, we have the moral and intellectual duty to accept that truth precisely as it presents itself, in other words, with all these difficulties. Insights into living realities are never mathematically or physically certain. They call for moral openness. Human possession of the truth is always delicate and precarious. It is completely the opposite to rationalism, which is convinced that we have the truth in our grasp. But, for us, truth is no more than a small light in the darkness. This idea that we have of the dead person leading a helpless, reduced and isolated existence, insofar as we can form any judgement of this existence from our human experience, in other words, the absurd end of human life, is confirmed in the light of faith and revelation. According to the view of life provided by revealed religion, death, although it is in itself normal and natural, is in fact a punishment for sin. The dead person's being dead is thus no more than an extension of this punishment, its inner consequence – the state of the so-called 'departed soul' thus shares in the absurdity of sin itself. This state can be understood in the light of humanity's situation in the absence of salvation.

The death of the person who nonetheless continues to exist and its consequence, his or her state of disintegration, thus essentially merges into a religious problem. Something is happening to a person. The problem presents itself naturally, but it is only revelation that can throw light on it. The natural immortality of the soul is certainly a victory of the spirit over matter, but at the same time it is also a fatal failure of the human person. Revelation gives us insight into the religious backgrounds of this datum. It confirms the absurdity of death and of the undesirable state of disintegration of the 'departed soul'. In contrast with Platonic dualism, this means that the natural immortality of the soul does not imply any promise or expectation of salvation. This immortality is the ultimate failure of human life. The absurdity of the 'departed soul' is the freely caused absurdity of sin itself in its anthropological consequences. In itself, the 'departed soul' is, of its very nature, an *unredeemed* soul – a situation of hell. Under the influence of Greek dualism, scholasticism completely overlooked this. The 'departed soul' is not a pure spirit, but an absurd situation of essentially incarnate human, a genuine 'imprisonment', a complete 'de-situation' of the human person – at least without redemption, since redemption makes everything quite different for the departed soul. There is, then, a radical difference between the wretched *natural* immortality of the human soul and its *Christian* immortality. Natural immortality is the implication of the human person and, as such, it is a guarantee of the transcendence of the human spirit. But, because this transcendence is essentially incarnate, the natural immortality of the human spirit is a state of disintegration for the dead person. Christian immortality, on the other hand, is the implication of the human community of grace with the living God. Whereas the only idea that we can form naturally of the continued existence of the soul after death is that of a wretched, inferior existence that is thrown back on itself, we know, in the light of revelation, that the post-terrestrial life of the person who has died in the community of grace with the living God is above all a redemption of the soul of the dead person. This redemption does not consist of a redemption *from* the body – this would be non-Christian, platonic dualism – but of the human soul's participation in the life of God. Through grace – and only by grace, not naturally

– the departed soul is taken into the arms of God the Father and is thus capable of personal activity in grace. The growth of the naturally immortal soul beyond death towards true life and indeed towards life in abundance is therefore attributable only to God's redeeming grace. It cannot be traced back to a dualistic view of humanity. The tragic aspect of 'being dead' and thus of the 'departed soul' no longer applies to the soul that is justified by redemption. It is, however, true that this divine life of the departed soul is still not fully human until the resurrection has taken place. Direct relationships between human persons and with the world are still not present for the saints. Perfect redemption at the end of time will not take place until the general resurrection, when all these truly human relationships will once again come about and the deified soul communicates its divine mode of being to the body which is thereby glorified. The dogma of the direct beatific vision of God that the holy soul enjoys after death thus confirms the primacy and the transcendence of the soul over matter. But the emphasis placed by faith on the 'hope of resurrection' and the coming *parousia* of Christ also stresses human being's essential incarnation and therefore strikingly contradicts any dualistic view of humanity. Both dualism and monism are contradictory to faith.

Impossibility of theorising ultimate meaning and of a universal hermeneutic horizon[27]

Particular experience of meaning, it has been argued, is logically possible only if based on an inevitable implicit demand for total meaning because of the logical implication of a potential total meaning. Hence the meaning of historical events becomes fully and definitively evident only in the perspective of the universal, ultimate meaning of history as a whole – if that actually exists. Particular experiences of meaning only imply the demand for universal meaning. But they do not logically imply that 'universal history' necessarily has to signify final, positive meaning, hence salvation. Logos and actual fact are locked in an irresolvable contradiction, and history remains ambiguous: we cannot rationally and theoretically anticipate universal total meaning. Since historical evolution has not been concluded, every particular experience of meaning is subject to fundamental uncertainty which neither philosophy nor science can resolve.

Now the question of universal meaning, implied in all partial experiences of meaning as well as in protesting contrast experience in the same history, is confronted with the phenomenon of 'religions'. In religious experience a specific, universal ultimate meaning – the *eschaton* of history – is formulated and confessed. Thus Christianity speaks of Jesus Christ as the ultimate meaning of all history. That is a profession of faith. The question is whether human reason is open to a critical, rational understanding of this divine revelation – and in such a way that faith, for

---

[27]Selected from: Edward Schillebeeckx, *Jesus: An Experiment in Christology*, trans. Hubert Hoskins and Marcelle Manley, Collected Works of Edward Schillebeeckx vol. 6 (London: Bloomsbury T&T Clark, 2014), 579–86 [616–25].

its part, cannot entrench itself in a storm-free zone and exempt itself from critical inquiry.

Elsewhere, in an admittedly unfinished essay, I postulated that in theological thinking what religious faith posits as a conviction and a thesis functions as a 'hypothesis', which in some way needs to be tested on the material of human experience.[28] This means that the at any rate implicit demand for total meaning emerging from the analysis of particular historical experiences of meaning is not identical with the Christian affirmation of total meaning in Jesus Christ. It is an open question, because the implication of total meaning does clarify any demonstrable, specific form in which that meaning is realised and is not merely a logical implication. Reflecting on it, the theologian, hypothetically at first, identifies the Christian creed as a response corroborating the logically implied ultimate meaning as a reality, a specific answer to the demand for universal meaning. From the standpoint of theology as a scholarly discipline this initial identification is provisional and hypothetical. The theologian must verify (or falsify) the hypothesis in terms of the concrete data of human historical experience.[29] That is the only way that theologians as scholars can rebut the charge of reasoning in a closed 'hermeneutic circle' which presupposes what still has to be critically tested. For nothing is taken for granted: as in every scholarly discipline, one simply works with a hypothesis which needs to be tested. Naturally this testing will differ from the verification of hypotheses and theories in the physical sciences; it is not direct and will never be apodictically cogent; nonetheless it has to be verifiable if theology is to make meaningful, non-ideological pronouncements and qualify as a scientific discipline. There must be a method to ascertain whether the hypothesis finds support in our experience and whether in so doing it opens up a future for all.

Whether God's saving activity in fact takes place in Jesus of Nazareth must to some extent be experientially provable and expressible in religious language. For if, as Christianity confesses, God is the ultimate all-determining reality (for now still in a broad sense without specifying its actual substance, e.g. almighty love displayed in 'weakness'), then in this worldview no earthly reality can be fully understood without reference to God; then God opens up a deeper understanding of all reality. It follows that the theologian's 'hypothesis' (the thesis of faith) must in some (non-apodictic but meaningful) way be testable and find support in human reality, the human world and society in short, in our historical experience.

I realised some time ago already that this entails a clear break with the 'implicit intuition' of the totality of meaning propounded by classical philosophers like D. De Petter, L. Lavelle and the French *philosophes de l'esprit*. This tradition (not without solid grounds in Thomas Aquinas's worldview) brilliantly analyses the participation of total meaning in every particular experience of meaning. Thomas could blithely – and rightly, at the time endorse this view in medieval (patristic) society, where a single (Christian) destiny for human life – the beatific vision of God – was a self-

---

[28] See *Geloofsverstaan: interpretatie en kritiek* Bloemendaal 1972, 211–16, esp. 214; trans.: *The Understanding of Faith*, Collected Works of Edward Schillebeeckx vol. 5, 131–5 [150–5].

[29] What in particular brought me to state explicitly the implications of my own essay was an article by W. Pannenberg, 'The Nature of a Theological Statement', in *Zygon* 7 (1972), 6–19.

evident social truth with (sociologically) appropriate plausibility structures. Today, in our society where divergent ideologies and worldviews compete in the 'common market' of world history, that is not possible. Hence the concept of participation has to be replaced by the idea of anticipation of total meaning in the midst of a history still in the making. The result is that each specific or identificatory, anticipated total meaning (whether of the Christian eschaton, the classless society of the future or J. Habermas's ideal democratic society with its non-coercive communication) can only present itself to the forum of critical reason (in the first instance) as a 'hypothesis', whose cognitive value – hence reality and truth value – has to be tested on the material of human historical experience. These experiences will prove or disprove the provisional anticipation of total meaning (Christian, Marxist, critical social theory, etc.) before the forum of critical reflection, in an, at any rate, rationally meaningful if not rationally cogent way (as is the case in the physical sciences; but they have no monopoly on scientific status). In saying this I am aware that a scientific approach is only one of many human potentialities and strengths, and certainly not the only effectual one – even relatively. But it is an inalienable right of critical reason; and therefore no faith can evade it by invoking the pseudo-argument that God and religion belong to a super- or extra-scientific plane of human existence without losing its plausibility. In essence they actually belong to such a plane; and one cannot define the heart of a religion in terms of its functional meaning for a human being and his society. No direct verification, therefore, is possible; but indirectly it is, in the decisive impact of faith in God on human experience: that is to say, religion is tested on its own implications (hence indirectly, yet in no sense 'extrinsically'). Thus demonstrating the personal, socio-political, secular, historical relevance of the Christian faith (in a critical approach to society and culture) becomes an indirect test of faith-motivated statements.

So the question of the universal significance of Jesus of Nazareth finds its proper context in the universal hermeneutic horizon which, although in itself resistant to theorising, is included (as a logical implication) in negative contrast experiences and particular experiences of meaning – hence in the horizon of the question forced upon us by history itself concerning the ultimate sense or non-sense of our human history and the nature of that sense or non-sense. That is our question, because the process of our history evokes it in our minds, a process which is, after all, a variegated, pluralistic record with a potential unity (whatever concrete verbal expression one may give this fundamental existential theme; for there are many possible approaches to what presents itself as the crucial problem of human life). Of special importance, it seems to me, is the fact continually confronting us – that of unaccommodated, innocent suffering, in short, the story of human suffering, those dark stains that cannot be assigned any rational or theoretical place. Human suffering and the problem of evil go hand in hand with our history as a permanently thriving 'epiphenomenon' of our 'situated' freedom. Philosophy and theology alike are left speechless and confounded by the complexity of evil and human suffering caused by nature, persons and structures. There is too much innocent and senseless suffering to rationalise this calamity ethically, hermeneutically or ontologically. And history testifies to the human inability to realise his dream of a pristine society free from suffering.

The salvation that Jesus offered was rejected, moreover, because of our age-old yet ever new human and social praxis, which sweeps away everything and everyone that does not fit into its pattern. The offer of religious salvation is – paradoxically – the condition of its potential rejection. Only thus was the *religious* implication of such rejection revealed in its ethical profundity that cannot be rationally plumbed or measured. We rightly speak of a demonic strain in our history which, despite occasional partial amelioration, constantly recurs: a fundamental human impotence dogs our finest intentions and achievements. The hard facts of history offer no guarantee or hope that ultimate shalom and reconciliation are possible. We humans are capable of making our history flourish or founder. Given our negative contrast experiences, shalom, universal meaning and reconciliation can only be articulated in parables and eschatological symbols, in images of promise and wrath, ultimately of God's kingdom or reign, of forgiveness and *metanoia*. The rejection of proffered salvation is not theoretically explicable, because in the final analysis profound evil is incomprehensible and eludes every theory; it will not fit into any ontological or philosophical unitary system. The only adequate response is a *praxis* of resistance to evil, not a theory about it. Hence belief in a universal meaning of history cannot be pinned down in a philosophically interpreted, 'universal history'; it is only realised in a praxis that tries to overcome evil and suffering on the strength of the religious promise that things can be otherwise. Evil and suffering are a dark stain on our history which no one can remove or explain, which we cannot reconcile with a theodicy or ever erase with social critique and the resultant praxis (however necessary). How then can we rationally and hermeneutically analyse and express the 'universal meaning' of history, of which evil and suffering are such massive components?

Contrast experience, however, especially in memories of the actual history of accumulated suffering, has its own critical, cognitive value and force,[30] which are not reducible to a purposive *Herrschaftwissen* (the controlling knowledge typical of science and technology) or to diverse forms of contemplative, aesthetic and playful, 'aimless' knowledge. The proper cognitive value of the contrast experience of unjust suffering is critical of all forms of premature contemplative as well as exclusively scientific and technological knowledge. It is critical of purely contemplative total perception and every theoretical unitary system, because they already start from universal reconciliation; but it is equally critical of the world-manipulating knowledge of science and technology insofar as they postulate a human being only as the controlling subject and disregard the ethical priority to which the sufferers among us are entitled.

The distinctive cognitive value of suffering is not only critical of the two positive forms of human knowledge; dialectically it can also form a link between the contemplative and actively controlling cognitive potentialities of the human psyche. I even believe that only the contrast experience of suffering (with its implicit ethical demand) can forge an intrinsic bond between the two, because it alone possesses characteristics of both forms of knowledge. For on the one hand experiences of suffering befall human beings, even though this form of 'lived' experience is negative,

---

[30]E. Schillebeeckx, 'Naar een "definitieve toekomst": belofte en menselijke bemiddeling', in *Toekomst van de religie: religie van de toekomst?* (Bruges, 1972), especially 48–53; and the well-known memoria articles by J. B. Metz, in particular: 'Zukunft aus dem Gedächtnis des Leidens', in *Concilium* (1972), n. 6, German ed. 399–407.

very different from the equally 'lived' but positive joyousness of contemplative, ludic and aesthetic experiences. On the other hand, with respect to contrast experience or critical negativity, suffering lays a bridge to potential praxis aimed at removing both the suffering and its causes. Because of this intrinsic affinity, albeit critically negative, with both contemplative and nature-regulating knowledge, I call the cognitive force of suffering practico-critical, that is, a critical faculty prompting a new praxis, which opens up a better future and actually realises it (even though one cannot be sure that it will succeed).

This means that –given our human condition and our concrete social culture – only ethical critique of humanity's accumulated history of suffering can, paradoxically yet truly and intrinsically, connect contemplation and action with potential realisation of meaning. After all, as a contrast experience, the human experience of suffering presupposes an implicit yearning for happiness, for salvation or healing; and as unjust suffering it implies at least a vague consciousness of what human integrity or positive wholeness should entail. In other words, as contrast experience it implies indirectly a positive summons from and to the *humanum*. Anyone who examines the conditions that permit contrast experiences, which engender new, imperative tasks, can confirm that such negative experiences include a positive, if as yet unarticulated, sense of value, at the same time disclosing it and demanding its expression in good conscience, which begins to protest. The absence of what ought to be is indirectly apprehended in the negative experience, and so one gets a glimpse of what has to be done here and now, still hazily but nonetheless unmistakably. In that sense acts designed to overcome suffering are only possible by virtue of an at least implicit or confused anticipation of possible universal meaning yet to be realised.

In contrast to the goal-directed knowledge of science and technology and the 'goal-less' knowledge of contemplation (intrinsically meaningful, not pointing beyond itself), the cognitive value of contrast experience of suffering is knowledge that demands a future and opens it up. Besides the foregoing concepts 'goal-directed' and 'goal-less' (in the sense of intrinsically meaningful), the notion of 'future' now enters into our quest for a universal pre-understanding in which the question about Jesus can find a comprehensible answer. The history of human suffering also possesses critical cognitive force that calls for a praxis that will open up a future. Contrast experiences of suffering, then, are negative, dialectical awareness of a longing and a demand for meaning and real freedom, salvation and happiness to come.

In this as yet unfinished human history of suffering in quest of meaning, liberation and salvation, Jesus of Nazareth presented himself with a message and praxis of salvation, a fellow human being who nevertheless, through his new praxis and innocent suffering and death on the cross, gave us a new and renewing reading of our old history. Its effect is to reveal that the factor linking the historical person Jesus with his significance for us now is, concretely, a Christian life praxis in ongoing human history. Without the churches' solidarity with suffering human beings, whoever or whatever they may be, their gospel becomes implausible and incomprehensible. A universal hermeneutic horizon of understanding, therefore, demands a human liberated freedom, a praxis that is actually liberating. This does not tell us what real freedom and humanity consist in. The universal horizon within which the question and answer concerning Jesus of Nazareth become generally accessible to all is a very concrete demand for the *humanum* – a demand which no doctrine (not even that of

Christianity) can satisfy by anticipating the future. (It can only be answered by way of searching, largely empirical initiatives. Whether humans will succeed in this is not inscribed in our history.)

How does Jesus of Nazareth fit into this history of human suffering in quest of meaning, liberation and salvation? From the foregoing it is clear that Jesus' universal significance cannot be affirmed directly by objectivising an abstraction without considering the concrete effects of his history. Those effects are discernible mainly in a historically demonstrable, hope inspiring, liberating Christian praxis. In addition we must not only inquire into the universal preconception, shared by all human beings, of what Jesus conveyed, but should also stress that the church, the vehicle of the Jesus tradition, must listen to the world if it is to get its gospel message across. It is not just a matter of determining humanity's universal preconceptions so that everyone might heed Jesus' message as something that concerns them profoundly; the churches of Christ must also respect the world's right to be 'world' and must note what the world has to say and is already doing for human wellbeing and happiness. Then 'the world' may have the freedom to listen to what the Christian gospel has to say to it. Historical humanity's concrete question to the gospel today is: what do Jesus' message and praxis contribute to the overall effort of liberating humanity in the full sense of the word?

Human freedom is not a purely inner affair. It is a bodily, extroverted freedom, realised only in an encounter of truly free people in liberating social services and structures. Of ourselves we are just a potentiality for freedom; the freedom is still void, without substance. Culture fills the void creatively, but no single form or degree of culture can fill it completely. Freedom concretely realised is constantly interiorised; that is to say, inner freedom depends on encounter with free persons in social structures that permit it and protect it. The social dimension is an essential component of inwardly free action; it helps to constitute our experience of ourselves and of the world. Liberated freedom thus surmounts the dualistic distinction between inward and outward. There is a constitutive relation between personal identity and collective consensus or recognition, between inner freedom and liberating social structures.

Liberation or salvation, then, is the conquest of all human, personal and social alienation: it is the wholeness of the human person, human life and human history. Individuals and society are interrelated in an irreducible dialectical tension. The 'void' of our freedom is never totally filled by culture. There always remains a further possibility, an openness. On the one hand we cannot say that society is the transcendental, all-encompassing horizon of reality, for that would disregard the unimpeachability of the human person, who is not simply a product of the social process. But neither is personal interiority with its necessary privacy and intimacy a transcendental, all-encompassing horizon. As a result human alienation cannot be fully overcome on a personal or a social plane; 'liberated freedom' or true wellbeing transcends both person and society. There is human hurt for which no socio-political cure exists; the best of social structures may still be fragmenting and alienating; optimal structures do not automatically turn human beings into good, mature, humane people. Nature can be humanised and yet remain largely and ineluctably alien (think of death!); and finally there is our inescapable finitude, which can be a source of faith in God, but also of loneliness and anxiety. Hence making some worldly factor lord and master of human's total wellbeing is the beginning of tyranny.

Ultimate reconciliation of the dichotomy of our existence can only be achieved by an operative reality that *includes* person and society, that is, all of reality, without violating it.[31] That makes it possible to link the question of salvation and liberation with the question of God, of salvation imparted by God. Only absolute freedom that is at the same time creative love seems capable of realising universal reconciliation. That brings us to the question whether acknowledgment, in practice, of God 'being God' is not also recognition of someone's humanity, which is the core of Jesus' message: God's rule or lordship oriented to humanity. Despite the historical failure of this message Jesus attested his indestructible assurance of God's salvation, grounded in an exceptional *Abba* experience. For us it entails a promise from God that human salvation and wholeness are possible and that human life is ultimately meaningful. Thus faith in Jesus makes it possible to affirm simultaneously the two theoretically irreconcilable aspects of human history: evil and suffering, *and* salvation or wellbeing. That enables, allows and obliges us to give wellbeing and goodness the final say in a way that is grounded in Jesus, because the Father is greater than all suffering and greater than our inability to experience ultimate reality as a trustworthy gift.

Selected literature

- The Concept of Truth; Selected from: Edward Schillebeeckx, 'The Concept of "Truth"', *Revelation and Theology*, trans. N. D. Smith, Collected Works of Edward Schillebeeckx vol. 2 (London: Bloomsbury T&T Clark, 2014), 189–91 [II 5–9].
- The Relationship Between Experience and Concept in Modern Catholic Theology; Selected from: Edward Schillebeeckx, 'The Concept of "Truth"', *Revelation and Theology*, trans. N. D. Smith, Collected Works of Edward Schillebeeckx vol. 2 (London: Bloomsbury T&T Clark, 2014), 196–200 [II 17–22].
- The Biblical View of the World: The Cosmos; Selected from: Edward Schillebeeckx, 'Religion and the World: Renewing the Face of the Earth', *World and Church*, trans. N. D. Smith, Collected Works of Edward Schillebeeckx vol. 4 (London: Bloomsbury T&T Clark, 2014), 4–7 [5–9].
- Human Beings in Thier Bodily World: Death; Selected from: Edward Schillebeeckx, 'Man and His Bodily World', *World and Church*, trans. N. D. Smith, Collected Works of Edward Schillebeeckx vol. 4 (London: Bloomsbury T&T Clark, 2014), 188–92 [245–50].
- Impossibility of Theorizing Ultimate Meaning and of a Universal Hermeneutic Horizon; Selected from: Edward Schillebeeckx, *Jesus: An Experiment in Christology*, trans. Hubert Hoskins and Marcelle Manley, Collected Works of Edward Schillebeeckx vol. 6 (London: Bloomsbury T&T Clark, 2014), 579–86 [616–25].

---

[31] Sharply formulated by W. Kasper, *Einführung in den Glauben* (Mainz, 1972), in these terms: '... eine Größe... welche das Ganze umgreift und eint, ohne es zu vergewaltigen' (110).

3

Nouvelle Théologie

The question proper to dogmatics: The contemporary context of God's word[1]

Dogmatic theology is not possible without exegesis of biblical theology. It is not that the dogmatic theologian looks in the Bible for references in support of his own theses. The proper relationship is precisely the other way around – Christian exegesis and biblical theology have a critical task with regard to the contemporary propositions of dogmatic theology. Of course, Scripture is not the only source of dogmatics, but, as the original archives of the mind of the church, it is the constant and inviolable norm for every theological activity, even though it must be read *in* and *with* the church whose Scripture it is. In this respect, dogmatic theology implies Christian exegesis and biblical theology. The dogmatic theologian, then, is at the same time also an exegete and a biblical theologian.

On the other hand, however, dogmatic theology is more than biblical exegesis or theology. The content of faith is the content of God's address to humanity. God's word is directed through the medium of salvation history and the church's scriptural teaching authority to the whole of humanity, including people who are alive today. God's word must again and again be related to the contemporary spiritual situation of the people who listen to it here and now. This listening to the one word of God here and now – the Bible itself testifies to this contemporary reception of the word – is so intimately connected with revelation that it to some extent coincides with revelation itself. Despite the newness of its formulation in comparison with a scriptural affirmation, the definition of a dogma is a reflection of the original word of revelation. When, for example, the Council of Chalcedon expressed the saving reality which is Christ in the affirmation: 'two natures, one person',[2] the community of the faithful at that time heard the same in these words as the apostles had heard

---

[1] Selected from: Edward Schillebeeckx, 'The Bible and Theology', *Revelation and Theology*, trans. N. D. Smith, Collected Works of Edward Schillebeeckx vol. 2 (London: Bloomsbury T&T Clark, 2014), 124–7 [I 192–7].
[2] See DS (*Denzinger 'Enchiridion Symbolorum'*) 301–2 (=DR 148) [DH 301–2].

from the reality of Christ, but their manner of appropriating this same word of God was different. This appropriation nonetheless forms part of the dogma – it is the dogma itself. A dogma is a correct, although never exhaustive listening to a reality or a word of revelation. The *manner in which* revelation and Scripture are heard again and again by human beings *who make history* is precisely what is called 'tradition'. Tradition is simply the constant and always contemporary listening in grace to the reality or word of revelation which found its constitutive expression in the apostolic church with its Scripture. It is therefore possible to claim, along with other exegetes, that Scripture has, as it were, a double context. The first is the biblical context proper, which is established by exegesis and biblical theology. The second is the context of each period of the church's history – in other words, the contemporary context. This is the context which is investigated by the dogmatic theologian and which is connected with what is known as the 'development of dogma'. It is important to note that there is no question of trying to find the later dogma *as such* in Holy Scripture. An exegesis of this kind would in fact be 'ento-egesis'. But the word of God, proclaimed in Scripture, was not simply addressed to the Jews and to the early apostolic church – it is addressed to people of all times. The exegete attempts to establish precisely how this word was spoken to and heard by the Jewish people and the early church. The dogmatic theologian, on the other hand, attempts to establish how this same word, heard by Israel and the apostolic church but nonetheless addressed to us as well, should be heard in a pure form by us in the twentieth century. A study of this kind must be preceded by the establishment of precisely how God spoke to Israel and the apostolic church, and how these understood and experienced his word. That is why there can be no dogmatic theology without exegesis and biblical theology. The Old-Testament and apostolic listening to the word of God belongs to the constitutive phase of revelation. It is therefore *ephapax*, once-for-all – a unique, unrepeatable event, acting as a constant norm to the obedient listening of the post-apostolic church. Exegesis has consequently a position of honour in all theological speculation.

On the other hand, however, although public revelation is closed, God's address to humanity is still a *present* reality. His revelation in Christ is a personal giving of himself by the living God. In it, he gives himself in a personal gesture to be intimately known and experienced by us. He comes forward in this gesture to meet human beings, inviting them to share a living communion with himself. That is why the saving reality of revelation, as directed towards us, includes not only God's historically datable saving acts with their prophetic interpretation (the so-called 'public revelation'), but also an inward address by God in and through the grace or 'light' of faith, by means of which we can also personally perceive and assent to God's gracious offer of salvation with our hearts. As de la Potterie has so painstakingly pointed out, the Bible has itself expressed this in the phrase *to chrisma tou hagiou* – 'the chrism (unction) of the holy one (Holy Spirit).[3] This *chrisma* is the

---

[3] See 1 John 2.20, 27; and I. de la Potterie, 'L'onction du Chrétien par la foi', *Biblica* 40 (1959), 12–69. This article provides an outline of the scriptural basis of the Thomist doctrine of the *lumen fidei*. In my opinion, certain adjustments need to be made to de la Potterie's exegesis: see J. Ysebaert, *Greek Baptismal Terminology: Its Origins and Early Development*, Nijmegen, 1962, 263ff.

word of Christ himself, the *fides ex auditu* ('faith as listened to and heard'), as called to mind by the Holy Spirit, the *locutio interna* ('inner voice'). The inward *chrisma* is intrinsically linked with the *fides ex auditu*. The church's listening to the word of God has, expressed figuratively, a horizontal and a vertical dimension. There is an inner confrontation with God who proclaims himself here and now as well as proclaiming himself an anamnesis, a memorial and commemoration, of that to which Scripture and tradition testify concerning God's speaking to humanity.[4] In connection with the scriptural doctrine of the 'unction of the Holy Spirit', the great medieval theologians, such as Aquinas, for example, imitating the fathers of the church, also refer to an 'inward, divine instinct that invites us to believe'.[5] An early council of the church, the Council of Orange, also mentions an inner impulse and illumination.[6] God's intervention in history, culminating in the person and the life of the God-man, is intelligible to us in and through the public word of the divinely inspired prophets and ultimately of Christ himself. Scripture provides us with an inspired account of this and finally the heart of every believing Christian is opened to the divine content and meaning of this revelation by the grace of faith. One of the fathers of the Council of Trent alluded to this reality of grace when he said:

> Because he was not always to remain among us physically the Son of God sent the Holy Spirit who will reveal God's secrets in the hearts of the faithful and will instruct the church every day until the end of time, and will settle any doubts that may arise in the minds of people.[7]

Divorced from public revelation, the inward grace of faith or the 'inward speaking of God to a person' would be in no way explicit, and the word of God would thus not be heard. On the other hand, however, listening to outward, public revelation without this inward light of faith could not bring about a true surrender in faith to the word of God, as in that case it would not be heard according to its divine content. It is clear, then, that faith in the church is determined by the historical event in Israel and in the human person Jesus, as proclaimed in Scripture. It will also be clear that this faith is the result too of the *present* self-revelation here and now of the heavenly Christ *through* his Spirit in the church.

This also means that dogmatic theology, if it wishes to hear the pure word of God, must study first Scripture and then past tradition. But, because this same word is also spoken to us, the dogmatic theologian will have to ask different questions of Scripture and tradition from those asked by the exegete or the historian. Among the questions asked by the exegete and the biblical theologian are, for example: What did Israel, inspired by God, think about itself as the people of God and about Yahweh as the God of Israel? What did Christ think about himself and about man? What did the

---

[4] For the *anamnesis* character of Christianity, see Nils A. Dahl, 'Anamnesis: Mémoire et commemoration dans le christianisme primitif', *Studia Theologica* 1 (1948), 69–95.
[5] See, for example, *EJ* c. 6, lect. 5; *ST* II-II, q. 2, a. 9, ad 3.
[6] See DS 377 (=DR 180) [DH 377], quoted in the *Constitution on the Catholic Faith of the First Vatican Council* (DS 3010=DR 1791) [DH 3010].
[7] *Concilium Tridentinum.*, ed. Goerres, V, 11; see also XII, 508.

early church, confronted with the risen Christ, think about itself and about Christ? Assuming all this, the dogmatic theologian goes further. It is not that she or he aims to extend the results of Christian exegesis in human, philosophical ideas and build a superstructure on to what the exegete, guided by the church, has heard of this divine speaking. But, governed by the norm of what Israel and the apostolic church have heard of the word of God, the dogmatic theologian (in other words, the present-day believer who listens in holy obedience to the word of God from the vantage-point of his own, contemporary situation and meditates on it in holy reflection) has, as it were, the task of listening to the same word of God in all its inner associations in a new way and of formulating it for his or her own time. It is really nothing new that he or she does, but it is something quite different. It is precisely this which indicates the difference in perspective between Christian exegesis and dogmatics, and at the same time establishes the connection between the results of the two studies. This is because it is precisely this listening in grace to the word of God, that is, faith, which is the guarantee of the identity that exists between Scripture and dogma, between Scripture and tradition, and between Scripture and a theology that is subject to the norm of the church and does not aim to be a superstructure built on to the heard word of God, but a reflection about it.

The difference between the point of view of Christian exegesis and that of dogmatic theology should therefore not be seen as though the exegete is *outside* the faith of the church and studies biblical texts in the manner of a specialist studying secular literature. There is of course a radical difference between the point of view of pure biblical criticism or philological and literary exegesis and that of Christian exegesis proper, although the latter does make use of the critical method. The difference, however, is that, like the dogmatic theologian, the Christian exegete listens to the word of Scripture in his research as a believer and, like the dogmatic theologian, tries to understand this word with his intellect illuminated by faith. In scholastic terms, it is possible to say that the *lumen quo* of Christian exegesis is the same as that of theology or of dogmatics. Both exegesis and dogmatics are critical sciences and both are also sciences of faith which employ critical thought. What is more, the object that is studied in this light is also materially the same in the case of both of these sciences of faith – it is the revealed word of God, as it is heard and accepted in the reaction of the believer. This, however, is the formal distinction between the Christian exegesis and dogmatics. The manner in which the exegete hears and examines this revealed word of God in faith, systematises it, and synthesises it, differs from the manner in which the dogmatic theologian studies this same word of revelation in faith and attempts to synthesise it in accordance with its inner structural divisions. The Christian exegete and the biblical theologian examine God's word as it was given to and hear d by the Old Testament people of God and the early apostolic church in its precise biblical context. The manner in which exegetes appeal to human reason is therefore also different from that of dogmatic theologians. They seek first and foremost to understand a given type of thinking about the faith, such as that of Paul, and is not concerned with speculative reasoning. The dogmatic theologian, on the other hand, examines the same word of God, but rather as it is addressed to all people at all times and as it should be heard by them here and now. We may indeed say, in the concrete, as it is addressed to *us*, the people of today.

This topical note – 'as it is addressed to us, the people of today' – is not added because of a subjective feeling for contemporary needs, but in the knowledge that God does not simply address humanity in the abstract, but speaks to people who are making history, people in the concrete – human beings in biblical and in patristic times, medieval people, modern people and people today. This does not in any way place a relative value on the word of God. In faith, human beings in the concrete – human beings as they are at every period of history – are always in search of the objective content of God's revealed word. But, however absolute and unchangeable supernatural truth, like every truth, may be, it nonetheless shares, as a truth known by us in faith, in the characteristics of everything that is human – in the imperfection, the relative value, and the evolutive or historical aspect of every human possession of truth. The same meaningful datum can be approached and illuminated from various sides, with the result that different, but correct and complementary, views of the same reality are possible. This vision of truth from different perspectives is an essential factor in all human knowledge. It can be found in Scripture itself. We rightly speak of a synoptic, a Johannine, or a Pauline view of Christ, and recognise the difference between the eschatological vision of the Johannine writings and that of the Pauline epistles, and so on. Listening to Scripture and tradition, deciphering the many studies made in the history of the church of the word of revelation, and devoting his attention to the proclamation of the faith by the church of today and to the various tendencies in the modern church, dogmatic theologians are always trying to hear this same word of God in its totality and to synthesise it in accordance with its inner structural divisions – and to do this, moreover, ever more adequately, even though their work is essentially relative, in that they always leave much for future generations to accomplish. They do all this so that God's word may speak to the present and the next generation concretely in present-day and future preaching. That is why their use of human reason and understanding is rather more an appeal to speculative reasoning, whereas that of the exegete is more an appeal to critical positive reasoning. This term should not, however, be wrongly understood, as sometimes happens. Speculative reasoning is not an ability to 'build something up' on to a datum, but an ability to grasp the data of faith as meaningful according to their inner intelligibility and their interrelationship, as, for example, Paul himself attempted to do. What was done by Paul, who had the guarantee of the charisma of inspiration and was within the constitutive phase of revelation which had, at his time, not closed, is also done by dogmatic theologians, who work in a purely scientific and thus fallible way – they try to penetrate more deeply into the meaning of the given realities of salvation, by tracing their mutual relationship and their saving significance for human life and by attempting to throw light on their meaning by human analogies.

It is possible to object to some of the contributions made by exegetes and biblical theologians on the score that, although they do accurately reproduce the original conviction and ideas of the biblical authors, they (perhaps unconsciously) allow this description to pass as a normative description and neglect to use the critical element essential to dogmatic theology. The biblical theologian can, of course, only make use of this critical element when he functions not only as a biblical theologian, but also as (simply) a theologian – in other words, when he does not only listen to the Bible (although he will do this first and foremost), but when he also listens to the church's life and thought in the light of the Bible throughout the whole history of the church. No study of the dogmatics of the angels is, for example, complete when the New Testament teaching on the angels has been accurately set out, and similarly no study of revealed Mariology is complete simply by providing a full-length outline of the image of Mary in the gospels. But, on the other hand, the objection can be raised that certain dogmatic theologians are not acting as speculative theologians if they look for biblical evidence for already established theological arguments. It is precisely because of the identity that exists, within Christian development, between the word of God as testified by Scripture, and the word of God as dogmatically defined, that there must be in Scripture itself an objective dynamic force which can only be established by Christian exegesis and dogmatic theology and not by the philological and literary method. This does not mean that we make Paul or John say what the church now states explicitly to be true. It means that we point out the 'limits' of Pauline or Johannine thought in Scripture as seen from the vantage-point of later dogmas. These limits are, as Lévie has rightly said,[8] not purely negative – they indicate an imperfect state, a beginning, a tendency or, as Auzou expressed it, they are 'des réalités en marche'.[9]

Biblical theology: The point of departure for dogmatic theology[10]

It will be clear from the foregoing that it is a constant duty for the dogmatic theologian, as it was for the apostolic church, to re-read Scripture retrospectively, assuming the results of Christian exegesis. As Aquinas correctly observed, 'Even the true prophets did not perceive everything that the Holy Spirit intended in their visions, words, and actions'.[11] The divinity of this inspired human word can only be made fully and explicitly conscious in and through the life of the church under the guidance and protection of the church's teaching authority that acts as the instrument of the Holy Spirit who spoke through the prophets. According to the New Testament, and especially the gospels of John and Luke, the Holy Spirit was sent partly in order to give the church a Christian understanding of Scripture. The Acts testify to this deeper insight in the case of Peter, Stephen, Philip, and Paul after Pentecost, when they 'spoke', full of the Holy Spirit (Acts 4.8; see also Acts 6.5; 7.55; etc.). For dogmatic theologians, Scripture is not just one of the many documents that they have to study. It has for them as well a unique, primary and irreducible meaning. It is true that Christians receive the word of God from the church, but in so doing they

---

[8] See 'L'Ecriture Sainte, parole de Dieu, parole d'homme', *Nouvelle revue théologique* 78 (1956), 561–92, 706–29; 'Les limites de la preuve d'Ecriture Sainte en théologie', *Nouvelle revue théologique* 71 (1949), 1009–29; 'Exégèse critique et interprétation théologique', *Recherche de Science Religieuse* 39 (1951), 237–52.
[9] G. Auzou, *La parole de Dieu*, Paris, 1956, 92.
[10] Selected from: Edward Schillebeeckx, 'The Bible and Theology', *Revelation and Theology*, trans. N. D. Smith, Collected Works of Edward Schillebeeckx vol. 2 (London: Bloomsbury T&T Clark, 2014), 135–7 [I 212–14].
[11] *ST* II–II, q. 173, a. 4.

receive the word of God to which Scripture testifies. Biblical and dogmatic theology cannot be set against each other, even though each has a different way of viewing things directly. The church, tradition, subject to the guidance of the Spirit, can only suggest to us what Christ himself has said and done and what he was when he was still on earth. And this is an event to which the apostolic *kerygma*, as this comes directly to us in holy Scripture, bears immediate witness. Just as the post-apostolic church is built on the authority of the apostles, the sacraments, and the proclamation of the faith, so too is it built on Holy Scripture, which stands on the altar next to the chalice in the form of a Missal. At one time, anti-protestant tendencies in the church made it seem as though the vital significance of the Christian reading of Scripture was pernicious. That time is, however, past, and as a consequence of this dogmatic theology has in recent years acquired a fresher and more authentic character. Because it is a testimony about the origin of the reality which we call in theology 'tradition', Scripture is really the *caput divinae traditionis* ('source of divine tradition'). The church does not derive its dogmas from theological conclusions drawn from Scripture, but it recognises its own living dogma in Scripture. Congar was therefore right when he said:

> I respect and I never cease to study the science of the exegetes, but I challenge their supreme authority.[12]

Christian exegesis does not have the last word to say on the subject of revelation. Although this comes to us through the medium of the history of salvation of the Old and the New Testaments and the inspired testimony about this, it is after all directed to all people at all times. What believing humanity, guided by the Spirit working in the church, personally makes its own of this revelation can differ, at the explicit level, from what Holy Scripture has explicitly made its own. But the scriptural expressions continue to be expressions of the same faith that the church now confesses. There is therefore, at the explicit level, an acquisition, in the course of the history of the church, in comparison with Scripture, viewed in its explicit character. In this acquisition and progress, dogmatic theology plays a subordinate part which cannot and may not be left exclusively to Christian exegesis and biblical theology. On the other hand, however, the exegete has, as I have already said, a critical function with regard to dogmatic theology, because it is he who studies the origin and beginning guaranteed by God and the tendency first set in motion by God which, because of its original direction, is bound always to have an authoritative critical function with regard to the further course of the movement. In this sense, we may with Rahner call Scripture the *hegemonikon* (i.e. critical ruling principle) of dogmatic theology.[13]

Let me conclude by saying, in the light of this brief argument, that dogmatic theologians frequently draw both too much and too little from Scripture, for the simple reason that they only consult it in order to find evidence for really or supposedly established theological theses. They ought instead, proceeding from the starting point of faith, to follow and to experience themselves at close quarters the

---

[12] Y. Congar, *Vraie et fausse réforme dans l'Eglise*, Paris, 1950, 498–9.
[13] Rahner, 'Biblische Theologie', *Lexikon für Theologie und Kirche*, part 2, Freiburg, 1958^2, cols. 449–51.

movement from the Old to the New Testament. They ought also to follow personally the searching tendency of the early apostolic church which approached the Christian mystery of salvation from the Old-Testament themes in the light of the incarnation, and at the same time let itself be absorbed in this tendency of *fides quaerens intellectum*, of faith searching for understanding, for which the New Testament itself so clearly provides us with the example.

The place of the church fathers in theology[14]

Already by the time of the rabbinical writings there was constant reference to the 'tradition of the fathers'. This meant that the law, interpreted and expounded by different generations of teachers, was handed down to the living generation. The idea of the 'elders' was echoed in the word 'fathers'. In the ancient world, a teacher was usually called 'father' and his pupil or disciple 'son'.[15] The Christian teachers were also automatically called 'fathers' in the patristic period. To begin with, this title had no special meaning. In the fourth century, however, this typically Christian concept of 'father' developed until it had a clearly defined meaning, and this growth went together with the development of the idea of the 'tradition of the church'. It was in this century that a very clear distinction was made between Scripture or the apostolic *kerygma* and the 'tradition of the fathers'. In its content, tradition is the same as the apostolic teaching. This was called 'tradition' insofar as it had not come directly to the generation living at the time in Holy Scripture, but had been passed on 'from hand to hand' by previous generations – with their own elucidations but nonetheless with the original inheritance faithfully preserved – to the subsequent generations. Thus the *traditio patrum* was the 'tradition of the older generations'. The subject of the teaching church was, however, the college of bishops. Tradition was therefore even earlier – for Irenaeus, for example – than the apostolic *kerygma* itself, insofar as this was preserved and passed on (in a mature, but at the same time in an essentially unchanged, form) to the living generation of people via the links in the chain of successive bishops.

The technical term *church father* came about for the first time in the fourth century as a result of this view. Christians were by this time already removed by a distance of several centuries from the immediate witness of the apostles. From the time of Athanasius onwards, it was therefore becoming less common to refer directly to Scripture and more common to refer directly to the 'authority of the fathers'. There was a firm conviction of the responsibility of the episcopate in each generation for the 'received doctrine' which, after having been clarified in the light of contemporary problems, was handed down to the next generation. The fathers, that is, the teaching bishops of previous generations, formed the link between the apostolic faith and the latter generations.

---

[14]Selected from: Edward Schillebeeckx, 'The Place of the Church Fathers in Theology', *Revelation and Theology*, trans. N. D. Smith, Collected Works of Edward Schillebeeckx vol. 2 (London: Bloomsbury T&T Clark, 2014), 139–43 [I 215–22].
[15]See, for example, 1 Cor 4:5; 1 Pet 5:13; and Irenaeus, *Adv. Haer.* IV, 41,2.

This was, then, the patristic idea of 'father of the church'. The 'fathers' were in this case quite concretely defined. As far as the local churches were concerned, they were the founders of those churches.[16] As far as each individual Christian was concerned, the father was the 'baptising bishop' by whom he was initiated into the mysteries of salvation.[17] Thus two streams of faith came about – 'inspired Scripture' and the 'tradition of the fathers'.[18] Together with Scripture, the fathers formed the norm of faith.[19] The legitimacy and truth of a proposed new doctrine was tested against its conformity with the doctrine of the earlier fathers. The very fact that these fathers held a different opinion was sufficient (at least at the time of Athanasius) for the proposed new doctrine to be condemned.[20] The authority of the fathers was decisive.[21]

The bishops of the local churches who enabled Christians to live from the apostolic faith by their teaching, especially in connection with the Christian initiation, but also on other occasions, were therefore regarded in the fourth century as fathers of the church whose teaching was, with Scripture, normative for the Christian faith. The normative principle that already held good in the fourth century and was a guiding thought in the great councils of the fifth century (the idea that what was 'patristic' was apostolic) shows that in those days the concept *Father of the church* was really formulation of what we now call the 'living tradition of the church', at least insofar as this is formally vested in the college of bishops. This explains why one of the essential elements in the modern concept *father of the church* is 'approval by the church'.

Nonetheless, the idea of 'father of the church' was enlarged even in the patristic period, especially in the west (Augustine, Jerome, Vincent of Lérins), to include all ecclesiastical writers, even if they were not bishops. All Christian writers therefore came to be regarded as fathers of the church insofar as they were representative of the church's tradition of faith.

In his *Commonitorium* (chapter 41), Vincent of Lérins formulated this in the following way:

> Whenever a new question arises to which no answer has yet been given, reference must be made to the views of the holy fathers, to those who, each in his own time and place and in the unity of faith and the community, were tried and tested teachers [*magistri probabiles*]. And everything that they have held, one in spirit and in consent, must without any doubt or scruple be regarded as the true and catholic teaching of the church.

As time passes, the links between the early apostolic *kerygma* and the living generations in the church become more numerous. The concept *father of the church*

---

[16] Basil, *Epist.* 210, 3 (*PG* 32, 772).
[17] Basil, *Epist.* 204, 2 (*PG* 32, 746).
[18] *Epist.* 5, 3 (ed. Pasquali, p. 90).
[19] Cyril, *De recta fide ad reg.* 2 (*PG* 76, 1204); *Epist.* 39 (*PG* 77, 177).
[20] Athanasius, *Contra Apoll.* I, 20 (*PG* 26, 1128); *Ad Serap.* I, 28 (*PG* 26, 593–4); *Contra Arian.* I, 8 (*PG* 26, 28); I, 3 (*PG* 26, 17).
[21] See also Basil, *Hom. c. Sab.* 4, 5 (*PG* 31, 609, 642); *De Spiritu Sancto* X, 25 (*PG* 32, 112).

is thus bound to include more generations than those of the time before the fourth century. In itself, then, the 'fatherhood' of the church could be as long in duration as the apostolic succession, which originally meant more or less the same as the concept *church father*. In later centuries, however, a limit was set to the extent in time of the idea of father of the church, and the name *church father* was reserved for those who were closest in time to the apostolic church. *Antiquitas*, or the fact that they were active in the period of Christian antiquity, thus became one of the essential characteristics of the church fathers. The patristic period was regarded, more or less correctly, to have ended with John Damascene (749) in the east and with Isidore of Seville (636) in the west. Aquinas called these fathers the *sancti*; their works had an 'authentic' value, whereas the later theologians were only called *magistri*, and their works had no decisive authority (*robur auctoritatis*).[22] This change is, in my opinion, partly connected with the historical fact that theology came, with the passage of time, to be less and less directly the concern of the bishops themselves, because of their increasing administrative activities. This gave rise to the so-called 'theological argument', dissociated from the teaching function of the hierarchical church, and this argument *ipso facto* acquired a value which was different from the *patristic* 'theological arguments'. It was perhaps this change which determined the somewhat arbitrary limit set to the period of the church fathers.

In the technical language of the church, then, the term 'church father' acquired a classic, clearly defined, and permanent meaning, which may be recognised by four essential characteristics.

1. *Christian antiquity*. The fathers of the church are representatives of Christian antiquity – they formed the first link between the apostolic period and later periods, and they are for this reason accorded a position of special privilege. This qualification might in itself seem arbitrary, like the limits that mark off the patristic period, but a very profound idea is in fact contained in it. The fathers were the first Christian writers to attempt, after the closing of revelation, to solve the problems brought about by the confrontation between the apostolic *kerygma* and the post-apostolic age by means of theological reflection. They were, in other words, the initiators of the church's theology, of conscious thought about faith within the church – it was they who laid the foundations of the theological 'faith-in-search-of-understanding' for later generations of Christians. They have a special value, then, in that they laid the foundations of theology. As bishops teaching within the church, they cannot be regarded as in any way superior, for example, to the church's hierarchy today.

2. *Orthodoxy in doctrine*. To say that they were orthodox does not mean that individual fathers did not commit error in doctrine. The orthodoxy of the patristic doctrine should rather be seen in their collective testimony of the church's doctrine – the *consensus patrum*. Aquinas called their testimony 'arguments from the proper sources of theology, but with only probable evidence'.[23] The value which is ascribed to them is theirs not as private theologians, but as active witnesses of

---

[22] See M.-D. Chenu, 'Authentica et magistralia', *Divus Thomas* 38 (1925), 3–51.
[23] *ST* I, q. 1, a. 8, ad 2: 'argumenta ex propriis sed probabiliter'.

the living tradition of the church. This brings us to a third characteristic of the fathers.

3. *Explicit or implicit ecclesiastical approval.* 'The authority of the teaching of the Catholic teachers is derived from the church. We are therefore bound to place more trust in the church's authority than in that of Augustine, Jerome, or any teacher'.[24] The church fathers drew their doctrine from the church and were witnesses of the apostolic *kerygma* only as representatives of this living tradition. This inner communion with the church is implied in their works, but it is only the church's teaching authority that can give official recognition to this. In fact, this official recognition was also accorded to many individual church fathers by the church's appointment of some of them as doctors of the church (*doctores ecclesiae*). The term *father of the church* and *doctor of the church* thus coincide only partially. Not all the fathers have been made doctors of the church, and there are also medieval and modern doctors who could be called 'fathers of the church' were it not for the fact that they lack the attribute of 'Christian antiquity'. But this characteristic is in fact one of the essential attributes of the concept *father of the church*. The patristic *doctors* of the church are the leading figures among the fathers. The church's universal and implicit regard for the fathers was only given concrete *expression* by the church's raising them to the rank of doctors of the church. Basil the Great, Gregory Nazianzen, and John Chrysostom have been the eastern doctors of the church from the very earliest times, and later Athanasius was also accorded this distinction especially by the western church. Since the eighth century Ambrose, Jerome, Augustine, and Gregory the Great have been regarded as the four great patristic doctors of the western church, and later other fathers have been created doctors of the church. The only factual difference between the fathers of the church and the patristic doctors of the church is that some of the fathers are regarded, because of the clearly universal orthodoxy and the influence of their doctrine in the church, by an 'explicit declaration of the church' (by the pope or the Congregation of Rites) as authentic teachers of the church's life of faith.

4. *Holiness of life.* Only those patristic writers who have from the earliest times been venerated as saints (even if they have not been 'canonised') are regarded as fathers of the church. This is less a question of their personal holiness than of the holiness of their testimony. Like the church fathers themselves, these characteristics must be seen as a whole. It is not a question of eminent individual figures, but of a single great community, scattered in time, but equally inspired, of greater and lesser personalities, whose voices echo each other so that the whole sounds like one great choir singing in unison. This ensemble alone guarantees the catholicity and apostolic nature of their teaching. For all these reasons, modern theological speculation, in addition to making a fundamental study of Scripture, cannot neglect the compelling need to study patristics, as this will always have an authoritative critical function with regard to the solutions that the theologian attempts to provide to contemporary problems.

---

[24] *ST* II–II, q. 10, a. 12.

Selected literature

- The Question Proper to Dogmatics: The Contemporary Context of God's Word; Selected from: Edward Schillebeeckx, 'The Bible and Theology', *Revelation and Theology*, trans. N. D. Smith, Collected Works of Edward Schillebeeckx vol. 2 (London: Bloomsbury T&T Clark, 2014), 124–7 [I 192–7].
- Biblical Theology: The Point of Departure for Dogmatic Theology; Edward Schillebeeckx, 'The Bible and Theology', *Revelation and Theology*, trans. N. D. Smith, Collected Works of Edward Schillebeeckx vol. 2 (London: Bloomsbury T&T Clark, 2014), 135–7 [I 212–14].
- The Place of the Church Fathers in Theology; Selected from: Edward Schillebeeckx, 'The Place of the Church Fathers in Theology', *Revelation and Theology*, trans. N. D. Smith, Collected Works of Edward Schillebeeckx vol. 2 (London: Bloomsbury T&T Clark, 2014), 139–43 [I 215–22].

4

Dominican Spirituality

What is Dominican spirituality?[1]

For the most part people live by stories. I myself live by my own story. When I became a Dominican I linked my life story with the family story of the Dominicans; as a result, my life story took on a new orientation and I picked up the thread of the story of the Order in my own way. So my own life has become part of the Dominican family story: a chapter in it. Through the story of the Order I have attained my own identity. Stories of the Dominican Order keep us together as Dominicans. Without stories we should be deprived of remembrance, fail to find our own place in the present and remain without hope or expectation for the future. Thus as Dominicans we form a group precisely as our own storytelling community, which hands down its own traditions within the wider story of the many religious communities, within the all-embracing story of the great community of the church, and within the even greater community of humankind. This makes us our own special family, recognisable from all kinds of family characteristics, some major, some minor, but none of which can be hidden.

In saying this, I have already said something about 'Dominican spirituality'. This can only be my own life story in so far as it has become a chapter of the Dominican family story. My own life story extends and enriches the history of Dominican spirituality, while as a small – almost infinitesimally small – chapter in it, it is at the same time relativised and criticised by the already older and wider story of the Dominican family. This makes me ask whether I really am not distorting this family story. So I am already sceptical towards all those who would suggest 'one's own insight' or 'one's own experience' to others as a norm for Dominican spirituality. Furthermore, thank God, there are still Dominicans alive today. In other words, our story is not yet exhausted, completely told; there is still something to be said.

A first conclusion already follows from this: a definitive all-round definition of Dominican spirituality cannot be given. You cannot make a final judgment on a

---

[1]Selected From: Edward Schillebeeckx, 'Dominican Spirituality', *God Among Us: The Gospel Proclaimed*, trans. John Bowden (New York: Crossroad, 1983), 232–7.

story which is still in full swing. We can only trace some of the main lines in the plot of the story, which has now been handed down for seven centuries in constantly different ways: the one basic story has been told in countless other languages and tongues with a view to constantly different listeners, and especially with a view to their cultural, historical circumstances and the nature of their church.

The basic story which stands at the beginning of our own Dominican storytelling community is of fundamental importance here. But the origin of any relevant story usually blurs into an obscure past which is difficult to reconstruct historically. Dominic (1170–1223), the origin of the Dominican family story, did not write any books. Through laborious historical reconstruction which extracts the 'real Dominic' from all kinds of legends (so typical of the Middle Ages), we nevertheless have sufficient firm ground under our feet. In particular, though Dominic may not have left behind any books or documents, what he did leave behind as a living legacy was the Dominican movement, the Order, a group of people who wanted to carry on Dominic's work in his footsteps. The Dominican story therefore begins with Dominic and his first companions; together they stand at the beginning of what is to become the Dominican family story. They gave the story its theme: they set its tone.

However, this story, often retold and sometimes rewritten, is in itself a particular way in which the thread of an already older story, that of Jesus of Nazareth, is taken up and continued in a new manner. This already brings us to a second conclusion. Dominican spirituality is only valid in so far as it takes up the story of Jesus and brings it up to date in its own way. In its Decree on the Renewal of Religious Life, the Second Vatican Council said that 'to follow Jesus' is the ultimate and supreme norm of any form of religious life (*suprema regula*, no. 2). Dominican spirituality is therefore subject to the criterion of the sources of all Christian life. This also means that even the 'Dominican spirituality' of Dominic and his first followers is not directly an absolute law for Dominicans. A fuller and more sophisticated knowledge of the 'story of Jesus' which has become possible since then (e.g. through new devotional experiences based on the Bible or through more refined exegesis of Scripture) may therefore lead us to different emphases from those of Dominic and his followers. For according to the council's Decree on Religious Renewal, this renewal must happen in the first place through a return 'to the sources of all Christian life' (no. 2), the Gospel of Jesus Christ (Mark 1.1), and this is the source which is never exhausted and always offers new possibilities, for which even Dominic himself did not know the all-embracing 'Open Sesame'.

At the same time this implies that the story of every Order must be judged as a part, or better as a modulation, of the greater story of the 'community of God', the church ('a participation in the life of the church': ibid., no. 2). Here the council points to the 'present-day projects' of the church: biblical, liturgical, dogmatic, pastoral, ecumenical, missionary and social. That is, Dominican spirituality essentially presupposes a critical involvement in the very specific needs and problems of today's church in its historical circumstances; it cannot be an isolated cultivation of our own 'Dominican' garden alongside the ongoing life of the world and the church.

Given all this, however, as governed by the gospel and subjected to the constant historical criticism that it exercises, and at the same time as a concrete historical feature of the necessary major projects of the church in the world here and now, in fact 'the original inspiration of one's own religious institution' (thus the council's

Decree on Religious Life, no.2) is the basic theme of the Dominican family story, and is therefore normative. Here the council decree points not only to the original 'specific project' (propria proposita) of the founder, but also to the order's 'own religious traditions', at least in so far as these are sound (*sanae traditiones*), that is, to the 'spiritual heritage' of a religious order: its spirituality.

The third conclusion may therefore run: Dominican spirituality is valid as a special modality of the church's task 'to follow Jesus', especially – for us – in the footsteps and the inspiration of Dominic, as this inspiration has constantly provided new light and direction in the best moments of the history of the Order. Therefore we must clearly bring this basic historical story to mind, for in the course of time the Dominican community has also had a broken relationship to its own origins. When the Inquisition brought, for example, Joan of Arc to the stake, the Dominicans involved were essentially contradicting Dominic's inspiration and orientation. People had become deaf and blind to the origin of new charismata: this was an essentially un-Dominican attitude.

As a third criterion for renewed religious life, the same decree of the council gives the relationship of the story of Jesus and the original basic story (for us, of the Dominicans) to the altered circumstances of the time (no. 22). This implies that Dominican spirituality cannot be defined purely by a reference to the original story or purely by a reference to the further modulations and updating of this basic story in the course of the history of the Order, though this is presupposed. Dominican spirituality also involves the way in which we live out this Dominican family story here and now, in our time. Dominican spirituality does not indicate simply how things were 'at the beginning' or in the course of the history of the Order. In that case we would simply be writing a historical report of the way in which Dominicans were inspired in former times. But historical knowledge is not yet spirituality. Thus someone who was a good historian but not a Dominican could reconstruct it better than we could. If it is not to be purely the 'history' of a spirituality (and furthermore, if it is not to become an empty ideology), Dominican spirituality is a living reality today; it is handed on (or distorted) by Dominicans living now, who reshape the Dominican family story here and now with an eye to the situation in the world and the church, the cultural historical situation of the moment.

Thus the fourth conclusion runs as follows: without a living relationship to the present, any talk about Dominican spirituality remains a purely historical preoccupation with the past of the Order (often an excuse for neglecting tasks which are urgent now). Dominican spirituality is a living reality which is to be realised among us now. Otherwise we simply repeat stories which others have told for a long time, as though we ourselves did not have to write our own chapter in what is of course a story which had already begun before us. Whereas now we do have to write a new chapter which is still unpublished, if after us anyone else is going to think it worth taking up the thread of this Dominican story again. If in fact we can, may and will write that new living chapter, I am certain that many young people, men and women, will again be drawn to continue the Dominican tradition after us. For any meaningful story has a power of attraction; it is retold, and no one can stop its snowball effect. Whether that happens, however, depends on the tone in which we write our chapter in the great Dominican family story and the tension it contains. Will it be a dull, unread little paragraph? Or will it be an alien story which does not take up the thread of the family story that has already begun, and so allows the Dominican story to die out, perhaps for good? Or will it become an attractive episode, attractive perhaps only because all that the hearer notices is that we are zealously in search of the real thread of the story, which for the moment we have lost track of? That too can also be an important part of the already old Dominican family story.

Should you now reread my previous 1954 duplicated article on 'Dominican Spirituality' in the spirit which I have just described, I think that you may find that it still provides sufficient inspiration and orientation in its historical reference to the 'golden thread' which runs through the Dominican family story from Dominic down to the present day. As may become evident, this golden thread sometimes runs across the fabric of Christianity – a fact that we may not obscure when we are writing our share in the great history of the Order. Provided that this golden thread is woven into our life story, however different it may be in content, we have in fact realised Dominican spirituality. 'Spirituality' is not spirituality so long as it is only described, whether in an assertive or an authoritarian tone. It is spirituality to the degree that it is realised in practice – as a completely new rendering of an older Dominican melody.

How does this older melody go, this constantly recurring theme, this basic story?

I would say that it is a cross-grained story! In the twelfth century and at the beginning of the thirteenth there were two burning points at issue: a need for renewal in the priestly life and a need for renewal in the monastic life. The Fourth Lateran Council in 1215 dealt with these two problems separately, without any relation between them, and without connecting the two. This Council was not without its influence on Dominic who, as an Augustinian canon of Osma, on a journey to the south of France had already gathered round him a group of fellow workers to provide for the pressing needs of priestly care in the see of Toulouse, which had severe pastoral problems. Dominic saw the signs of the times. In the twelfth century, religious movements had arisen: a great many lay people joined them. The basic tendency of these movements was to combine gospel poverty with preaching, but they often had an anti-clerical tone. All kinds of clerical abuses had prompted the question: does Christian preaching require the permission of the church (the bishop), and involve commissioning and sending by the church? Or is not religious life, and life according to the gospel in the footsteps of the apostles (at that time called the *vita apostolica*) itself a qualification for Christian preaching? This last view was the standpoint of many religious movements, whereas it was officially regarded as 'heresy' by the councils. We could say that the heretical movements of that time were inspired by the gospel and Christ, while the official preachers, though orthodox, did not lead a life in accordance with the gospel – at least to all outward appearances – and were completely embedded in feudal structures. All manifestations of this new religious movement – above all in France, Italy, Germany and the Netherlands (the rich countries of that time) show striking common features (independently of each other): living out the gospel sine glossa (without compromises). Its spirituality was characterised by a deep devotion to the humanity of Jesus: following the poor Jesus. (This happened under the influence of the Cistercian movement and the Gregorian reform.)

At the same time there was clear influence from the contemplative, Greek Byzantine East (through the crusaders and cloth merchants). The situation became more serious when these gospel movements came into contact with dualistic Eastern movements which arrived in the West through the Slav lands of the Danube; they were called Cathari, a collective term for gnostic and dualistic trends. As a result the whole of the 'gospel movement' became even more suspect to the church. The problem became that of saving the gospel movement for the church and mobilising it against heresy. We must set the phenomenon of Dominic against this historical background of all kinds of enthusiastic revivals of evangelism, but on the periphery of the official church. Dominic was not alone in seeing the problems in the situation: Pope Innocent III, Bishop Diego, with whom Dominic travelled to the south, and Francis of Assisi also saw it. With outspoken realism, Dominic formulated a clear rescue programme. He saw that an enormous potential for the gospel was being lost to the church. Though trained in the already traditional canonical priestly life, he was nevertheless sympathetic to these new counter-experiments. But he saw quite clearly why they either kept failing (splitting off into 'heretical' sects), or came to be incorporated once again into traditional monastic life (e.g. the Premonstratensians). He wanted to make these counter-movements authentic alternative forms of the church's evangelism, a church movement: he wanted as it were to 'live like the heretics' but 'teach like the church'.

The history of Dominican spirituality[2]

Evangelism must be a challenge within the church; in other words it must be the church and not a sect. Dominic's own vision came near to this in that he saw the solution of the problems of the time in the combination – in one institution – of apostolic preaching (that is, preaching with a critical remembrance of the need for a proclamation endorsed by the Pope or by the episcopate), and the *vita apostolica* (that is, radical evangelism: following Jesus like the apostles). He brought together organically, in one programme, the themes treated separately by the Fourth Lateran Council. Because this same Council, to some extent contrary to the personal views of Pope Innocent III, had forbidden all new forms of religious life (Mansi 22, 1002) and 'banned' unauthorised preaching (Mansi, ibid., 990), Dominic combined the best of traditional monastic life with the basic trends of the new counter-movements which had arisen all over Europe and which, to make the Christian proclamation credible, required a life commensurate with the gospel from those who proclaimed it. In so doing he broke down the feudal structures of the old monastic life: thus there arose a new form of religious life, the Order of Preachers, the Dominicans. Hence our earliest constitutions are largely made up of elements from the constitutions of traditional religious life, especially from the Norbertines and Cistercians (at that time the most lively religious institutions). However, Dominic and his first followers transformed these elements by the very purpose of the Order: apostolic itinerant

---

[2]Selected From: Edward Schillebeeckx, 'Dominican Spirituality', *God Among Us: The Gospel Proclaimed*, trans. John Bowden (New York: Crossroad, 1983), 237–44.

preaching; that is, the new spirit of what were then modern, experimental gospel movements brought into the perspective of the church.

Dominic had been caught up in this spirit through his contact in the south of France with all this heretical gospel enthusiasm, which was shared by a broad spectrum of people, high and low. Through the structure of his Order, Dominic had weakened the economic stability which had been the basic principle of the older monastic institutions. On the basis of a religious criticism Dominic thus attacked the foundations of the feudal system (in church and society). Furthermore, the association of the contemplative monastic element with itinerant preaching resulted in a basic difference from the traditional form of monastic life. The new 'corporative' idea (a particular form of organisation, as in the official guilds) was adapted to the religious institution: no 'monarchical' authority from above but a democratic form of government with a range of choices (democratic and personal). Paradoxically, Dominic's evangelism led to a new incarnation in secular structures, especially those of the rising democratic mediaeval bourgeoisie.

By thread and cross-thread, Dominic wove a new fabric, created a new religious programme. Thus the Dominican order was born from the charisma of the combination of admonitory and critical recollection of the spiritual heritage of the old monastic and canonical religious life with the 'modernistic' religious experiment of the thirteenth century. Dominic had a fine sensitivity both to religious values from the past and to the religious promise for the future emanating from the modern experiments of his time. The Dominican Order was born out of this two-fold charisma. With Pere Cormier, a modern Magister General of our Order (see my 1954 duplicated article, p.7), I would say that this is our *gratia originalis*, the grace at the origin of our Order.

Dominican spirituality is therefore in the first instance to be defined as a spirituality which, on the basis of admonitory and critical reflection on the heritage left behind by the past religious tradition, takes up critically and positively the cross-thread provided by whatever new religious possibilities for the future keep emerging among us. Therefore it can never be a material repetition of what our Dominican forebears have themselves done admirably; nor, however, can it be an uncritical acceptance of whatever 'new movements'(in the mystical or political sense) are now evident in our midst. For Dominic, the essential thing was the question of truth. In his heart Dominic was ultimately one hundred per cent behind the new apostolic experiments of preaching combined with poverty, but – remembering the good achievements of the previous patterns of religious life – he unconditionally observed the guidelines laid down by the Fourth Lateran Council (1215) for any renewal of both priestly and religious life. His charisma was organically to combine two divergent guidelines and thus personally to extend the aims of this Council.

On the basis of this spirituality, which found expression in our very first Dominican Constitutions, the further history of the spirituality becomes understandable. This brings the historical, changing, cross-grained, new element into the very heart of Dominican spirituality. For example, the Constitutions from the years 1221–1231 said: 'Our brothers may not study the books of pagan writers (referring above all to Aristotle) and philosophers (what is meant is Arabic philosophy, the great modernism in the Middle Ages); far less may they study the secular sciences.' However, only about twenty years later, Albert the Great and Thomas Aquinas were to regard the study of secular sciences and the 'pagan philosophers' as a necessary condition of the preparation and formation of an appropriate Dominican apostolate. Thus on the basis of an authentic Dominican spirituality these two Dominican saints boldly went against a Dominican constitution set up in earlier times and were therefore in opposition to what was then in fact called official 'Dominican spirituality'. They did this – inspired by what Dominic did in his time – so successfully that the definition was later removed from the Constitutions by a General Chapter; indeed, later Constitutions urged Thomas as a model (Raymond of Penafort had centres for the study of Arabic built in Nursia and Tunis). That is an authentically Dominican development, after the heart of St. Dominic, who himself tried to reconcile 'the past' and new 'possibilities for the future'. (This brought with it the new danger that Thomas would later cease to be a beacon pointing towards the future and would become a closed frontier.) If no cross-thread can be seen in the story that the Dominican perceives and takes up again himself, there is every chance that Dominican spirituality will fade; worse still, that on the basis of an 'established' Dominican spirituality – a contradiction in terms – we shall wrongly write off as apocryphal talk new attempts at a truly Dominican spirituality. The greatest moments in the history of our Order are when at the same time this history becomes anti-history or a cross-thread: Dominic himself, Albert and Thomas, Savonarola, Eckhardt, de las Casas, Lacordaire, Lagrange, Chenu, Congar, to name a few. However, at the same time Dominicans have sometimes (in the first instance at least) run into difficulties with the already established Dominican story when in an un-Dominican way it has refused to take up the new cross-thread. Without mistaking the fundamental worth, by which we are all supported, of the many anonymous Dominicans who have quietly lived a successful Dominican religious life (though their tranquillity can have a broad influence and produce cross-grained stories within the Order), nevertheless it only becomes clear what is typically Dominican when Dominicans sometimes, following the example of Dominic, reshape 'the old' and combine it with the dynamism of constantly new and different forms. If this does not happen at regular intervals, then there is every chance that the well-known Dominican concern for truth is dishonoured in an Inquisition and the new 'Dominican possibilities' are rejected. They may then come to life outside the Dominican family. I would not want to include this less rosy story – which is also part of our Order – in the golden thread of our family story, which is always in a state of constantly taking up the cross-thread again. However, the cross-thread sometimes ensures the continuity! The history of this cross-thread is the golden thread of the Dominican family story, woven into a broader, as it were more serene, whole. That St. Ignatius of Loyola was shut up in the cellars of one of our monasteries because he shocked the people of his time with a new charisma is one of the many stories in which 'Dominican spirituality' has perversely become its opposite; it now shows us to be guilty of un-Dominican chauvinism. In other words, this is typical of times in which the Dominicans were no longer 'Dominican' and on the basis of their own 'established' position had already dubbed the new counter-thread heretical. The constantly new forms which Dominican spirituality must take in accordance with Dominic's basic story will emerge even more clearly precisely through the moments in which we have failed in the past.

It is essential for Dominican spirituality to attend to God as he has already revealed himself to us in the past and to attend to the present-day 'signs of the time' in which the same God, who is faithful to us, makes his appeal. Any one-sidedness – in one-track, uncritical judgment either of the past or of what prove to be symptoms of the future in the present – is un-Dominican. Dominic submits the present, with its own possibilities of experiment, to comparison with the dangerous recollection of certain events and legacies from the past, just as at the same time he opens up the global past and gives it the stamp of the cross-grained experimental present: it is out of this kind of attitude that the Order was born. This must remain its 'genius'. The *presence a Dieu* and the presence au monde (as Lacordaire puts it) describe the very nature of Dominican spirituality throughout the history of the Order. And perhaps today we are going to see clearly that – in recollection of the religious past – the 'presence au monde' or critical solidarity with the human world is the only possible mode of our *presence a Dieu*. At the same time this insight confirms the need for a critical recollection of the religious past in which the same *presence a Dieu* is always revealed in the communication of what were then the contemporary signs of the time. The 'modernism' of the Dominican order lives on dangerous memories from the past. After what was almost a centuries-long sleep, it was Père Lacordaire and Master General Jandel who in the nineteenth century recalled the Dominican Order to its original charisma and brought about a break with the serene traditionalism to which the 'established order' had fallen victim. 'Lacordaire' (and everything connected with that within our Dominican history) was in fact the rediscovery of the Order by itself. For the Lacordaire movement was nourished by the original charisma of the order and as a result again raised the problem of 'Dominican spirituality'.

Some consequences of Dominican spirituality are clear from this.

1. Belief in the absolute priority of God's grace in any human action: the theologal direction of the Dominican life and its programme in relation to ethics, the world, society and the betterment of people. No cramped self-concern but trust in God: I can trust God more than myself. Therefore a tranquil and happy spirituality. God still gives an unexpected future to the limited meaning and scope of my own actions.

2. Religious life in the light of the gospel (*vita apostolica*) as the atmosphere in which the Dominican is apostolic (*salus animarum*, salvation as the aim of the activity of the Order): through preaching in all its forms. The result of that is *contemplari et contemplata aliis tradere* (i.e. the agreement between what a person proclaims and their own life, see Thomas, II-II, q.188, a.6 and a.7, in which he contrasts the character of the Mendicants with that of other religious institutions and at the same time connects this with 'poverty': being free from financial worries). This general mendicant view became typically Dominican through the essential insertion of study into the structure of this Dominican evangelism. This particular clement was not characteristic of the mediaeval evangelical movements. 'Study is not the aim of the order but an essential instrument for this work' (says Humbert of Romans in his commentary on the Constitutions). The failure of many gospel movements was also brought about by a lack of thoughtfulness. Furthermore, while the universities, which were only established at that time, had intensified the element of scientific study, at the same time they had concentrated it and centralised it so that there

were no intellectuals in the dioceses. Dominic saw this, and therefore he incorporated study as an institutional element in the very organisation of his order. He would not have any monastery founded 'without a doctor in theology', and any monastery had to be a 'school of theology': a Dominican monastery is 'permanent instruction'. The distinction between study monasteries and pastoral monasteries is un-Dominican; both must be monasteries for study and pastoral ministry. (See Thomas' defence of a religious institution 'founded for study': II-II, q.188, a.5.)

3. The 'Jesus spirituality' of the order – the 'humanity of Jesus' (Albert, Thomas, Eckhart, Tauler, Suso, etc.) (here directly connected with the only two Dominican devotions, to Mary and to Joseph), but this humanity experienced as a personal manifestation of God's love for humanity – is the centre of Dominican spirituality and mysticism without any predilection for 'derivative devotions'. All this is typically twelfth century; along with all the other characteristics it is also typically Dominican.

4. *Presence au monde (la grâce d'entendre ce siècle*, as Père Lacordaire says): openness for constantly new charismata which the different circumstances require of us. Hence the need for structures which do not hem us in but are democratic and flexible, through which it becomes possible for Dominicans to accept the rise of new stories which go against the grain. It is characteristic that the Dominicans never had their Constitutions approved by the Pope, so that they themselves could adapt them to new circumstances (see P. Mandonnet, *Saint Dominique*, Paris 1937, I, 237; L. Moulin, 'Les formes du gouvernement local et provincial dans les ordres religieux', in *Revue Internationale des Sciences Administratives*, nos. 1–3, 1955, 9 n.l).

5. (As a consequence of 4.): Since Albert and Thomas, Dominican spirituality has been inwardly enriched by the inclusion of the Christian principle of secularisation within the essentially religious, gospel trend (Dominicans at first rejected this, but soon they generally accepted it): this involves first coming to know things (objects, inter-personal relationships, society) in their intrinsic characteristics and their own structures rather than prematurely defining their relationship to God. In modern times this has enormous consequences over against all kinds of forms of pseudo-mystical supernaturalism, which often ends up as a sense of superiority masquerading as piety.

To begin with, the Order agonised over the introduction of 'natural sources' into Dominican evangelism. The traditional rejection of the 'profane sciences' by the monks continued to have its effect, though this was limited by the Dominican principle of dispensation. The first Dominicans were 'anti-philosophical' (thus running the risk of an evangelical supernaturalism). The *Vitae Fratrum* (G. Frachet) reeked of 'holy naivety'. Albert and Thomas changed the direction, Albert even arguing fiercely against fellow-brethren 'who thus again want to become the murderers of Socrates'. The dispute was over the consequences of integral evangelism which Albert and Thomas wanted to be enlightened, not naive. In the Chapter of Valenciennes (1259), the trend supported by Albert and Thomas won through: the study of the 'profane sciences' became obligatory in Dominican training.

6. The other elements: a liturgical choral office, monastic observances and community life, are traditional and generally religious, and in this sense not typically Dominican. That was the dangerous recollection of the monastic and canonical past to which Dominic continued to give expression in his new religious and apostolic programme – albeit in critical, reduced and more modest form.

7. The 'principle of dispensation' (historically this seems to go back to Dominic himself in person), i.e. respect for the particular personal charisma of a fellow Dominican within the Dominican community, bearing in mind the purpose of the order. Of course this is an extremely dangerous principle, which has been abused to disastrous effect. However, Dominic would rather take that risk than give up the human and Christian significance of the dispensation principle because of the threat of abuse. As a general principle this was a completely new Dominican discovery in the Middle Ages. In furtherance of study in the service of the 'salvation of souls' (*salus animarum*) and in furtherance of the apostolate, it is, paradoxically, possible to be a Dominican (if necessary) on your own. This presupposes having been trained as a Dominican, but it is in no way understood as a matter of standing outside the law: on the contrary, dispensation is a constitutional Dominican law. Conformity is alien to original Dominican legislation. Even now, this original Dominican principle opens up broad possibilities for 'modern experiments' in our time, even experiments which some people accustomed to an 'established' Dominican spirituality cannot stand. (However, these experiments also always need to happen from and within the dangerous recollection of a tradition which is already centuries old. This tradition prefigures permanent perspectives which are always worth thinking about – without it all experiments seem doomed to religious failure.) Although there are countless examples of this characteristic from our rich family archives, I want to point to just one event in the first redactions of our Dominican Constitutions. The striking 'democratic structure' of our Order has been said by experts in administration to be unique among Catholic monastic institutions. This feature can be understood precisely as a result of the typical cross-grained spirituality of the Order (along with its respect for all that is good in the tradition). The Constitutions were 'reformulated' during a revision at a time when great canon lawyers from the universities of the time had entered the Order (for example, Raymond of Penafort). This reformulation took place at a General Chapter in Bologna. Shortly before and during this Chapter, social protests were voiced in the university and city of Bologna, and in addition there was already a dispute between the Ghibellines (the conservatives) and the Guelphs (the progressive popular party). Dominicans were involved as advisers throughout this conflict. The 'co-responsibility of all' required by the progressive party had its influence on our Dominican Constitutions. 'What affects all must also be resolved on

by all'. This new civic principle called for at that time was also supported by the Dominicans and later sanctioned in our Dominican Constitutions (under the influence and as a result of the civic experiences in Bologna). New 'secular experiences' thus came to exercise a substantial influence on our earliest Constitutions. The emancipatory social movements of that time left a substantial mark on our Constitutions, differing completely from the traditional administrative model then current. Following the example of Dominic, these Dominicans did not just raise a warning finger and point to what had been the custom from earliest times, but at the same time listened to the voice of God in what came out of the human secular emancipatory movements of the time (however turbulently). As a result of these experiences they rewrote the Dominican monastic structure, barely twenty years after Dominic. That is just one case of the cross-thread that the Dominican family story keeps showing as its 'own theme' down the ages.

I have only recalled a few Dominican characteristics: more could be mentioned. Furthermore, I should point out explicitly that I am in no way denying that perhaps non-Dominicans do the same things. In that case Dominican spirituality can simply say with delight: all the better! It is not our concern to maintain an unparalleled exclusiveness. It is a question of what we, as Dominicans, do here in any case, and do in the strength of the charisma of the Order and our Dominican commitment (through our profession). If others also do the same thing, this can simply confirm the validity, the correct intuition of our view. When a typical view is universalised, it in no way loses its value: quite the opposite.

The person who was once an Augustinian canon, Domingo de Guzman, while trusting in the original direction of his life nevertheless gave it a new course (which became the beginning of the Dominican Order), thanks to a living contact with the needs of people and of the church of which he was unaware when he was first called. One cannot accuse Dominic of betraying his first calling, which was meant to be irrevocable. His change of course was a new way of life (in contact with what then appeared to him to be better possibilities), in order to remain faithful to the deepest sense of his calling, when confronted with new needs. (According to Dominic's earliest biographers he could be moved to tears at the sight of the needs of others. Hence the desire of this realistic organiser – which remained with him all his life – to go to the Cumani, somewhere in the Balkans, evidently the place where the dualistic heresy crossed from East to West.) The Order came into being from such an amazing change of course in trust. A change of course in trust is therefore part of the essence of the Dominican charisma.

No theologian, canon lawyer, professional psychologist or sociologist can work out at his study desk or in his armchair what we must do now. This must be tried by way of concrete experiment, by charismatically inspired religious, albeit bearing in mind the sometimes dangerously cross-grained element – the golden thread – in our Dominican family story. In so doing it will adopt, with due criticism, the successful attempts in the context of our past, gratefully rethinking them and making them fruitful in the context of the new programme. With Thomas Aquinas, who clearly followed the matter-of-fact and brilliant temperament of Dominic here, we can say, 'The excellence of a religious institution does not lie so much in the strictness of its observances as in the fact that these observances are designed with greater skill towards the purpose of the religious life' (II-II, q. 188, a.6, ad 3). And in the circumstances of our time this calls for a renewed and skilled religious decision in which all have a share, both high and low, so that the structures themselves remain open to this new cross thread.

This question is our duty. For in our profession we also opt for a particular community, a Dominican community and its ideals. There can be such faults and defects in a particular community (whether through betrayal of the Dominican family story or because this story is no longer alive there and has become ossified and dead) that out of faithfulness to his or her Dominican ideal the professed religious is ethically permitted (and in some cases may even be obliged) to leave the Dominican community because it does not give him or her the support to which they have a right by virtue of their profession. For paradoxically, here we expose ourselves to the danger that as Dominicans we may expel a 'Dominican charisma' from our ranks. The Dominican family story gives us adequate pointers if we also listen to God's voice in the characteristics of contemporary movements and trace their lines of force, so as to enrich this story with a new chapter which is still to be published. Many people think that the Dominican family story is exhausted, because hardly anyone still comes under its spell. All of us who are Dominicans today, men and women, are the only ones who can give it a new twist so that the story flourishes again (not as a stunt or a sensation but as an authentic Dominican family story), so that others in turn will join the Dominican storytelling community and continue to hand the story on. Here we may also happily pass on the folklore which each Order has alongside its own great story: that simply points to the fact that the great Dominican family story is made up of, and told by, ordinary, very human, people, though they transcend themselves through the strength of God's unmerited and loving grace. However, it would be fatal for the Dominican family story if this greater story eventually became narrower and was reduced to the story of the folklore of Dominican houses.

I am aware that I have said a great deal and very little. That is perhaps the most appropriate thing for the chapter which we are all adding, here and now, to the story of a great family tradition. I hope that it will become a serial which lasts longer than the stories which have entranced the whole world on television, but which have not in any way renewed the face of the earth: Peyton Place, the Forsyte Saga or Dallas. May the Dominican story be a parable which in an unspoken, but compelling, way ends with the words of Jesus: 'Go and do likewise' (Luke 10.37).

Domingo de Guzmán: Founder of the movement of 'the Dominican family'[3]

In the south of France, in Vence, in a quite beautiful chapel of Dominican sisters, last year on Maundy Thursday I saw the famous Matisse pictures. On the wall of

---

[3] Selected from: Edward Schillebeeckx, *For the Sake of the Gospel*, trans. John Bowden (New York: Crossroad, 1990), 119–23.

this simple chapel Dominic was depicted in a few strokes, but you could not say that the portrait was 'abstract'; it had just a few very evocative contours: very concrete and at the same time incomplete, figuratively abstract. If you look closer, you are impelled to fill in this sketch of Dominic yourself and yet you feel that your own interpretation is under the spell and the norm of this drawing. With gentle pressure the drawing itself indicates the direction of your colouring of it, while you yourself need not give up your own Dominican experience, from which you fill it in.

I thought, that *is* a full-length portrait of Dominic. Dominic was himself and granted others their space and freedom. We do not have a hymn to the Sun from him, as we do from Francis of Assisi; nor even a Rule, like those of Benedict and Francis; we do not have a single writing from him, a single document in his own hand – which is also typical of Jesus of Nazareth. But we trace his spirit, we hear his 'logia' or sayings, and even his very own words, in some texts from the Fourth Lateran Council of 1215, very clearly in the first constitutions of the order, and finally above all in his living heritage: the Dominican movement. The French *Larousse Encyclopaedia*, which is not a specifically Catholic work, calls Dominic the first 'minister of education' in Europe and another non-Christian historian calls him the first democrat in the church system.

It was on the initiative of Dominic that the Master General of the Order was not called abbot, prelate or any such title, but constitutional master, a leader who has no legislative power, but only executive power in respect of everything that the brethren of the annual General Chapter had laid down as guidance each year. It was also an extremely distinctive decision of Dominic to abolish the law then applying in all religious orders which made the Rule and Constitution obligatory on pain of sin so as to encourage the brothers and sisters. One has to be a religious from the heart, not under the threat of sin. The third Master General, Humbert of Romans, relates that he had heard Dominic say through others: 'If anyone of our brothers (or sisters) thinks that the monastic rule is obligatory on pain of sin, then I will run round all the monasteries with a sharp knife to carve out every rule of the Order.'

Dominic has always seemed to me to be someone who is *par excellence* 'inwardly free', without complexes, liberated from concern for his own identity and therefore sovereign himself. *He* was an eminent administrator who, wary of all complicated legislation, simply gave his followers some rules of thumb, defined the direction and within that left space for others. As a personality Dominic was a kind of harmony of contrasts. On the one hand he was notable for an incredible lack of concern, in the sense of an almost audacious trust in God. The first Dominicans formed a happy community in the monastery of Saint-Romains, but Dominic abolished this monastery and scattered the members, apart from a few inhabitants, two by two round the world: to Paris and Spain, to Rome and Bologna. For a new religious foundation this seems to be one of Dominic's most reckless decisions. Moreover he was assaulted with doubts and advice from powerful sympathisers: Count Simon de Montfort, the Bishop of Toulouse, the Archbishop of Narbonne and many others urged Dominic not to do this. But Dominic's answer was brief but friendly: 'Don't contradict me, I'm well aware of what I'm doing.' History proved him right.

Moreover the same untroubled Dominic was an acute and purposeful organiser and strategist: he was as watchful as a fox, on his guard at every step. He calculates and calculates again, knows how to influence people for his apostolic projects, also under the impact of his human charm and natural authority. Sister Cecilia seems to have observed him closely. She testifies of Dominic: 'He was small in stature, rather slight in build, with a somewhat ruddy face, rather red hair and beard, attractive eyes. On his face, above all between eyes and eyebrows, there was a glance which cast a spell on many. He was always cheerful and alert, except when confronted with someone else's suffering. He had very long hands and a very resonant voice. Even when he grew older, he was not bald, but he had a short crop of light-grey hair' (Cecilia, ch. XV, p.30). So a woman can tell you something more about the outward aspect *of* a male saint.

Through cunning politics Dominic assured himself of the friendship of popes and other church and political authorities *for* his mission and apostolate. So he mobilised both the Fourth Lateran Council and the authority of the Pope for his project of 'the Dominican preaching'. Already through his financial administration, at least in the first period of the rise of the Order, he was one of the most stringent economists that the Order ever had. Many historians have been amazed at the way in which he acquires foundations and income; holds on to and expands, secures, leases out and develops what he has acquired; and does all this to free the brethren for study and above all *for* preaching the gospel. He would go back on that later. As he became older, Dominic made his views more radical and he then compelled all Dominican priories to cede all the property and collective possessions that they had gained, apart from humble dwellings with a small garden round them, to the Cistercian monks. In place of security of existence for the benefit of preaching, from now on Dominic wanted insecurity of existence out of solidarity with the poor and *for* the sake of the credibility of the preaching. That was the consequence of his acquaintance with Italian cities. In contrast to Spain and the cities in the south of France, Dominic now got to know the rich cities in Italy. He saw the greed and avarice in the cities which led to the building of rich palaces, but also to the impoverishment of many others which increased as a result.

Historical documents relate how Dominic's more radical approach by siding with the poor made many brothers leave the Order after the first General Chapter of Bologna in 1220. Dominic was resolutely opposed to the building of so many great priories because of the mass arrival of novices, and they remained incomplete until his death. Dominic was anything but a contemplative dreamer; he was God's fox, for God was the heart and soul of all that he did, and of his clear insight into what was going on in the church and the world. Although in my opinion (historians argue over this) he was not in agreement with the war which Count de Montfort *waged against* the Albigensians, he nevertheless *calculated the* fluctuating chances of this army in order to be able to exert skilful apostolic influence on the changing situation. Dominic built his house, his Dominican family, as an architect who calculates all the vicissitudes and takes them into account beforehand. Our first constitutions admonish us: 'Think of the rock from which you are hewn'.

Dominic was a charismatic, but with a very rational attitude, and I think that this combination was his success. Again there is a harmony of contradictions: evangelical sagacity coupled with a crystal-clear rationality. His rapture of spirit, his thoughtful practical wisdom, his well-known affable serenity: all this was paradoxically enough the work and the attitude of one prone to stomach ulcers who consequently had severe migraines, from which according to Jordan of Saxony he probably died. Psychologists assert that instability and moodiness, disquiet and lack of peace, chagrin, are all part of the psychology of those with stomach trouble and migraines. Jordan of Saxony, Dominic's friend and brilliant successor, nevertheless says of Dominic: 'The balance of his humour was remarkable.'

I could apply to Dominic what has been said of the apostle Paul in a way which is true to life but somewhat poetical: 'I am the Lord's singing bird. I build my nest in the mountain of my contemplation of God and I flop down there when I see a soul, as though Almighty God cast me down. I have long wished to ascend to the eternal tent on the heavenly plain. And hardly have I got up to the area of my desire above temple and obelisk than in the rarefied light such sorrow seises hold of me that, heavy with mercy and compassion, I descend below again, and each time I there get a passionate love and hope of again becoming all to all' (here I am quoting from memory Fr. Molenaar's, *In a Cool Shadow: Saint Paul* [*In koele schaduw: Sint Paulus*]. That is also a complete portrait of Dominic. They are the real saints; they no longer know whom they love best, God or human beings, because they can no longer distinguish between the two, so much are they 'of God', who is also a *God of human beings*.

Dominic was a person with a fine sense of the essentials in the great Christian tradition of experience, the essentials of the apostolic movement around the preaching brother Jesus of Nazareth. He was also a person with a fine sense of all the contemporary developments in the Middle Ages, in a period in which the old feudal system still predominated but was gradually being broken up by the rise of the free cities with their autonomous trades of free citizens. For the social and church system of the time, and also for many older religious orders, all this new development was 'of the devil', above all because in it a degree of emancipation of the laity was coming about which was furthered by the new techniques. People are often afraid of new developments; at that time for many people technology was a black and magic art, and cultural developments were disturbing the naïve faith of some people. However, Dominic saw in this new social constellation a possibility of proclaiming the gospel in a new way: no longer for the benefit of a small elite but at least for a greater number, even if these were still primarily limited to the cities. Dominic too, is a child of his time.

Selected literature

- Dominican Spirituality; Selected From: Edward Schillebeeckx, 'Dominican Spirituality', in *God Among Us: The Gospel Proclaimed*, trans. John Bowden (New York: Crossroad, 1983), 232–7, 237–44.
- Domingo de Guzmán: Founder of the movement of 'the Dominican family'; Selected from: Edward Schillebeeckx, *For the Sake of the Gospel*, trans. John Bowden (New York: Crossroad, 1990), 119–23.

PART TWO

The Second Vatican Council and Its Aftermath

Introduction

Daniel Minch

On 26 January 1958, Edward Schillebeeckx moved from his native Belgium to the Netherlands to take up the chair of Dogmatics and the History of Christianity at the Catholic University of Nijmegen (today called Radboud University Nijmegen). This came just a year before important news would come from Rome: Pope John XXIII would announce on 25 January 1959 that he intended to convene an ecumenical council. That the announcement of the council and the installation of Schillebeeckx in Nijmegen coincided became seemingly providential. Schillebeeckx would go on to be deeply involved in the preparations of the Dutch church for the coming gathering, even ghost-writing a pastoral letter from the Dutch bishops that was read at Christmas in 1960 and published in January of the next year. The fact that he was thanked by name in a postscript to the letter had the double effect of placing him in the theological spotlight and under the scrutiny of the magisterium. Translations of the letter appeared in several European languages, but the Italian translation was quickly banned in Rome and it attracted the attention of the Prefect for the Holy Office, Cardinal Alfredo Ottaviani (1890–1979). Schillebeeckx became an unofficial advisor to the Dutch bishops at the council, having been denied the status of a *peritus* likely thanks to his notoriety and the influence of Ottaviani. Despite this, however, he was generally in demand as a speaker for groups in Rome and gave many talks to groups of bishops at the first session of the council. His commentary on the first Schemas was widely available in Latin, French, and English and, along with those composed by Karl Rahner and Joseph Ratzinger, helped to shift the conversation in that first session away from the prepared texts and towards a more open debate.

Vatican II was certainly a turning point in Schillebeeckx's life and career. It led to his increased contact with other rising stars in twentieth-century theology, and placed him in contact with the world-church in a very concrete way. The journal *Concilium* which he co-founded in 1965 and helped edit would continue the theological trajectories that began at the council. The direction of Schillebeeckx's theology also changed rather markedly as a result of and after Vatican II. One of the main questions that was debated in the preparation of the Dogmatic Constitutions on the Church, on Revelation, and the Pastoral Constitution on the Church in the Modern World, was precisely the relation between God and the world – in essence, the old debate on nature and grace had once again re-emerged, but in drastically different circumstances and a rapidly changing world. It is in the mid-1960s, therefore, that we see a shift in Schillebeeckx's work away from his previous focus on more traditional dogmatic topics in his teaching, and especially his prior work on the sacraments, to fundamental theological method and considerations of the role of new approaches to philosophy for theology. The debates in the Dutch church over the Eucharist and the real presence of Christ in 1965–66 provide an interesting key to his evolving thought process. In his book, *The Eucharist* (Dutch: 1967; English: 1968), he begins with a historical consideration of how the Tridentine doctrine of Eucharistic change emerged, what it was responding to in the sixteenth-century context, and what the text means *for us* in light of these reflections and the wider continuity of tradition. He then turns an adapted phenomenological analysis of Eucharistic presence, which explains the '*transsubstantiatio*' in terms of what God does in and for the gathered community of faith. The centre of the reflection is not the 'objective' elements that are transformed, as though through a physical or even magical process, but the subjective and personal transformation effected by God and the church as Body of Christ. Experience here is key to the liturgical, and ultimately ecclesiological argument. Experience is a *locus theologicus*, and interpretation, rather than being something that, as an additive element, either clarifies or distorts the objective fact of revelation, is actually an intrinsic part of the event of revelation itself. This turn to experience, and ultimately a turn towards the world, took different forms. Certainly, in the late 1960s it manifested in essays and collected volumes on method, and specifically the application of hermeneutics and critical theory in theology. From here, Schillebeeckx turned in what was at the time a rather unexpected direction: towards Christology and to a systematic theological synthesis of historical critical research on Jesus. This resulted in his first two revolutionary *Jesus* books in 1974 and 1977, as well as the slim volume *Interim Report on the Books Jesus and Christ* which appeared in 1978. These books also brought controversy and renewed scrutiny by the Congregation for the Doctrine of the Faith. This process began in 1976 and only concluded, without condemnation, in 1980. From there he turned his gaze to matters regarding ministry, ecclesiology, and revelation. His writings in this area once again attracted the attention of the CDF, now led by Ratzinger, and after informal 'conversations', a notification, but no condemnation, was issued in 1986. After this, the final *Jesus* volume, *Church: The Human Story of God* appeared (1989) which updated and synthesised his understanding of experience and revelation, and then applied this to the formation of tradition and the future of the church.

The chapters included in this section of the *Reader* include Vatican II and primarily the methodological innovations adopted by Schillebeeckx after the council. Ecclesiology, a topic generally either covered under Dogmatic Theology or the History of the Church in theological faculties, is treated here precisely because of its intrinsic connection to method: the nature of human experience and interpretation is foundational to the ability to perceive divine revelation and therefore also for the formation of Catholic tradition. As such, there is a direct line that can be drawn from the revolutionary impact of *Gaudium et spes* and the debates that formed it in which Schillebeeckx was active, to his constructive integration of philosophical hermeneutics with neo-Marxist critical theory, to the evocative title of Chapter One of *Interim Report* – 'It Began with an Experience', to the opening reflection of *Church* that affirms '*extra mundum nulla salus*' – outside of the world there is no salvation. After all, where else would salvation occur, if not *in the world* where God reaches us?

Vatican II

Chapter Five explicitly addresses the Second Vatican Council and includes writings contemporaneous with the council as well as his reflections on the results both immediately following and nearly thirty years after the event. In the selected texts, Schillebeeckx outlines the two theological 'wings' at the council: the 'open' and Roman viewpoints and their positions. He explores the meaning of the word 'pastoral' as it was taken up in the debates at the time. This relates intrinsically to the evolution of tradition and doctrine in the church, and it leads Schillebeeckx to consider the importance of the Pastoral Constitution on the Church in the Modern World, particularly for how the church can be said to exist in and for contemporary and their political reality. Finally, we have included a systematic reflection on how Vatican II changed the fundamental understanding of what it means to be 'church' and how the church is organised and constituted. Ultimately, Schillebeeckx would come to regard the council as 'a catching-up manoeuvre of the church which came too late (in relation to what was happening in the world)'.[1] Even so, it remains an important paradigm for the church with regard to the contextual evolution of tradition and doctrine as well as a font of inspiration for theology. Schillebeeckx is clear that, despite the shortcomings of the council, it definitively attempted to change the church's self-understanding as the People of God and *sacramentum mundi*.

Hermeneutics

In Chapter Six, a number of selections present the full range of Schillebeeckx's considerations on the problem and use of philosophical and existential hermeneutics for theology. We begin with sections from 'Towards a Catholic Use of Hermeneutics' (Dutch: 1967) that set out the contemporary problem of understanding and interpretation in light of historical consciousness. This is followed by Schillebeeckx's attempt to integrate ideology critique – the critical unmasking of elements of oppressive ideology inherent in linguistic structures – with a strong tradition hermeneutics. Central to these issues is the nature and role of experience as the source of human understanding of the divine. Such experience only occurs, however, in a given socio-historical situation which is informed and preconditioned by a multitude of cultural, religious, political and linguistic traditions. Thus, revelation appears to us within the framework of normal human experience, and yet mediates something that does not originate from our own finitude. We have included important later reflections that outline his synthesis of the evolution of tradition and the proportional

---

[1] Edward Schillebeeckx, *Church: The Human Story of God*, trans. John Bowden, Collected Works of Edward Schillebeeckx vol. 10 (London: Bloomsbury T&T Clark, 2014), 205 [206].

identity between past and present tradition in preserving the 'understanding of faith' throughout Christian history.

Church and world

Schillebeeckx's ecclesiological reflections span his entire career, and it is certainly extremely telling that his dissertation was on the sacraments in the theology of Thomas Aquinas and his final major work was explicitly about the church as 'the human story of God'. The sacramental nature of the church was a topic already present in his first bestseller, *Christ the Sacrament of the Encounter with God* (1959). Chapter Seven begins with the sacramental constitution of the church and then continues with selections from the 1960s that deal with the changed relation between 'church' and 'world'. In particular, the texts on the 'social teaching of the church' and on *Gaudium et spes* are especially thought provoking, especially given that the former was originally about the draft text of the Pastoral Constitution known as 'Schema 13'. Later, it was revised for new audiences and 'Schema 13' was substituted in most cases by 'the church's social teaching' and in one case (not included here) 'the magisterium'.[2] Finally, in an important selection from *Church*, Schillebeeckx explains the connection between the church in the world and the eschatological nature of the 'four marks' of the church.

Historical-Critical Method

The evolution of the historical critical method as a tool for investigating the biblical texts, and above all the 'historical Jesus', has a long history, beginning with the creation of 'critical' editions of the Bible and the *Textus Receptus* by Erasmus of Rotterdam in the early sixteenth century, then evolving in complexity in the Enlightenment through the efforts of Hermann Samuel Reimarus and Gotthold Ephraim Lessing. In the nineteenth century, new forms and standards of scientific historical research were developed under the banner of German '*Wissenschaft*' and progress. The 'Life of Jesus' by David Friedrich Strauss (*Das Leben Jesu, kritisch bearbeitet*, three volumes 1835–6) truly created a new genre of literature and inaugurated the first 'quest for the historical Jesus', which generated even more public attention thanks to the controversy surrounding the French scholar, Ernest Renan's *Life of Jesus* (*Vie de Jésus*, 1863). The second quest began in the 1950s with the work of Ernst Käsemann and which followed on the Kerygmatic theology of Rudolph Bultmann. Schillebeeckx's *Jesus* books and his engagement with the historical critical method followed this 'second quest' and brought the available research together in a truly impressive theological synthesis. His methodological studies in hermeneutics and the structure of experience provided a framework for him to utilise historical critical research as well as to evaluate it on the basis of ideological-critical considerations.

---

[2]See Edward Schillebeeckx, 'Church and World', *World and Church*, trans. N. D. Smith, Collected Works of Edward Schillebeeckx vol. 4 (London: Bloomsbury T&T Clark, 2014), 82 [109]. Cf. 'Kerk en wereld', *Tijdschrift voor theologie*, 4 (1964), 395.

PART TWO: INTRODUCTION 93

The selected texts in Chapter Eight all come from Schillebeeckx's landmark volume, *Jesus: An Experiment in Christology* (1974). The sections presented here are meant to help understand Schillebeeckx's use of the historical critical method, since he is not a historian but a Catholic theologian. In order to see Jesus of Nazareth as the object of historical research, Schillebeeckx finds it necessary to situate historical critical images of Jesus within the long line of other images of Jesus that preceded it. This is itself a hermeneutic undertaking, as is every interpretation of Jesus and his life and message, meaning that historical critical work is no less laden with presuppositions and abstractions than previous 'non-historical' methods of interpretation. A short an interesting selection on John the Baptist gives some insight into how Schillebeeckx worked with historical and biblical sources, and the likely pre-New Testament traditions that they represent. In a final selection, we present what is essentially a narrative evaluation of how Jesus deals with a sinful woman (Lk 7.36–50) as part of the presentation of him as the 'eschatological messenger' who announces and mediates salvation, and the 'eschatological prophet', which is Schillebeeckx's preferred lens through which he views the 'historical Jesus'. It was this 'eschatological prophet', the prophet who announces the Kingdom of God (or, more actively translated, the 'rule of God'), that Schillebeeckx believes to be one of the earliest layers of Jesus-tradition, underlying the later credal formulae that are more readily visible in the New Testament.[3]

Questions for discussion

1. How did Vatican II change the church's self-understanding of its own constitution and mission? What implications does this shift have for other areas of theology or religious life?
2. According to Edward Schillebeeckx, what role does interpretation play in human experience and how is are experience and interpretation related to revelation?
3. How does Schillebeeckx argue for continuity and change in the Christian tradition? Based his model, how can we say that the hermeneutical 'situation' has changed since he proposed his argument?
4. What are the 'four marks' of the church, and what does it mean for the visible church in the world if we accept Schillebeeckx's argument that these are to be understood and applied eschatologically?
5. Why is it important to understand and research 'the historical Jesus' and how does this task differ for historians and for theologians? Can one interpretation of Jesus – whether past or present, historical or theological – be said to be 'definitive' or absolutely true?

---

[3] See also Chapter Seventeen, *Eschatology* ('Eschatological Revolution: Jesus' Beatitudes'); also related is Jesus' '*Abba* experience', his unique experience of God as loving father. See Chapter Thirteen, *Christology*.

5

The Second Vatican Council

Vatican II: Misunderstandings at the council[1]

We can only rejoice that after the turn taken by the Second Vatican Council during its first phase we may justifiably hope for greater freedom for what is, somewhat erroneously, called the 'new theology'. In an earlier article[2] I have already commented on that aspect of the council. Since then I have given some thought to related aspects of the council.

When we examine more closely the speeches of the council fathers in St. Peter's we have to admit that some of the utterances of the so-called 'open wing' strike us as less felicitous, and such as might evoke, during the second phase of the Council, reactions of a kind that could easily cause confusion in the ranks of this 'open wing'.

The 'Open Wing's' gain – We are all convinced that the 'open wing' carried the day (and how mundane we are when we represent events in such terms, when in reality the whole of the world episcopacy is aware of the impulse of the Holy Spirit in God's Church). But I am convinced that the 'open wing' has won, not simply because it represented 'progress', but because it brought to the fore aspects of reality which had, apparently, remained unnoticed by the so-called 'closed wing'. It is always the germ of truth behind a certain trend, in profane matters too, that gives it its dynamic force and power of appeal. Untruth as such has no force of appeal whatsoever. But that is precisely why we must not forget that the 'germ of truth', upheld by the 'conservative wing', also possesses dynamic forces which might well, during the second phase of the council, assert their appeal. And if in that case it is the truth, even only in germ, that elicits our response, we can only acclaim it. It is only the truth that sets us free. But there exists a very real danger that the bias of the 'closed wing' position would gain credence among many council fathers alongside the germ of truth it represents, just because this truth is vested in what I have called a one-sided 'essentialist' attitude. So it may be necessary for the 'open wing' to reconsider its own positions if on 8th September 1963 'conservatism' is not to start off with a new force

---

[1] Selected from: Edward Schillebeeckx, 'Vatican II: Misunderstandings at the Council', *Life of the Spirit* 18, no. 203 (1963): 2–4.
[2] *Life of the Spirit*, June 1963 (Both articles appeared originally in the Dutch weekly *De Bazuin*).

of appeal. Similarly the most entrenched elements should rethink their positions and move to 'catharsis' or purging.

The term 'ecumenical' – Undeniably there were misunderstandings during the council debates, inside and outside St. Peter's, especially regarding the terms 'ecumenical' and 'pastoral'. In my opinion the word 'ecumenical' should describe an attitude of mind attuned visible unity, not only of love and hope, but also of faith among all people who confess Christ as Lord, and in fact more generally among all people who acknowledge the value of the religious in human life. Because of their belief in the *Una Catholica*, however, attitude of Catholics has acquired a particular stamp. To them the term 'ecumenical' expresses the mind of Catholics who want to do full justice to the totality of their belief. This attitude has introduced a certain distinction between the uncontaminated essence of the Church, as Christ instituted it under the leadership of the apostolic office of the college of bishops headed by the Pope, and the empirical outward form of that same Church in which, through the ages of church history, all forms of one-sidedness could gain access, at least in its manifestations. As a result certain Catholic values have become obscured in the Church's teaching, and more particular in its practice. And it is precisely these obscured or neglected truths and values which (partly also by the inner logic of contrasts) are retained in their original authenticity in the practice of the non-Catholic Christian Churches, even indeed in some large non-Christian world religions more fully than they are practised by the average Catholic. And that is why it is rightly the ecumenical concern of Catholics to emphasise those suppressed truths and values. In my opinion it was precisely this aspect of Catholic ecumenical thinking that, during the first phase of the council, achieved an unmistakable break-through, more-so than the 'new theology' as such. Not that one can really make a distinction, for the 'new theology' itself is motivated by an ecumenical spirit, and the re-integration of suppressed or overgrown truths into totality of the theological synthesis is its hallmark. A break-through for this ecumenical thinking is in fact a break-through for the so-called 'new theology'. We should realise, moreover, that the new theology is just as much concerned with the 'consolidation of positions' with regard to the deposit of the faith – but by a renewal which, since it seeks to reintegrate by means of a return to the sources, calls for a shift of emphasis. For the new theology holds that the Catholic Church, in order to hold its own today as a reality which appeals to people's minds and hearts, should overhaul its entire outward form a itself. This was indeed the basic intuition that made Pope John XXIII decide to hold a general council.

The Roman viewpoint – 'Roman theology' on the other hand (I realise this is a simplification, but in view of the bishops' own terms of reference in their interventions in the council we might as well keep the classification, for lack of a better one) seemed to put quite a different interpretation on the word 'ecumenical' during the council. Somewhat to my surprise I heard this expressed most strikingly when a bishop in St. Peter's complained pathetically: 'But where is all this going to lead, if we are to suppress one Catholic truth in order not to offend our disunited Eastern brethren, and another so as not to upset the Anglicans and finally if we have to preserve a mysterious silence about yet another truth to avoid further alienating the Protestants'. This intervention speaks volumes. Apparently, to Roman theology thinking means 'eirenics': suppressing or at any rate soft-pedalling some Catholic truths, which might put the Orthodox, the Anglican, the Protestant off Catholicism.

Truth as possession and growing truth[3]

Cardinal Ottaviani, in an interview with a journalist of *La France catholique*, said quite rightly: 'Theology today is in a ferment, and there is a great deal that is by no means ready yet; nothing should be included in a dogmatic that is not yet ripe'. I fully agree with this. But it is another matter whether a fossilised truth (which, I repeat, in so far as it is true and remains true) still appears in a true light in our time, when it is presented with all its original circumscription. Here, I thought, lies a deep-rooted misunderstanding. Whatever earlier Councils, Trent and Vatican I, for instance, decided dogmatically rightly remains (now and in a hundred years' time) a norm for the Catholic faith. But a complementary truth passed over in silence perhaps at Trent, because of reaction or simply because this truth was not a matter of controversy, might well imply a more important and from a religious point of view more valuable aspect of truth than what Trent decided. Moreover the Tridentine aspect of truth might reveal its uniquely Catholic significance only within the totality of this complementary religious truth. Surely then it is a concrete 'untruth' to go on repeating and re-affirming this Tridentine aspect, while concealing again the complementary truth? Consciously stating a part truth outside its totality always make it a heresy, an excision. It is quite possible to place truth in an untrue light. To prevent this was often the sincere intention of the so-called 'open' wing, who were blamed for being in league with non-Catholic Christians, and for concealing truth from this motive. At this Council the Church finally broke with her counter-reformation attitude of mind, but not with her catholicity. And this is where the tragic misunderstanding arose in connection with the so-called 'two sources' of revelation. Admittedly the 'progressive wing' was at times compromised by what was written on all sides in inferior publications in the way of biased comments on various questions. But crisis of Modernism should have taught us that all who used so-called modernist terms (for instance 'collective religious experience', said of the Church) did not necessarily interpret these in a modernist sense. And yet the judgement of Modernism was passed on unorthodox as well as orthodox. The Church should beware of repeating such painful mistakes.

That Pope John XXIII should state that this Council must not reaffirm what has formerly been decided seems to have been an intuition on the part of a person who, especially through his priestly feeling for pastoral care, helped by his attitude of mind as a historian, is particularly sensitive to the complementary aspects of a particular truth. Truth as a human 'possession' is never outside time and place. A denial of this (making one interpretation of truth absolute) betrays its fatal effect in what we have called essentialist thinking. This, I maintain, is the basic conflict that came to the surface during the first phase of the council. The misunderstandings surrounding the ecumenical and pastoral attitudes of the council are merely the outcome of it. And I trust that I am not exposing myself to the reproach of denying the value of human concepts.

---

[3]Selected from: Edward Schillebeeckx, 'Vatican II: Misunderstandings at the Council', *Life of the Spirit* 18, no. 203 (1963): 10–12.

If people would think all this over carefully I would be in complete agreement with Professor Tromp when he says: 'I am hopeful that both sides will grow nearer together, that they will have a better understanding of each other and that they will find that their viewpoints are not as widely separated as they thought'. Nevertheless I think that those beyond the Alps first need to understand what we mean when we attack the 'essentialist way of thinking' and that those on this side of the Alps should with a good grace learn to accept the sincere anxiety of 'Roman theology' to preserve the faith in its pure form. I fully recognise that the Church has need of a body which (at any rate by helping the Church's teaching authority, the college of bishops, headed by the Pope) is concerned with the *particular* care (I say particular, for every believer has this duty) of preserving the faith intact. But this purity does not only, not even primarily, demand the maintenance of what at one time has been dogmatically stated, but an increasingly shaded integration of what has been defined in the balanced totality of the faith. Without this it is impossible to keep the faith pure, because people will become obsessed with a part truth to the detriment of the whole.

Reflections on the final results of the council[4]

A real appreciation of this religious dimension of life as a gift from God raises the problem of humanity's earth. My future and of its absolute future, i.e. of the relation between the organisation of the earthly life and the kingdom of God, announced by the church and confirmed by her among the nations[5] – the field covered by the Pastoral Constitutions on the Church in the World of Today (until its promulgation known as Schema 13).

Of that kingdom the church on earth is the germ and the beginning.[6] 'In her slow process of development, the church longs for that kingdom in its final fulfilment and strives hopefully and with all her powers towards the final union with her King in glory.'[7] This eschatological dynamism of the church,[8] in other words, this striving for the final fulfilment, naturally raises a problem now that present-day humanity has itself discovered its historical, dynamic dimension – has taken its earthly destiny into its own hands and looks ardently to a better future on earth for all people without distinction. Here the problem of 'church and world' rises up life-size. Lost somewhere in Schema 13 are meaningful words: 'The church is the sign and the safeguard of the transcendence of the human person.'[9] This can be regarded as the pastoral constitution's basic outlook: a human being with a transcendental, absolute destiny, though living in an earthly history with its own plans for the future.

---

[4]Selected from: Edward Schillebeeckx, 'Reflections on the Final Results of the Council', in: *The Real Achievement of Vatican II*, (New York: Sheed and Ward), 69–77.
[5]Constitution on the Church [*Lumen gentium*], ch. I, no. 5.
[6]Church in World [*Gaudium et spes*], ch. I, no. 5.
[7]Church in World.
[8]See also the Constitution on the Church, ch. VII. no. 48.
[9]Church in World, pt. 2, ch. IV, no. 76.

Many confusing things have been said about the realities of church and world and various tendencies became noticeable even in the council hall. All kinds of misunderstandings rose to the top and divergent views could be found in the schema itself. Some had in mind a dialogue between the church and the world – as 'non-church' – which could only mean 'non-believers' – and this at once made humanist and Marxist atheists partners in the dialogue. Others regarded the 'world' as the whole secular dimension of life, as all people are called to shape the religious dimension of this same human life within the church of Christ. Again these two views converged in the main intention of this pastoral constitution: the church, i.e. God's people led by its pastors united in council, tries to express in a few fundamental themes her thoughts about the phenomenon of a human beings as beings who, through their own embodiment, realises themselves in company with their fellow human beings in this world, and yet at the same time is personally addressed in the community of his fellow believers by the living God, the bearer of history, who is therefore in his Son made human alpha and omega of humanity's stirring history. This formulation summarises not only the material content of the constitution but also the deeper meaning. In the words of its council the church expresses to all who are ready to listen its view of humanity from the historically conditioned *kairos* of humanity's twentieth-century situation. In this sense the pastoral constitution is a *kerygma* applied to the twentieth-century situation: the evangelically inspired answer to humanity's empirical question about present-day problems, expectations and aspirations. The fundamental answer to this double problem of world and church was given in the *Dogmatic Constitution on the Church,* to which reference is also made in the Pastoral Constitution.[10] Its text has already been quoted: 'In Christ the church is as the sacrament, that is, the sign and instrument, of the intimate union with God and of the unity of all humanity.' The church is the effective sign of the mutual unity or fellowship of all humanity through, and in her union with, God; she is a community among people by virtue of their communion with the living God. In this universal fellowship the church fulfils a sacramental role: she is its effective sign. Effective: it is not the church herself that is in question, but unity among people; the church is only an 'instrument' of God's redemptive actions in this world and therefore bound to serve. A sign: this effect is achieved through the church in a sign, i.e. in this world the church herself is the pregnant visibility or meaningful presence of an already accomplished (still accomplishing) community of people in and through their express communion with God in Christ. In this sense the church already is the presence of salvation in our midst, and thus conceived she also has a value of her own. But, sign and mediating realisation are one. As a sacrament the church experiences In advance what still needs to be given concrete shape in the whole human fellowship. That means the church achieves a fellowship of human beings because she herself is already a community: God's people and, therefore, a community of brothers. She is 'a sign set among the nations'. *The Pastoral Constitution on the Church in the World of Today,* as the intrinsic consequences of the *Dogmatic Constitution on the Church,*

---

[10]Introduction, no. 2. The text from the Dogmatic Constitution is quoted in full in the Pastoral Constitution, Pt. 1, ch. IV, no. 42.

has recognised the existential link between the religious Christian and the world as a link which is essential to the church yet fades into an unfathomable mystery.

Though still undeveloped, this *Pastoral Constitution* touched the most fundamental problem of our time, popularly presented by John A. T. Robinson, for instance, as well as by many others. Its basic aim is to bridge the gulf between world and religion: 'The breach which many bring about between the faith they confess and the lives they lead must be counted among the most serious failings of our time.'[11] Reference is here made to the cutting accusation of the prophet Isaiah against 'churchy pietists', who 'seek (God) daily, and delight to know (his) ways', but do not choose 'to lose the bonds of wickedness, to undo the thongs of the yoke, to let the oppressed go free... do not share (their) bread with the hungry, and reject their own brother...'[12]

Again and again the constitution hammers home that it is precisely through his faith that a Christian bears special responsibility for secular matters and for his or her fellow human being.[13] Its final reflection is reminiscent of the words of Christ that it is not he who prays 'Lord, Lord' in orthodox fashion, who will enter into the kingdom of God, but he who also gives real effect to his prayer in concrete fellowship. There were some who accused Schema 13 of being too optimistic, while others went so far as to speak of 'Teilhardism'. But the council document warns against the tendency to identify the development of a world fit for people to live in with the expansion of God's kingdom.[14] The constitution regards the appearance of God's kingdom in worldly features not as coming 'from below' but as a gift from above. 'Because the mission of the church is a religious one, it is, by that very fact, a highly humanising factor.'[15] In this connection the council opposes representations of God and human beings as competitors.[16] Indeed, 'although the same God who redeems us is also our creator, the same Lord of human and of salvation history, not only does this divine policy preserve the rightful autonomy of the creature and especially of human beings, but it also restores and confirms it to its own value'.[17] God's kingdom cannot, therefore, be contrasted with the care for humanity in his concrete historical situation, a care which is, after all, the mainspring of all worldly activities.

> The longing for a new world must not hinder the concern to make this earth fit for people to live on but rather stimulate it; for it is on this earth that lives the community of the new human family which is capable of foreshadowing even now the eschatological kingdom; this kingdom is, therefore, already present on earth in a mysterious form.[18]

---

[11] Pt. 1, ch. III, no. 43.
[12] Is 58.1-12, to which ch. III, no. 43 refers.
[13] See, among others, Pt. 1, ch. III, nos. 34 and 43; in connection with the atheistic dilemma of God or humans, also ch. I, no. 21.
[14] 'Progressus terrenus a Regni Christi augment sedulo distinguendus set' (Pt. 1, ch. III, no. 39).
[15] Pt. 1, no. 11.
[16] Pt. 1, ch. III, no. 34.
[17] Church in World, no. 41.
[18] Church in World, no. 39.

Accordingly the consequences of this mysterious presence are clear: 'the values of human dignity, of brotherly fellowship and of freedom [note the allusion to *egalité, fraternité, liberté*], all good fruits of our nature and efforts, we shall, after fighting for them here on earth in the spirit of Christ and in accordance with his command, find again later but purified of every blemish, transparent and transfigured – namely, when Christ shall return to his Father the everlasting and universal dominion, "a dominion of truth and life, of sanctification and grace, a dominion of justice, charity and peace".'[19]

As a visible community of believers who have expressly gathered around Christ under hierarchic at leadership (Pt. 1, ch. IV), the church 'to whom has been entrusted the manifestation of the divine mystery, humanity's deepest meaning in life', must, through this manifestation, 'disclose to human beings the meaning of their own existence'.[20] This is the very reason why in Christianity a believer also becomes 'more of a human being'.[21] By its preoccupation with humanity, the church stands right in the centre of this world: 'Therefore the church proclaims, by virtue of the glad tidings which were entrusted to it, the rights of humans and the dynamic energy of the present tide of life, whereby these rights are everywhere promoted, recognised and greatly appreciated' (no. 41). It must, I think, be conceded that these sounds are different from those formerly heard in devotional books on the subject of the world's course. Nonetheless, the council also warns against misconceptions:

> We are, however, exposed to the temptation of considering our personal rights safeguarded only if we cut ourselves adrift from the bonds of divine law. But along that path the dignity of the human person, far from finding salvation, comes to grief.

After discussing the relation of the visible church with the world, the constitution turns its attention to what the religious community in its turn receives from the world. Indeed, for the first time in conciliar history there is a break in the one-way traffic and the church considers not merely the blessings it gives the world, which would apparently know only darkness without and stand outside God's active grace. Now it is also said that the church's religious community develops and grows inwardly richer thanks to a growing self-awareness and to humanity's new valuable experiences to which it owes much itself – though sometimes rather belatedly.[22] In this connection the council cites, among others, modern social dynamism, the socialising process and the growing concern for the world's unification; the chapter on culture refers, moreover, to what the development of religious expression owes to the contributions of evolving human awareness.[23] From these worldly contributions the church has learned that she is not bound to a definite culture or political,

---

[19]Church in World.
[20]Pt. 1, ch. IV, no. 41; see also no. 40.
[21]Church in World, no. 41.
[22]Church in World, no. 42.
[23]Pt. 2, ch. II, nos. 58 and 62.

economic or social system.[24] Therefore, the council now affirms that there can also exist Christian pluralism in secular options. (Pt. 1, ch. IV) One of the consequences of these views has been formulated by the council:

> Let not the laity imagine that their priests are always so expert that they have a solution to hand for every question, even a most important one, that arises, or that they ought to have one, as if that were their assignment. [Pt. I, ch. IV, no. 42]

This *Pastoral Constitution on the Church in the World of Today* puts an end to medieval conceptions of the state and of politics.

Post-conciliar difficulties[25]

In closing the balance of this council, I cannot refrain from pointing out at least a few of the difficulties which the post-conciliar era will have to face in its effort to perpetuate and enliven what has been called 'the spirit of Vatican II'.

1. A careful watch will need to be kept to ensure that no misunderstanding arises around the considerable change of meaning given by Pope Paul VI in his address during the public session of 18 November 1965 to the concept of *aggiornamento* compared with the significance attached to it by Pope John XXIII. To quote Pope Paul: 'Henceforth *aggiornamento* will mean to us: enlightened penetration into the spirit of the council and the faithful application of the directives so happily and firmly outlined by the council.' Before and in the early stages of the council, aggiornamento meant throwing open the doors and setting out on a journey of discovery. But in the meantime the council has reached definite decisions, so that from now on the *aggiornamento* is channelled. Herein also lurks the danger of a 'post-Vatican Catholicism', just as the Council of Trent led to a rigid 'post-Tridentine Roman Catholicism', at least if only the second half of the pope's sentence ('faithful application of the council directives') is pounced upon while the first half ('penetration into the spirit of the council') Is ignored. Because this means that the criterion of every aggiornamento is the apostolic spirit of Holy Scripture, of which every council – Vatican II included – can only draw a historically situated profile.

2. A second difficulty is connected with the council's keyword: the pastoral character of the council. 'Pastoral' was a very ambiguous term in this assembly. During the first session the minority undeniably opposed the pastoral character which the majority wanted to give it. This opposition was due to the rather peculiar meaning of what they understood by 'pastoral'. Their pleas for a 'doctrinal' council soon showed that they

---

[24] Pt 1, ch. IV, no. 42.
[25] Selected from: Edward Schillebeeckx, 'Reflections on the Final Results of the Council', in: *The Real Achievement of Vatican II*, New York: Sheed and Ward, 83–90.

regarded an interpretation 'doctrinal' and 'pastoral' as opposites; which was further confirmed by the interventions from 'pastoral' bishops. They held 'pastoral' to mean: a practical, apostolically affected attitude which is less concerned with dogmatic or moral truth than with a soothing and encouraging approach to human persons.

During the second session, the minority became reconciled to the 'pastoral' character of the council. But this constituted a threat to its doctrinal value ever since, and even succeeded in making it ambiguous. There was general surprise when, at given moment, the qualification 'dogmatic' disappeared temporarily from the title 'Dogmatic Constitution on the Church', after the concept of collegiality had already been approved, at least by an official opinion poll. In other words, an attempt was made to level out the new dogmatic aspects by appealing to the council's pastoral character. Thus the impression was created that the actual doctrine of the church was not to be sought in this council but in earlier ones as well as in the papal encyclicals of this century. This makes it possible to have divergent interpretations of the council documents.

This ambiguity was further increased when representatives of the majority view themselves took to playing with the concept 'pastoral'. There is no historical sense in trying to deny this. In order to obtain the passage of certain formulations with a modern tendency, they, too, pointed now to the council's pastoral character. And the process was successful. On many points the minority too, convinced that 'it was, after all, only a pastoral council', accepted 'modern formulations'. This gap between 'doctrinal' and 'pastoral', which was used as a pawn, will continue to have a bearing on the interpretation of the council and is, in my opinion, one of the most important shadows cast on the council debates, to which I have never been able to resign myself. On the other hand, it brought a happy balance in conceptualising the formulations and definitions of the faith.

3. A third difficulty lies in the 'diplomatic choice' of some of the council formulas. These were often selected so as to allow both the majority and the minority to slip in their particular divergent conceptions. One instance will suffice: the council has chosen the expression 'unauthorised practices against procreation' in preference to 'anti-conceptional techniques'. Now, in accordance with the modern viewpoint, it is clear that periodic abstention too can and must be counted among the 'anti-conceptional techniques'. However, since periodical abstention has already been expressly approved by the hierarchy as a method of birth control in accordance with human dignity, the expression 'anti-conceptional techniques' could not be maintained. In consequence, the finally approved formulation 'unauthorised practices against procreation' can cover several meanings. Some have approved the formula because they do not want to condemn periodic abstention, others because they want to leave the door open (for instance, for the birth pill) and because, through the formula, they also want to condemn purely egoistical application of periodic abstention. The text is 'open', but could be abused.

4. The two preceding difficulties will be weighty ones particularly in the composition of the new code of canon law. Canon law needs to be guided by faith and theology, not the other way about. The church's past shows that the outward forms of the religious life are really influenced more by current canon law than by living theology. The new composition of the code is therefore of central importance. Owing to the ambiguity of some of the council formulas, even important ones, there is a danger that the translation of council doctrine into canonical laws and forms will start out from the significance attached to it by the minority and not from what the majority meant by it. For this reason, the working commission entrusted with the drawing up of the new code should have a very wide composition and include some theologians.

5. Another difficulty in post-conciliar period is undoubtedly the possibility of an integralist reaction, which is, in fact, already springing up in several countries, especially in connection with the so-called Schema 13. Whether this reaction will, in fact, take on violent proportions, depends, in my view, on two factors: for convenience we can call them 'progressives' and 'conservatives'. On the progressives, in the measure that their legitimate renewed reflection on the faith may neglect the value of obedience as a form of loyal self-surrender. The faith is, after all, a liberating bond, not a liberation from all bonds, however difficult it may be here and now to establish in precise detail where the bond lies. On the conservatives, in the measure that they, legitimately concerned for the soundness and the authenticity of this bond, identify the treasury of the faith with traditional representations which they cannot give up, with the result that they constantly make their fellow believers suspect. The unavoidable outcome of a clash between these two extremes is integralism. This is why an examination of conscience – their own, not the others' – is called for from both.

6. In connection with the so-called underground theological currents, the soundness of the catholic life will, from a theological point of view, depend in part on whether catholic theologians are in practice given their legitimate freedom of publication and research. If such confidence in theologians does not become a reality, there will be no chance either of their retaining by their dialogue among themselves and by mutual criticism the equilibrium necessary for the reassessment of doctrinal interpretation. For this will lead them, from a sense of brotherly love, to grow intellectually shy of attacking the theories of fellow theologians because of their suspicion that this may lead them into difficulties. The reformed Holy Office or new 'Congregation for the Doctrine of the Faith' will, therefore, also need to follow the development of theological thinking in positive ways and allow more room in its own management for free discussion among theologians. A mere reference to the letter of Vatican II and its consideration as the final norm for the appreciation of theological thinking in the future can only have reactionary results. It can, after all, be regarded as significant that, apart from the Constitution on the Liturgy (which had

been drafted by a working group of wide composition), the other pre-conciliar schemas in which the contemporary thinking of the Roman centre was largely prevalent, were all written off. Nevertheless, all theological writings of that time were judged from that theological standpoint. Though the council has made up this leeway, the faith naturally remains alive, i.e. theological thinking goes on. If, therefore, the Congregation for the Doctrine of the Faith does not think along the same lines as the faithful, the same distorted relationship will again be revealed in a few years' time.

However, I will not end up in a minor key. It is not in a spirit of what has been termed *'le triomphalisme du contretriomphalisme'*, but in sober assessment of the mentality which came about during the council, that I reach the conclusion: while fully recognising the right of existence of the 'Roman viewpoint' within the church, the council has nevertheless clearly shown that this is no longer representative of what is alive in the entire church. The council has laid bare a deep disorder of spiritual communication between the centre and the periphery of the Catholic Church; it has itself already partly removed and in principle healed it on the basis of the permanent bishops' synod and the announced reform of the curia. Thus it is no idle hope that in a not too far distant future both periphery and centre will move on the same wash of the waves, in accordance with the vision of St. Ambrose of Milan who saw the whole church as a little boat floating on the waves of world history.[26] *Pusillus grex*, a small flock, but a sign and the forerunner of God's all-embracing mercy.

The mystery of the church according to Vatican II[27]

According to this third draft of the Constitution [on the Church: *Lumen gentium*] it is this church of which the creed confesses that it is 'one, holy, catholic and apostolic'. It is then said of this same church: 'This church, constituted and ordered in the world as a community, exists in the Catholic Church, which is governed by the successor of Peter and the bishops in communion with him, although many elements of holiness and truth are found outside its framework (*compago*), which as the distinctive gifts of the church of Christ contribute towards Catholic unity.'[28]

The 'identification' of the biblical mystery of the church with the Catholic Church was formulated carefully, diplomatically and as a result somewhat ambiguously, in a way worthy of a senator politician (it was also a felicitous phrase of the Flemish priest, senator and theologian, Mgr. Prof. G. Philips of Louvain), as follows: '*Haec Ecclesia* subsistit in *Ecclesia Catholica*'. Philips in no way gave this *subsistere in* a specifically scholastic significance (although the minority swallowed the formula precisely because of the scholastic aura surrounding it. *Subsistere, substantia*: in scholasticism these two words were heavily ontological, which is why the minority

---

[26]See Dominican breviary, fourth Sunday after Pentecost: Homilia S. Ambrosii Episcopi (PL, 14, 1633).
[27]Selected from: Edward Schillebeeckx, *Church: The Human Story of God*, trans. John Bowden, Collected Works of Edward Schillebeeckx vol. 10 (London: Bloomsbury T&T Clark, 2014), 190–3 [192–5].
[28]*Schema Constitutionis de Ecclesia*, Vatican City 1964 (n. 8), 15.

yielded). However, it emerges from the Acts of the council that *subsistere in* was chosen as a weaker version of the first, stronger expression '*Haec Ecclesia est Ecclesia Catholica*'.[29] The weakened expression is used precisely so as not to blot out the reality of elements of the church in the other Christian churches. The reasons given for the acceptance or rejection of relevant amendments to this *subsistit in* make it clear that the aim of the commission was to indicate that 'the church, of which the inner and concealed being was described as 'the mystery of the church', is *concretely found* here on earth in the Catholic church',[30] but in its explanatory memorandum the commission betrays its second intention, which is hidden behind the main aim by the choice of the terms *subsistit in:* 'This empirical church reveals the mystery (of the church), but not without shadows, and it does so until it is brought into the full light, as Christ also reached glory through humiliation.'[31] This is all put very carefully; people were as it were anxious to admit to outsiders that there is sin even in the church. At all events, in this final redaction it becomes clear that (in contrast to post-Vatican attempts subsequently to give the word '*subsistere*' a heavily ontological significance) this word is used because of its suggestive power, in which the *sub* is not without its explosive significance: '*sistit sub...*'. In other words, what the New Testament envisages with its biblical mystery of the church is present in the Ecclesia Catholica under all kinds of historical veils and distortions: the mystery is present, but...! It is also present elsewhere, in other churches, but...! In this formula the uncritical, almost exclusive, identification of the mystery of the church with the Catholic Church is put aside.

The Commission's justification for refusing to accept particular amendments in this connection went like this: the church is unique, 'although ecclesial elements are also found outside it'.[32]

In the same Council's Decree on Ecumenism it is stated not only that many ecclesial values are present 'outside the visible limits of the Catholic Church', but at the same time that this can be for our edification – Catholics can learn from it – and moreover that through the existence of different Christian churches it becomes more difficult for 'the church to express the fullness of its catholicity in all its aspects in the reality of life'.[33] The process by which 'the mystery of the church in the catholic church' becomes transparent in fact takes place 'both in power and in weakness', 'in sin and in purification'.[34]

This amended last preliminary version was approved by 2,144 votes out of 2,189. The last possibility of improving this text or shifting it in a conservative direction by introducing *modi* or final amendments as it were at the eleventh hour (a situation in which in the last instance the official commission could decide on a free and autonomous basis whether or not it would accept the final proposals for amendments – unless a veto intervened 'from above', as had been the case with other

---

[29]'Loco *est* dicitur *subsistit in*, ut expressio melius concordet cum affirmatione de elementis ecclesialibus quae alibi adsunt', in *Relationes de singulis numeris*, Relatio in no. 8, 25.
[30]*Relationes* (n. 13), Relatio in no. 8, 23.
[31]Ibid.
[32]Ibid.
[33]Ibid.
[34]*Decretum de Oecumenismo*, Vatican City 1964, ch. 1, no. 4.

issues), did not bring any changes (at least in connection with this theme). The text I have just analysed then in fact became the final text and thus the authentic rendering of the Dogmatic Constitution itself.

But it is interesting to note that in the last instance there were still some bishops who wanted to add further qualifications to the formula which had already been broken open ecumenically (*subsistit in*), in order to put yet more stress on the ecclesial character of the non-Catholic Christian churches.[35]

The purpose of this Dogmatic Constitution is clear: the mystery of the church of Christ, 'the community of God', as the Constitution had sketched this out in broad outline in its first chapter, is not an idealistic or unreal vision, nor a coming reality which is not in fact present in any way now. No, according to this constitution that mystery is really present in our history, in a very concrete community, in the Catholic Church, though that presents this mystery in shadows, distortions and deficiencies, and through this distortion sometimes or often makes it almost unrecognisable. However, these blemishes do not make it downright impossible for that mystery to be manifested or made transparent in this church. That was the view of Vatican II, and also the spirit of this council. The council here wanted to go a long way towards the other Christian churches without being unfaithful to the centuries-old self- understanding of the Catholic Church.

It cannot be denied that the Dogmatic Constitution on the Church stands in a notably different climate from that of Catholic church theology prior to the council. The rejection by Vatican II of the pre-conciliar draft in particular was a specific reaction against the one-sided and indeed triumphalist accents of the encyclical *Mystici Corporis*. Here I would like to indicate three clear differences.

1. The clearly marked distinction between the church on earth and the kingdom of God is striking, though the intrinsic bond and connection between them is maintained.

2. Equally striking in comparison with pre-conciliar ecclesiology is the carefully qualified identification of the biblical mystery of the church, the mystical body, with the Roman Catholic church (though this is formulated with almost prudish care). But this conciliar declaration implies (though this is said only in a minor key) that the same biblical mystery of the church, albeit under yet another veil and distortion than the empirical distortions within the Catholic church, is also present in other Christian churches in a varied way.

3. Finally, it emerges from the whole of this Dogmatic Constitution on the Church, although it is not said in so many words, that this Constitution accepts a distinction between the church as a 'saving institution', and the

---

[35] *Modi a Patribus conciliaribus propositi, a Commissione doctrinali examinati*, 1964, Chs. 1, 6. The commission did not want to go into this. On the other hand, the meaning of *subsistere in* is not to be rendered by a rather weak version as 'is actually found in' the Catholic Church. It is clearly meant by this council in a stronger sense: 'is *de iure* found in this church'. This is the wording of the draft of an amendment: 'Quod spectat ad additionem *iure divino* ex contextu paragraphi patet sermonem esse de institutione Christi' *(Modi,* ibid., 6).

church 'as the fruit of divine redemption', in other words between the institutional element in the church and the eschatological community of faith and grace, although this distinction remains inadequate.[36]

In Chapter 2 of this Constitution, which deals with the people of God, it is said of this people of God: 'All those, who in faith look towards Jesus, the author of salvation and the principle of unity and peace, God has gathered together and established as the church, that it may be for each and every one the visible sacrament of this saving unity.'[37]

Selected literature

- Misunderstandings at the Council; Selected from: Edward Schillebeeckx, 'Vatican II: Misunderstandings at the Council', *Life of the Spirit* 18, no. 203 (1963): 2–4.
- Truth as Possession and Growing Truth; Selected from: Edward Schillebeeckx, 'Vatican II: Misunderstandings at the Council', *Life of the Spirit* 18, no. 203 (1963): 10–12.
- Reflections on the Final Results of the Council; Selected from: Edward Schillebeeckx, 'Reflections on the Final Results of the Council', in: *The Real Achievement of Vatican II*, New York: Sheed and Ward, 69–77.
- Post-Conciliar Difficulties; Selected from: 'Reflections on the Final Results of the Council', in: *The Real Achievement of Vatican II*, New York: Sheed and Ward, 83–90.
- The Mystery of the Church According to Vatican II; Selected from: Edward Schillebeeckx, *Church: The Human Story of God*, trans. John Bowden, Collected Works of Edward Schillebeeckx vol. 10 (London: Bloomsbury T&T Clark, 2014), 190–3 [192–5].

---

[36]'Alii... volunt apertiorem distinctionem inter Ecclesiam medium salutis et Ecclesiam fructum salutis. Quae distinctio iam satis videtur clara in textu', in *Schema Constitutionis de Ecclesia*, 1964, relatio in no. 8, p. 24.
[37]*Lumen gentium*, ch. 2, no. 9.

6

Hermeneutics

The hermeneutical problem for the Catholic faith[1]

The Catholic theologian is also aware of the hermeneutical problem presented by the Bible, magisterial pronouncements and the tradition of faith, although he is probably conscious of the opposite question as of even greater urgency – the hermeneutical problem as a *dogmatic* matter. In the Catholic practice of the 'development of dogma', a mass of hermeneutical material has been collected experientially, but Catholic theologians have practically never brought this hermeneutical material that is actually present in their own Church to light or attempted to thematise its content. Part of the reason for this has been a rather careless interpretation of one of the canons of the Council of Trent which was believed to have laid down the following hermeneutical principles for Catholics: 'Ecclesia, cuius est iudicare de vero sensu et *interpretatione* Scripturarum sanctarum' ('It is the Church's prerogative to judge the true sense and *interpretation* of the Sacred Scriptures').[2] Actually, this statement does not in any sense imply that the Church's apostolic office is the *hermeneutical* principle. What it does say is that this office is the judge of our *hermeneia* or interpretation of faith and the Bible. The relationship between the 'calling to mind' of the Holy Spirit, who guides the Church in her unanimous confession of faith, and the faith of the whole community of the Church together with the magisterial pronouncements of the apostolic office (which functions in the community as a *diākonia* and is, at the same time, the judging, authentic exponent of the whole faith of the Church) is undoubtedly a datum which the Catholic must take into account in his hermeneutics as a *dogmatic* problem.

It would, however, be naive to assume that this solves the hermeneutical question: it does no more than simply raise the question. This is, of course, generally applicable – the author of a historical text may be completely trustworthy and we may have absolute confidence in him, but precisely *what* he is saying to us

---

[1]Selected from: Edward Schillebeeckx, 'Towards a Catholic Use of Hermeneutics', *God the Future of Man*, trans. N. D. Smith, Collected Works of Edward Schillebeeckx vol. 3 (London: Bloomsbury T&T Clark, 2014), 12–13 [17–19].
[2]Denzinger, *Enchiridion Symbolorum*, ed. A. Schönmetzer, 1507 (786) [DH 1507].

needs to be understood interpretatively. A text is a document, the real meaning of which can only be understood beyond its literal meaning because it tells us about something, a 'matter', which we too are trying to understand and about which we ask questions in the light of our present-day experience. This applies equally to conciliar texts and other magisterial statements, even though a believer has complete confidence in these declarations. The magisterial statement may in certain cases (according to the subtle distinctions of the First Vatican Council) even be infallible, but the important point is to know precisely what (maybe in an infallible way) is said to me in that statement. *What* precisely is expressed and to what can we and may we bind ourselves in obedience to faith? The fact is that whole volumes of commentary have to be written in order to establish what the Council of Trent, for example, meant; a whole series of articles to enable us to know precisely in what respect the Church's apostolic office binds believers to the word of God. The interpreter is, after all, in history himself. Our patterns of reading are different now and our questions are different from those answered by the Fourth Lateran Council, for example, when it spoke of angels and devils or by the Council of Trent when it spoke of original sin and the Eucharist. And the answer to the questions asked in the thirteenth or the sixteenth century – in other words, the literal repetition even of unambiguously dogmatic definitions, such as those of Trent – is not an answer to our contemporary problems in which we are trying to come to an understanding of faith. Without the *Tridentine* answer to *my questions now*, I shall not understand what Trent means and my obedience in faith will fail to be authentic, so that a short-circuit will inevitably occur. Anyone who maintains – as some do – that Trent, because it is formulating a *dogma*, is, in what it explicitly says (*das Gesagte*), *a priori* an answer to my present-day question is radically misconceiving the historicity of human existence, of human questioning and of all human understanding. Authentic orthodoxy is seldom to be found in those who simply repeat literally what has already been said, with Denzinger in their hands as material to prove their point. Fortunately, however, their Christian faith transcends the inauthenticity of such thematic orthodoxy. A modern theologian, on the other hand, may feel *secure* as a believer and yet *hesitant* as a theologian – in this, he is respecting the mystery. One is sometimes bound to wonder whether the certainty of some theologians does not conceal a hesitant *faith*.

Understanding: Text and tradition[3]

The importance of the present as the hermeneutical situation is clear, for example, in the difference between the Old Testament interpretation and the Christian interpretation of the same Old Testament texts. In both cases, the Old Testament remained unchanged and valid as a sacred book, but the Christians reread and reinterpreted the Old Testament in the light of the new hermeneutical

---

[3] Selected from: Edward Schillebeeckx, 'Towards a Catholic Use of Hermeneutics', *God the Future of Man*, trans. N. D. Smith, Collected Works of Edward Schillebeeckx vol. 3 (London: Bloomsbury T&T Clark, 2014), 20–2 [29–32].

situation (the eschatological kerygma of Christianity). The New Testament thus found itself in a different frame of reference from the one which the Jews, or an Old Testament scholar, would take as their basis. In this way, a distinction between the Old Testament and the New Testament understanding of the same Old Testament books came into being. The New Testament texts were, after all, to a great extent only the literary expression of a Christian rereading of the Old Testament in the light of the new hermeneutical situation – the encounter with Jesus, the Lord. Even within the New Testament itself, a theological process of reinterpretative understanding of initial Christian interpretations took place on the basis of the gradually changing social context of the earliest Church. The difference that is apparent between the translation of the Septuagint and the earlier Hebrew texts is equally indicative of the importance of the socio-cultural context as a hermeneutical situation. We have here in two distinct texts what can be separated in the synoptic 'history of traditions' only by comparison and analysis of the three synoptic gospels – earlier, normative *logia*, dialogues and texts are reinterpreted in, and in the light of, a new context in life. This is an ordinary human hermeneutical process *within* the life of the Church. For a Christian, however, the eschatological kerygma of Christ is a situation that is constant and cannot be superseded. That is why it acts as a constant norm to every age's understanding of biblical faith – the identity in faith must therefore be preserved *within* the *Christian* reinterpretation itself.

The result of this analysis is extremely important. It is that understanding of a traditional text takes place only in its application to the present, and not in a kind of interpretation 'in itself', in a historical reconstruction or in a return to the original period. Christian understanding of the Bible is therefore different from what is known simply as exegesis. If an earlier truth is to be preserved in accordance with its original intention, it must be reformulated in the light of the present and interpreted differently. With reference to Jesus' logion that what God has joined together, no human must put asunder, for example, the text of Matthew 19.1-9 said that a man may not divorce his wife. In Oriental and Jewish society a wife was never allowed to take the initiative and divorce her husband. In Greco-Roman society, on the other hand, the situation was different – according to Hellenistic custom women as well as men were able to take the initiative. The formulation of this truth was consequently revised, brought up to date and translated into contemporary terms, so as to preserve the intention of the logion in its pure form in the new social environment. Therefore, according to Mark 10.10-12 Jesus said that neither the husband nor the wife may divorce. A literal repetition of the earlier formulation of the truth would have been most ambiguous in the new situation, since an initiative taken by the wife to divorce her husband would have been regarded as legitimate, and this would have been flagrantly contrary to the deepest intention of the original statement. It was only in this contemporary application – in the reinterpretation, in other words – that it was clear that Christians had genuinely understood the 'earlier' truth. Similarly, our understanding of the Tridentine dogma of transubstantiation comes about, not in a literal repetition of the dogma, but in a contemporary interpretation and a new formulation. On the basis of the filled distance in time, a text is understood only if it is understood in a *different* way – which does not mean a better or a worse way – from the way in which it was understood in its past social and cultural context. Understanding must change in changing situations, otherwise the same thing cannot continue to be understood.

Understanding is therefore intimately bound to the text which has to be understood. The text has a normative value, but we can understand it only in its application to the present. Exposition of the text may never replace the text itself, but the historical survival of the tradition (the text) consists in a new appropriation which of necessity takes place again and again. The past will remain unintelligible to us if we do not incorporate its meaning into our contemporary existential experience. If we do not do this, we shall not understand what the past really has to say to us. But the fact that our present frame of reference inevitably plays a part in our interpretation of an earlier text does not mean that we can first enter completely into the life of the past, so as to understand it, and only then, as it were in the second place, translate the result into terms of our present frame of reference. The two phases run parallel to each other, and our understanding is a product of their interaction. The task of interpretation therefore involves finding the right phraseology to convey the real, essential meaning of the text, as there is no interpretation which 'in itself' – that is, independent of human concepts – holds good for all historical periods. It is within the context of the present, with its particular insights, that the traditional text finds its own inner fulfilment. Our productive creativity and our bond with tradition therefore interact in forming our understanding of the text, since in bringing his present understanding to bear on a traditional text the interpreter is not free with respect to the distinctive meaning of the text but is bound to it. We can say that by definition tradition receives from the interpreter of another age a different reading from the one called for by the texts in themselves. Bultmann's distinction between 'what is said' and 'what is intended' is simply insufficient to explain what occurs here, since the divine truth which the author of the traditional text intended to express must somehow (however inadequately) be expressed in the text. But this 'intended meaning' is included in a meaning which has not yet been consciously perceived by the author himself and has still to be unveiled – a meaning, that is, which is implicit in everything that is expressed in this 'saying and intending' and which discloses itself without having been thematically intended.

The new critical theory and theological hermeneutics[4]

In the light of the salutary challenge presented by critical theory to theology, I should like to state explicitly that hermeneutic theology must be inspired by a practical and critical intention.[5] This implies that the orthopraxis that has been discussed repeatedly

---

[4]Selected from: Edward Schillebeeckx, 'The New Critical Theory and Theological Hermeneutics', *The Understanding of Faith: Interpretation and Criticism*, trans. N. D. Smith, Collected Works of Edward Schillebeeckx vol. 5 (London: Bloomsbury T&T Clark, 2014), 116–18 [132–5].
[5]See my report to the congress held in September 1970 under the auspices of *Concilium*, 'Het kritisch statuut van de theologie', published in *De toekomst van de kerk. Verslag van het wereldcongres Concilium te Brussel*, Amersfoort/Bussum, 1970, pp. 56–64.

in previous chapters of this book is an essential element of the hermeneutical process. Although it is, of course, possible to dispute precisely what may be called *orthos* in our praxis, it is in any case certain, on the basis of both human and Christian motivation, that any praxis which manipulates human freedom and brings about alienation is both wrong and heterodox. If this criterion were taken seriously into account, we should make considerable progress!

It is therefore clear that a theologically actualising interpretation is not possible without a critical theory which acts as the self-consciousness of a critical praxis. If the unity of faith takes place in real history, in other words, if it is itself really history, then we must not hope to be able to attain unity in faith either purely hermeneutically or by means of a purely theoretical theological interpretation. History is a flesh and blood affair and what has come about in history – the divisions in the Christian church, for instance – can never be put right by purely theoretical means. History is an experience of reality which takes place in a series of conflicts, which can only be resolved if the theory used is really the self-consciousness of a praxis. I would therefore agree with J.B. Metz's contention that the historical identity which Christianity has lost cannot be regained by making Christian traditions present and actual again purely theoretically.[6] Christianity is, in its very being and therefore also in its history, much more than simply a history of interpretation. A purely theoretical interpretation of Christianity, an 'orthodoxy' based on an idealist view of history, will in our own times inevitably come into conflict with the problems with which the reality of history itself confronts us. The churches are really the 'community of God' and the 'temple of the Holy Spirit', with the result that we are bound to speak about this in the language of faith. At the same time, however, the churches are also historical and contingent. 'The earthly church and the church enriched with heavenly things ... are not to be considered as two realities' (*Lumen gentium* 8).

Cultural revolution or social and economic structural change?

Is it possible to claim that a universal subject – an individual, society, 'humanity' – within history contains the course of its development and directs that development? Anyone who does assert this can nowadays expect to be sharply criticised by philosophers, who have shown that ideology and totalitarianism inevitably result if we take as our point of departure the fact that history is governed by a secular universal subject and that a total meaning, which can be embodied in a system or a programme of action, is contained in the individual, in human society or in history itself. This idea can also be defined by affirming that the individual, society and history do not have their ground and their total meaning in themselves, in other words, that they are contingent. The individual, society and history cannot put themselves forward as absolute; they are not identical with themselves. The Christian

---

[6]J.-B. Metz, *Reform und Gegenreformation heute*, Mainz, 1969, p. 15.

believer will, of course, interpret this fact in the light of his faith in God's creation and say that the individual, society and history have their ground and their total meaning in the living God, who puts them forward in their autonomy. This faith implies that the believer entrusts himself and the whole of history to this source, who transcends from within the active and passive capacity of our freedom in the world to make history.

The Christian's refusal to accept a universal subject of history has far-reaching consequences. On this basis, we would have to refuse to sacrifice one generation for the benefit of another – for example, the present generation in favour of the next. We are, however, also bound to conclude from this that the present generation and its established practices and structures cannot be an absolute norm. Ultimately too, the Christian's view extends even into the past, with the result that not even the dead are excluded from the better world of the future. If we take the primacy of the future as our point of departure – and the first importance of the future is rightly emphasised nowadays – then we should not go so far as to make the demand for radical revolution legitimate: this would be a modern form of Manicheanism, for which, in the social sphere, good and evil are irreconcilably opposed to each other. It is therefore already apparent that those philosophers and theologians who have rightly emphasised the primacy of the future have also begun to eliminate the rather menacing one-sidedness of this idea by rehabilitating the past. E. Bloch, H. Marcuse, T. Adorno, P. Ricoeur and J.B. Metz have all in turn elaborated the idea of the 'past as a subversive memory'.

I am personally convinced that, on the basis of the same inner dynamics, the present has also to be rehabilitated, without denying the primacy of the future and, what is more, the present has to be rehabilitated in its critical power. If this is done, then it will be possible to reformulate in a very clear way the old problem which can be summed up in the contrast between Marx and Feuerbach; must we, like Feuerbach, aim at a revolution brought about by a 'conversion of the heart', a cultural revolution from which all the rest would follow, or should we, like Marx, aim at social and economic structural changes, from which all the rest would follow? Since the time of Marx, however, the situation has changed fundamentally and it has become clear from the different forms that the cultural revolution has assumed that the basic concern of the younger generations is not material or economic, but rather a preoccupation with 'personal liberation'. In America, for example, many of the younger critical spirits, who are inspired by Marxism, are emphasising the priority of a 'new consciousness', because they are convinced that this will have an effect on politics and ultimately lead to a change in structures. On the basis of the change that has already taken place in the situation since the time that Marx was writing, these critics believe that their adaptation of Marx's insights is fully justified in the light of Marxist principles. They therefore affirm that a cultural revolution necessarily precedes any structural change.

These American critics probably base their arguments too much on the contrast between Feuerbach and Marx in the sense outlined above, but the fact that radical movements are so often rendered impotent in a highly developed country such as the United States also plays a part in opening people's eyes to the reality of the situation. People are becoming more convinced that, in the West at least, only a cultural revolution, a 'new consciousness', can bring about a gradual change in the political situation and ultimately undermine and transform from within the Moloch of unfree structures. This idea has, of course, still to be worked out in detail, but it is already sufficiently clear for us to be able to ask seriously whether critical theory is not based on a contrast that has outlived its usefulness.

The authority of new experiences[7]

If the authority of experience is an authority gained from a many-sided and yet directed process of experience – which does not, however, mean *anarchic* openness to the future, specifically without critical recollection of past experiences – and at the same time directed openness for new experiences, then the widening possibility of the integration of new experiences, which does not manipulate but reinterprets what has already been attained, is a pointer towards the power of a particular tradition of experience. Humanly speaking, this is a demonstration of plausibility, of its meaningful authenticity and its foundation in truth. In that case the credibility of the given tradition is strengthened, or it gains force. For the virtues of a particular tradition emerge more clearly from the way in which the tradition is able to accord a real place to new and above all 'divergent' experiences – dynamically remaining itself, without eclecticism or false *aggiornamento*. On the other hand, a (religious) tradition which cannot cope with new experiences and therefore negates them, avoids them or brands them *per se* as 'diabolical modern temptations' forfeits moral authority, even if this refusal is based on age-old and honourable traditions (the presuppositions of which are not, however, explored). Furthermore, in that case there is a danger that this traditional community becomes a 'holy remnant'; it asserts itself by forming ghettoes and aggressively asserting its own group identity. At that point, it is not in fact swearing by the authority of its own tradition of experience but by the letter of what was once the expression of authentic experiences in a particular historical situation. Climaxes then become points of stagnation.

All this is also true on the individual level. Anyone who has come to experience of life or a conviction about life which is lived out in practice will try to digest new experiences within his own experience of life. Sometimes this proves successful; sometimes less so. In the long run, however, one can be compelled by the resistance offered by constantly new experiences to revise some presuppositions of one's own convictions about life. Initially this usually happens by giving way or correcting one's own view of life to some degree. Only when all attempts at integration fail is one confronted with the possibility of a collapse in one's convictions about life, at least if it is a matter of remaining true to oneself. (For it is also possible to assert one's rights more and more stubbornly and aggressively against increasing evidence from experience.) This proves once again the authority of critical experiences (quite apart from the question whether they have been formulated properly or wrongly). We can, however, still ask whether

---

[7]Selected from: Edward Schillebeeckx, *Christ: The Christian Experience in the Modern World*, Collected Works of Edward Schillebeeckx vol. 7 (London: Bloomsbury T&T Clark, 2014), 24–6 [38–40].

an accumulation of negative experiences will in fact bring the committed believer to change his convictions about life. The Christian and even the Stoic will say: Neither death nor life nor anxiety nor tribulation, *nothing* can separate us... Suffering and a number of empirical proofs do not seem to be able to shift the believer from his faith that God loves him. No accumulation of empirical indications to the contrary will cause such faith to totter. This has to do with the force of non-cognitive, emotional elements in human experiences and conviction of life. The experience of faith is capable of living with doubt. Within his own varied projects for life everyone can give good reasons for his convictions about life, despite experiences to the contrary: the history of our human experiences is not so clearly negative or positive. Above all, religious and para-religious and even atheistic convictions about life are highly resistant to falsification from negative experiences. But if anyone wants to maintain the relevance of experience for faith, then negative experience cannot be the last word. Moreover, in the last resort the emotional elements must draw their strength from the cognitive element or the evidence of experience in the conviction of faith. If the particular value of the aspect of knowledge or the evidence of experience were irrelevant, there would be no way of distinguishing illusion from reality. If existing convictions about life are not in any way connected with actual experiences, they become empty and irrelevant, even if it seems that someone only gives up the conviction when more meaningful alternatives present themselves.[8]

As will become even clearer as we proceed, to have come this far is to say that experience of something new and surprising will always also be an experience of the familiar, though of a different kind from what we might have imagined. We discover the familiar through alienation or negative experiences and nevertheless see it in a form that surprises us. Discovering something new is also a rediscovery. This does not do away with alienation from oneself, which in fact becomes an essential element in the real knowledge of truth; it brings the new element into view as something that is to a degree familiar and expected, even if this also goes beyond all our expectations. The new is never *radically* the 'wholly other', for the simple reason that in our experiences we ourselves are part of this reality which reveals itself to us. Reality has already revealed itself, albeit in such a way that we only recognise this revelation as something that is already familiar to us as a result of alienations from ourselves.[9]

Tradition and situation: A definition of concepts[10]

On the one hand the Christian tradition is a tradition of meaning. In fact, within all the great and above all the classical religious traditions of humanity[11]

---

[8] I. Barbour, *Myths, Models and Paradigms*, London, 1974, 130.
[9] If the experience were radically of the 'wholly other', it would in fact have no hermeneutic significance whatsoever for revelation.
[10] Selected from: Edward Schillebeeckx, *Church: The Human Story of God*, Collected Works of Edward Schillebeeckx vol. 10 (London: Bloomsbury T&T Clark, 2014), 33–7 [34–8].
[11] See W. Oelmüller, *Fortschritt wohin? Zum Problem der Normenfindung in der pluralen Gesellschaft*, Dusseldorf 1972, 99.

there is a force which discloses meaning: through all the rises and falls of these traditions their history is a cumulative disclosure of meaning and truth down the ages (apart from possible ideological misuse). That is the way in which all these traditions understand themselves. Moreover in these great traditions meaning-and-truth is expressed precisely as an authentic possibility of life which can be actualised or become a reality which is alive even now in changed circumstances in the world and the church. The tradition of faith opens up a horizon of possible experience for us, too, now.

On the other hand this tradition of faith is a tradition of religious meaning with renewing, liberating or redemptive power. The tradition of faith which discloses meaning is at the same time a call to a well-defined practical way of life. Whatever the specific name given to the liberation in which divergent human and religious traditions can also be involved, these traditions promise salvation and liberation for men and women through their own disclosure of meaning, truth about life as human beings. In the end we have here the convergence of two stories, the story of the gospel tradition of faith and the story of our personal and social life which in the best instances has itself as it were become 'gospel': a fifth or umpteenth gospel.

So primarily such great traditions are not concerned with a theoretical disclosure of meaning but with a way of life, a praxis, and thus with witness: a narrative revelation of meaning which even in the Old and New Testaments is constantly accompanied at least by an incipient theological reflection.

On the basis of these two facets – a tradition of faith which discloses meaning *and* does so with liberating power – faith, which also leads to theology, is an undertaking which on the one hand is interpretative and on the other hand, as a theory of faith, is related to a particular praxis of liberation or redemption, of healing men and women and bringing them to fullness. So the interpretation of faith and theology cannot be reduced to a purely theoretical interpretation of the Christian past. There is a dialectical relationship between the present, the past and the future still to be made, a relationship between praxis and theory.

The term I use for what stands over against tradition is situation, in a general sense: the cultural, social and existential context of men and women to whom the gospel is proclaimed here and now; the concrete situation in which the tradition of faith is handed on by Christians to new generations: to contemporary people, living in a modern culture with its good things and its bad, with its new insights and its own particular sensitivities, but also its own blind spots, one-sidedness and prejudices. So 'situation' is not an unequivocal concept; it covers divergent realities which, moreover, time and again call for an appropriate analysis. Situation is thus a complex totality of contingencies which can partly be analysed but are never completely clear. So no theory can cover the situation as a whole; here all totalitarian theories fall short.

In a more specific sense I use the word situation to describe the present 'Christian situation', i.e. the answer or variety of answers to the question how Christians stand *qua* Christians in this modern society and culture and how far they should take over modern categories of experience and thought. In a conformist way? To legitimise them? Critically? Or rejecting them all without further ado as being of the devil? In other words, what is to be their praxis and understanding of faith here and now? In what way are they to follow Jesus or perhaps diverge from his way of life? Identity with (or perhaps deviation from) the Christian tradition of faith is already given *in* the specific action of believers. In this sense the situation is itself already a bit of 'new' Christian tradition, a new chapter in the story of the Christian experiential tradition, though this may be (as always) in an orthodox or a somewhat divergent direction. That is already to say that the subject of the interpretation of faith is not really the theologian but the Christian communities of faith themselves – the church in its broad spectrum and its cultural distribution over many centres. Here theology is merely a help to the community of faith. Academic theology then tries to integrate the new experiences, the new praxis and the reflections of local communities into the totality of the 'church's recollection' and into the great reserves of the experiences and faith of the whole church down the ages. Theology thus at the same time prevents these new experiences from remaining sporadic or ultimately causing disintegration. Thus academic theology 'mediates' to the base the rich experiential traditions in the churches down the ages, and prevents the base from being cognitively isolated. Theology itself is enriched by the new experiences and reflections from theology which grows in and from the life of the communities of faith.

Encounter between different cultures and traditions of faith

The subject of our closer attention now is the interrelationship between the Christian past and the Christian present.

I have chosen the term 'interrelationship' deliberately: it is vague enough to cover the broad spread between clear identity on the one hand (it clicks) and unmistakable non-identity on the other (it clashes): from correlation to conflict and confrontation, from complete identification to partial recognition and finally to non-recognition. Here we have very delicate problems in which both the Scylla of fundamentalism and the Charybdis of modernism have to be avoided.[12] For there is a danger on the one hand that church leaders bind believers to particular forms of faith where God leaves them free; and on the other hand that the interpretation of faith in fact given by believers and their theologians distorts the authenticity of the gospel.

On the one hand the fundamental tendency and power of 'the gospel' is transcendent and universal, and in this sense 'trans-cultural'; by that I mean only not bound to one culture, not that there is a substance of faith which is timeless and in that sense transcultural. On the other hand, precisely this universal message, open to all cultures and a challenge to all men and women, can be found concretely only in the forms of particular cultures (Jewish, Jewish-Hellenistic, Hellenistic; later the culture of late antiquity, Carolingian culture, Celtic, Romanesque, contemporary African, Asian and Latin American culture, and so on), never neat, above or outside any culture, and therefore never in an 'abstract substance of faith', stripped down

---

[12]This is the problem already posed by G. Tyrrell, which certainly is not solved by Peter Berger, who discusses a similar problem in *The Heretical Imperative*, New York and London 1979.

and free of any culture. So there is a constant dialectic between the universality of the gospel, through which it challenges every culture critically and transcends it, and its nevertheless constant appearance in particular cultures. Only in concrete particularity can the gospel be the revelation of the universality of salvation from God, because men and women are cultural beings with their own particular cultures and can only be reached as human beings in them. In this sense not only all forms of theology but also the biblical and magisterial expressions of faith are contextual and cultural, while they nevertheless seek to express the universal message of the gospel. So there is the constantly young, abiding 'offer of revelation', but on each occasion this is acclimatised in a particular culture, while that offer can never be found in an unhistorical and supra-cultural form. What we have is a historical identity of what remains, precisely *in* what gets forgotten and passes away because of its contingency. Here we have the problem of the interpretation of faith, and this problem cannot be argued away with any amount of authoritative statements.

What is important here is the insight that 'the situation' is no longer purely the channel in which the transmitted faith flows to meet us. The situation, the context of faith, is itself also theologically relevant. For according to my analysis above, the whole of history stands under God's liberating and redemptive will. The interpretation of faith is not concerned with the adaptation of a normative Bible and an authoritative tradition of faith to a 'theologically free' situation, but rather with the encounter of different cultural forms of the same understanding of faith and the practices that go with it: that of the Bible with all the forms of Christian understanding of the faith which came later, in diverging periods of culture within one cultural tradition and within divergent cultures. What we have here is a theoretical *and* practical, mutually critical encounter between faith cultures and therefore between different faith traditions, an encounter (or better, a long series of encounters) which allows us here and now (with all the limitations of the encounter) to catch sight of the 'offer of revelation', the Christian gospel, that we can never catch hold of and never objectify. In the interrelationship between the two poles there is therefore never any question of an obvious correlation, not even in the sense that one could call one pole (past Christian tradition of faith) the only source, while the other pole (the situation now and then) is not the source but, for example, only the area of dissemination. The contingent situation of the past is already present *in* the Christian tradition, twisting it, and in our contemporary situation God is as creative in liberation as he was before: he has not ceased to be 'the biblical God' in the meantime. I have already said above that we cannot simply set 'experience' and 'tradition' abruptly over against each other, because the tradition is the experiential horizon of all new experiences. So if we may speak of two poles, these poles lie in the past cultural forms and the present cultural forms which have to be sought today for the one gospel, which is itself the real source of both the earlier and the contemporary cultural form and expression of the faith. Of no single period of the tradition of faith, not even that of the Bible, may the cultural forms and historical context be absolutised. But this certainly does not mean that these historical and socio-cultural mediations are worthless for faith or to be neglected. On the contrary, they have a very positive function, for all their relativity, since they are the only possible vehicles for the meaning of the offer of revelation to which an answer is given in faith, precisely because the gospel, which is not bound to one culture, can nevertheless be seen and found *in* the special features of particular, culturally limited structures of understanding (only there and precisely there). Anyone who claims that the historical mediations are theologically irrelevant because of their relative specialisation, so that they relate only to the particular situation, is depriving the concrete history of Jesus of its specific importance for our history today. The Christian constants are expressed *in* many historical mediations which change down the ages, and are not as it were 'abstracted' from these concrete events.

Tradition and situation: A definition of concepts 2[13]

The problem of the interpretation and transmission of faith is thus: how do we build a bridge between the past tradition of faith and our existence as Christians in new situations? In the last resort the Christian message is preached *now*, no longer to the old citizens of Corinth, Ephesus and Thessalonica; it is preached to men and women who are our contemporaries, with their own understanding of themselves and the world, living in an almost post-modern social and economic social system and labour system, with their own, albeit uncertain, political plans. Consequently, believing now means bringing the Christian tradition of faith and experience to life and making it understandable in the present, in other, different historical situations and with other categories of thought and experience. This calls for a mutually critical and nevertheless continuous relationship between the past Christian tradition and our understanding of faith in our contemporary socio-historical and existential situation and our present-day praxis – in such a way that our presentation of the gospel today does not damage the identity of the liberating tradition of the gospel which discloses meaning and truth; in other words, by preserving its dynamics and orthodoxy. As a result of all this, the living interpretation of faith, expressed schematically, comes about in two phases, which together form one dialectical whole.

First, any believing attitude must be capable of being justified with reference to the Christian tradition of faith. This means that believing is also an *interpretation* of faith. (I shall not enter here into the technical possibilities, difficulties and 'methodological dispute' in contemporary hermeneutics, which I hope to work out technically in another book.)

Secondly, the attitude of any believer must also be capable of being justified with reference to an analysis and interpretation of the present situation in which we live. (This makes any interpretation and praxis of faith, *in* its intention of being universal, at the same time nevertheless contextual.) Otherwise there would be a short-circuit between categories of experience and thought from the past and those from the present.

However, these two stages of the one process of interpretation form a dialectical whole. For we only understand the Christian tradition in the light of questions which are addressed to us by the present situation; the understanding of our past already implies an interpretation of the present. And conversely, our Christian critical understanding of the present is itself also influenced historically by the Christian tradition.

This constant looking in two directions by the believer means that the process of interpretation in faith will consist in bringing the earlier phases of the tradition of

---

[13] Selected from: Edward Schillebeeckx, *Church: The Human Story of God*, Collected Works of Edward Schillebeeckx vol. 10 (London: Bloomsbury T&T Clark, 2014), 39–42 [39–43].

faith as we understand them into relationship with our analysis of the contemporary situation, in the twofold sense analysed above: the situation both in the general cultural and in the specifically Christian sense.

Present-day society and culture enters the understanding of revelation

From the analyses given in this first chapter we have already understood that experiencing-and-understanding revelation is also a constitutive element in the process of revelation itself. Precisely for this reason, perhaps paradoxically, revelation can also be handed down to others. For the personal and collective faith experience of decisive salvation in Jesus which his first followers had could be communicated to contemporaries and to later generations because these first followers described their experiences by means of their socially shared system of communication (a semiotic system, one conveying meaning). This was initially in the Jewish language, later in the Greek language, in the understanding of reality characteristic of Asia Minor, and so on. In each instance we have a culture-specific appropriation of the message of the gospel: living contact between the gospel and the changing, culturally-shaped understanding of reality by believers in a particular cultural period. Think, for example, of the Christian message as this is translated by the authentic letters of Paul and the same message again translated into the cultural climate of the understanding of reality in Asia Minor at that time in the letters to the Christians of Colossae and Ephesus! The continuity and the difference here become quite clear. Because each time a different semiotic cultural system (i.e. one conveying meaning) is involved, a history of socio-cultural historical mediations comes into being: specifically, a history of Christian believing in a variety of tongues and languages. Moreover, the distinctiveness of these historical mediations, then and now, begins to play a greater role in this conception of what the interpretation of faith and thus the specific form of Christian faith is than Christians were formerly aware, though they did the same thing spontaneously and often without reflection in an instinctive Christian way.

If all this is the case, then it already emerges that for us the identity in the meaning of the gospel cannot primarily lie at the level of the Bible and the past tradition of faith, at least as such, and therefore cannot be found in a material repetition of that past (in any kind of 'fundamentalism', whether in conservative or in progressive forms). Far less, however, can it be found at the level of the situation, then and now, *as such* (whether in a biblicist or a modernist direction). This identity of meaning can only be found in the fluctuating 'middle field', in a swinging to and fro between tradition and situation, and thus at the level of the corresponding relationship between the original message (tradition, which also includes the situation of the time) and the situation, then and now, which is different each time. The fundamental identity of meaning between the successive periods of Christian understanding of the offer of revelation is not to be found in corresponding terms (e.g. a parallel between the situation of the Bible and our situation, on the basis of which one could then, for instance, use Jesus' cleansing of the temple to justify the action of squatters in Amsterdam) but on corresponding relationships between all the terms involved (message and situation, then and now). Moreover there is a fundamental unity and identity: this has no relation to the terms of the factors involved, but to the *relationship* between all these terms. The following diagram may clarify it to some extent:

the given articulation or relationship

$$\frac{\text{Jesus' message}}{\text{the socio-historical context of Jesus}} = \frac{\text{the New Testament message}}{\text{the socio-historical context of the NT}}$$

is reproduced, for example, in the relationship:

$$\frac{\text{patristic understanding of faith}}{\text{the socio-historical context then}} = \frac{\text{mediaeval understanding of faith}}{\text{the socio-historical context then}}$$

and this relationship, given and reproduced, must ultimately be reproduced once more in the following relationship or articulation:

$$= \frac{\text{the present understanding of faith in the year 1990}}{\text{our socio-historical and existential context in the year 1990}}$$

The identity of relationship between these articulations of nevertheless completely different terms bears the Christian identity of meaning. The equal proportion of relationships down through the Christian tradition of faith is a norm, an orientation and an inspiration; it is the model on the basis of which now, loyal to the gospel, we can nevertheless also make its message comprehensible here and now.

So we never have a direct view of the Christian identity of meaning; moreover it can never be laid down once and for all. But this does not mean that it is arbitrary. Christian identity, which is one and the same, is never complete identity, but proportional identity. In their differing interpretations of the one gospel, particular historical and cultural mediations sometimes contradict one another, in the sense that they cannot all be harmonised on the same level. But that one level is a fiction. The unity is a unity in depth in which some things stand out. Therefore we cannot look at what is called 'the development of dogma' (the life of the Christian tradition in various cultures or at different periods of the same culture) in the same way as the Scholastics or neo-Scholastics, nor even as in the more sophisticated approach of Newman, namely as a permanent explicitation of a substance of faith which was always already implicit, a making explicit from the implicit to the explicit; from the Bible in roughly a straight line to the present day. For although the offer of revelation with its non-objectifiable meaning and content is indeed present from the beginning, this meaning as assignable and expressed is to be found only in the believing interpretations of men and women in a particular social and cultural context. The periodical twists in the cultural understanding of reality rule out a purely explicative process. Something else is involved. What we have is, rather, the process of a constantly new inculturation of a gospel which is not bound to one culture, but which is not given in the Bible, either, apart from a limited, particular cultural form.

The relationship between past and present as an encounter between different cultural forms of Christian understanding[14]

This process of interrelating tradition and situation can be called a 'correlation method', although the term strikes me as ambiguous: by 'correlation' I simply mean interrelationship in a very general sense. The word permits various possible meanings, ranging from similarity and correlation to conflict and confrontation – in short, the whole broad spectrum between identity (clicking) and non-identity (clashing).

Here we are up against an extremely delicate problem. On the one hand the fundamental tenor and power of the gospel are transcendent and universal, and in that sense trans-cultural, that is not tied to any one culture. On the other hand this very universal, trans-cultural gospel that challenges all humans is only to be found in the form of particular cultures (Judaic, Judaeo-Hellenistic and late antiquity, Carolingian, Celtic, Roman, African, Asian, etc.), never above or beyond these, never in distilled religious substance. Thus there is a perennial dialectics between the universality of the gospel, which challenges every culture critically and transcends it, and its concrete manifestation in particular cultures. Only *in* concrete particularity can the gospel reveal the universality of salvation coming from God. In that sense biblical and official ecclesiastic religious statements are equally contextual, local and particular, while still actively conveying a universal message. Thus there is an enduring religious substance that is always actualised in and acclimatised to particular cultures, whereas it is not accessible to us a-historically or supra-culturally. It is a *historical identity* of that which is rooted in the evanescent reality that eludes its contingency. That is the very core of theological hermeneutics.

Thinking on these lines one perceives the real hermeneutic problem as one of encounter between diverse Christian cultures. Besides, the present-day situation is not merely the *channel* for the transmitted religious current. The secular situation itself has *theological relevance*, for according to our interpretation all history falls under God's scheme of liberation and redemption. What is at issue is not the application of a normative biblical and ecclesiastic tradition to a 'theology-free' situation, but rather an encounter between different cultural embodiments of the same religious understanding with its corresponding existential praxis: that of the Bible, along with all subsequent forms of Christian religious interpretation in diverse cultural eras and cultures. What is at issue is a critical encounter, both theoretical and practical,

---

[14]Selected from: Edward Schillebeeckx, 'Theological Interpretation of Faith in 1983', *Essays: Ongoing Theological Quests*, Collected Works of Edward Schillebeeckx vol. 11 (London: Bloomsbury T&T Clark, 2014), 57–61.

between different cultural embodiments of Christian religious understanding, which enables us to conceive of a substance of faith that can never be encountered in isolation. Hence the interrelationship of the 'twin poles' does not imply a self-evident correlation, not even in the sense that the one pole (Christian tradition) is considered the sole source, whereas the other pole (the present situation) is not treated as a source at all but only as, for example, the area to be irrigated. *In* Christian tradition the erstwhile situation has already been taken into account, and *in* our present situation God is no less creatively and liberatingly active than he was then. Hence if one can speak of twin poles at all, they lie in *bygone* cultural forms as well as in *contemporary* cultural embodiments of *the same religious substance*, which is the actual source of both past and present-day cultural forms and expressions of faith. In a manner of speaking correlation is a metaphoric, even a misleading term. We should rather speak of an encounter of cultures living by the substance of the Christian faith and 'acclimatising' it to their own cultural reality.[15] That seems to be the only way of avoiding two to my mind illegitimate extremes: on the one hand a kind of positivist notion of revelation (or rather tradition), in which only one pole is normative – the vertical imperative of what is known as God's word in Scripture – and on the other the 19th century liberal model, in which 'modernity' in fact becomes the norm determining present-day religious interpretation, thus declaring just one cultural form (the modern one) absolute. Because of the trans-cultural character of the universal gospel (albeit manifested only *in* particular cultural forms) the cultural forms of no given period – neither the biblical era nor that of ecclesiastic segments of the church's living tradition – can ever be absolute.

But that does not mean that the historical, socio-cultural vehicles of tradition must necessarily be denigrated. On the contrary, as the only possible vehicles of the manifested substance of faith they have a positive function for the very reason that the transcultural component of the gospel is only to be found in the particularity of cultural hermeneutic structures. Those who denigrate historical transmission in all its relative particularisations – that is, relate them exclusively to the situation at that time – rob Jesus' history of its significance for our present-day history. It is in historical transmission that the Christian constants emerge,[16] not as it were 'abstracted from' concrete history.[17] Just as one can compare biblical theology in Christian history with that of Augustine, and Augustine's (and the Bible's) with, say, that of Athanasius, Thomas Aquinas or Bonaventure, and these (and the Bible's) with that of Luther, Karl Barth, Wolfhart Pannenberg or Karl Rahner, so contemporary

---

[15]In Chicago's Theological Union Robert Schreiter is researching the cross-cultural problem of encounter between different religions and cultures. See e.g. 'Issues facing contextual theologies today', in: *Verbum* (SVD) 1980, 267–77. See C. Geertz, *The Interpretation of Cultures*, New York, 1973; L. Luzbetak, *The Church and Cultures*, Divine Word Publications, 1963, and: 'Signs of progress in contextual theology', in: *Verbum* (SVD) 1 (1981), 39–57; D. Von Allmen, 'The birth of theology. Contextualisation as the dynamic element in the formulation of the New Testament theology', in: *International Review of Mission* 64 (1975), 38–52; E. Leach, *Culture and communication*, Cambridge, 1976.
[16]See E. Schillebeeckx, *Christ*, London/New York, 1980, part III, 629–45.
[17]In a review of the preceding book (*Christ*) Leo Bakker rightly formulated my exact meaning more precisely than I did, thus preventing misinterpretation of these pages. See 'Gerechtigheid en liefde', in: *Bijdragen* 39 (1978), (70–7) 75.

hermeneutic theologians compare the 'present Christian situation' with forms of theology and Christian praxis in the Bible, in patristics, in the Middle Ages, in modernity, etc.

Hence belief in God's revelation always has its point of departure in our world of today: *there are historical vehicles*. Revelation is transmitted in various places and eras but still takes on the features of the religious interpretation advanced in each instance. Thus every conceivable religious interpretation is based on and couched in the medium of people's understanding of the world, which is peculiar to their culture. That understanding is historical and culture specific; it is but one culturally determined, particular understanding of the world (despite a universally human, even logical basic structure). Hence the hermeneutic problem of Christian identity throughout the ages can be solved only by comparing the various cultural forms of religious experience and religious interpretation, in which the substance of the gospel is articulated in diverse ways. The only difference between Christian tradition in the past and the new tradition we are shaping today is that our comparisons of past interpretations are *post factum*: history has already weathered the dangers of actualising theology; that still lies ahead for us, who are in the midst of the actualising process with all its dangers of success and failure, conjecture and error – of orthodoxy and 'heresy'.

Two poles, one source

So when we speak of two poles and one source we need to differentiate this elliptic expression precisely. In discussing my theological hermeneutics Hans Küng does not refer to two sources or poles. Instead he recognises a single source (the Bible and Christian tradition) on the one hand; on the other he does not regard the situation as a source but calls it a pole and a horizon.[18] But that entails a risk of creating a *theology-free zone*: the situation. For my part, on closer scrutiny I would identify the 'two poles' as, firstly, the substance of faith embedded in the Jewish and Judaeo-Hellenistic culture of the Bible (and in the various cultures of the church's tradition in the past), and secondly, that same substance that we need to apply to our contemporary situation, hence a contemporary piece of 'Christian tradition'. Thus the question could read: how do we bridge the divide between the old religious tradition and our new situations?[19] After all, nowadays the Christian message is no longer proclaimed to the people of Corinth, Ephesus or Thessalonica, but to present-day people with their own understanding of themselves and the world, living in a modern socio-economic order with its own political dispensations. Actualised faith and – at the level of thematic, critical reflection – actualised theology in effect mean *representing* the Christian religious and experiential tradition intelligibly and vibrantly in other, historically altered

---

[18]H. Küng, E. Schillebeeckx et al., *Consensus in Theology? A Dialogue with H. Küng and E. Schillebeeckx*, Philadelphia, 1980, (1–17) especially 16–17.

[19]The reciprocal critical 'interrelationship' between religious documents from the past and the present situation requires prior structuralist or semiotic work, namely (a) a theory explaining how meaning is produced; and (b) structurally analyses differentiating between possible meanings of a text and impossible ones. But understanding a text cannot be reduced to an exposition of the text.

situations and other experiential and thought categories, That requires critically yet continuously relating past Christian tradition and our contemporary socio-historical and existential situation to the concrete praxis of present-day Christians, in such a way that the actualisation does not impair the liberating disclosure of the truth of the Gospel tradition – in other words, whilst preserving orthodoxy.

As a result authentic theologising proceeds in two phases, which together constitute a dialectic whole. Firstly, every theological proposition must be justifiable in terms of the theologian's religious tradition. That implies that all theologians are engaged in *interpretation*. Theology is a *hermeneutic enterprise*. It means that theologians use manifold and divergent interpretive methods derived mainly from the literary sciences (e.g. historical literary criticism, structuralism and semiotics, so-called materialistic exegesis, etc.). They also have to explicate and justify their chosen method. After all, every method has a 'philosophy' of its own and is not 'innocent'; each has a highly focused intention. Finally, they have to devise criteria according to which interpretations of the Christian tradition can be publicly and critically evaluated. Orthodoxy needs a coherent set of criteria.

Secondly: every theological proposition also has to be justified in terms of an analysis and interpretation of the 'current situation'. Otherwise one creates a short circuit between past and present experiential and thought categories.

Yet together the two steps constitute a dialectic whole. After all, we can only interpret the Christian tradition in terms of questions arising from our real-life situation. Understanding the past in itself presupposes interpretation of the present. Conversely, our understanding of the present is partly determined by the historical influence of the Christian tradition.

The theologian's constant two-way scrutiny means that the theological hermeneutic process consists in 'relating' the (exegetic and historical) interpretation of religious tradition to an interpretation of the critically analysed present situation, in both a profane cultural and a specifically Christian sense. Even a positivist-style theological interpretation, where one pole (the Christian religious tradition that propounds revelation) conflicts with the second pole (the current situation), still correlates tradition with the situation here and now, even if only by categorically rejecting 'modernity'. If that rejection is to be critically substantiated, the modern situation in which we live has to be analysed and interpreted. Hence whether positive or negative, for theology interpretation entails analytical involvement, not only with the Christian past but also with the present situation. In that situational analysis the theologian is dependent, albeit critically, on the human and social sciences and their scientific models. Only after such interdisciplinary exploration of the field on which the believer wishes to comment 'theologically' can an autonomous theological discourse get under way, primarily and especially in response to the question why we aver that the situation has a 'religious' dimension and hence is open to theological discussion.

Interconfessionally, this could lead to differences. Because of the fundamental prominence of the Christian belief in creation Catholic theologians in particular will confess both the world and history in every affirmation of God, despite the ambivalence and sinfulness of that history. In Catholic tradition, trust in humanity and its history leads to the affirmation that, regardless of all ambiguities, the present situation remains an authentic *locus theologicus* or location where theological reflection finds its data in light of the Christian tradition. Protestant Christian theologians, by contrast, would be more inclined to accentuate the brokenness of our situation; they will concentrate on 'the demonic' (itself a 'religious' category) in our situation, hence will usually produce negative correlations between religious tradition and present situation. Both approaches entail a risk, the former of underplaying the senseless aspects of history (and of the massive tradition of the churches) and the autonomous rationality of the socio-economic order, and the latter by overlooking God's ongoing liberation history in and through human deeds ever since the creation.

Selected literature

- The Hermeneutical Problem for the Catholic Faith; Selected from: Edward Schillebeeckx, 'Towards a Catholic Use of Hermeneutics', *God the Future of Man*, trans. N. D. Smith, Collected Works of Edward Schillebeeckx vol. 3 (London: Bloomsbury T&T Clark, 2014), 12–13 [17–19].
- Understanding: Text and Tradition; Selected from: Edward Schillebeeckx, 'Towards a Catholic Use of Hermeneutics', *God the Future of Man*, trans. N. D. Smith, Collected Works of Edward Schillebeeckx vol. 3 (London: Bloomsbury T&T Clark, 2014), 20–2 [29–32].
- The New Critical Theory and Theological Hermeneutics; Selected from: Edward Schillebeeckx, 'The New Critical Theory and Theological Hermeneutics', *The Understanding of Faith: Interpretation and Criticism*, trans. N. D. Smith, Collected Works of Edward Schillebeeckx vol. 5 (London: Bloomsbury T&T Clark, 2014), 116–18 [132–5].
- The Authority of New Experiences; Selected from: Edward Schillebeeckx, *Christ: The Christian Experience in the Modern World*, Collected Works of Edward Schillebeeckx vol. 7 (London: Bloomsbury T&T Clark, 2014), 24–6 [38–40].
- Tradition and Situation: A Definition of Concepts 1; Selected from: Edward Schillebeeckx, *Church: The Human Story of God*, Collected Works of Edward Schillebeeckx vol. 10 (London: Bloomsbury T&T Clark, 2014), 33–7 [34–8].
- Tradition and Situation: A Definition of Concepts 2; Selected from: Edward Schillebeeckx, *Church: The Human Story of God*, Collected Works of Edward Schillebeeckx vol. 10 (London: Bloomsbury T&T Clark, 2014), 39–42 [39–43].
- The Relationship between Past and Present; Selected from: 'Theological Interpretation of Faith in 1983', *Essays: Ongoing Theological Quests*, Collected Works of Edward Schillebeeckx vol. 11 (London: Bloomsbury T&T Clark, 2014), 57–61.

7

Church and World

The Church, earthly sacrament of Christ in heaven[1]

We have said that Jesus as person and Messiah is unthinkable without his redemptive community. Established by God precisely in his vocation as representative of fallen humanity, Jesus had by his human life to win this community to himself and make of it a redeemed people of God. This means that Jesus the Messiah, through his death which the Father accepts, becomes in fact the head of the People of God, the Church assembled in his death. It is thus that he wins the Church to himself, by his messianic life as the Servant of God, as the fruit of the sufferings of his messianic sacrifice: 'Christ dies that the Church might be born.'[2] In his messianic sacrifice, which the Father accepts, Christ in his glorified body is himself the eschatological redemptive community of the Church. In his own self the glorified Christ is simultaneously both 'head and members'.

The earthly Church is the visible realisation of this saving reality in history. The Church is a visible communion in grace. This communion itself, consisting of members and a hierarchical leadership, is the earthly sign of the triumphant redeeming grace of Christ. The fact must be emphasised that not only the hierarchical Church but also the community of the faithful belong to this grace-giving sign that is the Church. As much in its hierarchy as in the laity the community of the Church is the realisation in historical form of the victory achieved by Christ. The inward communion in grace with God in Christ becomes visible in and is realised through the outward social sign. Thus the essence of the Church consists in this, that the final goal of grace achieved by Christ becomes visibly present in the *whole* Church as a visible society.

It was the custom in the past to distinguish between the soul of the Church (this would be the inward communion in grace with Christ) and the body of the Church (the visible society with its members and its authority). Only too rightly, this view has been abandoned. It was even, in a sense, condemned by Pope Pius XII. The

---

[1] Selected from: Edward Schillebeeckx, *Christ the Sacrament of the Encounter with God*, trans. Paul Barrett, N. D. Smith, Collected Works of Edward Schillebeeckx vol. 1 (London: Bloomsbury T&T Clark, 2014), 33–7 [56–62].

[2] 'Moritur Christus ut fiat Ecclesia'. (St. Augustine, *In Joh. Evangelium*, tr. 9, no. 10 (PL, 35, col. 1463).)

visible Church itself is the Lord's mystical body. The Church is the visible expression of Christ's grace and redemption, realised in the form of a society which is a sign (*societas signum*). Any attempt to introduce a dualism here is the work of evil – as if one could play off the inward communion in grace with Christ against the juridical society of the Church, or vice versa. The Church therefore is not merely a means of salvation. It is Christ's salvation itself, this salvation as visibly realised in this world. Thus it is, by a kind of identity, the body of the Lord.

We remarked that this visibility of grace defines the whole Church; not the hierarchical Church only, but also the community of the faithful. The whole Church, the People of God led by a priestly hierarchy, is 'the sign raised up among the nations'.[3] The activity, as much of the faithful as of their leaders, is thus an ecclesial activity.[4] This means that not only the Hierarchy but also the believing people belong essentially to the primordial sacrament which is the earthly expression of this reality. As the sacramental Christ, the Church too is mystically both Head and members. When the twofold function of Christ becomes visible in the sign of the Christian community, it produces the distinction between hierarchy and faithful – a distinction of offices and of those who hold them. Even though the Hierarchy, on the one hand, are themselves part of the believing Church, and the faithful, on the other hand, share in the lordship of Christ and to some extent give it visibility, the sacramental functions of hierarchy and faithful differ within the Church and show the distinction.

The ecclesial character of the office of hierarchy and laity

How are we to understand this distinction in office? The sacramental manifestation of the Lord in his role as head of the People of God is realised formally and functionally in the apostolic office, the ecclesiastical hierarchy. In this aspect the hierarchical Church is sovereign with regard to the community of the faithful. On the other hand, the whole community of the faithful, or the People of God, is the sacramental realisation on earth of the Lord as representatively the People of God. In this aspect the faithful themselves are the Church. In its entirety – apostolic office and community of the faithful – the Church is the sacramental or mystical Christ. And in its entirety it is at the same time both community of the redeemed and redeeming institution. In and through the visible activity of the Church – that is, of the apostolic office and of the faithful who are signed with the Christian character – the Lord brings to fulfilment the work of redemption for which he laid the foundation as the historical Messiah. The Church on earth is the visible presence of the work of fulfilment in which Christ

---

[3] Thus the First Vatican Council. (*Denzinger-Banwart*, no. 1794 [DH 3013–14])

[4] It is necessary for a clear presentation of the argument to adopt this form of the adjective. In everyday usage 'ecclesiastical' has become so closely linked with all that concerns the hierarchical element in the Church; this currently more common word would therefore be misleading here and in the pages to follow, and circumlocution would not only prove cumbersome but also obscure the already compact text. 'Ecclesial' is used to signify all that is proper to the Church in its entirety, a synthesis of hierarchical and lay elements.

is now engaged in his glorified body and so also in his Spirit. This visible presence of grace and consequent bestowal of grace in the Church is achieved in a twofold manner: through the apostolic office in virtue of the character of the priesthood, and through the faithful in virtue of their character of baptism and confirmation.[5] What Christ is doing invisibly in this world through his Spirit, he is at the same time doing visibly through the mission of his Apostles and of the members of the Church community. These two missions (of the Spirit and of the Church) are organically connected. What the Hierarchy does in virtue of its apostolic office, and the faithful do in virtue of their baptismal and confirmational mission, each in the sphere of the objective visible life of the Church, the Spirit of Christ does inwardly in this visible activity and in the hearts of people.

In his article on the Church in the Epistle to the Ephesians H. Schlier says that according to St. Paul the glorified body of Christ is the Church of heaven, which comes on earth through the Spirit and becomes the earthly Church.[6] We have come to the same conclusion by a different route. The body of Christ in heaven is also the enduring sign of the messianic redemption or of the mystery of saving worship which Christ is; a sign that contains what it signifies, for it is this messianic act of redemption itself in visible form. But for the time being, until the *parousia*, this sign remains invisible to us earthly beings. Therefore the Lord gave this external sign of the Redemption a visible prolongation on earth: the visible Church. Through this visible prolongation the Redemption is revealed in this world in which we live as something that is for us, and thus it is precisely through this that the Redemption is offered to us.

Office and charism in the Church

The Church in its entirety is not only a saving institution; as such it is also a saving and sanctifying community. As the earthly representation of the sign of salvation in heaven, the Church in its entirety is itself a sign already containing the redemptive reality of Christ. The Church's own inward invisible communion in grace with God in Christ becomes visible in its saving activity. This earthly body of the Lord, the Church, is at the same time the Lord's *pleroma*; being filled with Christ, it in turn fills the faithful. For this reason the sacramental Church, in the Hierarchy and in the community of the faithful signed with the sacramental character, is not only the earthly visible form of the activity of Christ as High Priest, but at the same time is a sign that in its sacramental or visible saving activity it is itself filled with the reality to which it is giving form. This means that the Church in its institutional existence as a society manifests not only Christ in himself but also its own communion of grace and life with Christ. As earthly representative of Christ, the Church too is the

---

[5] We do no more than mention this point here. At a later stage in this work the significance of the character of baptism and confirmation and, in contrast to them, of the priesthood, will be analysed. It has been found necessary to anticipate this analysis to a certain extent, for otherwise the present exposition might be incorrectly interpreted, as reactions to earlier editions have shown.
[6] 'Die Kirche nach dem Briefe an die Epheser', in *Die Zeit der Kirche*, Freiburg (1956), pp. 159–85.

'child of the Father'; being supreme worship of the Father, and also the one who at Pentecost was 'established in power', the Church bestows the Spirit whom it has itself received in prayer from Christ. Therefore in the Church too there is the twofold movement we have already discovered in Christ: the movement down from above and up from below.

Thus the Church in its own proper activity is a historical manifestation of God's own love for people in Christ (bestowal of grace) and, at the same time, of its own love and adoration of God in the same Lord (worship). Because the Church, as the bride Christ won to himself, is itself 'full of grace', it is an offer of grace to those who approach it, and the bestowal of grace upon those who open themselves to it. In this way the Church is a community of salvation and of worship.

Thus the grace of redemption becomes visible in the Church in a twofold manner: through office and through charism. The grace of redemption becomes visible, in other words: (1) Through office, or institutionally: both through the priestly activity of the Hierarchy (that is, through the administration of the sacraments, through the administration of the word, ecclesiastical preaching or authority to teach, and through pastoral government or the care of souls), and through the ecclesial office proper to the laity, that is, through their activity in virtue of the characters of baptism and confirmation. (2) Through charism: that is, through the activity of both Hierarchy and laity, in so far as this activity is an outward manifestation of inward communion in grace with God.

Both the institutional and the charismatic elements are genuinely ecclesial. We must not lose sight of the fact that the Church is a mystery, a sign bearing within itself the reality of inward union with God in Christ. The consequence of this is that both Hierarchy and laity must carry out the functions of their office in virtue of the charism associated with it. Office and charism could never be dissociated within the Church as a whole, but they are dissociated at times in individual members of the Hierarchy or laity, creating a distorted situation in which the Church is deprived of something proper to herself.

'The world' as the objective expression of the life of grace[7]

The *locus theologicus* or source of all reflection about faith and also of the theology of the relationship between church and world is the historical event of salvation in which God gave himself to us in an absolute and gratuitous manner in Jesus Christ. The person Jesus is the absolute and gratuitous proximity of the divine mystery. Jesus' *humanity* is the objective expression of God's communication of himself in grace and at the same time the objective expression of the free response of this person, the Son of God, to the Father. Christ's human existence, with all its historical conditions and implications, is the personal life of God himself, the Son. The deepest

---

[7]Selected from: Edward Schillebeeckx, 'Church and World', *World and Church*, trans. N. D. Smith, Collected Works of Edward Schillebeeckx vol. 4 (London: Bloomsbury T&T Clark, 2014), 75–8 [98–103].

unsuspected possibilities of being human are thus disclosed, possibilities which only become intelligible in the light of Christ. Thanks to Christ, our being human is the possibility of the self-manifestation of the life of grace or of life in union with God. Christ's 'hypostatic union', on whose riches we can draw, teaches us that the whole of the history of humanity is contained in the love of God. The history of this world is therefore not sacralised, because it preserves its specific quality, but sanctified, included in the absolute and gratuitous presence of the mystery.

Although people have various ways of expressing it, it is a universally human datum that our existence as human beings is steeped in mystery. Christianity only throws light on this datum in its promulgation of the word, which proclaims that the mystery in which our life is grounded has come closer to us in an absolute manner, not only in mystical inwardness, but also in historical tangibility. The whole of the Christian kerygma, the whole of dogma, from the Trinity, the incarnation and the life of grace to the church with her sacraments, her ministers and her proclamation of the word and faith in individual and collective 'last things', can be traced back to this fundamental religious affirmation. In her proclamation of the word, the church discloses the implications of this absolute nearness of God in Christ, a nearness in grace which is actively present in the lives of all people as the revelation of reality even before they have been historically confronted with the phenomenon of the church. Acceptance of this nearness is, moreover, the very essence of all saving faith, since believing is placing one's confidence, in and despite everything, in this mystery which has come near to us. This simple reality is of the greatest importance, because it means that the acceptance of actual human existence with all its responsibilities is an act of theologal[8] faith, since it has become clear to us in Christ that human existence can be made the objective expression of the life of grace. The reader may have the impression that I have strayed from my theme of 'church and world'. I believe, however, that I have come closer to the central core of the question, because two things have been made clear by this brief analysis.

In the first place, the absolute nearness of the mystery has reached an explicit, historically recognisable epiphany (as a given reality and at the same time as a task) in the church of Christ. In the second place, it is precisely this epiphany of the church with its concentrated presence of grace that makes explicitly clear and explicitly confesses the wealth (which is perhaps not reflectively conscious) present in the reality of every human experience of existence in the world, namely, security in God's grace. Even in our life on earth, we are with God and, what is more, we are with him not only in prayer and in the worship and the sacraments of the church. Ordinary everyday life with its secular concerns and its work for and with the world is therefore the immediate sphere within which Christian life has to be objectivised and its source of strength and inspiration is the direct expression of the life of grace given by the church. Christianity, in other words, acceptance of God as the mystery which comes forward to meet us in Christ, normally has to be accomplished in the context of secular life with its tasks and responsibilities in the world. Paul expressed this idea in a masterly though negative way:

---

[8]The English translators used the term 'theologal' for that which is infused by God, e.g. the theological (in Dutch: *theologaal*) virtues, faith, hope, and love. In English, however, this term is hardly used.

> For I am sure that neither death, nor life, nor angels, nor principalities, nor things present, nor things to come, nor powers, nor height, nor depth, nor anything else in all creation, will be able to separate us from the love of God in Christ Jesus our Lord. [Rom 3. 38-9]

What else does this text mean, other than that true Christianity is faith in the absolute and gratuitous nearness of God, in Christ, in all the circumstances of life in this world, and that acceptance of the security of all human history in God's grace is the very substance of Christianity? Does it not mean that we are with the living God precisely in and with our world of people? The reality that we call 'world' is given a distinctively theological significance by this insight. 'World' is the reality which, while remaining a profane reality with its own laws and structures and a secular aim of its own, was nonetheless included by God in Christ in the absolute and gratuitous nearness of God. We should not, moreover, regard this world as static – it is something that has been given to human beings for them to humanise and make a place fit for humans to live in, in the service of the whole of humanity. We should not, of course, ignore the fact that the world is marked with the sign of transience and of the creature. Like everything that is touched by the hands of people, the world too is affected by sin. The building up of the world and the development of peoples is therefore a *finite* work of humanity, participating in the ambiguity of everything that is human and material. The world is non-God, a creature – this is an affirmation of the secular nature of this task. As such, however, creation is a divine placing of realities in their profane, non-divine distinctiveness. It is a divine act which, in contrast to the mythological accounts of creation of Israel's neighbours, was depicted in the account given in Genesis as a demythologised and desacralised act of God, who gave the world to itself, into the hands of people, for the glorifying of God's name. This implies that the history of humanity will always display, in and through God's continuing act of creation, a constant desacralisation of the structures and functions of the world.

Nonetheless, only one aspect of reality is intended in all this, since the bearing, desacralising, silent divine ground of all creatural being has come nearer to us in an absolute and gratuitous manner in Christ. This world, with its profane distinctiveness, is borne into the theologal sphere of the life of grace by human beings, whose anthropology can ultimately only be fully understood in the light of Christ. This means, in other words, that 'the world' is, in the contemporary saving situation of the incarnation, *implicit Christianity* – a distinctive, non-sacral, but sanctified expression of the living community with the living God – while the church, as the institution of salvation with her communal confession of faith, her worship and her sacraments, is the 'set aside', sacral expression of this implicit Christianity. Speaking about the church's relationship with the world is therefore not a dialogue between what is distinctive to Christianity and what is alien to Christianity, between the religious and the profane, between what is supranatural and what relates strictly to this world. It is, on the contrary, a dialogue – and here we are confronted with the very essence of the whole problem – between the *two complementary forms of experience of the one Christianity,* a dialogue between the set aside, sacral expression *by the church* of the theologal life of those who explicitly believe and the secular expression that has not been set aside, *within the world,* of the same life of faith. It is only insofar as this theologal life itself remains implicit and anonymous and is not given its appropriate expression in forms that are specifically those of the church that these two forms of experience of the one Christianity can be indicated by the two words implicit and explicit Christianity.[9]

Anonymous but real Christianity therefore means in this context the secular reality of life within this world which is taken up, in its profane distinctiveness, in the absolute and gratuitous nearness of the mystery, that is, of the theologal life which is in itself the beginning of eternal life and which thus through humanity involves the secular itself in the definitive eschatological salvation and enables it to participate in this salvation. Within this absolute presence in grace of the mystery and thus within the theologal sphere, which may perhaps be simply anonymous, the building up of the world and work for a better world in the future for all people becomes an activity which *inwardly,* and not only in its intention, has something to do with the dawning of the eschatological kingdom. It goes without saying that the final eschatological consummation of everything on earth will, precisely because of the absolute and gratuitous nature of this consummation, transcend all our expectations and all our building up of this world. Nonetheless, because it is included in the life of grace, everything on earth really shares, in the present plan of salvation, in the mystery of eternity, as the dogma of the resurrection of all flesh and the kerygma of the 'new heaven and the new earth' affirm. There is something irrevocable in commitment to this world, which extends concretely much farther than its purely temporal dimensions might lead us to suppose. God, after all, loves humanity unconditionally and humanity is not abstract 'human nature', but a being who, together with his equals in this world, takes the fate of humanity on earth into his hands. It is this human being whom God loves eternally and this ultimately gives a divine significance to the building up of the world and the development of all people. After all, if it is true that human beings are the subject of grace by virtue of their 'receptivity to grace' which is grounded in his spiritual being, then their receptivity to grace means simply this – what is included in theologal intimacy with the living God and thus, transcending themselves, participate in 'eternal life' are human beings themselves in their distinctiveness and totality who, as beings who make history, humanise themselves in their humanisation of the world. This total reality receives grace. In the past, an anthropologically false and dualistic view of the conferment of grace and redemption frequently led to our regarding this as a matter of God and the human *soul.* This meant that the whole of human activity within this world – and quantitatively this was ninety-nine per cent of the factual activity of the majority of people – lay outside Christianity. If this view were to persist, it would inevitably encourage the estrangement between church and world, especially at a time when the distinctive meaning of the world is being discovered.

---

[9] It is clear that the status of implicit Christianity can be destroyed by the refusal of human beings to accept grace. I am therefore not saying that all those outside the church are in themselves implicit Christians. Only God can judge the state of a person's conscience. It is worthwhile placing this on record, however, as the objection that all people who are outside the church cannot justifiably be called implicit Christians is certainly valid, just as the opposite is also true – that all explicit, practicing Christians are not in themselves authentic Christians.

The social teaching of the church[10]

The starting point for the church's social teaching cannot be a 'dualism' between church and world in which the latter is regarded as a kind of 'outboard' world which can only be meaningful to Christianity as providing an opportunity and the matter for the practice of Christian charity. The significance of theologal hope, its cosmic significance as well, must be clearly understood, and the close connection between the great expectations for this earth and the coming of the kingdom of God must be the dynamic idea that sustains and supports everything. In this sense, it is valuable to refer to the theological reflection that was given great prominence years ago at the World Council of Churches when it met at Evanston in 1954, in connection with 'Christian hope in the modern world'. Here too, a dialogue with the other Christian churches could have a fruitful effect on the precise formulation of the Catholic view in this respect.

Furthermore, the real problem, that of humanity's future on earth in connection with Christianity, must be central. A certain Augustinianism, and certainly an Augustinian attitude with regard to precisely those aspects that Albert the Great and Thomas, for example, attacked in the Middle Ages because they were more aware of secularity and the real meaning of 'second causes', must not be allowed to dominate our thinking, even unconsciously. We must be bold enough resolutely to affirm the contemporary meaning of 'apostolic secularity' and, in this context, the whole collective and historical dimension of humanity as well, so as to avoid giving the impression that the special significance of the socialising history of the world is not taken sufficiently seriously.

Finally, we should not take as our point of departure a theological and theoretical conception of the traditional problem (which is, in itself, correct) concerning the relationship between 'nature and supernature'. Our starting point must be the existential experience of lay Christians who, from the vantage-point of their involvement in terrestrial realities and responsibilities, question the place of religion and of the church in their lives. Only in this way will we be able to express in a liberating manner, on the one hand, the church's being non-world, *separata a mundo*, and, on the other, how the 'recapitulation of everything in Christ' within the human life of grace with the living God, the constantly present mystery of grace, inspires a secular holiness and an apostolic secularity which, however, find their source of nourishment within the experience of the church.

To stress the transcendence of grace at the expense of its immanence is always a depreciation of transcendence, or at least a one-sided limitation of this immanence to the sacral, set-aside forms of grace within the church. Nature and history are not, after all, sacralised or deprived of their profane significance by the active presence in grace of the mystery in humanity and the human making of history. They are *sanctified,* included in God's embrace of humanity. As Thomas said, 'to diminish the excellence of the creature is to diminish the excellence of God'. In this context, we

---

[10]Selected from: Edward Schillebeeckx, 'Church and World', *World and Church*, trans. N. D. Smith, Collected Works of Edward Schillebeeckx vol. 4 (London: Bloomsbury T&T Clark, 2014), 83–7 [110–14].

should not lose sight of the fact that, thanks to Christ, the aspect of creation *(creatio)* is, in the present plan of salvation, only an aspect of the *assumptio*. As Augustine said, *ipsa assumptione creatur,* in other words, in being situated creatively in his distinctively earthly quality, a human being, the creature, is in Christ included in the nearness in grace of the God of the covenant, who definitively loves humanity in an absolute manner even in his historical attempts here on earth to provide humanity with a better world and a better place to live in.

There is no doubt that this dwelling-place on earth is not outweighed by the personal love of God which comes to us in Christ Jesus. This is why stepping outside ourselves in sacrifice and 'emptying ourselves' will always be a vital reality for all Christians. The ambiguity of humans building up of the world indicates that it is human making. But, on the other hand, it is precisely this finitude that is taken up into the grace and redemption of God. We know therefore that the future of humanity on earth has already been redeemed in advance by Christ. Its transient, earthly aspect has in principle already been superseded by Christ and, as such, it is only a truly human and meaningful future insofar as it is de facto included in the mystery of Christ (though without losing its earthly, profane character by this inclusion).

The church's social teaching must be the proof of the extent to which she understands herself as the eschatological community of salvation. Human beings in the world have also received, in his distinctively profane quality, the gift of the definitive character of the 'eternal life' which comes, in Christ, to those who step outside themselves in love and who expect salvation, even in its cosmic dimensions, only from God as a gratuitous gift. This gift has, however, already taken possession of us now through the *Pneuma* and therefore, living and active in humanity on earth, also makes this material, terrestrial world, as the space and the sphere of experience of the human spirit, long eagerly for the revealing of the sons of God (see Rom 8.19-22).

The church must in the first place extend the line that she began so clearly in the Vatican II Constitution on Revelation, *Dei verbum* – just as there is a development of dogma in the church's tradition, so too can the church's attitude towards the world evolve recognisably in the course of history. The church does not, after all, perceive all the implications of redemption from the very beginning. She learns from the real development of human world-history with its constantly changing situations. In this way, she herself also makes salvation-history – faith's dialogue with concrete humanity allows this faith, itself governed by the norm of Christ's unique and non-recurrent appearance in the world, to enter history in a process of development that only gradually, tentatively and in seeking discloses the inner riches of faith clearly. Viewed in this light, it is more understandable that there was a time when the world was under the guardianship of the church and there can be no doubt that this situation made a definite contribution to the well-being of humanity on earth. But, although we should never judge the past by modern criteria, the church must humbly admit that mistakes have been made with regard to the legitimate emancipation of this world and that these have partly been the cause of the world's alienation from the institutional church.

It is furthermore strikingly apparent to historians that the church has recourse especially to secular means and positions of power in this world for her mission to the world whenever she becomes alienated from the world at a given period in history. Whenever this alienation is absent or disappearing, however, she abandons these positions of power and chooses to appear as the truly evangelical church, without key positions and points of support and, from the point of view of the world, standing helpless in the world and, precisely because of this, as a powerful and irresistible sign. The power of Jesus Christ, God's servant, now raised by God himself to be Lord of the world, was also present in the impotence of the cross. The church's renewed awareness of herself and the new human and Christian appreciation of what 'world' is require the church to take up a new position with regard to the secularised world.

The church sees the human ambitious attempt to transform the world situation into a truly human situation and she also sees the wonderful success of these ambitious undertakings today and their failure tomorrow. Yet, despite this cycle of success and failure, humans always continue to set about this task again and again and to begin anew the arduous work of building up the world. A veiled *hope* seems to sustain and strengthen this world in spite of certain signs of despair on all sides and a sense of the absurd in the history of the world. In its teaching the church, 'always prepared to make a defence to anyone who calls you to account for the hope that is in you' (1 Pet 3.15), must seize hold of this concealed hope and invite the world to its explicit expectation: 'If you knew the gift of God' (John 4.10) from which you, world, are unconsciously living! If only you recognised God's gift!

Although it must guard against false human optimism, Christian social teaching must also include, in its dynamism, all human expectations. The church loves the world, not only insofar as it is receptive to the life of grace, but also as the world. She loves the world as it is, which means that this love is creative. Therefore, the church equally desires for the world the great human values that it needs so much – freedom of conscience, the personal value of marriage and family life, cultural values, a social, economic and political system in which human and Christian life is possible and finally a human world community living in order and peace. The concrete relationship between the structure of the world here on earth and the heavenly social environment transcends all human thought, even when this is inspired by faith: 'What no eye has seen, nor ear heard, nor the heart of man conceived, what God has prepared for those who love him' (1 Cor 2.9). Thus, the ultimate meaning of the building up of this world merges into the mystery which is only accessible to the faith that makes hope live:

> Behold, the dwelling of God is with people. He will dwell with them, and they shall be his people, and God himself will be with them; he will wipe away every tear from their eyes, and death shall be no more, neither shall there be mourning nor crying nor pain any more, for the former things have passed away (Rev 21.3-4).

The church must confess and proclaim this and it is in this perspective of ultimate fulfilment that believing Christians, who already possess the earnest-money, the pledge of the Holy Spirit and thus of the eschatological gift, must work for the restoration of this world, despite the reality of sin, which never ceases to undermine the work of redemption that is aiming to make this world into a dwelling-place worthy of humanity, and even worthy of sons of God. In the meantime, the modest but nonetheless splendidly practical result of this process of humanisation within life in union with God will be that we build up the world in such a way that, in it, people can live a life that is both truly worthy of humanity and at the same time Christian and in this way more easily accomplish the will of God. In and through this love for the world, included in human personal love for God, God's name is glorified and salvation is brought to people. 'God's glory – living humanity'.

The church as the epiphany and historical completion of God's plan of salvation[11]

Without denying the legitimacy of a more technical concept of sacrament that has become current since the theology of the middle ages,[12] the council nonetheless went back to the richer and more dynamic and universal concept of the Bible and the church fathers. The Greek word *mystērion* – in the Latin of the church *sacramentum* and *mysterium* – denoted the divine decree, or God's plan of salvation, insofar as this is and has been manifested in a veiled manner in time and is accessible only to faith. In this sense, the concept of sacrament embraces the whole of the Christian plan of salvation, visibly prepared in the old testament, but given a completing manifestation in the life death and resurrection of Jesus, the Christ, of whom the church is the visible presence in this world, although 'under shadows' and 'under the assumption of constant purification' (Constitution on the Church, 8). According to this concept, then, sacrament is the history of salvation itself as the active manifestation of God's plan of salvation.

What the council meant precisely by the word sacrament is most profoundly expressed in the decree on missionary activity, although the word itself is unfortunately not used in this context: 'Missionary activity is nothing other and nothing less than the revelation of epiphany of and the completion of God's plan of salvation in the world and in the history of the world, in which God, through the mission visibly completes the history of salvation'.[13] But because 'the church on the way is, by virtue of her being, orientated towards mission', one is quite justified in replacing words like 'mission' and 'missionary activity' in this conciliar text by the word 'church'. Consequently, the text that I have quoted might just as well have read: 'The church is nothing other and nothing less than the revelation or epiphany of and the completion of God's plan of salvation in the world and in the history of the world in which God, through the church, visibly completes the history of salvation.' In yet other words,

---

[11] Selected from: Edward Schillebeeckx, 'The Church, the "Sacrament of the World"', *The Mission of the Church*, trans. N. D. Smith (New York: Seabury Press, 1973), 44–50.
[12] It is for this reason that this idea of the church as sacrament was expressed with a certain reserve in at least one conciliar text ('as it were the sacrament'; see Constitution on the Church, 1), because of pressure exerted by the minority group at the council.
[13] 'The church as the sign of herself' – we should not forget that the church is not the kingdom of God or ultimate salvation. She is subject to the promise of the kingdom which is to come, 'Sign of herself' thus means the sign which foreshadows the kingdom of God that is present in Christ.

using the concept 'sacrament': 'In Christ, the church is the universal sacrament of salvation which manifests and realises the mystery of God's love for man' (*Pastoral Constitution on the Church in the Modern World*, 1, 4. 45), 'God's love for man' being 'for all people and for each individual' (*Constitution on the Church*, 2, 9). The church, then, is the universal and effective sign of the salvation of all people. She is the epiphany, in other words, the active and historically tangible form of God's plan of salvation, a form which makes the source of salvation, Christ, present for us. The church is the 'instrument of redemption', because she is the 'visible sacrament' (*Constitution on the Church*, 2, 9) of this redemption on earth – 'she is the germ and the beginning of the kingdom of God on earth'(*ibid*, 1, 5). But the church is this only 'under shadows' – is always in need of purification' (cf. pp. 1–19 above). Indeed, the *Relatio*, the justification of this text provided by the commission during the council, makes this even clearer: 'This empirical church... reveals the mystery (of the church), but she does not do this without shadows' and the mystery in the catholic church becomes visible 'both in strength and in weakness'. Partly in her *metanoia* and conversion, the church is therefore the historically visible form of salvation, in other words, salvation itself becoming visible in human history and, as such, the way to salvation for all people.

The church, sacrament of salvation for the whole world[14]

According to the first aspect that I have considered, the church is the active presence of God's salvation in the world, in a veiled, but nonetheless perceptible form. It is precisely in this quality that the church is the sacrament of salvation offered by God to the whole world. In other words, salvation, which is in fact actively present in the whole of humanity, is given, in the church, the completed form in which it appears in the world. What God has already effectively begun to bring about in the whole of humanity in an activity of grace that is not clearly expressed and recognised as such, is expressed and accomplished more clearly and recognisably as the work of grace in the world in the church, although this expression and accomplishment are to some extent always deprived of their lustre because of our human failure.

The council did not state explicitly that the church is the visible sacrament of that salvation which is already active wherever people are to be found, but so many conciliar texts point in this direction that it is even possible to say that a dialectical tension exists which is not resolved in the texts themselves and which consequently calls for further theological clarification. Indeed, the *Constitution on the Church* says, on the one hand, with reference to the church as the 'messianic people', that 'although this does not yet in fact include all people and often seems to be a small flock', it is nonetheless 'the most powerful germ of unity, hope and salvation for the

---

[14]Selected from: Edward Schillebeeckx, 'The Church, the "Sacrament of the World"', *The Mission of the Church*, trans. N. D. Smith (New York: Seabury Press, 1973), 46–9.

whole of humanity' (2,9). This small flock, then, is the sacrament of salvation for all people. On the other hand, however, the same constitution also explicitly states that 'the church on the way is necessary for salvation' (14). Other conciliar texts intensify the dialectical tension between these two statements. This tension is illustrated, for example, by the statement: 'Even those who, through no fault of their own, remain ignorant of the gospel of Christ and the church, but who are nonetheless honestly seeking God and, the influence of grace, are really trying to do his will, which they recognise in the voice of their consciences, are able to achieve eternal blessedness' (16). The *Pastoral Constitution on the Church* is even more emphatic. After having depicted the Christian as the 'new human in Christ', it states explicitly that this new humanity is present 'not only in Christian believers, but also in all people of good will, in whose hearts grace is active in an invisible manner' (1, 22). The council's declaration on the non-Christian religions, moreover, says that Christianity is the 'fullness of the religious life' for all these other religions (2), thus indicating clearly that the relationship between the church and the non-Christian communities is not a relationship between a religion and a non-religion, but a relationship between a fullness and something that simply does not possess this fullness. Finally, the *Decree on Missionary Activity* states clearly: 'God's all-embracing plan for the salvation of the whole of humanity is not only realised in, so to speak, a hidden way in the hearts of people or by initiatives, including religious initiatives, through which they seek God in many different ways, "in the hope that they might feel after him and find him; yet he is not far from each one of us" (Acts 17.27)' (1, 3).

These texts – and there are probably others which could be quoted – show that the council has made two fundamental statements which are to some extent dialectically opposed. On the one hand, we have the statement that the church is necessary for salvation and, on the other hand, that those who are 'outside the church' not only are able to achieve salvation, but also frequently do in fact share in it. What, then, we are bound to ask, is the real meaning of the conciliar statement that the church is the 'universal sacrament of salvation'? Does it mean that God's salvation cannot in any sense reach the world except in and through this world's gradual and historical confrontation with the church? Or does it mean that universal salvation, which has already been offered to the whole world on the basis of God's universal will to save all people, and which is already active in the church, only reaches its completed appearance in the church? It is, I believe, abundantly clear from the texts than I have quoted that the council tended to think in the second direction. What God's grace, his absolute, gratuitous and forgiving proximity, has already begun to do in the lives of all people becomes an epiphany in the church, in other words, completely visible. There is no doubt that, because she is the completed manifestation of God's saving grace, the church is a very distinct and separate gift of grace and opportunity for grace. There is, equally no doubt that the other, non-Christian religions are not, as such, special and distinctive in this sense, because they need this completing grace. In order to fill this gap, the church, as the 'universal sacrament of salvation', is, by virtue of her very being, truly missionary – she is orientated towards mission.

From this, then, a certain 'definition' of the church according to the Second Vatican Council becomes crystallised, namely that the church is the completed and active manifestation, confessed explicitly in thanksgiving and praise to God, of that salvation which is already actively present in the whole world of people. In other words, the church is the 'primordial sacrament' of salvation which is prepared for all people according to God's eternal decree, the salvation which is, moreover, not a monopoly of the church, but which, on the basis of redemption by the Lord who died and rose again 'for the sake of the salvation of the whole world', is already in fact actively present in that whole world. The church is therefore both the sacrament of herself, in other words, the visible appearance of salvation that is present in her, and, at the same time, the *sacramentum mundi*: in other words, what is present 'outside the church' is everywhere, whenever people of good will in fact give their consent personally to God's offer of grace and make this gift their own, even though they do not do this reflectively or thematically, is audibly expressed and visibly perceptible in the church. The church is the 'sacrament of the world' precisely as the sacrament of the salvation which is offered to all people – she is hope not only for all who belong to her; she is also, quite simply, *spes mundi*, hope for the whole world. The mystery of salvation which God is always bringing about in the whole of history of humanity and which he will never cease to bring about – the enduring fact of the living prophecy of the church bears witness to this – appears fully in the church and is present in her as in a prophecy. It is possible to say that the church is the making public of existential salvation in the world. She reveals the world to itself. She shows the world what it is and what it is able to become by virtue of God's gift of grace. Because of this, she hopes not only for herself, but also for the whole world, which she serves.

Since the conciliar texts can only be interpreted in this light, the council has in fact, with its key statement, 'the church is the universal sacrament of salvation', laid the foundation on which a new and practical synthesis can be built up, a synthesis which may help to banish 'the discrepancy which exists in the case of many believers between the faith that they confess and their daily lives', a breach which 'must be regarded as one of the most serious errors of the present time' (*Pastoral Constitution on the Church*, I, 4, 43). This will be a synthesis in which the church and the actual world no longer confront each other as strangers. On the contrary – in this synthesis, the church, as the sacrament of the world, will clearly express, for the benefit of the human world, the deepest meaning which people have already experienced, in tentative search and without being able to express it, in the world, even though this meaning does not have its origin in the world. The world will then see, in grateful recognition, its meaning and hidden inspiration fully expressed as a sign in the church.

The specific historical face of the church[15]

According to the biblical admonition, 'judgment begins at the house of God', in Israel and the church (1 Pet 4.17-18). Therefore Vatican II took over the Reformation concern for the *Ecclesia semper reformanda* almost literally, *Ecclesia semper*

---

[15] Selected from: Edward Schillebeeckx, *Church: The Human Story of God*, Collected Works of Edward Schillebeeckx vol. 10 (London: Bloomsbury T&T Clark, 2014), 193–6 [195–8].

purificanda.[16] For of the church on the way, the mystery of which is described in the first chapter of *Lumen gentium,* the same council says: 'Advancing through trials and tribulations the church is comforted (in the biblical sense, strengthened) by God's grace, promised to her by the Lord so that she may not waver from perfect fidelity, but remain the worthy bride of the Lord, ceaselessly renewing herself through the action of the Holy Spirit until, through the cross, she may attain to that light which knows no setting.'[17] The conquest of weakness takes place only 'through the power of Christ and love'.[18] Here in its own way the council is accepting a Reformation view when it says that the church is *sancta simul et purificanda:* it is holy, but must constantly be purified; it must arrive at *metanoia,* repentance and renewal.[19]

This promise does not rest only on the church as a whole but on a particular, i.e. ministerial, way on ministerial service in the church,[20] especially – in both its function of proclamatory teaching –[21] and of cultic and sacramental healing through presiding in prayer and sacrament[22] – and finally in its function of pastoral guidance.[23] However, given that the biblical admonition constantly to renew oneself in the weakness of the flesh is addressed to the people of God as a whole, even before there is any mention (in this Dogmatic Constitution) of the functional or ministerial or official differences between believers and ministers, both the hierarchy and believers stand under the constant admonition to incessant renewal and a Christian 'return to the sources'. From this it may be concluded that the church as the community of salvation and as a saving institution stands under the powerful promise of the Lord, who will not tolerate its becoming unfaithful. Nevertheless this church must constantly renew itself in the power of the Spirit.

The synchronic affirmation of the *Ecclesia indefectibilis* (i.e. a church which cannot fall away from its basic inspiration or cannot come loose from its original roots) and the *Ecclesia semper purificanda* (the church which must always purify itself) poses serious and delicate problems. Precisely on the basis of the support promised it by the Lord, 'The gates of hell shall not prevail against it' (Matt 16.18), and thus on the basis of the Lord's powerful promise, the firm stand of the church on its indefectibility takes the historical form of a constantly renewed *metanoia,* renewal and self-correction. It already emerges from this that this is an indefectibility

---

[16]*Lumen gentium,* ch. 1, no. 8. See *Schema constitutionis de Ecclesia,* 1964, ch. 1, no. 8. The choice of the word *purificanda* above other suggested expressions is determined by the liturgical use of the formula *purificatio Ecclesiae* in the Roman Missal, e.g. on the first Quadragesima Sunday and the fifteenth Sunday after Pentecost. See *Schema Constitutionis de Ecclesia,* 1964, *Relationes de numeris,* in no. 8, p. 25. Of course many people here were influenced by a reluctance to take over directly the Reformation formula *Ecclesia semper reformanda.*
[17]*Lumen gentium,* chs. 2, 9. It sounds over-pious and unctuous, remote from the prayer of most people, even Christians. If it is to be understandable and capable of being experienced, what is meant must be expressed in everyday language, even for Christians.
[18]*Relationes de singulis numeris,* Relatio in no. 8, p. 23.
[19]Ibid.
[20]'Munus autem illud, quod Dominus pastoribus populi sui commisit verum est servitium quod in sacris libris diakonia seu ministerium significanter nuncupatur', ibid., ch. 3, no. 24.
[21]Ibid., ch. 3, no. 25.
[22]Ibid., ch. 3, no. 25.
[23]Ibid., ch. 3, no. 27.

not in triumphalism, but in weakness in which God's grace triumphs. This implies that there is no indefectibility *despite* weakness, i.e. automatic indefectibility, but in and through constant renewal in faith, hope and love.

The indefectibility of the church is therefore not a static, as it were fixed, essentialist property of the church which could by-pass the constantly precarious, existential faith of the church in obedience to God's promise. The promised indefectibility becomes effective only in the faith, trust and constant self-correction of the church. The term 'divine guarantee' does not fit in with this. It is at least misleading, though it can be used as an extrapolation of the overwhelming power of grace into the juridical sphere, grace so powerful that it is at work *in* the response of the church in faith. But a juridical objectification of this indefectibility at work in faith and in believing self-correction is impossible, because the nature of the church called to life through the mission of Jesus Christ implies the existential experience of the community of salvation, precisely as the fruit of redemption.

We must also see the so-called four marks of the church in this perspective. With the creed of the Council of Constantinople in 381 (often wrongly called the Nicene Creed), all Christian churches confess: 'I believe the one, holy, catholic and apostolic *ecclesia* or community of faith'. In the Second Vatican Council this is said of each local church in which, provided it is living in community with the other local churches, the universal church is present. But we know that this unity does not exist: the Christian churches are divided. We all suffer under our own sinfulness and that of our churches. So the four marks do not describe our real churches in their historical forms, while on the other hand no church can achieve a mystical distillation of the essence 'church': churches exist only in historical forms.

This does not mean on the other hand that the four marks of the church are purely eschatological, a reality of the final kingdom. It means that all the Christian churches now already contain elements which call for this unity, particularly the church's belief in one God and one Lord, one baptism and one table. Because these four marks are present in all churches defectively and in a mediocre way, in particular or restrictive compartmentalisation, they are nevertheless internal imperatives of change within all the churches: a summons really to go on the way to the final ecumenical fulfilment. The dynamic of these structural elements in all the churches does not call for this break. The gospel does not legitimise mediocrity. And the message that is proclaimed is in no way the basis for shutting oneself off in different hiding places to provide protective security from 'the other'! The four 'properties' of the church issue a summons for conversion to all Christian churches. One cannot just ask for the conversion of other Christian churches. All local and confessional churches are 'church' to the degree that they can affirm, encourage and further *communio*, communication, with other local churches.

The scandal is not that there are differences but that these differences are used as an obstacle to communion (though on the other hand people rightly do not want to make a comedy of unity; they take the differences seriously). But richly diverse unity-in-communion in no way calls for a formal, institutional and administrative unity, nor a super-church. Even for the Roman Catholic church the four 'properties' confessed are not a description of its specific form of the church but an imperative for it, as they are for other churches. The *ecumene* is not a private annexation of the gospel by any confessional church, but the 'self-dispossession' of each and every

Christian church. Although there is historical plurality as a system of exclusion, there is also multiplicity which need not arouse opposition and can be experienced within communion and mutual recognition. Difference is positive only within communion with the other: in respect of the other who is other and yet not alien to us.

There can be no authentic *ecumene* without the attempt to understand and experience the plurality of churches theologically: we must be able to experience and understand it… in mutual difference. There is no uniform, eternally valid model, nor is there an historically pre-existing model of unity to which all churches must convert themselves. We need all Christian churches for the *ecumene* as the true church of Jesus, the Christ. All Christians must strive for a unity the model for which does not fully exist in any single church. Unity is future for all the Christian churches, not a return to any old situation. Moreover there is no community without internal conflicts except in Utopia (i.e. nowhere, except in wishful thinking) and eschatologically, in heaven. But this final consummation judges our present by the human and Christian revolt against the unredeemed present of the churches and the world.

Selected literature

- The Church, Sacrament of the Risen Christ; Selected from: Edward Schillebeeckx, *Christ the Sacrament of the Encounter with God*, trans. Paul Barrett, N. D. Smith, Collected Works of Edward Schillebeeckx vol. 1 (London: Bloomsbury T&T Clark, 2014), 33–7 [56–62].
- 'The World' as the Objective Expression of the Life of Grace; Selected from: Edward Schillebeeckx, 'Church and World', *World and Church*, trans. N. D. Smith, Collected Works of Edward Schillebeeckx vol. 4 (London: Bloomsbury T&T Clark, 2014), 75–8 [98–103].
- The Social Teaching of the Church; Selected from: Edward Schillebeeckx, 'Church and World', *World and Church*, trans. N. D. Smith, Collected Works of Edward Schillebeeckx vol. 4 (London: Bloomsbury T&T Clark, 2014), 83–7 [110–14].
- The Church as the Epiphany and Historical Completion of God's Plan of Salvation; Selected from: Edward Schillebeeckx, 'The Church, the "Sacrament of the World"', *The Mission of the Church*, trans. N. D. Smith (New York: Seabury Press, 1973), 44–5.
- The Church, Sacrament of Salvation for the World; Selected from: Edward Schillebeeckx, 'The Church, the "Sacrament of the World"', *The Mission of the Church*, trans. N. D. Smith (New York: Seabury Press, 1973), 46–9.
- The Specific Historical Face of the Church; Selected from: Edward Schillebeeckx, *Church: The Human Story of God*, Collected Works of Edward Schillebeeckx vol. 10 (London: Bloomsbury T&T Clark, 2014), 193–6 [195–8].

8

Historical-Critical Method

Images of Jesus as object of historical inquiry[1]

From what we have said it is evident that every period has its own way of representing Jesus. That was already the case in the various phases of early Christianity, but the process continued well beyond that. Just as the letter to the Hebrews already depicts him as the heavenly high priest; the early fathers as God 'who became human in order to make humans divine' and give him everlasting life; Byzantium as 'Christus Victor', Pantocrator and Sun God, 'Light of light'; so in the Early and High Middle Ages he became the one who makes reparation or satisfaction, who has ransomed us, and simultaneously the 'Jesus of the *via crucis*' and the Christmas manger. Later on, for Luther, he was the one who achieved reconciliation with God in a free and sovereign act that absolves our guilt and invites us to rely unconditionally on God's favourable verdict; then came the Christ mystique of the incarnate Word in seventeenth century French spirituality, the veneration of the 'childhood of Jesus' and of 'Christ, the Sacred Heart'; the Enlightenment saw in him the prototype of human morality, the basis of true human community; the Romantics felt he was the model of a genuinely human personality; and our twentieth century with its now fully fledged *raison d'état* proceeded to extol him as Christ the king; then, after this triumphalism and the experience of two world wars, came Jesus 'our brother', our fellow human being, whose example shows us what we have to do, the 'man for others' and the contemporary 'Jesus of human liberation' (in some quarters even 'Jesus the combatant and revolutionary'); et cetera. Just as in the course of history people have continually given God new names as inventive love alone knows how to do, while his name has also been sullied and besmirched in many different ways, so Christian love has enabled each and every period to find its own endearment, even though his name is forever being horribly misused: in his name brothers have been slaughtered, and in ships with the name 'Jesus' emblazoned on their standard black slaves have been stowed away like cattle destined for the white man's territories. Our 'Jesus images' indeed call for criticism, indispensable though they are for our decisive choice to follow Jesus. This surely

---

[1]Selected from: Edward Schillebeeckx, *Jesus: An Experiment in Christology*, trans. John Bowden, Collected Works of Edward Schillebeeckx vol. 6 (London: Bloomsbury T&T Clark, 2014), 45–51 [64–71].

applies to nonbelievers as well: not just belief but unbelief, too, has its own dogmatic Jesus image. The Jewish authorities and Pontius Pilate condemned Jesus because they had formed a certain picture of him for themselves. Even prior to the Eastertide events there were 'images of Jesus', both positive and negative. It is only once a person has been interpreted that he becomes part of history.

The question emerging from this cursory survey of Jesus images is whether all these Christological patterns are simply projections of our currently prevailing, constantly changing worldview. Once somebody has found ultimate salvation in Jesus, it is natural (and proper) that he should project his own expectations and conceptions of 'true humanity' onto Jesus. Correlatively, of course, this means that a real facet of Jesus' life must at least point in that particular direction if we are not to turn Jesus into a mere receptacle for our own predilections, an arbitrary 'cipher' that we manipulate; in that case, surely, Jesus might well be left out of it. He becomes indispensable only if and when the really crucial point of our human existence and its proper destiny are actually defined by the historical phenomenon of the real Jesus of Nazareth, and our own projections of true humanity are corrected by that; in that context there is legitimate room for human projections always subject to the corrective and directive criterion of what and who Jesus actually was in history. Thus the historical truth in the quest for Jesus of Nazareth becomes a vital issue.

Old and new: The critical approach

The fact of the matter is that in the past the faithful the Christian community, theologians, the church's teaching office have seen all the New Testament traditions about Jesus as directly reflecting actual historical occurrences. The responses from theology and believers were based on a pre-critical, purely biblicist interpretation of the Jesus event, ignoring, for instance, the different literary genres. Every period inevitably suffers from the limitations of its own historical context which in no way rules out the possibility of authentic belief. It only goes to show that Christian belief has a real history and that the faith cannot be fixed once and for all, as it were, super-historically.

In our modern period historical consciousness with its own critical methods has made quite a dent in the pre-critical or biblicist interpretation. Only then – and not before did the possibility arise of what one might call a rigid and conservative interpretation of the Bible. For as we see, despite a pre-critical consciousness of history, the church fathers, for instance, and the Middle Ages as well did not in any way insist on what now passes for conservative biblical interpretation: through their allegorical interpretation of what appear to be historical narratives in the Bible they permitted themselves liberties to which the most progressive exegete would never concede nowadays. 'Conservative' biblical interpretation, therefore, is a strictly modern option, that is, a 'no' to the newly arisen challenge posed by historico-critical consciousness; in that sense it is 'modernistic', a new phenomenon in the history of biblical interpretation.

But the historico-critical approach to the Bible is also a new, modern possibility. To some extent the ways in which the faithful had come to represent the concrete Jesus of Nazareth did not tally with the results yielded by a historical approach to scientifically assured data. For that reason many people feel that their Christian faith compels them to oppose the critical results of scientific studies. That is always a hopeless and fruitless enterprise, because it is impossible to live with a 'double truth': you cannot deny something as a historian which you are bound to accept as a believer. Faith cannot hold back what is scientifically evident, but neither can scientific evidence contradict faith's *representations*. Although there is a large body of established data commanding the general agreement of historians, there is undoubtedly still a lot of uncertainty about details. But to belittle historical science from a religious standpoint or to point to uncertainty in the sciences as grounds for setting them aside is unfair and unworthy of the believer. This in itself discloses a false conception of faith. Of course, historically speaking we know much less nowadays about Jesus of Nazareth than our forefathers did, but what we do know is scientifically vouched for. Besides, it is still more than enough to situate the historical basis of Christianity and enable us to understand the Christian interpretation of Jesus better.

At any rate, nobody will deny that, especially in the nineteenth century, historical and critical study often had an underlying anti-dogmatic or anti- ecclesiastic purpose, and once there is such a religious intention those who seek to popularise these new insights often have too little feeling for the accustomed ways of the faithful and their powers of assimilation. On the other hand in the best interests of the Christian faith one cannot remain silent about the results of criticism. Christian faith has nothing to lose and much to gain from new, empirical truth.

Modern historiography and Jesus of Nazareth

From 1774 to 1778 onwards the work of Reimarus dramatically changed traditional religious images of Jesus. The very idea was so novel that Reimarus did not publish his work. Later on Lessing, though still with some misgiving and therefore 'anonymously', published seven fragments of Reimarus's manuscript, which proposed that the actual historical Jesus presents a very different picture from that of the Bible and Christian tradition. L. Ranke (1795- 1886) formulated the new historical concept which emerged during that period, namely that the image people had formed of Louis IX, for instance, or of other celebrated persons in the past, does not tally with the picture we get from a critical study of the historical sources. Thus a distinction was introduced between, for example, the current notion of Alexander the Great and the 'Alexander of history', between Napoleon and the 'Napoleon of history', between the Christian Jesus image and the historical 'Jesus of Nazareth'. Inevitably it became a question of 'the way things really were' (Ranke), a critical force in the study of history not previously known in that sense. Unhappily, this premise was given a positivistic interpretation, partly modelled on of the so-called exact sciences: it was considered feasible to prise a fact loose from the interpretation given it by people living at the time, from the course of later tradition, and from one's own hermeneutic horizon. So by surrendering their own presuppositions in order to submit the historical data to critical analysis based on the principles of the exact sciences, people thought, it should be possible to arrive at an un-dogmatised, purely historical Jesus. On closer inspection, however, this Jesus of the historians turned out to be a nineteenth century projection of idealised notions of humanity: Jesus became a kind of mascot, a symbolic X or cipher onto which the nineteenth century could project its utopian evolutionist optimism; or else he was seen simply as representing first century Palestinian apocalypticism.

Even so, this uncovered a real problem: the 'historical Jesus' indeed differed in many respects from the Christ of faith. The term 'historical Jesus' here refers to that which the methods of historical criticism enable us to retrieve of Jesus of Nazareth, that is, the 'earthly Jesus'. However, nineteenth century liberal positivism tended to identify 'being' with 'being aware of'. Consequently historical reality was taken to coincide with what we can know on the basis of a science of history. History became synonymous with its scientific study, hence 'historical' is whatever has been ascertained by systematic research. That in itself narrows the field of vision; for there is a real difference between the 'historical Jesus' and the 'earthly Jesus': what can be reconstructed historically (the 'historical Jesus') naturally does not coincide with the full reality of Jesus, the person who lived when the beginning of the first century was still the 'present time'.

Of course, one could fairly say that in practice this distinction, however real, is now irrelevant, because what escapes the historical net does in fact vanish into oblivion as far as we are concerned. (With finer meshes or more refined historical methods we can, of course, catch more in the historian's net; but the result will never be identical with what the living reality had been: 'what was going on' at the time.) In the study and writing of history we are dealing only with historically knowable happenings; and although these do not coincide with what actually happened, it is futile to peer 'behind' historically accessible facts, or to think that a religious angle will somehow give us access to further *historical* aspects. Faith does not of itself supply any new and real facts; it can reveal their real significance, which a purely historical assessment fails to discover. Yet the idea that only the historical method can get at the facts often implicitly lays claim to ontological exclusivity. Not only are there events which are accessible to the historian but have not yet been investigated, but the science of history can never recover everything that really occurred. Less pretentiously, then, we may call those events 'historical' which are ascertainable by means of the historical method. This means that the actual stuff of all historiography is 'abstract', a slice excised from the real past; it formalises and yields only images. Thus the so-called historical Jesus is no less a Jesus image than the Christ of the believer. This at once mitigates the sharp contrast supposed to exist between the 'Jesus of history' and the 'Jesus of faith'. Via images, they both derive from the 'earthly Jesus'.

As an epistemological category, that is methodologically, historical abstraction is perfectly legitimate, provided one does not turn it into an ontological category. In the latter case one insulates oneself in advance against everything that may be said, also in non-scientific terms, about historians' findings. In other words, one still cannot deny reality to the 'non-historical' (in the sense of what is scientifically inaccessible in past events). In interpreting the past allowance may indeed be made for 'history' which, however real, is no longer accessible to the historian or is even in principle irrecoverable. Thus the historian cannot, in principle, ascertain whether 'history' is the locus of God's saving activity, whereas this may be a reality in the dimension of the actual events and for the believer is truly so. Occurrent reality (='the course of historical events') is broader than what 'history' (=professional historians) is able to recover of it, without denigrating the 'interpretation' as purely subjective and, in that sense, speculative.

In regard to Jesus of Nazareth this means that, 'historically', that is, in the occurrent reality of his earthly existence, there is something which is fundamentally inaccessible to purely historico-critical methods: the real-life individual who in himself (like everyone else) eludes a purely scientific approach. In Jesus' case this 'something', experienced in the encounter with him, was expressed by Christians in images such as Son of Man, messianic Son of David, and so forth. The only question, then, is whether this articulation is indeed partly *determined* by the concrete reality that they encountered in Jesus, or derives solely from the socio-cultural context in which these people were situated. One is bound to ask, therefore, whether their image of Jesus, arising out of their faith, is both the product of the real historical offer constituted by Jesus and (naturally) the result of their tradition the process in which they interpreted and assented to this concrete offer and consciously appropriated it.

The post-liberal 'New Quest', the renewed historical search for Jesus of Nazareth, is engaged in this second, new inquiry. Of course, the sole reason we go in quest of the historical Jesus is that we cannot ignore two thousand years of Christendom: the context of our inquiry is the Christianity of the churches today. So we are really inquiring into the historical basis and source of what we have called the 'Christian movement', which still constitutes the distinctive reality of the churches. And we do this because with the passage of time the Christian churches have evolved a fractured relationship with their source. Because of that fracture, the initial effect of a historico-critical interpretation of Jesus will be to startle and even perturb: it endangers our Christian identity, shaped but also distorted by the course of history. Yet the disconcerting experience of surprise is a first and necessary stage in the hermeneutic process that leads from the biblical answer to the question of who Jesus is to our answer. Even in the Bible itself we see this sense of surprise at pre-canonical traditions in the community. Of course we can never pinpoint the authentic gift of Jesus 'in itself': Jesus' offer to people some two thousand years ago is concretely not the same as his nonetheless permanent offer of salvation to twentieth-century people; after all, our need for deliverance and salvation derives its historical content from our real-life circumstances. As I said before: if Jesus is God's definitive act of salvation for us now, as he was for the people of his day, then this entails that his relationship to the ever new present must partly determine the concrete form of his offer. I think that some endeavours by proponents of the so-called 'New Quest' retain liberal vestiges, so that they are still really looking for a 'phantom', a sort of Jesus of Nazareth *an sich*. And this seems to me not only a futile enterprise but one devoid of any prospect for theology, for a critique of church and society and above all for religion itself.

All the same, acceptance or non-acceptance of the historico-critical method is a matter of life or death for Christianity. If, for instance, Jesus either did not exist (as was sometimes argued) or was quite different from what faith affirms of him (e.g. a *sicarius* or guerrilla, a Zealot or Jewish nationalist resistance fighter), then the faith or *kerygma* is obviously implausible. A radical disparity between the knowledge imparted by faith and that imparted by history about what after all is a single phenomenon, namely Jesus and his first believing disciples, is untenable. Such dualism inevitably leads to repudiating one of the poles (or at any rate its theological relevance), whether one proceeds, with Kierkegaard and Bultmann, to deny all *theological* significance to knowledge of the historical Jesus, or whether, following D. F. Strauss, one dispenses with *kerygma*-centred knowledge, or like H. Braun locates the biblical 'constant factor' in anthropology and the variable factor (the diverse *kerygmata:* Son of Man, Son of God, messiah, etc.) in Christology (which then becomes superfluous).

If Christian faith is faith in Jesus of Nazareth, in the sense that our attitude to him definitively settles our choice for or against God, or to put it in biblical terms, if it is faith in Jesus of Nazareth *confessed as* the 'Christ, the only begotten Son, our Lord', then religious knowledge and confession are indeed limited by our knowledge of the historical Jesus; and that knowledge in its turn is limited, that is, put in its place or kept within its proper bounds, by religious interpretation.

Jesus of Nazareth and Jesus Christ[2]

The moment we human beings inquire into the significance of a historical happening, it reveals itself as complex, ambiguous, susceptible of multiple interpretations, while as an occurrent phenomenon it intrinsically had a very specific form: that which it is, and nothing else, thus an unambiguous fact (definitively, only after a person's here Jesus' death). The Christian faith (a particular interpretation of Jesus) makes a decision when faced with this ambivalence, which remains open to historico-critical inquiry, and on religious grounds actually repudiates the rightfulness of a non-Christian (e.g. Jewish, secular or atheistic) interpretation of Jesus. The believer will base this decision on trust, thus affirming the unequivocal interpretation that of the Christian faith as the only true one, that is, the answer which (albeit expressed in different forms) faithfully responds to the historically complex reality of Jesus. This interpretive response surpasses the purely historical evidence about Jesus, yet the latter is not excluded from a decision made in faith.

Historical criticism certainly cannot lay a foundation for faith in Jesus. At the same time its task is not purely negative, that is, to prevent the foundation from crumbling under our feet (which would be the case if it were demonstrated that Jesus never existed or was a quite different person from what the faith says). In a positivist era the fact that reality is more than what can be discovered through 'objective observation' and scientific analysis pre- supposes openness to faith; on the other hand (given our modern historical consciousness), historical inquiry is *essential* for faith to gain access to the authentic gospel. The result of historical investigation is objectively observed material in which the believer sees more, experiences a disclosure. The believer in fact sees God's saving activity realised in Jesus' life, which would not be possible without the material about Jesus recovered by the historical method. This, then, is the importance of historical study of Jesus for determining, concretely, the content of faith. Again, the historical approach serves to show that the existential question which Jesus poses for us only acquires its full force as is the case with every human life when his life has run its course to the end, that is, after his death; only then is a definitive verdict possible. Before his death even the disciples acclaim him only as a prophet; the 'higher' honorific titles emerge in the period after his death.

This is why a modern theology or Christology cannot ignore the historico-critical data. To deny these is to fail to take seriously the historical basis of Christianity and to

---

[2]Selected from: Edward Schillebeeckx, *Jesus: An Experiment in Christology*, trans. John Bowden, Collected Works of Edward Schillebeeckx vol. 6 (London: Bloomsbury T&T Clark, 2014), 55–6 [74–6].

see its power to elicit a life commitment located in a purely formal kerygma. I would not deny that such a kerygma-without-Jesus may still open up new existential options and can still have challenging power. But Christianity would lose its historical basis and become a purely fortuitous phenomenon in the life of religious humans, liable to vanish as readily as it appeared. One cannot go on forever believing in an idea, whether it is abstract (D. Strauss's notion of 'God become man' without Jesus) or is given existential content (such as Bultmann's kerygma). In that way Christianity loses its universal purport and forfeits the right to continue speaking of God's ultimate saving activity in history: one would let the world be regulated by an *Ideengeschichte*. Ideas so often let us down or end up functioning as ideologies. I can only believe and put my trust in persons (even though I am sometimes betrayed by them as well). That is why for me the Christian faith entails not only the personal, living presence of the glorified Jesus, but also a link with his life on earth; for it is precisely that earthly life that was acknowledged and empowered by God through the resurrection. For me, therefore, a Christianity or kerygma minus the historical Jesus of Nazareth is ultimately vacuous not Christianity at all, in fact. If the very heart of the Christian faith consists in an affirmation in faith of God's saving activity in history decisively accomplished in the life history of Jesus of Nazareth for the liberation of human beings (in other words, if we must use the language of faith even when speaking about the historical Jesus), then the personal history of this Jesus cannot be lost sight of, nor can our talk about it in the language of faith degenerate into ideology.

Thus Jesus of Nazareth turns out to be, *theologically*, the antipode of the Christ-confessing churches, constantly present even though this antipode criterion and norm can never be grasped in itself but only apprehended *in the course of* our letting ourselves be defined by Jesus. The difficulty with reaching a scrupulous interpretation of Jesus, therefore, is the ambit in which it has to be achieved. What I mean is that we have to express the reality of Jesus in our contemporary hermeneutic categories, which are given in advance (albeit open to criticism) and accessible to all; at the same time we can only recognise what that reality signifies *for us* in and via those categories. In other words, the critical disharmony between the actual offer of salvation that Jesus is and the interpretive response of the believing community is a problem typical not only of New Testament forms of expression but of our own as well.

Eschatological messenger of God's openness towards sinners[3]

In no fewer than four traditions we hear of Jesus consorting and even (forbidden to Jews) sharing a meal with sinners;[4] there are also many parables telling about

---

[3]Selected from: Edward Schillebeeckx, *Jesus: An Experiment in Christology*, trans. John Bowden, Collected Works of Edward Schillebeeckx vol. 6 (London: Bloomsbury T&T Clark, 2014), 181–3 [206–8].
[4]Markan tradition: Mark 2.15-17, pl. Luke 15.2; Q tradition: Luke 15.4-10, pl Matt; SL (peculiar to Luke): Luke 7.36-50; 15.11-32; 19.1-10; SM (peculiar to Matthew): Matt 20.1-15. See also Lk. 11.19, pl. Then too the Johannine tradition: John: 4.7-42.

going in search of what has been lost and, finally, of God's kingdom being promised 'to tax collectors and prostitutes' (Matt 21.31b) – passages in which the Christian community is expressing realistically what these people had experienced of Jesus' dealings with sinners. The memory of that impression is captured most vividly in the story (albeit reworked by the church and even liturgically) in Luke 7.36-50 (proper to Luke) about the 'woman who was a great sinner' – perhaps an instance where, besides Jesus' telling of a parable, we are also given the concrete circumstances that prompted him to tell it.[5] A Pharisee had invited Jesus to a meal (apparently because of his fame as a prophet). 'And behold', a woman held officially to be of ill repute (thought with good reason to be a prostitute) hears that Jesus is there; she comes up to him, washes his feet with her tears, dries them with her hair and kisses his feet (also anointing them with oil). It dismays the Pharisee to see how Jesus dares to let himself be touched by a sinful woman; such a person cannot be a prophet. It occurs to the Pharisee that Jesus does not realise he is dealing with a sinful woman; if he did, he would certainly rebuff her – so he has no prophetic gifts. But the point of Luke's story is that the Pharisee 'thought to himself', he did not speak out, and as he was talking Jesus divined his secret thought and mentioned, almost in passing, that of course he knew he was dealing with such a woman and was prepared nonetheless to submit to the washing. That is the point. And then Jesus tells a parable: 'A certain creditor had two debtors...' (Luke 7.41-43). He absolved both of them from their debt, the greater and the lesser. 'Now which of them will love him more?' (7.42). 'Therefore, I tell you, her sins, which are many, are forgiven, for she loved much' (7.47). Only at this point in the Lukan story does it appear that the woman has fulfilled the duties of the host, who (somewhat improbably!) neglected them; and that she did so unstintingly – being in that respect like the debtor who had had the greater debt forgiven him: thus she loves all the more. This makes the actual host, who had skimped on his duties, the debtor who had had the lesser debt remitted. The Pharisee's attitude here, as in the parable of the Pharisee and the publican (Luke 18.9-14) – despite his legally correct aloofness from sinners – turns out to be negative when compared with the behaviour of the sinful woman. 'Your faith has saved you' (7.50). Faith is suddenly associated with forgiveness of sins, thus affirming once again (see above: 'faith and miracles') that faith entails an attitude of *metanoia* towards the (saving) fellowship offered by Jesus. The woman's display of love and the forgiveness promised by Jesus are explicable in the context of the saving fellowship brought about by this event. Jesus's presence itself is an offer of saving fellowship, which is grasped in faith by the sinful woman. Jesus let the woman do what she was doing, not because he failed to realise that she was a sinner but for that very reason: to open up forgiving communion with a sinful person. That was what prompted the woman's prodigal devotion. Exegetes disagree fiercely – also on confessional lines – whether the woman's faith and love are a consequence

---

[5]Thus J. Jeremias, *Die Gleichnisse Jesu* (Göttingen 1965[7]), 126-7. The church's revision for liturgical purposes is discussed from his own standpoint by U. Wilckens, 'Vergebung für die Sünderin', in *Orientierung an Jesus* (Freiburg 1973), 394–424, who also accepts a historical basis (404). A survey of the exegetical positions up to 1966 is provided by J. Delobel, 'L'onction par la pécheresse', in *Ephemerides Theologicae Lovanienses* 42 (1966), 415–75.

of or a condition for Jesus' forgiveness. Luke's account is indeed complicated by contamination from another tradition – that of Jesus' anointment Jesus by a woman (Mark 14.3–9). This anointment is not part of the tradition on which Luke 7.35–50 is based (it does not actually fit in with it). Luke 7.44–46 also appears to be secondary,[6] in view of the introduction of the anointing incident from Mark 14. Luke himself wants to highlight the contrast between the Pharisee and the sinful woman, but according to the parable's particular tenor the difference in remission of (a great or a small) debt results in greater love by the person who has had the greater debt forgiven. The measure of forgiveness is the measure of the responding love, not vice versa. Both are forgiven everything, without limit; therefore the greatest sinner has the greatest love. That is the shock effect of the parable (also see the parable of the workers in the vineyard, Matt 20.14) – and that is said in view of the Pharisee's implacable legalism. The sinful woman recognises the kingdom of God in Jesus, which is precisely what the Pharisee does not do. So she has the greater love; for the least in the kingdom of God is even greater than John the Baptist! Letting Jesus convert her to God makes this woman greater than the Pharisee, who is indeed law abiding and only slightly in debt with God (see the parable of the elder brother of the prodigal son, Luke 15.12–32, and of the Pharisee and the publican, Luke 18.9–14; cf. also the parable of the two sons, Matt 21.28–31). It may fairly be said (on the strength of Jewish parallels) that this narrative belongs in the Christian tradition as a 'conversion story' (and acquired its *Sitz* in the liturgy of Christian baptism), but in substance its source of inspiration is Jesus' saving interaction with sinners.

Selected literature

- Images of Jesus as Object of Historico-critical Inquiry; Selected from: Edward Schillebeeckx, *Jesus: An Experiment in Christology*, trans. John Bowden, Collected Works of Edward Schillebeeckx vol. 6 (London: Bloomsbury T&T Clark, 2014), 45–51 [64–71].
- Jesus of Nazareth and Jesus Christ; Selected from: Edward Schillebeeckx, *Jesus: An Experiment in Christology*, trans. John Bowden, Collected Works of Edward Schillebeeckx vol. 6 (London: Bloomsbury T&T Clark, 2014), 55–6 [74–6].
- Eschatological Messenger of God's Openness towards Sinners; Selected from: Edward Schillebeeckx, *Jesus: An Experiment in Christology*, trans. John Bowden, Collected Works of Edward Schillebeeckx vol. 6 (London: Bloomsbury T&T Clark, 2014), 181–3 [206–8].

---

[6]Thus Wilckens, 'Vergebung für die Sünderin', 399; also Roloff, *Das Kerygma und der irdische Jesus*, Göttingen 1970, 162, n. 204, who moreover thinks it unlikely that a law-abiding Pharisee would have ignored his obligations as a host.

PART THREE

Theological Themes

Introduction

Julia Feder

The foundation of Edward Schillebeeckx's theology is an insistence that God is one who authors good and opposes evil. This starting point may deceptively appear obvious, yet many Christians consciously or unconsciously imagine that God is one who saves through violence and pain. Schillebeeckx opposes this view. As he puts it – God is indeed a fire, but one that does not burn up those who are enflamed; God is indeed a soaring eagle, but one that does not consume smaller birds. In other words, God does not use violence to accomplish God's aims, not even toward God's own son: Jesus Christ. It is nothing less than blasphemous to claim that God required the death of Jesus as compensation for human sin; such a claim would paint God as the author of evil. Whatever causes evil cannot be God. Jesus proclaimed a God whose cause is the human cause, not providing us with a new understanding of God but rather reminding us of a traditional insight that God liberates humanity. Schillebeeckx argues that it is better to not believe in God at all than to believe in a distorted God who harms human beings. The goodness of God is a theological starting point that informs Schillebeeckx's understanding of salvation, the significance of Jesus, and the role of the church.

Salvation

Salvation is the restoration of God's creation to wholeness. For human beings, salvation includes the restoration of the whole human person – materially, spiritually, interpersonally, socially and politically. In other words, salvation is holistic human freedom. This kind of freedom is fundamentally eschatological – that is, we experience seeds of salvation wherever human beings experience freedom and fullness of life. Nevertheless, the fullness of freedom has not yet been experienced in history. This is not because comprehensive salvation is impossible on earth, but rather because salvation is so far incomplete. Human salvation is brought about in the cooperation of God and human beings for the well-being of humanity. Contrary to what some pious Christians may believe, human action is not competitive with God-given salvation. The person of faith recognises God-given salvation *in* human self-liberation. Yet, contrary to what some humanists may believe, human action is not enough to bring about the fullness of salvation. Salvation exceeds that which human beings are able to imagine or accomplish. Thus, human beings cooperate with God in bringing about salvation, never acting alone.

God entrusts humanity with responsibility for history. Thus, Schillebeeckx's idea of 'creation faith' points just as much to God's faith in humanity as humanity's faith in God as a creator. In the person of Jesus, God's unconditional trust in human beings is finally 'not put to shame' since Jesus is one who announced and enacted the restoration which God intends for all of creation. Our own belief in the integrity of creation can set us free for our intended tasks in the world: to love creation as creation and to love God as creator. To love ourselves and our fellow human beings as creation is to reverence human beings *as* human beings – i.e., to love them as finite and contingent creatures who are invited to growth and who are capable of mistakes. To fail to accept our finitude and contingency is sinful and not a mark of salvation or some kind of enlightened state. Our finitude is not a wound of which we need to be healed or an original sin from which we need to be freed. Rather, finitude is the condition of being created and, therefore, the condition for the possibility of our relationship with the Creator God. The fullness of restoration of creation for which we await will never discard our finitude, but rather fully restore the communion with God and with others that this finitude allows.

Because the Creator God has entrusted creation with its own capacities and responsibilities, God does not direct human history in any straightforward way. God does not control historical outcomes or the details of personal lives in any way that might eclipse our own agency. Yet, God does linger lovingly with us as Creator and Sustainer. God's creative work is incomplete and will culminate with the full restoration of the world in and through love. Jesus referred to this restored world as 'the Kingdom of God'. Yet, the path to this Kingdom is not preordained. Jesus did not have a 'blueprint' for the Kingdom. There is no pre-packaged salvation waiting in the wings for the right moment to enter the stage of history. Instead, salvation is made in the cooperation of creation with God and, therefore, truly not yet (not even in God). Though we cannot conceptualise all that the Kingdom of God involves, we can be assured that the Kingdom is on the way because evil and oppression can have no transcendent future. Goodness and evil are not equal forces. Only goodness can have a future beyond death.

Jesus

If, in the Catholic imagination, a sacrament is a visible sign of an invisible grace, then Jesus Christ is the 'Primordial Sacrament' who makes visible both divine love for humanity and human love for God. In the way that sacraments symbolise a reality by actually and effectively bringing that reality about, Jesus symbolises God's love for humanity by actually and effectively bringing about God's grace for humans. And, Jesus symbolises humanity's love for God in authentic religious worship, committing himself unconditionally to God in his mission and ministry. Jesus preached the Kingdom of God as his vision of the future in which healed human persons will live with each other in the freedom of egalitarian relationships and he worked to bring this reality about through his life work. Jesus proclaimed that God's cause is the human cause and, thus, God both desires and promises comprehensive human good. Specifically, Jesus's manner of life was characterised by his presence with suffering people. As one who healed and ate with others who were otherwise socially alienated, Jesus' presence brought others freedom and deep joy.

Jesus' table fellowship and healing activities were directed toward those who were normally considered beyond God's hospitality and nurturing care – Gentiles, sex workers, those working in collaboration with Roman imperial authorities to oppress the Jews, etc. – and, thus, symbolised God's own openness to friendship with all of humanity. Therefore, Jesus did not just talk about the Kingdom of God as an abstract intellectual idea, but rather *enacted* his vision of the Kingdom of God in his ministry. As a healer, Jesus ushered in a new social order where those who were weak, socially isolated, and impoverished might be enveloped and restored by God's loving care. And, as host, Jesus practiced open fellowship meals at which all might eat freely nourished by God's own hospitality. The Kingdom that Jesus announced is still yet to come, but, at the same time, it also already present (in germ) wherever love is practiced.

For Schillebeeckx, Jesus' death was not the will of God but the result of sinful violence. Yet, God responds to this evil by raising Jesus from the dead. The resurrection is 'God's amen' to the life and mission of Jesus – i.e., the resurrection signifies God's endorsement of Jesus and God's refusal to allow evil to have the final word. Jesus' own life anticipated the resurrection, especially insofar as he preached a God who is the author of good and the opponent of evil and as he refused to regard evil on the same footing as good. With the resurrection, God confirms Jesus' theological and metaphysical insights. Yet, the resurrection is still not yet complete: it has an eschatological character. The resurrection is a prophecy to us who still experience evil and it is a promise that evil is ultimately impotent.

Church

The church is the community of those who remember Jesus' teachings, embody his enduring mission, and follow his example of entrusting their lives to God even when vindication may only come beyond death. Faithful followers of Christ bend history into salvation history, making a good God visible in the world.

Human beings cannot encounter God in an unmediated fashion. God must be mediated by the material world, interpersonal relationships, and social-political structures. For this reason, the church is of vital importance: the church bodies-forth God's grace. Yet, some of the ways that the Roman Catholic church has made God visible for human beings misses critical opportunities to live into the richness of Jesus' liberating mission. Schillebeeckx is critical of what he sees as a historical overemphasis on the Eucharist outside of the eucharistic celebration, making the Eucharist an object to be adored rather than a meal (i.e., an *action*) in which Jesus appears in the midst of community. Additionally, ecclesial anxieties about more democratic forms of church governance mistake subjection to God for subjection to earthly hierarchical authority. And similarly, patriarchal oppression of women in the church creates structural forms of violence that obfuscate the liberating hope of the Gospel. The only remedy to these ecclesial missteps is to re-centre the goodness of God whose cause is the human cause and to recognise that anything which issues evil or oppression truly cannot be of this God.

Questions for discussion

1. If history is not prescribed ahead of time but rather, for Schillebeeckx, human beings have to make history into salvation history along with God within the limits of finitude, does it make sense to say that 'God has a plan'? If so, how? If not, then what is faith? Does faith necessitate belief in God preordaining historical events?
2. Schillebeeckx maintains a belief in the 'real presence' of Christ in the Eucharist, yet he rejects what he calls a 'crudely realistic physicalism' with regard to the Eucharist. Why does he make this argument?
3. Schillebeeckx frames the rejection of finitude and limitation as sin rather than as salvation. What is at stake in this argument? Does this align in anyway with his views on the Eucharist? In other words, how does Schillebeeckx's view of the Eucharist prioritise the finitude and limitation of the sacramental elements as that which can be transformed (and not discarded or replaced) by God?
4. Schillebeeckx argues that humanity is still in the making, yet he also outlines seven parameters for human salvation (i.e., the restoration of humanity). What are these seven 'anthropological constants'? Do these parameters effectively avoid overdetermining human nature? How?

9

God

The search for the living God[1]

Even human history does not show us God. Precisely because he demonstrates his effective presence in this world in it his own way, he seems to be absent. He is, after all, totally different from all experienced reality. On the natural level, we experience him precisely as the one who exceeds all experience. Human beings can thus reach out to God only as to someone who is absent from the normal totality of created things. The transcendent significance he gives to history is beyond any of our conceptions of human finality and purpose precisely because of its transcendence. Indeed, history strikes us as lacking sense in any human understanding of the word. This is, in fact, so much the case that history looks to us like a motley collection of arrant nonsense complicated by abrasive suffering. Thus all appearances speak against the existence of God. Our human insight finds it impossible to justify his providence. In consequence some people regard the idea of divine providence as the utmost absurdity, more absurd certainly than a flagrant denial of his existence. Where humans are concerned God is powerless precisely because of the divinity of his existence, which can manifest itself only in absence. It is precisely the divine nature of his presence and his activity that makes him seem absent from us.

Whenever we try to grasp and take hold of God as an object, we find ourselves still in this finite world and never in the presence of God. However, there are forms of presence which draw our attention only as the result of a certain orientation of a conscious ignorance. We are concerned with a purely personal presence which can nevertheless not be situated amongst all those other things that manifest themselves to us directly by their presence. The impossibility of our accounting for our existence ourselves, and the fundamental experience of our wholly contingent presence in this world, brings us face to face with the invisible but real mystery of a personal Giver whose heart is greater than his gifts which surround us and of which we ourselves form part. Divine liberality forms the intangible background of our inner and outer

---

[1] Selected from: Edward Schillebeeckx, 'The Search for the Living God', *Essays: Ongoing Theological Quests*, Collected Works of Edward Schillebeeckx vol. 11 (London: Bloomsbury T&T Clark, 2014), 38–40.

world whose reality and contingency constantly betrays its vital source, but which always stands in the gap between him and us. Only when human beings show sufficient courage to see themselves and the world truthfully, as a fact, as a reality thrown at his feet, as a presence in itself unexplainable, can they begin to regard this tangible presence as the evidence of a very different Presence manifesting itself in an indirect fashion therein. Only when we face the world in our simple quality as human beings – as neither *homo faber* nor *homo oeconomicus* – and approach these realities in their simple, artless truth, can we realise our secure existence in a deeper mystery of a personal absolute freedom. But to this end we must first accept the fact that truth is something more than the eager grasp on tangible data. The natural affirmation of God's existence is no more than a critically confirmed affirmation on the basis of this world of our secure existence in the personal mystery of God, a mystery, however, that we cannot encounter on that same basis. Any arrogant attempt to seize God's presence merely confines us still more definitely in the isolation of our life in this world since it deprives us of that interiority which is secured only when we become conscious of ourselves within the security of the divine creative mystery. When God reveals his presence to us only through the act in which he founds our existence, whilst remaining transcendent even in this act,[2] this means that he is there not *because* we exist, although it is only through our own existence that we have come to realise his divine existence; it means that we are there only as a function of him. Thus the natural affirmation of God's existence is completed only in the willing surrender to the divine mystery which lies at the accepted origin of what we experience in this world. In this sense the existential experience of God's absence, combined with our own profound interest in the inner problematics of one's own existence and that of the world, represents the 'experience' of our secure being in an all-embracing mystery of transcendental but personal love. In this love we would willingly take a personal part, but in the nature of things we cannot, although on the basis of the creative act through which God draws our attention, as an essential requirement of our existence, to his presence as a loving person, we already have an inner consciousness of his *appeal to surrender*.

The direct personal relationship with the divine mystery of life, and in consequence the actual religiousness in which the presence of God develops into mutuality and encounter, becomes possible, however, only when God, acting from beyond the cloud of that mystery in which we already consciously exist, completes what he began in his creative act, and begins talking to us as one person speaks to and treats another. In the natural affirmation of God, human beings have already come to realise that although in free relationship to the world God is not, in the last resort, of this world, though he is not on his own able to give a *personal* significance to this free relationship which transcends the world. Regarded as the absolute bedrock of human and objectively unlimited freedom, God necessarily eludes all merely human attempts at understanding. But God himself now personally accomplishes this miracle, since it is precisely at that point where human beings face the world in free subjectivity that they are directly approached by the living God in order

---

[2] D. De Petter, *Begrip en werkelijkheid: Aan de overzijde van het conceptualisme*, Hilversum-Antwerp, 1964, 150–67.

that they may rise above themselves, step outside themselves, and live in personal intimacy with God. This supramundane personal loneliness of human freedom is just the point at which the question of personal communion with God arises, because it is there, at the summit of his transcendence over his worldly relationship, that on the basis of God's creation, and precisely because of his freedom, human beings are directly attuned to the mystery of the living God, even though they are incapable of reaching it by their own resources. By its very nature, therefore, religion is a personal act of human freedom which abandons its lonely outlook and lets itself be taken up by grace into the mutuality of God's presence, and thus into the intimacy of the divine life.

But from this personal communion with the living God we must now retrace the way we have already come, since as a result of this personal communion everything now takes on a much more profound dimension. Thanks to this personal living relationship with God enabling humans to step outside themselves and outside his earthly relationships towards a personal God, these earthly relationships themselves are given a divine significance. They develop into signs of a closer divine presence, of a presence that develops in mutuality into a personal encounter. For the *religious* person, the world of nature and history becomes a passage in his dialogue with God. At the same time, it develops into God's instructions to humanity, and the visible form of God's answer to human prayers.

However, the fact that the world of human history-creative freedom is now taken into personal living relationship with God also means that within this religious relationship humans make history into salvation or into judgment. Since human freedom is the factor which gives significance to history, intramundane relationships are thus directed and determined by the intimacy in which God and human beings have found each other, or by the rupture which is brought about when human beings in their freedom deny their God. In consequence, therefore, the whole of humanity's profane history is transformed either by the worship of God or by the denial of his existence, since even in his apostasy human beings remain subject to the living God by a personal transmundane relationship to him.

Thus because it is part and parcel of the divine dialogue that human existence in this world also becomes an anonymous medium of revelation and at the same time a sphere in which religious significances are established. Everywhere, history becomes either salvation or judgment. Despite, or rather *in*, its earthly nature, it also becomes an empirical manifestation of the religious relationship to God in faith or apostasy.

God the living One[3]

To talk about God-given salvation is a second discourse, namely a discourse on the basis of a first discourse that e.g. talks about self-liberation. The theologian 'elaborates' from his formal object, that is God as ultimate and absolute meaning

---

[3] Selected from: Edward Schillebeeckx, 'God, the Living One', *New Blackfriars* 62, no. 735 (1981): 364–6.

of human beings and society, the given reality of 'self-liberation' and sees precisely therein *God-given* salvation. He, then, produces the theological affirmation: 'that liberation *is* salvation'. Of course, this must be justified (on the level of concept, of proposition and of theory).

If God, as the belief in God implies, is the absolute meaning of history, there is nothing in history that cannot and must not be related to God.[4] So, everything in reality can become material object of theology, or one can theologise about everything.

It is the task of theology to search for that relation between everything and God. In order to be able to do that, the theologian has to accept beforehand that, that relation is present in the objective consistency of every event, independent of whatever *awareness* that would project that relation into that event. So, what happens *in* reality makes theology possible. The relation of salvation is located in reality itself and does not coincide with *religion*, for the religion is the *awareness* that *thematises* God's universal saving activity. Religion is the 'symbolic order' of the salvation that is realised in history, in the world, but is not itself the universal salvation. Theology is not in the first place the voice of institutional religion or church, but it is the voice of the universal salvation, that God is realising in the world-history. Theology can only be theology if it, first, listens to the non-religious voice of daily experiences, of the sciences and philosophy; if it, secondly, breaks off these ties, that is to say if it transcends these in the right moment and if it, thirdly, plays a different language game. On the level of theological language itself, interdisciplinarity is not necessary: it is even impossible. Interdisciplinarity is necessary, though to understand the material object, about which theology has to say something that cannot be determined accurately and that is where the interdisciplinarity comes in: it belongs to the terrain of that one can theologise about, it does not belong to the terrain of theology. To accept it there would result in squinting or talking double Dutch. Whatever happens inside the absolute limit, that is: inside the world and history is the material object of theology. This means that there is an essential difference between the theological theory of self-liberation seen as God-given salvation and the sociological theory of the same self-liberation.

Important here is the distinction between: (1) the reality and the whole of history as place where salvation is fought for over and against disaster and evil; (2) the awareness of salvation, thematised in religion: the faith or belief in God; the history of the awareness of the salvation; (3) the theory or theoretical awareness of the order of salvation: namely theology.

It should be clear that one is not permitted to identify the reality of salvation simply with the *awareness* or knowledge of it in the religions. Otherwise one would be the victim of a theological idealism. Liberation is God-as-salvation. For the believer in God there is no 'natura pura' in reality, but only nature and history in the light of the God of salvation (the concept of 'natura pura' is of course thinkable, as a limit-concept, but that does not say anything about it is possible existence).

---

[4]Theology is 'principaliter de Deo' but also it concerns everything 'secundum quod referentur ad Deum' (1, q. 1 a. 3 ad 1). The isotopy of the 'unitas scientiae' is not destroyed by this. See also I. q. 1 a.7: 'secundum ordinem ad Deum'. The identity of the pertinency, of the objectum formate quo.

In everything there is a reference to salvation and on this reference the specific theological objectivity is founded. It is a reference which constitutes reality either by acceptance or refusal. That relation with God is concretely *grace*. God's absolute presence full of promise, or *sin*. God's initiative to salvation is thus a reality to a certain extent independent of our *awareness* of it; that is so to say, that reality of salvation is not constituted by our awareness of it, and is thus independent of our activities and deeds, in which none the less it is realised. This does not result in the acceptance of the distinction between salvation *and* revelation, for salvation can only be 'God-given salvation', and in that sense 'revealed salvation'. For, without revelation there is for us no God and thus no salvation. But there is a difference between salvation *and* faith, although faith is conceptually closely related to revelation, since faith is essentially 'revelation-faith'. Faith is the explicit awareness of the God-given salvation, but this awareness does not coincide with God's factual saving activity and the already realised salvation in history. In this respect, one can limit the concept 'revelation' to 'the religious awareness of' the reference, the relation of salvation in all things and all events (not without humanity's practice of *charity*). Considered in this way, there is a real distinction between the history of salvation in the world *and* the history of *faith in salvation*. There is salvation outside religion and Church: one even has to say that salvation – which is not identified with the *awareness of* salvation – is properly realised *outside religion and Church*, that is, in the so-called profane world-history; everywhere where people are set free and live: the praxis of love or *agape*. Paradoxically, I might say: 'Extra *mundum* nulla salus'. Because it is the world of God, as far as people in this world are the promoter of good and the enemy of injustice and evil.

Nevertheless, on the other hand *salvation* is an *experiential* concept, and therefore it must reflect at least partially what humanity *experiences* as '*saving*'. The experience or some knowledge of salvation as saving and liberating is part of the concept of salvation. That does not mean that salvation is everywhere and fully and completely a reality of experience, but it must *at least partially* and *at least sometimes* be experienced specifically by those affected *as saving*. No salvation-reality without at least *some revelation!*

However, not everything that people pass off as their own salvation is *in fact saving and liberating*; thus salvation is in fact announced to us *in the name of God*. God and salvation are not exhausted by our *particular* experience.

The absolute limit[5]

At least in our modern times, believers and non-believers have the basic experience of an absolute limit, of radical finitude and contingency. I am not talking here about particular 'limit situations' in human life to which philosophers and theologians sometimes refer in order to 'give religion' to men and women at moments in which

---

[5]Selected from: Edward Schillebeeckx, *Church: The Human Story of God*, Collected Works of Edward Schillebeeckx vol. 10 (London: Bloomsbury T&T Clark, 2014), 75–8 [77–8].

they feel most vulnerable and hopeless: in sickness and death, plagues, AIDS and so on. There are also evidently people who do not recognise any kind of absolute limit: they are champions of an unlimited belief in progress in a world of inexhaustible possibilities. But the economic crisis and the destruction of our natural environment stand in radical contradiction to this naive optimism.

Of course, the simple and abstract notion of a limit does not take us any further. Confronted with limit-experiences primitive people believed in a fantastic kingdom beyond the absolute limit within which we live, and filled this 'other world' with mysterious powers and forces which intervened from above in human life and kept this world under their control. But if we are confronted with an absolute limit to all our experiences and knowledge, with what right can we then speak of the existence of something that lies beyond this absolute limit? In that case is not agnosticism not only a modest but also a more reverent attitude?

Recognition of radical finitude as such is no longer a religious concept, as it used to be, but is usually a generally recognised reality of human experience. No one has analysed this radical finitude of being human in this contingent world better than an agnostic who was originally in fact a militant atheist, Jean-Paul Sartre. There is both an atheistic and a religious experience of our radical finitude. The experience of contingency is the unexpressed heart of human life, but it is not a 'direct experience', as is that of someone who comes up against a wall at full speed, experiences a relative limit in a painful way and collapses with concussion. The radical experience of a limit is mediated through all kinds of experiences of relative limits in our life. Here I am rejecting Schleiermacher's direct datum of a 'feeling of absolute dependence'; this theological concept is too much a reflection of nineteenth-century liberal and social circumstances.

Far less is the experience of an absolute limit a kind of generalisation or extrapolation of immediate experiences of very specific limits. Rather, in my view it is an experience of an absolute limit *in* the constant experience of all our relative limits, in all kinds of sectors and at all human levels. In each particular experience of a limit, in the long run we experience that we are neither lords nor masters of ourselves, far less of nature and history. There is a radical contingency or finitude at any moment of life within what are nevertheless many kinds of positive possibilities. Since the experience of transition from relative limits to an absolute limit is above all a philosophical problem, here I shall leave any technical analysis on one side. For I am not concerned to provide a so-called 'proof of God', but to make sense to some degree of what believers call God.

The question then is: are we imprisoned this side of an absolute limit, like prisoners within their relative limits, the walls of their cell? Or is this imprisonment purely fictitious? In other words, is an absolute limit something that really bounds us and thus keeps us as it were captive within this limit? Do we have to say metaphorically, but really, that the absolute wall around our limited existence in the world is a reality, for believers and agnostics? Can we say anything more about this absolute limit than that we ourselves are radically finite? We ourselves are this limit. The absolute limit is our limit, not a human product, not a human projection, but a real fact. In whatever way, we ourselves are posited as finite beings, as Heidegger puts it. Our finite existence in the world is not itself a human product or project. In other words, if God exists, the boundary between God and the finite is not on God's side, but on the side of the finite. Agnostics like Horst Richter, a Marxist- Freudian psychotherapist, see unreadiness to accept our absolute limit or 'finitude' as the cause of the sickness of modern Western men and women and also as the foundation of all reasons of state and dictatorships: finitude and all human limitations, including the possibility of suffering, are argued away and smothered. But the reality of the absolute limit remains, despite all human boasts of greatness, and this then introduces neurosis into a culture.

The real fact of this limit also compels us to interpret it. What is the structure of such an interpretation, whether in a religious or an agnostic sense? Because of the absoluteness of this limit, our interpretation of it, however it is made, is at the same time a particular view of humanity and the world, a particular understanding of reality. In other words, here, in and with the great silence, in the vacuum of the absolute limit, not only all religious but also all other non-religious, agnostic views of humanity, the world and history arise, which on the whole are enclosed within this absolute limit or, more correctly, are themselves this absolute limit. For the modern concept of 'absolute openness to the future' is also subject to optical illusions. In that case, the surface or the perimeter of the absolute limit is stretched, perhaps to infinity. But that does not remove this absolute limit. Present, past and future fall within the absolute limit of all that is finite.

This absolute limit is thus a basic condition of our whole human existence; the divine and eschatological proviso is simply its religious expression. As experience, however, this proviso is secular, human and universal. The structure of any human interpretation of this boundary that we experience seems to me to be the same for the two directions that human beings can take. The situation is often, wrongly, put like this: there is a fundamental and universal datum of experience (experience of contingency, experience of an absolute limit); the unbeliever accepts this and leaves it at that, while those who believe in God also envisage a completely new 'other-worldly kingdom', a kind of superstructure above experience. Imagined in these terms, this is a false estimation of the interpretations of both believers and unbelievers.

Is the experience of contingency by the person who believes in God and the atheist really a fundamental experience for both, a concrete experience which both share in common? Some say, 'There is no neutral basis of experience which can be interpreted in both a theistic and an atheistic way',[6] since the interpretation is an integral part of experience itself and can never be detached from it. That is true, but it is only a half-truth, for it is clear that the believer's experience of contingency is fundamentally different from that of the agnostic. For the believer, this is concrete, albeit mediated through this experience of contingency or absolute limit, an experience of God's absolute saving presence throughout his or her life, while the agnostic is shut up alone with fellow men and women within this absolute limit. These are certainly two fundamentally different experiences. But it in no way follows from this that one cannot speak meaningfully of the same sort of experience with two possible interpretations. It does not mean that there is a neutral common experience which is simply interpreted in two different ways. It means that there is no uninterpreted

---

[6]Thus H. D. Lewis, quoted by J. J. Shepherd, *Experience, Inference, and God*, London, 1975, 13.

experience of contingency, but in the whole of this interpretative experience there is a pre-linguistic element of experience which is universally human, although the specific totality of this experience is experienced and interpreted in a religious way by Christians and in an agnostic way by humanists. Both interpretations are specifically part of the experience itself. But although both interpretations are an intrinsic part of the experience of contingency and thus colour this experience as a whole, the experiential aspect of contingency *qua* contingency is not as a matter of course identical with the interpretative element and is thus human and universal.

Contingency, accessible to both a believing and an agnostic interpretation, is thus itself positively an experience which is held in common. Here we have an experience which in its pre-linguistic experiential element (at which we can never arrive separately) is accessible to everyone. Therefore, this religious interpretation can be tested by our dimension of experience which is shared by all men and women. We do not develop the divine out of ourselves, but the divine freely manifests itself in profoundly human experiences.

The mystical 'direct experience of God' also ultimately has to do with the experience of God through the mediation of our 'absolute limit'. Hence Ruusbroec's brilliant religious talk of the experience of God as dark light, mediated immediacy!

Selected literature

- The Search for the Living God; Selected from: Edward Schillebeeckx, 'The Search for the Living God', *Essays: Ongoing Theological Quests*, Collected Works of Edward Schillebeeckx vol. 11 (London: Bloomsbury T&T Clark, 2014), 38–40.
- God the Living One; Selected from: Edward Schillebeeckx, 'God, the Living One', *New Blackfriars* 62, no. 735 (1981): 364–6.
- The Absolute Limit; Selected from: Edward Schillebeeckx, *Church: The Human Story of God*, Collected Works of Edward Schillebeeckx vol. 10 (London: Bloomsbury T&T Clark, 2014), 75–8 [77–8].

10

Creation

Kingdom of God: Creation and salvation[1]

Via a long history, Jesus' message and person is linked to the great Jewish expectation of salvation in the approaching kingdom of God, also linked to Israel's royal messianic expectations as a model of general human expectations and finally linked to creation as the starting point of this coming event in which God entrusts to human beings his struggle against the chaotic powers. In this struggle, human beings are God's own viceroys on earth. In spite of everything, and without any basis in the humans self, that is, as a free gift and unconditionally, God entrusts it to human beings. 'The human being' or 'the Son of Man' – first the king, after that every human being – is ultimately 'Jesus of Nazareth' (see this movement from 'human being' to 'Jesus Christ' in Heb 2.8–9 also). In him God's risky trust in human beings is not disappointed. In spite of everything – even in spite of the execution of the eschatological prophet of God's approaching kingdom of salvation by and for humanity – this kingdom is still coming: resurrection! The creation promise is repeatedly contradicted by the actual course of history, but it is brought to completion. Israel's old dream of the coming kingdom as *shalom* for humanity, placed in the hands of human beings, is in that case also the horizon of expectation and experience in which Jesus must be seen and interpreted: the human person in whom the creation assignment has been successful, albeit still within the conditions of a history of suffering. The consequence of this is that trust in this human person is the specific form of faith in God, creator of heaven and earth, who through his creative action places unconditional trust in humanity. Without this divine trust in humanity, creation would indeed make no sense! This human person Jesus makes it possible for us to believe that God indeed places his unconditional trust in humanity – while for many precisely what happens in our history of suffering is the reason why they no longer can believe in God. After Auschwitz and the like, belief that God trusts people is severely tested. And nonetheless! says the Jewish-Christian tradition of experience.

---

[1] Selected from: Edward Schillebeeckx, *Interim Report on the Books Jesus and Christ*, trans. John Bowden, Collected Works of Edward Schillebeeckx vol. 8 (London: Bloomsbury T&T Clark, 2014), 97–102 [111–16].

This expresses that faith in God is impossible without faith in humanity. Christianity expresses this in its creed: 'I believe in God, the creator of heaven and earth, *and* in Jesus: the Christ, his only Son, our Lord.' This faith in God's trust in human beings as well as in *this* human person Jesus is so paradoxical that it is only possible in the power of the Spirit of God: 'I believe in the Holy Spirit.' The paradox of this lies in our faith that God trusts humanity, while we hardly have any reasons to trust 'human beings', others and ourselves. Repeating many Old Testament echoes, Paul expresses it like this: 'God proves his love for us in that while we still were sinners Christ died for us' (Rom 5.8).

This makes the New Testament message universal, for by means of this it is anchored in the universal happening of creation: faith in God, creator of heaven and earth, who therefore will judge all, the 'living and the dead', – everyone. Creation and salvation, therefore, shed light on each another, mutually and essentially. Any other, alienating vision of creation, as an act of God's trust in humanity, will therefore distort the Christian vision of Jesus, or even make it impossible. For creation faith is only liberating – this only becomes fully apparent from Jesus' trust in his creator, the Father – if we understand creation neither dualistically nor as an emanation.

In this context, dualism came into being from humanity's scandal at suffering and evil, injustice and meaninglessness in our world, nature and history. Therefore it denies that God, when creating, willed the world precisely as world, and men and women precisely as human beings. In that case, finitude is not the normal condition of creatures, but is traced back to a fault in creation or to a mysterious primal sin. In the light of creation interpreted in this way, salvation or being whole, i.e. the true, integral form of our being human, is then also placed either in a past and lost paradise or in an apocalyptic new earth and new humanity which is coming. God will bring about this new state of affairs only secondarily, and on top of the terrible mess of this world, in an unexpected and sudden future which, given the terrible mess in which we live, is imminent. In this vision, the world of creation is a sort of compromise between God and one or another dark power.

Emanationism, for its part, is not so very different in essence from dualism, but it does come from a very different sentiment towards life, namely from the concern to safeguard God's transcendence. God is so great and so exalted that it is beneath his dignity to meddle directly with creatures and to compromise himself. He entrusts creation to a representative, a principal viceroy of a somewhat lower order. From this perspective, world and people are degradations of God – divinity reduced in rank, because this flowing forth of things from God is seen above all as a necessary process.

In both cases – dualistic and emanationist conceptions of creation – humanity's salvation or well-being logically consists in raising themselves above their human and worldly conditions and their own specific human character in order thus to reach a super-creaturely status. This distorts the entire good news of creation. The Old Testament story in Genesis sees the so-called primal human sin not in the fact that people want to be just a people in a world which is just a world, but rather in the fact that human beings do not want to accept their finite or contingent condition, that they crave infinity: immortality and omniscience, in order to become like God.

In deliberate contrast to such ideas about creation, the Jewish-Christian belief in creation says, after a long history of maturing, that God is God, the sun is the sun, the moon is the moon and a person is a person, and moreover that God's blessing rests precisely upon this: it is good like this. It is good that a human being is just a human being, the world just the world, i.e. not-God, contingent: they could just as well not have been there and nonetheless they are said to be worth the difficulty and the cost. They are there without any explanation or foundation in themselves or in anything else in this world, nature or history. Precisely for this reason, belief in the creating God cannot be an explanation either, for from his side God's act of creation is unconditional and absolutely free. In that case, finitude means that the creature has no prior necessity at all and does not find any explanation in any connection with this world: it is there, inexplicable, as pure gift. Nowhere – not even in God – is it prescribed how humans, society and the world should turn out. How the world, which is there, will turn out, is something human beings themselves will have to discover in good conscience; they will have to devise it and implement it within the limits of the material universe in quite precarious situations – in the condition of a creature.

The basic fault of many misconceptions regarding creation lies in this: that one senses finitude as a wounding, which as such really need not and should not adhere to the things of the world. Therefore one begins to seek a separate cause of this finitude and finds this in some dark power of evil or in some kind of original sin. In other words, finitude is identified with the improper, with a disorder, even with sinfulness or apostasy, a wound in the existence of humanity and the world. As if coming and going, mortality, failing, mistakes and ignorance need not belong to the normal condition of our being human and as if people would originally be equipped with all kinds of 'preternatural' gifts such as omniscience and immortality, things which humanity would have lost due to the primal Fall. Close reading shows that the Genesis story, albeit in mythical terms, wants to register a protest against precisely such representations. If God is creator, then he does indeed create the non-divine, that which is wholly other than himself, in other words, finite things. Creatures are not copies of God. The Jewish-Christian belief in creation has quite keenly grasped this, even though one must admit that, under foreign influence, much distortion has often been introduced into the representations of creation, by many Christians as well. I would like to elucidate the unique characteristics of this Christian belief in creation, in two respects.

First of all, this belief implies that we in no way have to transcend or escape our contingency or finitude, or to experience it as a wound. We may and must just be people in an environment which is just the world: fascinating, but also mortal, failing, suffering. To want to transcend the finitude is megalomania, which alienates human beings from themselves, the world and nature. Humanity and the world are no fall, no apostasy from God, no fiasco and thus in principle neither a test in expectation of better times. If God is Creator, then the creature is indeed not-God, other than God; then it may be different, and this also includes the burden of subjection and ignorance, of suffering and mortality, of coming and going, of failing and mistakes. Finitude or contingency means that human beings and the world, in and of themselves, hang in a vacuum, above absolute nothingness. There is nothing between the world and God that can be added for the interpretation of their relationship. This is what one means when one uses symbolic language to speak of 'creation from nothing'.

But the reverse side of this belief in creation is that the anguish of this dangling above absolute nothingness at the same time has as a counter-balance the absolute presence of God in and with the finite. Finite beings are a mixture of solitude and presence, and therefore faith in the creating God does not take away the finitude, nor distort it as sinfulness or decay, but makes it take up this finitude in God's presence, without divesting the world and human beings of their finitude or regarding these as hostile. In this respect Christian belief in creation distinguishes itself from pantheistic conceptions as well; for if God's presence were to mean that everything else outside God were to be explained in some way as an illusion or as belonging to the proper definition of God, then God does not seem to be able to be present with sufficient power to be able to bring autonomous and nonetheless non-divine beings into existence. From a Christian point of view, the world and human beings are utterly different from God, but within the presence of the creating God. Therefore, this other-than-God can never emigrate from the divine act of creation; in other words, God remains beside and with the contingent, the other-than-God – the world in its worldliness and human beings in their autonomous but finite humanity.

It follows from this twofold character that (in contrast to the vision of dualism and emanationism), salvation from God never consists in God's saving us *from* our finitude and *from* all that this involves. For a creating God, this is precisely where God's own powerlessness lies. In that case he also wills this powerlessness, absolutely freely. However, this also means that he wants to be our God in our humanity and for our humanity, in and with our finitude. It means therefore that we may be humane people, albeit also in mortality and suffering. But this, in itself very oppressive, burden at the same time means that God is beside us and with us, also in our failing, also in our suffering, also in our death, just as much as in and with all our positive experiences and sensations. It also means that he is present to the sinner, forgiving. Indeed, the boundary between God and us is our boundary, not God's. This has considerable consequences. In acknowledging and accepting our limits and those of nature and history, we acknowledge the divinity of God; and to acknowledge the finite condition of humanity and the world is to acknowledge what gives human beings and the world their own specific character, and at the same time to acknowledge that they are not divine and are therefore limited, and to act in accordance with this.

Because it is only possible to talk of God, that is to speak of God as creator in the indirectness of worldly intermediaries, namely our contingent nature and history, this means that these conditions are experienced as non-divine; they may not be absolutised or idolised. Here, *inter alia*, lies the critical power of belief in creation, which for that reason at the same time signifies salvation by and for humanity and the world, and their judgment. To want to annul this boundary from our side towards God is what the Bible calls the fundamental human sin, continually repeating itself in the course of history. On the other hand, this belief in creation sets us free for our own task in the world. Enjoying and loving what is worldly in the world, what is human in a person, is enjoying and loving what is divine in God. God's honour lies in the happiness, in the well-being of human beings in the world, who seeks his honour in God: this seems to me to be the best definition of what creation means. Then this creation is no one-time event somewhere in the beginning, but a sustained dynamic event. God wants to be the origin, here and now, of the worldliness of the world and of the humanity of human beings. He wants to be with us, in and with our finite task in the world.

Belief in the creating God is never an explanation; neither does it want to be according to its own understanding of itself. This faith is good news which says something about God, the human person and the world, and indeed in their mutual relationship. It is a message which the human person does not hear about primarily from some authoritative body foreign to his own experience. On the contrary, it is an invitation, an echo which he can listen to from his own familiar world of experience: from nature and history. Nature and history are authoritative sources in and through which God reveals himself as creator in and through our fundamental experiences of finitude.

The inexhaustible surplus of creation[2]

The fact that what, in the past, was only a matter for religions and Christianity, seems to be experienced today as a common task of all people, in no way weakens the Christian faith vision; quite the contrary. Since when does a particular vision of reality become less true because it ultimately becomes universalised, i.e., begins to be shared by a great many others as well? This argues, rather, for its accuracy. But one could reason in this way: admitting that the introduction of many ideas about values, especially in the West, is partly due to the Christian tradition of experience, these have now become the common property of all and, for this reason, we can now say farewell to this Christian faith, while thanking Christianity for services rendered – a saying that does receive attention, right and left. I believe that we then think too little about the inexhaustible potential of the Christian belief in creation for expectation and inspiration. The so-called tendency towards secularisation, understood as a gradual universalising of originally religious inspirations, which I regard as correct, seems to me however, as a totality thesis, to be a disastrous short-circuit, and this for two fundamental reasons. The first reason is finitude itself. Finitude, which is really the definition of all secularity, can indeed itself never be fully secularised, for in that case the modern world would nonetheless have to find a magic potion to nullify the essential finitude of humanity and the world. The second reason has to do with how religions understand themselves, especially Christianity. Humaneness, the orientation of 'worldly' experience, is, at least in the Christian tradition of experience, not intended only as ethical but rather as theologal or God-centred orientation (*virtus theologica*, says the tradition). Therefore, the Christian tradition sees a religious depth-dimension in humaneness which has to do precisely with the insight of faith that finitude is not left in its solitude but is borne by the absolute presence of the creating God. And this presence continues to be an inexhaustible wellspring which can never be secularised.

---

[2]Selected from: Edward Schillebeeckx, *Interim Report on the Books Jesus and Christ*, trans. John Bowden, Collected Works of Edward Schillebeeckx vol. 8 (London: Bloomsbury T&T Clark, 2014), 106–8 [122–4].

I believe that precisely the critical and productive power of authentic belief in creation is that whatever element concerning value, inspiration and orientation that proceeds from it and that can unceasingly be universalised, and in this sense secularised, that is liberated for the benefit of all people, and so, as it were, 'escapes' the monopoly of the particularity of religions and Christianity, can never catch up with the inexhaustible potential for expectation and inspiration which belief in creation possesses. For secularity says finitude. And although non-religious secularity sees only finitude in this, religious and Christian secularity sees, together with this finitude, God's presence, inexhaustible because it is absolute. On this basis, finitude or secularity will continue to point to the wellspring and basis, inspiration and orientation which surpasses all secularity, which believers call the Living God and which is not susceptible to any secularising. Precisely for this reason, belief in creation is also the foundation of prayer and mysticism. There is a surplus in creation which cannot be derived from any secularity. That is also why the fullness of salvation cannot be reduced to what people do with it. The salvation of humanity is God himself, as humanity's wholeness. This implies that the experience of God – call it 'mysticism', without thereby intending extraordinary things – is the core of all human salvation – mysticism, however, which with and from the experience of God in the heart, goes out to humanity. Thus, according to the testimony of a mystic such as Eckhart, the model of all mysticism is not Mary, preoccupied with mysticism, but Martha, industriously caring for her fellow human beings. Thus mysticism is indeed the source of continuing improvement of human life and of society, the source of salvation of and for humanity.

Eschatological surplus

Even though Christian salvation also includes earthly salvation, this salvation from God in Jesus is indeed indefinable in the upward direction; earthly salvation gradually slips into a greater mystery. We cannot pin down God's possibilities to our limited expectations of salvation. Whatever positively fills in definitive salvation runs the risk of becoming human megalomania or of belittling God's possibilities and, by means of this, also of restraining human beings, keeping them smaller than God dreamed them.

Because this definitive salvation, that is, the perfect and universal wholeness of all and every person, living and dead, cannot be defined, no one within the narrow limits of our history can complete the end of this story of God in Jesus with humanity nor recount it to the end. After all, in the best case, each one's death time and again breaks the thread of a liberating narrative. Is there, then, no more salvation, not even for the one who has passed on the torch of this story and kept it burning among the living, and perhaps has been martyred for this reason? That is why the final consummation of God's way of salvation with humanity must be 'not of this world', while the liberating involvement of God with humanity, whom he rescues and makes whole, nonetheless may and must receive a recognisable content in forms which in our history will nevertheless constantly be transcended.

Although definitive salvation is eschatological and obviously, as such, cannot be experienced as already present content of experience, the faith-inspired knowledge of the promise of a definitive perspective of salvation is nonetheless actually given in an experience-now, namely in fragments of particular experiences of salvation, thanks to Jesus Christ. The church's proclaimed 'notification and promise' of definitive salvation proceeding from the story of and about Jesus as the Christ takes on real meaning for believers only if it is based on such partial experiences of salvation. Without this religious story about Jesus Christ, we are at most confronted with a liberating utopia which perhaps arouses some chances of life and salvation for people who appear on the far horizon of our history, but which has just written off the rest of humanity of this 'prehistory' for the benefit of a dreamed-of utopia to be realised someday. Definitive salvation does indeed substantially exceed our present experience – ultimately no one among us experiences being whole now – but in so far as that promise-filled proclamation of salvation can and may be said to be valid, it does have its basis in a connection of experiences here and now; of Jesus and of those who 'follow after him' in this world, as well as of all those who actually do what Jesus did. This eschatological promise cannot rest purely on a verbal revelation – by the way, anthropologically, 'word' is an expression of human experience and praxis – thus, not on a purely proclaimed notification of a coming, definitive and complete salvation. For on what basis would such a 'notification' have real value? As God's exegete and a practitioner of one who acts in accordance with God's kingdom, neither did Jesus work from a blue-print or a well-defined concept of eschatological and definitive salvation. Rather, in and through his own historical and thus situationally limited praxis of 'going about doing good': of healing, liberating from reigning demonic powers of the world, and of reconciliation, throwing light on a distant vision of definitive, perfect and universal salvation: 'See, the home of God is among mortals. He will dwell with them as their God; they will be his peoples, and God himself will be with them; he will wipe every tear from their eyes. Death will be no more; mourning and crying and pain will be no more, for the first things have passed away' (Rev 21.3-4); this is how the Christian Apocalypse interpreted, correctly, the vision of Jesus' ministry: the kingdom of God in its final form, which Jesus Christ already positively guarantees now.

Selected literature

- Kingdom of God: Creation and Salvation; Selected from: Edward Schillebeeckx, *Interim Report on the Books Jesus and Christ*, trans. John Bowden, Collected Works of Edward Schillebeeckx vol. 8 (London: Bloomsbury T&T Clark, 2014), 97–102 [111–16].
- The Inexhaustible Surplus of Creation; Selected from: Edward Schillebeeckx, *Interim Report on the Books Jesus and Christ*, trans. John Bowden, Collected Works of Edward Schillebeeckx vol. 8 (London: Bloomsbury T&T Clark, 2014), 106–8 [122–4].

11

Sacramental Theology

Sacramental and extra-sacramental grace[1]

A question often arises concerning the purpose of the sacraments: Are they needed for our approach to Christ? Those who put this question make a distinction between the normal and the unusual ways in which grace is given. They then argue that when the sacramentality of the Church is disregarded inculpably through ignorance, the grace of Christ, though coming in an unusual manner, can produce the same wonders of holiness as when it comes through the sacraments. But this we cannot grant.

We must remember that the essential factor in ecclesial sacramentality is Christ's eternally-actual redemptive act, made to concern each one of us personally. This comes about through Christ's Church, the earthly manifestation of his will to redeem us. Now this heavenly act can affect and influence people outside the sacraments, although it will not then be *visibly* present among them. This may indeed be called an extra-sacramental bestowal of grace, but nevertheless the Church will always be involved in it even if only through the daily sacrifice of the Eucharist for the good of all people. When we too receive grace apart from the sacraments it comes through Christ the Mediator in and through his Church the primordial sacrament.

It is from these facts that we must begin to investigate the relationship between the sacramental and the extra-sacramental bestowal of grace. We should first notice that in the natural order, alongside the decisive and central acts of life, there are everyday actions which call for a personal involvement of a lesser kind. In the same way there are decisive Christian acts and everyday ones. There is moreover another psychological aspect which must not be neglected. The human body and its contacts with the world around are the realities through which and in which the soul grows to personality, just as they are the realities through which the soul expresses its personal development. In human activity a person's own bodiliness is an aspect of the active subject. The bodily expression is not merely the manifestation of a free spiritual act after it has already been fully achieved in pure inferiority; the spiritual act can only

---

[1]Selected from: Edward Schillebeeckx, *Christ the Sacrament of the Encounter with God*, trans. Paul Barrett, N. D. Smith, Collected Works of Edward Schillebeeckx vol. 1 (London: Bloomsbury T&T Clark, 2014), 143–5 [244–8].

be achieved in incarnation. Because it is only an imperfect revelation of the inward personal act, the outward element is only a sign of that act. Every personal act is one and undivided; in it the interior element is made visible at the same time as it is given its fully personal and human character by its opposite pole, the bodily element.[2]

There is a similar relationship between a religious act which is sacramental and one which is not. That which is lived out in an everyday manner outside the sacraments grows to its full maturity in them (this, at least, is the purpose of the sacramental system of salvation). Seen from Christ's point of view the sacraments are the express taking-hold of the person who receives them, because they are the earthly manifestation of the heavenly act of redemption. But the response to Christ's willing availability in encounter must therefore grow in the recipient to a culminating point which is personal and decisive. It is partly on human grounds that this response is possible, since the recipient humanly realises his desire for grace in the visibility of the Church which is full of grace. This desire for grace is made manifest in a definite and tangible form in which the human person is entirely involved in concentrated action, taken hold of as he is by a tangible action of Christ. The anonymity of everyday Christian living is removed by the telling power of Christ's symbolic action in and through his Church.

The fact that the sacraments are (or should be) culminating moments in a personal Christian life is something that rests on more than merely human grounds (on these alone the sacraments would only be of relative importance). The supremely important character of the sacraments derives from the fact that they bring a person's desire for grace to ecclesial manifestation (this fact does of course include psychological elements). So through the sacraments the individual's desire for grace is linked with the redemptive power of that mystical body which is one with Christ. Again they are culminating moments because they are a special divine contact with a person in a situation which, for the Christian view of life, is decisive. The sacraments bring about the encounter with Christ in exactly those seven instances in which, on account of the demands of a special situation of Christian life, a person experiences a special and urgent need of communion with him. They are the divine act of redemption itself, manifest in the sacred environment of the living Church, making a concrete appeal to human beings and taking hold of them in a living way, as really as does the embrace of a mother for her child. And it is not enough for the child merely to know that its mother loves it; it needs the actual embrace to perfect the experience of love.

On the other hand, these special moments are prepared for, depend upon, and can be intensified by growing maturity of soul in the everyday acts of life, just as they may be weakened by everyday acts in which all fervour is lacking. Therefore, the sacraments cannot be isolated from the organic unity of a whole persevering Christian life. Thus it may also happen that experiences of God may be more intense outside the sacraments than during their actual reception. The sacraments determine the objective importance of certain moments in life, to which we personally and in a religious spirit must give full value. But besides these moments which are decisive

---

[2] Cf. Karl Rahner, 'Personale und sakramentale Frömmigkeit', *Schriften zur Theologie* 2 (Einsiedeln 1955): 115–41 – although we cannot entirely agree with the many passages in which the author makes the constitution of a personal act – and not merely its human character – depend on the bodily element.

objectively, in the life of a religious person, there can be others which are of vital importance subjectively. These extra-sacramental bestowals of grace can in fact raise the Christian to greater heights than the grace received in the sacraments themselves. The sacraments are necessary as markers, milestones on the way, so that by living the Christian life *as a whole* we may become more and more one with Christ.

Again, we should not forget that every grace coming to a baptised person bears, in the last analysis, a relation to his sacramental status as baptised. Baptism is a blessing on the whole of life. In the same way in marriage the strength to face all the moments of difficulty and decision in life comes from the sacramental grace of matrimony. The practice of religion in the Church – the regular reception of the sacraments – is therefore a vital and necessary condition for a living awareness of communion with God.

The church as the sign of God's grace on earth[3]

We have already said that the Church, as the visible presence of grace among us, is made up of both clergy and laity, the priestly hierarchy and the faithful People of God together. It is this whole community of the faithful which is the 'sign raised up among the nations'. The ecclesial (i.e., the sacramentally visible) presence of grace is not something which merely proceeds from the ecclesiastical hierarchy and from the characters of baptism and confirmation in the faithful; it is something which also arises, and proceeds visibly, from the inward communion of the faithful in grace with Christ the Lord. In this connection, many of the faithful have a kind of totalitarian notion of the Church, and confuse the absolute claims of a Church in which the Hierarchy does hold the office of administration of Christ's visible grace with a sort of secular dictatorial power arrogated to itself by the Church, and making of the laity nothing more than a group of subjects who can carry out only what the Hierarchy decides they must do. This notion is not only incorrect; it is completely alien to the true character of the Church and in fact heretical.

The Spirit of Christ, the active principle of the entire Church, leads and guides her not only through the Hierarchy, from above, but also through the faithful, from below. Both office and charism are essential to the whole of the Church, and both come under the guidance of Christ the Lord. Both are ecclesial. When we look for the way in which the Church is a sign raised up among the nations to show to all the victorious Christ, we must look not only to the teaching authority of the Church, and to its pastoral government but also, and as essentially, to the Christian lives of the faithful: to their constancy, to their unselfish love and goodness, to the humility and faith and resignation with which they bear life's difficulties, to the living Christian example and the responsibility of a father and a mother, to the courage and purity of heart which is visible in their actions, to the virginity of those who consecrate themselves wholly to Christ, to the 'old maids' who, though they may not have wanted to remain unmarried, nevertheless do not become soured by their lot but know how

---

[3]Selected from: Edward Schillebeeckx, *Christ the Sacrament of the Encounter with God*, trans. Paul Barrett, N. D. Smith, Collected Works of Edward Schillebeeckx vol. 1 (London: Bloomsbury T&T Clark, 2014), 146–9 [249–54].

to give it the meaningfulness of a new vocation. All of these are true manifestations of the Church, the visible presence of grace among us. So are the various forms of desire for grace: the appearance among the laity of a variety of Christian movements, of hopes and trends towards new forms of Christian life and activity – in all this the Spirit of Christ is guiding and governing the Church. The works that Christian artists and thinkers achieve through the strength of their life in the eucharistic communion in grace, the forces they release in the context and in the mind of all Christendom – all this is a true part of the reality of the Church, all this is the visible activity of grace among us, a sacrament of God's love for people. In some periods of the Church's history the movements created by Christian writers and thinkers and the results they have produced have done far more to manifest the presence of grace than has the hierarchical government of the Church. These various, constantly renewed and often surprising activities, all having their source in the charisms of the ecclesial communion in grace, should in our own times be getting much more attention than they are. To live as a member of the Church means much more than simply to practise one's religion in the narrow sense of the word 'practise'. Beside regular reception of the sacraments, and no less essentially than this, it means giving a visible reality in our everyday life to our faith, our hope and our love; to our holiness itself.

The Spirit of Christ breathes where he will, not only on the Pope and among the ranks of the bishops, but also among the people and their priests. The assistance of the Spirit which Christ has granted to his Church is not only for the exercise of the hierarchical office in the Church, but for the life of the Church in every other aspect too. It is granted to the whole community of believers. True, the whole life of the Church remains under the control of the Church's authority, which is supreme and from which there is no possible appeal. But it is of the essence of the ecclesial character of the Hierarchy that it allows the true ecclesial character of the laity its proper scope. All sorts of tension can arise from this double aspect of ecclesial character. We do not want to examine them now. We want simply to point out that what we believe in is this Church as it is in the concrete, the living Church of Christ, and not an abstract ideal. We believe in the visible presence of grace among us, a communion in which nevertheless we still find sin. This is the Church that is the object of our faith. Throughout its history there have been individuals who have allowed themselves to be so scandalised by its weakness that they became blind to its strength and grace, visible and untarnished, constantly living and spreading. Again and again, people have fallen into the heresy of regarding the Church as merely the invisible communion of those who truly live in the union of grace with Christ. They deny the Church its incarnation. They take away not only its weakness and sinfulness but also the visibility of its grace, which means that they take away grace itself. We must be able to achieve that strength of faith which will enable us to believe in the Church as it is; that is to believe in it as manifestation of Christ's redeeming grace, and by the same faith to accept that in head and in members all is not yet wholly what is proper to it as Church; there is still some human weakness, lack of understanding, impersonal mechanical routine, and especially in past times – why should we be shy of historical fact? – earthly lust for power and crass covetousness. Let us say again, the Church as such is holy. That belongs to its essence. In this sense St. John says, 'Whosoever is born of God commits no sin... he cannot sin because he is born of God' (1 John 3.9), and he says this because the Church is a reality, not something ethereal, divorced from the facts of experience.

'We know that whosoever is born of God does not sin' (1 John 5.18). And yet, when the same St. John is speaking of Christians, he says, 'If we say that we have no sin, we deceive ourselves' (1 John 1.8). If this does not involve a contradiction, what does it mean? It means that in the Church all is not yet wholly what should belong to it as such. The Church is the visible shape of salvation, the sign filled with the reality it signifies. Its members can therefore sin only to the extent to which they positively withdraw themselves from its sanctifying influence. To the extent that a person sins, he is outside the Church; in himself, and thus in his place in the Church, he brings about a rupture between the sign and the reality it signifies. All of this implies that the Church has not yet reached its final state. For we cannot hold that it will cease to exist at the end of time, and make place for a purely spiritual communion of the saints in grace. In virtue of Christ's incarnation, the bodily visibility of grace is not a provisional and temporary measure but the definitive reality. Only in heaven will the Church reach its full maturity, still as a visible saving society. The resurrection of all flesh establishes and perpetuates in glory the earthly history of the Church, just as the personal holiness which the saints have fought for and won in this life will be visible in their bodies when they rise again. All that is weak and sad and troublesome will have disappeared from the Church in heaven, but it will continue to show us the face of its holiness in the visibility that comes of incarnation. Indeed, only in heaven shall we see this to the full.

The Church, as the earthly sign of the triumph of Christ's grace, still remains in a state of weakness, needing to purge itself of all that is sinful. This fact shows us two things; first, that the glory of the Church on earth is a veiled glory, for around it there is still a broad margin of weakness and shortcoming; and second, and more especially, that the power of God is fulfilled in and through the weakness and poverty of the Church. The Church is great and glorious, but not on account of its earthly strength and achievements; in it Christ's redeeming grace always triumphs in spite of human weakness. It is in this weakness that the divine power comes into its own and, becomes visible as divine. The Church is therefore not only the object of our faith; it is also the test of our faith. It can become an obstacle and a danger to faith. For belief is not a conviction to which a person is forced by the glory of the Church manifest in his experience of her. We always believe in the midst of darkness. And if we look at it in this way, the weakness of the Church is a *felix culpa,* for it makes us realise that our only boast is in the powers of God. Just as Christ was a scandal to the Jews because to the Jewish mind he set himself up in opposition to Yahweh, so too the Church must pass through its pilgrimage, poor and despised, for the power of redeeming grace alone will bring the victory. This is the real strength of our faith in the Church.

The sacramental life of the church[4]

We must show a real love for our fellow human beings, and this love must truly be the sacrament of our love for God. But this sacramentality in its turn has an effect

---

[4]Selected from: Edward Schillebeeckx, *Christ the Sacrament of the Encounter with God*, trans. Paul Barrett, N. D. Smith, Collected Works of Edward Schillebeeckx vol. 1 (London: Bloomsbury T&T Clark, 2014), 151–4 [258–64].

upon our human love for our fellow human beings, for however much we as believers can and should share the problems of unbelievers in order to retain side by side with them a solidarity in human experience, we cannot share their lack of redemption. A Christian's *presence au monde*, which is the great motive of credibility for the Christian faith, is always motivated by redemption. The Christian lives in the world because he lives in and with the living God; his is a redeeming presence.

For this reason not only may we not, in our human solidarity with unbelievers, go so far as to share with them those situations of life which are sinful (as the 'priests of the poor' in Coccioli's unfortunate novel, *Le Ciel et la Terre*), but even in those situations, the common lot of all people, in which the disturbing results of the Fall are most clearly felt, our experience is essentially different from theirs. The tension and the suffering are not lessened for the Christian, but he knows that God 'who gives joy to his youth' is with him. All this gives to the visible Church its persuasive power of drawing people. The miracles which, with fairly regular irregularity, occur in the life of the Church, are after all a quasi-normal phenomenon accompanying the presence of truly holy people in this world. They are a motive of credibility not so much of themselves, but insofar as they point to the visible presence of grace in the midst of the world. Miracles spring from grace incarnate as normally as do sparks from a fire.

There have been some who have looked for the whole of salvation in human encounter (even though their actual approach to such encounter made it far too little of a sacrament). That they did so came from their acute awareness that Christianity possessed true doctrine and redemption, yet like treasure in a chest to which the key had been lost. The key is indeed a real approach to people, but it must be the expression of our love for God. We do not merely toss out dogmas to people who are crying out in dire need. We begin to teach Christian truth successfully by ourselves beginning to live for our fellow human beings. Our life must itself be the incarnation of what we believe, for only when dogmas are lived do they have any attractive power. Why in the main do Western people pass Christianity by unnoticingly? Surely because the visible presence of grace in Christians as a whole, apart from a few individuals, is no longer evident.

If Christianity is to be offered to people as something really worthy of their serious attention, this collective witness is once again urgently required. It is only then that the Church, the visible mystery, will come to occupy a central position in the ordinary everyday lives of people, and the others who are without faith will not be able to escape the challenge of Christianity, which will then be irresistible. There are so many people who are swept along by the world's current and who have never encountered, in their own particular environment, anyone whose life has suddenly brought them up against the idea that it is really possible to transform life into something more beautiful. People do discover their potential depths in the eyes of other people. The murderer was converted when he looked into the eyes of Christ on the Cross, and learned from them the depths of which his own heart too was capable. It is up to us as Christians to make the Church appear as visibly present to those people who are carried along by the current in this world, by providing the simple direct evidence of our Christian behaviour and way of life. We can thus give them a real desire for salvation, and make it possible for them to come to believe. This belongs essentially to our Christianity not only as apostles but in our total life in the Church. It often seems, in this world, that people only want to make things difficult for each other, and consequently everyone is deeply impressed whenever he comes across truly disinterested generous love – charity, like a bright ray of light breaking through from another, higher world into our own. The result often is that a person is disarmed, and compelled to admit defeat. It is in cases like this that the essence of the Church, as the visible presence of grace in this world, is to be found, and that the Christian faith is seen, in concrete terms, to be worthy of human acceptance. Whenever saints and sanctity are no longer visible in the world, we begin to live in darkness. None the less, however painful this may be, we should not forget that even though there may be an insufficiency of visible grace present in and through the whole of Christian society, grace is all the same present and is able, as we have already said, to exert power in circumstances of impotence and misery. In this way the Church can be seen to be the lowly and submissive sacramental sign of the triumphant Christ. It is possible by means of this continual challenge to our faith to direct attention to the fact that the Church is not the work of human beings, but was instituted by God for humans' salvation, and this can even act as a motive for becoming a member of the Church.

Let us express our answer to the problem we have posed in the following way. There are only seven official sacraments, but there are numerous forms of sacramental expression within the life of the Church. It would be wrong to identify the life of the Church with that life which is confined within the bounds of the priesthood and the official sacraments. It is not exclusively from the sacraments that we derive grace – it also comes, for example, from fraternal contact between Christians and their treatment of each other and their fellow human beings; all this is included in practising the Church's pattern of life, and even 'receiving a sacrament'. Such contacts are certainly able to develop into a true conversion – a 'confession'. The seven sacraments are there precisely so that the sacramentalism of the Church, in its more extended sense, can be fully realised in everyday life. The truly Christian life in the midst of this world is – for other Christians – an external and meaningful supply of grace, dogma and preaching. Similarly, when non-Christians come into contact with those whose life is truly Christian, they are in fact coming up against the Church, as the visible and effective presence of grace in the world. It is through this kind of contact that they can be led to the full sacramental practice of Christianity, in which the Eucharist stands out as the point of centrality. It is true to say that, in one respect, there is a greater and more pressing need today for grace to be present and embodied in Christian life in this way – visibly present among people – than there is for a new and more modern form to be given to the Liturgy, in order to narrow the gap existing between it and the people. I feel sure that the first will lead to the second – that the visible presence of grace, embodied in the Christian way of life, will create a positive and dynamic force which will result in liturgical reform. After all, liturgies are not constructed – they develop organically from a renewed spirit. When this point has been reached, the sacraments will be able to exercise once again their true influence, which is of central importance in the life of the Church.

Since we have deliberately emphasised an aspect of the Church's pattern of life which is not usually stressed, it is important to bear in mind that the sacramental experience of Christian life, and thus the practice of Christianity in the more narrow sense of the word, occupies a central position in this way of life; the sacraments are at the very heart of Christianity. They are the centre core from which the Christian life stands out in relief. It is by these central sacraments too that the level of Christian experience which has already been reached is raised. It is also vital for day-to-day Christian activity to keep in close touch with the sacraments, if it is to be prevented from becoming grey, featureless and quite anonymous. Once the sacramental way of life is abandoned Christianity itself and, in the long run, any kind of 'ecclesiality' whatever, will be lost. Thus an element of truth can be found, deep down, in the rather colourless phrase so often used when referring to a Christian – 'a person who still practises his faith'. The sacramental experience is potentially the culminating point of all Christian experience. It is the apex of human contact with God, in the shape of a contact with human beings – in this case, a priest – for it should not be forgotten that no-one administers a sacrament to themselves, but that a sacrament is always administered by and to another person, a fellow human being. The sacrament thus forms the culminating point of the Church's appeal to us and bestowal of grace upon us, through the heavenly Christ who is present within her. Our stand as Christians in the world, our encounter with living Christianity through our contact with our fellow human beings, in other words our way of life as practising Catholics in the wider (but no less essential) sense of the word – all this has the effect of increasing our desire for the fullness and perfection of sacramental contact with the Church. What we must infer from this is, then, that it is the Christian way of life followed by the layfolk and priests within the Church – insofar as they also act as believers in their contact with each other and with their fellow human beings – which in fact leads to the hierarchical and liturgical way of life of the sacraments.

Everything is 'grace made visible'[5]

Christ's visible and efficacious presence in the Church calls to mind the image of a stone thrown into a pond, making ripples spread out in continuous concentric circles. The ripples flow in all directions from this one central point. This point is the Church, the visible presence of Christ's grace on earth, and from it all movement can be seen to flow. The sacrament of the Eucharist is situated at the heart of this central point – the Eucharist is the focal point of Christ's real presence among us. Around this focal point can be seen the first radiant lights – the other six sacraments. This central mystery is, however, revealed to us only through the medium of the Church's preaching. Instructed and enlightened by this sacrament of the word, our vision is extended, and we can see the whole wide, continuous sphere of the Church's sacramental life. Grace is made visible for us in the Christian life itself of the faithful members of the Church and comes forward to meet us, within this life, offering itself to us. These sacramental ripples, however, continue to spread still further, though they gradually become less and less clearly defined – at this stage they are the sacramentals. Still further away from the centre they merge into the reality of the

---

[5]Selected from: Edward Schillebeeckx, *Christ the Sacrament of the Encounter with God*, trans. Paul Barrett, N. D. Smith, Collected Works of Edward Schillebeeckx vol. 1 (London: Bloomsbury T&T Clark, 2014), 156–7 [267–8].

material and historical world of human beings, but this too is still under the influence of the triumphant *Kyrios*. In Christ, God ensures that everything will ultimately be for the good of those who love him. The sacraments, the word, all human conduct which proceeds from grace, the entire world of human beings – all these are, in their various ways, visible realities in this world of which the Lord avails himself, using his rich fund of inspiration in the most diverse means, to orientate human beings existentially towards God in Jesus Christ. The result of this, then, is that the grace of Christ does not make itself felt in us only in an inward manner; it comes to us also in a visible form. This is the abiding consequence of the incarnation of the Son of God, the mystery of God made human. The veil which conceals this mystery is drawn aside in the Martyrology at Christmas-time – *voluit consecrare mundum*. The Son's incarnation admits the world into a personal relationship between God and humanity and humanity and God. A close unity exists between 'inward' and 'outward' grace, but the whole created world becomes, through Christ's incarnation and the God-man relationship which is consequent upon it, an outward grace, an offer of grace in sacramental form. As a result of Christ's visible manifestation of himself in the world – a manifestation which embraces the whole world – the preaching and the sacraments of the Church can be regarded simply as the burning focal points within the entire concentration of this visible presence of grace which is the Church, for thanks to the Eucharist Christ is really *somatikos* – physically – present in her, and because of this physical presence also personally present.

Some modern perspectives on the Eucharist[6]

In my concluding section I now intend to examine, within this sacramental framework, the core of the theories called 'transfinalisation' and 'transignification' as interpretations of transubstantiation.[7] I will clarify the position of these theologians by referring to the well-known classic distinction: *sacramentum, res et sacramentum*, and *res sacramenti*. Applied to the sacrament of the eucharist, *sacramentum* is the consecrated bread and wine: these are *sacramenta-signa*. *Sacramentum et res* is the real presence of Christ in these *sacramenta-signa*. The *res sacramenti*, as the leading scholastics say, is the *communio ecclesiastica*, that is, the unity of the mystical body:

---

[6]Selected from: Edward Schillebeeckx, 'Transubstantiation, Transfinalization, Transignification', *Worship* 40, no. 6 (1966): 334–8.

[7]R. Masi ('Transustanziazione, transsignificazione, transfinalizzazione', *Osservatore Romano*, November 4, 1965, p. 5) affirms that according to these modern theologians the eucharistic change is only a psychological phenomenon, in such a way that the eucharistic presence is merely a symbolic presence. This is an implicit admission that he has not read the authors in question, and, even more, that he seems to identify the ontological with the physical. In *Osservatore Romano*, 13 September 1965, the Pope was reported as saying that these new theories were not 'vere e proprie eresie', but only that the encyclical 'avverte del grave pericolo cui le nuove opinioni espongono la retta fede'. But R. Masi concluded that they were true heresies because he himself interprets the anthropological approach of these theologians in the gnoseological perspective of the scholastic theory of sign, which is quite different from the modern 'anthropology of sign'.

the life of the community in Christ and, for the individual, the life of Christ in his soul, manifesting itself by an intimate sweetness, the *dulcedo eucharistica*.

Holy Scripture, the writings of the patristic age, and medieval scholasticism, in contrast to the theology of the post-Tridentine era, always emphasised the *res sacramenti*. Obviously, this presence of Christ in our hearts (*res sacramenti*) is brought about through the medium of the sacred host, and this implies the real presence of Christ in the host. Yet, the emphasis is placed not on the eucharistic presence but upon the purpose of this presence, the presence of Christ *in us*. It is for this purpose ultimately that the sacrament of the eucharist was instituted by Christ: *Institutum ut sumatur* (Council of Trent). Forced by circumstances and already preceded in this by medieval piety, post-Tridentine theology shifted the emphasis. The *res sacramenti* was pushed into the background, while the *res et sacramentum*, that is, the real presence in the sacred host, was emphasised so much that it seemed to be an end in itself and not a *res et sacramentum*, that is, totally oriented toward the *res ultima*: the growth of Christ in the heart of the Christian and in the community.

The consequence of this transfer of emphasis was that in popular piety devotion to the blessed sacrament was almost isolated from the context of the eucharistic celebration or of the holy mass. The blessed sacrament was adored; it was no longer eaten. Modern theologians, while accepting the real presence in the eucharist as well as the legitimacy of the adoration of Christ in the blessed sacrament, want only to replace the emphasis where the New Testament, the fathers, and the great scholastic theologians placed it, that is, on the *res sacramenti*, the end for which Christ instituted it. In my opinion, that is the central point of this whole new theology regarding the eucharist; and to a certain degree it is acknowledged by the *Constitution on the Sacred Liturgy*. What preoccupies these theologians is the eucharistic celebration and the active participation of the faithful, culminating in holy communion.

But this shift of emphasis has its repercussions on the concept of the eucharistic presence. Because the 'new' emphasis is concerned with the intimate presence of Christ in the hearts both of the individual believer and of the community of Christians, the eucharist must remain on the level of interpersonal relationship: of the presence of one person to another person. For human beings, each interpersonal presence is communicated by means of a spatial, visible, tangible, and even tasted presence. But in this case the spatial presence is integrated into the personal presence, that is, the body and the corporeal elements receive a new dimension: they become signs of a person who is present, signs which effect this presence, and signs which are real because they 'realise' this presence.

This is what is effected, in an infinitely, ontologically deeper way, in the intimate presence of Christ in our hearts by means of his real presence offered to us in bread and wine become sacramental food and drink. The 'real presence' must be viewed against the background of the saving act of Christ, who in this sacramental bread gives himself to us. Christ remains truly present in the sacred host before being received in communion, but always as an offer; it is a *praesentia oblata*. The presence becomes reciprocal – that is to say, presence in the full and completive human sense – only in the acceptance of this offered presence, and in that way it becomes the presence of Christ in our hearts, which is the very purpose of the eucharist. Only a eucharistic presence that is personally *offered and accepted* becomes an altogether complete presence. The presence of Christ in the tabernacle is therefore real, but as such it is only offered, and in this sense it is secondary in relation to the complete, reciprocal presence to which it is directed as to its end and perfection.

From this it follows that these theologians accept the real presence proper to the eucharist, but they do not want to place it outside of the context of an interpersonal relationship, even though this relationship is in fact accomplished by means of earthly things transformed in such a way that these things become a sign effecting the offer of this real presence. Here these theologians invoke an analogy or a comparison. When a housewife gives a party and serves her guests food and drink, the nourishment and beverages are assumed into an interpersonal relationship. They become a sign of the love and hospitality of the hostess. And she would take pains to see that the coffee or tea, for example, would be delicious so that in the excellence of the drink one might, so to speak, savour the love and the hospitality of the hostess. Recall how, especially in the Arab countries on the occasion of a visit, the preparation of tea or coffee becomes a ceremony in which honour and hospitality are at stake.

As a matter of fact, it was particularly these analogies and comparisons which raised many questions in Holland. Without any doubt analogies always limp. Still they express something of the symbol-making activity of man; in a practical way they give us an 'anthropology of sign'. But in the eucharist this anthropology is assumed into the dynamism of the Holy Spirit, the *Spiritus Creator* who effects the ontological depth of Christ's gift of self in the sacramental sign of bread. This gift of himself in and through the bread and wine transsubstantialises the bread and wine in their proper being.

Some persons ridiculed these theologians, saying that the eucharist means no more to them than the loving gesture of someone who gives his friend a piece of chocolate! However, these theologians have only reacted against a eucharistic materialism, whereas in the eucharist we ought to be concerned with an interpersonal relationship between Christ and us, an interpersonal relationship in which Christ gives himself to humanity by means of bread and wine which, by this very gift, have undergone a transfinalisation and an ontological and therefore radical transignification. The bread and wine have become this real presence offered by Christ, who gave his life for us on the cross; offered by Christ in order that we might participate in this sacrifice and in the new covenant which is life for us all. The chemical, physical, or botanical reality of bread and wine is not changed; otherwise, Christ would not be present under the sign of eatable bread and drinkable wine. Eucharistic sacramentality demands precisely that the physical reality does not change, otherwise there would no longer be a eucharistic sign. But in its ontological reality, to the question 'What is this bread ultimately, what is this wine ultimately?' one can no longer answer, 'Bread and wine', but instead, 'The real presence of Christ offered under the sacramental sign of bread and wine.' Therefore, the *reality* (that is, the *substance*, because that is the meaning of 'substance') which is before me, is no longer bread and wine, but the real presence of Christ offered to me under the sign of food and drink. This is precisely what the Holy Father said in his encyclical *Mysterium Fidei*: 'After transubstantiation has taken place, the species of bread and wine undoubtedly take on a new meaning and a new finality, for they no longer remain ordinary bread and ordinary drink, but become the sign of something sacred, and the sign of a spiritual food. However, the reason they take on the new significance and this new finality is simply because they contain a new 'reality' which we may justly term ontological.'[8] In other words, the encyclical admits transfinalisation and transignification on condition that they are not considered as an extrinsic designation or as a peripheral change, but rather as having a profound and ontological content. That is the very meaning of the dogma of transubstantiation. *Vanum videtur contendere de nominibus ubi constat de rebus* (S. Thomas, *Responsum 9 ad Lectorem Venetum*).

Opus operatum and opus operantis[9]

My main aim in this subsection is to find a new way of closing the traditional gap between the *opus operatum*, the objective side of the sacrament, and the *opus operantis*, its subjective side, even more fundamentally than I tried to do in 1952 in my book, *De sacramentele heilseconomie*.[10] The *opus operantis* is intrinsically part of the *opus operatum*, for the two aspects combined are the actual performance that mediates God's gratuitous condescension and are not tagged on to it afterwards. The *opus operantis* is the *opus operatum*, though I would not put it the other way round, as if the *opus operatum* were the work of whoever performs it. In the first place I want to avoid the casuistry of the distinction between a 'valid' and a 'fruitful' sacrament that can lead to disastrously over-generalised conclusions. Secondly, I want to uphold the insight that in the *opus operatum* (of which the *opus operantis* is an essential part) God's free, gratuitous gift is decisive: through devoutly experienced, human ritual performances – independently of human merit – it allows participants in the liturgy to share in the abundance of God's goodwill.

The traditional division between the objective and subjective sides of a sacrament actually derives from Augustine of Hippo, who made a sharp distinction between a valid (*validum*) and a fruitful (*fructuosum*) sacrament. That happened at a time when his reaction to the doctrinal aberrations of the Donatists (who maintained that the personal integrity of the officiant affected the quality of the sacrament) put him in a dilemma and he could find no solution other than this distinction. At the time, in view of its theological potential, it was an extremely opportune solution and served its purpose. Historically, however, it led to a gradual, almost magical attenuation of the sacraments, especially in the eucharistic liturgy. In the tenth and eleventh centuries, for instance, farmers used to take a consecrated host with them from church to bury in their fields, expecting it to ensure a bounteous harvest. The

---

[8] 'Peracta transsubstantiatione, species panis et vini novam proculdubio induunt significationem, novumque finem, cum amplius non sint communis panis et communis potus, sed *signum rei sacrae signumque* spiritualis alimoniae; sed ideo novam induunt significationem et novum finem quia novam continent realitatem, quam merito ontologicam dicimus'. (Encyclical Letter *Mysterium Fidei* [3 September 1965]. English translation published by the National Catholic Welfare Conference, Washington, D.C.)
[9] Selected from: Edward Schillebeeckx, 'Towards a Rediscovery of the Christian Sacraments: Ritualising Religious Elements in Daily Life', *Essays: Ongoing Theological Quests*, Collected Works of Edward Schillebeeckx vol. 11 (London: Bloomsbury T&T Clark, 2014), 200–3.
[10] See *De sacramentele heilseconomie: Theologische bezinning op S. Thomas' sacramentenleer in het licht van de traditie en van de hedendaagse sacramentsproblematiek*, I, part II, section I, 561–619 (tr.: *L'économie sacramentelle du salut*, Fribourg, 2004, 455ff.).

theology current at that time, based on a crudely realistic physicalism, offered only vague, if far-fetched, legitimation for this practice; at any rate the local church leadership, often with minimal theological training, tacitly permitted it.

Linking 'sign' with causation: a categorical error

Some empirical anthropological studies of ritual rightly criticise the physicalist approach of traditional Catholic sacramental theology, at any rate as it was practiced since the Middle Ages. The fact that Thomas Aquinas in particular made his own contribution in this regard, however, is often overlooked. To be sure, one must concede that he, too, used categories derived from physics. One need merely recall his use of hylomorphic theory, with its distinction between *materia* and *forma*, as a framework to make Augustine's famous proposition, *Accedit verbum ad elementum et fit sacramentum* (by adding the word to the element – e.g. water or oil – a 'sacrament' comes about), intelligible in Aristotelian terms. In this hylomorphic philosophical framework a human ritual action, with or without the use of an object (laying on of hands, sprinkling with water), linked with a ritual formula (e.g. 'I baptise you in the name of...') becomes, through the objective operation of the rite (*ex opere operato*), the instrumental 'cause' of grace, in the same way that a physical cause has a physical effect. If one faults Thomas for this, one is forgetting the traditional premise of his entire sacramental theology, namely that sacraments belong in the category of signs (*sacramentum est in genere signi*), that is of symbolic reference and representation – though one must concede that, particularly in his eucharistic theology, Thomas did not consistently adhere to this premise because of his choice, all but unavoidable in his day, of the physicalist model of matter and form, especially in regard to the conjunction of cause and sign. At the very least locating sacraments in the category of signs implies that their salvific action has nothing to do with physics or physical change. Even what Thomas calls eucharistic transubstantiation – indeed philosophically non-Aristotelian, in the sense that 'substance' is divorced from its 'accidents' – he considers proper to the category of symbolic signs, hence not referring to any physical changes in the bread and the wine. It shows that, whereas he does use the hylomorphic model, he prefers to interpret the instrumental causation of the sacraments non-physically, that is, analogously. In the Middle Ages there was simply no alternative to such an identification of the operation of the sacraments with physical instrumental causation. To complicate matters further, in our late modern era the use of both these concepts – causation and sign – have become philosophically suspect, especially among analysts of language.

This critical suspicion and semiotic difficulty are compounded by the fact that theology – as was almost unavoidable in the Middle Ages, given the lack of phenomenological and semiotic insights – conjoined the two problematic concepts in a formulation, brilliant for its day: '*significando causant*'; that is to say, through the dynamism of their signification the sacraments 'causally' mediate God's readiness to extend grace and the resultant forgiving, healing and sanctifying blessedness. In a different philosophical framework, however, the performative signification of a religious ritual as a whole is sufficient; anthropologically the sacraments have no need whatever of a supplementary instrumental cause transcending the efficacious ritual of the Christian faith. The meaningful ritual in its entirety, being the human expression and vehicle of (ecclesial and individual) religious inspiration of all participants, *is* the actual gift of grace.

In later times Thomist epigones, and subsequent modern theological textbooks even more so, have by no means interpreted the application of hylomorphism to the sacraments analogously. Some textbooks went so far as to look for some mysterious transformation of the atoms and molecules in the eucharistic bread and wine. In the process the distinctive character of metaphoric action and symbolic speech was totally disregarded. In short, the peculiar meaning, structure and 'aim' or intention of symbolic activity and ritual were overlooked, particularly the fact that one has to invoke symbolic language and metaphoric actions to articulate and actualise the reality of grace;[11] after all, we can never express that dynamic reality in terms of our meagre terminology or our conceptual, controlling and 'objectifying' knowledge. The ritual event as a significatory expression surpasses pure reason not downwards from above, but upwards from below: rituality has its own logical rationality, but that rationality cannot be located or pinned down with a measuring rod. Hence rather than speak of 'healthy irrationality', as has been proposed, one could call it trans-rationality.[12] The 'operation' coming from God and the 'operation' upwards from below (coming from the faithful believers) is one and the same *opus operatum*, for the ecclesial and personal faith of the Christian participant in the sacramental liturgy is still embedded in the 'ritual performance' itself.

Sacraments and rituals[13]

Hence the sacraments have two dimensions: one anthropological, the other – merging with it – a 'theologal' one, focused on God. In the *sacramenta fidei ecclesiae* the vision of God's active kingdom – our letting God's work be done in our daily living – is ritualised. There God's world and the human world are intended, as one reality. Our spatiotemporal human world is God's world. But to us God's cause is a

---

[11] Some scholars hold the view that metaphors do not deal in truth, but to my mind metaphors are very much concerned with the relation between meaning, thought (in concepts and images) and reality. In religious (especially Christian or sacramental) ritual, too, the cognitive relationship remains a vital ingredient, which should not be papered over, under pressure from the new notion of performative efficacy, with 'anti-intellectualist' emotion. Concern about the 'cognitive relationship' of propositions, metaphoric or otherwise, has nothing to do with intellectualism; that would be the case only if it entailed suppressing all other relations or not giving them their due.

[12] This debate can also turn into a battle of words. What many scholars now call trans-rationality is worked out by Thomas as *intellectus*, the antithesis and implicit basis of conceptualizing and analytical ratio. In Thomas's thinking *intellectus* (hence intellectualism) means something very different from rationalism and even includes more than 'intentional knowing'. It also embraces all inner life, which in the medieval classification of human faculties was not included under *ratio*, even though Thomas was sufficiently familiar with the interrelationship or *circuminsessio* of human faculties. One would have to circumscribe the current usage of 'intellectualism' somewhat more accurately.

[13] Selected from: Edward Schillebeeckx, 'Towards a Rediscovery of the Christian Sacraments: Ritualising Religious Elements in Daily Life', *Essays: Ongoing Theological Quests*, Collected Works of Edward Schillebeeckx vol. 11 (London: Bloomsbury T&T Clark, 2014), 205–8.

human cause. What is close to people's hearts is also close to God: it is his concern. Thus, on the one hand, there is the so-called profane level of everyday life where people and the world converge, in which we perceive flashes and facets of the active God – what we call our day-to-day Christian life with its worldly tasks. And on the other hand there are the sacraments and the liturgy as a whole, in which we ritualise what transpires, both every day and not every day, both joyous and tragic. Ordinary actions are 'interrupted', in the sense that, at given times, such everyday behavioural complexes are stylised and, up to a point, fixed in symbolic movements. The ritual material is intrinsic to our very humanity; Christian faith is its soul and dynamic inspiration

Scholarly studies of ritual have shown me that rituals are an existential, ludic interpretation of existentially relevant actions, whether religious or profane – postures, gestures, forms of behaviour, protocols, eating customs, marriage customs – expressed in a culturally specific manner and embedded in specific cultural, social and even political structures. To my mind these scholars – because of understandable irritation with presumptuous intellectualism – lose sight of the fact that in its own way the dynamics of a ritual performance also refers to knowledge. After all, the logic of metaphoric, symbolic actions is not the same logic that forms the premise of modern, scientific manipulation of matter, and hence of relations of cause and effect.

As mentioned already, ritual has two components: the *legomenon* or words in many forms – messages, promises, admonition and exhortation, stories of the living Jesus, et cetera – and the *drômenon*, comprising gestures, music, chanting, silence, objects like bread, wine, incense, candles, light as well as spatial arrangement and the liturgical order or *taxis* which, as Paul tells us in 1 Corinthians 14.40, should prevail in any authentic, proper liturgy. These two components jointly constitute ritual or, in a Christian sense, sacrament. Hence the latter is a single, indivisible, performative, dynamic and meaningful happening executed in word and actions, in silence and song, in light and incense – in short, in playful earnest. *To Christians this ritual totality itself is God's means of grace, actualised at a cognitive, emotional and aesthetic level, in and via the inherent performative power of liturgical celebration inspired by the Christian faith.* Just as the performance of, say, a musical score can, *via the performance*, evoke and genuinely bring to life something in the performers, so in sacramental liturgy the salvific action accomplishes efficaciously (*efficax*) what it intends! Only then the ambiguous and abstract classical axiom that a sacrament is an efficacious sign of grace (*signum efficax gratiae*) is truly justified. This interpretation is indeed far removed from so-called physical, instrumental causation, however analogously it is understood. Both anthropologically and religiously causation in this sense falls wholly outside the richly textured signification that is peculiar to (sacramental or other) ritual. This active signification with its performative efficacy is operative already at the anthropological level of a genuine liturgical performance.

Hence the gift of grace is not a vertical addendum to the liturgical celebration, in the sense of a sort of superstructure. Human symbolic celebration of the church's faith by a celebrating community and being supported by it are God's gift of grace, not something that is added to it. The Christian faith of all participants in ritual liturgy (as the local representation here and now of what, fundamentally, the universal church confesses worldwide) is nonetheless the essence of all this, and at the same time the conduit of God's act in Jesus Christ; he, after all, is the 'pioneer and perfecter of our faith' (Heb 12.2), the faith of God's church in the sense of the assembled religious community, the *ecclesia,* aptly expressed by the term 'congregation': God's congregation as gathered in the church for liturgical celebration.

A perception of the sacraments based on the ideas of semiotics, the linguistic sciences and ethno-cultural anthropology has far-reaching implications, particularly for pastoral theology. It also explains why, by and large, traditional sacramental practice no longer works, and why the Christian faith is increasingly questioned by Christian believers themselves – the result not so much of declining religious feeling or religious needs as of outdated religious images, because neither religion nor the sacraments are embedded in a socio-cultural environment that is authentically rooted in the here and now (even though critical detachment from, and even protest against, that real-life environment may sometimes be warranted). Sacramental phenomena cannot be reduced to physical events. Sacramental grace is not designed for physical consumption. Sacraments belong in the category of symbols or signs, but in the full compass of height and depth, length and breadth of the wealth of meaning – cognitive, emotional and aesthetic – that the cultural human sciences have deciphered in what is known as ritual or symbolic activity: a playful yet serious activity that approximates the concrete density of reality more accurately than dogmatic formulas and doctrinal pronouncements (which does not mean that the latter are not also needed as always provisional – being culturally and historically restricted – definitions of certain uninfringeable horizons, especially when the church's religious life is in crisis).

Only when the contributions of the various cultural anthropological sciences have been interpreted theologically does it become clear – unlike in the past – that sacraments are an existentially emotive encounter with God in Christ Jesus. Such an approach is primarily a way of deepening symbolic praxis as a special way to 'knowledge of God' that is more accurate than purely theoretical, thematic knowledge of God (even though the church cannot do without such knowledge either). Over the centuries the gospel message has, on the whole, been communicated to believers more emotionally, more sensitively and especially more vividly by sacramental liturgy and depictions in the liturgical space of churches and cathedrals than by theoretical doctrines. The sacraments involve both the expression and the construction and growth of a fundamental identity of Christians and Christian communities or churches, and of the 'ecumenical', universal church.

In sacramental liturgy we celebrate the Christian dream of God's kingdom proleptically, in anticipation. That kingdom, the basis of the celebrations in the Christian community, is also actualised fragmentarily in an openness to eschatological liberation and salvation, which entails more than individual or socio-political liberation. In fact, ritual celebrations show how God's footmarks in Christians' profane engagement are the *presupposition* of their sacramental celebrations, and how these celebrations – the occasions when Christians are *nourished by God* in and via Jesus in the power of Christ's Spirit – in their turn give courage, orientation and inspiration for their earthly endeavours, to which the liturgy returns them. Thus the eschatological vision of God's kingdom transcends both actual Christian praxis in the world and Christian ritual or sacramental celebration. Yet the anticipatory or proleptic realisation of the eschatological kingdom through both profane endeavour and liturgical celebration falls under the proviso of God's surprising judgment, which in this respect, too, is always new to us.

The Christian sacraments effect an encounter with God in a special way. To Christians that truly makes Jesus Christ the 'sacrament of the encounter with God', thus endorsing Tertullian's dictum, '*caro salutis est cardo*': corporeality is the pivot of salvation. This applies particularly to sacramental ritual, as a protest against the evil, absurdity and sinfulness in our worldly lives, and at the same time a festive celebration of the encounter with God already realised in that 'profane' life, *especially* in encounters with fellow human beings. That, at bottom, is the meaning of Tertullian's dictum.

Selected literature

- Sacramental and Extra-Sacramental Grace; Selected from: Edward Schillebeeckx, *Christ the Sacrament of the Encounter with God*, trans. Paul Barrett, N. D. Smith, Collected Works of Edward Schillebeeckx vol. 1 (London: Bloomsbury T&T Clark, 2014), 143–5 [244–8].
- The Church as the Sign of God's Grace on Earth; Selected from: Edward Schillebeeckx, *Christ the Sacrament of the Encounter with God*, trans. Paul Barrett, N. D. Smith, Collected Works of Edward Schillebeeckx vol. 1 (London: Bloomsbury T&T Clark, 2014), 146–9 [249–54].
- The Sacramental Life of the Church; Selected from: Edward Schillebeeckx, *Christ the Sacrament of the Encounter with God*, trans. Paul Barrett, N. D. Smith, Collected Works of Edward Schillebeeckx vol. 1 (London: Bloomsbury T&T Clark, 2014), 151–4 [258–64].
- Everything is 'Grace Made Visible'; Selected from: Edward Schillebeeckx, *Christ the Sacrament of the Encounter with God*, trans. Paul Barrett, N. D. Smith, Collected Works of Edward Schillebeeckx vol. 1 (London: Bloomsbury T&T Clark, 2014), 156–7 [267–8].
- Some Modern Perspectives on the Eucharist; Selected from: Edward Schillebeeckx, 'Transubstantiation, Transfinalization, Transignification', *Worship*, 40, no. 6 (1966): 334–8.
- Opus operatum and opus operantis; Selected from: Edward Schillebeeckx, 'Towards a Rediscovery of the Christian Sacraments: Ritualising Religious Elements in Daily Life', *Essays: Ongoing Theological Quests*, Collected Works of Edward Schillebeeckx vol. 11 (London: Bloomsbury T&T Clark, 2014), 200–3.
- Sacraments and Rituals; Selected from: Edward Schillebeeckx, 'Towards a Rediscovery of the Christian Sacraments: Ritualising Religious Elements in Daily Life', *Essays: Ongoing Theological Quests*, Collected Works of Edward Schillebeeckx vol. 11 (London: Bloomsbury T&T Clark, 2014), 205–8.

12

Theological Anthropology

Unique universality: universal appeal of 'what is worthy of humanity'[1]

For a reality to have universal significance means that it affects every person's definition of the ultimate purpose of his life, in other words that his or her destiny is determined by a real and – given our freedom freely accepted reference to this universal value. It is a reality that imparts universal meaning, but one has to experience it as meaningful if it is to have that effect. In other words, the universal meaning which may emerge in a real-life situation has no concrete substance if we fail to recognise it personally as an appeal directed to our inquiring minds. Through personal motivation that universal value can become fascinating in its own right. Thus we ourselves decide the meaning and purpose of our lives on the basis of universal values manifested in real life.

The problem confronting us is this. Can such unique universality be found and identified in one historical person, Jesus of Nazareth? Put differently, does this person, Jesus of Nazareth, confessed by his disciples in his lifetime as the Christ, Son of God and Lord, still have meaning for us today in the sense that we, too, can find definitive, ultimate wellbeing and salvation in him? The underlying problem is bound up with the question of how a particular historical event can have universal significance for all human beings, hence also for us today. If this is at all possible, it seems to require a historical intermediary.

Finding the meaning of one's life in constitutive reference to Jesus of Nazareth is manifestly a religious quest, that is, a way of determining the overall meaning of life. 'Religious' refers to humanity's relation to the whole and, ultimately, to the living God; it also refers to God in his relation to humanity. A religious statement, then, always entails both anthropological and theological discourse: it is a way of speaking about humanity and God, all in one. This intrinsically implies that a religious statement can only have universal significance for everyone if it can be verified at least to some

---

[1] Selected from: Edward Schillebeeckx, *Jesus: An Experiment in Christology*, trans. John Bowden, Collected Works of Edward Schillebeeckx vol. 6 (London: Bloomsbury T&T Clark, 2014), 565–7 [602–4].

extent, that is, if it can be showed that the believer's affirmation of God's universal love for people a directly non-empirical reality – also discloses true humanity – an empirical, demonstrable fact.

Thus the question of Jesus' unique universality encompasses two interrelated poles: on the one hand, unveiling the true face of God, on the other disclosing the true nature of humanity, in such a way that the former is achieved via the latter. The one true, living God becomes a shadowy abstraction, universally unattainable, unless at the same time the true face of humanity emerges in the religious reality and the discourse about it. Only by respecting this fundamental structure of religious discourse can a claim to universality have intrinsic evidential value which distinguishes it from ideological pretension. In that case the best approach to the distinctive nature of Jesus of Nazareth and his universal significance seems to be not to approach him either from a preconceived notion of what it means to be God or of what it means to be human, hence a human person. It is not a matter of fitting together two models or concepts – 'human being' and 'divine being' so as to arrive at a conceivable (or inconceivable) 'amalgam' of a God-man, at the perhaps abstractly conceivable model of 'God made man', for which Jesus of Nazareth might have been a historical occasion. Turning to Jesus to find salvation in him means approaching him in a state of not knowing, or rather of 'open knowledge' of the true meaning of humanity and divinity alike, maybe to learn from him the true nature *via* their interrelationship as manifested in Jesus. Naturally we have certain conceptions of both God and a human being, as the Jews had when they encountered Jesus. Jesus himself belonged to the tradition of the Yahwistic, Jewish experience of God. This preconceived understanding is in no sense denied. But we are required to be open to Jesus' own interpretive experience of the reality of God which he manifests in his humanity.

Of course, the question about Jesus' unique universal significance can only be answered in faith, either positively or negatively. Hence a positive answer essentially has theological relevance; it cannot be simply historical. On the other hand religious statements must have some basis in the history of Jesus; if not, they would be unrelated to reality and therefore ideological. Hence the historical reality of Jesus must have communicated something which people could, might and in the end were compelled to articulate in those religious statements. That something must have been historical, namely that anyone who saw Jesus had indeed seen the Father. Had the gap between these two planes been too great, Christianity would never have stood a chance.[2] On the other hand religious affirmations are always vulnerable in the face of historical findings. Put differently, Jesus' unique universality cannot be historically demonstrated either on the basis of Jesus of Nazareth or through systematic comparison of the world religions. What we have is an affirmation of Christian faith which claims to accord with reality although that claim is itself an act of faith.

Yet if we affirm a reality, albeit in religious language that is, something which is not constituted by us (as believers) but which actually evokes our affirmation and

---

[2] J. A. T. Robinson, 'Need Jesus Have Been Perfect', in *Christ, Faith, History: Cambridge Studies in Christology* (London: Cambridge University Press, 1972), 39–52, 48.

constitutes it as an act of faith then this historical reality must form the basis of what we say in religious language and at the same time give substance to it. Otherwise our claim would be ideological. In my view, then, the plausibility of the Christian creed can be proven in two ways only: (a) through historical study of Jesus' baptism, his words and deeds, life and death and establishing their possible meaning, and (b) by showing how the Christian claim to universality is actualised in the true humanity that confronts us in the person of Jesus of Nazareth. Although 'true humanity' is not a concept that can be fully rationalised since its actual substance implies a specific option and viewpoint, one can say that the Christian claim to universality will have to be proved on the evidence of a real-life manifestation of such humanity. What is at issue is the intrinsic relationship between Jesus of Nazareth and the kingdom of God *and* the salvation and happiness of humanity. In modern terms, the point at issue is the transcendent manifestation of what sociologists call 'significant others'.

The humanum we seek[3]

An inquiry into a particular fellow human being's existential significance for humanity immediately calls for a distinction between (a) people who in whatever way have been confronted in history with the Jesus movement, and (b) people who have never heard of Jesus, or have heard something about him but in a social or personal situation that precluded any real confrontation. The real problem is with the first of these alternatives. If that can be meaningfully resolved, it would provide all the data necessary to find a (missiological) solution to the second alternative as well.

An anthropological truth that can hardly be denied is that every person is a fellow human being, receiving and giving in a larger whole of diverse widening circles which ultimately encompass all humanity. Ultimately, therefore, a person can only be understood in the context of the whole, where he has uniquely personal, irreplaceable meaning. The human face which we ourselves never see, and which seems to be there to be looked at by others and to prove our openness to the other, plainly symbolises our fundamental dependence on and orientation to others.

Christologically this in itself is an interesting fact; but it is a universally human structure, not a distinctive feature of Jesus of Nazareth. Being human for others is a task built into the structure of our 'human constitution' – which is not to say that we actually do much about it. Hence the question of the concrete realisation of this 'being human for others' is very pertinent to Jesus of Nazareth; but it becomes Christologically relevant only when the personally unique, particular realisation is of such a nature that it becomes a point of reference for the total or definitive meaning of every human life. That is why Jesus as a human being for others is an important presupposition and prerequisite for any meaningful, more precise qualification of his Christological uniqueness.

---

[3]Selected from: Edward Schillebeeckx, *Jesus: An Experiment in Christology*, trans. John Bowden, Collected Works of Edward Schillebeeckx vol. 6 (London: Bloomsbury T&T Clark, 2014), 568–9 [606–7].

An explanation which seeks insight into Jesus' Christological significance only in the fact that he verbalised and practised profound, universally human yet simple things accessible to all in such way that they continue to challenge and summon all people of goodwill in search of true humanity, is also correct; its claim is historically demonstrable and accepted even by non-Christians. It is also a presupposition and precondition for making Jesus' Christological or universal importance professed in the church's credal statements meaningful and intelligible. Yet other works in the world's religious literature by or about 'founders' of existing religions can make a similar claim. A call to authentic humanity indeed, every good deed manifestly has universal significance (with due regard to the inevitable pluralism and socio-historical situation in which that authentic humanity has to be realised here and now). The fact that everything of worth in a human being does not have to differentiate her from other people, but can actually unite her with them[4] is a truth which we often no longer dare utter aloud lest we seem 'odd'. But does such a universal appeal to humanity uniquely manifested in Jesus reflect his full historical reality? If it refers solely to his uniqueness, it may actually obscure his true originality and uniqueness. After all, our analysis of his message regarding God's reign and his praxis showed that Jesus' cause was certainly the cause of humanity but as the cause of *God*. In other words, we do not get to Jesus' real uniqueness if we ignore what was closest to his heart: a God mindful of humanity. Jesus' relationship with God, then, has to be an essential part of the argument.

God does not want humanity to suffer[5]

In theory, people may not be in a position to *explain* suffering and evil, but the *remembrance* of what has happened in very specific suffering in a particular historical context also belongs to the structure of human reason or critical rationality.[6] The story of these specific remembrances therefore remains an inner stimulus for practical reason which seeks to be liberating and active. Human reason may not simply brush aside these admonitory remembrances if it still wants to remain *critical* reason.

The only question is whether at the same time this implies that the practical task with which people find themselves confronted as a result of the many accounts of contrast experiences in our history of human suffering can also in fact be brought to a successful conclusion. For human action in resistance against evil is itself subject to criticism, at least in its claim to totality – not through any theory, much less through religious and Christian faith, but through a specific reality of experience, part of human life: the tension between 'nature' and 'history' which makes up human transitory life and can never be removed, a dialectic of which death is merely an

---

[4]Thus, rightly, P. Schoonenberg, in *Geloof bij kenterend getij: peilingen in een seculariserend christendom*, Roermond-Maaseik 1967, 178.
[5]Selected from: Edward Schillebeeckx, *Christ: The Christian Experience in the Modern World*, Collected Works of Edward Schillebeeckx vol. 7 (London: Bloomsbury T&T Clark, 2014), 719–24 [726–30].
[6]See J.-B. Metz, 'La théologie a "l'âge critique"', in *Le service théologique dans l'Église, Mélanges offerts à Y. Congar*, Paris 1974, 131–48, 145.

extreme exponent, the boundary situation. Thus at the deepest level, at the level of our outline of an earthly, human future, we are at the same time confronted with the final fiasco of our efforts at resisting evil. Death above all shows that we are deluded if we think that we can realise on earth a true, perfect and universal salvation for all and for every individual. However, human salvation is only salvation, being whole, when it is universal and complete. There cannot really be talk of salvation as long as there is still suffering, oppression and unhappiness alongside the personal happiness that we experience, in our immediate vicinity or further afield. All this means that we cannot look for the *ground* of suffering in God, although suffering brings the believer directly up against God.

Some theologians want to base the necessity of redemption by God on the theologically questionable insight that God himself is the one starting point of both the giving of life and the destroying of life; the permanent crisis of our human existence has its basis in the paradox of God – *fascinosum* and *tremendum*. The starting point for the justification of our life is at the same time also that for the endangering of our life, namely God himself.[7] I do not want to deny that this is a fundamental conception in many religions, beginning with that of Israel. Numerous texts from the Old Testament could support this conception: Yahweh is a God 'who kills and restores to life' (2 Sam 2.6). However, I pointed out earlier that in the long run Israel itself rejected this primitive conception of God. God is pure positivity; he wills the life of the sinner and not his death. In the beginning, God was regarded as the principle of life and death. The correct intuition here was that the believer was thus guarding himself against a metaphysical dualism which ascribed the good to God and the evil to a 'first principle' of evil. Such a view cannot in fact be reconciled with a generally religious belief in God and especially with Yahwistic belief. If God is defined as equally the 'power of life-giving' and the 'power of annihilation' in one, this undeniably cuts at the root of the critical and productive force of religion. For in that case, God's whim decides whether salvation or destruction has the last word. God's freedom, which is beyond human control, then becomes defined, in all too human terms, as a *finite freedom to decide* between good and evil.

If we recognise the correct intuition in the anti-dualism of this ancient Hebrew conception of God, which can also be found in religions generally, we must also recognise the correct intuition in Persian dualism, namely that 'God' cannot solely be pure positivity, the 'first principle' of good and in no way the *ground* of any evil. God is the author of the good and the opponent of evil, but in that case it becomes necessary to look for a non-dualistic 'ground' for evil.

It is well worth remembering that faith does not disqualify human reason and its liberating practice in order to claim the honour of being able to offer a correct solution once reason has conceded defeat. For religious belief does not blame human beings for their ultimate theoretical impotence and their practical failures in the face of evil and suffering. This bitter insight, this 'accusation', stems from our own human experience and critical reason. By contrast, religious belief seeks to rescue us from

---

[7]This is the main argument of R. Schaeffler, *Religion und kritisches Bewusstsein*, Freiburg-Munich 1973, which to my mind is incomprehensible. Of course it is a definition of God in certain religions, but it is certainly not the Christian concept of God.

this fatal experience and give our action new meaning by breaking its impotence in the light of a new possibility *from* God: thanks to the proclamatory reminiscence of Jesus as the story of a crucified person who is now alive, through whom a future is given to those who have come to grief in history, even those who (for the moment) are victors at the expense of the defeated.

The Christian message does not give an *explanation* of evil or our history of suffering. That must be made clear from the start. Even for Christians, suffering remains impenetrable and incomprehensible, and provokes rebellion. Nor will the Christian blasphemously claim that God himself required the death of Jesus as compensation for what *we* make of our history. This sadistic mysticism of suffering is certainly alien to the most authentic tendencies of the great Christian tradition, at the very least. Nor can one follow Jürgen Moltmann[8] in solving the problem of suffering by 'eternalising' suffering in God, in the opinion that in the last resort this gives suffering some splendour. According to Moltmann, Jesus not only shows solidarity 'with publicans and sinners', with the outcast and those who are everywhere excluded; not only, in this line, has God himself identified Jesus with the outcast; no, God himself has cast him out as a sacrifice for our sins. The difficulty in this conception is that it ascribes to God what has in fact been done to Jesus by the history of human injustice. Hence I think that in soteriology or the doctrine of redemption this approach puts us on a false trail, despite the deep and correct insight that God is the great fellow-sufferer, who is concerned for our history.

I think that at this point it would be good to resort to Thomas Aquinas. True, in reality on this matter he is seldom understood and little studied, and he did not apply his fundamental philosophical or theological principle consistently to Christian soteriology. However, he does seem to me one of the few people who can give us some reasonably satisfactory viewpoints which at the same time leave all the darkness in its incomprehensibility. More than anyone else, Thomas stresses the priority of the all-determining, positive 'first causality' of God. On the one hand as a theologian he dares to write: 'The first cause of the lack of grace lies in us';[9] and on the other, as a philosopher: 'Although God is the creative cause of our (human) will – i.e. the one who calls up out of nothing – this will has this 'being from nothing' from no one other than itself; and precisely for that reason the defects of the will which follow from a creaturely deficiency may not be carried back to a further or higher cause';[10] here we have finitude, as it were, as 'the first cause'. As soon as there are *creatures*, there is the *possibility* (not the necessity) of a negative and original *initiative of finitude*, if I can put it that way.

In a system of thought which seems somewhat alien to us, then, Thomas expresses deep insights into life which, without making the history of human suffering understandable in theory – i.e., without harmonising it with God's Godness or

---

[8] J. Moltmann, *The Crucified God*, London and New York 1974; it must, however, be conceded that here Moltmann argues in a very Lutheran way. See also T. van Bavel, 'De lijdende God', *Tijdschrift voor theologie*, 14 (1974), 131–50.

[9] "*Defectus gratiae*, prima causa *est ex nobis*' (*Summa Theologiae* I-II, q. 112, a. 3, ad 2).

[10] '*Quamvis Deus sit causa voluntatis faciens eam ex nihilo, hoc tamen quod est* ex nihilo esse *non habeat ab alio, sed a se; et idea defectus qui sequitur eam secundum quod est ex nihilo*, non oportet quod in ulteriorem causam reducatur' (in *II Sent.* d. 37, q. 2, a. 1, ad 2).

our positive humanity – nevertheless point to the unfathomable depths in which they have to be put: on the one hand the incomprehensible depth of the mystery of God, and on the other hand the negative depth of what finitude and finite freedom can involve. For Thomas, it is a senseless philosophical undertaking to look for a particular cause, a ground or motive for evil and suffering in God; these do not necessarily follow from our finitude, but they do draw their fundamental possibility from there. *Negativity* cannot have a cause or a motive in God. But in that case we cannot look for a divine *reason* for the death of Jesus either. Therefore, first of all, we have to say that we are not redeemed *thanks to* the death of Jesus but *despite* it.

On the other hand, it cannot really be claimed that the Creator God remains as it were without awareness of what finite and free people can make of their history in a finite world and nature. The enormity of the fact confronts us: a history of suffering which has broken many human hearts. The 'initiative' of finitude (I put initiative in quotation marks), namely an initiative which at its extreme origin, albeit in deficiency, *begins exclusively* from the finite without any contribution from God's side, such a negative initiative which plays an *incidental* part *in* human life that is positively supported by God, does not, however, checkmate God: in my view, at any rate, we do not know this from a general 'concept of God' but from the 'God of Jesus', namely from Christian belief in the *resurrection* of Jesus. For it emerges that God transcends these negative aspects in our history, not so much by allowing them as *by overcoming them*, making them as though they had not happened. By nature, and in addition to other aspects and meanings, the resurrection of Jesus is also a corrective, a victory over the negativity of suffering and even death. From the point of view of the Christian Bible, for anyone who thinks historically it is not a question of 'divine permission' for evil and unmerited suffering (this is the initiative of finitude), but of God's *victory* over this particular initiative of the finite. Only *in* the overcoming of it can we say that the negative aspects in our history have an indirect role in God's plan of salvation: *God is the Lord of history.* That is why Mark 8.31 could say intuitively, 'The Son of Man *must* suffer many things.' We shall never be able to give a reason (any more than Mark could) for the significance for salvation history of this improper expression 'the divine must'. On the one hand it contains the insight that humanity is redeemed by Jesus *despite* the death of Jesus, seen as negativity and the human rejection of Jesus from our midst, one of the many exponents of our history of suffering. On the other side, however, this 'despite' is so transcended by God, not because he permits it in condescension but because through the resurrection of Jesus from the dead he *conquers* suffering and evil and *undoes* them, that the expression 'despite the death' in fact does not quite say enough. However, the terms in which we could fill this unfathomable 'does not say enough' in a positive way, with finite, meaningful categories, escape us. What this 'does not say enough' might suggest is expressed most clearly in the refusal of Jesus to look for a *culprit*. When the Jews ask, 'Rabbi, who has sinned, this man or his parents, that he was born blind?' according to John 9.3 Jesus replies: 'Neither he nor his parents have sinned, but the works of God must be made manifest in him.' God overcomes the initiative of what 'finitude' can do purely of itself, without God's help – bringing suffering and evil into our history. The 'mystery of unrighteousness', which comes into tension with nature out of the unfathomable depths of our history of freedom, is evidently weaker than the 'mystery of the mercy' of the divine event that is God's nature itself: the Father who is greater than all suffering because he overcomes it in solidarity with our salvation. He is greater, too, than any theoretical and practical inability of creatures to experience the deepest reality in the last resort as an unconditionally reliable gift. But we are not in a position to arrive at a *theoretical* reconciliation of the two. For the depth of what the negativity of 'finitude' can (not 'must') mean, and the depth of what represents God's essential positivity, cannot be fathomed by human beings.

The insight that God does not want people to suffer but wills to *overcome* suffering where it occurs in our history (from a divine freedom of wisdom and will, whose divine nature and manner we cannot either define *a priori* or derive from his nature – do we know that so very well?), throws us back on *our own history* (in which Jesus himself also appeared), in order to be able to say something meaningful as Christians about redemption and liberation. God wants *people's salvation,* and in it victory over their suffering. The New Testament says with bold realism: 'Be imitators of God' (Eph 5.1), whom we have come to know in Jesus as the champion of all that is good, as the one who brings happiness – makes whole – and as the opponent of chaos, evil and injustice: as the Creator and warrior against the beast Leviathan, under whatever form this may be manifested in history. What this talk means for Christians here and now will have to find its inspiring and orienting impulse on the one hand in the gospel of salvation from God in Jesus, and on the other hand from an awareness of the problem at which by now we have arrived, of true and good, happy and free humanity.

The system of co-ordinates of human beings and their salvation[11]

Relationship to human corporeality, nature and the ecological environment

The relationship of the human being to his own corporeality – a human being *is* a body but also *has* one – and by means of his own corporeality to the wider sphere of nature and his own ecological environment, is constitutive of our humanity. So, human salvation is also concerned with this.

If we take no account of this human reference in our action, then in the long term we shall dominate nature or condition people in so one-sided a way that in fact we shall destroy the fundamental principles of our own natural world and thus make our own humanity impossible by attacking our natural household or our ecological basis. Our relationship with nature and our own corporeality come up against *boundaries* which we have to respect if we are to live a truly human life and, in an extreme instance, if we are even to survive. Therefore what is technically possible has

---

[11]Selected from: Edward Schillebeeckx, *Christ: The Christian Experience in the Modern World*, Collected Works of Edward Schillebeeckx vol. 7 (London: Bloomsbury T&T Clark, 2014), 728–37 [734–43].

not by a long way been an ethical possibility for people which makes sense for them and is well-founded.

This also applies to the physical and psychological limitation of our human strength. Although we may not be able (or perhaps may not yet be able) to establish by an empirical scientific method precisely where the *limits* of the mutability, conditioning and capability of humanity lies, we may be sure that such inescapable limits do exist. This certainty, which is *cognitive,* though it goes beyond the bounds of science, can also be seen manifested spontaneously in the individual and collective protests which emerge at the point where people feel that excessive demands are being made on them. The elementary needs of human beings (e.g. hunger and sex), their drives (e.g. aggression) and their corporeality cannot be manipulated at will without the *realisation* that there is an attack on human goodness, happiness and true humanity (which will express itself in spontaneous resistance).

This first anthropological constant already opens up a whole sphere of human values, the norms needed for a relationship between our own corporeality and the natural environment of human beings worthy of our true humanity – norms, however, which we ourselves must establish in the context of the particular circumstances in which we now live. This already opens up the perspective of the relationships of humanity to nature, which are not exclusively provided by the human value of the domination of nature, but are also provided by the equally human value of aesthetic and enjoyable converse with nature. The limitations which nature itself imposes on the way in which it can be manipulated by human beings to human advantage open up for us a dimension of our humanity which is not exhausted in the purely technocratic domination of nature.

On the other hand, the same constants warn us against the danger of an anti-technological or anti-industrial culture.[12] Scientists who reflect on what they are doing[13] emphatically point to the anthropological relevance of instrumental reason. Cultural philosophers have worked out that human beings are not really capable of remaining alive in a *purely natural* world. In nature human beings must create an appropriate human *environment* if they are in fact to survive without the refined instincts and the strengths which animals possess. A rational alteration in nature is therefore necessary. A 'meta-cosmos' (F. Dessauer) thus appears, which rescues human beings from their animal limitations and offers an opening for new possibilities. In times when this 'meta-cosmos' was hardly different from nature, only a small stratum of the population shared in the advantages of culture, and the mass of humanity had to work slavishly for the liberation of a few people

---

[12]This is the tendency of T. Roszak, *The Making of a Counter Culture,* New York and London 1969.
[13]See *inter alia* K. Tuchel, *Herausforderung der Technik,* Bremen 1967; C. P. Snow, *The Two Cultures and the Scientific Revolution,* London 1959; F. Dessauer, *Seele im Bannkreis der Technik,* Olten-Freiburg ²1952; id., *Streit um die Technik,* Frankfurt 1958; C. von Weizsäcker, *Die Einheit der Natur,* Göttingen 1971; G. Picht, *Wahrheit, Vernunft, Verantwortung,* Stuttgart 1969; W. Heisenberg, *Physics and Beyond,* London 1971. For the corporeality of human beings in nature see M. Merleau-Ponty, *Structure du comportement,* Paris 1949; id., *Phenomenology of Perception,* London and New York 1962; A. De Waelhens, *La philosophie et les expériences naturelles,* The Hague 1961; *De aarde is er ook nog,* ed. Hans Bouma, Wageningen 1974; A. Gehlen, *Der Mensch, seine Natur und seine Stellung in der Welt,* Frankfurt-Bonn 1966.

from material cares. (However, we can ask whether things are very different in a highly industrial 'meta-cosmos'. It emerges from this that the first, fundamental 'anthropological constant' is not enough in itself.) The meta-cosmos therefore offers human beings a better abode and a better home than the natural cosmos. So technology is not dehumanising in itself, but is rather a service towards liveable humanity; it is an expression of humanising and at the same time a condition for the humanising of human beings. Indeed, it is a fact that the establishment of a 'meta-cosmos' has been the historical presupposition for reflection on questions about the meaning of life. Furthermore, this humanisation of nature has not yet been completed, though that might easily be assumed, given the advance in technology. However, human beings can have an influence on his ecological position in nature, though he depends on it, as becomes clear above all when he destroys the conditions under which he lives. Now the concern on the one hand to emancipate human beings from nature without on the other hand destroying his own ecological basis is an eminently human task, which cannot be accomplished without 'instrumental reason'.

Moreover, it is evident that the outlining of meaning and of particular images of the world and humanity is also communicated through instrumental and technological reason, and is not just an immanent development of ideas. Ideas about marriage, love and sexuality have shifted in our time (e.g. from biblical conceptions), for the most part solely because science and technology have been able to provide means which were not at the disposal of people of former times. With technological possibilities available, intervention in *nature* in fact looks different from those times when any intervention was felt to be an irresponsible and therefore evil attack on the divine ordinances of creation. However, at the same time there arises the human danger that simply because of the availability of technological possibilities and capabilities, people believe that they can and may provide a *purely technological* solution for all their physical and psychological, social and general problems of life. However, the technocratic *interpretation* of the ideal of a liveable life worthy of human beings is not the same thing as the anthropological relevance of science and technology. What is in reality often the dehumanising character of technology does not come from technology itself, but from the question of meaning associated it, which has *already* been solved in *positivist* terms. It is not science and technology, with their potentialities for improving human condition, but their implicit presuppositions which are criticised.

Thus this first anthropological constant shows a whole series of partial constants – for example, that human beings are not only reason, but also temperament; not only reason, but also imagination; not only freedom, but also instinct; not only reason, but also love; and so on. Thus it is a matter not only of the active dimension of human beings and their control of the world, but also of their other dimensions, in contemplation, in play and in love.

If Christian *salvation* is in fact the salvation of human beings, it will also have essential connections with this first 'anthropological constant'. To cite only one aspect from the past: Christian salvation is also connected with ecology and with the conditions and burdens which particular life (here and now) lays on people. To say that all this is alien to the meaning of 'Christian salvation' is perhaps to dream of a salvation for *angels*, but not for *human beings*.

Being human involves fellow human beings

Human personal identity at the same time includes relationships with fellow human beings.[14] This, too, is an anthropological constant which opens up a sphere of human value in which people have to look for norms which will provide them with salvation here and now.

The element of being together, of contact with our fellow human beings, through which we can share ourselves with others and even be confirmed in our existence and personhood by others, is part of the structure of personal identity: authorisation by others and by society that we, that I, *may be*, in my own name, in my own identity, a personal and responsible self, however distorted this may be. A society which out of so-called self-protection (sometime euphemistically called 'the building up of society') leaves no room for the disabled person is not worth a fig.

This personal identity is only possible if I may be allowed by other fellow human beings, to be myself in my own inalienability, but at the same time in my essential limitation *(divisum ab alio,* as earlier philosophy put it), and if on my side I confirm the other. In this limited individuality the person is essentially related to other, to fellow persons. The human face in particular – a person never sees his *own* face – already indicates that human beings are *directed towards* others, is *destined for* others and not for himself. The face is an image of ourselves *for others*. Thus, already through quite specific manifestation, human beings are destined for encounter with his fellow human beings in the world. This lays on them the task of accepting, in inter-subjectivity, the others in their otherness and in their freedom. It is precisely through this mutual relationship to others that the limitation of human individuality is transcended in free, loving affirmation of the other, and the person himself arrives at personal identity.

The connection with social and institutional structures

There is, thirdly, the relationship of the human person to social and institutional structures.[15] While we bring these structures to life in the course of our history, they become independent and then develop into an objective form of society in which we live our particular lives and which again also deeply influence our inwardness,

---

[14]C. Waayman, *De mystiek van ik en jij*, Utrecht 1976; M. Chastaing, *L'existence d'autrui*, Paris 1951; L. Binswanger, *Grundformen und Erkenntnis menschlichen Daseins*, Zurich ²1953; I. Madinier, *Conscience et amour*, Paris ²1947; M. Nédoncelle, *La réciprocité des consciences*, Paris 1942; G. Gusdort, *La découverte de soi*, Paris 1948; E. Levinas, *Totalité et Infini*, The Hague 1961; F. Buytendijk, *Phénoménologie de la rencontre*, Bruges 1952; R. Kwant, *Wijsbegeerte van de ontmoeting*, Utrecht 1959; M. Theunissen, *Der Andere. Studien zur Sozialontologie der Gegenwart*, Berlin 1965, and the many works by G. Marcel (see R. Troisfontaines, *De l'existence à l'être: La philosophic de G. Marcel*, two vols., Namur 1955).

[15]Among others, especially P. Berger and T. Luckmann, *The Social Construction of Reality*, London 1967; J. Habermas and N. Luhmann, *Theorie der Gesellschaft oder Sozialtechnologie*, Frankfurt 1971; A. Schütz, *Der sinnhafte Aufbau der sozialen Welt*, Vienna ²1960; K. Raiser, *Identität und Sozialität*, Munich-Mainz 1971; H. Schelsky, ed., *Zur Theorie der Institution*, Düsseldorf 1973; A. Gehlen, *Studien zur Anthropologie und Soziologie*, Neuwied 1963; *Neue Anthropologie*, ed. H.-G. Gadamer and P. Vogler, four vols., Stuttgart-Munich 1972–73.

our personhood. The social dimension is not something additional to our personal identity; it is a *dimension* of this identity itself. When they become independent, these structures and institutions give the impression of being unchangeable natural regularities, whereas we ourselves can change them and therefore also their regularity. Independently of what people do, and independently of human reason and human will to preserve these structures, such highly praised sociological and economic regularities do not exist; in fact they are essentially subject to the *historical hypothesis* of the objectively given social and economic system. They are contingent, changeable and thus changeable by people (although sociologists and cultural anthropologists will perhaps be able to discover a deeper, almost immutable level and therefore structural constants in some perhaps even fundamental social changes).[16] The empirical sciences often do not take into account that this appearance of regularity depends on the hypothesis of our given (changeable) objective form of society: given the hypothesis, they rightly discover these sociological or socio-psychological regularities, but sometimes treat them as though they were a natural law or a metaphysical datum.

This constant, too, shows us a sphere of values, above all the value of institutional and structural elements for a truly human life. This is once again a sphere of values which needs concrete norms. On the one hand there can be no permanent life worthy of people without a degree of institutionalising; personal identity also needs social consensus, needs to be supported by structures and institutions which make possible human freedom and the realisation of values. On the other hand, actual structures and institutions which have grown up in history do not have *general validity;* they are changeable. This gives rise to the specific ethical demand to change them where, as a result of changed circumstances, they enslave and debase people rather than liberate them and give them protection.

The conditioning of people and culture by time and space

Time and space, the historical and geographical situation of peoples and cultures, are also an anthropological constant from which no human being can detach himself.[17]

Here, first of all, we are confronted with a dialectical tension between nature and history which cannot ever be removed, even by the best possible social structure. Nature and history come together in particular human cultures. Their dialectic is a given one, which is an element of our transitory human existence and of which death is only an extreme exponent, a boundary situation. That of itself means that apart from some forms of suffering which can for the most part be removed by humans, there are forms of suffering and threats to life on which human beings can have no influence through technology and social intervention. This is where the question of *imparting meaning* emerges. The historicity and thus the finality of a human beings, which they do not know how to escape so that they can

---

[16] See the three levels in social changes in *Jesus: An Experiment in Christology*, 537–42 [576–9], and the literature there.
[17] See especially, H.-G. Gadamer, *Truth and Method*, London 1975, 235–74.

adopt a standpoint outside time, makes them understand their humanity also as a *hermeneutical* undertaking, i.e. as a task of *understanding* their own situation and unmasking critically the meaninglessness that human beings bring about in history. Of course human beings can be helped in this attempt to understand themselves, which also involves the question of truth and falsehood, by a variety of empirical, analytical and theoretical sciences, but at the same time they are conscious of the experience that the truth for human beings is only possible as *remembered* truth which at the same time is to be *realised*. If understanding is the original way in which human beings *experience,* this understanding is just as universal as history itself. That means that the presumption of adopting a standpoint outside *historical* action and thought is a danger to true humanity.

Numerous other problems are given with this constant. I shall only point to some of them (within the theme of this book). There can be historical and even geographically conditioned attainments which, although they appear late in human history and in particular places, and thus cannot be called necessary or universal *a priori* presuppositions, cannot be regarded *here and now* as random or arbitrary.[18] Here values have developed requiring norms which apply, for example, to highly industrialised and advanced cultural conditions in which Western people live, and which need not apply directly in other cultures.

Some examples may be enough. Because of their general prosperity, Western people have a duty to international solidarity, above all towards poor countries, regardless of the historical question of how far they themselves are the historical cause of the poverty of these poor countries. This obligation also arises from the duties resulting from the second and third anthropological constants. It also follows on the basis of these same constants, which point to the historical and geographical limitations of any culture, that taking into account the limited potential of the imagination of people in one particular culture, critical remembrance of the great traditions of humanity, including its great religious traditions, will be a necessary stimulus in the search for norms for action which here and now further healthy and realisable humanity (this critical remembrance is an element in a hermeneutical enterprise, in which one seeks illumination for his coming action).[19]

Finally, this fourth anthropological constant also reminds us of the fact that the explicit discovery of these *constitutive constants* has only come about in a historical process: their coming to consciousness *is* already a fruit of human hermeneutical practice.

Mutual relationship of theory and practice

The essential relationship between theory and practice is likewise an anthropological constant. It is a constant in so far as through this relationship human culture, as a hermeneutical undertaking or an understanding of meaning, and as an undertaking

---

[18]W. Oelmüller, 'Die Grenze des Säkularisierungsbegriffs am Ende der bisherigen Neuzeitgeschichte', in H. Hommes, *Gesellschaft ohne Christentum?*, Düsseldorf 1974, 48–4.
[19]See above in this analysis, n. 5, p. 655.

of changing meaning and improving the world, gets *permanence*. On a sub-human level, i.e. in the animal world, permanence and the possibility of the survival of the species and the individual are ensured by instinct and the elasticity with which it can adapt itself to changed or changing conditions, and, finally, by the law of the survival of the fittest in the struggle for life. Now unless people want to make their own history into a kind of spiritual Darwinism, a history in which only will and thought, the power of the strongest and the victor, dictate to us what is good and true for our humanity, then on the human level a combination of theory and practice will be the only humanly responsible guarantee of a permanent culture which is increasingly worthy of humanity[20] – of what brings human beings *salvation*.

The religious and 'para-religious' consciousness of human beings

The 'utopian' element in human consciousness also seems to me to be an anthropological constant, and a fundamental one at that.

Here we are concerned with the future (see above). What kind of future does one want? Under this utopian element I would place a variety of different conservative or progressive all-embracing conceptions which make it possible for human beings in society in some way to make sense of contingency or finitude, impermanence and the problems of suffering, fiasco, failure and death which it presents, or to overcome them. In other words, I am talking about the way in which a particular society has given specific form to the hermeneutical process in everyday life (see the fourth constant) or looks for another social system and another future in protest against the existing attribution of 'meaning'. These are comprehensive approaches which teach us to experience human life and society, now or in the future, as a good, meaningful and happy totality for humanity – a vision and a way of life which seek to give meaning and context to human existence in this world (even if only in a distant future).

Here we find 'all-embracing views' of both a religious and a non-religious kind – views of life, views of society, world-views and general theories of life in which people express what ultimately inspires them, what humanity they choose in the last resort, what they really live for and what makes life worth living. All these can also be called *cognitive models of reality*, which interpret the whole of nature and history in theory and practice, and now or later allow it to be experienced as a 'meaningful whole' (yet to be realised).

In most, though not all, of these 'utopias' a human being is understood as an active *subject* who furthers humanity, interpreted as being good and true, and the establishment of a good human world, though on the other hand individuals are

---

[20]See above all M. Riedel (ed.), *Rehabilitierung der praktischen Philosophie*, two vols., Freiburg 1972 and 1974; W. Pannenberg, *Theology and the Philosophy of Science,* London 1976, and above all his discussion (156–224) with J. Habermas, *Theory and Practice*, ET London 1974. See also O. Schwemmer, *Philosophie der Praxis*, Frankfurt 1971.

not personally responsible for the whole of history and its outcome.[21] For some, this all-controlling principle is fate or *fatum,* for others evolution, for yet others humanity, the 'human person' as the universal subject of the whole of history, or, less definitely, nature. For religious people, this is the living God, the Lord of history. But no matter what form such a comprehensive view may take – unless one glorifies nihilism and professes the absurdity of human life – it is always a *form of faith,* in the sense of a 'utopia' which cannot be scientifically demonstrated, or at least can never be completely rationalised. And so in fact 'Without faith you're as good as dead.'[22] In this sense 'faith', the ground for hope, is an anthropological constant throughout human history, a constant without which human life and action worthy of humanity and capable of realisation becomes impossible: a human beings loses his identity and either ends up in a neurotic state or irrationally takes refuge in horoscopes and all kinds of *mirabilia.* Furthermore, faith and hope are strengthened as necessary human constants by the nihilistic claim which calls liveable humanity an absurdity and thus has no faith and no hope. That implies that faith and hope – whatever their content – are part of the health and integrity, the worthwhileness and 'wholeness' of our humanity. For those who believe in God, this implies that *religion* is an anthropological constant without which human salvation, redemption and true liberation are impossible. In other words, that any liberation which bypasses a *religious redemption* is only a partial liberation, and furthermore, if it claims to be the *total* liberation of humanity, clearly destroys a real dimension of humanity and in the last resort uproots human beings instead of liberating them.

Irreducible synthesis of these six dimensions

In so far as the six anthropological constants which we have discussed form a *synthesis,* human culture is in fact an *irreducible autonomous reality* (which cannot be reduced either idealistically or materialistically). The reality which heals people and brings them salvation lies in this synthesis (and therefore the synthesis itself must be called an anthropological constant). The six constants influence one another and go over into one another. They delineate a human basic form and hold one another in balance. It may sound fine and even right to talk of the priority of 'spiritual values', but such talk can in reality at the same time destroy the material pre-suppositions and implications of 'the spiritual', to *the detriment of* these spiritual values. Failure to recognise one of these profoundly human constants uproots the whole, including its 'spiritual' component. It damages human beings and their society and distorts the whole of human culture. Whether consciously or not – even under the flag of the 'primacy of the spiritual' – this represents an attack on true and good, happy and free humanity.

---

[21]*Geschichte, Ereignis und Erzählung,* ed. R. Koselleck and W.-D. Stempel, Poetik und Hermeneutik 5, Munich 1973, and esp. 'Geschichte, Geschichtsphilosophie und ihr Subjekt', 463–517, and here W. Pannenberg, *Theology and the Philosophy of Science,* 478–90; J.-B. Metz, 'La théologie à 'l'âge critique'', in *Le service théologique dans l'Église, Mélanges offerts à Y. Congar,* Paris 1974, 131–48.
[22]The English sub-title of H. M. Kuitert, *The Necessity of Faith,* Grand Rapids 1976.

On the other hand, it may have become clear from what has already been said that these anthropological constants, which open up a perspective on the fundamental values of 'humanity', in no way provide us with specific *norms* which must apply here and now, taking into account our objective form of society and given culture, in order to arrive at conditions more worthy of humanity As I said, these constants simply outline, as it were, the system of co-ordinates in which specific norms must be sought and found, through general considerations and after an analysis and interpretation of the position of the person in it. The minimum requirement for starting – and perhaps this too is an important factor in considering what is specifically 'worthy of the human person' – is that we should be at the *level of awareness of the problem which has already been achieved.* From that point we can then carry out an analysis of the gulf between ideal and reality, on the basis of negative experiences or experiences of contrast, and also on the basis of experiences which we have already had, *in the light of* what is seen to be 'utopia'. This differential analysis will show the *direction* which we must take (always considering different possibilities), a direction which together we have to agree in defining and for which we have to make urgent specific norms which are valid here and now.

I said that there would always be different possibilities. For people have very different views both of the details of this utopian element in our human consciousness and of the analysis and above all the interpretation of the result of this analysis (for a utopian consciousness with a particular direction is always involved *in* the manner of this analysis). This clearly also gives rise, even in scientific analysis (which takes place in a conscious or unconscious framework of interpretation), to *pluralism* in the sphere of specific norms – even when people recognise the same *basic values* to which the 'anthropological constants' draw our attention. However, the proposed norms which we ourselves adopt at our own risk must also be tested for inner logic and discussed in dialogue if we are also to challenge others with them. Even if their fundamental *inspiration* comes, say, from a religious belief in God, *ethical* norms, i.e. norms which make life more dignified, must be capable of being given a rational foundation and validity in intersubjective discussion, i.e. discussion which is accessible to all rational people. None of the conversation partners can hide behind a threadbare 'I can see something that you can't' and nevertheless compel others simply to accept this norm. All too often in discussions the initial situation can be of this kind: that one of the conversation partners sees something that others do not. But in that case the others must also be enlightened in a free and rational process of communication. No one can appeal here to a 'zone of tranquillity' (even if other conversation partners cannot *per se* arrive at a consensus on the basis of the arguments presented). One of the tasks of a liveable modern humanity will be that of learning to live with different conceptions of specific norms for a worthwhile human life which is called for here and now. The pain of this pluralism is part of our *condition humaine,* above all in modern times; we must cope with it, and not by means of the dictatorial rejection of other conceptions. This art is also an element of true, good and happy humanity within the limitations of our historicity and transitoriness – that is, unless we want to become 'megalomaniacs' who have got it into their heads that they can step out of their human *finitude*. However, the concern for the well-being of each and every individual cannot on the other hand simply begin from 'politics' as the so-called art of the possible, what can be done or achieved. Politics, rather, is the difficult art of making possible what is *necessary* for human well-being.

Thus *Christian salvation*, in the centuries-old biblical tradition called redemption, and meant as salvation from God *for humanity,* is concerned with the whole system of co-ordinates in which human beings can really be human. This salvation – the wholeness of humanity – cannot just be sought in one or other of these constants, say exclusively in 'ecological appeals', in an exclusive 'be nice to one another', in the exclusive overthrow of an economic system (whether Marxist or capitalist), or in exclusively mystical experiences: 'Alleluia, he is risen!' On the other hand, the *synthesis* of all this is clearly an 'already now' and a 'not yet'. The way in which human failure and human shortcomings are coped with must be termed one form of 'liberation' (and perhaps its most important form). In that case that might then be the all-embracing 'anthropological constant' in which Jesus the Christ was meant to precede us.

Selected literature

- Unique Universality: Universal Appeal of 'What Is Worthy of Humanity'; Selected from: Edward Schillebeeckx, *Jesus: An Experiment in Christology*, trans. John Bowden, Collected Works of Edward Schillebeeckx vol. 6 (London: Bloomsbury T&T Clark, 2014), 565–8 [602–5], 565–7 [602–4].
- The *Humanum* We Seek; Selected from: Edward Schillebeeckx, *Jesus: An Experiment in Christology*, trans. John Bowden, Collected Works of Edward Schillebeeckx vol. 6 (London: Bloomsbury T&T Clark, 2014), 568–9 [606–7].
- God Does not Want Humanity to Suffer; Selected from: Edward Schillebeeckx, *Christ: The Christian Experience in the Modern World*, Collected Works of Edward Schillebeeckx vol. 7 (London: Bloomsbury T&T Clark, 2014), 719–24 [726–30].
- The System of Co-Ordinates of Human Beings and Thier Salvation; Selected from: Edward Schillebeeckx, *Christ: The Christian Experience in the Modern World*, Collected Works of Edward Schillebeeckx vol. 7 (London: Bloomsbury T&T Clark, 2014), 728–37 [734–43].

13

Christology

The actions of Jesus' life as manifestations of divine love for human beings and human love for God: Bestowal of grace and religious worship[1]

'As the Father has sent me, I also send you. When he had said this, he breathed on them and he said to them: Receive the Holy Spirit; whose sins you shall forgive, they are forgiven them.'[2] Thus it is as a revelation of God's merciful redeeming love that we are to understand the sending of the Son on earth. By the incarnation of the Son God intended to divinise humanity by redeeming him; by being saved from sin human beings are brought into a personal communion of grace and love with God. This implies two things. First, the fullness of grace which properly belongs to the human person Jesus in virtue of his existence as God was intended by God to be a source of grace for others; from him all were to receive. Christ's love for human beings thus manifests God's love for human beings by actually bestowing it; it is the redeeming mercy of God himself coming to meet us from a human heart. But as well as this movement down from above, coming to us from God's love by way of Jesus' human heart, there is in the human person Jesus also a movement up from below, from the human heart of Jesus, the Son, to the Father.

The human actions of Jesus' life as they come from above show us their character as acts of redemption of his fellow human beings; these acts, in the mode of a human love, are the merciful redeeming love of God himself. As coming from below they show their character as acts of worship; these acts are a true adoration and acknowledgement of God's divine existence; they are a service of praise or cult, religion, prayer – in a word, they are Jesus' love of God. Thus Jesus is not only the revelation of the redeeming God; he is also the supreme worshipper of the Father, the supreme realisation of all religion. Jesus became the Redeemer in actual fact by freely

---

[1]Selected from: Edward Schillebeeckx, *Christ the Sacrament of the Encounter with God*, trans. Paul Barret, N. D. Smith, Collected Works of Edward Schillebeeckx vol. 1 (London: Bloomsbury T&T Clark, 2014), 12–14 [18–22].
[2]John 20.21-3.

living his human life in religious worship of and attachment to the Father. In Christ not only were God and his love for people revealed, but God also showed us in him what it is for a human being to commit himself unconditionally to God the invisible Father. In this way God revealed to us the embodiment of religion, the countenance of a truly religious human being. The living and personal relation of Jesus to the Father reveals to us what is meant by the majesty and mercy of God. In and through the religious service of Jesus, God has revealed himself.

If we now consider that this humanity of Jesus represents us all, then it also becomes clear that the movement up from below is a movement to the Father ascending, by way of Jesus' humanity, from the whole of humanity. Therefore Jesus is not only the offer of divine love to humanity made visible but, at the same time, as prototype (or primordial model) he is the supreme realisation of the response of human love to this divine offer: 'in our place' and 'in the name of us all', as Scripture repeatedly says. Whatever Christ does as a free human being is not only a realisation in human form of God's activity for our salvation; it is also at the same time the positive human acceptance, representative for all of us, of this redeeming offer from God. The human person Jesus is personally a dialogue with God the Father; the supreme realisation and therefore the norm and the source of every encounter with God. As a reality religion can only be understood in the context of the incarnation of God the Son. For since redeemed existence means that through the intervention of God humanity itself is once more turned towards God in close communion of life with him, then the whole of humanity is already truly redeemed objectively in Jesus, as in its Head.

The foundation of all this is the Incarnation. But this incarnation of God the Son is a reality which grows. It is not complete in a matter of a moment; for example, at Jesus' conception in Mary's womb or at his birth. The Incarnation is not merely a Christmas event. To be human is a process of becoming human; Jesus' humanity grew throughout his earthly life, finding its completion in the supreme moment of the Incarnation, his death, resurrection and exaltation. Only then is the Incarnation fulfilled to the very end. And so we must say that the incarnation in the Son itself redeems us. This mystery of Christ or of redemption we can call, in its totality, a mystery of saving worship; a mystery of praise (the upward movement) and of salvation (the downward movement).

This ascending and descending dynamism pervades the whole human life of Jesus. For although Jesus in his earthly life was always the humiliated 'Servant of God', he remained even in his humiliation the Son of God, the grace-abounding revelation of God.[3] And although in his glorification Christ can bestow grace in full measure, there too he remains a human person who, in religious and filial service, adores and honours the Father from whom he must receive all. None the less we can trace a development in the course of the saving history of the mystery of Christ. By the fact that he became human, the Son of God is fundamentally already the Christ. But we must also realise that it was only upon his rising from the dead that, because of the

---

[3] Therefore St. Thomas says repeatedly: '…thus by the power of his divinity his [Jesus'] actions bring salvation for us, seeing that they cause grace in us, both by merit and by a certain efficient causality'. (*ST*, III, q. 8, a. I, ad 2.)

love and obedience of his life, the Father *established* him absolutely as the Christ. We must look closely into this growth towards the fullness of redemption, for in it we are confronted with the mystery of Christ's life, which is this: Jesus, in his humanity, as 'Servant of God', by his life of obedience and love on earth, even unto death, earned for us that grace of salvation which he, in glory with the Father, can himself, as Lord and Christ, bestow upon us in abundance. This saving reality calls for the closest consideration, for in it we find the key to the sense of the sacramentality of the Church in its relation to the *Kyrios,* the risen and glorified Lord, and so also to the Holy Spirit.

God's message in Jesus[4]

Historically it is impossible to determine whether a human being bound by time and history has universal meaning for all humanity. But if what is said about Jesus' unique universality is not to be ideological, there have to be signs and traces, requiring identification and interpretation by others, within our human hermeneutic horizon. Historically Jesus of Nazareth must have appeared at least as a catalytic question, an *invitation* with respect to final salvation. Christians interpreted that question and invitation in a very specific way: they found the definitive promise of salvation and liberation imparted by God in Jesus and that gave them sufficient reason to commend him to others and to witness to Jesus Christ. This has continued right up to the present day; we, too, are still confronted with the possibility of the catalytic question and invitation which Jesus is; but... in an entirely new situation: for us Jesus raises the issue of God in an age which in most if not all sectors of life appears to do without God. It cannot involve a claim, substantiated or otherwise, that Jesus is the historical embodiment of an existential or socio-critical message. For such a message we in the 20th century are less and less inclined to turn to someone who lived in the first century of our era – and why should we? The historical Jesus was a person who continues to confront us with the question whether the reality of God is not the most important thing in human life, a question which, if answered positively, demands radical *metanoia:* a reorientation of our own lives. That is why the question which Jesus continues to put to us is, in the first place, fundamentally disorienting.

Especially in a modern situation we do well to distinguish between Jesus of Nazareth as a catalytic question and invitation, and the Christian churches' Christological answer to this question. It seems to me that this is also a consequence of the new pastoral situation in which we are living: namely that (besides acknowledging and celebrating the salvation imparted by God in Jesus) our proclamation (including our Christology) should present Jesus pre- eminently as a question which catalyses our greatest human, personal and social problem. The earthly Jesus was someone who in a very specific, historical situation presented

---

[4]Selected from: Edward Schillebeeckx, *Jesus: An Experiment in Christology*, trans. John Bowden, Collected Works of Edward Schillebeeckx vol. 6 (London: Bloomsbury T&T Clark, 2014), 599–601 [636–9].

the option to take a stand for or against him. Jesus himself never directly answered the question of who he is. His personal identity is somehow woven into his message, way of life and death. Hence the question raised by his message, ministry and death can only be fully answered by responding to his person. After all, like every historical event the earthly Jesus shared the ambiguity of history, requiring interpretation and identification.

Jesus confronts us with an assured promise of a 'future from God', based on his personal *Abba* experience, and in his ministry he actually proffers it. Without the reality of this original *Abba* experience his message is an illusion, an empty myth. To put one's trust in Jesus is to ground oneself in the ground of his experience: the Father. It implies acknowledging the authentic, non-illusory reality of Jesus' *Abba* experience. This is only possible in an act of faith which, although not dependent on rationality, advances sufficient rational motives to consider the faith justified. The historical Jesus allows the Christian response as an interpretation which, because of the ambiguity of all historical phenomena, is never cogent but still rationally and morally justified, recognisable in the historical phenomenon, and as such surpassing rational motives without excluding them.

In our modern situation the startling implication of Jesus' praxis, his message and its historical failure in his death is that we have to rethink the contemporary notion of total emancipation through self-liberation. For us his death by execution, which did not shake his confidence in the human focus of God's coming reign he continued, in the face of immanent death, to proffer salvation from God – is the challenging message that historical failures do not have the last word, that even in utter fiascos we may continue trusting in God. Jesus' message is essentially intended to be a message about God and from God, a message which he maintained to the end, throughout the successes and failures of his life up to the historical fiasco on the cross, a seal on the authenticity of his life and message. This life summons us to *metanoia,* to this effect: whatever happens, put your trust in God; then – how? *I* don't know, just look at the cross! – humanity's liberation, eschatologically fulfilled salvation will come. This is Jesus' challenging message, which on the one hand permits and stimulates human liberation and emancipation, and on the other hand surpasses it in unshakable confidence in total salvation that only God can give; and that is his transcendent answer to human finitude, the necessary index and exponent of every emancipation and critical praxis. Because of their finitude (the metaphysical fissure in human nature) a human being is a being whose salvation, wholeness and fulfilment depend on the grace and mercy of his creator. The realisation that God accepts us in Jesus Christ proleptically heralds the victory of grace, even in the historical, no longer comprehensible defeat of human finite autonomy.

Even when dying Jesus did not desperately hang on to his own identity and self-preservation, but remained intent on God's reign which, although receding as his eyes grew dim, was sure to come. Thus Jesus' message, sealed by his death, calls us to revise our self-understanding by referring to God, who silently reveals himself in Jesus' historically defenceless failure on the cross. God directs himself to humanity, but in a world which does not always share his concern; as a result his love for humanity in Jesus is coloured by our way of thinking. In his love for humanity, however, God overrides all our contortions and distortions without violating our finite autonomy.

Significantly, it was a Jewish thinker and philosopher, E. Levinas,[5] who spoke of the irresistible power of the 'defenceless other' who goes on trusting. But that shows that ethics and religion, although interrelated, cannot simply be equated.

One might ask, why not look for the same sort of inspiration in other figures in world history? The question could be debated endlessly, but it overlooks an accomplished fact: Jesus' concrete appearance in history cannot be disregarded, so it continues to address an ineluctable historical challenge. The response to this challenge, identified as Christian, has adequate grounds to continue propounding trust in Jesus and witnessing to it, not just verbally but primarily through concretely enacted testimony, in which the praxis of God's kingdom as proclaimed by Jesus seeks to embody itself. In a modern situation a message without real-life praxis simply does not work. It becomes ideological propaganda, not a challenge or an inviting witness. That is why even a 'new' theological Christology will be ineffectual if it is not a theological reflection of the praxis of God's kingdom, of Christian orthopraxis, actually demonstrated in the life of the churches in prayer and care for our fellow human beings. Only then does deeper reflection on Jesus' identity become fruitful.

The continuity between Jesus of Nazareth and the risen one[6]

By sending Jesus to Israel, God fulfilled the promise of the old covenant, thus saying 'yes' to creation and covenant. Only when Israel rejected the definitive offer of salvation in Jesus did God bring about a 'new creation' in and through the resurrection. So Jesus of Nazareth is at once the completion of the Old Testament and, as the rejected yet risen one, the start of the New Testament. Despite the continuity between our human history and the new creation based on Jesus' resurrection, the rejection of Jesus as the fulfilment of creation and covenant creates a discontinuity that no human act can bridge. This is intrinsically conjoined with continuity through God's startling new saving act which surmounts the fiasco of the rejected and crucified fulfiller of creation and covenant, and installs the rejected one in his role as universal saviour. Jesus' integration of his own rejection and death with his real offer of salvation (the meaning of his whole life) in our history is the intra-historical index of this victory: 'It was God who reconciled us to himself in Jesus Christ' (2 Cor. 5.19).

Because God confirmed Jesus' belonging to him whom he called *Abba* in the resurrection, the resurrection is God's endorsement of Jesus' message and praxis. It means, too, that the 'content' of the eschatological liberation expressed by the religious term 'resurrection from the dead' has to be filled in from Jesus' historical ministry from his words and deeds which are 'endorsed' by it. Hence the dilemma of salvation in Jesus of Nazareth or salvation in the risen crucified one is a false

---

[5]E. Levinas, *Totalité et infini* (The Hague 1961); see also *Het menselijk gelaat* (Utrecht 1969).
[6]Selected from: Edward Schillebeeckx, *Jesus: An Experiment in Christology*, trans. John Bowden, Collected Works of Edward Schillebeeckx vol. 6 (London: Bloomsbury T&T Clark, 2014), 603–5 [641–3].

dilemma, since the second expression affirms God's validation of Jesus of Nazareth, while the first gives substance to what God is validating. Put differently, the risen crucified one without the concrete Jesus of Nazareth is a myth or a gnostic mystery, while without what Christians call the resurrection the historical Jesus, despite his astonishing message and conduct, would have been just one more failure in the long line of innocently convicted martyrs in the history of human suffering a fleeting hope which each time seems to confirm a surmise that a lot of people do not *accept* human suffering, yet at the same time experience hope's utopian character in light of the distinctive nature and pressure of our own history.

Thus there is no discontinuity between Jesus of Nazareth and the risen crucified one. Because of the life which preceded it, Jesus' death does confront us with a fundamental question about God, with only two possible answers: either that God that is, the God whose reign Jesus proclaimed was an illusion on Jesus' part (and for his followers a disillusion); or that his rejection and death obliges us radically to revise our understanding of God, our God concepts and our understanding of history, and abandon them as invalid, since God's true nature was validly manifested only in the life and death of this Jesus which opened up a new perspective on the future. God, whose utter reliability Jesus attested, is either a tragic farce or we are invited to confess this God of Jesus, both in his preaching and in his historical failure. Faith in Jesus can only take the form of this confession of God.

The discontinuity in the Christian faith, then, is not Jesus' death – after all, he experienced it as related to his mission to proffer salvation, and as a historical consequence of his caring, loving service of people (this is the minimum, but also the most assured element that we have to retain as the historically solid core of the Last Supper tradition). The discontinuity lies in the rejection of his message and praxis, culminating in the rejection of his person. That is why God's validation in the resurrection pertains to the very person of Jesus inherent in his message and conduct. Both the rejection of and God's 'amen' to the person of Jesus validate the specificity of the Jesus event, in which both person and project – that is, person, message and praxis are indissolubly conjoined. For the Christian creed, therefore, God's reign assumed the aspect of Jesus Christ; and it was possible to speak of the 'Lord Jesus Christ' as synonymous with the reign of God proclaimed by Jesus.

When we talk about God's 'amen' to Jesus' person, message and praxis we must remember that this, too, is a profession of faith not a ratification or legitimation in the ordinary human sense. The resurrection confirms that God was constantly with Jesus throughout his life right up to the human forsakenness of his death on the cross, the moment also of God's silence. One religious conviction – the resurrection – cannot serve to legitimate another religious conviction, namely, that of God's saving act in Jesus of Nazareth. Hence the real legitimation, evident to all, remains totally eschatological (that is the meaning of the *parousia*). Thus our faith in the resurrection is itself still a prophecy and a promise to this world – and as such unsheltered and unprotected, defenceless and vulnerable! So a Christian life is not visibly 'justified' by historical facts. But those who believe in Jesus' resurrection are freed by this belief from any compulsion to justify themselves and from any requirement that God should publicly take human beings and their world under his protection here and now, and should ratify them. The servant is not greater than his master. Like Jesus, the Christian risks entrusting himself and the vindication of his life to God; he is prepared to receive that vindication as Jesus did: beyond death. And so, reconciled to God's way of doing things, he is also reconciled with himself, with others, with history, in which he tries nevertheless to realise emancipation and justice. This is why Christians can exert themselves to the full, without violence or rancour, in order to improve this world, to make it a happier and more just world without alienation. Yet no more than Jesus can Christians present any legitimating credentials except by actually putting into practice God's kingdom in this human history of ours.

Christology: Concentrated creation[7]

After a number of Christian generations, the ancient church intuitively put this article of belief within the context of belief in God as the creator of heaven and earth. Both articles of belief provide mutual clarification, just as in the Old Testament the originally independent traditions of covenant and creation already influenced and enriched each other, resulting in refinement, correction and mutual reinforcement.[8]

Christian belief in creation implies that God loves us unconditionally, without limits: boundlessly, without merit on our part, and without qualification. Creation is an act of God which, on the one hand, unconditionally gives us our own particular character – finite, not divine, and destined for true humanity. Simultaneously, on the other hand, creation is an act in which God presents himself in selfless love as our God: our salvation and happiness, the supreme content of what it means to be true and good humanly. God creates men and women freely for the salvation and happiness of themselves; however, in the very same act, with the same sovereign freedom, he wills himself to be the deepest meaning of human life, its salvation and happiness. He is a God of humanity, our God, the creator. This is the Christian belief in creation. But how?

How this is so has to emerge from a history shaped by people, for better or for worse. Belief in creation means that God's nature reveals itself. In other words, who God is, the way in which God is really God, is not conditioned or determined, but is revealed in and through the whole of our history. Christians call God 'Lord' in the light of this history of the world. On God's part, to dare to create human beings and call them into being is a vote of confidence in humanity and our history, without any conditions or guarantees being offered from the side of humanity. Creation is a blank cheque for which God himself and God alone stands surety. It is a vote of confidence which gives those who believe in God the creator the courage to believe in word and in deed that, despite many experiences to the contrary, the kingdom of God, i.e. human salvation and happiness, is in fact in the process of being realised for humanity by the power of God's creation, which calls on human beings to realise it. God's battle against all the powers of chaos and alienation will be victorious. In

---

[7]Selected from: Edward Schillebeeckx, *Interim Report on the Books Jesus and Christ*, trans. John Bowden, Collected Works of Edward Schillebeeckx vol. 8 (London: Bloomsbury T&T Clark, 2014), 110–14 [126–32].

[8]That is why I usually speak of the 'Christian belief in creation' without separating the Christian and the philosophical aspects.

their belief in creation, Christians bear witness to their belief that God's innermost being, in total freedom, is one of love for humanity and human deliverance: happiness, salvation, even enjoyment for men and women. As a result, the one who is trustworthy in all his freedom is a constant surprise for humanity: 'He who is and was and is to come' (Rev. 1.8; 4.8). By virtue of its eternal and absolute freedom, God's unchangeable being, unchangeable because it does not share in the nature of created beings, presents itself to finite humanity as permanently new. This newness can nonetheless be recognised on every occasion as the action of the selfsame God: 'Here he is again!' Because God's act of creation is his eternal, absolutely free being, his absoluteness or non-relativity is at the same time relational,[9] i.e. relating itself to his creation, humanity in the world, in an absolute freedom, not conditioned by anything. By creating, God takes the side of all his vulnerable creation. For anyone in the Jewish-Christian tradition who believes in the living God, a human's cause is the cause of God himself, without that in any way diminishing human responsibility for our own history.

As a result, 'Christology' – the second article of belief: salvation from God in Jesus – can only be understood as a specific way of making belief in creation more precise. It does make belief in creation more precise, gives it specific content, in terms of our human history and the historical appearance of Jesus of Nazareth in it. Thus, in Christian terms, belief in creation shows those who are non-divine or vulnerable that God's nature is liberating love in Jesus the Christ.

People evidently find it difficult to believe in a divine being which in utter freedom determines what and who and how 'it', 'he', 'she' (here human words fail completely!) really is. Nevertheless, this is what belief in creation is. We ourselves, in accordance with our own vision of life and our plans for it, can only determine who, what and how we want to be in a very limited degree, dependent on all kinds of conditions. And even then, to a large extent we still fall short. In contrast, God's being is utterly and precisely as God wills it to be, without any remainder. He determines freely what he wills to be, as God, for himself and for us, not in arbitrary sovereignty, but in unconditional love. For those who oppose death, injustice and alienation, and dare to choose life, this Christian belief in creation offers a secure footing. 'God is love. In this the love of God was made manifest among us, that God sent his only Son into the world, so that we might live through him' (1 John 4.8–9). According to the New Testament, the Word which, in the Old Testament, had already spoken above all of love, has become flesh in Jesus of Nazareth: incarnate love.

Therefore 'Christology' is concentrated creation: belief in creation as God wills it to be. It is not a new divine plan for a creation which has gone wrong, which is the way in which some religions interpret particular human experiences; it is the supreme expression of God's eternally new being which we can perceive to some degree only from ongoing creation and its history. In the creed, in which belief in creation is essentially bound up with belief in the person of Jesus as God's definitive salvation for men and women, we bear witness to our readiness to accept that we are loved 'for nothing' by a God who takes the side of humanity, unconditionally and

---

[9] I deliberately use the somewhat pedantic word 'relational' here to avoid the ambiguity of 'relative'. Relative is opposed to absolute, but that is not necessarily the case with the word 'relational'.

without our deserving it, a God who stands up for the humanness and humanity of men and women. This is expressed most strongly in the words of St. Paul: 'He loved us when we were still sinners' (Rom 5.8), or in Johannine theology: 'In this is love, not that we loved God but that he loved us' (1 John 4.10).

Only through Christ do we begin to realise clearly that there is more to God than might otherwise have been expected. God, the creator, the one in whom we can trust, *is* liberating love for humanity, in a way which fulfils and transcends all human, personal, social and political expectations.

We can and even must ask why, for what sound reasons did people who call themselves Christians arrive at the conviction that it is God's nature to love humanity, and not, as was often said earlier, even in the older strata of the Old Testament, that he is a God who has arbitrary and sovereign control over human life and death. Christians have learned this through their experience of the life of Jesus: from his message and from the way in which he lived in conformity with that message, from the specific circumstances of his death, and finally from the apostolic witness to his resurrection from the dead.

The message and praxis of the kingdom of God

It is striking that there is no mention in the creed of the message and lifestyle of Jesus, which are the foundation of his death and resurrection (see below). In the Bible, and above all in the New Testament, 'kingdom of God' is the expression used to indicate the nature of God – unconditional and liberating sovereign love – in so far as this makes itself felt and is revealed in the life of men and women who do God's will. It is enough to choose one text at random from the rich store of New Testament stories about Jesus' message and praxis, viz., Luke's account of the calling of Peter (Luke 5.1–11). In it we hear of two boats drawn up on the shore and a number of fishermen who are mending their nets after an unsuccessful, indeed quite useless night of fishing. Jesus 'happens' to pass by. He simply gets into one of the two empty boats and says to a fisherman, Peter, 'Come on, we're going out on the lake.' Peter looks at this man, who is still a stranger, and without knowing precisely why, accepts his suggestion: he gets into the boat with Jesus. The others follow. Then Jesus begins to talk about a mysterious kingdom which nonetheless seems to be something quite definite, 'the kingdom of God', a kingdom for poor fishermen, joy for those who weep, satisfaction for those who are hungry. Suddenly he changes the topic again and says, 'Let's go out into deeper water, and then we will catch big fish.' And indeed, a short while later there are so many fish that the nets seem likely to break. After what Peter had just heard about the coming kingdom of God, especially for the poor, for fishermen with empty nets, Peter felt the approaching nearness of God, and said in great anxiety, 'Go away from me, Lord, for I am a sinful man'. To perceive God in their everyday lives seems to make people anxious, just as small birds are terrified at the approach of the great eagle which is going to devour them. But Jesus says, 'Do not be afraid.' And the story goes on, 'They brought their boat to shore, left everything and followed him.' The text runs, 'Do not be afraid, from now on you will be catching people.' For Peter however, this was not the heart of the matter at that moment. It did not have to do with his one day becoming a great apostle; the important thing for Peter at that moment was Jesus' reassuring remark, 'Do not be afraid.'

People's deepest feelings do, in fact, make them expect the most grotesque things from their God. They expect that if they were to give themselves to God completely and to concern themselves only with God's cause, nothing would be left but God, the great eagle who swallows up all the smaller birds, and that they would, therefore, have to do without themselves and the whole marvellous world of God's creation. The fact that the human cause is God's cause, and vice versa, and that this is what Jesus means when he talks about the kingdom of God, transcends all our human expectations of God. People imagine God in a very different way from the way in which he sees himself and presents himself. 'Does not even the sparrow find a home? Does not the swallow have its own nest?' In that case, will the small birds fall victim to the Great Eagle? When people think of God in human terms it can indeed lead to bizarre ideas. At one time people offered human sacrifice to honour their God. Are things any different in our day? Does not a great deal of evil and suffering come about in our world in the name of God? But Jesus says, 'Do not be afraid'; do not be afraid when you feel God approaching. God is a God of humanity, a God who, as Leviticus says, 'abominates human sacrifices' (Lev 18.21–30; 20.1–5). God is indeed a fire, but a fire which does not consume the burning bush but leaves it intact. God's honour lies in human happiness.

The full content of this human salvation and happiness – the kingdom of God – transcends the power of our human imagination. We only get a faint idea of it, on the one hand, through human experiences of goodness, meaning and love; and on the other, as reflected in situations in which, whether as individuals or societies, we experience a threat to what is human in us, finding it oppressed and degraded in such a way that we rebel against it. However, these experiences only stand out properly against the background of Jesus' life, the way in which he went about Palestine 'doing good'. Here we have an expressive form of the vision of what the kingdom of God can be. The New Testament has recorded this in one of its earliest recollections, when it says that, with Jesus, the kingdom of God approaches us (Matt 12.28; Luke 11.20; see Matt 3.2; 4.17; 10.7; Mark 1.15). The kingdom of God is a new relationship of humanity to God, and the visible tangible side of it is a new type of liberating mutual relationship between human beings themselves, within a peaceful, reconciling society. The wolf and the lamb lie down together, and the child plays by the snake's hole. To believe in this at its deepest, i.e. to believe in Jesus as the Christ, means to confess and actually to recognise that Jesus has a permanent and constitutive significance in the imminent approach of the kingdom of God, and thus in the all-embracing healing of men and women and making them whole. Our Christian creed is essentially concerned with Jesus' own unique relationship to the coming kingdom of God as salvation for humanity. 'I tell you, everyone who acknowledges me before men, the Son of Man will also acknowledge as his own before God's angels' (i.e. at the last judgment)': this is the way in which the New Testament translates Jesus' own understanding of himself (Luke 12.8f. = Matt 10.32f.; see also Mark 3.28f.; Matt 12.32; Luke 12.10). For believers, the person of Jesus has worldwide historical significance. It is a fundamental Christian conviction that, with the coming of Jesus, 'God brushes up against us', so it has to be expressed in the creed in some way or other.

Of course we must remember here that (given the existence of the Jewish Yahwistic tradition) Jesus did not so much introduce a new doctrine of God; rather, he had a particularly sharp prophetic eye for the way in which this concept of God functioned in the society of his time, to the detriment of those who were already of no account. Jesus unmasked a concept of God which enslaves people; he fought for a view of God as a God who liberates humanity, a view which has to be expressed in specific actions. As a result, in the Christian gospel both 'God' and 'Jesus' take on a critical and productive, liberating force of their own. A religion which in fact serves to dehumanise people, in whatever way, is either a false religion or a religion which has a mistaken understanding of itself. This criterion of 'humanising' which Jesus proclaimed, a passion for the humanity of human beings, for its totality and wholeness, is not a reduction of religion, as Jesus' opponents feared (both then and now). It is the primary condition for human possibility and religion's credibility. Furthermore, it is the only logical conclusion from the Christian vision of the nature of God, confessed as love. Jesus Christ is the 'great symbol' of this God and no other, the 'image of the invisible God' (Col 1.15; see 2 Cor 4.3f.). Here Jesus is at the same time the image of what a human being really needs to be as well, a picture of true and good humanity. The fact that believers knew themselves to be confronted uniquely by God himself in Jesus, in some way or other, was expressed in the creed by the confession, 'I believe in Jesus: God's only Son'. For in Jesus we are not just confronted with God; in Jesus we are also addressed by God: in Jesus God confronts us with his own being. Jesus is therefore 'the word of God', i.e. not only the interpreter of humanity, someone who shows in word and deed what it can mean to be a truly human being, but at the same time the interpreter or exegete of God, someone who shows us in word and deed who and how God himself is. From the life of Jesus, Christians learn to give stammering utterance to the content of what 'God' is and the content of what 'human being' is. Within the context of their own, different questions of a later period of time, the fathers of the Council of Chalcedon had the same concern as the authors of the Apostles' Creed when they said that one and the same Jesus Christ is truly human and truly God. Salvation from God in Jesus. The spirit in which we prayerfully use the creed is not that of cramped orthodoxy, but the spirit of the gospel: 'Lord, I believe, help my unbelief' (Mark 9.23).

Parables of the kingdom of God[10]

Jesus clarified what he meant by 'kingdom of God' and thus by 'God' above all in the language of parables.[11] The originality with which Jesus talks about God

---

[10] Selected from: Edward Schillebeeckx, *Church: The Human Story of God*, Collected Works of Edward Schillebeeckx vol. 10 (London: Bloomsbury T&T Clark, 2014), 113–14 [114–16].

[11] For the distinctive image of God in the parables see W. G. Kümmel, *Heilsgeschehen und Geschichte. Gesammelte Aufsätze 1933-1964*, Marburg 1965; J. Dupont, *Études sur les Évangiles Synoptiques*, two vols., Louvain/Gembloux 1985; H. Merklein, *Die Gottesherrschaft als Handlungsprinzip. Untersuchung zur Ethik Jesu*, Forschung zur Bibel 34, Würzburg 1981; J. Zumstein, *La condition du croyant dans l'Évangile selon Mathieu*, Orbis Biblicus et Orientalis 16, Fribourg and Göttingen 1977, 407–16; H. Merklein and E. Zenger, 'Ich will euer Gott werden', *Beispiele biblischen Redens von Gott*, Bibelstudien 100, Stuttgart 1981, 152–76.

does not diverge substantially from the Old Testament image or concept of God. But particular accents above all from the prophetic proclamation of what and who God is take on such a distinctive profile in Jesus' preaching, to the point of almost being over-emphasised, that other aspects of the traditional picture of God are constantly forced into the shade. Generally speaking, we can say that according to Jesus, his God – the God of Abraham, Isaac and Jacob, the God of Moses, the God whom Jesus called his 'Father' – is a God who does not let himself be claimed by a caste of pious and virtuous people who know that 'they are not like the tax-collectors and sinners' and are sure of a commensurate reward for their faithful observance of the law. No, all parables rule out this view of God; Jesus shows that God comes to stand on the side of those who are pushed aside by the 'community which thinks well of itself': the poor, the oppressed, the outcast and even the sinful. But this 'God of the poor and sinners' is not an indulgent God: he lays claim completely on men and women and asks them to follow him with a undivided heart.

This already emerges from the parable of the lost sheep (Matt 18.12–14; Luke 15.4–7): the behaviour of the shepherd illustrates God's action as Jesus lives it out for us. Here is a God who is more concerned about one benighted sheep than about the ninety-nine who are safe. The parable of the 'lost son' further stresses this (Luke 15.11–32). The utterly surprising attitude of the father towards the prodigal son promptly provokes the indignation of the oldest son (Jesus' first listeners). But Jesus teaches them that the sinner remains their brother or sister and that they all must share in God's joy over the conversion of the sinner. In the parable of the Pharisee and the publican (Luke 18.10–14), the pious Pharisee who in fact keeps the law scrupulously and thanks God because he is not like this sinner is turned away by God. The publican who feels unworthy to appear before God goes away 'justified'. Moreover in the parable of the workers employed from the eleventh hour (Matt 20.1–15) Jesus presents a very provocative picture of God: God remains free in handing out his gifts and favours. No one is so justified before God through good works as to stand in the way of God's goodness to those who have no good works to offer, or at least have few 'merits'. This attitude of God then becomes all the more challenging for pious and virtuous people since it is really about sinners. To offer forgiveness to one sinner causes God more joy than the salvation of ninety-nine righteous.

The parables finally speak about God, although he is almost never named. They teach us that God does not mean to be a guarantor of privileged positions in bourgeois or religious society. In contrast to the dominant and conformist images of God in his time, Jesus presents a God who shows special love towards those who are handicapped, crippled, oppressed and marginalised, even sinful. For it is not the perhaps hidden spiritual or ethical nobility of the poor and outcast which moves Jesus to this special love. He looks around in the first place for particular people because they are handicapped, crippled, poor or seriously ill. It is precisely these people who accept his message, while the wise and intelligent elite rejects it. In the parables Jesus shows 'the other face of religion (or the church)': his way of being the 'God of men and women', of all men and women, makes him primarily the God of the outcast and the excluded. Anyone who cannot hear that from the New Testament, above all in the parables, has understood nothing of Jesus' message of the kingdom of God. It is perhaps our own bourgeois acclimatisation over the centuries, our membership of the 'community which thinks well of itself, that has made us blind to the plain meaning of Jesus' message and the parables which clarify it. The God of Jesus is a God who does not allow himself to be won over by the lobbies of pious people. That is one of the basic elements of Jesus' gospel. As followers of Jesus, we must follow God, 'who makes his sun shine on the good and the evil' (Matt 5.45). The behaviour that Jesus requires of his disciples must distinguish them from the tax collectors and Gentiles (Matt 5.46–47), and from the sinners (Luke 6.32–24). Therefore it is required of Christians that they should 'Be merciful, as your Father is merciful' (Luke 6.36); do not cast out even sinful brothers or sisters. Anyone who opposes any form of discrimination whatsoever has Jesus on his or her side. The commandment 'love your enemies' (Matt 5.44–45; Luke 6.35) is on the same wavelength as the radicalism of Jesus' love of the neighbour. Anyone who follows that commandment will be called son of God (Matt 5.9).

Jesus' praxis of the kingdom of God[12]

The kingdom of God is a new world in which suffering is abolished, a world of completely whole or healed human beings in a society where peace reigns and there are no master-servant relationships – quite a different situation from that in the society of the time. As things are there 'it may not be so among you' (Luke 22.24–27; Mark 10.42–43; Matt 20.25–26). However, the coming of this new world does not take place without human action, in which Jesus has preceded us.

For alongside Jesus' proclamation there is his action, and in particular the New Testament miracle stories. Historically there can be no doubt that in the time of Jesus and the early church phenomena were produced by religious preachers which their contemporaries adjudged to be miracles. The separate stories in the New Testament reflect the awareness of the narrators that Jesus did miracles, although they express this awareness in forms which do not correspond to our understanding of these events. It is certain that people experienced fullness of life in Jesus' company in a way that immeasurably transcended their everyday experiences. In this context the miracles are signs of the 'whole', healed and sound world of the kingdom of God which is made present in them. Moreover the proclamation of the nearness of the rule of God and the miracles of Jesus belong inseparably together.

By both the parables of the kingdom of God and Jesus' praxis of the kingdom of God it becomes clear how Jesus relativises the human, sometimes heartless principle of justice. Jesus' praxis and parables often offend our sense of justice even now. The worker at the eleventh hour gets just as much as the worker at the first hour (Matt 20.1–17), and from the person who has nothing will be taken away even what he has (Matt 25.29). Jesus here wants to teach us that the rules for the praxis of the kingdom

---

[12]Selected from: Edward Schillebeeckx, *Church: The Human Story of God*, Collected Works of Edward Schillebeeckx vol. 10 (London: Bloomsbury T&T Clark, 2014), 115–17 [117–18].

of God have nothing to do with the social rules in our societies; this is an alternative form of action. Jesus does not defend immoral or anarchical people, but he does go and stand alongside them. He unmasks the intentions of those who are zealous for God and righteousness; he takes from these zealots even what they have: a zeal for God and the law which excludes people. He points to the perverse effects of virtue like that of the oldest brother of the lost son (Luke 15.11–32) who is overbearing about the repentance of his youngest brother. Jesus reacts sharply against those who manipulate the social rules. Strict justice can involve the excommunication of men and women who are already public outcasts. The coming of the kingdom of God does not know the human logic of precise justice. Jesus wants to give hope to those who from a social and human point of view, according to our human rules, no longer have any hope.

There is something subtle and killing in a particular kind of virtue. The subtle vice of 'perfection' has not yet disappeared from church life. People defend so-called unassailable laws, and in so doing injure already vulnerable fellow human beings. Jesus showed that up. The effect of this zeal is often to deprive people of room to breathe. Jesus opposes worldly practice when the law has the effect of excluding the other person. If the law reduces people to despair, it forfeits all authority. For Jesus, the poor and the outcast are the criterion of whether the law is functioning creatively or destructively, as the will of God for the benefit of human beings. Even the tradition of Jesus' Jewish people, of Israel, is not the final authority for him. For him, this tradition has a human legitimacy, but he does not submit to it unconditionally.

The novelty of Jesus' attitude to law, to tradition, to the existing pictures of God, does not derive directly from his transcendent authority, which puts itself in the place of Moses. If that happens, the new features that emerge in Jesus are derived without any intermediary directly from his divinity, and the critical power of his human choice, the reason why he was condemned, is completely trivialised. For Jesus, God is not the guarantor of society, of prosperity, and of the family.

Jesus' picture of God is determined by the thirsty, the stranger, the prisoner, the sick, the outcast; here he sees God (Matt 25). In all his behaviour, Jesus rejects justice as the 'absolute imperative' (Matt 20.15–16). In his view justice is not the last word. Jesus takes the part of those who have no advocate but many accusers, who with their references to the law, pointing their fingers, expel men and women and thus kick them when they are down.

In all this Jesus is aware that he is acting as God would. In and through his life he relates God's action to human beings. In his parables he is concerned with the one lost sheep, a lost coin, a lost son. To fellow believers who are offended at his dealings with unclean people, Jesus seeks to make clear through his actions that God turns towards lost and vulnerable people; Jesus acts as God acts. So in him there is a claim that *God himself* is present in his actions and words. To act as Jesus does is praxis of the kingdom of God, and moreover a demonstration of what the kingdom of God is: salvation for human beings.

That Jesus' activity in healing and performing cures, along with all his conduct which frees men and women from need and misery, is part of his task is also shown by the fact that he sent out his disciples not just to hand on his message of the forgiveness of sins and eternal life but also with the task of 'curing and healing people' (cf. Mark 3.14–16; 6.7ff.). The kingdom of God includes forgiveness of sins, but it is more than that. The people who can experience salvation from God in Jesus are also themselves called to do this after Jesus, to an even greater degree (John 14.12), in unconditional love towards their fellow human beings. The foundation of the life of the disciples of Jesus lies in the life which Jesus himself led in his day.

Selected literature

- The Actions of Jesus' Life as Manifestations of Divine Love; Selected from: Edward Schillebeeckx, *Christ the Sacrament of the Encounter with God*, trans. Paul Barrett, N. D. Smith, Collected Works of Edward Schillebeeckx vol. 1 (London: Bloomsbury T&T Clark, 2014), 9–26 [13–43], 12–14 [18–22].
- God's Message in Jesus; Selected from: Edward Schillebeeckx, *Jesus: An Experiment in Christology*, trans. John Bowden, Collected Works of Edward Schillebeeckx vol. 6 (London: Bloomsbury T&T Clark, 2014), 599–601 [636–9].
- The Continuity between Jesus of Nazareth and the Risen One; Selected from: Edward Schillebeeckx, *Jesus: An Experiment in Christology*, trans. John Bowden, Collected Works of Edward Schillebeeckx vol. 6 (London: Bloomsbury T&T Clark, 2014), 603–5 [641–3].
- Parables of the Kingdom of God; Selected from: Edward Schillebeeckx, *Church: The Human Story of God*, Collected Works of Edward Schillebeeckx vol. 10 (London: Bloomsbury T&T Clark, 2014), 113–14 [114–16].
- Jesus' Praxis of the Kingdom of God; Selected from: Edward Schillebeeckx, *Church: The Human Story of God*, Collected Works of Edward Schillebeeckx vol. 10 (London: Bloomsbury T&T Clark, 2014), 115–17 [117–18].

14

Grace

The concept of *charis* or grace[1]

Corresponding to the key Old Testament concepts ḥesed and ḥānan, in the New Testament grace means, the benevolent and merciful (and at the same time free and sovereign) love of God for people. This is not, however, to be understood exclusively in an internalised sense, as a benevolent disposition of God and in God, but rather as a benevolence of God which in fact brings salvation that manifests or reveals itself freely in the favours of redemption and liberation shown forth in history and experienced by people in faith (for Jewish Christians the Old Testament concept of ḥesed and ḥānan rules out any dualism between inwardness and its outward expression).

Grace is a *new way of life* prepared for us by God in Jesus Christ, and offered to us on the level of our own earthly history, freely (Paul) and to make us glad (Luke) (see Heb 10.20; 2 Pet 2.15; John 14.6; a way of salvation: Acts 16.17; 9.2; 19.23; 24.14; 1 Cor 12.31; 'the way' is an oriental expression, also to be found in late antiquity, for a particular practice and viewpoint which leads to salvation). Thus grace is a new human possibility for life, a particular mode of existence through which and in which human beings really experience salvation and redemption, liberation and renewal of life, happiness and fulfilment. For the New Testament, 'the way' means following the life of Jesus with God, expressed in his concern for humanity, in solidarity with our experience of God's care for all: a way of life or mode of existence through which God's own concern, his merciful love and faithfulness – ḥesed and 'ᵉmet – on which we can rely, are continued by human beings in our earthly history.

God himself equips human beings for this. For although this new possibility for human living, proclaimed by Jesus in his preaching and in his parables, demonstrated and put into practice in his way of life and his death, is given a variety of names in the New Testament, they all fundamentally express a single reality. Pauline theology calls it adoption *(hyiothesia)*, Johannine theology *birth from God*. Both conceptions

---

[1] Selected from: Edward Schillebeeckx, *Christ: The Christian Experience in the Modern World*, Collected Works of Edward Schillebeeckx vol. 7 (London: Bloomsbury T&T Clark, 2014), 453–7 [465–8].

seek to express that the Christian has a share in the particular relationship which binds Jesus, in his humanity, as the Son, through the Spirit with the Father – three concepts (Father, Son and Spirit) which in the New Testament point to God, but *in* his attitude towards people.

The concept of grace therefore points primarily towards a *call* to this special living community with God: the Christian vocation as a consequence of a prior decision made freely and graciously by God, who calls people to the way of the gospel (Gal 1.6; 1 Tim 1.11). On the other hand, by virtue of this call, namely as the obedience of faith (Gal 3.5; 1 Cor 2.12; Rom 6.16; 5.15, etc.), the concept points to Christian life itself: existence in grace, in being and acting, through which this responsible action is experienced as being supported, guided and directed by the power of Jesus which, as divine *dynamis* (Acts 4.33; 6.8; 20.32; 14.26; 15.40; 18.27; 1.18; 6.14; 2 Cor 4.7; 12.9f.; 2 Tim 2.1; Rom 1.16; Eph 2.7f., etc.) 'fulfils everything in us' (Col 1.6f.), 'through faith which is at work in our love (of neighbour)' (Gal 5.6).

This divine calling has appeared to us personally in Jesus and has taken shape in his personal call: to be converted, to take a different course from the one that we have been on, since the kingdom of God is now near (Mark 1.14f.). Therefore for those who have not themselves heard this historical call of Jesus, the good news of this event is given by the Christian community in the world which is itself grace and power (Acts 5.20; 20.24,32; Luke 4.22; 1 Cor 15.2; James 1.21; 2 Tim 1.1; Eph 6.15, etc.). In addition, there is above all the event itself, Jesus' personal appearance in our history, the grace of which the New Testament particularly speaks. Individual texts, taken from a wide variety of New Testament writings, seek to express in brief formulations what these Christians have experienced as salvation from God and how they have experienced God as salvation.

> 'Grace and truth have come to us in Jesus Christ' (John 1.17)
> 'The great gift of the grace of God: the one man Jesus Christ' (Rom 5.15, with 5.17)
> 'God's saving grace appeared to all people' (Titus 2.11)
> 'The goodness and loving-kindness – *(philanthropia* as an exceptional Septuagint translation of *hesed)* – of God our saviour has appeared' (Titus 3.4)
> 'God made all fullness dwell in him' (Col 1.9)
> 'For in him the whole fullness of deity dwells bodily, and you have come to fullness of life in him' (Col 2.9)
> 'One mediator between God and a human being, the person Christ Jesus' (1 Tim)
> 'He is the access to the Father' (Rom 5.2) 'He has richly poured out the Spirit upon us through Jesus Christ our saviour' (Titus 3.6)
> 'In this the love of God was made manifest among us, that God sent his only Son into the world' (1 John 4.9); and, 'See what love the Father has given us that we should be called children of God; and so we are' (1 John 3.1)
> 'God who has called us... to receive a share in God's own being' (2 Pet 1.4c).

It is already clear from these texts how in the New Testament religious awareness, the religious experience of God, has its focal point in its connection with Jesus Christ, in his humanity. Is Jesus here the symbolic point of reference of a kind *of mysticism of being?* Or is a *historical* event really the specific Christian access to God? The New Testament defends the latter point of view, sometimes with great stubbornness. Johannine theology, which most markedly demonstrates a degree of God-mysticism, nevertheless attacks any *lyein ton Iēsoun* (1 John 4.3), that is, any attempt to do away with Jesus of Nazareth in favour of a heavenly or spiritual Christ principle (see also the deliberate use of 'Jesus' – not 'Jesus Christ' – in Eph 4.21). Here we find the same interest as that from which the first three gospels were written.

There is a previous history to this appearance of God's grace in Jesus Christ which gives us his and God's Spirit. But as the New Testament lives under the spell of Jesus' experience of grace, it shows less interest in God's revelation of grace outside Christianity. From a psychological point of view, this results in a certain narrowing of perspective and at a very early stage in a pattern of thinking in terms of thesis and antithesis. Nevertheless, at the periphery of this enthusiasm engendered by the Spirit over what has been experienced and continues to be experienced in Jesus Christ, these Christians are aware that universal grace had been revealed in a great many ways even before Jesus Christ: fundamentally in the history which embraces all people, as the event of people in nature, which arouses an ethical and even a religious consciousness (above all Rom 1.18–22), and especially through Israel's own history in the melting-pot of the history of the nations of the surrounding world (Heb 1.1; Rom 2.1–3.20). Jesus of Nazareth makes his appearance against this general and specific historical background (Rom 3.21–4.5), as God's 'amen' to all his promises to Israel and thus to all peoples (2 Cor 1.20).

Jesus as grace: The risen Christ as grace

All the parts of the New Testament assert that the earthly appearing of Jesus is the grace of God. But there are marked differences of accent. In the four gospels the whole event of and around Jesus is a sign of the grace of God. For Mark this is true from the baptism of Jesus on, and for Matthew, Luke and John from the first moment of his coming into the world (John 1.14; 3.16; 12.46f.; see also 1 John 4.9, 14). Not only his death and his resurrection but also his message of God's kingdom, intended for humanity, and his whole way of life are gifts of grace; his dealings with people, above all in eating with them, his care and concern and especially his contact with sinners, the poor and the oppressed who were despised by the religious and suffered the social consequences of this discrimination. It emerges above all from the supposition to be found even before Easter, that to take up an attitude for or against Jesus has to do with a decision about one's own destiny: a decision for or against the coming kingdom of God.[2]

The all-embracing manifestation of grace, however, both in the four canonical gospels and above all in the whole of the rest of the New Testament, is Jesus' love to the point of death: his suffering and dying as a breaking of the life which he entrusts to his God, in grief, but with all his heart (see Rom 5.9–11; 1 Cor 15.2f;

---

[2]See *Jesus: An Experiment in Christology*, 120–240 [140–271].

2 Cor 3.17f; Heb 10.29; 1 Pet 2.21; 2 Tim 1.10b, etc.): 'He who did not spare his own Son but gave him up for us all, will he not *also give us all things* with him?' (Rom 8.32). 'God so loved the world that he gave his only begotten Son that all who believe in him should not perish but have everlasting life' (John 3.16). Above all in Paul and in the New Testament traditions influenced by Paul, the grace of God in Christ is so strongly concentrated in the death and resurrection of Jesus that there is a tendency to concentrate and to limit *charis* as it has appeared in Jesus exclusively to his death and resurrection. So Paul himself never connects the term *charis* with the message and the appearing of Jesus of Nazareth, but only with Christ Jesus who has risen from the dead. Paul never associates *charis* with *Jesus* but only with (Jesus) *Christ,* the risen one (Gal 2.19; see 1 Cor 1.30; 2 Cor 5.21). Only the *Lord* Jesus is grace. Without the resurrection from the dead, the earthly appearance of Jesus in fact remains open, even problematical. However, the four gospels avoid this exclusively *kerygmatic* conception of the dead and risen Jesus; in their proclamation *of the gospel* they also recognise the grace to be found in the message of Jesus and his way of life (albeit in the light of the resurrection).

It is, however, true of the whole of the canonical New Testament that death and resurrection are the determinative climax of the grace of God in Jesus Christ. Only after Jesus, dying, has firmly held God's hand and in turn has known himself to be sustained in this impenetrable situation,[3] is he confirmed by God: 'By the grace of God Jesus tasted death for everyone' (Heb 2.9). Hebrews above all emphatically stresses that an exclusive divine act on the part of the Father gives 'perfecting' constitutive significance to the reality of Jesus' sacrifice. This in no way removes the element of Jesus' own love to the point of death, indeed it even presupposes it, as it is this that is confirmed and sealed by God in the resurrection or glorification of Jesus. Jesus' resurrection is thus a free and sovereign action on the part of God, even if it manifests itself as already beginning *in* Jesus' personal communion with God into which he has incorporated his suffering and dying. From God's perspective, this very communion is already a manifestation of *grace* to Jesus, a grace which simply reveals its inner dynamic in his exaltation or resurrection and is brought to a final consummation. Only at this final consummation – which Phil 2.9 expressly calls a grace for Jesus himself: *echarisato,* see also Heb 2.9 – can one say that Jesus 'is the cause (source) of eternal salvation' (Heb 5.9). In connection with the historical Jesus, the Gospel of John also says (while putting stress on the grace which already became manifest through the earthly Jesus): 'The Spirit was not yet because Jesus was not yet glorified' (John 7.39, a text which radically excludes the possibility that after his death Jesus again became a post-existent Logos *asarkos,* not incarnate as in his pre-existence).

Thus the New Testament conception conveys that only the risen Jesus bestows eschatological salvation: the *pneuma,* his, God's own Spirit (Rom 8.14-18; 8.29; Gal 4.4-7; Eph 1.3-5; Titus 3.6, etc. see below); the Spirit through which the Christian, thanks to the grace of faith and baptism (Rom 6; Gal 3.26f.; Titus 3.5), is conformed to God, i.e. receives a share both in his relationship to God and also in his radical service (like an 'elder brother': Rom 8.29) and his dedication to his fellow human being.

---

[3] E. Schillebeeckx, 'Jesus und das menschliche Lebensscheitern', *Concilium* 12, 1976, 189–95.

'To bring all to unity (peace)'[4]

The object of the investigation here is not biblical faith in creation as such, but the biblical theology of grace. As in the Christian tradition, however, so too in Holy Scripture the central question is that of the relationship between 'nature' (creation) and grace: creation and covenant. This group of problems is the subject of exegetical and theological dispute, and is often complicated by confessional prejudices.

Terminologically speaking, *nature* as opposed to *grace* is not an independent concept in the primal documents of the Jewish-Christian tradition of revelation. There is no Hebrew equivalent for *natura* or *physis* in the Tanach. In the few places where we come across the term nature, *physis,* in the deutero-canonical book of Wisdom (7.20; 13.1; 19.20), as indeed in the New Testament, it does not have any specific theological meaning. The term found an entry into Christian theology when theologians began thinking about the revelation of the grace of God with the help of categories drawn from Greek philosophy: first of all from the popularised concept of nature current among the Stoics, and later in systematic terms drawn from Aristotelianism. Terms like 'nature' and 'creation' (created nature) did not completely coincide. What God has created is not merely a neutral nature which human beings can analyse by means of natural science, but created nature, i.e. the expression of a divine plan which extends beyond 'nature'. In that case, this nature cannot, theologically speaking, be separated from the divine plan. To speak theologically about the natural world, therefore, does not just mean that this nature is contingent, did not need to be 'in and of itself', and could have been otherwise, in other words, that it is transitory; this nature is also the living expression of a divine decision which in the last resort proves to be a will for salvation. Creation and consummation are embraced by one great divine plan. In this sense the theological, philosophical and scientific usages of the term nature differ from one another.

People of earliest times and of antiquity, including the Hebrews, the Israelites, and the believers of the Tanach, lived in a world in which everyone began from the assumption that God – a god or gods – had made or created this world with the people in it. For them, this was something to be taken for granted, an ingredient of their world-view. There was no alternative at that time. However, this accepted state of affairs was misunderstood by the important studies made by G. von Rad; and with his conception of creation and covenant he marked the beginning of the development of a common view which is almost ubiquitous among both Protestant and Catholic exegetes and theologians. Belief in creation is said to be a derivative extrapolation of belief in salvation, and has only a marginal significance in the Old Testament: 'Creation is part of the aetiology of Israel.'[5] This conception, which has been widespread since Karl Barth and Gerhard von Rad, begins from the observation (which is substantially correct) that nowhere in the credal statements of the Tanach is there an expression

---

[4]Selected from: Edward Schillebeeckx, *Christ: The Christian Experience in the Modern World*, Collected Works of Edward Schillebeeckx vol. 7 (London: Bloomsbury T&T Clark, 2014), 503–5 [515–17].
[5]G. von Rad, *Old Testament Theology* I, London and New York 1975, 138. Karl Barth puts forward the same view (probably independently of G. von Rad). The works cited by H. Brongers, the authors of *Mysterium Salutis* and many others are dependent on von Rad.

of belief in creation. The experience of the covenant is said to be the origin of the constituent parts of Old Testament belief in creation. According to this explanation, to the Israelite consciousness Yahweh was not so much the God of creation as the living God, i.e. the God of the grace, election and the history of Israel. 'Thus obedience towards the commandments, precepts and requirements of Yahweh is not required because the Creator has the right to make certain demands of his creatures by virtue of his creation of them, but exclusively because in ancient times Yahweh redeemed his people from alien captivity'.[6] The fundamental creed of Israel is the confession of God's deliverance of Israel from Egypt (Deut 26.5-9). Israel explained its history and brought it up to date on the basis of this creed, and it was this that, not in the beginning but in the course of time, also gave rise to Israel's belief in creation. Only then were accounts of creation put at the beginning of the holy books. Of course, these also took up earlier creation narratives; but it was peculiar to Israel that this belief in creation was seen only in the perspective of the covenant of Yahweh with Israel. Thus creation was thought to be subordinate to the covenant, and not to be an independent theme in the Tanach. However, these authors concede that in a number of passages, above all in Ps 8, but also in Pss 19; 104 and throughout the wisdom literature, we find independent creation hymns; the explanation of these is either that they are litanies in which creation and covenant are celebrated side by side or one after the other, or that they are the consequence of alien influence on Israel. In fact, Ps 19 is certainly part of an ancient hymnic fragment from Canaan, and Ps 104 shows striking similarities to the famous Egyptian hymn to Aten. By and large, the same kind of Egyptian influence can be detected throughout the wisdom literature; the influence of Egyptian didactic poetry is especially discernible in the later wisdom literature. Instead of a theology of creation embedded in salvation history, we find there an almost metaphysical, independent concept of creation. Creation is treated as an independent theme, apart from salvation history, in Job 28; Prov 8; Sir 24.

God of Grace, Jesus Christ and the Spirit[7]

What the New Testament calls 'the gift of the Holy Spirit' (e.g. Acts 2.38; 10.38) presents a variety of problems. No difficulty is found in also ascribing to the Holy Spirit all the gifts of salvation which are ascribed to Christ – salvation, deliverance, redemption, justification, sanctification, access to the Father, etc. There is a *pneuma hagiasmou* (Rom 15.13, 16; 1.4; 2 Thess 2.13; Gal 5.6; Acts 26.18; 1 Pet 1.2), a spirit of sanctification; a *pneuma dikaiosyēs*, a spirit of justification (1 Cor 6.11; Tim. 3.16; 1 Pet 1.2); a *pneuma apolytrōseōs*, a spirit of liberation (Eph 4.30); a *pneuma zōēs*, spirit of life (Rom 8.2, 6, 10f.; 2 Cor 3.6; John 6.63; 1 Pet 3.18; Gal 5.25); a *pneuma tēs pisteōs*, spirit of faith (2 Cor 4.13; Acts 11.24). Grace is also a *koinōnia pneumatos*, communion of the spirit (Phil 2.1; 2 Cor 13.14) which (like Christ) 'gives access to the Father' (Eph 2.18) in 'a spirit of renewal' (Titus 3.5; Eph 4.23). This is the 'spirit of

---

[6]H. Brongers, *De scheppingstradities bij den profeten*, Amsterdam 1945, 116.
[7]Selected from: Edward Schillebeeckx, *Christ: The Christian Experience in the Modern World*, Collected Works of Edward Schillebeeckx vol. 7 (London: Bloomsbury T&T Clark, 2014), 523–5 [534–6].

joy' (Rom 14.17; Gal 5.22; 1 Thess 1.6), 'the spirit of peace' (Gal 5.22; Rom 14.17; 8.6) and 'the spirit of love' (Rom 15.30; 1 Cor 4.21; Col 1.8; see Rom 5.5; 2 Tim 1.7, etc.). Moreover, in the New Testament the spirit is understood on the one hand in terms of Christ (Rom 8.9; 1 Cor 15.45; Gal 4.6), while on the other hand Christ is understood in terms of the Spirit: Jesus is the fruit of the Spirit, who begets him (Matt 1.18; Luke 1.35); he is 'born of the Spirit' (Luke 4.18), which descends on him at his baptism (Mark 1.10 par.); Jesus is 'risen in the power of the Spirit' (Rom 1.4; 1 Tim 3.16). Finally, Christ means 'anointed with the Spirit' (Acts 10.38).[8] Hence the changing occurrence of expressions with the same content like 'in Christ' and 'in the Spirit', at least in Paul and the writings inspired by Pauline theology (this equation is impossible in Johannine theology because there the *pneuma*-paraclete has another significance and function). Finally, *hyiothesia* or adoption (Gal 4.5; Rom 8.15,23; Eph 1.5; see Rom 9.4, *hyiothesia* as the privilege of Israel) is a gift of the Spirit, above all if we compare Gal 4.5f, and Rom 8.15f. Christians receive the *hyiothesia* as they receive the Spirit (see Gal 3.2, 14; Rom 8.15; 1 Cor 2.12). The Spirit which we receive is the Spirit of the Son of God (Gal 4.6). Is the Spirit poured out on us because we are children of adoption, or does God pour out the Spirit so that we may become children? I do not believe that we should pose this question with excessive theological concern: to become children is receiving the gift of the Spirit; that becomes even clearer in Johannine theology which speaks of a spiritual birth from God. Sonship or adoption is realised specifically through faith, baptism and the gift of the Spirit; this forms a single (liturgical) event the elements of which can hardly be separated by analysis (hence the aorist: the Spirit is given at baptism). The 'spirit of the Son' is the Son himself in his 'spiritual' presence (see Rom 5.5). The Spirit itself therefore gives Christians the experience of the Father (Rom 8.14; Gal 4.6; see 1 John 3.24). The grace of the Father in Christ is the spirit of grace: *pneuma tēs charitos* (Heb 10.29; see Zech 12.10).

Through the grace of Jesus Christ, the *pneuma* is 'the Spirit that dwells in us' (2 Tim 1.14; Rom 8.9, 11; 1 Cor 3.16; James 4.5); thus the man of grace is 'an abode of God' (Eph 2.22; see 1 Cor 3.16; 6.19). The New Testament does not make more precise the relationship between the redeeming work of Jesus Christ and the same work of the Holy Spirit, and perhaps that is unnecessary. Apart from a few texts in the Gospel of John, it is therefore obscure whether the Spirit should be translated in the masculine or the neuter. The Johannine Jesus calls the Holy Spirit *'another* Paraclete' (John 14.16), while 1 John 2.1 evidently calls Christ himself 'our Paraclete with God', i.e. intercessor.[9] The identification of *pneuma* (Spirit of

---

[8] See *Jesus: An Experiment in Christology*, pp. 404–8 [441–4].
[9] Literature on the Paraclete-Spirit in connection with Johannine theology: H. Schlier, 'Der Heilige Geist als Interpret nach dem Johannesevangelium', *Internationale Kirchliche Zeitung* 2, 1973, 97–103; R. Brown, *The Gospel according to John*, London 1972, 2, 1135–43 (see also in *New Testament Studies* 13, 1966–67, 113f.); J. Schreiner, 'Geistbegabung in der Gemeinde von Qumran', *Biblische Zeitschrift* 9, 1965, 161–80; G. Johnston, *The Spirit-Paraclete in the Gospel of John*, Cambridge 1970; F. Porsch, *Pneuma und Wort*, Frankfurt 1974; F. Mussner, 'Die johanneischen Parakletensprüche und die apostolische Tradition', *Biblische Zeitschrift* 5, 1961, 56–70; A. R. C. Leaney, 'The Johannine Paraclete and the Qumran Scrolls', in *John and Qumran*, ed. J. Charlesworth, London 1972, 38–61; O. Betz, *Der Paraklet: Fürsprecher im häretischen Spätjudentum, im Johannesevangelium und in neugefundenen gnostischen Schriften*, Leiden 1963; P. Schäfer, *Die Vorstellung vom Heiligen Geist in der Rabbinischen Literatur*, STANT 28, Munich 1972; N. Johansson, *Paraklētoi. Vorstellungen von Fürsprechen für die Menschen vor Gott in der alttestamentlichen Religion, im Spätjudentum*

truth) with Paraclete is a feature of Johannine theology. John's purpose is perhaps to make the inter-testamental Paraclete completely dependent on Christ (see above). The concept of the Paraclete is the way and means by which John *Christianises* the concept of *pneuma;* the term Paraclete makes the *pneuma* Christocentric. So it is the Spirit which provides the connection between the historical Jesus of Nazareth and the contemporary life of faith of the Johannine community; the Paraclete provides the connection between the past and the present; he brings up to date the revelation which is accomplished in Jesus. The contemporary church is the place in which the saving work that God has begun in Christ is continued by the Spirit. The Father gives us the Son (John 3.16), and the Father gives us the Spirit (John 14.16). The Spirit is both *pneuma* of God (the Father: Matt 10.20; 12.28; Luke 11.13; Acts 5.32; Rom 8.9, 13; 1 Cor 2.11–14; 3.16; 6.11; 7.40; 12.3; 2 Cor 3.3; Eph 4.30; 1 Pet 4.14; 1 John 4.13) and the *pneuma* of Christ (or of Jesus, the Son, of Jesus Christ: Gal 4.6; Rom 8.9; 2 Cor 3.17f.; John 14.16f; 1 Pet 1.11; Phil 1.19). According to the New Testament, Christ and the Spirit evidently perform the same function. This raises the question of the relationship between *Christology* and *pneumatology*. Furthermore, God is also called *pneuma* (John 4.24); this is not an ontological definition, but a reference to his heavenly sphere of life and a way of denoting God in accordance with his active relationship to humanity, namely because he gives the Spirit (John 14.16; like 'God is light', 1 John 1.5; and 'God is love', 1 John 4.8, namely as the one who gives light and love to people). Like Christ, the Holy Spirit also 'brings about all things' (1 Cor 12.11). On one occasion Christ himself is called *pneuma* (2 Cor 3.17).

Selected literature

- The Concept of *Charis* or Grace; Selected from: Edward Schillebeeckx, *Christ: The Christian Experience in the Modern World*, Collected Works of Edward Schillebeeckx vol. 7 (London: Bloomsbury T&T Clark, 2014), 453–7 [465–8].
- To Bring All to Unity; Selected from: Edward Schillebeeckx, *Christ: The Christian Experience in the Modern World*, Collected Works of Edward Schillebeeckx vol. 7 (London: Bloomsbury T&T Clark, 2014), 503–5 [515–17].
- God of Grace, Jesus Christ and The Spirit; Selected from: Edward Schillebeeckx, *Christ: The Christian Experience in the Modern World*, Collected Works of Edward Schillebeeckx vol. 7 (London: Bloomsbury T&T Clark, 2014), 523–5 [534–6].

---

und Urchristentum, Lund 1940; G. Bornkamm, 'Der Paraklet im Johannesevangelium', *Festschrift R. Bultmann*, Stuttgart 1949, 12–35; G. Locher, 'Der Geist als Paraklet', *Evangelische Theologie* 26, 1966, 578ff.; J. Blank, *Krisis. Untersuchungen zur johanneischen Christologie und Eschatologie*, Freiburg 1964, ch. 9; 'Die Vergegenwärtigung des Gerichts durch den Geist-Parakleten', 316–40; J. Veenhof, *De Parakleet*, Kampen 1975.

15

Resurrection

The official apostolic tradition: 'We believe that God raised him from the dead' (1 Thess 1.10)[1]

The earliest testimonies to Jesus' death and resurrection are in Paul's first letter to the Thessalonians: 'We believe that Jesus died and rose again' (1 Thess 4.14), and: '(We are waiting) for his Son whom he raised from the dead, Jesus...' (1 Thess 1.10). Here Paul is citing, in quotation marks (Greek *hoti*; I believe *that*), the already traditional kerygma of the church: Jesus' resurrection from the dead is God's saving act, an event that will bring deliverance: 'his Son, whom he raised from the dead, Jesus, who delivers us from the wrath to come' (1 Thess 1.10). There is no mention of appearances of Jesus; everything centres on his imminent *parousia* ('We are waiting for his Son... who delivers us from the judgment to come').

In a different context, in which Paul takes the religious identity of the Christian churches as the premise of a theological argument, the tradition of Christian belief in the resurrection is conjoined with that of Jesus appearances actually, with a list of four key elements: (a) he died (*apethanen*); (b) he was buried (*etaphè*); (c) he has been raised (*egègertai*); (d) he has shown himself (*ôphthè*: 1 Cor 15.3–5). Although the appearances of Jesus are not one of the elements of the Christian kerygma and creed, Paul (or even before him, the confessional or catechetic document he is citing) associates the initiative of what is meant by appearances with the fundamental saving event of Jesus himself.

'He was dead and buried': this serves to underline not only Jesus' actual death but in all probability his final rejection as well.[2] After all, the fact that a Christian sympathiser in the Sanhedrin, Joseph of Arimathea, is said to have taken it upon himself to give Jesus a proper burial according to Jewish custom is difficult to place historically; it may be a Christian legend also known elsewhere, in Qumrân circulated

---

[1] Selected from: Edward Schillebeeckx, *Jesus: An Experiment in Christology*, trans. John Bowden, Collected Works of Edward Schillebeeckx vol. 6 (London: Bloomsbury T&T Clark, 2014), 315–17 [346–7].
[2] See U. Wilckens, *Missionsreden der Apostelgeschichte*, Neukirchen 1961, 135.

by pious Christians unable to bear the idea of Jesus being buried dishonourably.[3] Luke draws on a different tradition: the same people who had Jesus put to death 'took him down from the tree and laid him in a tomb' (Acts 13.27–29).[4] Thus Jesus' entombment is the seal, as it were, set on his rejection. In contrast to that final rejection by people there now stands God's saving act: God raised him up, and the risen one has shown himself. This tallies with the – very early contrast scheme: 'You killed him, but God raised him up' (see above).

Jesus 'showed himself' or appeared (*ôphthè* is the technical term for this 'paschal event') both in this pre-Pauline tradition and in Luke: Acts 9.17; 13.30–31; Luke 24.34 (three times, in Luke), and once (though repeated in a similar context four times) in 1 Cor 15.3–9.[5] The four instances mentioned in 1 Cor 15 relate to Jesus; what is called 'appearing', therefore, is clearly not to be characterised as deriving merely from human psychology; on the contrary, it is described as an initiative of Jesus himself, his gracious act: God in Christ is party to it.

Manifestation, preaching and act of faith[6]

Theologically it is worthwhile putting the four elements that Paul identifies – he died and was buried, but God raised him up and made him 'epiphanous' – in their Pauline context instead of objectivising them by lifting them out of it. In that way an important point emerges.

---

[3] J. Delorme, in *Lectio Divina*, n. 50, 118, n. 40.
[4] This in itself does not necessarily run counter to the other tradition; Joseph of Arimathea was after all a member of the Sanhedrin. But the gospels differ regarding him: for Mark he is 'a respected member of the Sanhedrin' and 'living in expectation of the kingdom of God' (15.43); in Matthew he is already 'a disciple' (27:57); for Luke a Hellenised and goodly fellow (Luke 23.50); for John a 'secret disciple' (John 19:38), hardly distinguishable from the Nicodemus figure (John 3.2).
[5] Luke 24.34; Acts 13.31; 9.17; 26.16; 1 Tim 3.16 and four times in 1 Cor 15.5–8. It is remarkable, too, that only in this pre-Pauline passage does Paul use the word in association with 'appearances'. The term comes from the Hebrew (niphal form of *ra'ah*), meaning 'he showed himself (let himself be seen)' as well as 'he is seen'. See L. Koehler-W. Baumgartner, *Lexicon in V.T. libros* (Leyden 1958), 865; H. Graß, *Ostergeschehen und Osterberichte* (Göttingen 1964³) (1956), 186–9 (the word '*ôphthè*' in itself settles nothing; it does however underline Jesus' own initiative). See especially A. Pelletier, 'Les apparitions du Ressuscité en termes de la Septante', *Biblica* 51 (1970), 76–9; 'He showed himself' or '*God* made him epiphanous' is preferred, as appears also, for instance, from the Septuagint: *ôphthè ho Theos tôi Abram* (Gen 12:7); see other Old Testament theophanies (Gen 18.1-2; Num 12.5; Josh 5.13) or angelophanies (Judg 13; Exod 3.2; 6.3; Gen 12.7). '*ôphthè*' is also frequently used in Genesis for revelations, even when no visual element at all is present (Gen 12.7; 17.1; 22.14; 26.2, 24; 35.9; 48.3 with 35.11), or when the visual elements are minimal (Judg 13.3; 2 Chron 3.1; 1 Chron 21.16; Judg 6.11–12, 21). '*ôphthè*' with the dative expresses God's initiative; it contrasts with '*ephanè*' and '*phainesthai*', which rather suggest a vision (Matt 1.20; 2.13, 19). The terminology comes quite clearly, via the Septuagint, from the Old Testament theophanies (a self-disclosure by God). Use of another word might evoke the idea of the reanimation of a corpse. This danger is already present in Acts 1:3 *(Ièsous...parestèsen heauton dzōnta)*, but nowhere do we read what Josephus says later on: '*Iésous...ephanè autois palin dzōn*' (*Antiquities*, 20, 64). Cf. J. Delorme, in *Lectio Divina*, n. 72, 143–4; Leon-Dufour, in *Lectio Divina*, n. 50, 167; R. Fuller, *Resurrection narratives*, 30; G. Delling, in W. Marxsen et al., *Die Bedeutung der Auferstehungsbotschaft für den Glauben an Jesus Christus* (Gütersloh 1966), 72; H. Braun, in *Theologische Literaturzeitung* 77 (1952), 533–6.
[6] Selected from: Edward Schillebeeckx, *Jesus: An Experiment in Christology*, trans. John Bowden, Collected Works of Edward Schillebeeckx vol. 6 (London: Bloomsbury T&T Clark, 2014), 320–1 [351–2].

In his letter Paul is in conversation with Christians at Corinth. In this discourse, couched in the present tense ('I remind you, brethren', 1 Cor 15.1), there are verbs in the perfect tense, while the style of address remains very personal: 'The gospel which I preached to you' (15.1, 2, 3), past history common to the Corinthians and to Paul enter into the narrative. In this 'I-you' discourse there is suddenly mention of a 'he': another story is thrust into the 'I- you' story, resulting in three intersecting levels: Paul addressing the Corinthians insertion of a biographical story: Paul preached, the Corinthians believed lastly, the insertion of a story about a third party, Jesus of Nazareth.[7] In that way three biographical stories are intrinsically conjoined: Paul's preaching activity, the Corinthians' conversion, and the story of Jesus, who is dead but who has been raised to life by God and has revealed himself to Christ's official witnesses. In other words, the present tense of the discourse is that of life renewed in Christ, both for the Corinthians and for Paul; what is more, this present has a future.[8] What Paul says about Christ and his resurrection cannot be dissociated from the personal tone of his speech, in which the Corinthians are involved. The insertion of '(died) for our sins' relates Jesus' death to the present of the Corinthians; Paul adds: Jesus 'appeared also to me'. On the one hand the appearances are a constituent of the basic story (Jesus died but was raised) and, on the other, the object of Paul's autobiographical story.[9] Grammatically the primary story is the object of verbs like evangelise, proclaim, receive and hand on, and believe (1 Cor 15.1-3, 11). Thus the text itself tells us how we are to understand the primary story: it is a matter of proclaiming Jesus' death, resurrection and appearance *as good news*. The primary story in the third person he died but has risen again only acquires its full significance in the context of this announcement of good, new and receptive faith. The preaching (1 Cor 15.1) as well as the receptive belief (15.11) are the effective outcome of the primary story. That is to say, the latter cannot be detached from the proclamation and faith; this Jesus story is the *raison d'être* both of Paul and of the Christians at Corinth; the primary story cannot be understood in an objectivised context. Affirming the resurrection in faith entails the believer's personal involvement in the story thus accepted: speaking of the risen Jesus implies a personal experience, interpreted as an initiative of the other, of Jesus himself.[10]

Jesus is presented as the risen one in a collective ecclesial experience. Hence the source of this talk about the risen Jesus as risen is the experience of a new life. The full meaning of what Peter and the eleven experienced becomes evident only in their mission, in what they do, proclaim, in their actual life and praxis. The origin of their faith is the abiding essence of the Christian faith itself. The gospel narratives will clarify this.

---

[7] J. Delorme, in *Lectio Divina*, n. 72, 107-13.
[8] 1 Cor 15.23-28; 15.19, 30-32, 58; 15.20-22, 42-53.
[9] Delorme, in *Lectio Divina*, n. 72, 110-11.
[10] Although in a complicated form the same kind of structural analysis is possible in the case of Acts 2.22-23; 3-15; 4.10; 5.30 and all New Testament passages referring to Jesus' death 'for our sins' and his resuscitation by God.

Jesus was the reign of God[11]

Was Jesus, who proclaimed the imminent arrival of God's reign, mistaken? People often try to circumvent the problem by arguing that Jesus was not speaking of God's final salvation as being 'near at hand' in a temporal sense, but of an ontological 'nearness' of the God of salvation. This distinction does not appear anywhere in the New Testament. Jesus did in fact speak of *God's* rapidly approaching *parousia*, probably in terms of the coming Son of Man. The temporal/linear aspect cannot be eliminated from his message; and it would be false hermeneutics to explain the temporal aspect as a historically variable 'metaphor' whereas 'ontological proximity' was the actually intended core of the message. Besides, that would neutralise one of the first Christians' motives to proclaim Jesus as the risen one. We have seen that Jesus preached the imminent arrival of God's salvation and that this certainty did not wane when he came face to face with death; also that uncomprehendingly, perhaps, but with heartfelt conviction he integrated his death with his offer of salvation, the meaning of his whole life. So when he died the disciples faced the question: was this person mistaken (the kingdom of God has not come) or was he right? In the latter case the *parousia* of God which he had proclaimed had indeed occurred in the resurrection of Jesus; which would make the resurrection the foundation of the coming *parousia* of Jesus the Son of Man. Thus the Christian conviction that Jesus was not mistaken in his *Abba* experience was one of the factors inducing Christians to identify God's coming rule, as proclaimed by Jesus, with the risen crucified one: in *him* the kingdom of God *had come*. That was the fundamental religious intuition which the first Christians expressed when they proclaimed that Jesus had risen from the dead. The kingdom of God which he proclaimed had come, just as he had said: in the risen crucified one. It should be noted that initially Christians interpreted Jesus' resurrection as the beginning of his immediately imminent *parousia*; this generation would live to see the great event. They were already living 'at the end of the times' (1 Pet 1.20; 2 Pet 3.3; Jude 18; also 2 Tim. 3.1; Mark 9.1). The earliest phase of the Q community is the sole witness to a period in which there was as yet no indication that Jesus' *parousia* might be 'delayed'. All other traditions that we know already confronted the new situation: the non-arrival of Jesus' glorious appearance (Mark 13.32; Matt 24.36; Mark 13.30; Matt 10.23; Matt 25.1–13; Luke 12.38; Matt 24.25–41; Luke 12.42–46). Although this 'tarrying' did result in a crisis, Jesus' resurrection supplied the irrevocable guarantee of the coming *parousia*, so that for the Christians nothing essential was altered by the delay; it merely enabled them to discern more clearly the tension between 'already' and 'not yet', between a present and a future eschatology.

The New Testament interpretation of Jesus' resurrection – under the impact of what had happened to Jesus and, after his death, to the disciples shattered the apocalyptic concept of resurrection. Although history continued as usual, God's final saving action had been accomplished in Jesus of Nazareth, the risen crucified one. Despite the contradiction of his rejection and death Jesus, who had proclaimed

---

[11]Selected from: Edward Schillebeeckx, *Jesus: An Experiment in Christology*, trans. John Bowden, Collected Works of Edward Schillebeeckx vol. 6 (London: Bloomsbury T&T Clark, 2014), 502–3 [543–4].

the imminent reign of God, had not been mistaken. By raising him from the dead, God identified with him, who in his lifetime had identified with God's cause, his coming reign; Jesus Christ himself was the reign of God. So Jesus, who proclaimed not himself but the reign and lordship of God, as it were and without suspecting it, was proclaiming 'himself': the proclaimer *is* the proclaimed one.

This ushered in the eschatological age, whose hallmark is experience of the eschatological gift of God's Spirit, referred to (with the likely exception of the Markan gospel) as the 'Spirit of Jesus' (Acts 2.33; 10.44ff; 19.5–6; Rom 8.9; Phil 1.19; Gal 4.6). And Jesus' Spirit is the Spirit of God (1 Cor 2.12; see 1 Cor 3.16; 6.11; 7.40; 12.3). The eschatological age would begin with the sending of the Spirit (Joel 3.1ff; Ezek 36–37) and be accompanied by forgiveness of sins and the new law, written in the hearts of the faithful (Jer 31.31ff). And: 'Where the Spirit of the Lord is, there is freedom' (2 Cor 3.17). People had encountered this freedom in the life of the earthly Jesus; it was human freedom, based on dedicated commitment to God's absolute freedom. The 'freedom of the children of God' (Rom 8.21) was characteristic of early Christianity, which had disengaged itself from the Law. The basic creed of the first Christians was: Jesus of Nazareth is the Christ, that is, the one completely filled with God's eschatological Spirit. He is God's end-time, final revelation and the paradigm of eschatological humanity.

The crucifixion[12]

In the Christian tradition, Jesus' crucifixion becomes a central kerygma and dogma, although in the New Testament there are a whole series of passages in which no believers' interpretation of Jesus' crucifixion is given.

However, we may say that the Christian proclamation of the saving significance of the crucifixion of Jesus goes back to the basic tenor of Jesus' own proclamation. This becomes clear in a subtle way from the Gospel of Mark. Many commentators rightly see the 'messianic secret' as a construction by Mark, but in so doing they sometimes forget that this construction does have a foundation in the life of the historical Jesus, viz., his restraint in connection with the title 'Christ', Messiah. Mark addressed his Gospel to a community which already believed in Jesus Christ. He had to make clear to this Christian community that Jesus had interpreted his own mission in a way which in no sense corresponded to existing messianic expectations. This title can be applied to Jesus only if what 'Messiah' means is defined afresh. It was in fact the crucifixion of Jesus which reverified this term Messiah: the crucified and rejected Jesus is the Christ. That is the first confession of faith. Therefore the crucifixion is central in the New Testament, and rightly so. Mark 8.27–33 is significant here.

The scene of the first 'passion prediction' is set near Caesarea Philippi in the context of Jesus' question, 'Who do people say that I am?' Peter replies and goes on to say, 'I myself believe that you are the Messiah.' But at that point, according

---

[12]Selected from: Edward Schillebeeckx, *The Church with a Human Face*, trans. John Bowden, Collected Works of Edward Schillebeeckx vol. 9 (London: Bloomsbury T&T Clark, 2014), 29–31 [31–4].

to Mark, Jesus immediately tells them to keep quiet about it (to shut their mouths!) and he himself fills in the concept of Messiah with the words, 'the Son of Man must suffer many things, be rejected and die'. The words come from after Easter, perhaps, but they are not without roots in the historical Jesus. Here, on the basis of the way in which it is given new content by Jesus' proclamation and lifestyle, we also have a redefinition of the term 'Christ': it is used of a person who dies in 'unconsecrated ground', outside the walls of the holy city. Even during his lifetime Jesus had broken through the walls separating the sacred from the profane. The fact that in the New Testament narrative of Jesus' passion, witnesses said something to the effect that this person had said that he would destroy the temple and rebuild it in three days, is clearly connected with Jesus' proclamation about the nature and person of God's own being and the nature of his own messianism. Like God, Jesus preferred to identify himself with the outcast and the rejected, the 'unholy', so that he himself ultimately became the Rejected, the Outcast.

This identification is indeed radical. So there is continuity between Jesus' life and his death. Precisely for that reason, Jesus' saving significance comes to a climax in his death. The *theologoumena* used in the New Testament and indeed later to describe this reality of salvation to certain people within their own culture should not be confused with the specific reality of salvation itself. The redefinition which Jesus gave of both God and humanity, in and through his proclamation and way of life, takes on its supreme and ultimate significance in his crucifixion: God is present in human life where to human vision he seems to be absent. On the cross God shared in the brokenness of our world.

This means that God determines in absolute freedom, from eternity, who and how he will be, namely, a God of human beings. In his own being he is a God for us! It is very difficult to find a distinction between God in himself and God for us in the New Testament. (This has theological consequences; it does not fit with the affirmations of 'process philosophy' and its theological adherents, although it fits in with their fundamental concerns.) Clearly there is a theological redefinition of various concepts of God in the New Testament; there is also a redefinition of humanity. God accepts humanity without any condition from our side, and precisely as a result of this unconditional acceptance he transforms human beings and brings them to conversion and renewal. His is love without conditions. Therefore the cross is also a judgment on our own selfish views; on our ways of experiencing what it means to be human and what it means to be God. Here we have an ultimate and definitive revelation of God's humanity, the heart of Jesus' message of the kingdom of God: God who comes into his own in the human world, for human happiness. God does not lay down any conditions for us human beings or for Jesus himself for his redeeming and liberating presence: 'God reconciled the world to himself in Jesus' (2 Cor 5.19). Human beings put Jesus to death, but this execution is at the same time God's supreme self-revelation.

Resurrection: reality and belief

Of course this Christology (=this Christian messianism) only became clear to the first Christians, who were all Jews, by virtue of, and within, the 'paschal experience'.

For all the continuity there is a break here. Only a new action by God can connect Jesus' historical life, over the break of his death, with 'the Christ of faith', with the confession, 'he is truly risen'. In the resurrection from the dead, God's end-time action over Jesus, the crucified one, God's own judgment on, and also his relationship to, Jesus and his message, his life-style and his death, become clear to the believer. Easter faith implies and presupposes a new action from God towards the crucified Jesus. Here in the first instance is an expression of the way in which God himself is related to Jesus – as received in and interpreted by his disciples. Paul in particular understood this well when he observed explicitly in connection with those in Corinth who denied the resurrection of Jesus: 'Some evidently have *no sense of God*' (1 Cor 15.34). Therefore the reality of the resurrection, which is the only way in which belief in the resurrection is called to life, becomes the test both of the understanding of God proclaimed by Jesus and our soteriological Christology (= messianism). Here it becomes evident that Jesus' way of life and death did not happen in vain. In the resurrection God authenticates the person, the message and the whole way of life of Jesus. He puts his seal on it and speaks out against the human judgment on him. Through and in this Christian faith in the resurrection of Jesus, the crucified but risen Jesus remains active in our history. Here, too, the principle applies (though in another way) that the 'in itself' and the 'for us' cannot be separated. Jesus' own resurrection, his sending of the Spirit, the origin of the Christian 'community of God' living from the Spirit and the New Testament witnesses of faith provide a mutual definition of one another and are indissolubly bound up together, although at the same time they are not the same things. One can say that the communities of God which came into being on the basis of the resurrection of Jesus are what is meant *at the deepest level* in the New Testament by 'the appearances of Jesus'. The crucified but risen Jesus appears in the believing, assembled community of the church. That this sense of the risen, living Jesus has faded in many of them can be basically blamed on the fact that our churches are insufficiently 'communities' of God (though of course there are other factors). Where the church of Jesus Christ lives, and lives a liberating life in the footsteps of Jesus, the resurrection faith undergoes no crisis. On the other hand, it is better not to believe in God than to believe in a God who minimises human beings, holds them under and oppresses them, with a view to a better world to come. In this heartbeat we can hear an echo of the message of Jesus of Nazareth in all his goodness and earnestness.

Belief in the resurrection of Jesus[13]

To begin with, any meaningful statement about the resurrection of Jesus must be of such a kind that Jesus' shameful death is not trivialised in the light of the resurrection faith. Jesus' death is historically beyond question a defenceless event. To talk of Jesus' atoning death, or of the redemptive value of this death, can become sheer ideology

---

[13] Selected from: Edward Schillebeeckx, *Church: The Human Story of God*, Collected Works of Edward Schillebeeckx vol. 10 (London: Bloomsbury T&T Clark, 2014), 125–30 [127–32].

without critical reflection. Paul says that the cross is not a sign of honour but a curse (Gal 3.13), an offence and a shame. The resurrection of Jesus does not do away with that. In Jesus' death, in and of itself, i.e. in terms of what human beings did to him, there is only negativity. In his case this is not an ordinary death, nor an instance of the universal human problem of death as a dialectic of death and life, as Bultmann and others assert, but of a shameful execution which is quite out of proportion to the actual life of Jesus – indeed is in flagrant contradiction to it. Thousands have been crucified, yet nevertheless their crucifixions have not been thought to have universal significance, nor have they been called atoning deaths. So the importance cannot lie in Jesus' death as such. Purely as the death of Jesus, this dying cannot have any redemptive or liberating force; on the contrary, death is the enemy of life.

My position is that if the life journey of Jesus does not show any anticipatory mark of the resurrection, his death is sheer failure and in that case resurrection faith is simply the fruit of human longing (as Jacques Pohier thinks). Without effective anticipations of the resurrection in the earthly life of Jesus, Easter is an ideology. The only subject of the statement of faith 'He is risen' is the historical Jesus of Nazareth who believed in the promise by giving it form in his message and above all in his way of life. Jesus' faith in the promise as the source of an original praxis is a historical anticipation of the significance of the resurrection and thus of God's overwhelming power over evil. In his life Jesus is an 'already', still of course within the horizon of death, but now that of a death which has already been overcome in hope. The power of God was already at work in the life of Jesus, and his death shares in that. Only on this presupposition is belief in the resurrection not an ideology! If only Jesus' death is a historical anticipation of his resurrection (this applies above all for Bultmann and to some degree also already for the apostle Paul), this resurrection is unavoidably the negation of the history of Jesus' life.

Thus we cannot detach the defencelessness of Jesus on the cross from the free power and the positivity which revealed itself in his actual life of solidarity with oppressed men and women on the basis of an absolute trust in God. God is concerned with the happiness of men and women who live under the threat of nature, social oppression and self-alienation. Jesus is so opposed to this that his concern for his own survival fades away and even plays no part. Oppression may not be; the right of the strongest may not apply in the life of the human community. Oppression is injustice and a scandal. So Jesus refuses to regard evil as being on the same footing as good and acts accordingly. Jesus' life itself is therefore praxis of the kingdom of God, a historical anticipation of the resurrection, and his death is part of this way of life. So we can speak of his death as a defenceless superior power, disarming evil. Moreover, it was already the insight of the first Christians that even the earthly life of Jesus has to show positive anticipations of the resurrection if faith in the resurrection is not to be ideological; and that insight is acutely expressed in the story in which the Synoptic Gospels speak of a transfiguration of Jesus during his earthly life. So we can understand why precisely at the place of the deepest disappointment, the cross, a liberating faith could break through among the disciples. Let us analyse its content more closely.

The psalm which Jesus prays on the cross and which begins with the words 'My God, my God, why have you forsaken me?' ends in a prayer of thanksgiving for God's abiding, albeit silent, saving presence. God was not powerless when Jesus hung on the cross, but he was defenceless and vulnerable as Jesus was vulnerable. The basic experience of the first disciples after Good Friday was that evil, the cross, cannot have the last word; Jesus' life journey *is* right and is the last word, which is sealed in his resurrection. Although the cross was on the one hand the sealing of the superior power of human beings over God, in the dying Jesus God is present, and indeed present as pure positivity, as he was with the living Jesus, In that case suffering and death remain absurd, and even in Jesus' case may not be mystified; but they do not have the last word because the liberating God was absolutely close to Jesus on the cross, just as he was throughout Jesus' life journey. But that was a presence without power or compulsion. Paul says that 'the foolishness of God is wiser than people, and the weakness of God is stronger than people' (1 Cor 1.25); God's presence was near in power, but without the misuse of power.

So God can be present in reconciliation and we may speak of the redeeming and liberating life *and* death of Jesus. God conceals his superior power over evil and at the same time expresses it in his defencelessness in order to give us room to become ourselves in solidarity with oppressed men and women. In this defencelessness, however, at the same time God uses his superior power because his defencelessness is the consequence of his fight against evil in a wicked world. The messianic 'must suffer' of Jesus is not a 'divine' must. It is forced on God through Jesus by human beings, yet God and Jesus are not thwarted by it, not by virtue of the resurrection as such, which would then be regarded as a kind of compensation for the historical failure of Jesus' message and praxis, but because his 'going around Palestine doing good' was itself already the beginning of the kingdom of God, of a kingdom in which death and injustice no longer have a place. In Jesus' praxis of the kingdom of God his resurrection is already anticipated. The Easter faith expresses the fact that murder – and therefore any form of evil – has no future. Precisely for that reason death is overcome. The crucified Jesus is also the Risen One.

Only when we have seen the defencelessness of the cross can we and may we also look for the significance of Jesus' resurrection. Only a new action on the part of God – although this newness is the eternally young, free being or the one act of God's being God, and not a 'second act' which as it were makes up for what has gone before – could link Jesus' historical life, through his death, with the 'Christ of the church's faith', with the confession 'He is risen indeed'. In the resurrection from the dead, God's eschatological action with reference to Jesus the crucified one becomes God's own verdict on Jesus, and only in this way does God's evaluation of Jesus and his message, life and death also become clear to believers. The Easter faith presupposes a new action by God relating to the crucified Jesus. In the first instance this expresses how God is related to Jesus – in the reception and interpretation of Jesus' disciples. Paul understood this well when he explicitly said to those Corinthians who denied the resurrection: 'Some evidently have no sense of God' (1 Cor 15.34).

Therefore the reality of the resurrection, through which alone the resurrection faith is brought to life, is the test of both the understanding of God preached by Jesus and our soteriological Christology. In the resurrection God authenticates the person, message and whole way of life of Jesus. He puts his seal on it and speaks out against what men and women did to Jesus.

Just as the death of Jesus cannot be detached from his life, *so* his resurrection cannot be detached from his life and death. To extrapolate the death and resurrection of Jesus so that they become the nucleus of the Christian message is ultimately to twist the prophetic content of the whole ministry of Jesus: that is a Pauline kerygma without the four Gospels, and Paul is canonical only within the New Testament as a whole. First of all we must say that Christian belief in the resurrection is in fact a first evaluation of Jesus' life and death, and especially a recognition of the intrinsic and irrevocable significance of Jesus' proclamation and praxis of the kingdom of God which nothing can undo, in the light of the gospel. We undermine the resurrection faith if we remove this first dimension.

But this belief comprises still more, and this 'more' is also connected with the life and death of Jesus. The resurrection of Jesus is in the second instance the breakthrough or manifestation of something that was already present in the life and death of Jesus, namely his living communion or communion of grace with the living God, a communion which could not be broken by death. This living communion is already on earth the beginning of what is called eternal life.

Thirdly, there is also in the resurrection an aspect of a divine judgment on what human beings did. Resurrection is not merely the extension of Jesus' living communion with God (beyond death); it is the germ of the establishment of the kingdom of God: the exaltation and glorification of Jesus to God. 'I believe in Jesus *the Lord*.' His message and life themselves have an eschatological significance and do not get this only from the resurrection.

But this threefold theological argument remains an abstraction which we cannot locate properly in theology if we leave aside the living, *pneumatic* presence of the glorified Jesus in his church. Through and in this Christian belief in the resurrection of Jesus, the crucified but risen Jesus remains effective in our history through his followers. Jesus' resurrection, his sending of the Spirit, the origin of the Christian community of God as the church of Christ which lives from the Spirit, and the New Testament witness to all this and thus resurrection faith, define one another reciprocally, though they cannot be identified with one another.

We can say that the 'church of Christ' which came into being on the basis of the resurrection of Jesus is what is meant most deeply in the New Testament by the appearances of Jesus: in the assembled believing community of the church the crucified but risen Jesus appears, i.e. is effectively present. Moreover, where the church lives by Jesus Christ, lives by praying and liberating men and women in the footsteps of Jesus, belief in the resurrection does not undergo any crisis. On the other hand, I feel very strongly that it is better that there should be no belief in eternal life than that a God should be presented who diminishes people in the here and now, keeps them down and humiliates them politically with an eye to a better hereafter.

This presence of Jesus in believers through the Spirit has consequences for Christian life. Just as positive anticipations of the resurrection and thus of the superior power of the grace of God could be seen in Jesus' life (and must be seen, if resurrection faith is not to become an ideology), so the same holds true for Christians. Within the defencelessness of our own lives we must be able to *experience* the superior power of God: otherwise we accept it with a faith which is presented as purely authoritarian.

Anyone who begins to look for this element of present experience must, I think, first be well aware of the difference between our timebound existence and God's eternity. As human beings, we know that silence is an element of any dialogue, of any talking. Now how is that to be understood in a dialogue between human beings and God? What is a human life of at most between seventy and ninety years to the eternal God? A fraction in his divine life; a sigh, a moment in which we can say barely a few words to the listening God. Therefore God is silent in our earthly life. God listens to what we have to say to *him*. God can answer only when our fleeting life on earth is ended. Should the living God not be extremely interested in us all our lives, listen silently to our life story until we have expressed everything and each person has communicated his or her own life to God? Do we not all dislike being constantly interrupted before we have finished? Nor does God interrupt us, but for him the whole of our life, however important, is just a breath, and God also takes it seriously; that is why he is silent: he is listening to our life story. Precisely because he is greater than our human heart, he never speaks as a tangible human voice in our innermost being but only as a 'divine silence', a silence that only after our death takes on a distinctive voice and face that we can recognise. As long as the Eternal One is still listening to our life story of fifty or even a hundred years, the eternal God indeed seems to us to be powerless and defenceless. In this there is both a desperate trial for our historical existence and at the same time an experience full of hope and expectation.

In the light of the Christian view of Jesus' life journey, death and resurrection, both 'God' and 'Jesus' take on a critical and productive, liberating power for us. The criterion of humanisation, proclaimed by Jesus and used by him in practice, beyond all human expectations of the *humanum* which people desire and which is constantly threatened, this desire for the humanity of humankind, for our soundness and wholeness, is something which is close to the heart of God, and not a reduction of the gospel. For the gospel is good news not just about Jesus but about the God of Jesus, creator of heaven and earth, the God of all men and women.

The message of Jesus embraces the kingdom of God in all its height and depth, breadth and length, not just the forgiveness of sins and eternal life, though it does comprise that, and indeed perhaps does so above all. Jesus proclaimed to the end the absolute, freely effective nearness of the God who creates and brings salvation to human beings in all their dimensions. We Christians learn, stammeringly, to express the content of what God is and the content of what men and women can be, in other words the content of human salvation, from the life of Jesus.

We are liberated to new, authentically human possibilities of life. From all that has gone before we can at least make the following list. Through Jesus' redemption Christians experience the freedom to accept that despite sin and guilt we are accepted by God; the freedom to be able to live in this earthly world without ultimate despair about our existence; the freedom to look death in the face as not having the last word; the freedom to commit ourselves disinterestedly for others in the confidence that such dedication is ultimately of decisive significance (Matt 25); the freedom to accept experiences of peace, joy and communication and to understand them as manifestations, however fragmentary, of the saving presence of the living God; the freedom to join in the struggle for economic, social and political justice; the freedom to be free from oneself in order to be free for others, free to do good to others. For Christians, all these experiences are a Christian experience of faith in the God who discloses himself in Jesus Christ as the sacred mystery of all-embracing love: experiences of salvation from God.

Christian redemption is indeed liberation from sin. But liberation from sin also has a cultural context. In our time the Christian understanding of sin also includes the recognition of systematic disruptions of communication like sexism, racism and fascism, antisemitism, hostility to and attacks on immigrant workers, and the Western cultural and religious sense of superiority. The Christian love which is the basis of community therefore also includes the necessity to recognise the need for deep involvement in present-day work of political, cultural and social emancipation.

Selected literature

- The Official Apostolic Tradition: 'We Believe that God Raised Him from the Dead' (1 Thess. 1:10); Selected from: Edward Schillebeeckx, *Jesus: An Experiment in Christology*, trans. John Bowden, Collected Works of Edward Schillebeeckx vol. 6 (London: Bloomsbury T&T Clark, 2014), 315–17 [346–7].
- Manifestation, Preaching and Act of Faith; Selected from: Edward Schillebeeckx, *Jesus: An Experiment in Christology*, trans. John Bowden, Collected Works of Edward Schillebeeckx vol. 6 (London: Bloomsbury T&T Clark, 2014), 320–1 [351–2].
- Jesus Was the Reign of God; Selected from: Edward Schillebeeckx, *Jesus: An Experiment in Christology*, trans. John Bowden, Collected Works of Edward Schillebeeckx vol. 6 (London: Bloomsbury T&T Clark, 2014), 502–3 [543–4].
- The Crucifixion; Selected from: Edward Schillebeeckx, *The Church with a Human Face*, trans. John Bowden, Collected Works of Edward Schillebeeckx vol. 9 (London: Bloomsbury T&T Clark, 2014), 29–31 [31–4].
- Belief in the Resurrection of Jesus; Selected from: Edward Schillebeeckx, *Church: The Human Story of God*, Collected Works of Edward Schillebeeckx vol. 10 (London: Bloomsbury T&T Clark, 2014), 125–30 [127–32].

16

Mary

Mary's place in God's plan of salvation[1]

Why did God choose Mary? What was his reason for giving her this particular place in his plan of salvation? This question synthesises the entire Marian mystery. It forms the culminating point of the mystery and of the doctrine of Mary.

We have already indicated where Mary was situated, the precise place which she occupies in God's plan of salvation, but this does not, of course, mean that our examination of the subject of the mystery of Christ and Mary is complete. We have still to penetrate even further into the very heart of this mystery. It is certainly true that God's reason is God alone. This reason is first and foremost an aspect of God's boundless love for humanity. It is also a reason which is quite independent of any created situation or of any kind of 'natural determinism'. God's will is free from any 'motive' which might move it either from within or from without, from any cause which might influence it or even from any inducement or postulated condition. His win exists in perfect, sovereign freedom and is, of its own nature, creative. God wills simply because he wills to will.

On the other hand, however, the God who so freely wills is good and omniscient. This means that any act of divine dispensation, in all its gratuitous freedom, is always a meaningful act. In the particular case which we are considering this not only resulted in Mary occupying the place assigned to her in the divine plan of salvation by God's will and at his discretion, but in this particular place at once becoming a meaningful moment in the whole economy of salvation. It is in this context that it is possible to refer to the divine motive for Mary's co-operation in the work of redemption. The core of the whole Marian doctrine is contained in this question and, although the divine reason for the choice of Mary will always remain an unfathomable mystery, it is nonetheless possible to make its interior, implicit meaning to some extent explicit.

---

[1] Selected from: Edward Schillebeeckx, *Mary, Mother of Redemption* (London: Sheed and Ward, 1964), 101–4.

One of the most useful of all the functions which the theologian can perform is, of course, to attempt to establish the organic connection which exists between the various mysteries of the Christian faith and, with particular reference to Mary, to make explicit, as far as he is able, the all-important and basic mystery. An explication of this basic mystery can make all the other mysteries intelligible within the context of faith and throw a clear light on the divine reason for the particular choice of Mary.

Before the Nestorian heresy, which denied Mary's divine motherhood, the Church Fathers tended to regard Mary principally as the 'new Eve' and as the 'prototype of the Church'. It was not until the Council of Ephesus that her motherhood came to be regarded explicitly as the central mystery of Mary. This view has been maintained until the present century. Theologians, from Scheeben onwards, have, however, felt obliged to define this motherhood more precisely, by qualifying it with adjectives such as 'bridal', 'spiritual and bodily' or 'adequate'. This fact indicates quite clearly that motherhood in isolation cannot serve adequately as the basic principle in Mariology. In recent years many theologians have gone even further than this. Basing their claims on conclusions drawn from a close historical study of the earliest centuries, they have not only reaffirmed the patristic definitions – 'Mary, the new Eve', 'the prototype of the Church' – but have also proposed such definitions as 'Mary, the prototype of redeemed humanity' and 'the sublime first fruit of the redemption'. Definitions such as these, it is maintained, should form the basic principle of all teaching on the subject of Mary.

We should certainly welcome this renewed vision of Mary, which goes back to the first Fathers of the Church and once again places great emphasis on Mary's act of faith: 'What the virgin Eve's lack Of faith had bound was once more loosened by the faith of the Blessed Virgin Mary.'[2] This concise statement expresses, in clear terms, a fundamental aspect of the teaching of the Church Fathers. What is more, this emphasis on Mary's act of faith does not, as we shall see, in any way affect the central position of her *concrete* motherhood.

Another reason why many theologians have felt compelled gradually to abandon Mary's motherhood as the basic Mariological principle is because they have found it very difficult to reconcile her virgin state with her later conversion to motherhood. If it is really impossible to find the organic connection between these two states, then it follows that the fundamental Mariological principle cannot be established solely on the basis of Mary's motherhood.

Finally, some modern theologians have claimed that Mary's motherhood with regard to us cannot be reconciled with her motherhood of Christ. Many have attempted to resolve their difficulties by basing Marian doctrine on two fundamental principles – Mary's motherhood and her participation in the Redemption. In their view, the two are sufficiently distinct from each other to be regarded as separate mysteries, but at the same time they were, at God's discretion, embodied, and thus united, in one person.

---

[2] St. Irenaeus, *Adversus Haereses*, 3, 22,4 (PG, 7, col. 959).

The anticipatory sacramental activity of Mary's motherhood and its sacramental consequences[3]

Human motherhood is not merely a biological function. The biological function of motherhood implies a personal and free commitment on the part of the mother. In Mary's case this free, personal involvement in motherhood meant that she freely and personally took upon herself a saving function which bound her both spiritually and physically, in the most intimate manner, to the God-man Christ, the head of the whole of humanity which he had come to redeem, and consequently to all of us. Mary's personal commitment – her sublime consent made in faith – and her motherhood were thus essentially related to each other. Her exceptional submission in faith was therefore, essentially and intrinsically, directed towards the exceptional offer of redemption made in the person of Christ, as the child of her own womb. Her motherhood, on the one hand, and her personal, sublime state of redeemed holiness, on the other, cannot be conceived in isolation from each other. Each is implied in the other, and this essential relationship existing between the two entitles us to claim that it is Mary's concrete motherhood which constitutes the fundamental principle of the entire mystery of Mary. Her concrete motherhood with regard to Christ, the redeeming God-man, freely accepted in faith – her fully committed divine motherhood – this is both the key to a full understanding of the Marian mystery and the basic Mariological principle, which is concretely identical with Mary's objectively and subjectively unique state of being redeemed.

In this way too, it is possible to achieve a reconciliation between the strong emphasis which the Church Fathers before the Council of Ephesus placed upon Mary's *fiat*, and the prominence given to her divine motherhood in the traditional thought of the Church since the council. Moreover, those modern theologians, on the one hand, who tend to situate the basic Mariological principle in Mary as the prototype of the Church, the new Eve or the sublimely redeemed, also tend to overlook the fact that the entire content and meaning of Mary's *fiat*, of her holiness and of her state of redemption, are determined objectively by the vital content of the Message: motherhood with regard to the Redeemer.

On the other hand, however, those who subscribe to the older view, which accepted Mary's motherhood as the basic principle, tend to see this motherhood in too abstract terms and even, in extreme cases, simply in terms of its purely biological function. The essential aspect of Mary's personal commitment in faith to the full implications of her motherhood is bound to be neglected in a one-sided view of this kind. Finally, the other modern tendency, that of accepting a double Mariological principle of motherhood and partnership, also overemphasises an abstract concept of motherhood and ignores the concrete implications contained in Mary's concrete motherhood with regard to Christ, the God-man, who was by vocation the head of the humanity he was called to redeem.

---

[3] Selected from: Edward Schillebeeckx, *Mary, Mother of Redemption* (London: Sheed and Ward, 1964), 105–9.

Mary, then, may be regarded both as 'objectively and subjectively sublimely redeemed' and as the subject of 'freely accepted and personally committed motherhood with regard to the Redeemer'. These two basic principles of Marian doctrine are different in formulation and particular accentuation, but fundamentally identical. It should therefore be possible to relate organically all the Marian mysteries both to the fundamental privilege of the 'sublimely redeemed' and to the same, but differently formulated, privilege of 'concrete, freely accepted motherhood', even though, concerning the former privilege, we have to bear in mind that the sublimity of Mary's objective and subjective redemption derives its concrete significance from her motherhood. Pope Pius XII showed that he fully accorded with the most profound tradition of faith when he called Mary's divine motherhood the foundation of all her privileges.

Taken in connection with the foregoing argument, our view can best be expressed in the following way. Mary was the Chosen One. She was redeemed by her immensely deep *fiat* made in faith, externally represented in her bodily *conception* of the universal primordial sacrament, the holy man Jesus Christ, the God-man. She was, in other words, redeemed by her motherhood, insofar as it was fully accepted as a personal and free commitment on the part of the mother. Mary's immaculate conception, the holy state in which she lived before the message, her exemption from sin and sinful desires, her entire relationship with and attitude towards God, in virgin dedication as the 'handmaid of the Lord' – all this was anticipatory sacramental activity, preceding her conception in faith (*fide concepit*) of the primordial sacrament, Christ.

On the other hand, all that followed this conception – her spiritual motherhood with regard to us, her specific share, as Mary, in the Redemption, her co-meritorious mediatorship of all graces, her universal intercession and finally her early physical glorification and her 'constitution in power' – all this constituted subsequent sacramental efficacy. Thus, the mystery of Mary, Christ's most beautiful creation, emerges as an organic mystery, based on the fundamental privilege of concrete motherhood freely accepted in faith. It is this privilege which provides us with the key to a full understanding, in faith, of the entire mystery of Mary.

It is possible to approach this mystery from two different points of view. On the one hand, if our point of departure is faith as the inspiration of every sacramental reception, we are bound to proceed from Mary's subjective redemption or free commitment in faith in order to arrive at the point where we can see how her personal appropriation of objective redemption was determined and given a specific meaning, peculiar to herself, by her motherhood. If we consider the mystery from this point of view, we are bound to accept, as our basic Mariological principle, that Mary is the new Eve, the prototype of the Church and of every redeemed life.

It is, on the other hand, possible to take the objective sacramental gift as the starting point from which to approach the mystery of Mary. In this case we are bound to proceed from Mary – her bodily conception of Christ – in order to throw light upon her subjective participation in her own redemption and in that of all people. These two different ways of considering the mystery are not mutually exclusive, since a true sacrament, in the fullest sense of the word – that is, a fruitful sacrament – contains in itself both a reception in faith and a total submission in hope and love.

This is why a comprehensive Marian doctrine, which aims to bring all the mysteries of Mary together into a single, organic whole under one basic Mariological principle, must at the same time always take both the objective and the subjective aspects of redemption into full consideration. The essential core of the Marian mystery is that she conceived in faith (*fide concepit*), that her motherhood was one to which she freely committed herself in faith. The mystery can consequently be seen as a concrete, though exceptional and singular, case of 'objective and subjective redemption' affecting one particular and special child of Adam. Because the heart and centre of Mary's unique quality is to be found in her motherhood, she, though within redeemed humanity, was at the same time infinitely elevated above the community of her co-redeemed fellows. She is therefore not only our sister but also our mother, the mother of the 'whole Christ, both head and members', the mother of the Creator, the 'fully committed' and therefore maternal mother of the omnipotent Creator of the universe.

The divine reason for Mary's election[4]

The goodness of God's redemptive love is both paternal and maternal. 'I have loved thee with an everlasting love', we read in the Old Testament (Jer 31.3). The prophet Hosea describes the maternal love of Yahweh for his people: 'When Israel was a child, I loved him. It was I who taught Ephraim to walk, I carried them in my arms: and they knew not that I healed them. I drew them to me with human cords, with the bands of love. I pressed them to my cheek like a nurse, bent over them to feed them' (Hos 11.1ff). In Isaiah too we find expression of the maternal love of Yahweh: 'Can a woman forget her infant, so as not to have pity on the son of her womb? And if she should forget, yet will I not forget thee. Behold, I have graven thee in my hands' (Isa. 49.15-16). In this last passage the prophet compares Yahweh to a betrothed virgin who, according to the custom of the times, has inscribed the name of her beloved on the palm of her hand. God, too, has written our names on the palm of his hand so that he will always be mindful of us loved ones.

These texts certainly indicate that God's love for humanity, as manifested in the Redeemer, is really a maternal love. This maternal quality of mildness, this particularly feminine tenderness, this *quid nesciam* which is the special mark of the mother cannot, however, be explicated as such in the human person Jesus. It can only become explicit in a mother who is a woman. God chose Mary so that this maternal aspect of his love might be represented in her person. At the deepest level this would seem to be the basic reason why a woman, a mother, should have a role in the Redemption. Mary's activity is essentially a maternal function. We may, however, be quite certain that Mary's saving intervention is beyond all doubt perfectly attuned to Christ and that it detracts in no way from his unique function as Redeemer. We should not lose sight of the fact that her virginity forms an essential part of her quality as a mother. She is a *virgin* woman and mother. As such, her love for her children is never demanding or possessive. Never does she claim their love for

---

[4]Selected from: Edward Schillebeeckx, *Mary, Mother of Redemption* (London: Sheed and Ward, 1964), 109–16.

herself. The sole object of her virgin maternal love is to lead her children to the love of Christ. All her motherly care is directed towards Christ. It would be possible to quote a thousand instances from the lives of the saints in illustration of Mary's virgin motherly love which always seeks to orientate her children's love towards Christ. All of us must also, at some time or another, be aware of it in our own lives. Many great sinners too, who have lost their faith in Christ, still remain open to the tenderness which is apparent in Mother Mary and, in spite of everything, never cease to be children of Mary. It is always possible, as long as they remain open to Mary, that they may perhaps find Christ again, in the nick of time. Another example of this is the characteristic tenderness of Catholic devotion, as opposed to the comparative severity of Protestant Christianity. It is, of course, true that a race or people, as for example those of the Mediterranean countries, may give their own particular shape or colour to Catholic practice, and that this may be, and frequently is, due rather to a hybrid than to a pure form of Marian devotion. But at the same time no one can possibly deny that Catholic devotion as such is marked by a tenderness, a mildness, even a childlike and loving simplicity – and the only adequate explanation for this is that the Catholic grows up in faith in the intimate company of the most loving and lovable of all mothers, the *Mater Amabilis*, the Virgin with the Smile.

Growing up in close intimacy with Mother Mary, the Catholic learns the meaning of generosity from the boundless and indeed almost wasteful goodness of Mary, who surrounds every offering, even the ultimate sacrifice of Christ – for Christ on the Cross was still above all the true Child of Mary and felt the soothing balm of his mother's love during his crucifixion – with her infinite tenderness and makes life easier and more bearable for the Christian. Christ's 'yoke is not heavy' – it cannot be disputed that Mary has a part to play in lightening the Christian's burden. It is surely not surprising that the cry which comes spontaneously to the Christian's lips when he is in need is 'Mary'. She it is who enables us to participate in Christ's sacrifice in a spirit of gentle submission. The creator of all goodness, the blessed Trinity who sent the Second Person to redeem us, and decreed that he should be born, in the real sense, as Mary's Child, had a profound knowledge and understanding of the human heart! It is only if we consider Christ and his mother together that we can fully grasp the idea of the 'gentleness' of the Cross.

Seen in this light, the Redemption, in its fully human sense, is traceable not solely to the God-man, but also to the virgin, feminine and maternal quality of the mother of the God-man. This perspective also enables us to see the Christian redemption as the highest exaltation of humanity. The Redemption, accomplished by God himself by way of human nature, is fully human because it was given to us by Jesus and his and our mother. Woman played an essential part in the first sin and the Fall. The new Eve fulfilled a sublimely feminine function in the plan of redemption. 'Male and female he created them.' Mary is the *dulcedo,* the sweetness in Christianity: 'Our life, our sweetness'.

Mary was Jesus' mother. This means that Jesus, as a human being, was brought up by Mary and Joseph. This is, of course, a great mystery and difficult for the human mind to grasp. Nonetheless, we must affirm the dogma that Christ was a true human being and, as such, had to be brought up and educated, in the strictest sense of the word, by his mother. His human qualities and character were formed and influenced by his mother's virtues. And when we read in Scripture that Christ went around in the land of Palestine doing good, and realise that this human goodness was God's love of people translated into human terms, we are bound to acknowledge too that Mary had a maternal share in this Christian interpretation of God's love. It is common human experience that the mother's features are recognisable in the child, and this was also true in the case of Mary and Jesus. Mary's function in the Incarnation was not completed when Jesus was born. It was a continuous task, involving the human formation of the young man, as he grew up from infancy to childhood and from childhood to adulthood. How this was accomplished is hidden from us. Only Mary knew the secrets of Jesus' upbringing, and kept them in her heart. She, his mother, kept the secret of the first childish word her Child ever spoke to her and meditated it in her heart. God, in his humanity, formed his first word, and there can be little doubt that it was 'Mama'.

Theologians are always anxious to tie down Mary's maternal activity and reduce it to theological formulae. They like to measure her share in the Redemption accurately and compare it in minute detail with Christ's redemptive activity. But how could you possibly answer me, if I were to ask: 'On whom can family life be said ultimately to depend – on the father or on the mother?' It would be quite impossible to give a clearly defined answer to this question. In the family the relationships between father and mother are so delicately interwoven that the individual parts played by both parents can never be precisely divided and accounted for separately. Father and mother are indivisibly united, and what God has joined together, others may not put asunder. The good father is always intimately affected by the nearness and activity of the mother. The mother is entirely absorbed in everything that the father does and is trying to do. She looks up to him in admiration and shares his life, doing what he does together with him in her own maternal way. The mother's influence so permeates the whole of the family's life that it can even be felt in an empty room. She is an atmosphere, but an atmosphere that is always active and busy. She influences all those who live and breathe in this atmosphere.

Something of this kind happens in the life of their family, which is the Church. Christ and Christ alone – and God in humanity – was responsible for everything, but, within the Holy Family, Mary became Christ's maternal partner, with the result that everything that happened in the family was affected by her maternal quality. Viewed in this light, we may also say that Mary too was responsible for everything, as the Mother of the Redeemer and of his redemption. Christ's redemption was offered to us by Christ in his Church, saturated, as it were, with this maternal quality. All Mary's being, all her activity, then, amounted to this: as a mother, she constantly converted into maternal terms everything that Christ thought, desired, felt and did concerning our salvation. This process of conversion is, of course, still continuing. Mary is the translation and effective expression in maternal terms of God's mercy, grace and redeeming love which manifested itself to us in a visible and tangible form in the person of Christ, our Redeemer. She derived her maternal power from being so close to Christ, her own Child, her and our Redeemer, who emanated power. This is in no way different from Christ's normal activity, but in Mary's case it contained a unique and irreplaceable element, since it involved her participation as his mother.

This can also help us to understand the dogmatic development of the Marian mystery. The concrete reality, expressed in utter simplicity by the bare scriptural fact 'Mary, the mother of Jesus', comprises the entire dogma of Mary. All the other definitions of faith concerning Mary merely serve to develop or set out in greater detail what is contained in this infinitely rich concrete motherhood.

To be a mother is, however, not simply a momentary fact – bearing a child. It is a long process of growth and development lasting the whole of life, in which full and mature motherhood is attamed only as a result of the continuous action and reaction which takes place between the mother and the child. We should, therefore, avoid thinking of Mary's motherhood with regard to Christ, and consequently of her spiritual motherhood with regard to all of us, as an act of faith and love which occupied no more than a single moment of time. Mary's motherhood was a progressive reality. Bearing in mind what has been said in the foregoing paragraphs, we can outline Mary's maternal development schematically as follows.

Her immaculate conception and virgin life prepared her for her later pure motherhood and her maternal activity in the service of the Kingdom of God. Her assent to the angel's message made her in the real sense the mother of the God-man, our Redeemer, and thus at once the spiritual mother of the whole of humanity awaiting Christ's redemption. Her maternal communion with her crucified Child, our Redeemer, made her at once the tender mother of the whole of redeemed humanity. As a result of her Pentecost experience, she acquired a mature awareness of her maternal task within the redeemed world. Finally, her assumption into heaven and her spiritual and physical glorification made her queen and mother. Now, as the glorified mother, she is 'in power'. Enjoying the beatific vision granted to her by the glorified Christ, she has a clear, intuitive consciousness of her maternal task and knows all people intimately in their individual circumstances and their concrete worries and cares. In heaven she is concerned for every one of them and uses her maternal love on their behalf, so that the kingdom of her Son may be fulfilled.

What we really mean, when we refer to Mary as the co-redemptrix, the mediatrix of all graces, or the one who dispenses grace and intercedes for all people, is nothing more or less than this: She is 'in power' as the glorified mother of the redemption brought by Christ alone, the mother who completely identifies herself, in maternal love, with the redemptive acts of her Child, our Redeemer. In other words, within the Communion of Saints, the Mother of Jesus enjoys the most intimate human communion with the sole Redeemer. The various titles given to Mary are but other expressions of this one fundamental reality. On the basis of this same reality, moreover, all these titles are reduced to their proportions.

The Church reveals the inexpressible wealth of the enormous reality contained in the image of the 'mother of the redeemer of the world' only in separate statements. The basic structural lines of this image of Mary, the mother, the first lines from which this portrait has been built up, have emerged only very slowly with the passage of time. We have now reached the stage where nothing remains to be discovered as far as the basic structure is concerned. We shall, however, never come to the end of our search for the content and meaning of the essential maternal features of the image. This is surely comparable to our experience at the purely human level – our insight into the nature of our own mother here pa earth deepens as we grow older and our gradual understanding of her as our mother discloses new horizons of which we were not explicitly conscious during our early life. Scripture and the Apostles' understanding of 'Mary, the mother of Jesus' provided the basis for an intuition which has become more and more clear with the passage of time in the Church's life of faith. The later dogmatic pronouncements of the Church can thus be regarded as joyous words which have been suggested to us while what we were unable to express was on the tip of our tongues. In this way the holy possession which had hitherto been latent was able to achieve a greater clarity. 'Behold thy mother' – these words from the Cross form, as it were, Christ's dogmatic definition which the Church has since broken down, analytically, into richly varied, separate dogmas.

Catholics should have no cause to be astonished at the apparently tremendous development from the Gospel image to the dogmatic vision of Mary. The basic reason for the difference between the Protestant and the Catholic attitudes towards Mary in the sphere of worship is undoubtedly to be found in the different dogmatic views of Christ and in the fact that we, as Catholics, do not hesitate to call our Lady the mother of the redeeming God in humanity. Our Protestant brothers and sisters in faith, on the other hand, do not appear to grasp the deep and fundamental meaning of this great reality, 'God in humanity', and consequently fail to fathom the full depths of Mary's motherhood. At the same time, they misinterpret her essential maternal quality, by denying the human personal, meritorious co-operation in salvation. This particular misconception is probably the cause of their further misunderstanding of Mary's true greatness and sublime place in the event of the Incarnation. The characteristically Protestant attitude towards Mary, then, not only colours the Protestant's dogmatic vision of faith. It also forms the basis of Protestant, as distinct from Catholic, spirituality.

Mary, the type of the redeemed community of the Church[5]

The one, chosen out of the many in the human community, was redeemed in order to become the first fruit of the Redemption. That is to say, she was redeemed in order that she might, as a mother, represent in her own person and in a 'typical' manner what the whole of the Church was to be – virgin fidelity to Christ and maternal fruitfulness. In this context, what St. Paul had to say concerning the Church and Christ's relationship with the Church is strictly pertinent: 'Christ also loved the Church and delivered himself up for it; that he might sanctify it and cleanse it... that he might present it to himself, a glorious church, not having spot or wrinkle... but that it should be holy and without blemish' (Eph 5.25-27). Christ fully realised this, in the first place, in his mother Mary. The entire life of the Church throughout her history is nothing more nor less than a growth, an ascent, towards the image of the Mother of God.

What has been fully accomplished in Mary is still in a process of growth and becoming in the Church on earth. The *parousia* – the glorification and the spiritual and bodily togetherness of redeemed humanity with Christ in triumph – has already taken place for Mary and for Mary alone. In the words of St. Thomas, 'The true

---

[5]Selected from: Edward Schillebeeckx, *Mary, Mother of Redemption* (London: Sheed and Ward, 1964), 122–6.

Church, our Mother, is in heaven; we grow up towards her, and the entire reality of the Church Militant [on earth] is to be found in her conformity with the Church in heaven.'[6] The spotless Virgin Mother, which is the Church, is an eschatological reality, a vision of a future heavenly reality. This reality has, however, already been accomplished in the *Assumpta*, although on earth the Church our Virgin Mother, is still on pilgrimage. In this sense Mary makes the Church on earth a real Church, since the heavenly Church is, according to St. Thomas, the *true* Church from which the Church on earth is derived, and may be called a *real* Church.

Mary is therefore the prototype of the whole Church. Until now, it is only in her that the Church is in the fullest sense Church. The word *tupos* – type or prototype – which the Fathers of the Church use in this context, does not simply mean an example, a pattern or a model. It refers first and foremost to a human figure, a person from whose personal life-history or career and from whose ultimate state God's design to save his chosen people may clearly emerge. God clearly manifests his intentions concerning the Church in the perfect image of the Virgin Mother. The word 'type' does not, moreover, refer exclusively to a static image to which we should look up – a model which we should admire and upon which we should fashion our lives. It refers rather to something much more dynamic – a saving power. It should show us that Mary, as the 'type' of the Church, personally consecrated herself to the task of helping to bring about in the other members of the Church community what had already been 'typically' realised in her life by Christ. Since she is, as a mother, the type of the Church, she is able to co-operate maternally in the work of the Church built up and extended by Christ. Only in this sense can she be called 'Mother of the Church', that is, the Church owes her proper maternal character to Mary.

We are therefore bound to acknowledge the truth of St. Augustine's statement, 'Mary is a part of the Church, a holy member, an excellent and prominent member, but still a member of the whole Church.'[7] But in the Church she is the spiritual and physical womb of the Church. It should be possible, then, to define Mary's relationship to the Church more precisely from this point onwards.

Mary's place in the Church community of grace and her relation to the sacramental and hierarchical Church[8]

In any comparison between Mary, the Virgin Mother, and the Virgo et Mater Ecclesia, it is imperative for us to bear in mind one fundamental distinction. In calling Mary the prototype of the Church, it is necessary to distinguish between that aspect of the Church which we have characterised as the community of grace and that other

---

[6] St. Thomas, *In ad Ephes.*, c. 3, lect. 3.
[7] *Sermo XXV de Verbis Evang.* Matth. XII. XLI-L (PL, 46, col. 938).
[8] Selected from: Edward Schillebeeckx, *Mary, Mother of Redemption* (London: Sheed and Ward, 1964), 122–6.

aspect, the Church regarded as a sacramental, hierarchical institution. Mary can be considered as the type of the Church only in its first aspect. Indeed, she forms the culminating point of the community of grace with Christ in the Church. Her grace is the highest ideal in the redeemed Christian life. Such a high tide, such a flood of grace also contains a universal power, capable of exerting an influence over all people and capable, what is more, of doing this in a manner peculiar to this particular and sublime subject of grace. The influence exercised by this universal power of grace is a purely maternal influence, springing from and following the course of a mother's love. The grace which stems from the sacramental, hierarchical Church is, on the other hand, of a sacerdotal kind and is not in any way due to Mary, since she does not form part of the ranks of the Church's hierarchy. Mary is not a priestess. This is, however, not to say that the grace conferred by the sacraments is entirely outside Mary's influence. The grace given to us by the sacraments is always Christ's grace, and Christ was and is, as we have seen, imbued with Mary's maternal qualities. The Church, which, as the visible community, perpetuates the work of our redemption and distributes redemptive grace among us in an institutional manner, thus mediates the grace which was acquired by Christ and co-acquired maternally by Mary. We should not infer that there is something lacking in Mary because she forms no part of the sacramental Church as a structural principle. On the contrary, her not belonging to the sacramental Church as a structural principle results from the fact that she already fulfilled an essential and maternal function at the very inception of the redemptive act. The sacramental Church fulfils the function of communicating this redemption to us.

In this sense the whole of the Church's sacramental activity in the mediation of grace, considered as an act of Christ who is received by people in faith and love, can be seen to be foreshadowed in Mary's life. In faith she did not receive a specific sacrament, but the Primordial Sacrament itself, Jesus Christ in person. Mary's reception of the sacrament, anticipating both in time and in order of importance every subsequent case of personal reception, in the Church, of a specific sacrament, constitutes the prototype of the sacramental life of the Church, as seen from the point of view of the subject or recipient. In the words of Leo the Great, 'The principle of birth which Christ found in Mary's womb has been embodied by him in the water of baptism: *Dedit aquae quod dedit matri*. The power of the Most High and the overshadowing of the Holy Ghost, which brought about the birth of the Redeemer in the Virgin Mary, also make it possible for the water of baptism to bring about a rebirth in the faithful.'[9]

Christ alone and, in his power, the sacramental Church, are the ministers of the sacraments. Mary is not. She is on the side of those who receive the sacraments. Christ, however, is the principal minister of the sacraments, and the hierarchical Church distributes the sacraments in his power and is subordinate to him, as his servant, administering the sacraments through her priests. In precisely the same way, Mary, who personally received the Primordial Sacrament in sublime faith and love, is the principal recipient, and we receive the sacraments in her actively

---

[9] *Sermo XXV*, 4 (*PL.*, 54, col. 211).

receptive power. In this sense, Mary is completely outside the priestly distribution of the sacraments, although the hierarchical aspect of the Church is fully included in her universal, maternal and saving mediation. Her relationship towards the saving power of the sacraments can therefore provide us, if we consider it within the context of the sacramental communication of the grace acquired by Christ, with a clear understanding of Christ's unique position as the only Redeemer and Mary's maternal self-identification with Christ's work of salvation. The direct consequence of this is that Christ's grace is at the same time always Mary's, our maternal advocate's grace.

Selected literature

- Mary's Place in God's Plan of Salvation; Selected from: Edward Schillebeeckx, *Mary, Mother of Redemption*, London: Sheed and Ward (1964): 101–4.
- The Anticipatory Sacramental Activity of Mary's Motherhood and Its Sacramental Consequences; Selected from: Edward Schillebeeckx, *Mary, Mother of Redemption*, London: Sheed and Ward (1964): 105–9.
- The Divine Reason for Mary's Election; Selected from: Edward Schillebeeckx, *Mary, Mother of Redemption*, London: Sheed and Ward (1964): 109–16.
- Mary, the Type of the Redeemed Community of the Church; Selected from: Edward Schillebeeckx, *Mary, Mother of Redemption*, London: Sheed and Ward (1964): 122–6.

17

Eschatology

The Christian relativisation and radicalisation of the building of the 'secular city'[1]

Authentic Christians are people in whose lives the Spirit of Christ himself is visible – 'See how they love one another'. In the early church, this visible love functioned within the early image of humanity and the world. How must it function today? In other words, what is the relationship between Christian love and the building up of a better world for people to live in? Quite correctly, the pastoral constitution warns us of two dangers; firstly, the danger of our not taking, as Christians, the building of a better future on earth seriously and, secondly, the danger of our identifying, in an un-Christian way, a self-made future with the kingdom of God. Because of the promise of the kingdom of God, Christians are, in their commitment to this world, placed in the very centre of the mystery – every result achieved in this world is always questioned because of the Christian hope for the *eschaton*, yet this commitment to the world is never in vain. There is a tension between relativisation and radicalisation in the Christian commitment to the building of a better future on earth. I should like to conclude by throwing some light on this tension.

Every project to build a better future for human beings on earth has to come to terms with the problem of death, otherwise a utopia is planned without regard to real facts. The fact of death makes relative all attempts to build a better world for human beings to live in. On earth, humanisation has no definitive shape or form which can ultimately be called Christian in content. The Christian hope for the *eschaton* and faith in an eschatological 'new world', in which death no longer has any place, makes all humanisation here on earth and all human building of a 'secular city' relative. It is clear that the council understood this from the section in the pastoral constitution referring to the need to include all activity within the world in the mystery of Easter (*Gaudium et spes* 38). The ultimate world that dignifies humanity can only be given to us as a gift of God beyond the frontiers of death, that is, in the act in which we

---

[1] Selected from: Edward Schillebeeckx, 'Man's Expectation for the Future on Earth', *The Mission of the Church*, trans. N. D. Smith (New York: Seabury, 1973), 84–8.

ultimately confess our impotence to make this world truly human, in our explicit and effective recognition that the 'new world' cannot be the result of human planning, but must be a pure gift of God. It is only when human beings surrender completely to God that any real future lies ahead of them.

But, however fundamentally Christian this view may be, it is still not the whole of Christianity. If this – authentically Christian – aspect alone is emphasised, the objection raised by all those who are ready to lay down their lives in order to banish injustice and discrimination from the world still remains valid, namely, as Merleau-Ponty observed, if it ever comes to the point where there must be a revolution in order to banish injustice from the world, we can never rely on Christians, because they relativise every commitment to the world. This is a very real objection and, what is more, one which is not closely examined in the pastoral constitution.

Any attempt to answer this objection would in the first place have to throw a much clearer light on the fact that the Christian relativisation of human commitment to this world is not inspired by a flight from this world, nor is it prompted by a conviction that grace enjoys an absolute priority. Christian make this commitment to the world relative precisely because they hope for an eschatological completion, in which human beings will possess themselves and the world completely in a radical giving of themselves. This hope for a 'new world' makes every result achieved on this earth in the process of humanisation relative because the result achieved is not yet and cannot be this hoped for 'new world'. In the past, Christians drew the wrong conclusion from this correct assumption, namely that they had to be indifferent or even hostile to the building of a better world on earth. In fact, however, the only correct conclusion is that Christians can never reconcile themselves to an already 'established order' in the world, because it can never be Christian in content. In this sense, there is no such thing as a 'Christian' social order, civilisation or policy. What is precisely Christian in this context is the constant striving to go beyond the result achieved, the refusal to say, 'the result is satisfactory and everything is now in order'. Christianity is therefore the confirmation of a future which always remains open and this openness is not a static datum or a purely theoretical statement, but an active commitment to a better future.

The change that was made in the original text of the pastoral constitution from 'the form of this world insofar as it is characterised by sin, *will* pass' into the final version, 'is already passing', was quite justified. This passing of the form of the world does not, however, occur automatically, but through eschatological hope, which is already working for a better world here on earth. This may seem to some people to be an unjustified leap in the train of thought. But in this case they are forgetting the precise content of the 'veiled relationship' between the future on this earth and the eschatological future as affirmed by the council. This relationship certainly cannot be determined more precisely. Precisely because the Christian believes in an absolute future, the future which is God himself for humanity, he cannot describe the precise shape of this future meaningfully – any more than the non-Christian can – and he can never confuse or identify the result of human's historical striving on earth with the promised 'new world'. After all, if God is the intangible, incomprehensible mystery and human beings are embraced by this mystery, then their being is, by definition, also a mystery that cannot be comprehended by faith. But Christian hope in God, who is humanity's future, is not a theory but an active hope, which only becomes a reality in humans working for a better future on earth, in other words, in their care for their fellow human beings in concrete situations in this world. This radical commitment to our fellow human beings is an incomprehensible love and this love, because it is incomprehensible, makes the commitment completely radical. We do not know where this love is leading us, but we do know that it is not ultimately meaningless and will not be in vain. This makes Christian love incomprehensible for the world. It makes our commitment to this world thematically incomprehensible even to us Christians – we are a mystery even to ourselves and have, in all simplicity, to confess this to our 'non-Christian' fellow human beings when they ask us why we are committing ourselves to life in this world. This thematic incomprehensibility, however, does not mean that we commit ourselves any less to the world. On the contrary, it makes this commitment completely radical. Our commitment as Christians to our fellow human beings is completely radical because it is the other side of the coin of God's personal love for humanity. This commitment is radical because, even though it is not possible to realise here on earth a world that is truly worthy of humanity, it continues to work, in complete surrender to faith, towards a situation that is more and more human. It is a hope against hope, a hope against all despair that comes from our human experience, which continues to suggest that all our attempts to build a better world are in vain. The radical character of this Christian commitment and of the surrender to faith cannot be justified in the light of purely human experience. It is, of its very nature, a hoping in God (explicitly or implicitly) as the future for humanity. It is possible that many Christians have not yet drawn all these conclusions from the radical nature of this view and that they are consequently still hesitant in their attitude towards the social and political dynamism of the modern age and the struggle to build a world that is more worthy of humanity. They may therefore feel too satisfied in their own welfare state, while more than half of the world is still hungering and thirsting for a strict minimum of human dignity.

Nowadays, Christianity is discovering the 'political' dimension of Christian charity and the worldly dimensions of Christianity. The inspiration here comes from the present situation in the world and from contact with the Bible and especially with the old testament. In the past, Christians tended to live in a separate little world of the spirit, where God and the human 'soul' made asides to each other. The Bible, however, teaches us that God is active in the whole world and that the church is called to share in this activity of God in the world itself. In this age, God seems to be accomplishing more through people like Martin Luther King, for example, than through the church.

Eschaton as future[2]

When in our old culture, mainly concerned with the past, we thought and spoke about God's transcendence we almost naturally projected God into the past. Eternity

---

[2] Selected from: Edward Schillebeeckx, 'The Interpretation of the Future', *The Understanding of Faith: Interpretation and Criticism*, trans. N. D. Smith, Collected Works of Edward Schillebeeckx vol. 5 (London: Bloomsbury T&T Clark, 2014), 4–10 [4–11].

was something like an immobilised or immortalised past – 'in the beginning was God'. We knew of course quite well that God's eternity embraced humanity's present and humanity's future; that God was both first and last, and as such also a present that transcended our human present. On this point the older theology developed marvellous insights which have by no means lost their relevance. In a culture which constantly looked towards the past there existed obviously a powerful mutual attraction between 'transcendence' and eternity on the one hand and an immortalised 'past' on the other. Today, however, our culture is firmly turned towards the future as something that our culture itself must build. So the Christian notion of transcendence, supple and capable of more than one meaning, has to go through the same process. The meaning of 'transcendence' comes therefore closer to what in our time-bound condition we call 'future'. If divine transcendence transcends and embraces humanity's past, present and future from within, the believer will preferably and rightly link God's transcendence with the future as soon as human beings have recognised the primacy of the future in our time-bound condition. So they will link God with the future of humanity and, since human beings are communal beings, with the future of humanity as a whole. When we once accept the reality of a genuine belief in the invisible reality of God who is the true source of our understanding of God from within this world, this new understanding of his transcendence will lead to the new image of God in our culture.

In this cultural context the God of the believer will manifest himself as 'He who comes', the God who is our future. This implies a far-reaching change: he, whom we formerly saw as the 'wholly other' in our old outlook on humanity and the world, is now seen as he who is our future and who creates anew humanity's future. He shows himself as the God who gives us in Jesus Christ the opportunity to build the future, to make all things new and to rise above our own sinful history and that of all humanity. Thus the new culture becomes an inspiration to rediscover as a surprise the good news of the Old and the New Testament, the news that the God of promise has put us on the way to the promised land, a land which, like Israel of old, we ourselves must claim and cultivate, trusting in his promise.

If we see biblical history as an event handed down to us in a believing and critical interpretation, we can also see that the reference to the future is contained in the present of the people of God as it lives within the context of this history of traditions. 'Future' is an intrinsic dimension of present, is related to what must still happen in time without allowing us to see its future shape at present. This biblical structure of the prophecy of the future which sets the present within a living history of traditions rejects on the one hand any 'de-eschatologisation' of time (there is no room for a radical eschatology of the present) and on the other hand demands a rejection of all apocalyptic elements from the expectation of the future (apocalyptic thought thinks from the future to the present).

Because of humanity's essential historicity, 'future' means a future starting from the present and therefore from the past. Although its actual shape remains hidden, the future is an intrinsic element in human self-understanding. This hidden reality is therefore intrinsically related to the actuality. This has been insufficiently understood by Jürgen Moltmann.

In this sense there can be no true eschatology of the future without a certain eschatology of the present. Although the future has an element of 'not yet' in it we cannot neglect the element of 'already'. In fact, only the 'already' allows us to say anything meaningful about the still unknown future. It is therefore typical that the Old Testament never describes the unknown future in totally new and unexpected terms. Hope always looks for some ideal restoration, the particular features of which are supposed to be known from the past. The total picture, however, is always new. Expectation is not a state of hoping for a simple re-shaping of the past. Israel hoped for the fulfilment of what Yahweh had already done in its desire for the total achievement of it all. The re-actualisation of the past in the present with an eye on the future makes Israel expect with increasing tension that future which only Yahweh can bring, and which then will be definitive, once for all. Such an expectation has nothing to do with crystal-gazing or an unveiling of the future. It is rather an insight of faith, gained by the knowledge of God's dealings with his people. Only the unconditional surrender to Yahweh's faithfulness and the living traditions that are related to it can bring any certainty about the future. In terms of humanity's historicity, Yahweh's faithfulness is expectation of a future, certainty about the goodness of the plan of creation which is both the beginning and the *eschaton*, the ultimate end. It is 'very good' (Gen 1.31). In other words, human future as seen by God (the Bible puts these words into Yahweh's mouth) is 'very good', a future of salvation. The lack of salvation, temporary or possibly final, is of humanity's own doing. It is interesting here that biblical thought about the beginning (protology) is intertwined with eschatological thought. This protology, as formulated in the final draft of the creation story in Genesis, can only be understood on the basis of actual experience of God's faithfulness with its consequent eschatological expectations. The story of creation is therefore also an eschatological statement.

What, however, is the connection between future and *eschaton*? O. Procksch, G. von Rad and T. Vriezen[3] rightly maintain against V. Maag[4] that in the Old Testament the belief in God's dominion is not identical with the kingdom of God in the eschatological sense. Moreover, for centuries Israel practised its religion without expecting a hereafter. Apart from the late apocalyptic eschatology in the Old Testament, expressions such as 'the last days' do not refer to an existence beyond this earth, beyond history, but to a future within this world. The *eschaton* is marked by newness and universalism but it is all in a concept of history which remains on this side of the beyond. To this Ezekiel and Deutero-Isaiah add the idea of an approaching nearness. Throughout the prophetic tradition the picture of God's day of judgement is thrown on to the screen of earthly history; it is the picture of an expectation of a future in this world, this history. Only in Daniel and the very latest apocalyptic insertions into earlier prophetic traditions does the day of Yahweh put a full stop to history. The *eschaton* then refers to a situation beyond this earth, or at least to the time immediately preceding the end of time. But even in the probably late apocalyptic passage in Isaiah 24-7 the last days are still seen within the reality of the history of this world: the old people of God is then given its final eschatological

---

[3] O. Procksch, *Theologie des Alten Testaments*, Gütersloh, 1950, p. 591; G. von Rad, 'Basileia' in *Theologisches Wörterbuch zum Neuen Testament*, I (Kittel), pp. 566f; T. Vriezen, *Hoofdlijnen der Theologie van het Oude Testament*, Wageningen, ³1966.
[4] V. Maag, 'Malkût Jhwh', in *Supplements to Vetus Testamentum* 7 (1960), pp. 129–53.

status without mentioning whether history will still go on after that. Not until the book of Daniel is there question of a transcendent eschatology and is there talk of a post-historical existence, expressed in the powerful religious symbol of resurrection. That there will be a future for the historical past, and even for the dead, appears only very late in the Old Testament.

For centuries, therefore, the belief in Yahweh could be practised meaningfully without the assertion of a transcendent, post-historical and final fulfilment. This development in revelation shows that one does not live religiously for the sake of the hereafter. The development of Israel's faith shows that the unquestionable value of the covenant, the actual relationship between the historic Israel and God, provides the hermeneutic context for a belief in a transcendent eschatology. The *Sitz im Leben* of the eschatological expectation beyond this world is the temporal all-surpassing meaning of the actual relationship with the living God. This conceals the hidden urge towards a transcendent future. For some time devout Israelites had already had some inkling of the idea that even death has no power over him whom God loves. Most powerfully perhaps in Psalms 16, 49 and 73 that spiritual experience of relationship with God is expressed which would sooner or later destroy the idea of the state after death as one of excommunication from life, from life in this world with one's fellows in communion with God, and so pave the way for a transcendent eschatology. In these psalms Yahweh's faithfulness fosters the idea that love must be immortal and definitive, that through this love we know that we are in God's hand not only *in* but also *after* death. Beyond this vague hunch the psalmists had no appropriate terminology to express the certainty of this spiritual experience, and the concept of resurrection provided the first suitable formula.

The present, then, understood as the actual relationship with God and experienced historically as God's dealings with humanity, is not only the hermeneutic principle for the interpretation of religious expectations of the future, but also the principle which links the future of this earth with the transcendent *eschaton*. The Bible gives us no anticipatory historical report on this *eschaton*. We know nothing about the transcendent last things – judgement, Christ's return, heaven, hell, purgatory – except in so far as they are already indicated in the course of historical events expressing the actual relationship between the God of the covenant and humanity, particularly in Christ, 'the last Adam', or 'man of the *eschaton*' (1 Cor 15.45). Eschatology, therefore, does not allow us to withdraw from earthly history, because only in the depth of this history can eternity begin to take shape. The post-terrestrial *eschaton* is but a question of the manner in which what is already growing in the history of this world will receive its final fulfilment. This analysis seems to confirm Rahner's position: 'To speak from the present to the future is eschatology; to speak from the future to the present is apocalyptic.'[5] Eschatology is the expression of the belief that history is in God's hands, that the history of the world can reach its fulfilment in communion with God and that it will be brought to this fulfilment in Christ who embodies God's promise. Eschatology does not allow us to cash in on the hereafter, but it is something to be achieved responsibly by all the faithful within

---

[5] 'The Hermeneutics of Eschatological Assertions', in *Theological Investigations* IV, London, 1966, p. 150.

the framework of our terrestrial history. Faced with the real evil existing in history, eschatology expresses the belief that the true faithful can and must bend this history into the salvation of all. This must be done within the perspective of present world history, in newness and in the context of universality. This salvation must already be achieved now in our history, in this world, and so this history becomes itself a prophecy of the final and transcendent *eschaton*. It is the promise of a new world, a powerful symbol which sets us thinking and above all acting. The credibility of this promise lies in the renewal now of our human history. Through their justification the faithful themselves become responsible for the newness of this human world whose dimension in depth will be perpetuated into eternity. For this eternity does not come after our time or our history, but is both the transcendent and the intrinsic ultimate fulfilment of this history itself.

Eschatological revolution: Jesus' beatitudes[6]

What was the situation of the common people in these structures? They were 'the poor', that is, the actual poor in society. But the concept was acquiring a religious implication (Isa 29.19–21; Zeph 3; Prov 16.19; Wis 2.10–20). After the exile the repatriates in particular constituted the 'poor remnant', but nurtured and stimulated by ancient Yahwistic spirituality. The 'renewed people' came to be synonymous with 'the poor' (Isa 51.17; 54.13; especially 49.13), nourished by trito-Isaiahan spirituality (Isa 61.1–3; see 57.15). 'Poor' here (usually coinciding with social deprivation) refers to the devout and pious individual who in his poverty humbly waits on God (see also Ps 25; 34; 37.9–11). The 'poor' are victim of misfortune (of whatever kind), whose only strength and stay is to entrust themselves to God (Isa 52–53; Ps 22; Zech 9.9-10).

Grounded in this age-old tradition the popular conception persisted that the poor, the hungry and the sorrowful are those who have nothing more to hope for from human history and can only continue to wait expectantly on God, who is just. In Jesus' time, therefore, the 'poor' among the Jews were people who could not demand justice for themselves, hence could only trust in the justice of God.

Of course, some schools of thought (even religious ones) believed that this inability to demand justice for oneself was relative; they wanted to assist Israel's God by force of arms: the Sicarii and the Zealots. Although Jesus' time was a fairly peaceful spell between events thirty years previously (Judas the Galilean) and thirty years later (leading to the Jewish rebellion against Rome), the fact is that Jesus did not choose this way.

So when Jesus said: 'Blessed are the poor, the hungry, the sorrowful', the people understood what he meant. But Jesus did not repeat what they already knew, namely that given the concrete situation, they could not look for help to any earthly agency and that salvation and deliverance could come only from God. That *was* in fact the

---

[6]Selected from: Edward Schillebeeckx, *Jesus: An Experiment in Christology*, trans. John Bowden, Collected Works of Edward Schillebeeckx vol. 6 (London: Bloomsbury T&T Clark, 2014), 153–5 [176–8].

late Jewish concept of poverty and Jesus was not proclaiming a tautology. What, then, was he saying?

The eschatological prophet would come bearing glad tidings for the poor. That was a lively part of popular expectation, rooted in older traditions, among many of the poor and oppressed. Jesus' beatitude signifies that it was happening *now*: that is to say, the yearning expectation of divine succour was about to be fulfilled; promise and expectation were on the point of being realised. With Jesus the kingdom of God came upon them. Jesus felt compassion for these poor folk. God himself would move into action against humanity's history of incomprehensible suffering, insofar as there is no human remedy for it. Firstly, Jesus brings God's message of his radical 'no' to the continuing history of human suffering. The whole point of history, although only the *eschaton* will make this clear, is peace, laughter, satisfaction: salvation and happiness. Just as in earlier times people had tried to articulate the purpose of life and history 'protologically' with reference to the primeval history of all things, in Jesus' day it was described 'eschatologically' with reference to the end of the age. Despite everything, compassion is the deepest purpose that God seeks to fulfil in history. He wills people to live, wills their salvation, not their misery and death. Jesus undeniably expresses all this in terms of the mentality of his time – hence in temporally limited and conditioned terms. Neither can we deny, despite all sorts of necessary distinctions, that for him the end was very near. Hence preparing for the sudden coming of God's kingdom was the most urgent task. Jesus did not preach social revolution, although his eschatological message subjects the whole history of human suffering to God's critical judgment and so calls for an about-turn. This has fundamental consequences for continuing post-Jesus history implications which must be made explicit. Yet this is not the underlying purport of the beatitudes. What they quite unmistakably enshrine is a spiritual affirmation of the ultimate power of powerlessness a belief that however necessary it is to improve the world through human resources (that is, to make explicit God's 'no' to the history of suffering), at the deepest level there is a suffering, an impotence which no human being can alleviate and from which only God's future reign for the good of all people can free us. There is human helplessness which God alone can relieve. That was Jesus' own premise as well. If God wills universal salvation, as Jesus preached when he conveyed the message of God's lordship – if, therefore, God is love, creative love for humanity, then the poor, the hungry and grief-stricken may already rise up in hope, and say: but all the same... Laughter, not crying, is God's fundamental will for humanity. That implies, at all events, that he does not will suffering. On no account is Jesus prepared to blame God for suffering and evil. God's essential being is anti-evil, willing good. Later theological distinctions of God's 'positive' and 'permissive' will were introduced by theologians seeking a theoretical explanation for suffering, like the Greek attempts to describe all forms of evil as a 'non-being' so as not to have to fathom it – an escape route for people who could not locate evil theoretically. In Jesus' eschatological message we hear only God's radical 'no' to all forms of evil, all forms of poverty and hunger that lead to tears. That is Jesus' message; and it has enormous consequences. That in it God refuses to acknowledge the superior strength of evil and so with his own divine being stands surety for the defeat of evil in all its forms can in no way be turned to reactionary or conservative ends. The only message Jesus brings us from God is that God stands surety for us. Hence the poor, the suffering and the disadvantaged indeed have grounds for positive hope. How? Perhaps the rest of the story of Jesus' life, as well as the historical failure of his message and praxis, can tell us more about that. In particular his whole conduct should help to determine whether the overall picture of Jesus' message and preaching tallies with reality, more specifically whether Jesus was indeed the prophet of the imminence of God's kingdom how he conjoined this message with a praxis intended to change the existing situation radically (with all the attendant dangers) whether and how, inspired by the gracious mandate he received from God, he knew himself to be the saving instrument of God's approaching kingdom, which in his actions evidently became real among the people who came to him in trust.

The impossibility of defining humanity's complete salvation[7]

Precisely because a perspective on final salvation comes to us only in historically broken situations of experiences of meaning or meaninglessness, the awareness of final salvation is provisionally a 'negative awareness'. However, this can be a powerful stimulus towards achieving meaning in our history. I pointed out earlier that both meaning already experienced and the experience of refractory meaninglessness have an emotional force which can direct actions and prove productive. Experiences of meaningless suffering have a critical force because of the disturbing possibility that they may be repeated in the future; experiences of meaning, of love and joy, are meaningful only because they may be possibly established in the future, which is not automatically a given. Conceptions of an unthreatened, final, perfect salvation applying to all are on the one hand to some degree formulated in a positive way because of partial experiences of meaning already undergone; on the other hand, however, within the real history of suffering within which we stand they can only be expressed negatively, in parables and visions: a world in which righteousness and love prevail, a world 'without tears'. However, our situation never allows us to define in positive terms what this will ultimately imply for human salvation, given the spiritual openness and the human 'self-transcendence' still to be realised in history and, moreover, in view of the absolute freedom of God as the 'God of humanity', a God whose glory lies in human happiness. Any positive definition runs the risk of either becoming megalomaniac in human terms or belittling God's possibilities. The Greek fathers in particular spoke of a *divinisation* of human beings, in the sense of a gracious participation by human beings in God's own life.[8] But this was simply another way of expressing the impossibility of defining the final future of human life in grace. For we do not have any term to describe

---

[7] Selected from: Edward Schillebeeckx, *Christ: The Christian Experience in the Modern World*, Collected Works of Edward Schillebeeckx vol. 7 (London: Bloomsbury T&T Clark, 2014), 788–9 [791–3].

[8] '*Ekei paragenomenos anthrōpos esomai*': 'when I arrive there I will be human' (Ignatius of Antioch, *Rom.* 6.2). Here Ignatius says that he will only become really and fully human through and in his martyr's death. The death of the martyr is the birthday of his true humanity. True humanity is connected with the way through suffering through and for others. This is a unique statement in the patristic literature, not so much because of its content as because of the way in which it is put. It emerges from this also that the

the ultimate significance of our *humanity* which can be detached from our ongoing history, nor an appropriate unhistorical concept which means the Godness of God – as salvation for humanity. 'Divinisation of humanity through grace' therefore simply expresses something positive and undefinable, that *God is the salvation of humanity*. Therefore the Old and New Testament say, 'These are the things of which Scripture says, No eye has seen, no ear has heard, no man can imagine what God prepares for those who love him' (1 Cor 2.9; Isa 64.3, 65.17b).

That does not in any way mean that final salvation will come upon us *from outside*, detached from and regardless of what people in fact make of it in their history. Eschatological or final salvation – let us call it heaven – takes shape (heavenly shape) from what people on earth achieve as salvation for their fellow beings 'in mutual love, which heeds the things that must abide for ever' (Heb 13.1). We have biblical testimony to this effect: 'Come, O blessed of my Father, inherit the kingdom prepared for you from the foundation of the world; for I was hungry and you gave me food, I was thirsty and you gave me drink, I was a stranger and you welcomed me, I was naked and you clothed me, I was sick and you visited me, I was in prison and you came to me... Truly, I say to you, as you did it to one of the least of these my brothers and sisters, you did it to me' (Matt 25.34–40). The Last Judgment is as 'atheistic' as that! However, there was a point in Thomas Aquinas calling love of neighbour a *virtus theologalis,* a 'divine virtue' (and not just ethics). It is to the human action of doing good that God gives an unexpected future in which his forgiveness plays a major role: 'He loved us (already) when we were still sinners' (Rom 5.8). The fact that above all in Jewish-Christian spirituality the living God is witnessed to as merciful and ready to forgive, opens up a perspective of final salvation in which it would be presumptuous to attempt to provide a fixed and positive content. For in that case we run the risk of wanting to set limits to God's creative grace. Something of this undefinable mystery of God's mercy with our history is expressed in the practice of the Roman Catholic Church which, while it has the courage to call exemplary brothers and sisters among us saints, happily does not venture to call any of the children of humanity 'hellish' by name – not because no hellish things happen in our history, but because we people cannot fully fathom either human freedom or above all the freedom of the *creative* mercy of God. But that does not mean that we have to remain completely speechless about what happened to Jesus and what witness is borne to him through Christians. Faith in the risen Jesus gives us quite a *clear* perspective and not an indefinite one. Precisely here, the human person Jesus is the revelation of what is possible with God.

The kingdom of God: 'already and not yet'[9]

The seed of the kingdom of God already germinates and ripens here and now on earth. The kingdom of God is not an unearthly other world, but the completion

---

Greek patristic *theopoesis* or divinization at the same time denotes the full extent of humanity. To be human is in the last resort a grace.
[9]Selected from: Edward Schillebeeckx, *Church: The Human Story of God*, Collected Works of Edward Schillebeeckx vol. 10 (London: Bloomsbury T&T Clark, 2014), 131–3 [132–4].

of the restoration of this world, our world which is out of joint. Therefore the contemporary experience of men and women who as followers of Jesus place fragmentary signs of the kingdom of God in this world, our world that is out of joint, is also the foundation for a firm hope of a kingdom of God grounded in Jesus that will one day be completed. To what height and depth, to what length and breadth, will this ultimately completed kingdom of God, which began in this world 'as small as a mustard seed', finally grow?

The undefinable aspect of the *humanum*, i.e. the eschatological fullness and freedom of men and women, which is sought and constantly found in a fragmentary way, only to be constantly threatened again, can only be expressed in symbolic language, by speaking in parables and metaphors, though these reach further than the impoverished sharpness of our rational concepts (which we also need if we are not to lapse into chaos). Four great metaphors, presented in the Jewish and Christian Bible in many sounds and tongues, suggest to us the way towards what, according to God's dream for the happiness of men and women and all their fellow creatures, humanity will eventually be.

(a) The definitive salvation or the radical liberation of humanity into a brotherly and sisterly society and community in which there are no longer any master-servant relationships, in which pain and tears are wiped out and forgotten, and in which 'God will be all in all' (1 Cor 15.28), is called 'the kingdom of God'.

(b) In the Christian tradition of faith the achievement of the salvation and happiness of the individual (called *sarx*, body or flesh, in the Bible) within this perfected society is called *'resurrection of the body'*, i.e. of the human person including his or her human corporeality, this corporeality being the visible orchestration, the personal melody, of a person which others also enjoy (although this glorified corporeality has nothing to do with the body which is left behind, it has everything to do with the personal corporeality in which I lived on earth).

(c) The eschatological consummation of an intact ecological environment which human beings need for their life is suggested by the great biblical metaphor of *'the new heaven and the new earth'*. This is not another world (that would mean contempt for and rejection of the original good creation), but our earthly world redeemed from being out of joint – though I do not know how to imagine this. Anyway, whether or not we can imagine this here and now is quite unimportant; there are many surprises to come.

(d) Finally, the normative role or significance of Jesus (in fact a person from somewhere in Nazareth), whom many Christians confess as the Christ, will become evident to all, being established on the one hand now already from fragments of the kingdom of God and, on the other hand, also in the final eschatological consummation of this kingdom; this is something that we can express now as the deepest concern and interest only in the biblical image of 'Maranatha' ('Come, Lord Jesus'). This eschatological picture (*the parousia of Jesus Christ*), which cannot really be expressed in human language, is nurtured by the experience of and recollection of what Christians now already (see the following exposition), albeit with some hesitation, and in fact quite daringly, call the uniqueness of Jesus Christ. What in Christianity is called Jesus' *parousia* or second coming is, in the final consummation of the kingdom of God, ultimately the becoming transparent to all of the real significance of Jesus of Nazareth, in the midst of so many world religions, in the eyes of God himself.

These four metaphorical visions of the eschatological future[10] envisaged by God for human beings now already influence the action of Christians in the world: not in an indeterminate or undirected way, but in a very definite direction, namely through the dynamic of the direction indicated by these four symbols: concern for a better society for all, above all for the outcasts and those who are stand by their side, for vulnerable people; both a pastoral approach directed towards communication as an incessant criticism of society and culture where there is clearly injustice; concern for the human body, for human psychological and social health; concern too for the natural human environment; concern for a sound attitude of Christian faith, hope and love; concern for meaningful liturgical prayer and a meaningful sacrament; concern finally for the individual pastorate, above all to the lonely and those 'who have no hope' (1 Thess 4.13). The Christian spirituality with which Christians do all this draws both its power and its joy from this eschatological hope.

Heaven and hell[11]

Heaven and hell are asymmetrical affirmations of faith. You cannot consider them on the same level. Christian faith in eternal life in the form of 'heaven' has its foundation not in the Greek affirmation of the immortality of the human soul but in the living communion with God in grace (expressed in human solidarity) during earthly life. (People used to call it the 'state of grace'.) The bond of life with the living eternal God, sensed as being positive, cannot be destroyed by death. In Jesus God overcomes death for those who anticipate the kingdom of love and freedom in history. So there is a 'heaven'.

There can be no hell for evil people on the same symmetrical level. But those who are evil, oppressors, certainly punish themselves thoroughly for ever. If living communion with God is the foundation of eternal life, then the absence of this living community (not so much through theoretical denial of God as through a lifestyle which radically contradicts solidarity with fellow human beings and precisely in that way rejects God and living communion with God) is at the same time the foundation of non-eternal life for these people. That seems to me to be the 'second death' of the fundamental, definitive sinner (if there is such a person). That is

---

[10]Perhaps (though I am not sure, since biblical visions have something classical and immortal about them) in 1990 we must look for other more telling metaphors which suggest the same thing. For this we need poets who are tuned to the same wavelength as the sensitivity of the Bible.
[11]Selected from: Edward Schillebeeckx, *Church: The Human Story of God*, Collected Works of Edward Schillebeeckx vol. 10 (London: Bloomsbury T&T Clark, 2014), 134–7 [136–9].

'hell': not sharing in eternal life nor being someone who is tortured eternally, but no longer existing after death. That is the biblical 'second death' (Rev. 20.6). This sanction is the result of one's own behaviour and not a positive act of the punitive justice of God who sends sinners to an eternal hellish fire (however that may be imagined as an instrument of torture): there is just no ground for eternal life. These people have resisted God's holiness and are incapable of loving. No one in heaven will ever remember them. It is an unimaginable scenario for me as a Christian, familiar with the gospel, that while there is said to be joy among the heavenly ones, right next to heaven human beings are supposed to be lying down for ever, gasping for breath and suffering the pains of hell (however you imagine this – spiritually or physically). On the other hand, the idea of the second or definitive death respects God's holiness and his wrath at the evil that is done, to the detriment of the poor and the oppressed.

So ultimately no one is excluded from the kingdom of God; in that case there is only the 'kingdom of God', a kingdom of liberated and free people, who do not have next door to them a kingdom of those who have been definitively cast out. The evil do not have eternal life; their death is in fact the end of everything: they have excluded themselves from God and the community of the good, nor does any new heaven await them on earth. They no longer exist, and cannot sense the happiness that good men and women then enjoy. But there is no shadow kingdom of hell next to the eternally happy kingdom of God. That is inherent in the asymmetry between what we call heaven and hell. The blessed will be spared the fact that a stone's throw away from their eternal happiness, fellow human beings are being tortured for ever with whatever physical or spiritual pains.

Dante's 'sorrowful city' alongside the joyful palaces of the heavenly blessed ones is a pedagogical picture: especially destructive oppression and utter evil have no future; on the basis of their own logic they are without hope. There is nothing present in evil and wickedness which is to be marked out for eternal life. There is nothing here that can be integrated into a kingdom of freedom and love. Through its own emptiness and weightlessness the wicked world which was formerly so powerful and evil disappears by its own logic into absolutely nothing, without the blessed having to feel offended by some barracks next to heaven where their former oppressors are tortured for ever. They already had precisely this experience in their earthly life; to have it a second time, for ever, would be sheer blasphemy for them. This would seem to me to be the most plausible Christian solution, in contrast to the model by which the Christian tradition has usually proclaimed this insight in the past. But in the past no distinction was made between the rights of God's holiness, which were rightly defended, and the exercising of them in the concrete and definitive fate of stubborn sinners. In other words, people put good and evil on the same level; they forgot the asymmetry of the two. They also overlooked the grotesque finitude in the megalomania of evil!

Of course the good also has its own intrinsic logic. But it does not follow from this that we should demythologise heaven in the same way as 'hell' and look for heaven in the joy of virtue on earth without any perspective on an eternal life. Here too there is asymmetry in the relationship of God to evil and to good. As far as evil is concerned, there is no need for a transcendent factor; Thomas Aquinas himself dared to apply the term *causa prima* (first cause) to creatures where there was any question of negativity.[12] By contrast, the good finds its ultimate source (or *causa prima*) in God. The internal logic of evil therefore *terminates* in the finite mortality of human beings, while the internal logic of the good *culminates* in the, eternal love of God who sustains the good man and woman (despite their many failings) in death and draws them to him over the boundary which is inherent in humanity.

So there is no future for evil and oppression, while goodness still knows a future beyond the boundary of death, thanks to the outstretched hand of God which receives us. God does not take vengeance; he leaves evil to its own, limited logic! So there is in fact an eternal difference between good and evil, between the pious and the wicked (the deepest intent of the distinction between heaven and hell), but the pious continue to be spared having to rejoice over the torture of eternal doom being inflicted on their fellow human beings. God's unassailable holiness consists, rather, in the fact that he will not compel anyone to enter the kingdom of heaven as the unique kingdom of liberated and free people. The 'eschaton' or the ultimate is exclusively positive. There is no negative eschaton. Good, not evil, has the last word. That is the message and the distinctive human praxis of Jesus of Nazareth, whom Christians therefore confess as the Christ.

Selected literature

- The Christian Relativisation and Radicalisation of the Building of the 'Secular City'; Selected from: Edward Schillebeeckx, 'Man's Expectation for the Future on Earth', *The Mission of the Church*, trans. N. D. Smith (New York: Seabury, 1973), 84–8.
- Eschaton as Future; Selected from: Edward Schillebeeckx, 'The Interpretation of the Future', *The Understanding of Faith: Interpretation and Criticism*, trans. N. D. Smith, Collected Works of Edward Schillebeeckx vol. 5 (London: Bloomsbury T&T Clark, 2014), 4 [4–5], 4–10 [4–11].
- Eschatological Revolution: Jesus' Beatitudes; Selected from: Edward Schillebeeckx, *Jesus: An Experiment in Christology*, trans. John Bowden, Collected Works of Edward Schillebeeckx vol. 6 (London: Bloomsbury T&T Clark, 2014), 153–5 [176–8].
- The Impossibility of Defining Humanity's Complete Salvation; Selected from: Edward Schillebeeckx, *Christ: The Christian Experience in the Modern World*, Collected Works of Edward Schillebeeckx vol. 7 (London: Bloomsbury T&T Clark, 2014), 788–9 [791–3].
- The Kingdom of God: 'Already and Not Yet'; Selected from: Edward *Church: The Human Story of God*, Collected Works of Edward Schillebeeckx vol. 10 (London: Bloomsbury T&T Clark, 2014), 131–3 [132–4]. Heaven and hell, 134–7 [136–9].
- Heaven and Hell; Selected from: Edward Schillebeeckx, *Church: The Human Story of God*, Collected Works of Edward Schillebeeckx vol. 10 (London: Bloomsbury T&T Clark, 2014), 134–7 [136–9].

---

[12]'Defectus gratiae prima causa est ex nobis', *Summa Theologiae* I-II, q.112, a.3 ad 2.

18

Magisterium and Authority

Evangelical inspiration and the 'signs of the times'[1]

It is clear that when the Church's magisterium speaks about social and political issues, it is founded on the specific mandate of the Church to proclaim and promote the salvation of the concrete human person. Therefore, the Church speaks out of her own historical responsibility for humanity.

It is precisely this claim that creates problems. It hardly needs demonstration that, just as all fundamentalism is abhorrent in the interpretation of the Bible, so a biblical fundamentalism in political matters would have disastrous consequences. The Christian message does not provide us directly with any concrete program for political action. On the other hand, one cannot maintain that the choice of a particular social policy is an open question for Christians. Therefore, between the message of the Gospel and the concrete historical political decisions, some decisive element must intervene. This was clearly seen in the Pastoral Constitution: 'To carry out this task the Church must continually examine the signs of the times and interpret them in the light of the Gospel' (*Gaudium et spes*, nr. 4). In other words, the Church cannot directly rely on revelation in these matters. Human experience and 'nontheological' factors play a very important part here. Can we analyse the structure?

There is no need to insist here on the fact that if the Church cannot fulfil her mandate in this field except through dialogue with the world, this is by no means an exceptional case. It is not *in spite of* but precisely *because of* her claim to exclusiveness (*Ausschließlichkeitsanspruch*) that the Church *never* speaks exclusively from revelation, but is essentially a Church of dialogue, even in the witness to, and the proclamation of, the Good News. The actual situation, as the hermeneutical situation, is an essential element of the contemporary proclamation of the total evangelical message.[2]

---

[1] Selected from: Edward Schillebeeckx, 'Church, Magisterium and Politics', *God the Future of Man*, trans. N. D. Smith, Collected Works of Edward Schillebeeckx vol. 3 (London: Bloomsbury T&T Clark, 2014), 87–94 [146–56].
[2] I have tried to explain this in Chapters 1 and 4 of *God the Future of Man*.

I only recall this point in order to make clear beforehand that the contribution of non-theological information to the Church's magisterial pronouncements cannot be the immediate reason for the specific character of such ecclesiastical pronouncements about political matters. The same happens, for example, in a dogmatic definition where the Church tries to express the evangelical message in other than purely biblical words and concepts. The Church and the magisterium can never live *exclusively* on the 'data of revelation'. The relation of the Church to the world is not simply one of a 'teaching Church' to a 'listening world', but an exchange, a dialogue, where contributions are made from both sides and both sides listen to each other, even in the authoritative proclamation of the Church's unique message. There is no need to develop this further.[3]

In the case of a magisterial pronouncement on political matters, this dialogue character of the Church stands out because here directives are given for right conduct in *the field of the world as such* and not merely because the world is used to express truths of revelation in conceptual form, as is the case with doctrinal definitions. In this field of social and political action the Church takes up a position with regard to the world precisely as worldly. And this she does because of her function of service with regard to humanity's salvation. For example, she demands, or points to, agrarian reform. For this she can obviously not draw directly on revelation. Revelation does indeed impose on her a constant concern for people. But this concern must be expressed in terms of concrete history. That this expression of concern demands here and now this particular measure and not another (for example, whether she should emphasise the right to property or rather the need for fair distribution and socialisation), makes one wonder where the magisterium obtains this kind of knowledge, and on what the binding character of such of her directives would be based.

The particular structure of magisterial decisions

It is impossible to derive any concrete political plan of action *directly* from the Gospel message. Some think that this is possible when we combine this message with a scientifically conducted analysis of our present society. On the other hand, one may say that even such a scientific analysis still leaves a wide choice of alternative measures, and does not imply that only this or that political measure is ethically binding here and now, whether for a region or for the whole world. Often a number of possibilities stand open which then usually give rise to different answers according to different social tendencies, organisations or even political parties. And the fact is that the papal documents referred to and the Pastoral Constitution do not just leave room for various solutions but often refer to one particular concrete option. And here the problem becomes pressing: How can the Church justify an authoritative

---

[3]The council admitted this: 'The Church does not ignore how much she has received from the history and development of humanity' (*Gaudium et spes*, n. 44), and it applied this explicitly to the way in which she expounds her unique message (n. 58).

demand for specific options in political matters in such a way that, given the necessary conditions, it is no longer an open question for Christians but requires them to act?[4]

Without denying the charismatic assistance of the Spirit in the teaching, sanctifying and pastoral function of the Church, but rather accepting it fully, I nevertheless cannot see in this charismatic assistance the immediate explanation of the final concrete choice made in such ecclesiastical pronouncements. For this might create the impression that we invoke the Spirit on those difficult points which we cannot explain and that we try to bridge the unbridgeable distance between general Christian principles and the many-faced concrete situation by appealing to an intervening impulse from on high which would decide the definite choice from among the many possible ones. The Spirit of God does not work as a stopgap, but in and through humanity. In this sense we may say that an appeal to the Spirit cannot *explain* anything, while on the other hand, we emphatically maintain as believers that we see the charismatic assistance of the Spirit become historically manifest precisely when we have analysed the inner structure of such a concrete decision by the magisterium and have made it intelligible *(insofar as* free human decisions can be penetrated intelligibly). Thus, the factual analysis of this inner structure is also an homage to the Spirit.

Here we must discuss a general problem of ethics. Many start from a certain 'duality' in ethical norms because they *proceed from* an abstract and theoretical morality. Therefore, they talk of abstract norms that are generally valid and concrete norms that refer to a 'precise situation'. Thus, they draw the conclusion that general principles of ethics can never lead to a concrete situation by simple *deduction*. They are inevitably confronted with the question of how to bridge the gap between the abstract and generally valid norms and the increasingly complicated human social situation which can, as such, usually call forth a variety of possible human solutions and reactions. Moreover, while in some cases it may be of little importance what particular solution is found, there are many cases where only one particular answer is capable of promoting human dignity here and now and for that reason is truly morally binding.[5] If, therefore, on the one hand, the general principles cannot provide us with a concrete solution and, on the other, even a scientific analysis of the situation cannot give us an unambiguous and clear solution, it follows, in the opinion of those dualists (general norms *and* strictly situational norms), that there must be somewhere an unknown third factor to act as a catalyst and to release the one proper and obligatory option from among the many. This catalyst would then *either* be a 'supernatural' one, the guiding power of the Spirit, which breaks through the ambivalence of the problem, *or* some human, irrational factor such as intuition, or an un-rationalised sympathetic hunch, an imaginative sense of history, etc.

---

[4]The immediate obligation lies with the ecclesial community as such, and therefore on 'faithful at large', not all individual faithful. Not every *individual* faithful is, for instance, called upon to go to a developing country, nor need he be a theologian although there must be theology in the Church. I am taking this point for granted.

[5]The question is not that there is something relative and imperfect in *all* human decisions, also those of Church authorities. This is the mark of the human condition. I am referring here to the problem that specific historical decisions, however imperfect, can carry a moral obligation.

One may ask whether the starting point of such reasoning, the abstract norm *and* the concrete norm, is the right one for this problem. I do not deny the significance of abstract, generally valid norms in the total context of human life. The question is, however, whether we place them in the right context and see them in their proper function in such a way that they show at the same time that a mere situational ethics would provide no solution. I cannot fully deal with this here, and if I did, there would not be enough space left for the real problem, but some points have to be mentioned.

Abstract pronouncements cannot seise hold of the reality simply *by themselves*; if they nevertheless possess a realistic value, this can only be derived from our total experience of reality. For instance, 'to be human' is not a part of the real, i.e., individual and concrete human person side by side with another part which would constitute the individuality; for the individuality determines 'being human' from within. Only and exclusively as intrinsically individualised is 'being human' a reality and can it be the source of moral norms (which in religious parlance, we can rightly describe as the will of God). Therefore, there is only one source of ethical norms, namely, the historical reality of the value of the inviolable human person with all its bodily and social implications. That is why we cannot attribute validity to abstract norms as such. Moreover, no abstract statement can produce a call or invitation. The abstract and general nature of the norms simply shows up the human inability to express the concrete reality exhaustively. These abstract concepts appear in fact only as an aspect of a more integral human awareness of experience in which they obtain, due to the concrete existential contact with reality, the value of an inner objective reference to this experienced reality: only in that direction, indicated by the abstract conceptual pronouncement, lies the concrete reality, and in no other. But for the rest, the abstract content cannot determine this direction in the concrete.

Therefore, these abstract, generally valid norms are an inadequate yet real *pointer* to the one real, concrete ethical norm, namely, this concrete human person living historically in this concrete society. Ethical norms are requirements made by reality, and the so-called abstract general norms are but the essentially inadequate expression of this. Therefore, it is not the inadequate expression which, by itself, constitutes the ethical norm, but it is a pointer to the one and only norm: these persons who must be approached in a love that demands justice for all. The abstract expression can only indicate in a vague and general way the content of this one, concretely determined reality as it calls on me; therefore, I can never see in an abstract norm what I must do or not do here and now. For the same reason, namely, because these general norms express, however inadequately, at least something real about the concrete reality, my concrete decision must never fall *outside* the direction indicated by these norms (if, of course, correctly formulated). These general norms are directives, derived from earlier experiences and indicating a moral appreciation of basic human values without which human life would simply become absurd. And thus we overcome a morality that is either purely abstract or mere situation ethics.

If, then, for all practical purposes, the problem is not one of a confrontation between general norms and strictly situational elements, but one of respect for, and the promotion of, the concrete human person in their concrete society, the question is still: How do we know, or how does the magisterium know, what should be done in practice within the present society in order to contribute as a Christian to an existence that is more in line with human dignity for this particular part of humanity in this particular society? How does such a constructive ethical investigation proceed?

The Pastoral Constitution states that we must 'examine the signs of the times and interpret them in the light of the Gospel'; that means, we must interpret the concrete reality of society as the expression of a moral demand made on the Christian conscience. But human history shows that this is not primarily a matter of finding a theoretical interpretation of these 'signs of the times', because when we do that, the prophetic voice of a new moral imperative is usually heard too late. Elsewhere the Pastoral Constitution (46) speaks more realistically about a concern with urgent problems 'in the light of the Gospel and of human experience'. The past has shown that, long before the Churches had analysed the social problems, there were people who, in their commitment and in a pre-analytical dialogue with the world, had already reached the moral decision that fundamental changes were required. New situational ethical imperatives have rarely or never been initiated by philosophers, theologians, Churches or ecclesiastical authorities. They emerge from a concrete experience of life and impose themselves with the clear evidence of experience. Theoretical reflection comes afterward, and so do the critical examination and rationalisation, the philosophical or theological and official formulation. And so, after the event, such imperatives are put forth as 'generally valid, abstract norms'. All this brings out the essential need for a 'living presence in the world'. The Church cannot fulfil her prophetic task with regard to the worldly problems of humanity and society simply by appealing to revelation, but only by listening very carefully to that 'foreign prophecy' *(Fremdprophetie)* which appeals to her from the situation of the world and in which she recognises the familiar voice of her Lord.

When we listen to and analyse this voice of worldly prophecy, we discover that definite moral historical decisions and the initiation of new moral imperatives and directives are in fact not born from a confrontation between general principles and the result of a preferably scientific analysis of the social situation, but usually (though not necessarily exclusively) from those concrete experiences which may perhaps best be described as 'contrast-experiences'. The vocation, the concrete ethical decision of Cardijn (later Cardinal Cardijn) as to what he thought should be done here and now about some social problems, emerged, as he said himself, from such a 'contrast-experience': his fellow workers' bitter resentment of the fact that he, a worker like themselves, was lucky enough to get the money to study. There are hundreds of such cases. The contrast-experiences of the two World Wars, the concentration camps, political torture, the colour-bar, the developing countries, the hungry, the homeless, the underprivileged and the poor in countries where there is so much potential wealth, and so on – all these experiences make people suddenly say: 'This should not and must not go on.' And so develops the protest against war, social injustice, racial discrimination, the ownership of vast properties, etc.

In our present society moral imperatives and historical decisions spring, moreover, particularly from the experience of a collective evil, such as the too low income of certain sections of society, colonial exploitation, racial discrimination and other injustices. When we analyse these contrast- experiences insofar as they may lead to new ethical imperatives, we find that these negative experiences imply an awareness of values that is veiled, positive, though not yet articulate; that they stir the conscience which begins to protest. Here the absence of 'what ought to be' is experienced initially, and this leads to a perhaps vague, yet real, perception of 'what should be done here and now'. This experience is of course but the preliminary stage leading to the proper reflection of both a scientific analysis of the situation and of a new assessment of principles gained from experiences in the past. Yet, without this initial experience, which evokes a prophetic protest, neither the sciences nor philosophy or theology would have been stirred into action. (Such experiences often lead even to new sciences such as the 'polemological' – war- science – institutes and the sociology of religion.) Through these experiences human beings begin to realise that they are living at a level *below* that of their basic potential and that they are kept at this low level precisely by the pressure of existing social structures to which they are subject.

In the past, such contrast-experiences led conscientious people to the ethical imperative of charitable deeds in the private sphere of immediate interpersonal encounter (Vincent de Paul, Don Bosco, etc). Today, in contrast with 'medieval' people, we know that the social 'establishment' is not a divine creation, but a cultural and human-made situation which can be dealt with and reformed.[6] Historical imperatives that now emerge from such contrast- experiences immediately tackle the reform of the existing society itself. In other words, this type of contrast-experiences now lead to the moral imperative of decisions in the social and political field. This shows once again that the new moral imperatives, based on negative experiences, are part of human history; the science of ethics then begins to reflect upon this and in the course of time a whole framework of generally valid principles (basic and detailed) is built up.

Therefore, it is not this ethical formulation which is either the most important or the most decisive. And this makes it still clearer that the concrete ethical decision is not a mere application of a generally valid abstract norm. For these contrast-experiences show that the moral imperative is first discovered in its immediate, concrete, *inner* meaning, before it can be made the object of a science and then reduced to a generally valid principle. For that reason there is no need for an appeal to a 'third' factor which some want to introduce in order to bridge the gap between the 'general norm' and the 'strictly situational element'. The initial creative decision which discovered the historical imperative directly in its *inner* meaning in the very contrast experience *is,* for the believer, at the same time the charismatic element of this whole process. The general norms, on the contrary, are the mapping out of a long history of experience (full of contrast-experiences) in search of a society more worthy of humanity, and doing so precisely on the basis mainly of these negative experiences.

This should make it obvious that a Christian's life is not very much helped by the magisterium proposing merely 'general principles' for social and political issues because in that case the Church lags by definition behind the historical situation since such principles are the tail end of a preceding history, while the history of the future must be prepared by historical decisions and moral imperatives. To have seen this constitutes the real contribution made by such encyclicals as *Pacem in*

---

[6]See among others, H. Freyer, *Theorie des gegenwärtigen Zeitalters* (2nd ed., Stuttgart, 1963), who, in 1955, was one of the first to analyse the tractability of the world and of society.

terris and *Populorum progressio*. They deal really with definite moral decisions (though obviously against a background of basic principles already gained from past experiences).

The magisterium as negative theology[7]

Does the magisterium provide us, believers, with a guarantee that its specific indication is the only right one among many others? It seems to me that this can never be maintained in an *absolute* sense because concrete decisions in the field of politics can never have that kind of guarantee, not even when they proceed from ecclesiastical authority. We believe nevertheless that, functioning in and borne by the whole community of the Church, it stands under the charismatic guidance of the Spirit. We may say that this gives the Christian a moral certainty (within the limits of the 'hypothetical' element referred to above) that whoever acts accordingly will really act more in line with what the situation demands, and that the Christian can therefore face the consequences of such an action more confidently, even if it should lead to complications. All this, indeed, is not so much directly concerned with obedience to the Church's teaching authority as with obedience to her pastoral prophetic function. This function does not have the same precision but a more powerful prophetic ability to 'call forth', to stimulate a continuous search, and no Christian can close his ears, his heart and his inventive imagination to that. This leads us to the specific nature of the obligatory quality of these official directives. Because the concrete moral imperative grows mainly out of contrast-experiences, it has a primarily and principally *negative* character: 'this cannot go on'. What, for instance, peace may positively mean when we reject cold or hot wars, nobody knows. The Christian only has the vision of the 'eschatological peace' (which he can only describe negatively for a large part). But in the experience of the concrete 'non-peace' both our will to overcome this situation and the inventiveness of our informed love – seeking means to achieve justice for all – will grow apace.

And so this, perhaps somewhat abstract, yet significant analysis (so it seems to me) leads us to the conclusion that the obligatory character of a magisterial pronouncement on political and social issues lies rather in the 'negative' aspect (this *must* change) than in something positive. The specific obligation contained in this positive element *shares* in the absolutely obligatory character of the negative experience, but to a degree which the situation here and now will determine. The 'negative theology' in speculative matters shows us here the way to a 'negative theology' in practical matters, in which the eschatological vision of the future is the positive, 'utopian' and 'critical' norm for this particular concrete and changing situation. A Christian, therefore, who has read, e.g., *Populorum progressio*, without any noticeable change in his day-to- day life, is guilty with regard to the prophetic voice of this papal document. He is guilty particularly with regard to humanity

---

[7]Selected from: Edward Schillebeeckx, 'Church, Magisterium and Politics', *God the Future of Man*, trans. N. D. Smith, Collected Works of Edward Schillebeeckx vol. 3 (London: Bloomsbury T&T Clark, 2014), 99 [163–4].

and God because he obviously accepts the existing order which the Bible qualifies as disorder. All social structures will remain subject to the criticism of the biblical message for as long as history lasts.

Jesus and the Holy Spirit, source of all authority in the church[8]

The foundation of both the authoritative life of the community of faith and ministerial authority within the community of God is the Lordship of Jesus Christ in the church through his pneuma or Spirit and the Spirit of the Father. Let me put it this way: the general teaching authority of the people of God and the ministerial teaching authority in the church have a pneuma-Christological foundation: in so far as this is 'authority', it goes back to the activity of the Spirit of Jesus the Christ. The functioning of ministerial authority must, moreover, be organised in such a way that the liberating authority of the Lord Jesus, which is abidingly present, can come into effect time and again in the life of the Christian community of faith. Fundamentally, therefore, the norm in the church is not the formal authority of the ministry, but the *paratheke,* i.e. 'the entrusted pledge' (Tim 6.20; 2 Tim 1.14), namely the gospel (1 Tim 1.11; 2 Tim 2.8) as the apostles interpreted it, that is to say, 'the *didaskalia* or teaching of God our Saviour' (Titus 2.10).

Essentially it is a matter of the unbroken succession of the apostolic tradition of the gospel content of the faith. The teaching authority of the church is subject to this apostolic content as ministerial service, but the one calls for the other (the so-called 'apostolic succession' in the ministry). Moreover, this gospel content is the very life of the Christian communities in their local character and communion with one another, i.e. the life of the 'apostolic church'. As Paul says, it is imprinted as a letter, not just somewhere in canonical books, but on the hearts of believers. So the teaching authority of the ministry also has to rely on the actual life of the church communities of faith, at the grass roots, locally and in their mutual recognition of one another, here and now and through the ages, and under the direction of the searchlight of the first, i.e. biblical, normative documentation of the life of the first witnesses and followers of Jesus.

On the basis of this structure there may be no master-servant relationships in the church. There may not be any structure of domination in the church: 'You know that the rulers of the Gentiles lord it over them, and their great men exercise authority over them. It shall not be so among you' (Matt 20.25–26; Mark 10.42–43; Luke 22.25). Although there is authority and leadership in the church, there is really no *hierarchy*. Talk of church hierarchy in the sense of a pyramidal hierarchical structure of the church community is partly inspired by the social status symbols of the Graeco-Roman empire (of which the post-Constantinian church took over many features when the competition fell away) and from the sixth century was very

---

[8]Selected from: Edward Schillebeeckx, *Church: The Human Story of God*, Collected Works of Edward Schillebeeckx vol. 10 (London: Bloomsbury T&T Clark, 2014), 214–17 [216–19].

strongly influenced by the Neoplatonic works of Pseudo-Dionysius, who tried to legitimise all this in philosophical and theological terms.[9] Pastoral and sociological differentiations in the church were given theological clarification in this Neoplatonic view of the world. On this model the different services of ministry which grew up in the church over history became hierarchical: in multi-stage levels from the top down to the more inferior levels. The higher level thus has in a supreme way what the lower level has to a lesser degree and with limited power. The ministerial competences of all the 'lower' ministries were to be found in absolute completeness at the highest level: historically this plenitude of power was from an early time, the second half of the second century (say between 150 and 200), the episcopate in the current sense of the word. This pseudo-Dionysian principle of substitution devalued the pluriform specialised ministries in the church which came into being historically as a result of church needs, being thought pastorally necessary. This hierarchical development at the top of the church devalued the laity, 'at the base of the pyramid', so that they became merely the object of episcopal and priestly pastoral care. And in this situation pastoral care could at the same time be misused as a means of control, particularly in questions of power. In principle the clergy (among which the episcopate embodied the highest *status perfectionis* or state of perfection) realised in a perfect way a religious pattern of life and a religious unity with God which 'ordinary' believers could experience only indirectly and incompletely, purely in obedience to the *maiores*, the notables or prelates in the church.

Such a hierarchy inspired by Neoplatonism, which followed in the footsteps of declining late antiquity, no longer has anything to do with the nature of the church. If one wants to apply the term 'the hierarchy' to all those who legitimately bear authority and exercise leadership at the heart of the church and here, through the mediation of the church, even do so inspired by God, that is fine as far as I am concerned: no problem. But hierarchy conceived in this way has nothing to do with the concept which I analysed above and therefore in no way excludes *a priori* a democratic church government. However, in all official documents of the Roman Catholic church 'hierarchy' is used specifically as an argument for rejecting any democratic exercise of authority and thus democratic participation in the government of the church by the people of God on the basis of 'divine law'.

This refusal brings us to conflicting positions of the church hierarchy. For we can regularly establish from the Acts of the Holy See that the present official church commends and prefers democracy as a kind of ideal for any historical 'civil society', but that in terms of ministry, and indeed in principle, this same Roman Catholic Church presents itself as a non-democratic community. The argument for this exception for the church, which is said to be hierarchical and therefore already non-democratic, goes like this. The church, as founded by God, has its own specific social form. This is by divine right and therefore (the argument goes) is non-democratic. The arguments for this position amount to this: just as the Pope is not the delegate of the universal church, so the bishop is not the delegate of his see. Pope and bishops have their authority direct from Christ and not from a mandate which is given to

---

[9]See above all A. Faivre, *Naissance d'une hiérarchie. Les premiers étapes du cursus clérical*, Paris 1977; R. Hathaway, *Hierarchy and the Definition of Order in the Letters of Ps.-Dionysius*, The Hague 1969.

them by the people of God or by the diocese. Of course as 'hierarchs' they are at the service of the people of God, local and world-wide, but this service is a function of truth and love, the final aim of which is that the people of God should experience God's call. And this call is not dependent on the people. It is God's own absolute initiative.

Through its appeal to what it calls the hierarchical structure of the church the ministerial church seeks to demonstrate that the church (both believers and those in authority) does not exercise any rule, is not the owner of God's call or its institutional form. From this argument, which up to a point is theologically correct, the conclusion suddenly seems to be drawn that democracy 'thus' cannot be the model for the church, because the church lives from the word of God about human beings' 'ultimate concern', and no man or woman has any say over that. And in all this the same church, clearly without any sign of hesitation, has taken over for itself the civil forms of imperial-authoritarian, feudal and later absolute monarchical government as a matter of course and as such has regarded them as legitimate.

The 'category mistake' or false reasoning which goes astray in the argument that I have just mentioned is certainly subtle, but as false reasoning it is no less real. Precisely because (apart from its very beginning) the church traditionally has almost never experienced 'democratic' forms of government, at least in the modern sense of the word, the exercise of any form of democratic authority has been rejected, while the authoritarian exercise of authority has been, and is, approved with enthusiasm.

The mistake in all this false reasoning lies in the fact that democracy (which in fact is the fruit of the American and French Revolutions, now two hundred years in the past) stands or falls by respect for human rights. To look for the foundation of human rights is very different from the model of the functioning of these rights. Just as the state and civil society are not proprietors of human rights, so the church is not the proprietor of the word of God. The nature of a church community does not lie here. 'Not lording it over' does not exclude democracy! Why then should the church not be able to democratise its model of government and rule without in so doing harming its subjection to the word of God? As if an authoritarian government agrees better with the subjection of the church to God's word than a democratic government, in which the voice of the whole people of God is listened to more clearly and accurately!

However, that is the nub of the argument in all the official documents of the official Roman Catholic Church: democratic government harms subjection to God's revelation. Why? Such an argument is in my view a basically false argument, which has as its tacit ideology the view that the authority in power (because guided by the Holy Spirit) is always right; it does not need to be unnecessarily hindered in its actions by contributions from below. I recall the slogan of the war years 'Il duce ha sempre ragione' (the Duce, or the Führer, is always right). In the meantime the category mistake which is made here has not been cleared up at all, for what is under discussion is not whether or not the church is subject to the word of God, but how in practice the subjection of the church and hierarchy to God's revelation can be carried out in the most appropriate way. In other words, the supposedly non-democratic structure of the church is in no way rooted in the nature of the church, but can only be defended with a straight reference to the actual and contingent history of this church, which until recently moved in non-democratic civil societies and then to a large degree took over the non-democratic forms of government of the surrounding social and cultural milieu.

The only argument that is used to defend a non-democratic church is thus in fact merely a reference to twenty centuries of non-democratic cultures, from which the church, too, took the broad outlines of its own forms of government. History (including ourselves and everyone else) is a witness to that fact, so that immunising references to underlying mysteries are no longer any help. The rejection by the official church of the possibility of a democratically governed community of faith in fact has nothing to do with subjection to the Word of God, which is under no one's sovereign control (i.e. neither that of the community of faith or the hierarchy), whereas on the official side subjection to the word of God is and was the only constantly renewed argument against the democratic exercising of authority in the church.

The magisterium and ideology[10]

Because the Church's official teaching authority is pastoral in nature and not an institution for discovering truth, a purely theological teaching authority is necessary along with this pastoral, proclaiming teaching authority. The distinctive task of the theologian is accurately tracing the many interrelationships of the Church's official statements, while the magisterium in its direct pastoral care has other duties. Especially in times when the binding character of *formal* authority is restrictively over-emphasised and a certain suspicion exists regarding everything that comes down from the top in the Church, then there is the imminent danger that the magisterium, especially in its executive offices, will cling to the letter of some earlier definition given by the magisterium without paying much attention to the many forms of relativity or complication found in magisterial statements. Although at one time a definition by the magisterium really could have been the only proper way to articulate a truth of faith, we now have possibilities of expressing the same truth in other categories. Tragic interruptions in communication between the magisterium and the theologians can develop while both appear to be searching for an authentic fidelity to the Gospel of Jesus Christ. The question, 'What is the authentic content of Christian faith?' is much more complicated than a distinct 'theology of Church statements'.

The relationship between the magisterium and the theologians went through a great many changes in the course of the Church's history. These developments are helpful when it comes to gaining some insight into the theology of the relationship between the magisterium and the theologians. In the first millennium, we see that the Church's magisterium and the theologians' teaching authority usually overlapped. Although there were many lay and monastic theologians, the bishops were in fact the *ordo doctorum,* proclaiming the faith as both pastors and theologians. In the high Middle Ages, however, cathedral schools of theology came into existence in such

---

[10]Selected from: Edward Schillebeeckx, 'The Magisterium and Ideology', in *Authority in the Church*, ed. Piet F. Fransen, Annua Nuntia Lovaniensia 26 (Leuven: Leuven University Press, 1983), 14–16.

places as Chartres, Laon, and Paris; these schools were followed by the scientific, academic theology of a new class of '*doctores*', the guild of university professors in theology. During this period, bishops came mainly from the nobility and frequently were without adequate theological training. A sharp difference developed between the *magisterium episcoporum* and the *magisterium theologorum,* and this tense relationship led each side to intrude frequently on the other's territory. Besides the *imperium* and the *sacerdotium,* a third power emerged – the *studium* or the university, which had a great deal of autonomy.

Magister Gratianus, witness of a then-growing tradition, could say: 'The expositors of the Scripture (the theologians as *expositores sacrae paginae*) supported by *gratia*, with greater *scientia* and more *ratio,* stand above the *pontifices* (that is, the bishops and the pope) not in the (juridical) deciding of disputes, but in the interpretation of Holy Scripture'.[11] We also see that there were fewer conflicts between theologians and the Holy See at that time; more conflicts – and often stubborn ones at that – were found among the contending theological schools which fought their battles with mutual condemnations. In these disputes, one party frequently tried to use an appeal to the Holy See to its own advantage, seeking to have its opponent slapped with an excommunication and compelled to burn its denounced writings. We see, however, that such decisions by the medieval magisterium were hardly of any importance in advancing or arresting the development of theology. Bonaventure could bluntly say that in this or that matter the pope was off the mark. Thomas, who thought pretty much the same thing, solved the question more charmingly through the method of '*exponere reverenter*', drawing from a magisterial text a meaning opposite to the one intended by the pope. In the late Middle Ages, matters went so far that theological faculties themselves made magisterial decisions regarding orthodoxy-hence, '*superbia theologica*' was spoken about! Trent drew sharper lines: full juridical power belonged to the bishops alone. The bishops, however, needed theological advice to avoid making huge theological blunders. Theology, as a matter of fact, was really everywhere. The question is only what sort of theology. And that still holds today.

Since the nineteenth century, an entirely new type of theological model was developed alongside the older working model of the theologians as critical partners of the bishops. Malevolently, one could describe this model as follows: the theologians are servile, party ideologues, or, more correctly formulated, they are the perfect parrots of the magisterium. Under Popes Pius IX, X, XI, and XII a sort of totalitarian claim to the magisterium obtained. The magisterium became very doctrinaire regarding the theologians who were thought to have no teaching authority other than that doled out to them by reason of a *missio canonica*. It was a time for all sorts of 'mandates' and 'canonical missions', and the dominant image of the Church was one in which every gift from above came to the Church through the pope. With this image, many Catholics forgot that the community of faith, although never apart from its leaders, is itself the subject of the Church's being and so the subject of theological self-understanding. Theologians, therefore, are not theologians on the basis of a *missio canonica*, but on the basis of their baptism; they

---

[11] Ae. Friedberg, ed., *Corpus Juris Canonici*, 2 vols. (Leipzig, 1879–81; reprint, Graz, 1955), 65.

are theologians as members of a believing and thinking 'people of God'. Presently, however, the idea that theologians teach 'in the name of the Holy See' rules in Rome. *Sapientia Christi* is the most recent official documentation of this. I do not want to deny that special canonical institutes in which one teaches in the name of the Holy See can and may exist; such institutes, however, do not have anything to do with the proper ecclesiastical structures regarding Christian theology, which cannot be viewed as merely an extension of the papal magisterium.

The interplay of official teaching authority and the teaching authority of believers and their theologians (always in some tension)[12]

Theology, too, may share in the privilege of the whole of the people of God of being a channel of the Holy Spirit. It is a possible channel – for at the same time theology can also share in sinful neglect, if in the exercising of its function (which is one of the many organs which mediate the Holy Spirit) it is either unfaithful in tacit passiveness, or in self-assurance it neglects the working of the Spirit in other organs, for example those of the church's ministry.

Though the teaching authority of the ministry, in an exceptional case even infallibly, bears witness to the gospel of Jesus Christ and its implications, this witness in many ways remains 'relative', i.e. related to. In particular it is: 1. related to the coming rule of God as bound up with the whole appearance and person of Jesus Christ: the heart of the message which in one way or another must also resound in any particular ministerial statement (here I am thinking of the Vatican II 'hierarchy of truths') and the mediaeval theory of the *articulus fidei,* the *cardines* or main hinges which 'articulate' the whole of the doctrine of faith in fundamental, less central and finally even peripheral truths; 2. related to Scripture and all its prehistory; 3. related to history after Scripture, i.e. to the particular situations in the world and the church in which during the course of church history the church and the teaching authority of the ministry has borne witness to the gospel of Jesus Christ as the message of salvation from God which brings human liberation. Even a dogma has a history of its own and cannot be understood outside the process by which it developed; 4. related to our present, which is also an essential element in the understanding of the Christian tradition of faith – the present both of the people of God and the world situation.

In connection with this last criterion (the present), here and there one often finds the misunderstanding that present-day theologians use present patterns of thought as a norm for the Christian understanding of faith. However, the fact that there is a time-difference, or diachrony, between religion and the world in no way means that we need to remove this time-difference as quickly as possible in an attempt at *aggiornamento* which will bring Christianity up to date. The critical question here is

---

[12]Selected from: Edward Schillebeeckx, *Church: The Human Story of God,* Collected Works of Edward Schillebeeckx vol. 10 (London: Bloomsbury T&T Clark, 2014), 221–3 [223–5].

'up to which date?' That of our bourgeois and one-sidedly technological consumer society? In that case there would be a risk of our making Christianity into a 'civil religion' of the bourgeoisie. Alongside what is indeed an obstructive time-difference between old formulae of faith (which in their time were a successful expression of basic Christian experiences) and present-day Christian experiences, in the Christian religion there is also a time difference which is part of its being, a liberating time difference which believers must use creatively to change both our society and our bourgeois heart, our thought-patterns and our behaviour.

From all these mediations it emerges on the one hand that even the magisterial language of dogma must always be related back to the original Christian 'interpretandum', that which is to be interpreted: the appearance of Jesus of Nazareth in our history, interpreted in canonical Scripture as the Christ, the anointed Son of God who wishes salvation from God and in fact also offers it to all people. On the other hand what the ministry says, even in dogmatic statements, about this offer of salvation in Jesus can only be understood in the totality of the whole of human history. In other words, even a so-called Christian dogma is not an immovable rock; it has undergone a very changing history. Even this milestone in the life of the Christian history of faith and dogma cannot be understood outside the history of its development, as though precisely in being in fact a legitimate and even permanent milestone, it were a supra-historical pointer which in different cultural circumstances cannot tolerate any use of other categories of understanding which were still unknown earlier. This is not what happens in the life of the church guided by God's Spirit. Because the teaching authority of the ministry is pastoral by nature, and thus not a scientific institution for finding the truth or an academy, theology is also needed alongside the pastoral proclamation of the teaching authority: the 'theological teaching authority' as a scientific translation of the non-ministerial, general 'teaching authority' of the church's people of God. For there, in the faith of the church, lies the source of any authoritative statement even by the hierarchy, also in subjection to the Word of God. Precisely in listening to and standing critically by the specific faith which is alive at the grass roots – the people of God – the theologian is at the same time a servant of the authority of the ministry in the church, but not its cringing slave.

It is also the special task of the theologian to trace out accurately the manifold rationality of the statements of the ministry which I have just mentioned, whereas the teaching authority has plenty of other things to do in its direct pastoral concern. But above all in difficult times, in which emphasis is put on the binding character of formal authority in a rather desperate way and there is a certain mistrust of anything that does not come to life in the church from above, there is a danger that the pastoral teaching authority will keep to the letter of a statement made once in the past without much concern for the multiple matters involved and thus the relativity of the statements of the *magisterium*. This could in fact have been the one and only way of expressing a truth of faith in fidelity to the gospel at that time. In later times, however, on the basis of cultural developments Christians can be offered new possibilities of clarifying the same truth of faith through other categories which were not present earlier in culture, with equal fidelity to the gospel. Not to see or even not to want to accept this possibility, basically perhaps because of a static concept of the truth, can result in tragic disruptions of communication between the teaching authority and theology.

Selected literature

- Evangelical Inspiration and the 'Signs of the Times'; Selected from: Edward Schillebeeckx, 'Church, Magisterium and Politics', *God the Future of Man*, trans. N. D. Smith, Collected Works of Edward Schillebeeckx vol. 3 (London: Bloomsbury T&T Clark, 2014), 87–94 [146–56].
- The Magisterium as Negative Theology; Selected from: Edward Schillebeeckx, 'Church, Magisterium and Politics', *God the Future of Man*, trans. N. D. Smith, Collected Works of Edward Schillebeeckx vol. 3 (London: Bloomsbury T&T Clark, 2014), 99 [163–4].
- Jesus and the Holy Spirit, Source of All Authority in the Church; Selected from: Edward Schillebeeckx, *Church: The Human Story of God*, Collected Works of Edward Schillebeeckx vol. 10 (London: Bloomsbury T&T Clark, 2014), 214–17 [216–19].
- The Magisterium and Ideology; Selected from: Edward Schillebeeckx, 'The Magisterium and Ideology', in *Authority in the Church*, ed. Piet F. Fransen, Annua Nuntia Lovaniensia 26 (Leuven: Leuven University Press, 1983), 14–16.
- The Interplay of Official Teaching Authority and the Teaching Authority of Believers and Their Theologians (Always in Some Tension); Selected from: Edward Schillebeeckx, *Church: The Human Story of God*, Collected Works of Edward Schillebeeckx vol. 10 (London: Bloomsbury T&T Clark, 2014), 221–3 [223–5].

19

Ministry

Primary functions of the priestly apostolate[1]

The priest is, by definition, the 'steward of the mysteries of God' (1 Cor 4.1), the *oikonomos* of the mysteries of Christ. In St. Paul the text refers only to the fact that priests are the heralds, preachers and proclaimers of the mystery of Christ. But as early as the fourth century, the scope of the Pauline text was extended by the church fathers to include within the work of Christ's salvation not only the historical act of Christ's redemption, but also the celebration of this mystery, that is, the sacraments in which the mysteries of Christ remain accessible to us, people of all times, *in mysterio*. In the patristic period, then, the task of the priest, as the 'minister of the mysteries of God', consisted of preaching and liturgy – he was the minister of the word and sacrament (Augustine). Preaching and the sacramental apostolate remain the essential task of the priest. These two functions are therefore mentioned explicitly in the preface to the ordination of the presbyterate: 'So that the number of priests may be sufficient for the *offering* and the manifold celebration of the mysteries…; thou hast added *teachers of the faith* in order to be helped by them in the proclamation of the word throughout the whole earth.' We are not free to hold a different view from this if revelation, continued in the living tradition of the church, teaches us to see the priestly apostolate in this way.

The proclamation of the word and the ministry of the sacraments are, moreover, not separate activities – they are essentially related to one another. Just as the revelation of the word analyses, throws more light on and shows in greater detail the revelation of reality itself, so too does the proclamation of the word illuminate and explain more fully the sacramental presence of this revelation of reality and invite people to enter personally into this reality.

---

[1]Selected from: Edward Schillebeeckx, 'Priest and Layman in a Secular World', *World and Church*, trans. N. D. Smith, Collected Works of Edward Schillebeeckx vol. 4 (London: Bloomsbury T&T Clark, 2014), 28–35 [36–46].

1. The ministry of the word

In the apostolate of the priest we should always remember that preaching is a *paradosis,* a tradition. We proclaim the Christian faith – our preaching is a delivering of the Good News. As priests, we are only invested with authority to proclaim God, who appeared in Christ and lives in the church, together with the moral and religious consequences of this in the lives of people. We bear witness to the living God, to Christ. We should use no eloquence except in the ardour of our testimony. As Verlaine correctly said, 'take eloquence and wring its neck'. Our function in the *paradosis* is simply one of service and bearing witness.

There is a great need for adaptation in preaching. It is only by preaching the living God that we will strike home. And let us thank God for it! Our present age is crying out for the simple bread of religious truth – the redeeming presence of Christ and his new law. The church will be able to catch on again if we preach the visible coming of God and if we give people one single vision of the Christian plan of salvation. People cannot live from a hundred separate truths, but they can live from one single idea and, for us, that idea is the fact of Christ. Think of the political leaders and their propaganda – they do not present people with intellectual expositions of various ideas, they put forward one basic vision, one idea which is constantly cropping up in the various themes. Think of Augustine and his preaching to his people in *De catechizandis rudibus,* telling them that the mystery of Christ was the great history of salvation of a people in which the listener himself was personally involved. It is clear that he made his mark and that we do not with our preaching from manuals. Two and four make six – this arouses no emotions. But two days' paid holiday plus four days' paid holiday make six days' paid holiday – that is a meaningful addition sum! This is, after all, the whole task of the proclamation of the word – to preach inductively. People must be personally addressed by *their* God, we must speak to them about their God in their lives. Two conditions are presupposed in this:

a. I have said that we do not preach in our own name, but that we hand on the Good News. But this message is not something that is alien to us. The 'teaching' church is also the 'learning' church. We are not only teachers, we are also, first and foremost, *believers.* In preaching because it is our task to preach, we are expressing our own deepest experience. Our *paradosis* is a piece of our personal life: 'I believed, and so I spoke' (2 Cor 4.13). Lacordaire called the preacher 'a person who takes his soul and throws it into the soul of his listeners'. That is why Paul said, whenever he was speaking about the *paradosis* that he communicated in his preaching, he gave himself with it: 'We were ready to share with you not only the gospel of God but also our own selves' (1 Thess 2.8). The living God whom we preach is also *our* God, whom we are really only handing on – we are passing on the God who has become all in all for us preachers to people, 'being affectionately desirous of you' (ibid). It is precisely this personal aspect of experience which will bestow originality on our preaching the truths of faith and will call forth the only preaching that is really 'inspired'. All the rest is 'trickery', and this no longer has any effect on people who hear so many far better examples of clever, eloquent trickery on the radio and in the cinema that their hearing is deadened by it and their minds are saturated and stupefied by it.

b. In addition to this objectively oriented element of experience, there must also be what I shall call the 'element of social experience'. As a believer, I accept the whole plan of salvation as the reality which effectively concerns the whole of humanity. It is a question of our God and the listener is therefore personally involved. If we bring the word of salvation to people, then, we have to take care that people really can hear this as an *answer*. A preacher who is not humanly and socially (at least in affective interest and, in our own times, perhaps also really and in fact) involved in the needs, the miseries and the problems of these people will not, in his proclamation of the word, be able to preach the mystery of Christ as the making public of the word of salvation to specific people. To do this, we must have a sound knowledge both of people and of the *paradosis,* and not only a conceptual knowledge, but also a real and experiential knowledge. The great transformation takes place in preaching – putting contemporary people in contact with the supra-temporal mystery of salvation. The preacher who cannot play on those two keyboards of eternity and temporality will never touch the strings in the depths of the souls of his listeners, but will just be throwing eternal truths at random in the church like bricks that may land on the heads of his 'dear brethren', or else he will stay caught up in superficialities and not preach the living God. To be both God's and people's, with one's eyes fixed on their relationship with God – that is the fundamental condition of good preaching.

Adaptation in the apostolate has therefore, in the first place, to be concerned with the manner and the content of our stale preaching. Mgr. Dupanloup once complained ironically 'Every Sunday, there are thirty thousand sermons in France… and the people *still* believe!' We should not, however, lose sight of the sacramental significance of preaching in all this – the deeper mystery that is brought about by the power of the Holy Spirit in people's bearing witness through preaching. In the words of Augustine,

> See what a great mystery is accomplished here: the sound of our words strikes your ears, the Teacher, however, is in you… The external instructions are an aid, an invitation to devotion. But the one who teaches your hearts has his throne in heaven'.[2]

While we are preaching, the Holy Spirit is at work in the hearts of those who are listening by addressing them inwardly. Without our preaching this inward speaking is lost to people in the noise of life – the preacher is the radar, tracking it and bringing it explicitly to people's consciousness. As Sertillanges once wrote, preaching is 'revealing souls to themselves'. We elaborate what the Holy Spirit says inwardly to people. The priest has therefore to hear, in the sounding board of his heart, both people's questions and the Holy Spirit's answer to these questions and to elaborate this answer as a word of salvation and express it as a word of grace in his preaching – as the redeeming word, the Good News. That is preaching – 'the word of faith which we preach' (Rom 10.8). (Woe therefore to the priest who improvises – unless

---

[2] Augustine, *In I Epist. Joan,* III, 13 (PL, 35, 2004–5): 'Iam hic videte magnum sacramentum: sonus verborum nostrorum aures percutit, magister intus est… Magisteria forinsecus, adiutoria quaedam sunt et admonitiones. Cathedram in coelo habet qui corda docet.'

the circumstances are beyond his control – and fills up a quarter of an hour with a hit or miss sermon. He does not know what is God's! [Matt 16.23]). In good preaching, dogma and moral teaching are fused into a single connected whole. What people need from us is, if I may put it in this way, that we should, independently of scholastic treatises, preach the 'triune God', the God who 'creates and governs', the 'Word made flesh', the sacraments of the church and the 'last things' and that we should also, from these starting points, go on to preach Christian ethics as a life of grace, of unconditional love, ardent hope and surrender in faith, a God-centred life, something that is more than the ten commandments and yet always forges ahead in individual, family and social life here on earth. If we can link all this inductively with the facts of human life and with concrete human problems, we shall inevitably make people sit up and listen with interest. We must show people the way to the depths of God, but this way goes towards God through the depths of humanity itself! If we are in touch with life and have a fundamental view of the history of salvation from which the life of the living God is discernible and in which every human being is personally involved, we shall preach effectively.

Pure preaching therefore demands not only constant contact with the living God in prayer and human experience, but also the sustained practice of going back to theological sources. We must again and again reactivate our theological understanding so that we can continue to treat dogma in a free yet orthodox manner. Theology enables us to transpose, to rethink in intelligible language what is inwardly experienced, but ultimately cannot be communicated, in the life of faith as participation in the faith of the church. Then we shall be able to impart to people the reality of what faith is, without using scholastic terms that are incomprehensible to most of the faithful. The church is bound to confess in all humility that scholastic theology is to blame for the wretchedness of so many sermons. Theology is, of course, the science of the word of salvation that we have to preach. The fact is that all priests find out that it is in fact not true, probably, I feel, because they are not really familiar with Scripture, the fathers and the real Thomas Aquinas. The word of salvation is not patristics or scholasticism, nor is it even Holy Scripture – these are all only witnesses. No, the word of salvation is the living God himself, the God of our own times, our God who is eternal and yet visibly realised his definitive plan of salvation in Jesus Christ and accomplishes it in us in the sacraments of the church. In our preaching, we must above all be bold. Our respect for the dogma of faith, for the ineffable mystery of God and his plan of salvation, will give us, if we really take our theological studies to heart, a safe 'illative sense' and at the same time the firm certainty that God has revealed his plan of salvation for us, people of today. I agree that he revealed it too for people at the time of the apostles, but the apostles had to tackle that problem in their own times. Certainly I agree that God's plan is also revealed for people in a hundred years' time – but future priests will just have to tackle that task. We are the heralds of the reality of revelation for contemporary human beings. For us, God has revealed himself to people living in the next street, in the great city and in the 'missions'. Every dogma has a saving value for these people which we have to make clear to them. And if many people feel no deep need in their lives for the dogma of salvation, then we must try to make them long for it, that is, we must unleash that longing in them. If we fail, then we must go on preaching the message of salvation in season and out of season until they learn that, *at least for us*, Christian faith is our happiness, our salvation and our hope and that we can bear witness to our happiness and our redemption. It is not human life that gives value and meaning to dogma – it is dogma itself that brings this value and meaning with it. It gives an *answer*, even when there is no conscious question. 'Behold, the days are coming, says the Lord God, when I will send a famine on the land; not a famine of bread, nor a thirst for water, but of hearing the words of the Lord' (Amos 8.11).

What I have said here about 'preaching' should not, of course, be applied only to sermons, but should be taken in the broadest sense, with reference to instruction, catechising, house visits, spiritual guidance, conferences and retreats and ordinary contacts between priests and laypeople. 'Unless the Lord builds the house, those who build it labour in vain' (Ps 127.1). And the Lord is not God in his heaven, but God in our hearts. Our motto has always been, is now and should continue to be *contemplata aliis tradere*.

2. The sacramental apostolate and the priest as a 'personal sacrament'

I have dealt elsewhere[3] with the important problem of strict sacramentality and shall confine my attention here to the general and constant sacramental appearance of the priest. The apostolate and thus the 'apostolicity' of the priest as priest is distinctive in that it is he who has the task of realising, throughout the history of the church, the actual connection linking people with Christ's mysteries, his historical acts of redemption. The priest's primary function is thus mediatory and all the other work that he may undertake must be geared to this function. It is only by being directed towards this end that his other work will gain its distinctively priestly and religious significance. The priest is not a redeemer. There is only one redeemer, mediator and apostle (in the sense of one who is sent) and that is Christ, who, by the sacrifice of the cross, offered his body – that is, himself, together with his mystical body, which is potentially the whole of humanity – in complete self-emptying and in total dedication to the Father. The bond between Christ's body and his mystical body is the sacramental reality – the eucharist and, dependent on this, the other six sacraments – and the priest is, by virtue of his ordination, essentially the minister of this bond. He must always be fully conscious of this fact, that he is in this way in the fullest sense a priest and that his kerygmatic apostolate and all his other pastoral duties flow from this and must also flow into it. He will then also be conscious of the fact that it is Christ who redeems people and not he and that his function is one of service to people and not one of playing the little dictator over them. He will therefore not be intent on trying to tie people to himself, but will play the modest role of servant between God and people. The art of being a priest is that of 'attaching people to his person by *detaching them from his ego* and by leading them to the only master who is interior', as Jean Guitton

---

[3]*Sacramentele heilseconomie*, Bilthoven 1952; an abridged version of this work is translated as *Christ the Sacrament of the Encounter with God*, London and New York 1963.

once said, so strikingly, in a different context. God included priests above all as human assistants in humanity's personal ascent to God. The inner, divine teaching and supporting effect of God on the one hand and, on the other, the outward, human, priestly help of the priest as the human version of what God inwardly suggests are the two constitutive elements of the priestly apostolate. I can perhaps best define the priest's helping task with regard to the inner, spiritual life of people in the following way: (1) the priest is the silent, *reverent witness* of the work of the Holy Spirit in the lives of the people entrusted to him; (2) he is the *critical authority* of the reactions and the interpretations that people themselves give of the effect of the Holy Spirit in their lives and (3) he is also someone who makes explicit the unnoticed, hidden guidance of the Holy Spirit. The priest is therefore outside the sphere of his people's intimate, inner spiritual life and association with their Saviour, but from outside he does nonetheless have contact with this inward reality. He has a purely preparatory and episodic function especially in the theological life of the people entrusted to him. He has to teach these people to *believe* concretely, to *hope* concretely and to be the human version of Christ's saving *love* in their concrete environment. At the same time, he has also, in addition to giving objective guidance in this way, to take into account the concrete psychological and social possibilities of his people.

All the activities that the priest undertakes in his pastoral care must be personal acts of love, first of all his properly sacramental acts. As the minister of the sacraments – a personal sacrament – the priest is, so to speak, the first to receive the grace that God intends for the other people and he has to transform this grace in his heart and adapt it to specific people. If it is true that the sacrament is invalid without the intention of the minister of the sacrament, then it is also true that a sacrament which is not just valid but also priestly and apostolic must be an act of prayer and of apostolic love on the part of the priest himself. 'Do you not know that those who are employed in the service of the temple get their food from the temple, and those who serve at the altar share in the sacrificial offerings?' (1 Cor 9.13). This applies not only to the material needs of the priest, but also, and indeed in the first place, to his religious needs – his personal involvement in the stream of grace that comes from the altar. The sacramental life of the minister of the sacrament must be the very heart of his sacramental apostolate. Christ's apostolate was of its very nature sacramental – he transformed into human acts what he had seen, loved and experienced in the Father. As a human person, he sensed what was human and as God he sensed what was divine, after first having personally and sacramentally realised it in himself – in his very becoming human, which was not simply an event that took place at his conception, but was a continuous task throughout his entire life on earth, since he went on transforming the fullness of his high priestly grace into constantly new human acts. His entire appearance was one long drawn out administration of sacraments, a making visible and a giving of divine realities.

The sacramental appearance of the priest must be like this. Our humanity is the 'matter' and our divine life is the 'form' and our human, powerless approach to people thus becomes an epiphany of God, a translation of divine goodness into human goodness. It is only then that we priests will be not just valid, but also apostolic sacraments. Every priest who appears in the home of a believing family is a valid sacrament, but his appearance is fully apostolically fruitful, especially in the case of non-believers, only if it is not an 'empty' sign, but a transformation, a human version of God's merciful desire to save people. This also means that it is not really a question of us, but that we are simply a sacramental sign, a way through, people who point, from ourselves, towards the other, Christ himself, who is to come, and do so in such a way that this pointing out becomes a sign, in our priestly appearance. The authentic, real sacraments that we administer will then be simply the culmination of our entire sacramental and priestly appearance. That is why the formulae used in the rite of ordination do not provide any sublime theological reflections about the activities of the priest as proceeding from his ordination, but they do repeatedly admonish him that these sacramental acts should at the same time be 'acts of grace', that is, acts of prayer. The administration of the sacraments (in the strict sense), even though these may be valid apart from the priest's personal religious attitude, is only a personal and apostolic act if the administration becomes an act of faith, hope and love as intercession for the person to whom the sacrament is dispensed. It is only then that the priest's sacramental apostolate is fully an 'act of character and grace' and Thomas did not hesitate to call the sacramental grace of such an apostolic sacrament greater than that of a careless, un-prayerful administration of the sacraments. In this connection, it should be noted that, despite their apparent 'modernism', certain contemporary methods in the apostolate are nonetheless entirely in keeping with the deepest meaning of the sacramental apostolate. We are redeemed by Christ's sacrifice, in which the sacrifice of all humanity was virtually contained. Through the sacraments, and especially the eucharist, we must involve ourselves existentially in this sacrifice, so that the meaning of our sacrifice and the real sacrifices that we make in our day-to-day lives also form part of the *ratio sacrificii* of the mass. Christ offered *his and our* sacrifice on the cross, with the result that our suffering, and especially our act of dying, in principle participate *suo modo (mysterioso)* in the 'objective redemption'. Through our involvement in the sacrifice of the mass, 'Christ's sacrifice and ours', accomplished by Christ on the cross, also becomes really and personally *our own*. The priest accomplishes the celebration of this mystery, that of 'Christ's sacrifice and ours' on the cross, in a sacramental manner, but he must also, as a believer, together with the other believers, involve the sacrifice of his own life in a personal manner in this sacramental act. In this way, 'Christ's sacrifice and ours' on the cross will become *our* sacrifice of 'Christ and ourselves'. The priest's grace, the grace that is derived from the apostolic accomplishment of his ordination as priest, will therefore sustain the apostolic priest in the sacrifice of his life as a priest to the people entrusted to him. An extreme attempt, like that made by the worker-priests, who have left everything and become everything for their people, seems, then, to me to have been prompted by a profound understanding of the objective and the subjective form of Christian sacramentality and especially of the sacramental sacrifice of the cross, and it bears witness to their pure vision that we are redeemed only by *sacrifice*. It seems to me to be profoundly Pauline and, although we do not all need to put this particular solution into practice, their attitude of priestly sacrifice still makes us feel ashamed because we are far too much 'valid sacraments' and far too little sacrificing and fruitful sacraments.

Communication between the priest and lay people[4]

The essence of the problem is that the priest's task is religious and it is this and not the secular as such which determines his appearance and activity as a priest. It is, of course, true that the moral and religious aspects of a human being cannot be separated from all his other relationships. The religious element is transcendent, but it embraces and penetrates the whole of human life. In this sense, then, the priest is not a sacristy official. He is at the service of the members of his community in all the aspects of their religious lives – at the altar, in the pulpit, in the presbytery and in personal relationships in the course of his pastoral activity.

Since his office is carried out in a very special field, then, he will recognise and respect the special legitimate forms of secular life. He does not have to give meaning to his pastoral work by being present in every sphere in which lay people are active for the sake of maintaining communication with lay Christians. This would be a misunderstanding of the special nature of the lay apostolate. Through their baptism, which has enabled them to share in the universal priesthood of all Christians, lay people too have the task of bearing wittiness to their being Christians wherever they are. A transference of value has to take place between Christians. The lay apostolate is conditioned by the secular situations in which lay people are placed, whereas the priest renounces the secular situation to some extent in order to be free to carry out his distinctively priestly activities. The apostolate in face to face relationships is therefore above all a lay apostolate. In this, lay people carry out their apostolic work is informal relationships – for example, in a circle of friends, in the neighbourhood in which they live, in their leisure-time activities with others or in their sphere of work. Lay Christians are the obvious people to conduct this apostolate in the closed but informal relationships that come about spontaneously in the sort of sphere that I have described. Officially at least, the priest is out of place in this kind of relationship. In tending to take over the part played by lay people, he would be misunderstanding their special apostolic power and witness. Taking over from the layman in a sociological situation in which he is so frequently treated as an 'outsider' by a homogeneous group of lay people inevitably means that his priestly task is handicapped and made ineffectual. This is, I believe, what happened in the case of the worker-priest movement in France. The basic inspiration of this experiment was the conviction that it was necessary to communicate with the workers through the 'apostolate of presence' among them – by sharing their condition, the priests could bear witness to Christian love in informal relationships within industry. The priests, however, did this work anonymously – they did not appear as priests. What they did, then, as anonymous priests, was purely supplementary apostolic work – the work that Christian lay people ought to have done but did not in fact do. In other words, they replaced lay people in what was strictly speaking a lay apostolate. I think that this may, of course, be necessary from time to time, especially in order to stimulate lay people to take part in an essential activity of the lay apostolate, but in itself it is a substitute apostolate for the priest.

---

[4]Selected from: Edward Schillebeeckx, 'Communication Between the Priest and Lay People', *The Mission of the Church*, trans. N. D. Smith (New York: Seabury Press, 1973), 180–4.

The course followed by the worker-priest experiment is, I believe, characteristic for all forms of apostolate in which the priest plays the part of layman. This situation is indicative of the fact that the distinctively lay apostolate has not yet completely and explicitly penetrated into the minds of Christians. The priest, it should be remembered, does not occupy an all-embracing place in the lives of Christians – he does not have to be present everywhere. Both at the personal and at the social level, there is a sphere of mutual solidarity among Christians which does not as such form a part of the social organisation of the church. Even though the priest may not be excluded from circles of this kind, the part that he plays in them is not that of a priest as such.

The pastoral aspect of the priest's activity, insofar as it takes place in face to face relationships, is therefore very delicate. In any case, the priest should never intrude into natural or purely secular relationships, not even when he is visiting his parishioners homes. He must respect the natural basis of family life – in marriage it is the husband and wife who should, in the first place, care for each other in the pastoral sense. The priest should not intervene here as an 'alien' factor. He is bound to respect the natural structure of marriage and help both the husband and the wife, if necessary, in their moral and religious interests. But there has been more than one case of priests, in their so-called apostolate, unwittingly driving a wedge between husband and wife. The same situation applies too to all kinds of natural groups, communities and societies. The priestly apostolate is not furthered, in principle at least, by the priest joining in, as priest, these groups or communities.

The real difficulty is that the priest as a status-bearer is also forced, in modern society, into a social position. This social position makes him a stranger when confronted with others in different social positions. The priest is no longer 'among us' as 'one of us'. He will not, moreover, succeed in building a permanent bridge between himself and others if, as a priest and remaining within his social position, he tries to break through the impasse by spending his free time with lay people and doing what they do during their leisure – going to or playing football with them, for example, or with young people to their favourite haunts.

A person with whom one has confidential relationships is not always the person whom one sees most frequently. So it is with the priest. We should not exaggerate the importance of the modern concept of 'communion', at least not in the sense of the priest's becoming entirely absorbed in this 'communion' with others. Even though he may still be 'one of us', despite his social position, he is nonetheless the *segregatus*, the one set apart whom we visit if we have a real need to, if something important happens in our lives, not it we are troubled by some everyday trifle which we can just as easily sort out for ourselves.

It should therefore be clear from this that the distinctive task of the priest is not to be found, in principle, in purely secular functional relationships, in the informal relationships which often accompany these or in the face to face relationships of various closed groups. On the other hand, however, it should also be clear that all these relationships, insofar as they are a partial expression of a moral and religious attitude, do come within the sphere of the priest's pastoral activity. This in turn points clearly to the fact that one of the most important tasks of the priest in the pastoral sphere – in addition to his sacramental and kerygmatic activities – is to establish circles of trained Christian lay people so that a transference of value can take place via the Christian life of and witness borne by the laity to all these spheres in which the priest inevitably remains a stranger.

It has, however, to be stated explicitly that what I have said so far does not in any way mean that priests should by virtue of a special charismatic call, be apostolically active in, as it were, a non-conformist manner in sectors where they do not, 'according to the book', really belong. What is more, these charismas may, at certain times, have to become institutions. It is, for example, possible to ask whether the time has not come for certain 'natural group leaders' to be ordained priests in some circumstances (without making them follow the normal pattern of conventional training for the priesthood) and allowing them to remain in the same sphere of activity. The revealed essence of the priestly function is an 'unchanging' datum, but the way in which this is carried out can change according to historical circumstances. People are nowadays much more sensitive to the universal and immanent presence of grace in all people and consequently to the importance of their own personal decisions than, for example, to the concentrated presence of grace in the church. In the past, priests spoke almost exclusively about the sacraments – baptism, confessions, the mass and solemnising marriages. Now, people are much more open to the less institutional aspects of God's activity, with the result that the dialogue between the priest and the lay person will be more concerned with the personal insights and decisions of Christians and with the perspective that these open in the direction of the ecclesial character of grace. In my opinion, communication between priests and lay people should take place far more at this personal level. The priest will continue to bear witness to the orthodoxy of the church and to proclaim the law of the gospel and the sacraments, but he must learn to shed his dogmatic self-sufficiency and his frequently brusque and authoritative way of speaking. If he does this, he will be able, as a priest and at the same time a sympathetic person, to go along boldly with lay Christians in the search, without making discussion impossible by speaking too soon or too brusquely about the sacraments and Sunday mass. The priest has, in the past, too often identified himself with orthodoxy. Now, however, he must learn to look more carefully for the essential and immanent presence of grace in the Christians committed to his pastoral care, for the authenticity that is present in their personal lives in order to direct this more and more towards the church. There is no doubt that priests tended to deal too brusquely with people in the past by telling them to practice their religious duties and frequent the sacraments. In doing this, priests offered no solution to the problems of the laity and no orientation in their search. They must look, together with the laity, for an answer and not think that they already possess the truth and only have to apply it to whatever case arises. We can readily agree with Karl Jaspers' comment that humanity has 'lost its naivety' – human beings are no longer like a child and will no longer be put off with transcendent solutions which often do no more than simply cover up their difficulties.

Discontent among women[5]

At present, discontent in the church is fiercest among women. Moreover, it is no longer just discontent as a result of the negative experiences of women with

---

[5]Selected from: Edward Schillebeeckx, *The Church with a Human Face*, trans. John Bowden, Collected Works of Edward Schillebeeckx vol. 9 (London: Bloomsbury T&T Clark, 2014), 222–5 [236–40].

the institutionalised churches but a very conscious accusation. Above all in North America this discontent is organised into a deliberate 'Women's Church', a movement which intentionally accuses the patriarchal, masculine character of the church and its leaders, as indeed of society. This Women's Church seeks to 'weave' sisterhood between all the women in the world who are oppressed in one way or another by society and the church. Concentrated in this feminism is the awareness of all the situations of injustice which emerge from a particular social and economic system. It is not so much a matter of men oppressing women; the problem is structural violence, which moreover is given an ideological legitimation by philosophy and theology. Women and slaves, the old Roman Hellenistic house code had it, are possessions of men, and therefore they are subject to them and less than them 'in all things'. Against the basic tendency of the earliest Christian inspiration directly associated with Jesus, Christianity took over this pagan house code, brought it within the church and, moreover, later gave it theological legitimation (see above, Part One, Section 2).

I shall quote literally the suppressed complaint of women – finding expression in the consciousness, in faith, that they too are *subjects* of faith and being-the-church. This consciousness emerges in a liturgical prayer written by women and for women (it is a modest manifesto expressed in prayer):

> Spirit of Life, we remember today the women, named and nameless, who through the ages have used the power and the gifts which you gave them to change the world.
> We refer to these mothers who went before us to help us discover in ourselves this power, and how to use it in such a way that we help to advance a kingdom of justice and peace.
> We remember Sarah, who with Abraham responded to God's call to leave the land in which she was born and to put her trust in a covenant with God. We pray for her strength in faith.
> We remember Esther and Deborah, who saved their people through acts of personal courage. We pray for their strength to be bold, to act in the interest of the greatest good.
> We remember Mary Magdalene and the other women who followed Jesus and were not believed when they proclaimed the resurrection.
> We pray for their strength to believe against the temptation to doubt.
> We remember Phoebe, Priscilla and the other feminine leaders of the early church.
> We pray for their strength to spread the gospel and inspire communities.
> We remember the abbesses of the Middle Ages who kept faith and knowledge alive. We pray for their strength of leadership.
> We remember Teresa of Avila and Catherine of Siena, who strongly opposed the corruption of the church at the time of the Renaissance. We pray for their power of insight and bravery.
> We remember our own mothers and grandmothers, whose lives shaped us. We pray for the special power with which they try to hand things on to us.
> We pray for the women who are victims of violence in their own homes, that power will be given them to overcome their anxiety and look for solutions.

> We pray for the women who stand face to face with a life of poverty and undernourishment, that power be given them to hold fast and open possibilities for all women.
> We pray for our daughters and granddaughters, that power may be given them to seek their own lives.
> (Add here any woman whom you want to remember and for whom you want to pray.)
> Silently we dwelt on the power of many women from the past and present. Now it is time to stand by ourselves. In each of us there is the same life, light and love, and within us lie the seeds of power and glory. Our bodies can feel love, our hearts can heal, our spirits can go in search of faith, truth and justice.
> Spirit of life, be with us in our quest. Amen.[6]

The exegete Elizabeth Schüssler Fiorenza puts into words the discontent of women, which has become a deliberate self-definition, in the following way:

> For the first time in Christian history we women no longer seek to express our experience of God's Spirit within the frameworks of an androcentric spirituality but to attempt to articulate that we have found God in our soul in such a way that this experience of her presence can transform and break through the traditional framework of androcentric theology and patriarchal church.[7]

That this feminism has found expression in a confession of faith primarily in North America is a result of the sufficient economic and institutional independence that women have achieved there. They also have sufficient theological training not 'to be just the object of men's theologising and to be the initiating subjects of theology and spirituality'.[8] They fight against patriarchalism as a political, social and cultural system of domination which pervades all levels of life to differing degrees and has made women subject and deprived them of a voice.

> However, now those without a voice have achieved independence; the silence is broken and evidently for good.

Christian feminism painfully feels the dualism between the liberating hope given by the gospel on the one hand and, on the other hand, the enslaving patriarchal structures of the hierarchical church which keeps us to that gospel. Therefore many feminists no longer argue directly for the admission of women to the ministry.[9] In

---

[6] This prayer was written by Ann H. Heidkamp; unfortunately I no longer have a reference to the original.
[7] E. Schüssler Fiorenza, 'For Women in Men's Worlds: A Critical Feminist Theology of Liberation', *Concilium* 171, 1984, 32; see also her great work, *In Memory of Her*, New York and London 1983.
[8] E. Schüssler Fiorenza, 'For Women in Men's Worlds', 32.
[9] See Mary Dwyer, *New Woman, New Church, New Priestly Ministry*, Rochester 1980; D. Gottemoeller-R. Hofbauer (eds.), *Women and Ministry*, Washington 1981; Monica Furlong (ed.), *Feminine in the Church*, London 1984.

their eyes this would be the integration of women into patriarchal church structures. They demand their Christian birthright (in the power of the baptism of the Spirit), their right also to be the church *qua* women, fully endowed and responsible subjects of faith, of the expression of faith and of the reflection of faith. This also implies that as a matter of course they too can take a leading position in the church and also in the ministry.

This discontent of women is no longer just a complaint; it has become a sharp accusation. As long as women in the church are completely excluded from all the authorities which make decisions, there can be no question of the true liberation of women in and through the church. Perhaps the criticism expressed by women (more than half of the church community) is at present the most fundamental charge levelled at the churches, and one that they cannot avoid. Such a massive, and now overwhelming, call for liberation which cannot be stifled, from the other half of the whole church, can no longer be held back; in the long run it will change the face of the church, and its structures of ministry as well.

Selected literature

- Primary Functions of the Priestly Apostolate; Selected from: Edward Schillebeeckx, 'Priest and Layman in a Secular World', *World and Church*, trans. N. D. Smith, Collected Works of Edward Schillebeeckx vol. 4 (London: Bloomsbury T&T Clark, 2014), 28–35 [36–46].
- Communication Between the Priest and Lay People; Selected from: Edward Schillebeeckx, 'Communication Between the Priest and Lay People', *The Mission of the Church*, trans. N. D. Smith (New York: Seabury Press, 1973), 180–4.
- Discontent Among Women; Selected from: Edward Schillebeeckx, *The Church with a Human Face*, trans. John Bowden, Collected Works of Edward Schillebeeckx vol. 9 (London: Bloomsbury T&T Clark, 2014), 222–5 [236–40].

PART FOUR

Theology of Culture

Introduction

Elizabeth Pyne

The thematic focus of this final part of the *Reader* highlights not only a specific topic within Schillebeeckx's theological corpus but also a pervasive orientation in his life and work. From early on, an openness to culture – that is, to the world, to history, to human experience – characterised his personal disposition as well as his religious convictions and scholarly output. He seized on the relationship between the Christian tradition and the contemporary situation as an area of crucial concern, rich in possibility. Convinced that faith must be made relevant to the modern age and, reciprocally, that only in the midst of one's situation could one encounter God, his articles and lectures from the 1940s begin to articulate 'the basic principles for a theology of culture'. Theologically, Schillebeeckx was not alone in this interest. In the mid-twentieth century, 'culture' received attention from major Protestant thinkers such as Reinhold Niebuhr (*Christ and Culture*, 1951) and Paul Tillich (*Theology of Culture*, 1959). It was likewise a significant term in the Catholic developments leading up to and through Vatican II. As an influential voice in the pre-conciliar Dutch context, Schillebeeckx himself gained new impetus from the council's engagement with the modern world, especially in its closing pastoral constitution, *Gaudium et spes* (1965) [see Part two]. The texts gathered here in Part IV, originally published between 1966 and 1996, represent some of his efforts to hear, interpret, and reflect on 'the joys and hopes, the griefs and anxieties' (*GS* 1) of the world in the period following the council. It is a hallmark of Schillebeeckx's theology – evident throughout these excerpts – that faith in the abiding mystery of God aligns with a genuine immersion in and commitment to society. Thus it is a fitting achievement that he was the first theologian to be recognised with the prestigious Erasmus Prize in 1982, awarded annually to a person or institution on the basis of 'an eminent contribution to European culture'.

Culture

Culture is a complex term, which makes available a number of different emphases. While Schillebeeckx was more interested in exploring the significance of culture than its definition, it is important to be attentive to several valences on display in his writing. Occasionally he employs a narrow meaning to refer to particular forms of cultural expression (e.g., surrealist art). More often he has something broader in view, which may be akin to the world or society as such or may point to the spirit of the age – evident in widespread intellectual currents, values, and habits, as well as in institutions, like the university, that embody them. Culture is historically variable; Schillebeeckx's hermeneutical and historical-critical turns address the markedly different contexts of faith for Jesus and his first disciples as compared to modern and even post-modern people. The bedrock sense of the concept inheres in his overall aim to link what he comes to call the 'Christian experiential tradition' and the contemporary cultural situation. Yet, although 'culture' tends to signify the present, insofar as it is always bound up with the human experience that mediates faith it must be counted an integral element in the formulation of Christian tradition as well. Culture also has geographical resonances (e.g., Western vs. non-Western) that come to the fore in Schillebeeckx's later work as he continues to think through the relationship between the transcendent universality of the gospel and particular contexts.

Schillebeeckx's evolving approach to the tradition-situation dynamic emerged from the academic milieu in which he trained, where it is illuminated by several other sets of pairs, including: grace and nature; divine and human; church and world; salvation and history; religious and secular. A dualist presentation of neo-Thomist scholastic theology regarded each of the latter terms with some suspicion. (Note that, contrary to common usage, culture in this framing falls on the side of nature, i.e., associated with human nature in contrast to grace or the supernatural.) This oppositional reading was intensified by resistance to the declining role of the church in modern secular culture. Informed by his close study of Thomas Aquinas, however, Schillebeeckx retrieved a sacramental view of all reality wherein God's grace works in and through nature [see Part I]. Correlatively, while distinctions between, for instance, the church and the surrounding world remain operative to some extent, they are meaningful only in respect of a common human existence, a single history in which salvation is sought. The theologian must take culture seriously. For Schillebeeckx there is a pastoral and practical dimension to this insight: he is simply not persuaded that blunt appeals to scriptural or ecclesial authority are effective in a culture that praises rationality and freedom – indeed, such arguments may make matters worse. Yet, rather than being a concession to an unfortunate state of affairs, the task posed by a theology of culture positively reflects the fundamental structure of God's relationship with the world. As Schillebeeckx argues with various accents over the years, the imperative to understand culture and interpret its theological significance is a consequence of faith in the living God.

Secularisation

Whether regarded for good or for ill, the defining feature of Western modernity according to most commentators is its secularity. In selected texts from the 1960s, the project of articulating how, if at all, Christian faith could be credible in this environment appears as a major preoccupation for Schillebeeckx. His descriptions of the cultural situation of 'modern man' reflect the tenor of hostility and defensiveness around the question of religion; where it persists, belief in God seems to be a relic of a period that relied on supernatural explanations, a convenient crutch which has now been displaced – for thinking people, anyway – by scientific knowledge and human beings' responsibility for shaping their world. In his engagements with the overlapping issues presented by atheism, non-religious humanism, theology's relation to other academic disciplines, and the phenomenon of secularisation, Schillebeeckx simultaneously validates the paradigmatically modern impulse to centre human experience and challenges any claim to define the totality of that experience as necessarily excluding religion. Because the reality of truth exceeds all human ways of knowing, he argues, scientific reason and faith are better viewed as complementary partners than competitors in the quest for understanding. Likewise the interaction between human freedom and dependence on God is not a zero-sum game; by uprooting the mistaken assumption that these realities stand in competition, Schillebeeckx urges both believers and atheists to appreciate that the 'secularisation of faith' is not an oxymoron. Following his 1967 lecture tour in the United States, where the 'death of God' movement heralded the end of theism and embraced a post-Christian culture, Schillebeeckx responded with a new image of God oriented around the eschatological notion of 'promise', which enjoins Christians to actualise the possibility of a better future. Despite the appearance of a stark confrontation, then, the cultural revolution toward the secular – emphasising the products and process of human making, including self-making – in fact presents an opportunity for Christians to better appreciate creation's autonomy as a theological principle and 'purify' the tradition of reductive ways of speaking about God.

Politics of liberation

Awareness of the secular conditions of modern society remains a constant in the decades that follow, yet what Schillebeeckx considers the most salient points of engagement shifts in significant ways. His focus becomes the suffering and injustice that burden so many people; equally or more than the question of transcendence as such, it is their anguished questions, their cries for a God who seems absent, that challenge the meaningfulness of faith in the contemporary world. So, while Schillebeeckx had always shown an interest in social issues, and was buoyed by Vatican II's call to attend 'especially [to] those who are poor or in any way afflicted' (GS, 1), from 1968 his theological approach to modern culture took on a critical and political edge. His perspective developed alongside that of European colleagues, like the German J.-B. Metz, who criticised narratives of progress grounded in reason, science, and technology as they reckoned with Christian identity in the wake of the Holocaust. He was also in dialogue with liberation theologians such as the Peruvian Gustavo Gutiérrez and others globally who expounded the concrete historical relevance of Christian doctrine in light of people's struggle to overcome oppressive poverty. The deep ambivalence of culture – evident in modernity's horrific failures as well as its promise – calls for interpretation and discernment.

Schillebeeckx's major Christological works, penned in the 1970s, and subsequent essays reflect his exploration of the intimate connections amongst the theological concept of salvation, experiences of suffering, and earthly projects of liberation. He adopts the language of 'praxis' to describe Jesus of Nazareth's prophetic enactment of the Reign of God and the clear demand that follows for twentieth-century disciples to join in wholehearted commitment on behalf of the downtrodden and those who suffer. Always convinced that Christians' actions are the true measure of their faith, he now underscores the mandate to pursue social transformation at the level of political and economic structures. Yet, in critical dialogue with Marxism and with reference to participation in politics, Schillebeeckx cautions against taking any given order, party, or movement as an absolute goal, however revolutionary its intentions. Theologically, the fullness of salvation exceeds anything human effort can bring about; historically speaking, neglect of creaturely limitation harbours the potential for violence. Schillebeeckx contends that one enduring value of religion – despite historical failures of religious traditions including Christianity – lies in its capacity to continually spur recognition of the dignity of human beings and the reality of God: both motivate worldly transformations, but neither can be reduced to a system or program of ethics.

Attention to global injustice, politics and violence intersects with questions of pluralism in Schillebeeckx's explorations of the multi-dimensional complexity of a theology of culture. The core insight that theology always emerges *within* given contexts spells a need to attend carefully to cultural and regional differences. In this light, Schillebeeckx considers the responsibilities of European theology in relation to non-Western liberation movements. He also comments on diverse perspectives raised by theologians in the 'Third World', as Africans and Asians join Latin Americans in seeking to define their situation on their own terms. Across various continents, configurations of race and gender introduce further contextual specificity. In these discussions, 'culture' delimits spheres of social life that do not admit of a single political or economic analysis. Therefore, even where a shared allegiance to the salvific significance of liberation exists, there is no one-size-fits-all way of correlating Christian tradition and contemporary situation.

Pluralism

Cultural pluralism in turn opens onto the issue of religious pluralism. In line with the Second Vatican Council, Schillebeeckx rejects the notion that non-Christians stand outside the bounds of salvation. He joins a tide of Catholic thinkers interpreting how best to affirm the sociological and theological reality of other religions as ways of life and paths to truth. Schillebeeckx's position looks to the ministry of Jesus of Nazareth as the guide for appreciating how a unique and universal claim of salvation can coincide with cultural and historical particularity, thereby avoiding what he maintains are a number of pitfalls in contemporary Christian self-understanding relative to religious others (e.g., the absolutism of exclusivism and inclusivism, and the indifference of relativism). With these complex negotiations he integrates consideration of the world's multiple religious traditions alongside agnostic and atheistic interpretations of human life in his continuing explication of the intelligibility of Christian faith.

For Schillebeeckx, religion's embeddedness in culture – that is, in the products and process of human making, including self-making – represents a kind of constraint, too often a source of danger and failure, but is in principle 'an inexhaustible force field' for renewing hope and liberating possibility. Absent shared parameters of truth or a stable system of meaning, he proposes the foundational experience of indignation at suffering and injustice in 'negative contrast experiences' as a starting point for communicating the heart of Christianity's good news: that God is a God of human beings, a God whose graciousness goes beyond anything the world has to offer. Taken together, these snapshots of his theology of culture across three decades bear out the picture of a theologian who boldly expands and refines his ideas while demonstrating remarkable consistency in this core conviction.

Questions for discussion

1. What theological ideas or concepts guide Schillebeeckx's engagement with culture?
2. How and why does his interpretation of the key features of the contemporary situation shift?
3. Given Schillebeeckx's claim that theology is both conditioned by its particular context and expresses something of universal significance, what aspects of his writing do you consider most helpful or illuminating today? Where might his ideas need further development or correction?

20

Culture

The Catholic university[1]

We have come to realise, as a result of the present crisis in the university system, that any reaction against a connection between the 'university' and a view of the world, even though, in the past, this connection was frequently unscientific and therefore alien to the university, must be regarded, on purely scientific grounds, as superseded. Any division between the university and a view of the world is moreover a fiction, since the rejection of any world-view cannot be justified by positive science as such and is therefore an option which lies outside the realm of science and this implies, at least negatively, a view of the world.

1. Seen against this background, the idea of the Catholic university will cause less *a priori* surprise. All the same, we should not ignore the real problems that it presents. In the first place, we must try to clear the field in advance by dispelling various prejudices. The most persistent of these is undoubtedly that academic freedom and adherence to religious dogma are contradictory,[2] as though freedom and being bound had to be contradictory and freedom had to be identified with arbitrariness! The sense of knowing itself to be bound to truth and only to truth is the very charter of the university. It is from this adherence to truth that the university derives the whole of its academic freedom, even its freedom with regard to political powers.[3] Now, by definition, faith offers itself to us as a being bound to divine *truth*. This being bound to divine truth is certainly accomplished in surrender to faith, but

---

[1] Selected from: Edward Schillebeeckx, 'The Significance of a Catholic University for the World and the Church', *World and Church*, trans. N. D. Smith, Collected Works of Edward Schillebeeckx vol. 4 (London: Bloomsbury T&T Clark, 2014), 221–4 [287–92].
[2] See N. Luyten, 'Idee und Aufgabe einer katholischen Universität', *Universität und moderne Welt*, 593–609; see also *Theology and the University. An Ecumenical Investigation*, ed. J. Coulson, London 1964.
[3] We may even ask whether – and to what extent – state intervention in university teaching, however necessary this may be because, of subsidies and their just distribution among the various universities within the state, does not infringe this academic freedom and is therefore, to the same extent, a disservice to the population. In the medieval *universitas doctorum et studentium*, exemption from all authority apart from that of the university itself was a *conditio sine qua non*.

its ethically meaningful content is nonetheless critically justified in advance.[4] Despite their completely different character, faith and science are fundamentally very similar to each other in that they are both bound to truth and only to truth.

We may go further and say that the conviction that the world of human experience is the *only* access to all truth is shared by both faith and science. Outside human experience, there is no other mysterious source of knowledge. How could a divine revelation which took place outside our experience be heard? How could it, in other words, be a revelation to human beings? There can be no knowledge of realities of which no human experience of any kind is given. Human perception, as the basis of all knowledge, means that the *world* is, for us, the only access to explicit knowledge here and now of all other possible spheres of reality, in other words, of total reality. In this sense, we know primarily only the material world and *thus* everything that is connected with this material world and insofar as it has any connection with it – in the first place, me and my fellow human being, precisely *as* a being in the world, then God, *as* the creator of this world or, possibly, *as* manifesting himself in grace *in this world*. It is precisely because of this that divine revelation, according to the Christian view, takes place in human history, which thereby becomes salvation-history. Humanity's conscious being in the world is thus the basis and the matrix of science and of faith.

In certain scientific circles, there is, on the one hand, a tendency to limit truth to what is directly verifiable or, on the other hand, not to regard the 'world' as humanity's only access to all other realities, but rather to see it as the *enclosing horizon* of all human knowledge.[5] This is, however, a non-verifiable *postulate* which lies outside the realm of science and thus goes back to a pre-scientific interpretation of the world. Not only is this particular previously given view of the world open to criticism – the idea that faith or the religious view of the world cannot justifiably be accorded a place within the university system is also not scientific, but ideological. Why, then, should the acceptance of the transcendence of being and consequently of the transcendental range of the human spirit not have a place in the university when the denial of this transcendence does have a place, if both the affirmation and the negation of this concept lie outside the sphere of scientific thought – if, in other words, they both transcend positive science? The acceptance of the absolute openness of the human spirit to the totality of reality seems to me to be the real reason for the very existence of a *universitas scientiarum*, just as it is also the condition of the possibility of every branch of learning and science. This is precisely why I insisted, in the first part of this argument, on the central place of philosophy in the university – a position recently accorded to it in the Dutch law on higher education, in which philosophy was raised to the level of a separate faculty with the significant name of 'central interfaculty'.

Religious faith – and Christianity in particular – maintains that human beings in their absolute openness is always confronted by the absolute person of God who, because he is a person, can manifest himself in grace and has in fact done so. Indeed, it is even possible to say that this divine revelation is *necessary*, that it is

---

[4]See E. Schillebeeckx, *God and Man* (Theological Soundings 2), London and New York 1969, 162–79.
[5]M. Merleau-Ponty, 'La métaphysique dans l'homme', *Sens et non-sens*, Paris 1948, 165–95.

the very essence of God himself in comparison with us. Either God speaks or he is silent. But in view of the transcendental openness of the human spirit, God's silence, his non-revelation of himself, would acquire for human beings the significance of a revelation, because even God's possible silence would signify something for the absolute openness of the human spirit[6] and indicate something about an ultimate meaning – or in that case rather a non-sense – of human life. That is why, by virtue of the transcendental openness of his spirit – and thus on a *human* basis, not on the basis of a mysterious, unique and irrational source of knowledge – man must *a priori* take a possible speaking on God's part into account. If God positively speaks, this speaking is, on the basis of the transcendental openness of the human spirit, the highest fulfilment of humanity. This fulfilment is certainly transcendent, but it is nonetheless *inward* and through it human beings are at the same time *revealed to themselves*. Faith thus discloses a very special perspective, that of human beings who fully realise themselves only in a situation of salvation which God offers to him in the sovereign freedom of his grace.

Only then can human beings realise that without this grace, which they cannot claim for themselves, they are not so completely self-evident and that their deepest questions about human life and especially about their ultimate fate cannot be solved even by the *universitas scientiarum*, if faith and therefore theology are banished from it. The ultimate consistency of humanity would then be undermined. The *universitas scientiarum*, with its interdisciplinary approach and philosophy, therefore calls for a theological faculty, precisely because of the idea of totality and of humanity which dominates the university. The idea of humanity thus forms the inward link between religion and scientific thought in the university. This attitude is, in any case, just as scientifically justified as the attitude which accords no place in the university to faith. In other words, it is possible, if need be, to reject all religion and Christianity, but it is impossible ever to say that the integration of faith into the university system implies the destruction or violation of the idea of the university.

We can go even further. I have already referred to lived, simple experience as the prior datum for all scientific thought. If, according to the religious view, human beings are always confronted in the transcendental openness of their spirit by the God of grace, this implies that revelation in acceptance or refusal is present in every simple experience, either implicitly or anonymously, and that the concrete attitude of acceptance and affirmation of this mystery of life is already true faith, the unspoken primordial form of religious faith. Religion is the making public of the true form of a way of life which diffidently and reverently approaches the mystery of objective reality and allows itself to be directed by it. Faith thus takes hold of humanity in that transcendental openness of their spirit which is also the condition of the possibility of every branch of learning and science. Faith can therefore, in principle, not be violated in its existence and in its confession by any science. Just as science or learning cannot give me faith, so they cannot take my faith away either. If, then, science in one form or another is the critical explication of the lived experience in which I, as a person, associate with the world of things and other people, then this

---

[6]See, among others, Karl Rahner, *Hearers of the Word*, London and New York 1969, 94.

inexpressible reality which is the prior datum for all scientific thought also requires that scientific explication which we call *theology*.

This demonstrates, then, from the point of view of the presupposition of all sciences, that theology, as the reflection about faith and the reality of this world in the light of that faith, can occupy a meaningful and indeed a central place in the *universitas scientiarum*. Indeed, it also shows that, for the believer, theology, in addition to philosophy, must really be given the name of 'central interfaculty', since the theologian aims to penetrate to the deepest ground of all reality and humanity, although he does this by reflecting about *faith*. The theologian also needs to live in contact with the other faculties, because it is from these that the 'problems' which he has to consider come. A theological institute outside the university suffers from being placed in a predicament which is essentially precarious for theology itself. If theology is to be practised under the most favourable conditions, it essentially requires to be geared to and to form part of a *universitas scientiarum*, in which cross-fertilisation can also take place within the structure of the system itself. It is precisely this which is lacking in a separate theological institute since what is brought to light by scientific research is also of importance to our understanding of revelation, and the profane sciences in turn also need the light that can be thrown on them by the ultimate meaning of reality. If the theologian loses touch with the other, evolving branches of learning or science, he will inevitably fail in his Christian interpretation, for example, of the modern process of secularisation and of the new dimension in which human beings have come to live because of the increasing influence of science on human society.

Culture, religion and violence: Theology as a component of culture[7]

I think we are living in such a time when, as a result of changes mainly in our complex, fragmented or segmented Western society with its multiplicity of specialisms and autonomous sectors, all our fixed points of reference are disappearing (quite apart from oppression and exclusion in modern and postmodern society). Many people are totally at a loss, floundering. Our society, politics and institutions have grown too vast, too opaque. That also applies to those churches – nowadays merely components of society – in which authorities become implausible because of mistaken loyalties. Authoritative arguments can no longer drive home familiar, fixed points of reference as they once did; on the contrary, merely invoking authority has the opposite effect and arouses even fiercer opposition. There is widespread frustration because the traditional form of religion has become foreign to the new culture we are living in and, for that reason, culturally irrelevant, no longer speaking to people. That is not remedied by credal appeals (as often happens in Protestant churches), nor by

---

[7]Selected from: Edward Schillebeeckx, 'Culture, Religion and Violence: Theology as a Component of Culture', *Essays: Ongoing Theological Quests*, Collected Works of Edward Schillebeeckx vol. 11 (London: Bloomsbury T&T Clark, 2014), 172–82.

repeated authoritarian, even threatening warnings, prohibitions and bans (as is the case in the Catholic Church)! Still, despite or maybe partly because of secularisation, religion is thriving, albeit to my mind often in para-religious forms. In that case secularisation may alienate people from the institutional church, synagogue, temple or mosque, giving rise to peripheral membership, non-religiosity and alternative lifestyles; on the other hand its specialised fragmentation drives people towards a new, resurgent 'religiosity' and 'holism' in diverse (sometimes bizarre) directions.

Contemporary art perhaps makes us aware of this state of affairs, far more than cultural sociological, philosophical or theological analyses. "That's not a pipe!" I am convinced that Christian churches and other religions which *fail to use the medium* of humanism, humanitarianism and human solidarity, especially with wounded, beleaguered people, don't stand a chance in our evolving new culture.[8] To Christians living in the emerging culture it is a matter of reflecting the message of grace, salvation and deliverance in a *human form*. Anything that does not conform to the standards of authentic human dignity cannot claim to be Christian or invoke the name of God. Even in my days as a young Dominican theology student I was shocked when I read in a speech by Pope Pius XI to the staff of the Angelicum and the Master of the Dominicans: 'Especially in our time one should speak of "serving the church" rather than of "serving Jesus Christ".'[9]

A church that does not permit human rights in its own ranks, and thereby mutilates the human face in the name of a God allegedly transcending all humanity, has reached the end of its road in a culture gasping for genuine humanity: in that respect at any rate it is not a church, and is also not true to the gospel of Jesus Christ in his human manifestation that is the revealed form of the living God. In order to maintain the plausibility of divine transcendence Christian churches must radiate humanity, in terms of their own religious inspiration and as elements of a culture, because to Christians he is a God who cares for people. He is a 'God of human beings', many Old Testament psalms affirm repeatedly. When churches – both their leaders and lay members – do not display a genuinely human, ethical face they forfeit their plausibility as a religion and a religious culture. That is what is happening at present.

People are panting for a culture of justice and love. A human rights culture is a minimum and the beginnings of love, but it's not enough. People long to be accepted unconditionally by others, everyone wants to be accepted for their own sake, be they black, yellow, boss-eyed, handicapped or foreigners. Respect, forgiveness, love and trust are their due. Justice, like the law, is cold and forbidding. A human culture is a culture of love, and that cannot be pinned down in statutes and codified. That is why religious movements and religions, as long as they are not inhumanly alienated from

---

[8] To me that is the challenge of the at least 'agnostic' humanism that is resurfacing, albeit in a different configuration than formerly, in a book like *Humanisme: theorie en praktijk*, P. Cliteur and D. Van Houten (eds), Utrecht, 1993; also see the punchy, more differentiated article by the agnostic J. F. Glastra van Loon, 'Zoektocht naar de zin van het leven: een levensvervulling', in the newspaper *Trouw*, 18 Oct. 1996, 11 (Podium column). A Christian theist like Paul Ricoeur (throughout his oeuvre) would counter this by saying: 'There is meaning in life, but you have to look for it.'

[9] Rendering of a speech by Pius XI to a group of Dominicans, from my notes in my theological study years taken from the newspaper *La Croix* of 12 March 1931, 1.

their authentic roots, are among the most dynamic forces in any culture worthy of the name. Without Christian humanity Christianity will carry no weight in future, but without evangelically true Christianity humanity, too, is at risk. Christendom rooted in the gospel of Jesus the Lord, the coming Son of Man, is an inexhaustible force field, also for cultural actions aimed at human dignity for everyone, especially for the least among us.

Changes, even discontinuities in our worldview come about mainly when we are confronted with recalcitrance. That is no doubt why the incomprehensible, theoretically and practically intractable recalcitrance of suffering, especially when it is innocent or absurd, plays such a major role in human history and has meaning that we can never pin down in explanatory conceptions. Nowadays it is mainly artistic works that seek to convey that humans are up against an experience of final limits... against discontinuities.

On the threshold of the 21st century we have to recognise this experience of human beings as mystery in order to open up our culture to the transcendent mystery of God. If we confine ourselves to permanent horizontal, cultural human self-transcendence, we are still relying on the 19th century belief in progress, which is passé. It would lead to either a kind of nihilism or absolute relativism, or to a rediscovery (even if not mathematically or scientifically compelling) that the human mystery reflects the absolute mystery of what the world religions call God.

In a secularised world it is not the experience of final limits per se but examining it in light of major religious experiential traditions – which to many among us is Christianity – that can help us to hear the good news, retrieving our faith in absolute transcendence; and in the power of that faith we can fearlessly face our final limits and surmount them in prayerful surrender, opening ourselves to the undeserved gift that sets us free.

As we have seen, culture, art and language explore the limits of our finitude to the point of absurdity. It is up to us to transform every possible interpretation to be found in that foreign realm into kindly humanity, imbedded in the mystery of a living God who cares for people, a God who affirms human beings in their individuality and therefore stipulates justice and love as the supreme expression of culture and the art of living. No doubt many will miss that interpretation for now, until they miss the Mystery itself. I am quite sure that God's grace and mercy are at work and at a given moment will light up as that which opens up all limits, transcendently accommodating our finite human culture from the depth dimension of all cultures. After all, the reality that Christians designate the 'kingdom of God' is operative all the time – not merely fragmentarily but also as a golden thread of peace and righteousness throughout our history, despite the historical contrary of evil and suffering. It happens wherever God's silent, hidden presence in signs, language and sound surfaces in simple, sometimes supremely noble, brave human conduct: you encountered me when others were forbearing towards you; you encountered me when someone came to visit you on your sickbed; when you stood up for a marginalised or wounded fellow human being – then, then you encountered me!

These were the perspectives I had in mind when I kept writing that the gospel message only gets through to us in critical confrontation between the 'past' (the great Christian experiential tradition) and the 'present' (individual and collective new experience). That is why I can't agree with Erik Borgman's statement that

'Schillebeeckx in fact still proceeds on the assumption that the faith comes first, the church and its tradition come first, which he can then analyse and demonstrate their openness to the situation of contemporary people'. That is in fact what I have fought against with my hermeneutic approach since the 1960s. Certainly (obviously) the *solidified* Christian experiential tradition 'historically predetermines' our present, but it only becomes a living reality in the present, just as 'faith' is never 'objectively predetermined' for the Christian subject. What I didn't produce myself is only *realised* in my present-day religious experience, and highly contextually at that, in a series of fragmentary experiences. I must concede, though (and that may well be Borgman's objection), that so far I have analysed the reciprocal critical reflection between past and present (consciously, for that matter) purely formally: I merely wanted to show the coordinates within which one can theologise fruitfully and plausibly. Others, including Borgman himself, were to fill in the territory within those coordinates, and rightly, with concrete, fragmentary contexts. But to that end the system of coordinates first had to be clarified for everybody. At that time it was anything but self-evident! (Today it appears to be an *a priori* certainty.) Hence it was an essential prolegomenon to what others had to do after me.

Also, when I speak of proportionality in that context it has nothing to do with D. De Petter's epistemological notions of proportion and proportionality, but indicates hermeneutic proportionality, something totally foreign to De Petter's epistemological thought.[10] In fact I see no difference between Borgman's point and what I wrote then and continue to say. The difference, if any, is that I have never gone in for a consciously fragmentary approach, mainly because my interest lay, and still lies, in searching for and disclosing universally human features in fragments of every kind day-to-day encounters, novels, poems, scientific studies. I continue to believe in the 'great stories', which – like the Bible – comprise a series of highly fragmentary experiences, in which a later author or school of authors saw a sustained plot, and then turned a concatenation of minor histories of people or groups into a 'great story' – to trace a path for those who read that story with some sort of attention. Put differently, I keep looking for the Christian message that addresses all people, and that is only possible if one does not detach current fragmentary experiences from what (the so-called nonreligious) Walter Benjamin, who greatly influenced me in this respect, called the indispensable relevance of the 'great human traditions' to authentic humanity here and now. To my mind contemporary 'fragmentary stories' are merely a new, to me surprising and stimulating, part of these great traditions – in Christian terms, as I continually stress, a kind of 'fifth Gospel', which can make up an extremely variegated picture. But without an underlying continuity in that story (partly on account of many necessary discontinuities that keep the evangelical 'plot' moving) any talk of 'being a Christian' has no authentic meaning. I consider that to be the strength of (substantiated) faith in a major religious experiential tradition. One never starts from scratch, but is part of a long history, which for many entails

---

[10] The word 'hermeneutics' never crossed De Petter's lips; that was the source of the conflict between us towards the end of his life. The term 'proportionality', as Borgman points out, derives from J.-P. Jossua; I cited his article explicitly the first time I used the term in my hermeneutics, somewhat reluctantly, because his article was written from an epistemological rather than a hermeneutic perspective.

or signifies rebellion against real-life histories of suffering. That is not the lot of our generation only.

Relation to the transcendent and violence

To conclude my reflection, I have to point out a possible danger that always lurks when one sees 'religion', to my mind rightly, as a cultural form of divine salvation. Here ideological misinterpretation and abuse are a real hazard. The fact that religion itself, the concrete embodiment of both our relationship with Ultimate Transcendence and Ultimate Immanence, is part of culture is a caveat urging extreme caution.

If culture – both its horizontal and vertical (or depth) dimension of self-transcendence – is a ground-breaking movement in history, one immediately faces the phenomenon of violence, which therefore raises far more frequent objections than the introduction of the concept of transcendence (or the ultimate) into an exposition of our earthly culture. A glance at human history makes these objections painfully clear.

The sense of superiority that religions – and Christianity is no exception – have regularly displayed appears to be one of the greatest obstacles to the coexistence of diverse religions within the same political boundaries. That is increasingly evident in our time; thus Muslims and Buddhists, for example, daily rub shoulders with Christian neighbours. Such a sense of superiority poses a threat to a culture of human dignity. We must therefore own up to the history of encounters between religions – actually, between religious people – that have given rise to so much inhuman violence for the sake of an 'ideal' or 'great' cause, a professed 'only' truth, a specific religious relation to the Ultimate.

When we scrutinise this historical reality the question comes to mind whether there is an *intrinsic relation* between the essence of religion (i.e. a relationship with the transcendent, immanent Ultimate) and religious violence. If that is not so (which is my thesis), then the historical facts of interreligious encounter almost automatically raise a second question: is religion with its affirmation of truth not in fact packaged in all manner of nonreligious preconceptions, or covertly assimilated into a particular, false self- understanding? Such an entanglement betrays the innermost dynamics of an authentic relationship with the Ultimate, including a personal Christian or evangelical one, and as a result it turns violent.

Reading the Sermon on the Mount, 'Blessed are the meek and those who strive for righteousness...', one asks oneself how the history of Christianity could possibly have been so profoundly disfigured by religious violence, the more so because we Christians worship the living God, who (so we confess) seeks to be a God of people not of the dead but of the living, a God about whom even the Judaic roots of Christianity aver that he abominates human sacrifice (Lev 18.21-30, 20.1-5).

To some extent this contradiction between the behaviour of religious people and their relation to the Ultimate is humanly understandable. If religion is the supreme value in your life, as theists experience according to their self- understanding and may rightly profess, then any theoretical or practical abuse of that faith leads to the most inhuman cruelty. Here, too, corruption of the finest is the rock bottom of evil. In the course of history wars have been fought and people have been killed in the name of

God. Modern people who, many religious wars later, try to rationalise the problem often have difficulty accommodating a qualification such as 'understandably' and then, wrongly, conclude that there must be an intrinsic relation between religion and violence. I say, wrongly. On the other hand we cannot refute the allegation by trivialising the historical connection or reducing it to the weakness and inconsistency of believers. The perplexing fact that great, intrinsically tender-hearted theologians, including Thomas Aquinas, were children of their times and theologically legitimised violence, indicates that it is not so simple, especially not for people who experience their relationship with the absolute or incomprehensible mystery as the core of their existence: a matter of life and death.

I do not dwell on the thesis (nonetheless memorable) of a thinker like M. Merleau-Ponty, who saw religious violence as an unavoidable concomitant, inherent in religion. To this kind of atheism a relationship with the ultimate, the absolute, spells the death of everything relative and contingent, also of human autonomy. Many atheists and agnostics, notably humanists, also regard this view as outdated. While it no longer disfigures the praxis, it still mars the soul of most religions. Thomas expresses it forcefully in his doctrine of creation, which in effect says that the act of creation situates people in their human, albeit finite, autonomy and leaves them freely responsible for their ethical behaviour in this world and for their autonomous search for ethical criteria for their behaviour. God instated them in their proudly human personal rights; anyone who touches these touches God himself, says Thomas.[11] In principle this, quite rightly, subjects every religion to the critique of human dignity, on both humanitarian and Christian grounds. An authentic relation to the absolute or ultimate is in no way violent – on the contrary: it engenders intrepid courage to bring greater humanity to every domain of life.

The trouble is that the relation to the ultimate is never 'isolated': to believers nothing human escapes our creaturely bond with the ultimate. From our point of view the 'direct' bond with God is also invariably mediated. Clearly that allows for all sorts of healthy associations but also for false ones – between religious people and 'profane' mediations when these are elevated above their proper status and arbitrarily upgraded to 'God's will'. For then misguided alliances can incite them to religious violence in the name of their relationship with the ultimate.

Hence I see the problem of religious violence – including intolerance towards other religions and rejection of interreligious dialogue on an equal footing – as the only proper and necessary framework for posing the question concerning the true character of Christianity and of Jesus confessed as the Christ. Otherwise the answer to a painful, challenging question is diplomatically glossed over and becomes a civil gesture of religio-political gentility, formal courtesy towards the other. The real issue is whether the professed relationship with the ultimate, the transcendent – the 'mystery' – liberates or endangers humanity. From a human and Christian point of view, is violence in the name of religion essentially evil? I think it is, and want to show why. In so doing I realise that my answer entails a critical question about our traditional interpretation of Christianity's so-called claim to absoluteness, as well

---

[11]'Detrahere perfectioni creaturarum est detrahere perfectioni divinae virtutis' (Thomas, *Summa contra gentiles*, III, 69).

as Judaic and Christian concepts like predestination and covenant. I appreciate that this must lead to the conclusion that the notion of divine predestination includes 'mediation' but not anti-human partiality, hence can only be aimed at universality, not exclusion. That implies that predestination and covenant are subordinate to God's intention for creation, which is aimed at salvation for all people: *all humanity is God's chosen people*. All historical forms of belief in religious predestination must promote the belief in universal predestination; otherwise the self-understanding of individuals, nations and religious communities as being divinely chosen entails a danger of violence against adherents of other religions or 'unbelievers', which can result in a cauldron of violence.

Religious violence, hence also rejection of interreligious dialogue on an equal footing, has a dual basis of a nonreligious (and un-Christian) nature. The first has to do with professing to be the only true religion. In that case other religions will be consistently denied any right to exist, and in variegated societies such a refutation is in itself a virtual declaration of war, hence of violence. Religion, including Christianity, is subject to critique from a religious hermeneutics that 'does justice' to people on humanitarian grounds and, to believers, on Christian religious grounds of belief in creation. But the two bases cannot be aggregated as two separate ingredients. Humanity, human dignity is the *immediate ground* of human ethics (*etsi Deus non daretur*), and to Christian believers this is grounded in God's creation, which, being transcendently immanent, is ultimate or religious and not on a par with humanitarian grounds.[12] From this structure it follows that within the ambit of the autonomous sphere there are traces of this religious transcendence, at any rate if that which appears to be ethically 'humane' is also scrutinised in light of a given religious experiential tradition – to Christians the Judaeo-Christian tradition. There is no immediate self-evidence; here, too, the *redundance* of religious transcendence in human ethics only becomes apparent in light of a human religious tradition.[13] To Christians this insight implies that they cannot and may not interpret their confession of Jesus the Christ to mean that compared to other religions Christianity is the only true faith.

Even if one's own religion is not regarded as the only true one, a second pretention can cause religion to turn to violence. This second basis of religious violence is the belief that one's own religion is one's primary civic duty on the grounds that the God one confesses is the direct guarantor of the welfare of human society. This notion, even if it lays no claim to the absoluteness of that religion, also leads to religious violence. Even if a religion acknowledges that it is only one of many religions, it may

---

[12]Still, what constitutes human dignity here and now can only be determined democratically if everyone has a say in it; and even then democracy inevitably includes pluralism. Hence we need to apply criteria. See the problem of the struggle between the Right and the Good in J. Rawls, *A theory of justice*, Oxford, ²1973.

[13]Here I am reacting to the view of G. Steiner, *Von realer Gegenwart: Hat unser Sprechen Inhalt?* München, 1990 (original English: *Real Presences*), who professes to discern an immediate presence of the transcendent in aesthetics (and human ethics). I deny the reality of that immediate perception when it is said that it can happen without an accompanying, mediatory recollection of a pre-existent religious tradition. Here I share the criticism of both D. Mieth and J. Kuschel, in: *Theologie und ästhetische Erfahrung: Beiträge zur Begegnung von Religion und Kunst*, Hg. W. Lesh, Stuttgart, 1993, 111–24, 145–65.

still instigate violence because of diverse overt or covert alliances, hence because of an implicitly distorted God concept.

History offers many arguments to support this. It is evident in the classical concept of *religio* as defined in Roman law. *Religio* was the first, supreme patriotic or civic duty (*pietas*), any deviation being qualified as subversive and severely punished,[14] even though the Hellenistic Roman pantheon accommodated many kinds of gods. Despite this tolerant pantheon the early Christians were persecuted, since in the eyes of Latin-Hellenistic law they were 'a-theists', hence subversive because of their denial of the divine guarantee of the wellbeing of the Roman empire, thereby failing in their primary civic duty.[15] If, as in the Roman law concerning *religio* as a primary civic duty, one forges a direct link between the established or, alternatively, per se revolutionary socio-political order and a relationship with the ultimate as the guarantee of the established (or revolutionary) reason of state, interreligious, hence anti-human violence is a logically consistent outcome. In that case it was not even appreciated that such religious violence was 'inhuman', for in this view human beings, quite apart from their relationship with the ultimate, were even more inextricably enmeshed in all kinds of slavery and violence.

In the fourth century, in the latter days of the Roman empire, when Christianity became the official religion, the church adopted the Roman concept of *religio* (along with the associated concept of *Roma*) and applied it to the Christian relationship with the ultimate. In this way the Christian God became (in the West for centuries) the upholder of the established socio-political order, with all it implied for those considered dissident, 'heretical' or 'schismatic'. For according to this view all deviant ideas were simply lese-majesty.[16] That also allowed civil authorities to punish 'Christian heretics'. Thus reason of state stood four square behind the council that condemned Arius, because to the emperor anti-Arian dogma as the strongest weapon in his striving for the unity of the empire. Thus Arianism became subversive. Subsequently the church's adoption of the ancient Roman concept of *religio* permitted the Crusades, in which Muslims were slaughtered, and the Inquisition, in which dissidents from orthodoxy – the guarantee of political wellbeing – were handed over to the civil authorities as traitors and burnt at the stake.

In such cases religious violence is not rooted (exclusively) in a religion's claim – in this instance that of Christian churches – to being the only true faith, but in the false assumption that the religious relationship with the ultimate implies an essential connection with the concrete, humanly established socio- political order to which one belongs, in other words that the Christian God, for example, is the immediate guarantor of that order and hence of the wellbeing of the empire (*salus nationis,* the

---

[14]P. Stockmeier, *Glaube und Religion in der frühen Kirche,* Freiburg, 1972.

[15]J. Vogt, *Zur Religiosität der Christenverfolger im Romischen Reich,* Heidelberg, 1962; Th. Ulrich, *Pietas (pius) als politischer Begriff im Romischen Staate bis zum Tode des Kaisers Commodus,* Breslau, 1930; N. Brox, 'Zum Vorwurf des Atheismus gegen die alte Kirche', in: *Trierer Theologische Zeitschrift,* 74 (1966), 274–82.

[16]*Codex Theod.,* XVI, 1, 2; XIV 2, 25. See P. Stockmeier, 'Das Schwert im Dienst der Kirche: Zur Hinrichtung Priszillians in Trier', in: *Festschrift für A. Thomas,* Trier, 1967, 415–28; also see notes 16 and 17. The adoption of *religio,* already obliquely discernible in emperor Galerius' edict of tolerance in 311, is abundantly evident in emperor Theodosius the Great's law on religion (28 February 380).

'supreme law', guaranteed by God himself). The flipside is that not being a Christian is potentially subversive. After all, even tolerant modern states intervene forcibly to combat potentially treasonable elements and activities. Hence not the Christian religion as such but its association with the classical concept of *religio* accounts for its historical record of religious violence, as well as the historical fact that even critical theologians had no difficulty legitimising such violence.

The theological conclusion for us modern people is crystal clear: there is something wrong with the preconception that a relationship with the ultimate is associated with upholding an established order or (as a real, if less common alternative) with a directly religious summons to revolt. Put differently, directly linking the ultimate with a given (established or revolutionary) socio-political order is essentially to abuse religion and is therefore humanly and Christianly unacceptable. In my view that makes an actual 'state religion' anti-human and potentially violent. That applies equally to state recognition of a few privileged 'official religions', excluding or merely tolerating others (thought this still begs the question in how far religions in their relation with what they call the ultimate in fact liberate or threaten humanity).

Hence quite apart from theological and evangelical arguments it is unacceptable and discriminatory, also on humanitarian ethical grounds, to posit a direct relation between a religion and a given socio-political order. At its very core such a claim implies violation of human rights and therefore, in religious terms, rights grounded in God's creation. In a pluralist society it is tantamount to a declaration of war, that is to say, violence. This is not to deny what I have consistently pointed out, namely that the gospel is socio-politically relevant; it only refutes the existence of a *direct, intrinsic* link between the Christian confession of God and a humanly established or to be established socio-political order. Rejection of such a direct link moreover offers scope for Christians to engage in interreligious dialogue on an equal footing with all dialogue partners in the face of real religious differences and rejection of the view that all religions are 'equal' (known as indifferentism).

In reality Christianity is only reluctantly bidding the two forms of distorted religious self-understanding farewell, and then mainly under external social pressure, more especially from the modern secularised world a *Fremdprophetie* from which Christian churches can learn a great deal! Yet the pressure is salutary, even though it is imperative to keep looking for intrinsically religious, Christian grounds for non-violent religion and open interreligious dialogue, and for a distinctively Christian positive attitude towards religious people of other persuasions. But that analysis falls outside the scope of this article.

Selected literature

- The Catholic University, Selected from: Edward Schillebeeckx, 'The Significance of a Catholic University for the World and the Church', *World and Church*, trans. N. D. Smith, Collected Works of Edward Schillebeeckx vol. 4 (London: Bloomsbury T&T Clark, 2014). 221–4 [287–92].
- Culture, Religion and Violence: Theology as a Component of Culture; Selected from: Edward Schillebeeckx, 'Culture, Religion and Violence: Theology as a Component of Culture', *Essays: Ongoing Theological Quests*, Collected Works of Edward Schillebeeckx vol. 11 (London: Bloomsbury T&T Clark, 2014), 172–82.

21

Secularisation

God in dry dock[1]

I am well aware that the title I have chosen for this first chapter is blasphemous. To be in 'dry dock' is an expression originally used of a ship which needed such extensive repairs that it had to be withdrawn from service and put in a position in which its underwater parts could be examined at leisure: by extension it came to apply to anything that had become problematical and thus needed to be set aside for examination, and perhaps revision. The justification for using the expression here with regard to God is that it suggests precisely what a lot of people are thinking. If the title chosen had been 'The Idea of God in Dry Dock', it would have reflected the present-day situation even more accurately. But people today are not greatly enamoured of ideas. They prefer realities, and it is just these realities which represent their problem. Well, what is the situation where people today are concerned?

For one thing, people today are more aware than were any of their ancestors of their secular task in this world, and in striving to accomplish it they feel independent and very much on his own; hence they are often inclined to feel that religion is a specious hypothesis, and in any case a useless one. In fact, we even hear it suggested that religion is a hypothesis which is becoming more and more clearly untenable as time goes on. Surely, the argument runs, as human beings obtain a more and more profound understanding of life and the world around them, the ideological religious background fades away in a constantly diminishing perspective, so that ultimately it will reach vanishing point and disappear into thin air. Our scientifically slanted age seems to encourage this presumed disappearance of a religion whose shortcomings have been so exposed. In the natural sciences – sociology, psychology, depth psychology, and, finally, philosophy – and, indeed, in all other spheres, the human spirit has gradually advanced into those formerly hidden domains whose obscure inaccessibility for the human mind was once regarded as identical with the mystery in which God came into tangible contact with the world. But nowadays, for every step forward human beings take, God has to take a step backwards.[2]

---

[1] Selected from: Edward Schillebeeckx, 'God in Dry Dock', *God and Man*, trans. Edward Fitzgerald and Peter Tomlinson, Theological Soundings (New York: Sheed and Ward, 1969), 3–10.
[2] See the next chapter [in *God and Man*], 'The Search for the Living God'.

The whole process began, of course, in ancient times. Primitive people knew nothing at all about the direct causes of thunder and lightning, of fertility in the Nile valley, of inundations, of sulphur springs – or of life, sickness and death. Because they were ignorant of the causes of these things they believed that good or evil spirits were directly at work in the background in all such matters. In consequence it became what one might call lifemanship on his part to establish a favourable relationship between themselves and these higher and more powerful beings. But in the course of time, human beings gradually came into possession of the secrets behind these enigmas, and after that they were inclined to thank the spirits for services rendered and dismiss them for good. This was only a first farewell, however, the process was to go on in human history until the Great Spirit himself was compelled to beat a step-by-step retreat. Again and again 'he' was seen to lose ground, first in one sphere and then in another. However, it then turned out (and this has happened again and again) that there was still some point, somewhere or other in the world, which confronted the human mind with mystery, so that scope was left for the continued existence of the Great Spirit.

But our own day has ended even this – at least, that is what very many people seem to think. Modern people are observing the phenomenon of a constantly retreating God, and the shouts of exultation which go up from the unbelievers exceed in volume even that first triumphant shout that went up in the nineteenth century, recording the death of God. Some people here and there still believe, of course, but the trumpet has already sounded and it has given forth no uncertain note – fundamentally the retreat of God on all fronts is an accomplished fact. For example, the passage of the first Sputnik through space was reported in the Russian press as a sort of gleeful demonstration of God's complete debacle and the official certificate of his definitive death. The fact that some people nevertheless persist in believing in God is put down to their inability to realise that the historical process of expansion in human knowledge and experience is identical with the gradual shrinking of God's domain. Such people rely on the many problems of life and matter which still remain mysterious and reassure themselves with the thought that there is obviously still room in the world for God, that there is still a place in which his house stands foursquare. It is conceived as a sort of final line of defence; his domicile into which no human hand or eye, no human mind, can ever penetrate, however precise and accurate the scientific apparatus at its disposal. At world exhibitions dedicated to humanity, one still finds a 'pavilion of God'. The unbeliever looks down commiseratingly on such anachronistic ideas and deplores the backwardness and ignorance of people who fail to recognise the continuing dynamic of scientific progress and make themselves a God to fill the gaps in their knowledge. They are like the peasants who believed in God and got their priest to flourish the holy-water sprinkler over the fields to ensure a good harvest. Don't they really know that 'since the invention of artificial fertilizers' peasants no longer need the holy-water sprinkler and have therefore lost any sense of the Church? And the harvests still arrive on time as usual. Let's be reasonable: those problems which are admittedly still unsolved in the world will, in principle, find their solution as science progresses still further, developing all its practical possibilities for the creation and management of a secular order which will be truly human, intellectually and in the physically. God has already vacated the fields, and things are improving on their own. Social welfare is now in the hands of science, and in a few years scientific planning and technological achievements have done more for the sick, the poor and the aged than 'religious works of charity' managed to do in centuries. Where zealous missionaries bumble around – and have done so for ages – trying to improve the lives of backward peoples, scientific institutions under the aegis of governments work wonders in a very short space of time. God has therefore become a useless hypothesis. The world is really and truly in the hands of human beings – it is his field of action. No God is necessary to improve the scientific apparatus human beings have at their disposal.

Fine, but what about human beings themselves? Where do they come from? Do they perhaps come from God after all? At this point atheistic philosophy proposes to demolish the last refuge of the believer: It is true that I am alive without having asked to be born; that I am living in a world for whose existence I bear no responsibility. But at least I am living in it as a free human being, and this freedom may give life in this world a meaning and make it worthy of human beings. We must create the values which alone can make such a worthwhile human existence possible. It all depends on human freedom, and on that alone. It may well be that this secular mission will never be quite satisfactorily accomplished; that it is, in fact, a Sisyphean task. No matter. In that case it is the duty of human beings to accept this risk courageously, with their eyes open to all that it involves. Even when it cannot see beyond the horizon, human freedom must dare to tackle even what is preposterous and apparently hopeless. Where human beings are too fainthearted to accept this worldly task freely and gladly, along with all its sometimes-heart-breaking consequences, they are betraying their own human nature – that is to say, as free human beings in an uncertain world. To postulate a divine providence which must in the last resort eliminate all risk and lead everything to a good conclusion for those who love God is to seek a cowardly solution. Belief in the supernatural and in the supra-historical is the final remnant of a certain attitude towards life in which human beings do not dare to tackle life for themselves and therefore project a solution of the historical mystery into the hereafter – into eternity – since they lack the courage to accept its significance and face the fact that its problems defy solution.

Following on the above arguments the idea of God has been declared an offence to human dignity, an excuse for clinging to the past and for tolerating economic, social and political anarchy.[3] And indeed we must ask ourselves seriously whether the alleged 'cultural inertia'[4] on the part of believers is not an evident fact among us today. Isn't it a fact that 'the reactionaries' are found chiefly among religious people? And hasn't atheism perhaps got a point when it calls on the evidence of history to show that believers use their beliefs as an excuse for their own sloth and timidity and their refusal to face the urgent problems of the day courageously?

Aren't we constantly being reminded of the fact that, with all due respect to one or two minor pioneering attempts, the others were always ahead of us when it came to doing something practical – relieving, for example, the wretched condition of working

---

[3] For a searching inquire from the existentialist point of view in which the cowardice involved in religious flight from the world is opposed to the courage found in atheism, see the following: Simone de Beauvoir, 'Pour une morale de l'ambiguïté', in *Les Temps Modernes* 2 (1946), 193–211, and 3 (1947), 846–74; also 'L'existentialisme et la sagesse des nations', ibid. I (1945), 385–404. F. Jeanson, *Le problème moral et la pensée de Sartre* (Coll. Pensée et Civilisation), Paris 1947, and 'Athéisme et liberté', in F. Jeanson, 'Athéisme et liberté', in *Lumière Vie* 13 (1954), 85–96. M. Merleau-Ponty, *Sense and Non-Sense*, trans. Hubert L. Dreyfus and Patricia Allen Dreyfus, Evanston, Ill., Northwestern University Press, 1964.

[4] See also L. J. Rogier, *Het verschijnsel der culturele inertie bij de Nederlandse katholieken*, Amsterdam 1958. See also note 6.

people in the nineteenth century? And wasn't it only when we were shamed into action by their efforts that we believers finally and hesitantly made some attempt to join in? In addition, of course, the reproaches about Galileo are still with us. Even nowadays it still looks as though religious people are nervously fearful of anything that looks like progress in scientific, psychological, economic, social and political affairs.

For our part we must seriously ask ourselves whether it wasn't the believers themselves who brought atheism into being – not by their beliefs, of course, but by their distorted interpretation of those beliefs. And there we have it: it was through their erroneous ideas about God that believers gave atheism its real chance. However, we should not overlook the implication of this: that atheism is nothing other than a rejection of those erroneous ideas about God and a condemnation of a Christianity which is not being systematically lived and experienced. In short, the real atheists are probably not always to be found where we think we have encountered them. Because of all this it has frequently been pointed out that perhaps present-day atheism is, after all, a merciful dispensation, a new chance for salvation offered us by God, a chance to purify our beliefs of all the human dross and all the selfish distortions inevitably involved in any attempt to ensure ourselves a quiet life.

The fact that humanity was created by the living God means that they are constantly receiving themselves from God; that they are real in themselves, firmly fixed in his own inviolable independence, and nevertheless wholly from, in and of God both in their thought and their will and their essential existence in this world. I find myself in this mysterious state and I am unable to extricate myself from it: on the one hand I am really and truly myself; I stand freely and courageously in this world and take my life in my own hands, arranging it according to what I in my freedom choose to set as my aim in life, thus becoming more and more myself. On the other hand, in this whole being I am at the same time, and into the finest warp and woof of my being, wholly from God, from whom I derive myself and by whom I am constantly given to myself. In this dependence on God, I am nevertheless myself; that is to say, a being who possesses the power of taking his life freely into his own hands. Our whole life is lived within the vast sphere of the personal God who embraces us. It is therefore pointless to seek him in isolation *somewhere* in this world.

The world is *in* him. 'In him we live, move and have our being'. We have been inclined to seek an understandable and a tangible God with a resting place somewhere in this world as one of the many amongst the finite things around us. In consequence, when we found ourselves faced with an insoluble riddle we were inclined to suppose that we had come near to God's dwelling place. Or we sought after a God who would dry human tears, a God who would eliminate the risks attendant on our exposed existence in this world, alleviate our gloomy expectations and remove our insecurity. We have seen this sort of thing happening in our immediate environment only too often. Haven't believers 'enlightened' by 'the Fatima prophecy' – or, rather, misled by a distorted interpretation of it – relied supinely on what was going to happen in the mysterious year 1960, which was to bring such wonders to the world? They fail to realise that the only surprises are those which result from human free will in the world and its power to bring events about, or perhaps from natural forces not yet fully under human control. The fact that believers put their trust in God is not what brings grist to the atheist mill, but that in the meantime they neglect their secular duty and their worldly tasks. They sit back and wait for the year 1960, which seems so full of promise. And nothing happens but the events which result from their own slothful neglect. No, the real mystery of God lies in the fact that with their world, human beings live *in* God – in a godly or an ungodly fashion. The trouble is that human beings keep on looking for a God who will provide him with insurance against the injustices of this world, a God who, bypassing free will, would be prepared to intervene in the affairs of this world to ensure personal safety. We forget that our freedom to bring about events in this world is the revelation of God's action, and that this revelation is a charge imposed on our free will. We constantly seek God where he is not to be found, and for this reason unbelievers hold that believers themselves provide proof that God does not exist. But our belief in the existence of God should be a conviction, a divine certainty that our free, responsible and resolute behaviour in this world is secure in him who is Life. When scientific progress closes all the ways along which we thought we could come into contact with God somewhere in this world, in much the same fashion as we come into contact with the world itself, then all it is doing is to close off the approaches to a finite God, a non-God.

It is the paths which in any case lead into a blind alley which are thus being closed; and then, on the basis of an existence for which we bear no responsibility and in the midst of a limitless and problematical world, we suddenly realise that what we experience as deathly emptiness is only the breadth and depth of God's immeasurable inwardness. The fact that we can lose God in everything means equally that we can find him in everything too. The way to God leads straight through our ordinary everyday life and work. Our darkness, the chill darkness of our human loneliness in a world to which we – and we alone – must in our freedom give significance, is nothing but God's presence in unobtrusive activity. If we have the impression that this world and our human existence in it is in itself already sufficiently enlightened and needs no divine light, this merely comes from the fact that we, with our world, are living in God, whose approach casts no shadows. We stand in his light. Our being in this world is his light. The blind alley in which we live is itself the limitlessness of God, and therefore to search for ways in which we can find him *somewhere* will lead us away from him, since he is already with us. And yet again and again we feel this desire to seek him elsewhere, but when we try our hands grasp only the empty air and we hear behind us the loud laughter of the atheist. The air we grasp is empty because God is omnipresent.

Perhaps the prompt retreat of God each time human beings make a step forward in their history really shows us that it is only a pseudo-God which fades away, and not the living God under whose protection human beings have just made this very step forward. Again and again he walks one step further with us; and together, God and ourselves, we dislodge the pseudo-God.

Secularisation and Christian belief in God[5]

The twentieth century is experiencing the bankruptcy of all systems, including Christianity as a monological system. And so we are now all beginning a dialogue

---

[5]Selected from: Edward Schillebeeckx, 'Secularization and Christian Belief in God', *God the Future of Man*, trans. N. D. Smith, Collected Works of Edward Schillebeeckx vol. 3 (London: Bloomsbury T&T Clark, 2014), 40–2 [66–9].

with each other. The truth is not to be found in a system, but in a dialogue, in a sphere that is common to all of us, because we have become aware that no one has a monopoly of the truth and that the truth transcends all our thoughts and yet lives among us. It is experienced not in the soloist's song, but in the polyphonic chorus of all humanity. You may know the story of the four blind men who met an elephant. They touched the animal. The first touched its feet and said, 'This is a building with Doric columns.' The second touched its trunk and said, 'This is a snake.' The third felt its belly and said, 'This is the dried skin of a lion.' The last man felt its ears and said, 'This is a leaf of a palm tree.' They began to argue and finally to fight for their truth which left no room for the other person's truth. This is a parable of the history of the Western world, at least as far as its darker side is concerned.

The question that now poses itself is this: Is the present situation leading to the end of Christianity? Or to the end of what could be called 'conventional' or 'traditional' Christianity?[6] And, if the latter is the case, is there not a danger that authentic as well as inauthentic aspects of Christianity will be lost? The problem narrows down to the question of how we, as people of faith in a secularised world, can still speak of God. A quick survey would seem to indicate that the most obvious interpretation of the Bible in our secularised world would be an *atheistic* one. Unintentionally, radical theology has at least made clear once again that faith in God is not something that can simply be taken for granted, but rather something that demands essentially a fundamental *metanoia*, a conversion. In a so-called Christian world, we cheapened Christian faith into a condition of healthy human understanding of the obvious. Modern thought has thrust before our faces the inconceivable wonder of faith's interpretation of reality, based on a fundamental *metanoia* in relation to the evident worldly experience of reality. We are reminded of the words of Tertullian: 'Christians are made, not born.'[7]

Before we go more deeply into the question of speaking of and to God in a secularised world, we should be more precise about what we mean by the term secularisation, as the 'end-point' of the whole process. It seems to me that a distinction between two levels, that of the phenomenon itself and that of its interpretation, will help to clarify the problem. On the one hand, then, we must consider the process of secularisation as a socio-cultural and historical phenomenon, in which the world and human society are conceived within the rational sphere of understanding. This level is, I think, fundamental. Compared with the past history of Western civilisation, this implies that the world and human society have been withdrawn from the tutelage of the Church and religion. This results precisely in the positive secularity of the rational sphere of understanding, also including desacralisation.[8] Human beings are planning a future for the world, and themselves, which will be their own creation and, as a consequence of this, it cannot be denied that one of the sources which in fact nourished piety has disappeared. In the past, piety clearly drew much of its strength from humanity's impotence within the sphere of this world.

---

[6] W. van de Pol, *Het einde van het conventionele christendom*, Roermond and Maaseik (1966); see also the same author's *Op weg naar een verantwoord Godsgeloof*, Roermond and Maaseik (1967).
[7] Tertullian, *Apologeticum* 18, 4 (*Corp. Christ. Lat.* I, 118): 'Fiunt, non nascuntur christiani'.
[8] This secondary character especially (of an event with an essentially positive meaning) has been historically analyzed by H. Lübbe in his *Säkularisierung. Geschichte eines ideenpolitischen Begriffs*, Freiburg and Munich (1965). It should be borne in mind here that this secondary aspect may have acted as a stimulus to distinguish the essential aspect.

Secularisation is therefore not simply a cultural phenomenon – it at the same time also implies, when seen from the point of view of religion, the distinction between the 'God of faith' and the 'God of religion'. A *'religionless* faith' is therefore, seen from the socio-cultural and historical point of view, an implication of secularisation, in which by 'religion' (here intentionally distinguished from 'faith and divine worship') is meant religious experience at a cultural stage of human history when the rational sphere of understanding had not yet been explicitly discovered in its full extent, with the result that 'faith and divine worship' took over those *functions* of this world for which human ability was inadequate. 'Faith and divine worship' thus included a broad margin of 'religion'. Hence the process of secularisation seems to me to be fundamentally the discovery of the human rational sphere of understanding, a self-understanding which naturally takes place in history, with the result that secularisation is given with the growth of humanity *itself*. In this respect, the process of secularisation is clearly a positive achievement.

On the other hand, however – and here we come to an entirely different level, that of the *interpretation* of this cultural and sociological phenomenon – secularity is interpreted as atheism and is, furthermore, interpreted as such *because* many think that faith in God remains an obstacle to secularisation in the socio-cultural and historical sense. In other words, the idea of the 'God of religion' is historically so heavy with the customs of the past that for many people the end of the 'God of religion' is also the end of the 'living God', the God of faith. The cultural phenomenon – and secularity is this in the first place – is therefore often presented together with this atheistic interpretation. The whole – both the phenomenon and its interpretation – is thus called quite simply secularisation, and this word has consequently acquired an apparently inevitable ambiguity. It should therefore be made clear that this 'atheism' is an ideological interpretation and that the existing cultural phenomenon which is interpreted in this way can be made intelligible without recourse to this atheistic interpretation – that it can be integrated in a way that is meaningful from the Christian point of view.

The new culture as the point of departure for a new concept of God[9]

From the sociological point of view, 'secularisation' therefore refers to only one purifying partial aspect of a radical change in the experience of religion which takes place as soon as believers really want to take an active part in the present cultural transformation. It is permissible and correct to apply the statement 'God is dead' fully to this one partial aspect, which is indeed secularisation. But anyone who makes the mistake of applying the term secularisation to the total development will likewise – and quite wrongly – understand the term 'God is dead' in a universal sense. From the sociological standpoint they will have followed an unscientific course.

---

[9]Selected from: Edward Schillebeeckx, 'The New Image of God, Secularization and Man's Future on Earth', *God the Future of Man*, trans. N. D. Smith, Collected Works of Edward Schillebeeckx vol. 3 (London: Bloomsbury T&T Clark, 2014), 107–13 [178–87].

The objection can, of course, be raised here that sociology cannot provide an answer to the question of what is true. I should like to say first of all in reply that on precisely the basis of this sociologically unscientific designation of the whole process of social development as 'secularisation', the question of truth is already, in a considerable number of books and articles and in the spontaneous, unreflective conviction of many people, held to have been decided. Owing to this tendency to slip, quite unscientifically, from a sociological concept into a theological concept of secularisation, the sociologically unjustified use of the term 'total secularisation' has been increased twofold. This has been the cause of immense confusion – the question of truth is regarded as solved by the sociologically analysed facts! What has been forgotten in all this is, as Martin Marty has observed, that the statement 'God is dead', conceived as an all-embracing utterance, is the clearest *non-secular* affirmation to be found among the secularists – it is as unverifiable empirically, and as metaphysical, as the statement 'God exists'. And in any case, the sociologically analysed facts also show us that there are still religious people, not only as a survival from an earlier civilisation (in their factual experience of religion), but also as witnesses to a new experience of God.

In this chapter I do not intend to defend faith in God, on the basis of a new concept of God, apologetically against a secular interpretation of reality. I will simply take my own situation in the reality of the Christian faith as the point of departure and, on the basis of this, as a believer, clear up the problem of the cultural transformation in which believers are, of course, also involved. I will examine the possibilities of an experience of God that is really integrated into the new culture and of a new concept of God that really has its roots in this culture. Then I will investigate whether, on the basis of this, we can perhaps speak of the secularisation of faith in an entirely new, theologically justified sense. Finally, I will put the question as to whether this new concept of God has anything to tell us about the existential anxiety with which human beings, in their self-made world, is obsessed and which impels them to treacherous flight from the future whenever they come face to face with a future that they have to construct for themselves.

As far as experience of it and the forms in which it is expressed are concerned, religion is, of course, rooted in the culture in which it takes form. In our own period we are therefore seeing the emergence of a new concept of God which, as I have argued in earlier chapters, is nourished by the cultural soil of our historical situation, within whose structure the whole life of the believer is ordered. Hence the new concept of God is partly determined as to its explicit content and ideas by present-day culture – a culture not primarily directed towards the past but dynamically orientated towards the future. Philosophy, which is the reflective sifting of the spirit of the age, has therefore already begun to discuss the primacy of the future and a culture characterised by planning a better future for all humanity – the 'principle of hope'.[10]

Anyone who believes in God and is part of this culture will realise that their faith in God has lost its function as a substitute for human science. They will

---

[10] E. Bloch, *Das Prinzip Hoffnung*, Berlin (1954), the first attempt – in the light of Marxism – to conceptualise this feature of our culture.

consequently begin to reflect again and to change their ideas of God. They know that these are in part historically determined and therefore changeable, and they also know in advance that even the new ideas that they are seeking will not remain valid for ever. But, on the other hand, they know only too well that his idea of God cannot be relevant to their lives if it is entirely at odds with the pattern of their own society and that new ideas of God that are rooted in their own culture will make faith something capable of being experienced by, and of appealing to, modern people, with the result that the Church's confession of God will gain in credibility in the world of today. I should therefore like to give an initial outline of the new concept of God which is now taking shape and in which the believer is trying to express an idea of the living God of 'yesterday, today and tomorrow' that will be grasped and understood today. In doing this, I cannot, of course, go into all the implications of this concept of God.

In the older culture, orientated towards the past, whenever we thought or spoke of God's transcendence we used, almost automatically, to project God into the past. Eternity was rather like an unchangeable and petrified or eternalised 'past' – *'in the beginning* was God.' People knew very well that God's eternity embraced human beings' present, past and future and that God was not only 'the first', but also 'the last' and therefore the presence whose eternal present transcended our present. The older theology had wonderful things to say about this, things which have in no way lost their value. But in that older civilisation in which people's eyes were always turned towards the past, a powerful mutual attraction was felt between 'transcendence' and eternity on the one hand and an eternalised 'past' on the other. Now, however, in a culture which is resolutely turned towards the future as something that it means to make, what has in fact come about is that the flexible Christian concept of 'transcendence', which is open to more than one meaning, is also affected by this shift. 'Transcendence' thus tends to acquire a special affinity with what is called, in our temporality, 'future'. For, if divine transcendence really transcends and embraces, from within, the past, present and future, the believer will choose, as soon as they come to recognise the primacy of the future in temporality, to associate God's transcendence with the future, and they will be right in doing this. they will associate God with their future, and since this individual person lives within a community of persons, they will eventually also associate God with the future of humanity as a whole. This, then, is the real seed ground for the new image of God in our new culture – provided, of course, that the reality of true faith in the invisible God who is the source of the movement impelling to 'form a concept' of God in the light of his worldly experience has been accepted.

In such a cultural framework, the God of those who believe in him will obviously reveal himself as the 'One who is to come', the God who is *our* future. This, of course, brings about a radical change – the God whom we formerly, in the light of an earlier view of humanity and the world, called the 'wholly Other' now manifests himself as the 'wholly New', the One who is *our future,* who creates the future of humanity anew. He shows himself as the God who gives us in Jesus Christ the possibility of making the future – that is, of making everything new and transcending our sinful past and that of all people. The new culture thus becomes the point of departure for the surprising rediscovery of the fact that the God of the promise again gives us the task of setting out towards the promised land, a land that we ourselves, trusting in the promise, must reclaim and cultivate, as Israel did in the past.[11]

This 'new', eschatological concept of God is already radically changing 'theological treatises', and at an even deeper level the whole of Christian life is also changing. In answer to the contemporary question about the legitimacy of Christianity and to the increasingly urgent question about the 'verification principle' of the Christian faith that is asked by the linguistic analysts (and, faced with this question, a purely theoretical theology often seems to be completely impotent), all that we Christians can say, in the light of our faith in God as our future, is that faith is not based on what is empirically and objectively verifiable, but comes under the category of human existential possibility. For this reason, the verification principle of the Christian faith and its eschatological hope can only be stated *indirectly* – it is to be found in the fact that Christians, as the 'community of those who hope', show in practice in their lives that their hope is *capable* of changing the world now and of making our history a real history of salvation which brings well-being to all people, instead of a history without glory, opposed to salvation. A faith in God as the One who is to come, as the future of the individual person and the community of persons, must show its effectiveness in and to this world if it is to avoid being dismissed as incredible because of the pre-understanding of our contemporaries. Faith which has as its content the divine promise of an ultimate eschatological fulfilment for everyone and in every moment of our lives proclaims God as the One who is to come – and, what is more, as the One who is to come in the very history that he nonetheless transcends – has to make this believed promise come true in history and has to do this precisely by making this history *new*. Believers themselves will have to show, in their total commitment to life, where the richest springs are that can overcome the evil that deprives human beings of their joy and improve the world by really caring for others. In their total commitment, they will have to show who they are who have the power to protect the constantly threatened dignity of humanity and to bring salvation here and now. At this level, faith in God as the future for human beings and humanity will have to prove itself true.

---

[11]This trend is already discernible in many different theological works, although the theme in these is still, for the time being, worked out in very divergent ways. Among the best known of these works are: J. Moltmann, *Theologie der Hoffnung*, Munich (1965); G. Sauter, *Zukunft und Verheissung*, Zürich and Stuttgart (1965); J.-B. Metz, 'Nachwort', in *Der Dialog* (R. Garaudy, K. Rahner and J.-B. Metz), Reinbek (1966), pp. 119–38; *ibid.*, 'The Church and the World', in *The Word in History, St. Xavier Symposium*, New York (1966), pp. 69–85. According to the prospectus, there is to be an article by K. Rahner on 'Zur Theologie der Hoffnung', in connection with the dialogue between Marxists and Christians, in the new journal, *Internationale Dialog Zeitschrift*, the first number of which is to be published in 1968. H. Fries has written a number of sympathetic, but critical marginal comments, '*Spero ut intelligam*. Bemerkungen zu einer Theologie der Hoffnung', in *Wahrheit und Verkündigung* (M. Schmaus zum 70. Geburtstag), Paderborn (1967), pp. 353–75. What is more, the whole of W. Pannenberg's work can be interpreted in this light. See especially 'Der Gott der Hoffnung', *Grundfragen systematischer Theologie*, Göttingen (1967), pp. 387–98, and his contributions to *Theology as History* (New Frontiers in Theology, III), New York, Evanston and London (1967). Harvey Cox, who, in *The Secular City*, showed a strong inclination to join the 'death of God' theologians, has, in his latest book, clearly found his way towards a Christian 'theology of hope'. See *On Not Leaving It to the Snake*, New York (1967), and especially the first chapter, 'The Death of God and the Future of Theology', pp. 3–13. See also *Diskussion über die Theologie der Hoffnung*, edited by W.-D. Marsch, Munich (1968).

Of course, this new concept of God implies a criticism of the earlier idea of God and of the concrete practice of Christian life that resulted from this idea of God. Anyone whose entire being is, culturally and religiously, orientated towards the past inevitably runs the risk of leaving the world as it is, of interpreting it, but not changing it – this was Karl Marx's legitimate criticism of the religion of his time. This attitude also runs the risk of by-passing the terrestrial future and taking hold of the post-terrestrial directly. In our new culture, however, Christian faith in a post-terrestrial future can only be seen to be true if this eschatological hope shows itself capable of bringing humanity a better future here and now. Who could believe in a God who will make everything new 'later' if it is in no way apparent from the activity of those who hope in the One who is to come that he is already beginning to make everything new *now* – if in fact it is not apparent that this eschatological hope is able *now* to change the course of history for the better? Christian commitment to the world will therefore be the exegesis or hermeneutics of the new concept of God, in which God is really shown to be the 'wholly New One'. It will have to be clear from the concrete practice of Christian life that God *de facto* manifests himself as the one whose power can bring about the new future. It is only from the vantage-point of this exegesis of the new concept of God in and through total Christian commitment to life that we shall, in the second place, be able to reconsider the past so as to interpret or reinterpret it. In so doing, we shall understand how the earlier Christian experience of God was, in an older civilisation, justified, but is nonetheless subject to the criticism of the biblical 'God of promise' whom we have been permitted to rediscover as a result of the cultural change of today. The *identity* of the new concept of God with the original Christian message will have to come indirectly to light in the activity of Christians themselves. If a reinterpretation of the Christian message produces an activity in which its identity with the gospel cannot be discovered, this interpretation cannot be a Christian interpretation. It will therefore be apparent that there is a special kind of *understanding* which is appropriate to statements about faith – such statements, after all, have nothing to do with ideology.[12] Hermeneutics consisting of the very practice of Christian life are therefore the *basis* for the concrete exegesis of ancient, biblical or magisterial texts. The distinctive contribution that eschatological hope can make to truly human progress in the world for the salvation of all people itself interprets the dogma of the 'kingdom of God', in which 'neither shall there be mourning nor crying nor pain any more' (Rev 21.4). 'According to his promise we wait for new heavens and a new earth in which righteousness dwells' (2 Pet 3.13). This goal of Christian hope seems to have a positive content. It is certainly

---

[12] It may be felt that a Modernist influence can be detected here, but this is not so. In the first place, I have insufficient knowledge of the Modernist movement to have experienced its influence directly. I do, however, know enough about it to be able to say that the 'Modernists' were reacting against a view which regarded faith exclusively as a 'believing to be true' and that they consequently emphasised the existential aspect of faith. For this reason, they were wary of a *theoretical* orthodoxy 'viewed in itself' and regarded orthodox dogma more or less exclusively as a norm for the practical Christian attitude to life. I dissociate myself from this interpretation because it took into account only one aspect of faith and denied other aspects. The decree *Lamentabili* rightly dissociated itself from one clear tendency in Modernism, that is, that a dogma had, according to these thinkers, a purely pragmatic significance in orientating the activity of Christians. This is, however, obviously not the intention of my argument.

positive in its suggestive power, but on closer inspection it is first and foremost a powerful 'symbol that makes us think', a call to us to transcend what *we* have made – war, injustice, the absence of peace, the absence of love. We have, however, also been promised, in an example or prototype, that all this will pass away – the historical act of Jesus Christ and God's setting of his seal on this life by what we, in faith, call 'resurrection'. This reality is the most powerful religious symbol of what is truly possible as the future, the future which has *de facto* already commenced in Jesus as the Christ

In the Bible, the expression 'to *do* the truth' is used for the Christian attitude described. This gives emphasis to a concept of truth clearly different from the western idea of truth that was taken over from Hellenism, an idea which contains a fatal division because of the distinction that it makes, in spite of all the careful shades of meaning with which it is used, between theoretical and practical reason. It is certainly not necessary to accept all the implications of American pragmatism for one to be convinced of the truth of what I often heard at table in the United States – 'The proof of the pudding is in the eating.' One has, however, to be on one's guard against a short-circuit that often occurs here in Christian thought. Because God has promised us a future of salvation in grace *despite* our sinful history, it is easy for us to believe that this future in grace falls vertically into the terrestrial event, which would otherwise simply continue to take place as history without salvation. But eschatological hope implies faith that the Christian, by God's justification, is responsible for the terrestrial event itself becoming a history of salvation. In and through his attitude of faith, then, the Christian is already seeking to overcome all that is opposed to salvation in this world, to resist everything that has made and is still making our history a history without salvation and thus to make salvation triumph more and more. Just as our sinful freedom makes our human history into a history without salvation, so too will God transform this history without salvation into a saving event *in and through* our freedom into which we have been liberated in faith. The believer not only interprets history – he above all *changes* it. Anyone who disputes this is clearly forgetting that human freedom is the pivot of the historical event – via human freedom, grace is thus able to change history itself. This was the reason why I believed that it was possible to say that the credibility of the Christian promise must be *indirectly* apparent in the practice of Christian life. In our new culture, then, a theological treatise about God will be the culmination and completion of an exegesis which consists in the practice of Christian life. If this Christian practice is absent, the Christian faith will not be credible to modern people, who is sick of ideology, and is always ready to express the irrefutable reproach, 'Words, words, words'.

The new concept of God – that is, faith in the One who is to come, in the 'wholly New One' who provides *us* here and now with the possibility of making human events into a history of salvation through an inward recreation which makes us 'new creatures' dead to sin, thus radically transforms our commitment to make a world more worthy of humanity, but at the same time it reduces to only relative value every result which has so far been achieved. The believer, who knows of the eschatological fulfilment promised to humanity and to human history, will be unable to recognise in anything that has already been accomplished 'a new heaven and a new earth'. Unlike the Marxist, for example, he will not even venture to give a positive name to the ultimate fulfilment that is to come. The Christian leaves the future much more open than the Marxist: in his view, the Marxist tends to close the possibilities prematurely. For the Christian, it is an ideological misconception to call one concrete stage in the development of human history the ultimate point.

It is of course, possible to raise the following objection to what I have said – that it gives rise to a new identification which runs parallel with what has been objected to in the older experience of faith; in other words, an identification between faith in God and the new culture. In reply to this, I should like to say that no such identification has been made – all that I have done is to describe how faith must *function* in the new culture. My purpose in this has been to prevent anyone who is wholeheartedly taking part in the new culture from letting faith remain an attitude that cannot be realised, something that alienates him from the world because it forces him to live in two worlds, the world of science and technology, in which he carries out his secular task, and a world of fantasy which he has to enter in his faith. Objections such as the one expressed above give the impression that the questioner is of the opinion that the Christian faith must be made perfectly clear once and for all. I am unable to agree with this claim. I feel bound to say only this – that we, as Christians, can only expect to settle the problems of faith within our own society. Later generations will have to concern themselves with their own period, and we cannot anticipate their problems. It is not possible to provide a justification of the Christian faith that will be valid for all time, but it is possible to do so for the period in which we are living. The Christian authenticity of our present culture differs from that of other cultures, whether those which have become obsolete or those which may perhaps take form later on. Everyone must achieve Christian authenticity within the form of his own culture.

Selected literature

- God in Dry Dock; Selected from: Edward Schillebeeckx, 'God in Dry Dock', *God and Man*, trans. Edward Fitzgerald and Peter Tomlinson, Theological Soundings (New York: Sheed and Ward, 1969), 3–10.
- Secularization and Christian Belief in God; Selected from: Edward Schillebeeckx, 'Secularization and Christian Belief in God', *God the Future of Man*, trans. N. D. Smith, Collected Works of Edward Schillebeeckx vol. 3 (London: Bloomsbury T&T Clark, 2014), 40–2 [66–9].
- The New Culture as the Point of Departure for a New Concept of God; Selected from: Edward Schillebeeckx, 'The New Image of God, Secularization and Man's Future on Earth', *God the Future of Man*, trans. N. D. Smith, Collected Works of Edward Schillebeeckx vol. 3 (London: Bloomsbury T&T Clark, 2014), 107–13 [178–87].

22

Political and Liberation Theology

The influence of Third World theology on Western theology[1]

For the first time in history Western theology, which until a few decades ago considered itself universal, has come to realise that it has always been regional. This insight dawned as a result of various theologies in the Third World, notably Latin American liberation theology, which, although originally inspired by certain trends in central and north European theology, has matured and now goes its own independent way.

If I were to look into the heart of my friend and colleague J.-B. Metz, I believe I would find there the following wish: if only I had called my theology liberation theology all those years ago instead of political theology (however apposite), a term that has led to all sorts of (unintended and unwanted) confusions and misconceptions. On the other hand the term 'liberation theology' has given rise to misconceptions of its own. Besides, to my mind liberation theology and 'salvific theology' (*heilstheologie*), a term that I have been using ever since 1945) are synonymous. Theologically liberation and salvation have both mystico-theologal and socio-political significance. The problem centres on what we Christians would and may call liberation and salvation in the full sense of both words: mystico-theologal, socio-political, individual-corporeal, psychosomatic and ecological. Theology serves no purpose if it is not liberating. In this paper I raise some points that Western theologians should keep in mind if their theology is to be truly liberating.

For some years now Western theology, certainly as regards its themes, has been unmistakably influenced by the many forms of liberation theology. After a period in which only a handful of Western theologians took any interest in them, diverse forms of liberation pastoral ministry and theology, which originated mainly, albeit not exclusively, in Latin America as a result of Christian intellectuals' solidarity with spontaneously burgeoning basic communities of paupers, are currently very much in

---

[1] Selected from: Edward Schillebeeckx, 'Liberating Theology: Reflection on J.-B. Metz's Political Theology', *Essays: Ongoing Theological Quests*, Collected Works of Edward Schillebeeckx vol. 11 (London: Bloomsbury T&T Clark, 2014), 69–72.

the limelight among a broad spectrum of Western (European and North American) intellectuals. They have introduced a new, emotional polarisation into the discussion, in which their earlier political stances are recognisable. At the same time, inasmuch as Western theologians are in sympathy with liberation theology, they often have difficulty translating it analogously into their own Western situation. Yet in recent years J.-B. Metz for one has undeniably incorporated themes from Latin American liberation theology into his political theology project.

When listening to Latin American liberation theologians Western theologians may be wise to take note of Asian and African liberation theology as well. In 1976 Third World theologians took the initiative in Dar es Salaam, Tanzania in forming the Ecumenical Association of Third World Theologians' (EATWOT); the conference proceedings are regularly published by the North American Orbis Press, and the quarterly journal, *Voices from the Third World*, regularly furnishes information. At the fifth EATWOT conference in New Delhi (1981) G. Gutierrez was able to observe that for the first time in centuries a new kind of theological reflection has arisen outside the major European theological centres and their North American counterparts – a fact which still evokes surprise, even scepticism and animosity, or paternalistic condescension.[2] The first radical consequence of these conferences was growing awareness of the existence of a distinct Third World theology, which led some scholars to adopt an increasingly vehement stance against Western theology – after all, it was that of their erstwhile conquerors and exploiters.

For Latin American liberation theology, too, these conferences had significant consequences. Asians and Africans reproached the Latin Americans for using a typically Western product, the Marxist method, to analyse society, which, they claimed, reduced race and gender, culture and religion to essentially politico-economic factors. And indeed Latin American theologians disregarded the cultural role of women and ignored cultural and religious identity in their analyses of their society. The pioneer of Black Theology, James Cone, opposed the interpretation of the race issue in terms of Western categories of class analysis: it went far beyond that. In Asia (especially on the part of D.S. Amalorpavadass and A. Pieris from Sri Lanka) there was an outcry against the reduction of problems of exploitation to purely politico-economic domination.

Since then a powerful feminist movement has sprung up, especially in Central America. As far back as the second EATWOT conference in Accra (Ghana) in 1974 considerable attention was devoted to sexism, which permeated all culture, religion and theology in Africa, while the third conference (Sri Lanka, 1979) reproached Latin American liberation theology for allowing insufficient scope for culture and religion in society and focusing too exclusively on politico-economic dependence. Indian theologians put the accent on acquisitiveness and the need to oppose the power of money – Mammon.

The conclusion of the conferences thus far is clear: what has crystallised in the minds of Third World theologians is a sense that they represent a historical force that can subject the Western dominated 'international world system' to radical

---

[2] See the report of the EATWOT conference in New Delhi, 1981: *Irruption of the Third World*, ed. V. Fabella/S. Torres, Maryknoll, New York, 1983, 227.

criticism. EATWOT's principal criticism of Latin America was that (in contrast to the non-constructive, sometimes naïve criticism of the Roman Curia) its theologians were blind to the fact that the nature and method of Marxist class analysis were too narrowly Western for a proper analysis of the peculiar problems of the Third World; after all, they argued, the method was itself determined by Western culture and the situation of the emergent modern bourgeoisie. The Western imperialist instinct may have penetrated our scientific and epistemological notions to the core. Western scientific methods with their control over objects are not as value-free as they purport to be. They tend to entail (albeit often implicitly) a philosophy that is not altogether innocuous. We need not agree in every respect with Kurt Hübner's criticism of scientific reason,[3] but (like others) he rightly exposes the limitations of the scholarly approach. This criticism was particularly forcefully expressed at the EATWOT conference in Sao Paolo in 1980. But on one point there was consensus: the new movement was carried by people who were both exploited and religious, and who wanted to become subjects of liberating history.

To my mind the international, even intercontinental slant of EATWOT, in which diverse cultures and religions, including non-Western ones, converge, has been to the benefit of Latin American liberation theology; for some years now it has been revising some of its statements. EATWOT's dealings with invited Western theologians, on the other hand, have been somewhat strained, as evidenced by the Geneva conference.[4] Compared to the situation in the Third World, the West remains both exploitive and secularised, as opposed to exploited, religious people elsewhere! The difference is that all forms of Western liberation theology, theology of hope or political theology are concocted in an academic context; they are not supported by a concrete liberation movement or praxis, even though they do crystallise in the thinking of many progressive people and thus acquire a backing of their own. Yet they differ quite essentially from what is happening in Third World theology.

It has often been said that a Western liberation theology would have to be very different from that in, for instance, Latin America. While it contains a germ of truth, it conceals the fact that what happens on the East-West axis is to a considerable extent at the root of Third World suffering and protest. We cannot construct a Western liberation theology unless we Westerners acknowledge that our social structures necessitate Latin American liberation theology! In that sense we are part of their problem and must first listen to them before we can meaningfully speak to them in terms of our own, often academic traditions. Despite everything the West is not the incarnation of all evil. But considering the suffering that Western people have inflicted on virtually all cultures and the planet, we can only converse with Third

---

[3] K. Hübner, *Kritik der wissenschaftlichen Vernunft*, Freiburg/München, 1978; also A. Wellmer, *Zur Dialektik von Moderne und Postmoderne*, Frankfurt, 1985.
[4] J. van Nieuwenhove, 'Derde Wereld en de God van leven', in: *Tijdschrift voor theologie* 23 (1983), 253–69; also: 'De vele contexten in de Derde Wereld', in: *Tijdschrift voor theologie* 27 (1987), 21–36; Th. Witvliet, *Een plaats onder de zon: Bevrijdingstheologie in de Derde Wereld*, Baarn, 1984; E. Schillebeeckx, 'Theologie als bevrijdingskunde: Enkele noodzakelijke beschouwingen vooraf', in: *Tijdschrift voor theologie* 24 (1984), 388–402. Also see: E. Borgman, 'Bevrijdingstheologie als uitdaging aan de Westerse theologie', in: *Tijdschrift voor theologie* 27 (1987), 55–73, en: 'Theologie tussen universiteit en emancipatie: De weg van Edward Schillebeeckx', in: *Tijdschrift voor theologie* 26 (1986), 240–58.

World theologians penitently and humbly, even when we, maybe correctly, spot weaknesses in their theology.

In these circumstances, should a 'Western liberation theology' try to find its own way? Should the roles not rather be reversed so it forms part of Third World theology that looks at history 'from below', whereas we have been raised in the history of the powerful and the overlords? Apart from feminist theology, which is now being transplanted from the North American and North European West to the Third World, typically Western forms of liberation theology that are emerging – all aimed at liberating groups from social discrimination, such as homosexuals, minority groups, migrant labourers and the like – however imperative and crucial, are only comprehensible in the socio-historical context of affluent states. To Third World countries such theology remains a luxury for the time being. Food, clothing, housing and other primary needs may be material (materialistic, if you will) to the poor in the Third World; to affluent Westerners material poverty is a spiritual problem. That makes it even more apparent how inextricably a projected Western liberation theology is tied up with Third World theology, forms of liberation theology, Black Theology and feminist theology. Third World theology in particular should be seen as symptomatic of the flipside of Western history and what Europe has done to 'the world'. That is not sick self-pity but recorded fact.

Theological hermeneutics of radical contrast experiences[5]

I now want to radicalise what I have previously called important human experiences, to wit negative contrast experiences. They are foundational, and I therefore see them as pre-religious, basic experience – hence accessible to all people – vetoing the world as it is. It has nothing to do with dualism or opposition between a good and a bad world in the Hellenistic sense (even if we may need to reconsider that dualism in light of more profound human experiences at that time). At all events, we have to deal with this world of ours, which is the source of our troubles. What we experience as reality, what we see and hear about daily on TV and other mass media is patently *not* 'in order'; something is seriously amiss. Reality is full of contradictions. So human experience of suffering, evil and misfortune is the basis and source of a radical 'no' that people say to the actuality of their being-in-the-world. Such experience is also more definite, more manifest than anything that philosophy and science can offer us by way of verifiable or falsifiable 'knowledge'. Indignation (not even a scientific term) appears to be a fundamental experience of life in this world. Our world, unless we pass through it with our eyes shut, is intent only on consumerism, pleasure and oblivion... or power.

---

[5]Selected from: Edward Schillebeeckx, 'Liberating Theology: Reflection on J.-B. Metz's Political Theology', *Essays: Ongoing Theological Quests*, Collected Works of Edward Schillebeeckx vol. 11 (London: Bloomsbury T&T Clark, 2014), 78–80.

Undoubtedly there is also great beauty and goodness, much that is enjoyable in this world. In fact, there seems to be more joy and song among the oppressed than among the oppressors. But all these fragments of goodness, beauty and meaning are constantly being contradicted and crushed by evil and hatred, by manifest and muted suffering, by abuses of power and terrorism. This contradiction, so typical of our world, seems to render evil and good mutually 'harmless'. That is how cynics see it. To non-cynics this attitude is anything but a sign of decadence, which no longer finds anything worth living or dying for. For all their wretchedness people are too proud to put evil on a par with good. Meanwhile our world continues to be a baffling mix of good and evil, sense and nonsense. History does not tell us which element in the mix will gain the upper hand, not even whether, seen from the angle of the actual events, a last word will ever be spoken. As history it may also miscarry.

Still, a positive element is that indomitable human indignation, the second element of this foundational experience. It has an ethical dimension, maybe even more than that. (Personally I discern in it what was known in Catholic religious tradition as *theologia naturalis*, although the context at that time was differently oriented.) This refusal to acquiesce in the existing situation offers an illuminating perspective. It reveals openness to a different situation that does merit an affirmative 'yes'. It could be called consensus with 'the unknown', whose substance can never be positively determined: a new and better world which so far has never actually existed. To put it yet differently: simply positing the possibility of making our world a better place, openness to a nobler, unknown reality.

Thus people's fundamental veto of evil reveals an unspecified, hence open 'yes', as unshakable as the human 'no' – actually even more cogent, because an open 'yes' justifies and permits rebellion. Besides, from time to time there are experiences, fragmentary yet real, of meaning and happiness, be it on a limited or a grand scale, that revitalise the open 'yes', affirming it and keeping it alive. In such experience believers and agnostics find each other. It is also a ready basis for solidarity of everyone with everybody else and for a joint commitment to a better world with a human face.

Solid hope transcending all contexts

Believers in God give the single, two-sided foundational experience religious content. That puts the open 'yes' in sharper, more focused relief. Its origin is not so much – at least not directly – the transcendence of 'the divine' (the ineffable, as it were anonymous, inexpressible) but rather (at least for Christians) the recognisably human face of that transcendence that appeared among us in the human person Jesus, confessed as Christ the Son of God. Thus to Christians humanity's perpetual grumbling turns into solidly based hope. In the innermost depths of reality lurks a desire for mercy, compassion... in which believers hear the name of God. That is the Christian story.

To Christians this hermeneutics of negative contrast experiences has to do with the confession of all churches that God is the one who 'created heaven and earth' and, in its original state, found it 'good', as well as with the Christian belief in 'original sin' that tarnished creation, and in Jesus' life and death 'for the sins of the world', which kindled new hope in our blemished world. On that basis we can build a solid theology of liberation and also test it – at least in the real-life context of the world we live in and of the religious community here and now.

Theology is always 'in context'. Present-day theology owes this recently acquired insight to the manifold forms of liberation theology in non-Western countries. Nonetheless contextual Christian theology wants to say something that is not tied to just one context but is accessible to many – indeed, all – human contexts, even if that reality, which is not humanly conceived but is raised for discussion as a result of 'conversion experiences', transcends all contexts, although we can only find words for it in some historically specific context, never outside it. Regional forms of Christian theology are never purely regional. After all, they concern our – always specifically located – humanity in relation to our fellow humans in a world that ultimately is 'God's world'. All regional theologies want to proclaim the gospel in a concrete situation, especially in people's personal lives.[6] That calls for all sorts of socio-analytical, hermeneutic and practical interpretations (not to be analysed here).

Christian faith and politics[7]

The essence of all criticism of religion, no matter what form it takes, is really that religion proclaims the human inability to achieve his own liberation and in the face of that promises that God will bring salvation, while religion in fact is said only to confirm humans' inability to achieve their own salvation. In modern circumstances, Christians have often come to use this criticism for their own ends, by suddenly reinterpreting the Christian religion. They point to the stimulus it provides towards political emancipation and its relevance for liberation, although the past history of this religion can only show somewhat shoddy credentials (apart from the 'heretical' arguments, which were often suppressed).

First of all, we have to concede that it is a characteristic of the structure of the development of Christian faith that believers begin to catch a glimpse of significant new dimensions to their own Christian tradition, precisely as a result of the introduction of new stimuli from outside, stimuli which were in fact alien to their religion. At an earlier stage, these insights may have been suppressed or simply ignored because of the prevailing social system. The message of Jesus calls for freedom and love for each and every individual, without any exclusiveness. This can hardly be questioned historically. But the consequences of this message by no means revealed themselves automatically and all at once, but only gradually, in the ongoing history of developing human consciousness. Christian, critical solidarity with the emancipatory history of freedom[8] and a coalition of theology with critical

---

[6] See my farewell lecture, inserted in this volume (chapter 3): 'Theological interpretation of faith', expanded in: *Church: The Human Story of God* (Volume 10 in these *Collected Works*), 63–86 [65–88].
[7] Selected from: Edward Schillebeeckx, *Christ: The Christian Experience in the Modern World*, Collected Works of Edward Schillebeeckx vol. 7 (London: Bloomsbury T&T Clark, 2014), 770–3 [773–6].
[8] This is a basic argument of J.-B Metz, above all in J.-B. Metz, J. Moltmann, W. Oelmüller, *Kirche im Prozess der Aufklärung*, Munich 1970, 58–73.

social theories about humanity[9] can therefore become here and now a necessary demand of historically situated *caritas* or Christian love and theology – the need to create new traditions. But in that case we must investigate how far Christianity and theology here develop their *own* religious and critical force, and do not just repeat what human movements and critical theories have said already. Do they simply *take over* views which are alien to Christianity, though justified in Christian terms, or do they become aware of their own original Christian impulse precisely as a result of these views (and there is no disgrace in that)? We must raise the critical question whether contemporary theologies of hope, emancipation and liberation, all with Jesus Christ as their fundamental basis, do not again perform the function of stop-gaps – not in the old way, but with an eye for the on-going malfunctions of our particular personal, interpersonal and socio-political action. In other words, whether these modern Christian attempts might not represent a new *sacralisation*, this time no longer of the *status quo*, but of the political demand for *change* – and even revolutionary change.

However, the key question is whether believers and non-believers do not in fact *do the same thing*, namely renew the world. Perhaps the believer is simply giving another *interpretation* of this common action which *qua* interpretation has no consequences for what is done. For religion should not of itself make any contribution of its own to a practice which is indifferent to *religious* or *non-religious* interpretations. It follows from this that the claim of a religion to perform a unique and irreducible service for the world becomes problematical and seriously ambiguous to the degree that this service is understood in terms of *non-religious* goals. And vice versa, the claim of religion to offer its *own* interpretation of the world becomes just as problematical and seriously ambiguous to the degree that this interpretation remains irrelevant for *action*. Thus when we have a course of action which is *common to* believers and non-believers, and only with different theoretical interpretations of the world, we have mistaken the particular critical impulse which issues from the religious consciousness. For religion is not an interpretation of the world which remains alien to practice, any more than it is a practice without any reference to a particular interpretation of humanity and the world. Therefore in reality we often have the following experience. To begin with, people's inspiration provided by the gospel stimulates them towards solidarity with liberation movements (which are in fact socialist). In a second phase, people see more accurately the particular rationality of this emancipation. In a third phase, they recognise the priority of emancipation in their own rationality over the proclamation of the gospel; and in a last, fourth phase all this often ends up with the rejection of orientation on and inspiration from the gospel, as being irrelevant to liberation movements. This development, which can in fact often be noted,[10] indicates that – although it is in fact possible to misuse religion, for anything at all – religion is *not usable* by nature, for anything at all. God cannot be used as a means for human ends, any more than humanity can be used as a means for divine ends. Religion and humanity transcend the category of the usable and the functional – which does not prevent religion in this respect being 'highly

---

[9]See A. G. Geyer, H. N. Janowski, A. Schmidt, *Theologie und Soziologie*, Stuttgart 1970.
[10]Thus G. Girardi (I can no longer find the exact reference).

functional' for the advancement of human dignity generally. For religions are not inner dispositions; they *bring salvation*. They bring *salvation for people*. Only if we recognise the particular critical and hermeneutical force and impulse of religion as religion, can religion (as inner fullness, implication and consequence) show a service to the world which is both *specifically religious* and *practically effective* in the world (in political practice as well). If specifically religious interpretation-and-criticism is lost sight of, in other words, if religion is made to serve non-religious ends, then *either* religious means are offered as means for non-religious ends and in fact religion becomes magic, *or* religion is merely forced into the role of being a teacher and instructor in morality.[11] (At an earlier stage, this morality was seen primarily as individual ethics, but now it is the macro-ethics of political and social society.) In other words, if religion enters the service of projects imposed *from outside,* say by economic, social or political needs, it degenerates into magic, or it is undermined and reduced to mere ethics (though here it must remember that its specifically religious interest can be maintained only *within* the five *other* anthropological constants which were analysed earlier). True, religion implies an ethically good attitude, but it cannot be reduced to ethics. The only difference from the earlier position would then be that the alien service of religion to the world formerly showed a right-wing and reactionary tendency, whereas now it follows a left-wing and revolutionary course. In both cases, then, we have forms and manifestations of an out-dated 'Constantinian theology'. In that case, the appeal to Christian faith is often to serve the ends of a right-wing or left-wing policy, or to benefit a fluctuating, faceless party of the centre, merely an alibi for the lack of *rational arguments*. Therefore theology must stress the *specifically religious* form of the criticism of humanity and society; religion can do a service to the world in this respect if theologians do not just repeat and duplicate what critical sociologists have already said (perhaps rightly), but draw on *an experience of the holy*. Religions seek to bear witness to the holy, to God; it is there that they find the legitimation for their language and action. In their *service to God,* religions are also a *service to people*. If not, what we have is no more than a mere idealistic duplication.[12] For when we speak of religious consciousness (and its special critical force), we are speaking of a particular form of human consciousness. And the question then is, 'What is the *religious* element in this consciousness?' In other words, we then ask what knowledge and what reality so determine our consciousness that it becomes a religious consciousness. And at the same time, that means: how are we to judge the reality of humanity and the world in the light of the religious consciousness? Religion is concerned not only with God, but also with the *totality,* the support and hope of which is God.

---

[11] See R. Schaeffler, *Religion und kritisches Bewusstsein*, 155–8.
[12] In this connection one particular group of young theologians (see M. Xhauflaire and K. Derksen, *Les deux visages de la théologie de la sécularisation*, Tournai 1970) have rightly pointed to the idealism of this duplication: M. Xhauflaire, *Feuerbach et la théologie de la sécularization*, Paris 1970; F. van den Oudenrijn, *Kritische Theologie als Kritik der Theologie*, Munich 1972; L. Dullaart, *Kirche und Ekklesiologie*, Munich 1975; and earlier journals like *Tegenspraak* (Holland), *Kritischer Katholizismus* (Germany) and still existing ones like *Lettre* (France), *Imprimatur* and *Neue Stimmen* (Germany), etc.

Christian faith and political pluralism[13]

The Second Vatican Council recognised the legitimacy of a political pluralism among Christians. In fact this was progress in comparison with the monolithic or uniform politics which had previously been imposed upon Christians. On the other hand, it carried with it the danger of political liberalism, as though Christians could think that any political option whatsoever was commensurate with Christian faith. However, it follows from Christian faith that certain political options (whether of the right wing or the left) can in fact be at odds with the gospel and that – if the general insight into the political relevance of faith is still to retain a real meaning – a *minimal consensus* in the *political* sphere is naturally a consequence of common belief in the gospel, which is good news of *liberation* for *all* (though this consensus of faith cannot form the basis for a confessional party unless it cannot be made effective in the specific sphere of politics in any other way). However, this free consensus cannot be enforced unilaterally from above and has to be fought for by a common effort. In the light of the gospel, therefore, through their specific political choice – even if this is through neutrality – Christians may not be party to a political system in which structural or personal compulsion sacrifices the weaker, and injustice becomes a permanent state. The Second Vatican Council clearly pointed in this direction in the Pastoral Constitution *Gaudium et spes* (§§25–31; 34, 35). Christianity is essentially concerned with the progressive liberation of all people. In the light of the gospel, Christians must be partisans and advocates of the poor, those without rights, those who have no representatives anywhere. A political party which gives concrete expression to this aim in its programme will therefore be one of the first possible choices for Christians. The gospel summons Christians to show solidarity with the historical process of human liberation; therefore they will give their vote to political parties which want to remove any discrimination and slavery, any personal or institutional exploitation from the world by means of a political programme for the future which responds to the situation without at the same time making people less than themselves. True, these comments are very general, but they do provide a first orientation.

Christians who take seriously the prophetic message of the gospel and its call for liberation can, however, discover some elements in particular parties which call themselves progressive that they cannot recognise as progressive. Or they can decide on other ways and means within the same progressive programme. For there can be different alternatives, and because of the nature of his Christian belief, the Christian can show a preference in deciding between alternatives (e.g. violence or non-violence). Finally, there is the view of humanity, the image of humanity, the answer to the question: 'For what kind of humanity am I deciding in the last resort?', 'What conception do people have of a good life?' Explicitly or implicitly, but unavoidably, the answer to this question takes shape in the specific social context of the society which people make for themselves. Thus a particular view of humanity can be a fundamental reason why Christians do not join a particular party which calls itself

---

[13]Selected from: Edward Schillebeeckx, *Christ: The Christian Experience in the Modern World*, Collected Works of Edward Schillebeeckx vol. 7 (London: Bloomsbury T&T Clark, 2014), 781–6 [784–9].

progressive. For a conscious or unconscious view of humanity always underlies the particular organisation or articulation of a society and all its institutions, at any time. By analysing a particular society, one can in fact discover the image of humanity which serves as its model, and thus can unmask the limitations and constrictions of given social forms and institutions. This analytical and interpretative unveiling of an image of humanity which initially, at any rate, is often unconscious, and which underlies the divisions of wider social contexts, is even a necessary presupposition if we are to be able to transcend the limitations and constrictions of an established order with a view to a better future.

Now the picture of humanity which in fact exists, whether consciously or unconsciously, in a particular party-political programme for a future and in this sense progressive society can in fact seem to a progressive Christian to be no more than a torso, on which he does not really want to build a coming society. It is evident here that, after the analysis of social structures, fundamental differences can appear in their *interpretation* (as a basis for going beyond the *status quo* towards a better future). Anthropological conceptions and profiles of people play an essential role here. One example may be enough. For the Christian, a human being is not only a person, but is also essentially social; not only essentially social, but also an unassailable person. Therefore for a human being and believer, both individualism and liberalism, and also totalitarianism, are unacceptable politically, even if they should appear in a more progressive form. Furthermore, a human being is not only a *homo oeconomicus* but also a *homo faber;* not only a *homo ludens* but also a thinker and researcher, *homo philosophicus* and a scientist; not only a *homo eroticus* but also a *homo contemplativus,* a *homo ethicus* and often also a *homo religiosus,* etc. Therefore it is in fact possible to give form to the torso of an image of humanity in a political party programme. The decisive question for Christians, as for the political ethos itself, is moreover which values are given priority in the programme: a priority not following an abstract scale of values from above downwards, but as a humane requirement posed by particular situations of human need (thus for example the need for somewhere to live can claim a high level of priority). Furthermore, it is also possible to 'functionalise' human beings completely, to reduce them to a future programme of scientific and technological planning, and simply to call this scientific technocracy progressive without being at all critical, when in fact one-dimensional technology represents a dangerous threat to our humanity.

I conclude from this that no one can responsibly claim on a Christian basis that as a Christian one must vote for this *particular party* to be consistent with the Christian gospel. I will not deny that particular circumstances can arise in which to vote in a particular way may be historically necessary in the light of the gospel; to give one example, as a Christian one can hardly vote for a party which propagates hatred against humanity and nihilism (along the lines of contemporary Satanist movements). Faith does not go with everything. Furthermore, contemporary assertions that the Marxist movement *must* be the one consistent choice of a Christian who is a supporter of the poor seem to me to be empty slogans which cannot be put forward on Christian grounds. Moreover, it is outdated critical sociology to claim that the Marxist analysis of society is the only instrument for analyses. As Christians, we do not need to become Marxists; and to call oneself a supporter of the poor does not amount to 'Marxism', any more than Marxism is the best way of giving specific form to one's solidarity with the poor and the oppressed. One can only say that Christians and Marxists have to learn from one another, and that we have to respect the honest decisions of others.

Because Christianity points to the necessity of a general and complete liberation, it can introduce a certain 'personalisation' to the socialist struggle, and a resistance to hate, oppression and vengeance in this struggle. Christians can help to humanise this. The priest and Marxist Giulio Girardi remarks that Christians who decide for the revolutionary struggle often tend to stand on the extreme left. They no longer accuse the Communist party of being revolutionary, as they once did, but of being not revolutionary enough. One cannot deny the ambiguity which often lies in these hasty radicalisations, nor the ridicule to which people expose themselves who, on first becoming alive to the political dimension, think that they can give instruction in revolutionary purity to movements which have lived through a long and bitter experience.[14] However, Marxism has also made Christians aware that the privatising of religion has subjected it to the demands of society. Faith becomes 'ideological' when it is merely internalised, and thinks that it is then fully protected against science and political forces. It is certain that no one, including Christians, can ever decide for a party which corresponds fully to what they believe as a person and a believer in God to be true, good and happy humanity in the most just society. In that case one decides for a party which can present a mid-term programme in which the most pressing problems of humanity and society are given a more just and more humane solution for all, here and now, on the basis of *unselfish support* for those who are most oppressed. However, it is virtually impossible to find a party which does not describe itself as the supporter of violated and injured people! I spoke earlier of the need for a personalist and humanising socialisation. Of course this also includes a democratic socialisation. But we can see how wherever socialism seeks to give itself a democratic and human face in countries where Communism prevails, any attempt in this direction is nipped in the bud. At the same time, in all honesty it must be said that wherever attempts are made to achieve 'capitalism with a human face', this is also destroyed by a variety of subversive means. This of itself already demythologises the myth of 'subversive slogans'. For it can hardly be denied that the struggle for the *humanum* involves not only economic liberation from exploitation, but equally the democratisation of all decisions in which the future of humanity is at stake. Realism requires that any socialisation which limits human rights and freedoms already achieved (freedom of speech, freedom of the press, shared responsibility for political life and so on), even if these are not functioning as well as could be desired, can count on being resisted by people who have once enjoyed these rights and freedoms. Socialism without personalism and democracy is an attack on the possibilities of realising true humanity. At the same time, however, the call for freedom and democracy without socialism is in reality a disguised form of egotism and the expression of a requirement of free play for the greed motive. A Christian

---

[14]G. Girardi, *Dialogue et révolution*, Paris 1969, 236; see also his *Christianisme, libération humaine, lutte des classes*, Paris, 1972; id., *Chrétiens pour le socialisme*, Paris 1976, 64f. Cf the special number 'Chrétien marxiste', *Lumière Vie* no. 117–18, 1974, 1–198, and J. Guichard, *Marxisme. Théorie et pratique de la révolution*, Lyons n.d.

will therefore support those policies which in fact humanise economic conditions and for that very reason seek socialism for the advantage of all, while at the same time seeking to democratise social and political institutions. And democratisation by no means coincides with a large degree of state control. True, 'humanity' is not the universal subject of history in general, but human history is made by people, and so they themselves must be the people, the subject of their own history, and not dictators on the right wing or the left, who think that they have grasped the truth. The fact that Christians are often confronted with political parties who to a greater or lesser degree neglect one of these two demands often makes it difficult for them to choose a particular party. A Christian will often be unable to feel at home in any one political party, though he will have to join a particular party because they are driven on by the idea of a humanising, personalistic and democratic socialisation.

In this context, a word ought to be said about the anti-Communist instinct, which for some people seems to be a characteristic of the specifically religious. It is a fact that the churches with all their institutions are an integral part of bourgeois society, with which they are linked by countless threads. The sociological 'law of institutions' is particularly clear at this point. In given historical conditions these churches can only continue to exist, economically, if in fact they put up with this bourgeois society. In that case they become assimilated to prevailing political and economic systems. In this situation the possibility for development in any church institution, even if it means to be utterly in accordance with the gospel, is specifically dependent on the potentialities of late capitalism and is tied to those possibilities. That is a fact which is documented by the contributions made by capitalist sources towards so-called 'non-progressive' activities in the churches. The consequence of this situation is that it prevents these churches from speaking a liberating word at a time of crisis. Even if churches inwardly dissociate themselves from a system which makes the rich richer and the poor poorer, institutionally they are so tied up with the system that they have to keep their mouths shut. In order to be able to present their message, they have to keep quiet about this message! That is the vicious circle in this situation. In order to be able to continue to exist as a church, people keep silent about the demands of the gospel. Can the churches have forgotten that following Jesus can also cost them their lives? The primitive anti-Communism of many religious people (evidently there has to be a universal scapegoat somewhere) goes back to the same primal instincts of self-preservation: hang on to what one has. However, from a human point of view it seems to me to be just as much a basic feature of dogmatism as of primitive anti-Communism that 'anti-"anti-Communism"' is here systematically defusing and ignoring the flagrant violation of social freedom and human rights by the Communist system. I reject any 'dogmatism', whether it comes from the right wing or the left or from any church.

However, I must concede that it becomes a double test for Christians if they are confronted with the fact that particular *Christian churches* have welcomed attacks on a government which seeks to introduce a humanising socialisation as *God's answer* to the prayer of many anti-Communist Christians, thus identifying mammon with the living God. This seems to me to be one of the most grisly examples of primitive anti-Communism. Such reactions call for counter-reactions, of which 'Christians for Socialism' is doubtless one. On the other hand, they will have to remember that people cannot be *compelled* (except through a dictatorship) to more just economic conditions which are to the good of all. A dictatorship remains a dictatorship and is inhuman, even if it supports better economic conditions. I think that this was also the inner dilemma of the Enlightenment: can one compel people to emancipation and existence for others? To improve the world does not seem possible without an inner conversion! Perhaps here, too, the religions have an irreplaceable contribution of their own to make.

Selected literature

- The Influence of Third World Theology on Western Theology, Selected from: Edward Schillebeeckx, 'Liberating Theology: Reflection on J.-B. Metz's Political Theology', *Essays: Ongoing Theological Quests*, Collected Works of Edward Schillebeeckx vol. 11 (London: Bloomsbury T&T Clark, 2014), 69–72.
- Theological Hermeneutics of Radical Contrast Experiences; Selected from: Edward Schillebeeckx, 'Liberating Theology: Reflection on J.-B. Metz's Political Theology', *Essays: Ongoing Theological Quests*, Collected Works of Edward Schillebeeckx vol. 11 (London: Bloomsbury T&T Clark, 2014), 78–80.
- Christian Faith and Politics; Selected from: Edward Schillebeeckx, *Christ: The Christian Experience in the Modern World*, Collected Works of Edward Schillebeeckx vol. 7 (London: Bloomsbury T&T Clark, 2014), 770–3 [773–6].
- Christian Faith and Political Pluralism; Selected from: Edward Schillebeeckx, *Christ: The Christian Experience in the Modern World*, Collected Works of Edward Schillebeeckx vol. 7 (London: Bloomsbury T&T Clark, 2014), 781–6 [784–9].

23

Religious Pluralism

Christian, Jew, Buddhist, Muslim by birth, – or 'nothing'[1]

The Christian tradition says that belief in God is a gift of grace. On the other hand, we know from the previous chapter that religion is always a secondary discourse, i.e. speaking about something which in whatever way has already been expressed to some degree in our human experience. Belief in God includes worldly experiences in which something calls to be put into words, though it can only be expressed in the language of faith. The positiveness of revelation is in fact silent about precisely this mediation.

On the other hand, faith is not based on rational arguments which are meant to show the superiority of religion to other solutions of the questions of life. Such apologetic procedures overlook the fact that the fundamental orientation of the life of a person is based on a whole cultural history and not on a rational argument; they fall too short in their consideration of the self-awareness of belief in God as that has taken shape in a particular religion, for example in Christianity, which in fact acquired its knowledge of God from a specific history of salvation, from the life of a particular people and particular men and women among this people. Procedures to account for faith must rather be developed in close contact with the self-understanding of each religion and the social and cultural roots of particular believers. People never arrive at the deep decisions of life on their own. Hopefully critical, they stand and live within a particular cultural, religious or non-religious tradition, whether this is in a large-scale or a small-scale milieu (in the latter case, perhaps the family).

Human beings are 'cultural beings': they inherit and leave legacies; no one begins from zero as an absolutely certain starting point. We live in the present, from a past to a future. The structure of thought or memory in human life is striking here: we also allow our actions and experiences to be defined by the dialectic of present and

---

[1]Selected from: Edward Schillebeeckx, *Church: The Human Story of God*, Collected Works of Edward Schillebeeckx vol. 10 (London: Bloomsbury T&T Clark, 2014), 78–80 [80–3].

past, or past and future: memory and hope, tradition and prophecy. History is a process of learning, the handing down of culture, and at the same time it is planning: it is both tradition and experiment. Human beings are vehicles of culture and hand on the true, good and attractive humanity that has been offered them. But human beings also create tradition. Here the dialectic of theory and praxis plays a role. Human beings are never determined solely by their past; they also shape history to their desires and longings and create new traditions.

That for example a person is and remains a Christian because they were one originally and want to remain one out of a 'desire for the nest' is a social and historical fact that need not in any way be judged unfavourably. However, the fact that others turn away from their own desire for the nest, flee it and look elsewhere indicates that the real determining factor is not merely what is 'familiar from the beginning' (without further qualification). The determining factor is whether people 'feel happy' in this home, or whether it compels them to throw it off as an enslaving yoke. The determining factor is not 'the original', but the meaning, the dynamic and the enriching power which has emanated from this 'domestic tradition' to the individual (here one might also put up with painful recollections; in that case these are not determinative).

'Feeling at home (despite everything)' in a religious or non-religious tradition which one has inherited from the beginning is also a decisive factor in whether or not a person believes in God. (This standing in a religious tradition in which one has constructed one's own identity is then in fact the concrete form of what believers call a 'grace of God'. Grace does not stand as a dilemma in opposition to freedom and tradition!) The believer and the non-believer need not be judged here in different ways – the personal convictions of both are connected with the tradition in which they respectively stand. For the non-believer, too, this tradition (hopefully with the same critical attitude) has become his or her own flesh and blood. This tradition is also part of his or her personal identity. This applies to Christians, Buddhists and Muslims, and also to agnostics. The fact that a person is also culturally determined by a fundamental view of life does not in itself tell either for or against the truth of this conviction.

In a pluralistic society with conflicting and even diverse religious traditions of meaning, the necessity of a justification of faith in fact becomes more urgent. We need to be aware that no one can demonstrate by rational arguments that their conviction of faith is more 'rational' and better than atheism or other religions, unless the other's conviction contains confessional elements which injure and dishonour human beings (for example, a religion which called for human sacrifices) or plays down human values. Human beings cannot come fully into their own in just any religion or view of life. (Religious indifferentism on the basis that all religions are equal is therefore anthropologically already open to attack before it becomes a 'heresy'.)

However, apologetic under the sometimes sympathetic mask of 'open questions' is often a way of showing that, despite everything, one's own faith is unassailable. In that case, it is not an attempt, under the pressures of one's own time, to purge one's own belief in God of all kinds of historical accretions and distortions, which perhaps even have serious consequences for faith itself. The most responsible form of apologetic is to uncover the 'intelligibility' or the comprehensibility of faith. For 'mystery' does not mean an appeal to a truth which cannot be understood and is claimed ideologically to be immune from criticism – though it is often used in this sense by clergy as an excuse. A justification of faith is not a matter of looking for rational proofs, for faith, but of making understandable to fellow-believers and non-believers what is meant by talk about 'God'.

Good and bad questions in connection with the uniqueness of the Christian church[2]

In the history of Christianity, until recently it was generally accepted that Christianity was the vehicle of absolute truth. In fact, over the course of time the Christian churches have also behaved in this way. A justified claim to liberating uniqueness and universality was imperialistically twisted into a church claim to absoluteness.

Over against such absoluteness stand hard historical facts. The history of humanity shows us a collection of differing ways of life, a multi-coloured offer of 'ways of salvation': Judaism, Christianity and Islam; Hinduism and Buddhism; Taoism, Confucianism and Shintoism; animism, African and Indian ways to salvation and blessing. We call them all 'religions'; in other words we are convinced that there are essential resemblances between all these divergent phenomena. Therefore they are referred to by one term: religion.

Nostra aetate, a declaration of Vatican II, also says that human beings 'look to their different religions for an answer to the unsolved problems of human existence. The problems that weigh heavily on the hearts of people are the same today as in ages past' (no. l). In other words, through the offer of a message of salvation and the opening of a way of salvation, religions answer a fundamental question which men and women ask about their lives. Modern sociologists (e.g. H. Lübbe) speak in the same tone (but they do so functionalistically, and this does not correspond to the true nature of religion as gratuitousness), in very general terms, but correctly, about religions as 'systems of ultimate orientation' or 'systems for learning to live with contingency':[3] all-embracing systems which impart meaning or systems which help us spiritually, emotionally and above all existentially to cope with our vulnerable, changeable existence in an ambivalent society. But there are misunderstandings about what we call 'religion' among cultural scholars and philosophers of religion. These go in two directions, taking either an essentialist approach or a nominalist approach via 'general terms' ('universals') to what is called 'religion'.

Using a term of Wittgenstein's, we would therefore in my view do better to say that there are 'family likenesses' between the many religions. In that case we are really not talking of one or more 'common characteristics' nor speaking of 'ideal types'. Then, phenomena which show similarities and on the basis of this are denoted by one and the same term (religion) are (Wittgenstein would say, as members of a

---

[2]Selected from: Edward Schillebeeckx, *Church: The Human Story of God*, Collected Works of Edward Schillebeeckx vol. 10 (London: Bloomsbury T&T Clark, 2014), 158–67 [159–68].
[3]H. Lübbe, 'Religion nach der Aufklärung', in H. Lübbe (ed.), *Philosophie nach der Aufklärung. Von der Notwendigkeit pragmatischer Venunft*, Düsseldorf 1980, 59–86; id., *Religion nach der Aufklärung*, Graz and Cologne 1987.

particular family), item for item, unique in their specific combination or figuration of characteristics. But on the basis of 'family likenesses', despite their uniqueness, they can be compared with one another (semiotics also thinks in a similar direction).

As a social and cultural phenomenon and system providing meaning, Christianity, too, is one religion alongside other religions: one of many. However, Christians find salvation for themselves only in Jesus confessed as the Christ. Therefore in the course of history (on the basis of their own view and attitude to life) they begin to ask how pagans, non-Christians, can achieve salvation. For their confession of the uniqueness of Jesus was not simply an expression of a subjective conviction. According to the Christian confession this view refers to reality: in other words, it is true (although that is an affirmation of faith and not a truth that can be demonstrated and verified scientifically; so one can never use it as a weapon against non-Christians).

On the basis of this conviction of abiding in the truth, sooner or later Christians had to raise the question of the possibility of salvation for non-Christians. Indirectly this already happened from the beginning of Christianity: the second (or New) Testament says that God wills the salvation of 'all' people (1 Tim 2.4); moreover he wills it in an effective way, adapted to the human situation (even if people do not know Christ). And in a sermon of Peter's Luke says this even more clearly: 'Now I know that with God there is no respect for persons, but that out of every people anyone who fears him and does good is well-pleasing to him' (Acts 10.34-35). However, the real elaboration of this problem, how people 'can be blessed' if they have never learned to know Jesus Christ, began above all in modern times, and only in our time is it becoming a fundamental, central and even crucial theological problem.[4] Here Christianity does not drop its claim to universality – Jesus' message of universal liberation – but its exclusivist and inclusivist claim to absoluteness.

Broadly speaking, that was clearly a new way in comparison with the previous tradition extending over centuries. But it was not a break, because both the first and the second Testaments and church traditions (though these never spoke out loudly or from the heart) also recognised good things in the other religions.

In recent times Karl Rahner went even further. He not only recognised the individual possibility of salvation for the adherents of other religions, but also attached saving worth to these religions as such; they too are 'ways of salvation' to God. Daniélou and de Lubac have also made comments to this effect. But the already open statements of the Second Vatican Council in *Lumen gentium, Nostra aetate* and *Ad gentes* (texts to which the works of Rahner and Ratzinger, Daniélou and de Lubac were not foreign) do not go as far as this, at least in what they actually say. Implicitly H. Waldenfels seems to think that this modern position (inspired by Rahner) goes too far when he writes that if non-Christians also find salvation, 'then that does not take place "despite" but at all events "in" their religion'. And he explicitly adds: 'Christians should avoid the formula "through" their religion.'[5] I myself do not find

---

[4]In Germany it was above all O. Karrer, *Das Religiöse in der Menschheit und das Christentum*, who dealt extensively with this question as early as 1934. In France it was above all L. Caperan, *Le problème du salut des infidèles*, also in 1934! See also K. Adam, *The Spirit of Catholicism*, London 1928.
[5]H. Waldenfels, 'Ist der christliche Glaube der einzig wahre? Christentum und nichtchristlichen Religionen', *Stimmen der Zeit* 112 (1987), 470.

this reserve towards a religion as social system very satisfactory: evidently there is a fear here that a grain of truth in the old absolute claim of 'imperialistic' Christianity is being attacked.

But we must concede to M. Seckler that the saving value of all religions cannot be posited abstractly and globally.[6] Item by item we will have to examine each religion in a very specific way to discover its own values and the picture of human beings and the world that it implies. On the latter question everyone has something to say: how do you want and see your own humanity? Inevitably in a very schematic way, Vatican II nevertheless tries to describe the specific value of Judaism and Hinduism, Buddhism and Islam; moreover, finally in *Lumen gentium*, par. 16, the council speaks of the possibility of salvation even for agnostics and atheists. Here we are already close to the position which I defended in the first chapter: 'outside the world there is no salvation'. In world history God brings about salvation through human mediation, and human beings also do obnoxious things. This is the struggle with which we are involved.

In recent years some writers have gone even further than Rahner. So H.-R. Schlette reverses the categories used previously: for him Christianity is not the 'normal' or 'usual saving way' to God; that is true of the other religions. Christianity is the 'extraordinary' or 'exceptional' way to God.[7] This could even be confirmed by world statistics. According to 1982 surveys there are 1.4 billion official Christians in the world (a third of the world's population); there are 723 million Muslims, 583 million Hindus and 274 million Buddhists.[8] The number of non-Christians exceeds the number of Christians; and almost two-thirds of all Christians live outside the Western world. Although statistics are not the last word, they nevertheless warn Christians to be modest: there are more people of other beliefs than there are Christians in the world. And these others are not dumb or blind.

And we still have not finished with the shift in the self-understanding of modern Christians. Recently the Catholic Paul Knitter went one stage further than Schlette: he denies any form of claim to universality on the part of Christianity, but without lapsing into religious indifference.[9] Among Christians in our time there is indeed a particular new form of modern 'indifferentism': the view that all religions are equal. Of course they are not, since even their views of what it is to be human are different, and a religion which, for instance, condemns the firstborn son to death as a sacrifice to God is certainly not of equal value to a religion which explicitly forbids it. Here too criteria of humanity apply.

If their own religion is also involved in any comparison of religions, in the end men and women cannot avoid the question of truth. But this question of truth is in fact raised within a 'hermeneutical circle', and the definitive answer to it can only be eschatological. The question is thus whether in the meanwhile there are

---

[6]Seckler, 'Theologie der Religionen mit Fragezeichen', *Theologische Quartalschrift* 166 (1986), 178–81.
[7]Schlette, *Die Religionen als Thema der Theologie. Überlegungen zu einer Theologie der Religionen*, Quaestiones Disputatae 22, Freiburg 1964, 66–112.
[8]D. Barrett et al., *World Christian Encyclopedia. A Comparative Study of Churches and Religions in the Modem World, AD 1900–2000*, Nairobi and Oxford 1982.
[9]Knitter, *No Other Name? A Critical Survey of Christian Attitudes towards the World Religions*, Maryknoll and London 1985.

not many open questions here which cannot be solved speculatively, and moreover whether we are asking the right questions and not the wrong ones (which can never be answered). Moreover the outcome of the question of truth with relation to one's own religion need in no way entail discrimination against other religions. No single religion exhausts the question of truth. Therefore we must leave both absolutism and relativism behind us in religious matters.

Our age has 'liberated' itself in many ways from the distinctive post-Enlightenment modern claim to truth and universality. Logically and practically, multiplicity now takes priority over unity. The old and Neoplatonic Greek ideal of unity is in no sense still a norm for modern or postmodern people. The monotheism of Judaism, Christianity and Islam which lays claim to all humanity is regarded by many people (or some) as totalitarian.[10] Some see it as one of the causes of the shift of many Westerners to Asian religions. The statement 'All religions are equal' is understandable in terms of this modern spirit of the time, although this expression is cheap and basically wrong.

The question, however, is whether monotheism with its claim to universality cannot also be a criticism and provocation of this spirit of the time. The spirit of the time is certainly not a norm in itself! The universal claim of salvation in Jesus and the human reason which recalls the suffering of humanity can also provide a criticism of the liberal pluralism of the spirit of our time. There is also a cheap form of tolerance.

Christianity has, of course, often interpreted its own truth and uniqueness (which are not to be denied) as a claim to absoluteness through which all other religions are seen as having less value, while the good that is to be found in them is already thought to be present in an eminent way in Christianity itself. 'Christian values' were indeed discovered in other religions, but by the same token these are deprived of their own identity. The consequence of this religious and cultural 'imperialism' was that the modern history of colonialism and mission was to a large extent also a time of oppression by foreign cultures and religions, not just in the sixteenth-century missions but also from the time of and during the Enlightenment.[11]

However, Asia and practically all countries in which Islam is dominant shut themselves off from Christianity; these universal religions also discovered their own claim to uniqueness.[12] Therefore in the open world of the West, Christianity is increasingly regarded as one religion among many and, moreover, historically as a religion under which many non-Christian cultures and other religions have suffered heavily. This change of climate in Western thought was almost automatically coupled with a privatisation of Christianity as a religion: in their hearts people could happily respect Christianity as the one true religion, if only this had no consequences for others and for the public, bourgeois world.

So given this history, we shall have to look in a direction in which both absolutism and relativism are avoided in connection with what is called 'religion'. The question

---

[10]For monotheism as a political problem see E. Peterson, *Theologische Traktate*, Cologne 1951, esp. 45–149.
[11]See E. Wolf, *Europe and the People without History*, Berkeley and London 1982.
[12]See e.g. J.-M. van Cangh (ed.), *Salut universel et regard pluraliste*, Paris 1986; also Mensching, *Toleranz und Wahrheit in der Religion*, Heidelberg 1955, 162–8.

of the truth of Christianity is by no means the same as the question of the superiority of Christianity, as was often thought earlier. The issue is one of Christian identity, which recognises and respects the other person's religious identity, which allows itself to be challenged by other religions and which, on the basis of its own message, also challenges other religions. In short, we are confronted with other questions than those raised earlier, with more productive questions which are more fruitful for all sides.

So we now ask other questions, though it continues to be true for Christian believers that they find salvation 'only in the name of Jesus of Nazareth'. And in this Christian perspective questions then emerge as to whether and how, for example, one can be a Christian as a Hindu, in other words whether there can be a Hindu version of Christianity. There is no question of this being a speculative approach to one another's religions; it is a perhaps centuries-long attempt to arrive at a 'common experience', for only a common experience can lead to a similar hermeneutical interpretation. At present we are still far from having a 'common experience'. Therefore in my view the question for us is whether the pluralism of religions is a matter of fact or a matter of principle. How we answer this question of course has important consequences for our own view of the *ecumene* of world religions and finally for world peace, which over the centuries has been and at present still is being sorely put to the test through religious intolerance and thus on the basis of the claim to absoluteness, whether inclusive or exclusive, which is sometimes made.

The universality and historical contingency of Jesus' life

In contrast to the earlier Christian claim to absoluteness, which was also governed by the dominant spirit of the time, in my view the positive acceptance of the difference between religions is implicit in the nature of Christianity.[13] The problem is no longer the one formulated at the level of the earlier awareness of the problem: is Christianity the one true religion, or is it (in a milder version) a better religion than all the rest? In these comparisons the term 'religion' is borrowed from the one making the comparison (from whatever religion) in terms of his or her own religion, and thus by Christians in terms of Christianity. The problem is, rather, how can Christianity maintain its own identity and uniqueness and at the same time attach a positive value to the difference of religions in a non-discriminatory sense? Put in this way, what is relevant to Christianity is not what is common to many religions, but precisely that difference between them which forms their uniqueness and distinctive-ness. If this is the case, then we must be able to point to a foundation within Christianity itself for this new, Christian, open and not- intolerant attitude to the other religions of the world.

In my view this foundation lies in Jesus' message and praxis of the kingdom of God, with all its consequences. At any rate in its uniqueness and distinctiveness

---

[13] This is also the view of [Christian] Duquoc in his book *Dieu différent*, but see the following note.

as a religion, Christianity is essentially bound up with an unavoidable 'historical peculiarity' and thus is regional and limited. Therefore (like all religions), Christianity too is limited: limited in means of expression, perspective and specific praxis. Christians sometimes find it difficult to see this reality plainly. But this limitation is part of the nature of Christianity (and is indeed expressed above all when Christians use the 'incarnational model' in their tradition – which after all is regarded in this tradition as the dominant paradigm).

The special, distinctive and unique feature of Christianity is that it finds the life and being of God specifically in this historical and thus limited particularity of 'Jesus of Nazareth' – confessed as the personally human manifestation of God. In it there is a confession that Jesus is indeed a 'unique', but nevertheless 'contingent', i.e. historical and thus limited, manifestation of the gift of salvation from God for all men and women. Anyone who overlooks this fact of the specific humanity of Jesus, precisely in his quality as a human being, which is geographically defined and socially and culturally recognisable and therefore limited, makes the person Jesus a 'necessary' divine emanation as a result of which all other religions are volatilised into nothing-ness. This then seems essentially to conflict with the deepest sense of all Christological councils and confessions and ultimately with the very being of God as absolute freedom. In this view, Jesus' humanity is reduced to a docetic pseudo-humanity, while on the other hand the identity of all non-Christian religions is trivialised. Nevertheless, in the course of time Christians have absolutised precisely this historical and thus limited character of Christianity. This has led to the historical wretchedness of empirical Christianity in contrast to the original authenticity of the gospel.

But the revelation of God in Jesus, as the Christian gospel preaches this to us, in no way means that God absolutises a historical particularity (even Jesus of Nazareth). We learn from the revelation of God in Jesus that no individual historical particularity can be said to be absolute, and that therefore through the relativity present in Jesus anyone can encounter God even outside Jesus, especially in our worldly history and in the many religions which have arisen in it. The risen Jesus of Nazareth also continues to *point to* God beyond himself. One could say: God points via Jesus Christ in the Spirit to himself as creator and redeemer, as a God of human beings, of *all* human beings. God is absolute, but no single religion is absolute.

The particularity of Jesus, by which the origin, character and uniqueness of Christianity are defined, thus implies that we should leave the differences between the particular religions and not do away with them. The manifestation of God in Jesus does not fence off 'religious history', as emerges for example from the origin of Islam as a post-Christian world religion. And no one, not even Islam, can fail to recognize that further new world religions can and will arise after Islam. For all the critical questions here, particular present-day neo-religious movements are support for this hypothesis.

It is clear that there are in fact points of both convergence and divergence between all religions. However, differences must not be judged *per se* as deviations, which have to be remedied by ecumenical action; they must be regarded in a positive light. (On the basis of what criteria could we judge such deviations anyway?) However, God is too rich and too over-defined for it to be possible to exhaust him in his fullness through a particular and thus limited religious experiential tradition.

Certainly, according to the Christian perspective, 'the fullness of God dwells bodily in Jesus'. New Testament texts bear witness to this for Christians (Col 2.9; see Col 1.15; Heb 1.3; 2 Cor 4.4). But this 'corporeality' – or 'this dwelling (of the fullness of God) in Jesus' humanity' – denotes precisely the contingent and limited form of Jesus' appearance in our history. (Otherwise we would be practising the Docetism condemned by all Christian churches, i.e. the view that the divine appeared in Jesus only in phantom form.)

As a consequence of all this we can, may and must say that there is more religious truth in all the religions together than in one particular religion, and that this also applies to Christianity. There are therefore 'true', 'good', and 'beautiful' – surprising – aspects in the manifold forms of relationship with God (present in humanity), forms which have not found any place in the specific experience of Christianity and are not finding one now. There are differences in people's experience of their relationship to God, differences which cannot be smoothed over, for all the inherent similarities to other experiences. There are different authentically religious experiences which Christianity, precisely because of its historical particularity, has never thematised or put into practice. Moreover, *perhaps* (I say that cautiously, but assertively), it is the case that because of the specific and distinct accents which Jesus brought, Christianity cannot thematise such aspects without robbing these distinctive accents of the sharpness which Jesus gave them and ultimately of their specific Christian character.

From all this I learn that (even in the Christian self-understanding) the multiplicity of religions is not an evil which needs to be removed, but rather a wealth which is to be welcomed and enjoyed by all. That is in no way to deny that the historical plurality of religions which in principle is not to be removed is inwardly nurtured and supported by a unity which cannot be made an explicit theme within our history and cannot be practised: i.e. the unity of God (the trinitarian God confessed by Christians) in so far as this transcendent unity is reflected in the immanent family likenesses between these religions and allows us to give the one name 'religion' to all these different religious phenomena.[14]

The unity, identity and uniqueness of Christianity over against these other religions then lies in the fact that Christianity is a religion which associates a relationship to God with a historical and thus a very specific and therefore limited particularity: Jesus of Nazareth. This is the uniqueness and identity of Christianity, but at the

---

[14]In contrast to Duquoc, I do not refer to 'trinitarian symbolism' in order to provide a basis for this Christian view of other religions. I limit my argument to the uniqueness and at the same time historical contingency and thus limitedness of Jesus of Nazareth. Duquoc's position that the unity of the triune God is founded on a trinitarian multiplicity, through which the priority of pluralism over unity is said to be shown, seems to me to be philosophically and theologically unacceptable. For my view is that the oneness of the divine nature is the source and ground of the tri-'personality' of the one God, not that the three persons form the basis of the unity of the divine nature. Moreover, how far can one call the three 'persons' a plurality in a monotheistic view of God? (In certain French theological tendencies the divine Trinity is in fact a kind of family.). Is this not a nonchalant handling of the analogous character of categories like 'one' and 'many' as applied to God? And is not too little account taken here of a dialectical perichoresis – or mutual indwelling – in which unity and plurality hold each other in a mutual equilibrium? In that case for me pluralism in principle takes a different turn from the direction taken in Duquoc, for whom there seems to be no question of an implied though not thematised unity.

same time its unavoidable historical limitation. It becomes clear here that (on the basis of Jesus' parables and praxis of the kingdom of God) the God of Jesus is a symbol of openness, not of closedness. Here Christianity has a positive relationship to other religions, but at the same time its uniqueness is nevertheless maintained, and ultimately at the same time the loyal Christian affirmation of the positive nature of the other world religions is honoured.

This in no way rules out the question of truth, but the truth here is that no one has a monopoly of the truth and that no one can ask for the fullness of God's riches for himself or herself alone. This insight, which for Christians is to some extent new, derives from the fact that we are now also asking questions which people could not ask earlier, purged as we are by past (and constantly new) meaningless wars of religion and fruitless discrimination. In entertaining it we are not advocating the cheap liberal modern principle that all religions are equal, or all equally relative, or all equally wrong (as some atheists claim).

Christology is an interpretation of Jesus of Nazareth: it explains that the God of Jesus is the redeemer of all people and in this sense is the exclusive redeemer. But what redeems, what brings liberation and redemption, is not the interpretation but the means of redemption itself. The Sri Lankan theologian Aloysius Pieris in particular has pointed out, more strongly than I did in my *Jesus* book, that we are not redeemed by the honorific titles of Jesus but by the means of redemption itself, regardless of the linguistic framework within which that means is experienced and expressed.[15] 'Jesus' redeems us, not 'Christ'. Honorific titles emerge from a particular culture and often cannot be used in others. Moreover redemption through Jesus is unique and universal only in so far as what happened in Jesus is continued in his disciples. Without any relationship to a redeeming and liberating practice of Christians, redemption, brought by Jesus, remains in a purely speculative, empty vacuum. It is not the confession 'Jesus is Lord' (Rom 10.9) which in itself brings redemption, but 'he who does the will of my Father' (Matt 7.2). One has to go the way of Jesus himself; then Jesus' life journey concretely takes on a universal significance (Matt 25.37–39, 44-46). In fact a fragmentary but real making whole of humanity is the best evidence of liberation.

The claim that Jesus is the universal redeemer entails that Christians in our history should begin to bring forth the fruits of the kingdom of God. So Christology derives its authenticity from the concrete praxis of the kingdom of God: the history of Jesus' life must be continued in his disciples; only then is it meaningful to talk of the uniqueness and distinctiveness of Christianity. Pieris therefore speaks rightly of 'a co-redemptive function of the corporative Christ',[16] the community of God. As I said above, this way of life, following Jesus, has two essential characteristics: it is the way of the rejection of any messianic power on the basis of a sovereign inner human freedom (the bold human commitment to the poor and oppressed, the solidarity of

---

[15] A. Pieris, 'Christentum und Buddhismus in Dialog aus der Mitte ihrer Traditionen', in A. Bsteh (ed.), *Dialog aus der Mitte christlicher Theologie*, Beiträge Religionstheologie 5, Vienna, Munich and Lucerne, 131–78, esp. 174–8. In the meantime two books by Pieris have appeared in the original English, *An Asian Theology of Liberation*, New York and London 1988, and *Love Meets Wisdom*, New York 1988.
[16] Ibid., 177.

love, lies in this opposition to oppressive powers), and this way of life implies the *via crucis,* the cross. This is where the uniqueness of Jesus lies. The 'proof' of this is that down the centuries Christians bear witness to this way of life by going along it, even to the point of martyrdom. 'In my body I fulfil what is still lacking in the sufferings of Christ' (Col 1.24), as it was put in antiquity. Opposition and surrender.

Selected literature

- Christian, Jew, Buddhist, Muslim by Birth, – or 'Nothing'; Selected from: Edward Schillebeeckx, *Church: The Human Story of God*, Collected Works of Edward Schillebeeckx vol. 10 (London: Bloomsbury T&T Clark, 2014), 78–80 [80–3].
- Good and Bad Questions in Connection with the Uniqueness of the Christian Church; Selected from: Edward Schillebeeckx, *Church: The Human Story of God*, Collected Works of Edward Schillebeeckx vol. 10 (London: Bloomsbury T&T Clark, 2014), 158–67 [159–68].

INDEX

Abdul-Masih, Marguerite Thabit   18 n.44
Adam, Karl   345 n.4
Adorno, Theodor W.   14, 27, 113
Albert the Great   36–8, 41, 77–8, 80–1, 134
Alexander the Great   37–8, 146
Allmen, Daniel von   123 n.14
Alpers, Christiane   17 n.42, 18 n.47
Amalorpavadass, Duraiswami Simon   330
Ambrose of Milan   70, 104
Aquinas, Thomas   13–14, 27–8, 30–3, 35–7, 38 n.22, 39–41, 45, 46 n.9, 54, 62, 65, 69, 77, 82, 92, 123, 186, 196, 264, 267, 287, 300, 312
Aristotle   41, 77
Athanasius of Alexandria   67, 68 n.20, 70, 123
Augustine of Hippo   37, 68, 70, 123, 127 n.2, 135, 185–6, 252, 284–5, 286 n.2
Auzou, Georges   65 n.9

Bakker, Leo   123 n.16
Barbour, Ian   115 n.8
Barrett, David Brian   346 n.8
Barth, Karl   30, 123, 227 n.5
Basil the Great   68 nn.16–17, 68 n.21, 70
Baumgartner, Walter   232 n.5
Bavel, Tarsicius Jan van   196 n.8
Beauvoir, Simone de   318 n.3
Benedict of Nursia   84
Benjamin, Walter   310
Berger, Peter   117 n.12, 201 n.15
Betz, Otto   229 n.9
Binswanger, Ludwig   201 n.14
Blank, Josef   230 n.9
Bloch, Ernst   113, 323 n.10
Blondel, Maurice   30, 44
Boeve, Lieven   2 n.2, 9 n.20, 16–17 n.41, 19
Bonaventure   36–8, 41, 123
Borgman, Erik   2, 5 n.8, 5 n.11, 6, 14, 15 n.36, 16 n.37, 17, 309, 310 n.10, 331 n.4

Bornkamm, Günther   230 n.9
Bouillard, Henri   29, 44
Bouma, Hans   199 n.112
Braun, Herbert   148, 232 n.5
Brongers, Hendrik Antonie   227 n.5, 228 n.6
Brown, Raymond E.   229 n.9
Brox, Nobert   314 n.15
Buber, Martin   11
Bultmann, Rudolf   93, 111, 148, 150, 230 n.9, 238
Buytendijk, Frederik J. Johannes   201 n.14

Cangh, Jean-Marie van   347 n.12
Caperan, Louis   345 n.4
Casas, Bartolomé de las   78
Chagall, Marc   11
Chastaing, Maxime   201 n.14
Chenu, Marie-Dominique   6, 13, 17, 28, 30, 32 n.2, 69 n.22, 78
Chia, Edmund Kee-Fook   18 n.46
Cimorelli, Christopher   17 n.2
Cliteur, Paul   308 n.8
Congar, Yves   6–7, 13, 30, 66 n.12, 78, 194 n.6
Considine, Kevin   18 n.46
Cooper, Jennifer   17–18 n.43
Cormier, Pere   77
Coulson, John   304 n.2
Cox, Harvey   325 n.11
Cyril of Alexandria   68 n.19

Dahl, Nils   62 n.4
Daniélou, Jean   29, 345
Dante Alighieri   267
De Lubac, Henri   29–30, 345
De Paul, Vincent   274
De Petter, Dominicus   5, 8, 20, 29–30, 42, 44–5, 46 n.7, 50 n.26, 54, 160 n.2, 310 n.10
De Pol, Willem Henrik van   321 n.6
Delobel, Joel   151 n.5

Delorme, Jean   232 n.3, 232 n.5, 233 n.7, 233 n.9
Denzinger, Heinrich Joseph Dominicus   60 n.2, 108 n.2, 109, 128 n.3
Depoortere, Frederiek   2 n.2, 16
Derksen, Karl   336 n.12
Descartes, René   5
Dessauer, Friedrich   199 n.13
De Waelhens, Alphonse   199 n.13
Dolphin, Kathleen   17–18 n.43
Dominic (Saint)   13, 73, 75–82, 84–6
Don Bosco   274
Dondeyne, Albert   44 nn.2–3
Dullaart, Leo   336 n.12
Dupanloup, Félix Antoine Philibert   286
Dupont, Jacques   218 n.11
Duquoc, Christian   348 n.13, 350 n.14
Dwyer, Mary   295 n.9

Eckhart, Meister   80, 172
Eggensperger, Thomas   17 n.40
Engel, Ulrich   17 n.40
Erasmus of Rotterdam   92
Erp, Stephan van   1, 2 nn.1–2, 9 n.20, 12 n.33, 13, 16 nn.38–9, 17 nn.41–2, 27

Faivre, Alexandre   277 n.9
Feder, Julia   14, 155
Feuerbach, Ludwig   113, 336 n.12
Frachet, Gerald de   80
Francis of Assisi (Saint)   76, 84
Freyer, Hans   274 n.6
Friedberg, Emil Albert von   280 n.11
Fries, Heinrich   325 n.11
Furlong, Monica   295 n.9

Gadamer, Hans-Georg   27, 201 n.15, 202 n.17
Galerius   314 n.16
Garaudy, Roger   325 n.11
Garrigou-Lagrange, Réginald   29
Geertz, Clifford   123 n.14
Gehlen, Arnold   199 n.13, 201 n.15
Geyer, Hans-Georg   335 n.9
Ghellinck, Joseph de   32 n.2
Girardi, Giulio   335 n.10, 339 n.14
Gottemoeller, Doris   295 n.9
Graß, Hans von   232 n.5
Guardini, Romano   11
Guichard, Jean   339 n.14

Gusdort, Georges   201 n.14
Gutiérrez, Gustavo   22, 301

Habermas, Jürgen   8, 11, 14, 27, 55, 201 n.15, 204 n.20
Hathaway, Ronald F.   277 n.9
Hebblethwaite, Peter   19 n.49
Heffernan, Brian   16 n.38
Heidkamp, Ann H.   295 n.6
Heisenberg, Werner   199 n.13
Hilgers, Bernhard Josef   36
Hilkert, Mary Catherine   2, 4 n.4, 16
Hofbauer, Rita   295 n.9
Horkheimer, Max   14
Houten, Douwe van   308 n.8
Hübner, Kurt   331
Humbert of Romans   79, 84
Husserl, Edmund   5

Ignatius of Antioch   263 n.8
Ignatius of Loyola   78
Innocent III (Pope)   76
Irenaeus of Lyon   67 n.15, 244 n.2
Isidore of Seville   69

Jandel, Alexandre Vincent   79
Janowski, Hans-Norbert   335 n.9
Jaspers, Karl   293
Jeanson, Francis   318 n.3
Jeremias, Joachim   151 n.5
Jerome (Saint)   68, 70
Joan of Arc   74
Johansson, Nils   229 n.9
John XXIII (Pope)   6, 89, 95–6, 101
John Chrysostom   70
John Damascene   69
Johnston, George   229 n.9
Jong, Marijn de   18 n.44
Jordan of Saxony   85, 86
Jossua, Jean-Pierre   310 n.10

Kant, Immanuel   5, 44
Karrer, Otto   345 n.4
Käseman, Ernst   92
Kasper, Walter   59 n.31
Kenis, Leo   10 n.20
Kennedy, Philip   2, 4 n.5, 16
Kierkegaard, Søren   148
King, Martin Luther   257
Knitter, Paul   346 n.9
Koehler, Ludwig   232 n.5

Koselleck, Reinhart   205 n.21
Kuitert, Harry   205 n.22
Kümmel, Werner Georg   218 n.11
Küng, Hans   7, 10, 19 n.49, 124
Kuschel, Karl-Josef   313 n.13
Kuyper, Abraham   11
Kwant, Remigius Cornelis   201 n.14

Lacordaire, Henri   78–80, 285
Landsberg, Paul-Ludwig   50 n.26
Lavelle, Louis   54
Leach, Edmund   123 n.14
Leaney, Alfred L. Clare   229 n.9
Léon-Dufour, Xavier   232 n.5
Lessing, Gotthold Ephraim   92, 146
Lévie, Jean   65
Levinas, Emmanuel   201 n.14, 212 n.5
Lévi-Strauss, Claude   11
Lewis, Hywel David   165 n.6
Locher, Gottfried W.   230 n.9
Lombard, Peter   39
Loon, J. F. Glastra   308 n.8
Lübbe, Hermann   321 n.8
Luckmann, Thomas   201 n.15
Luhmann, Niklas   201 n.15
Luther, Martin   123, 144
Luyten, Norbert Alfons   304 n.2

Maag, Victor   259 n.4
McManus, Kathleen   17–18 n.43
Mandonnet, Pierre   80
Marcel, Gabriel   15 n.36, 53 n.27, 201 n.14
Marcuse, Herbert   113
Maréchal, Joseph   44, 45 n.5
Marsch, Wolf-Dieter   325 n.11
Marty, Martin   323
Marx, Karl   113, 326
Masi, Roberto   182 n.7
Matisse, Henri   83
Mensching, Gustav   347 n.12
Merklein, Helmut   218 n.11
Merleau-Ponty, Maurice   29, 199 n.13, 256, 305 n.5, 312, 318 n.3
Metz, Johann-Baptist   7–8, 18 n.44, 56 n.30, 112 n.6, 113, 194 n.6, 205 n.21, 301, 325 n.11, 329 n.1, 330, 332 n.5, 334 n.8
Mieth, Dietmar   313 n.13
Minch, Daniel   1–2 n.1, 9 n.20, 14, 16, 19 n.48, 89

Möhler, Johann Adam   36
Molenaar, Paul   86
Moltmann, Jürgen   196 n.8, 258, 325 n.11, 334 n.8
Montfort, Simon de   84
Montoya, Angel F. Méndez   17 n.40
Moulin, Leo   80
Mussner, Franz   229 n.9

Napoleon Bonaparte   146
Nazianzen, Gregory   70
Nédoncelle, Maurice   201 n.14
Newman, John Henry   30, 121
Niebuhr, Reinhold   299
Nieuwenhove, Jacques van   331 n.4

Oelmüller, Willi   115 n.11, 203 n.18, 334 n.8
Ottaviani, Alfredo   89, 96
Oudenrijn, Frans van den   336 n.12

Pannenberg, Wolfhart   54 n.29, 123, 204 n.20, 205 n.21, 325 n.11
Paul VI (Pope)   101
Pelletier, Anne-Marie   232 n.5
Peterson, Erik   347 n.10
Philips, Gerard   104
Picht, Georg   199 n.13
Pieris, Aloysius   330, 351 n.15
Pius IX (Pope)   280
Pius X (Pope)   280
Pius XI (Pope)   280, 308 n.9
Pius XII (Pope)   127, 280
Porsch, Felix   229 n.9
Potterie, Ignace de la   61 n.3
Poulsom, Martin G.   17 n.41, 18
Procksch, Otto   259 n.3
Prümmer, Dominic   35, 36 n.20
Pseudo-Dionysius   277
Pyne, Elizabeth M.   15, 299

Rad, Gerhard von   227
Rahner, Karl   7, 18 n.44, 44, 66 n.13, 89, 123, 177 n.2, 256, 306 n.6, 325 n.11, 345–6
Raiser, Konrad   201 n.15
Ranke, Leopold von   146
Ratzinger, Joseph   10, 22, 89–90, 345
Rawls, John   313 n.12
Raymond of Penafort   78, 81
Reimarus, Hermann Samuel   92, 146
Renan, Ernest   92

Richter, Horst   165
Ricoeur, Paul   113, 308 n.8
Riedel, Manfred   204 n.20
Robinson, John A. T.   99, 192 n.2
Robinson, Mary   11
Roderborn, Steven M.   18 n.44
Rogier, Lodewijk   318 n.4
Roloff, Jürgen   152 n.6
Roszak, Theodore   199 n.12
Roy, Édouard Le   47
Ruh, Ulrich   16 n.38
Ruusbroec, Jan van   166

Sartre, Jean-Paul   164, 318 n.3
Sauter, Gerhard   325 n.11
Savonarola, Girolamo   78
Schaeffler, Richard   195 n.7, 336 n.11
Schäfer, Peter   229 n.9
Scheeben, Matthias Joseph   244
Schelsky, Helmut   201 n.15
Schlette, Heinz Robert   346 n.7
Schlier, Heinrich   129, 229 n.9
Schmidt, Alfred   335 n.9
Schoof, Ted Mark   2, 9 n.20, 12 n.33, 15 n.36, 19 n.49
Schoonenberg, Piet   194 n.4
Schreiner, Josef   229 n.9
Schreiter, Robert J.   2, 3 n.3, 4 n.4, 15 n.36, 16–17, 123
Schüssler-Fiorenza, Elisabeth   295 nn.7–8
Schütz, Alfred   201 n.15
Schwemmer, Oswald   204 n.20
Scotus, John Duns   44
Seckler, Max   346 n.6
Sertillanges, Antonin-Gilbert   286
Shepherd, John J.   165 n.6
Sison, Antonio D.   18 n.45
Snijdewind, Hadewych   12 n.35
Snow, Charles Percy   199 n.13
Steiner, George   313 n.13
Stempel, Wolf-Dieter   205 n.21
Sterkens, Carl   2, 15 n.36

Stockmeier, Peter   314 n.14, 314 n.16
Strasser, Stephan   42
Strauss, David Friedrich   92, 148, 150
Strazzari, Fransesco   5 n.7, 5 n.9
Suso, Henry   30, 80

Tauler, Johannes   80
Tertullian   190, 321 n.7
Theodosius the Great   314 n.16
Theunissen, Michael   201 n.14
Thompson, Daniel Speed   17, 18 n.43
Tillich, Paul   299
Troisfontaines, Roger   201 n.14
Tromp, Sebastiaan   97
Tuchel, Klaus von   199
Tyrrell, George   117 n.12

Ulrich, Theodor   314 n.15

Veenhof, Jan   230 n.9
Verlaine, Paul   285
Vincent of Lérins   68
Vogler, Paul   201 n.15
Vogt, Joseph   314 n.15
Vriezen, Theodorus   259 n.3

Waayman, Kees   201 n.14
Waldenfels, Hans   345 n.5
Weizsäcker, Carl Friedrich von   199 n.13
Wellmer, Albrecht   331 n.3
Wiesenthal, Simon   11
Wilckens, Ulrich   151 n.5, 152 n.6, 231 n.2
Witvliet, Theo   331 n.4
Wolf, Eric   347 n.11

Xhaufflaire, Marcel   336 n.12

Ysebaert, Joseph   61 n.3

Zenger, Erich   218 n.11
Zumstein, Jean   218 n.11

www.ingramcontent.com/pod-product-compliance
Ingram Content Group UK Ltd.
Pitfield, Milton Keynes, MK11 3LW, UK
UKHW062306220426
470268UK00009B/357